W9-CLB-426

URBANISM, URBANIZATION, AND CHANGE: COMPARATIVE PERSPECTIVES

Edited by

PAUL MEADOWS

Department of Sociology and Anthropology
State University of New York at Albany

and

EPHRAIM H. MIZRUCHI

Department of Sociology, Syracuse University

ADDISON-WESLEY PUBLISHING COMPANY
Reading, Massachusetts · Menlo Park, California · London · Don Mills, Ontario

This book is in the
ADDISON-WESLEY SERIES IN SOCIOLOGY

Printed in the United States of America. Published simultaneously in Canada. Library of Congress Catalog Card No. 69–11629.

CONTRIBUTORS

Milton I. Barnett, *Department of Anthropology, University of Wisconsin*
Wendell Bell, *Department of Sociology, Yale University*
Robert O. Blood, Jr., *Department of Sociology, University of Michigan*
Robert Bogdan, *Department of Sociology, Syracuse University*
Guillermo Briones, *Facultad de Sociología, Universidad Nacional, Bogota, Colombia*
W. Buikhuisen, *Department of Sociology, University of Groningen, Netherlands*
Alan K. Campbell, *Department of Political Science, Syracuse University*
Theodore Caplow, *Department of Sociology, Columbia University*
David B. Carpenter, *Department of Sociology, Washington University*
Robert C. Cook, *Population Reference Bureau, Inc., Washington, D. C.*
Oliver C. Cox, *Department of Sociology, Lincoln University*
Otis D. Duncan, *Population Studies Center, University of Michigan*
Jack C. Fisher, *Department of City and Regional Planning, Cornell University*
Herbert Gans, *Department of Sociology, Teachers College, Columbia University*
Jack Gibbs, *Department of Sociology, University of Texas*
David Godschalk, *Department of Urban and Regional Planning, Florida State University*
Nathan Goldman, *Department of Sociology, Illinois Institute of Technology*
Fred I. Greenstein, *Department of Political Science, Stanford University*
Peter C. Gutkind, *Department of Sociology, McGill University*
F. William Howton, *Department of Sociology, City University of New York*
Alan B. Kirschenbaum, *Department of Sociology, City University of New York*
Louis Kriesberg, *Department of Sociology, Syracuse University*
Theodore Lowi, *Department of Political Science, University of Chicago*
William Mangin, *Department of Anthropology, Syracuse University*
Walter Martin, *Department of Sociology, University of Oregon*
Paul Meadows, *Department of Sociology, State University of New York at Albany*
Walter B. Miller, *Joint Center for Urban Studies of M.I.T. and Harvard University*
William E. Mills, *Vancouver, British Columbia*
J. Clyde Mitchell, *Department of Sociology, University of Manchester*
Ephraim H. Mizruchi, *Department of Sociology, Syracuse University*
Vatro Murvar, *Department of Sociology, Mount Mary College*
Peter Orleans, *Department of Sociology, University of California at Los Angeles*
Robert Perrucci, *Department of Sociology, Purdue University*
William Petersen, *Department of Sociology, University of California at Berkeley*
Zygmunt Pióro, *Institute of Town Planning and Architecture, Warsaw, Poland*
David Popenoe, *Department of Urban Studies, Rutgers University*
Lee Rainwater, *Department of Sociology, Washington University*
Leonard Reissman, *Department of Sociology, Tulane University*
Seymour Sacks, *Department of Economics, Syracuse University*
Miloš Savić, *City Planning Commission, Novi Sad, Yugoslavia*
Leo F. Schnore, *Department of Sociology, University of Wisconsin*
Manfred Stanley, *Department of Sociology, Syracuse University*
Charles Tilly, *Department of Sociology, University of Toronto*
F. B. Waisanen, *Department of Sociology, Michigan State University*
S. Kirson Weinberg, *Department of Sociology, Portland State College*
Sidney Willhelm, *Department of Sociology, State University of New York at Buffalo*
Charles V. Willie, *Department of Sociology, Syracuse University*

PREFACE

The last two decades have seen an impressive revival of interest in urban research. Studies by economists, historians, geographers, political scientists, and anthropologists join those by sociologists. Funded by both public and private agencies, these investigators have examined literally every major aspect of urban life—housing, family organization, government, personality disorganization, population trends and movements, and so on. The present political emphasis on the city promises an even greater attention to the patterns and problems of the metropolis.

This collection of readings is intended primarily for college students in courses in urban sociology, urban studies, and metropolitan studies. Hopefully, it will be of interest to the fast-growing group of urbanists, those urban practitioners who are to be found in such varied settings as urban renewal offices, community councils, neighborhood centers, boards of education, and urban parishes. This volume of readings does not propose to constitute a manual of action; it provides a review of general social theory as reflected in (if indeed not guiding) contemporary urban studies. Most of the readings are by sociologists, but political science, demography, anthropology, history, and economics are represented. Moreover, just as the readings are interdisciplinary, so likewise they are cross-cultural. The reader will find here presentations of urban patterns and problems in Europe, Africa, South America, and Asia as well as in the more familiar contexts of the United States. The limitations of space made it impossible for this volume to be more fully cross-cultural—a pity in view of the outstanding research and interpretative studies now available.

The focus of this volume is on urbanization as a complex but identifiable social process—on social change, in other words, on its patterns, trends, complexities, and problems. Mingled in the presentations of this volume are both objective and quantitative data and intuitive and phenomenological materials. This, we feel, is as it should be; for the city is now, as it has always been in history, sight and sound and touch as well as feeling and thought and purpose. Urbanism, that rich compound of thought and things, that index and epitome of the civilized life of man, is the theme and the intellectual concern of these representative studies by contemporary social scientists.

The editors wish to express their indebtedness to their colleagues and to editors and publishers for their willingness to permit the reprinting, or the publishing for the first time, of the papers in this volume. We thank also Mr. James O'Hair, who located materials for us and expedited the administrative aspects of preparing this book; Mrs. Janet McNair and Mrs. Mary Belle-Isle for typing; and our colleagues at Syracuse University, particularly Mark Abrahamson, Sandor Halebsky, William Pooler, and Manfred Stanley, for suggestions and comments on our selections.

These papers, which are reprinted in full, have been arranged according to the fairly conventional organization of courses in urban sociology and urban social studies in American colleges. Some well-known papers have not been included here because they are rather generally available. The various introductory sections by the editors have sought, by emphasizing developmental and common themes, to give this volume some of the coherence and unity of a text.

Syracuse, N. Y.
November 1968

P.M.
E.H.M.

CONTENTS

INTRODUCTION

The rapid and profound transformations characterizing man's social condition in the world today are emergents of urban processes. Cities have become the loci of ever-increasing communication between nations and among the various regions within nations. Cities provide the social contexts for political decisions affecting both world and country. Cities are arenas of interaction not only for political elites, but for intellectual and technological elites as well. In short, cities are where the action is.

Interest in city life is as ancient as the written history of man. It is reasonable to assume that the beginning of city life came about when the first surplus harvests released some agrarians from obligations to work the land. There arose the priests, the tradesmen, the intellectuals, and the recorders of the deeds of their civilization. Although the villages which emerged were a far cry from the kinds of centers we think of as cities today, they could be differentiated in terms of activities. The village provided the locus for the proliferation of activities which were distinctly urban in character.

There is little doubt that in the West the cities of old and the large urban centers of today have everywhere dominated both village and countryside. As residential centers for the various elites, they have provided opportunities for the concentration of power, wealth, and prestige. Cities have been centers for transforming raw materials into manufactured goods and for transporting and marketing these goods both intranationally and internationally. Since these activities have been concentrated in urban areas, it is not surprising that cities have come to dominate whole nations.

It would be an error, however, for us to project our Western image of cities into the conception we have of cities in newly developing countries. Indeed, as Breese tells us, "In studying urbanization in newly or rapidly developing countries, it is important to divest oneself of the Western image of urbanization. This process is absolutely mandatory, though difficult."

Sociologists have always shown particular interest in urban life. The emergence of sociology as a distinct field of study may be thought of as a concomitant of the industrial-urban revolutions which began during the seventeenth and eighteenth centuries in Europe and England. Saint-Simon, Comte, Tönnies, Durkheim, Simmel, and Weber were some of the founders of modern sociology who responded directly to the societal transformations associated with the industrial-urban revolutions. The interplay of technological forces stimulated the movement of populations into cities, creating a social milieu which required description and explanation. This perceived and societal need was concurrent with the outcomes of the intellectual revolutions which had been unfolding in Europe. Thus sociology was born in a world in ferment. The fermentation process was nurtured in the cities of the West.

Urbanism and Urbanization. Although sociology is primarily Western in origin, city life has been characteristic of societies the world over. The central ideas which provide a broad perspective for the student of city life are *urbanism* and *urbanization*. These terms must be used with much care and qualification. Like many other concepts in sociology, they derive not from careful, scientific assessments and observations, but from the day-to-day usages of laymen for whom precision may not be critical.

The complexities associated with the concepts are clearly delineated by Meadows in our first selection. With these caveats in mind, let us view urbanism as a cultural phenomenon, the outgrowth of interplay between technological and social processes. It is a pattern of existence which deals with (1) the accommodation of heterogeneous groups to one another; (2) a relatively high degree of specialization in labor; (3) involvement in nonagricultural occupational pursuits; (4) a market economy; (5) an interplay between innovation and change as against the maintenance of societal traditions; (6) development of advanced learning and the arts; and (7) tendencies toward city-based, centralized governmental structures. Urbanism refers to a number of values which can be intuitively perceived as a whole, but which have not yet been adequately dissected by the social scientist. Indeed, one of the major objectives of this book is to help clarify these values.

Urbanization refers to the processes by which (1) urban values are diffused, (2) movement occurs from rural areas to cities, and (3) behavior patterns are transformed to conform to those which are characteristic of groups in the cities. These are the basic processes to which American urban sociologists are addressing themselves.

The most dramatic developments in urbanism and urbanization are currently associated with Africa, South Asia, and Southeast Asia. In number, the cities of the non-Western nations dwarf those of Europe and the United States. Furthermore, in the future, particularly in terms of population, it is estimated that the largest cities in the world will be found not in the West but in the East. With the acceleration of urbanization all over the world, the interest in urban problems, particularly in urban sociology, is intensifying.

Detribalization and Stabilization. When we move beyond the American urban scene other *sensitizing concepts* are useful in our attempts to describe and understand urban processes. J. Clyde Mitchell, in a paper which has been revised for this volume (see Chapter 6), distinguishes between *urbanization, detribalization,* and *stabilization.* In urbanization, as we suggested above, our focus is on movement to cities, changes in occupational pursuits, and changes in behavior patterns. By and large, our attention is directed toward what is happening in the process as society becomes urban.

When we address ourselves to the processes associated with detribalization, however, we are concerned with problems surrounding movement from *tribal* units rather than from agricultural areas and, perhaps more important, changing relationships with chiefs, kin-groups, and fellow tribesmen. Concern with detribalization, for example, leads us to seek out the organized patterns by which fellow tribesmen bridge the gap between former ties and obligations and current urban challenges. Indeed, as anthropologists have already shown, voluntary associations emerge in urban areas for the guidance and protection of people experiencing detribalization (see, for example, Kenneth Little, "Voluntary Associations in West Africa," *American Anthropologist,* **59,** August, 1957; and the articles in this book by Mitchell, Gutkind, and Bogdan). The similarity is notable between these organizations and the various *Landsmannschaften* and other ethnic orders in the United States in the late 19th and early 20th centuries.

Stabilization, however, focuses on the process by which the detribalized assume relatively permanent urban residence. Like the concepts of acculturation and assimilation, the notion of stabilization sensitizes us to ongoing processes which are both complex and open-ended. Just as it is difficult to know when the activities to which assimilation and acculturation refer have ended, so is it difficult to determine when a population has become stabilized.

The Rural-Urban Dimension. In addition to the shift from tribal to urban, sociologists have been concerned with differences between rural and urban settlements. This distinction has created images of discrete societal units which have existed side-by-side for long periods of time, each having little influence on the other. Contemporary social scientists now realize that in complex societies such distinctions cannot be made. What is somewhat more closely related to the facts are categories of settlements which are more or less rural or urban. (That it is difficult to postulate such a continuum is noted by Otis D. Duncan in "Community Size and the Rural-Urban Continuum" and in Paul Hatt and Albert Reiss, eds., *Cities and Society,* New York: The Free Press, 1957, revised.)

Three primary factors play a role in our designation of settlements as more urban or rural: size, density of population, and life style. While variations in size and density of population can be easily determined, variations in life style are difficult to ascertain. In mass societies, where there is much standardization of products, entertainment, and education, there is a similarity of life style which tends to reduce differences between urban and rural. There are marked and conspicuous differences in life ways between Chicago, Illinois, and Kokomo, Indiana, but differences between middle-sized cities and small cities on the one hand, and small *cities* and large *towns* on the other, are more elusive.

Regardless of the quantitative and qualitative characteristics of settlements, it is important to understand that more general societal features play a role in how people respond to urban and rural life. Loci of life are influenced by larger societal currents. When most of the population and the life style tend to be rural, rural values play a much more important role in influencing the activities of the larger society than when larger proportions of the population are located in more urban areas. Thus, as suggested by Mizruchi (Chapter 4), urban activities in primarily rural societies have different consequences for populations than do urban activities in urban societies. In more technical terms, urbanization may be viewed not only as an independent variable but as a dependent variable in relation to larger social structures. (See Gideon Sjoberg, "The Rural-Urban Dimension in Preindustrial, Transitional and Industrial Societies," R. E. L. Faris, ed., *Handbook of Modern Sociology*, Chicago: Rand McNally, 1964.)

Community and Mass Society. Interest in the shift from rural and tribal ways to urban ways inevitably turns to questions of community, mass society, and their relationship to urban life. Although the concern with decline of community has been primarily associated with Western urban processes, it has been implicit in many studies of nonwestern populations as well (see Chapter 3).

The conceptual contrast between community and society in the sociological literature is most notably attributed to Ferdinand Tönnies, whose book *Gemeinschaft and Gesellschaft* (*Community and Society*), first published in 1887, is a classic work. Emile Durkheim's *The Division of Labor in Society*, 1893, another classic, was also directed to making distinctions between processes of community and those of societies. Still others which are equally noteworthy were works by Georg Simmel, Max Weber, and Robert Redfield (see Mizruchi, Chapter 4).

While each one of the above abstracted a specific aspect of social life which he felt was sufficient to understand the central processes by which traditional social structures were being transformed, all of them were explicitly or implicitly concerned with the fundamental existential problems of reconstructing meaningful forms of community in the midst of complex, heterogeneous, urbanized collectivities. The quest for community, to borrow Robert Nisbet's phrase (*The Quest for Community*, New York: Oxford, 1953), has not been ignored by the sociologists. However, the ambiguities associated with community as an idea, and the romanticism which permeates speculation about it as a phenomenon make it difficult to specify what it is that sociologist and layman are seeking to understand (Mizruchi, *op. cit.*).

Like urbanism and urbanization as conceptual tools, community cannot be adequately defined. let us suggest, however, that the idea of community from the perspective of the actor is usually *subjective*, that is, it refers to feelings of attachment to and identification with a collectivity which can be located in time and space. Thus, one may describe oneself as "a member of this community now," but "I grew up in that community."

From the perspective of the observer, a community is a locus of collective and social action. It is a general term which does not refer to part of a place, like a neighborhood or suburb, but rather focuses on the whole. As such, attention may be directed to units as small as hamlets and as large as metropolitan areas. Community in this sense refers to the inclusive units which ordinarily participate in the social and economic activities of a distinguishable area. The difficulties in clearly distinguishing community sentiment and behavior from other forms is largely attributable to both the homogeneity and heterogeneity of life in mass societies. As we noted earlier, there are serious complexities in attempting to characterize human settlements as falling on a continuum from rural to urban. A significant aspect of the problem is the lack of objective discreteness in life ways and even in physical boundaries which make it possible for us to designate the end of one form and the beginning of another. The lack of *objective* discreteness also contributes to some degree of *subjective* confusion regarding whether one can identify with one community or another. The emergence of megalopolis, for example, provides dramatic evidence of the elusiveness of boundaries between rural and urban settlements and between one city and another.

What appears to be occurring in American society, for example, is a tendency for some aspects of socially organized life to become homogenized while other aspects remain somewhat differentiated. Looking at American society macroscopically, we can see great similarities among human settlements. Federal financing of uniformly built roads and highways, the diffusion of architectural forms, and the manufacture of similar types of building products are all examples of the increasing standardization at certain levels of societal activity. These similarities are concomitant with greater homogeneity in occupational performance, education, and consumer products. All these processes suggest that social differentiation in American life is negligible. However, as Reissman suggests (Chapter 3), there are aspects of social life in the United States today which will probably continue to be differentiated for a long time to come.

When we take a microscopic view of an urban settlement, the social life suggests great heterogeneity. Because cities are loci of exchange of influence, information, products, and services, they bring people together whose interests, training, and talents are extremely varied. As a result, most of the economic activities of urban dwellers, to select one area, are diversified, and this diversification tends to be greater as settlement size increases. The heterogeneity which is the primary component of the division of labor in society is most characteristic of urban activities.

As societies become more industrialized and urbanized, the internal structural units which characterized them apparently undergo change toward greater diversification and complexity while at the same time tending toward standardization and simplicity. Questions dealing with the discrepancies between processes at various levels of society must be answered by the urban sociologist. Similarly, questions dealing with the activities contributing to the emergence of common denominators which provide the appearance of homogeneity in urban life must be explored. Understanding these processes will add immeasurably to our understanding of the balance between homogeneity and heterogeneity in urban life.

Sociological Perspectives on Urbanism and Urbanization. A number of more or less discernible perspectives have emerged in the field of urban sociology. Although there is always much overlap between one approach and another, and although variables and attributes judged to be peculiar to one viewpoint may be differently assessed by researchers holding to another, important implications derive from looking at societal life in different ways. More specifically, the *independent* variable (or variables) or *attribute* which tends to be selected for explanatory purposes is the one that reflects a given perspective. For example, if we make an assumption (i.e., state an hypothesis) that a change in the values which urban dwellers hold regarding personal property will be followed by a change in the probability that they will sell their houses to Negroes, we would be limiting our explanatory strengths to one independent variable, values. Similarly, if we make an assumption that increasing the *market* value of a house, an economic variable, will increase the likelihood that people will sell to Negroes, we would again be limiting our explanatory power to one variable. The use of either one or both of these variables to predict the likelihood of selling property to Negroes is methodologically valid. However, past research and our intuitive knowledge of the complexities of responses to similar occurrences suggests that there are more variables affecting these responses than the above hypotheses would suggest. Isolating a given independent variable or attribute would provide us with a picture of the impact that this factor would have on another factor or factors, but it would tell us nothing about the relative impact of other factors on the phenomenon being observed. The relatively sophisticated methodologist has certain techniques (e.g., factor analysis) at his disposal which aid in understanding some aspects of the differential interaction among variables. For the most part, however, appreciating the interplay among variables and attributes means intuitively grasping the elements of a situation as a complex whole. Our capacity to understand in this fashion varies directly with our knowledge of the independent effect of selected variables. What we are suggesting, in sum, is that while we remain aware of the limitations of single perspectives and our methodology, we appreciate the contributions they can make to our fundamental understanding of important urban processes.

At least three major perspectives appear to be significant in appreciating the divergent orientations associated with contemporary urban sociology: (1) the urbanization-disorganization approach, (2) the ecological approach, and (3) the value-orientation approach. (See Gideon Sjoberg, "Theory and Research in Urban Sociology" in Philip Hauser and Leo Schnore, *The Study of Urbanization*, New York: Wiley, 1965, pp. 157–189). While it is possible to isolate still other categories of theoretical and methodological perspective, as Sjoberg has done (*loc. cit.*), we shall limit ourselves to the three perspectives of the foregoing classification.

The fundamental distinction among perspectives depends upon whether the independent variable a theorist-researcher selects is primarily objective or subjective. The more *objective* factors involve variables which are presumably *external* to the actors under observation, variables like population size, age, place of residence, and male-female ratios. The more *subjective* factors involve variables which are more or less *internal* to the actors under observation, although they share such values and norms with others and are thus not idiosyncratic. A cursory review of the selections in Chapter 2, compared with those in Chapter 4, markedly illustrates this point.

The *urbanization-disorganization* approach has until recently been the most influential perspective in urban sociology, particularly in the United States. Growing out of the work of Tönnies, Durkheim, Simmel, and Weber, the most representative developments have been advanced by Robert Park and Ernest Burgess, Louis Wirth and Robert Redfield. Treating urbanization as an independent variable, the proponents of this school saw certain forms of urban social organization and disorganization as emergents of an ongoing process of transition from traditional to complex societies. (See Gutkind, Chapter 3 and Mizruchi, Chapter 4.)

Several critical points must be made here; we have already suggested that urbanization may be treated as a dependent variable. Industrialization and the normative elements of the larger society, including values for example, may play an important role in the quality of life which characterizes urban settlements (see Chapter 1). In addition to this criticism, the tendency to confuse deviant behavior with social disorganization has been a major weakness of the urbanization-disorganization perspective. Sociologists have come to realize that what appears to be disorganized behavior, e.g., crime, is in reality well organized. Furthermore, some sociologists, following Durkheim, assume that there are normal and abnormal amounts or rates of deviant behavior which are characteristic of given types of societies. Deviant behavior per se is not an index of social disorganization.

The *ecological* school is of relatively recent vintage, but its roots can be traced to some of the representatives of the urbanization-disorganization approach. The most prominent contemporary members of this school, Duncan, Schnore, and Hawley, are well represented in Chapter 2. They tend to focus on the objective-external factors as their independent variables. Although they do not explore more than a few interacting variables at a time, their approach reflects an appreciation of multi-factorial causal analysis. As Willhelm suggests in his criticism of this school (Chapter 2), some of the valuational attributes which are rejected by the proponents of this perspective inadvertently crop up in their research.

The *value-orientation* school, in sharp contrast to the urbanization-disorganization and ecological schools, holds that shared values are the most significant of the independent variables used to explain urban phenomena. As Sjoberg reminds us (*ibid.*, p. 171), Max Weber selected the values of socio-cultural systems as his independent variable, and the social structure of cities as his dependent variable. Although there are few urban sociologists who share this perspective—Willhelm and Firey belong in this group (see Willhelm, Chapter 2)—a number of sociologists whose names are not associated with urban research are inclined toward this approach. Talcott Parsons, William Kolb, the late Florian Znaniecki, Robin M. Williams, Jr., and other members of the "functionalist school" tend to focus on values as independent variables in relation to urban processes.

Among the problems associated with this approach is the difficulty of describing common value orientations in mass societies. If we cannot determine the qualities of the common denominators in complex societies, we cannot discern the nature of the independent variable. In addition, Sjoberg suggests (*loc. cit.*), a concern with value orientations as independent variables tends to direct us to seeking the unique aspects of cities in various cultures rather than the common, thus drawing our attention from more universal properties of urban phenomena. It is the common aspects which are particularly important for cross-cultural research.

In addition, although not a major school in terms of number of adherents and research output, *social area analysis* is a perspective which is becoming more influential in urban sociology. Eshref Shevky, Wendell Bell, Scott Greer, Marilyn Williams, and Peter Orleans (see Chapter 2) are representatives of this approach which stresses the significance of the economic factor as an independent variable in urbanization.

Given the nature of the kinds of problems with which urban sociologists must deal, particularly those dealing with cross-cultural analysis and social change, there is some serious doubt whether any one of these perspectives, taken alone, can contribute adequately to our understanding of pressing urban problems. In addition, there tends to be overemphasis on urban problems in the United States. Thus, as in other areas of sociology, it is likely that our most meaningful perspectives will be based on thoughtful, reflective eclecticism.

This collection and our introductions represent the various viewpoints described above and a number of others which cannot be classified into schools. The book is organized into seven chapters which emphasize the significance of historical and ecological factors, the varieties of social organization of urban life and the effects of organized activities, the problems and socially structured strains which are an aspect of urban living, social and cultural change, and planning and reform.

Wherever possible, we have selected materials from both the United States, on which the literature is voluminous, and other developed and developing societies. We have surveyed many areas of the world and many of the problems of urban life. A special effort has been made to provide descriptive materials which reflect depth and breadth. Originally we planned to include an extensive bibliography of articles and books dealing with urban sociology. Since there are so many excellent and easily available sources, however, we felt that such a listing would be superfluous. Extensive footnotes do accompany the various papers and our own contributions to this work. These should provide adequate leads to significant publications in urban sociology.

CHAPTER ONE

HISTORICAL AND CROSS-CULTURAL PERSPECTIVES ON URBAN LIFE

INTRODUCTION

Urbanisms—city-centered cultures—have attracted a great variety of scholars over the years: anthropologists, historians, economists, philosophers, political scientists, and sociologists. Although the city is not so old as human society, and although there have been and still are cultures without cities, the city has been widely recognized as central to any understanding of the phenomena and problems of social organization and change. These scholars—perhaps the word "urbanists" does not quite accurately describe them—have made us aware of the fact that there are different "kinds" of urbanism: agrarian, feudal, commercial, and industrial. They have shown us that the pre-industrial city differs from the industrial, and the oriental from the occidental, or so they have usually maintained. In like manner they have made it clear that "urbanization," that is, all the processes involved in the emergence, growth, and ultimate life-history careers of cities, varies from one kind or type of urbanism to another.

Moreover, the major focusses of interest vary considerably among the scholars interested in the urban scene. Some are concerned with the city and its total physical and social environment. Others find themselves attracted to the city as a problem of human settlement: its morphology, the natural history of its land uses, or the relationships between spatial location and urban phenomena. Still others are fascinated by the style, pattern, and ethos of the city as "a way of life" in different historical contexts: one thinks here of Max Weber and Lewis Mumford. And still others view the city in its many historical settings in terms of the processes and the variables of cultural origins, growth, and change.

In the articles which are included here, there is a brief presentation of some of these interests: Meadows, combining history and technology in a cultural interpretation of the city; Cox, challenging the familiar Childe and Turner thesis (which is set forth in the article by Meadows) concerning the emergence and role of the city in the early history of man; Cook, surveying the global distribution of cities and making it amply clear that urbanism is by no means singularly or even perhaps most significantly (at least in human numbers) a phenomenon of the industrial West; and Murvar, critically reexamining the Weberian contrast between Asian and European cities. Each article displays the familiar and fundamental characteristic of the city in history, its "capacity for modal organization," to quote Eric Lampard's very appropriate phrase. Cities are organizations of a variable number of people in areas of variable sizes, profusely distributed across the face of the globe.

THE CITY, TECHNOLOGY, AND HISTORY

Paul Meadows

The Approach through Intra-Urbanism

Over two decades ago a leading United States urban sociologist, Professor Niles Carpenter, opened a discussion of urban sociology with this statement: "Recent trends in the field of sociology might be epitomized in a four-word phrase—'the quest for data.'" [1] In retrospect, one might, while accepting the importance of this empirical bent, still ask the elementary question, data about what? So far as urban sociology is concerned, it is perfectly obvious that so long as it is data about some relationship concerning social life within the American city—whether trend, stage, cause-effect, fact-implication, problem-policy—which is to be discovered, nothing else has ever seemed to count. Urban sociology has been and is yet literally (and without reservation apparently) the sociology of life *within* the city.

This approach to urban sociology, which we may designate as the sociology of intra-urbanism because of the manner in which social phenomena are interpreted solely in terms of the city itself, has been characterized by both purely intellectual as well as markedly pragmatic interests. As an intellectual curiosity, urban sociology represents the emergence of the city as in itself a legitimate object of sociological study. The city is *sui generis:* hence, the sociology of city life. This perspective was proclaimed in an extraordinarily influential volume of papers published by the University of Chicago Press in 1924: *The City,* edited by R. E. Park, E. W. Burgess, and R. D. McKenzie. The theoretical position taken by these authors is indicated in the initial paper by Professor Park: "The City: Suggestions for the Investigation of Human Behavior in the Urban Environment." The subsequent ecological, personality, and institutional investigations of a generation of urban sociologists are foreshadowed in some of the other papers in this volume: McKenzie's "The Ecological Approach to the Study of the Human Community"; Park's "The Mind of the Hobo," and his famous paper on the metropolitan daily newspaper. Since then, the classroom texts in urban sociology [2] follow rather closely this thematic organization of this field. The much later, masterful essay by Professor Louis Wirth, summarizing and organizing the theory of a sociology devoted to the study of intra-urbanism and significantly titled "Urbanism as a Way of Life," [3] has been one of the most commonly quoted and cited papers in U. S. sociology.

However, this intellectual curiosity about the city was complemented by another kind of interest, one which perhaps was not so welcome among the ranks of theoreticians, but nonetheless widespread and popular. This pragmatic interest grew out of the necessity felt by many urban leaders to find more adequate

---

Reprinted by permission of the publisher from *Social Forces,* **36** (December, 1957), pp. 141–147.

solutions to human problems in the city. Prompted by social workers, municipal administrators, and institutional managers, teams of sociologists and other social scientists, armed with questionnaires, notebooks and maps, invaded city streets and engaged in comprehensive social surveys and social anthropological studies of U. S. cities. This monumental quest of empirical facts has been described by a number of writers, notably by Pauline Young in her *Scientific Social Surveys and Research.*[4] Besides yielding up great quantities of data, this practical search for the policy-relevant fact served to highlight the enormous vitality of the city along with the tragic loss of human values occurring in the disorder uncouthly hardened, as Lewis Mumford has observed, "in metropolitan slum and industrial factory district," [5] and in the widening circles of social derangement accompanying the residential and commercial exodus into the urban fringes. Urban sociologists in the United States owe a huge debt to these students of urban disorganization, a debt being slowly paid off in the form of newer patterns of community organization and municipal policy.

However, it is a contention of this paper that the prodigious empiricism of this double-barrelled investigation of urban life during the interwar and postwar years in the United States was an incomplete venture. Indeed, incompleteness marks any scientific enterprise, for investigation is a function of problems, and problems are unfortunately, even among scientists, a function of perspective. To be specific (but not exhaustive), consider the following limitations on any urban sociology which is content to be only a sociology of intra-urbanism.

In the first place, such an approach cannot possibly formulate universals and cannot, therefore, achieve universalism. It is no accident, for example, that some of the most popular sociological texts in the United States are emphatically American in scope, as even their titles indicate.[6] And even when their titles omit this fact, the contents do not.[7] There is, methodologically speaking, nothing amiss in the use of urban data which happen to be at hand. But the methodologists of science are constantly bewailing the failure, among many fields of scientific inquiry, to formulate problems which can lead to the development of trans-cultural or cross-cultural generalizations. This failure to arrive at arresting and provocative generalities cannot be compensated for by the abundance of attractive and stimulating, even limitedly useful, particularities.

In the second place, these American intra-urbanists have, following Wirth's crystallization of the conceptual field, worked with a very limited set of variables. For Wirth, urban social phenomena are a function of such variables as size and density of population, heterogeneity and mobility of population, secondariness and anonymity of population. This is a strictly sociologistic approach, eminently correct; but this merit does not—or should not—blind us to the narrowness of this circumscription of the field. Surely urbanism is not entirely a function of merely this handful of social variables operating neatly within the confines of the city boundary! Surely there are historic urbanisms—non-Western and non-industrial in character [8]—in which these variables are perhaps not even relevant! Moreover, it should be noted that the quality or state of social life which Wirth called the urban way of life seems to have little relationship to the historian's perception of the city as synonymous with civilization, and the artist's observation of the city as a qualitatively unique world which separates the urbanite from the primitive and the peasant in any era or area.

Fully appreciative of the importance and of the necessity of an intra-urban sociology, this paper proposes, however, to examine some of the work of urban sociologists (and others, mainly others) for whom the central concern has been less the phenomena within the city than the developmental and other regularities to be noted in the relationships between cities and their cultures, between cities and the cultures of many eras and areas—in other words, cities as intercultural phenomena. This second approach to the city, which does not deny but supplements the first, we may call, for want of a better name, an inter-urban sociology.

The witticism which states that sociology is what sociologists do is quite far off the mark as a description of urban sociology in this latter sense. For the plain fact is that some of the most valuable urban sociology has come from the pens of persons not usually identified with sociology—from historians, anthropologists, economists, and architects, among others. At least what they have written is sociology if one is sufficiently tolerant to conceive of the data of this field as consisting of invariant, or at least relatively stable, relationships between and among social and other phenomena. For these observers of the urban scene and role have been tremendously impressed by the abiding importance of (a) the relationship between technology and society, on the one hand, and the emergence and development of urbanism, on the other; and (b) the opposite relationship—that between urbanism and the emergence and development of technology and society. What we are really formulating here is in fact a reversible functional equation which sees these variables as functions of one another:

1. urbanism = f (technology and society); and
2. technology and society = f (urbanism).

It is proposed to explore during the remainder of this paper various aspects of these formulas, and to do so in terms of a major proposition, which reads as follows: *Urbanization represents the process by which urbanism emerges and develops out of the interaction of technology and society.* This proposition will then be restated and discussed: *Change and development in technology and society occur in and through urbanism.* Expressed as questions and not as assertions, this basic thought may be put thus: How do technological and social change encourage the rise of urbanism (urbanization)? Conversely, how does urbanization affect the processes of technological and social change?

Urbanism As a Function of Technology and Society

It might be helpful to state at this point the general theory of urbanism which expresses what is styled here the "inter-urban" approach to the sociology of the city. This theory may be formulated in a set of functional propositions somewhat as follows:

1. urbanization = f (economic surplus);
2. economic surplus = f (technology of surplus);
3. urbanization = f (technology of surplus).

Hence also:

4. the volume and rate of urbanization = f (the development and expansion of technology of surplus); and
5. great periods and epochs of urbanization = f (cycles of technological and social development).

The most perceptive—and probably the original—statement of the functional relationship between urbanization and technology-society was made by V. Gordon Childe, Australian-born professor of prehistoric archaeology, in his volume, *Man Makes Himself* (London, 1937). Subsequently, American historian Ralph Turner published his two-volume *The Great Classical Traditions,*[9] in which the Childe thesis receives further development and documented elaboration in terms of other culture situations. Together, these volumes constitute a full restatement of urban sociology in the direction of a theory of inter-urbanism.

The Childe-Turner discussions stipulate three major revolutions in history—the food-producing, the urban, and the industrial revolutions. Clearly, each is in point of fact a technological revolution, for each involves the development of skills and tools (techniques and technics) by which environmental resources are converted into economic goods and services. The nature of this conversion process is, of course, a function of the society and the technology, such that the type of economic organization and the level of technical theory (technology) determine the type, the rate, the volume, and the direction of resource utilization.[10]

Cities emerge historically when a technological complex (tools, skills, and theory) creates an economic surplus. The routes and scope of this exchange of the economic surplus develop an everwidening network of communities, and with the growth of trade and transportation there is a corresponding increase in the size and complexity of the urban net which contains and utilizes the surplus. Cities become linked with cities, cities in different cultures are related by trade and culture contacts generally with each other; the city becomes a cross-cultural emergent. Turner has expressed the relationships involved here in this manner:

> Since urban cultures appeared only with the formation of an economic surplus, they advanced largely as the economic surplus increased. In general, it is evident in the development of the ancient-oriental urban cultures, such increase has been brought about in three different ways: (1) by technological advances, such as the introduction of irrigation and metal-working, (2) by the expansion of economic enterprise, such as the Babylonian and Egyptian penetration of Syria, and (3) by the development of new forms of economic administration, such as gang slavery and the estate system of cultivation.[11]

It is clear from their accounts of the great ancient and classical empires of the Mediterranean and Middle East that Childe and Turner do not adhere to any simple technological interpretation of urbanization, particularly of technology conceived of in limited terms. This point is well demonstrated in Turner's concept of a natural history of urbanism. Throughout, he indicates two variables in urban change and development, technology and social interaction. Stated as a formula, his conception might read thus: urbanization = f (technology, interaction). Examining his depiction of urban cultural development stage by stage, we may note schematically, the correlatives as presented in Table 1.

TABLE 1. SCHEMATIC PRESENTATION OF TURNER'S CONCEPT OF A NATURAL HISTORY OF URBANISM

Phase	Technology	Interaction
I. Emergence of Urban Culture	Agricultural and handicraft technics; appearance of economic surplus.	Primary social specialization: a power-holding group, and industrial group.
II. Social Specialization and Integration	New lands, new tools higher productivity; new raw materials.	Distinction in power-group: secular-military and priestly sections; compact work groups.
III. Internal Crisis	Systematic application of wealth-producing technics; new tools; resources; expansion of transportation technology; intensified craft specialization.	Acculturation with outgroups; intergroup struggle to control economic surplus; ascendance of the military.
IV. Urban Imperialism	Commitment of wealth to arms; military utilization of technology for greater resources.	Byzantine pattern of social organization; slavery; network of intercity contacts; new leadership unbound by tradition; conspicuous waste.
V. Decline	Failure of integration of masses possessing technical skills with markets; hence, loss of productivity and production innovations.	Political regimentation; lack of interest among power group in technological innovations; wasteful exploitations of resources and organization through war, etc.

Acknowledging in passing the Spenglerian pessimism of this natural history conception,[12] one may observe that this scheme furnishes an excellent instance of the interpenetration of technology and society which an economic realism has always insisted is characteristic of any form of social organization. It spotlights the symbiotic dependence, the vital interdependence, which denotes the functioning of any urbanism. Urbanism depends upon the appearance and growth of an economic surplus. But that growth is clearly the function of interactional forces formulating and executing social policy with respect to the direction of the dominant technology and the disposition of the economic surplus. The fate of urbanism is bound up with the resolution of this problem.

Implicit in this reconstruction of the urban history of early periods is a Ricardian principle which further underscores the symbiotic dependence of urbanization on the interplay of technology and social interaction. The Ricardian principle of diminishing returns has been the setting of a number of discussions by the noted American author and urbanist, Lewis Mumford.[13] There are, he holds, the physical limits on the city of water supply, sewage disposal, traffic control, physical distance. There are the economic limits of increasing costs, frozen "price-pyramids" of land rents and mortgages, civic depletion, urban blight. There are the social limits of population density, complexity of organization, loss of social control, institutional impoverishment, and negative vitality. Here again the functional dependence of the city, in this case of the modern industrial city, is seen against the limited possibilities of a given stage of social interaction and technological development.

It is helpful to recall at this point that Mumford's own classification of the stages of modern industrial urbanism was based on this lively interplay of technological and social forces.[14] The fast shift which occurred in Western urbanization under the impact of industrialization Mumford ascribes to the changing pattern of productive technics and productive relations. Eotechnical," "paleotechnical," and "neotechnical" urbanisms represent for Mumford emergent cultural styles in which the transforming city is seen as an intricate and complex inter-urbanism—literally, if a new term may be permitted, an "urbanicism" [15]—of tools and institutions.

Technology and Society as Functions of Urbanism

Up to this point this discussion has focussed on the view that the city is an *organon*—literally a tool, an implement, or instrument—of a given technology and society. From this point of view the city is the creature and creation of technological and social processes. This thought has perhaps never been more eloquently phrased than by Mumford himself, who, though mindful of the fact that the city is an integral part of a larger functioning unity, nonetheless sees the city as the stage setting of a great and magnificent drama.

> The city, as one finds it in history, is the point of maximum concentration for the power and culture of a community. It is the place where the diffused rays of many separate beams of life fall into focus, with gains in both social effectiveness and significance. The city is the form and symbol of an integrated social relationship: it is the seat of the temple, the market, the hall of justice, the academy of learning. Here in the city the goods of civilization are multiplied and manifolded; here is where human experience is transformed into visible signs, symbols, patterns of conduct, systems of order. Here is where the issues of civilization are focussed; here, too, ritual passes on occasion into the active drama of a full differentiated and selfconscious society.[16]

However, the inter-urban approach to the sociology of the city also sees it as an independent variable shaping, fashioning, limiting, directing and otherwise influencing the total culture of which it is a part, and indeed of many other cultures. To bring out some of the salient themes of this theory of urbanism, it is proposed here to refer to some of the contrasts between peasant and urban cultures; to note the impact of urbanization on the social and technical processes; and to suggest something about the role of the city in the future development of the now "underdeveloped" areas of the world.

Inter-urban sociology, holding that the city is itself an independent variable in the functional nexus described by the terms technology and society, finds the urban revolution to be a major shaping force in the ascendancy of the technical order (to use at this point the excellent analysis provided by anthropologist

Robert Redfield).[17] The city, with its occupational and technological interests subordinating the earlier kinship organization of social life, presents us with the social reality which is indeed civilization itself. Here in the city the tools and the institutions which constitute the apparatus of civilized living are coordinated, rationalized, and integrated. Urban and civilized, urbanism and civilization: these are, one discovers, interchangeable terms. The city is the matrix and the carrier, the mirror and the stage of that form and level of organized social living which historically may be recognized as civilization.

The city, then, may be said to have an index value, indicating, measuring, and summarizing the civilization. Childe suggests this theme when he notes the typical traits of urban societies, all of them characteristics of civilized life, and most of them plainly denoting the technical order. The traits he points to include: (1) the great increase in the size of the settlement (the material equipment for human association becomes far larger); (2) the institution of tribute or taxation with resulting accumulation of capital; (3) monumental public works; (4) the art of writing; (5) the beginning of such exact and predictive sciences as arithmetic, geometry, and astronomy; (6) developed economic institutions making possible a greatly expanded foreign trade; (7) full-time technical specialists, as in metal-working; (8) a privileged ruling class; (9) the state. Following Redfield, then, we may say that the urban setting provides the facilities, the impetus, the spirit for the emergence and perfection of the formalized institutional and status systems which signalize the transformation of folk cultures into civilizations. The city thus becomes one pole in a continuum which has as its center the peasant village and culture and at its other extreme the primitive tribal community. With the emergence of the urban culture the old pre-urban society in which the technical order is subordinated within the moral order is shaken, often destroyed, always to some extent transformed by the new urbanism in which the moral order is embedded in the technical order, is seldom distinct from it, and often attains a superb adaptation to it. In fact, the mixing and mingling of many moral orders through trade and communication in the emporium which is the city usually subordinates (where it does not negate) the moral to the technical order. Meantime, the outward push of the city as the nucleus of the new world-order transforms country people into peasants: they become, as Redfield has suggested, part-societies with part-cultures, maintaining a tenuous autonomy in uneasy dependence on the city.

The historic novelty of this new order of things which the urban culture in fact is, which civilization indeed is, may be represented in many ways. Perhaps the most startling, certainly one of the most provocative, depictions of urbanism was drawn by the late Professor H. A. Innis, Canadian historian and political economist, who identified the central theme of civilization—of urbanism—with the conquest and monopoly of time.[18] By means of the symbolic and technical skills which the technology of economic surplus made available and concentrated in the city, human beings in many an early historic civilization fashioned their controls over time, resulting, in the course of time, in agricultural and craft technologies, public administration and military regimentation, and all the arts and skills of production and economy. State clashed with Church for the control of time, and ultimately into the interstices of weak control of time by the State came an invading industry which slowly became, in the industrializing cities of the West, "the first among equals" in the competition for the control of time. Time sits enthroned in the city, which links the ever-extending past with the ever-widening present and foreshadows relentlessly the future. Thus it is that a technological order in which social time is standardized, mechanized, packaged, priced, and merchandised in the strictest possible conformity to the time-patterned demands of the engineer and the accountant describes contemporary industrial urbanism in the West, an urbanism which promises to achieve, fairly soon, a universalism the scope of which no other historic urbanism has ever been able to approximate.

The historic novelty and uniqueness of the city as the collective utility and symbol which we call civilization is often misunderstood and misinterpreted as a result of the confusion created by two quite contradictory modes of thought about urbanism. There is, on the one hand, the tendency, as in the case of cultural primitivism, to treat the city as if it were a diabolic contrivance, stifling, corrupting, distorting the supernal moral and social values of a pristine social order identified with the primitive or peasant way of life. Thus, indigenous primitive or peasant cultures are often fervently acclaimed as good and fair beyond words; civilization is then earnestly dismissed as bad and deteriorating. This dichotomic moralism, which often passes for science in the hands, for example, of an eager anthropology or a subservient agricultural extension service, has often led, as George Dixon has observed,[19] to the interesting conclusion that " 'essentially human' social behavior is a function of the least 'civilized' social structures. 'Civilization' and social change . . . are invested with an inherited predisposition to engender 'problems.' " The Rousseauan cast of this view is unmistakable; its ideological or propagandistic values unmeasurable.

An equally misleading view of urbanism, glamorizing and glorifying the city with the same intemperateness and zeal with which the preceding view debases and discounts it, may be thought of as the heroic theory of the city. Here the city is seen as an abstract culture hero, creating, sustaining, elaborating, refining, often rescuing fundamental, significant human values. In its more academic guise this view regards the city as the dominant center in a gradient of power and influence extending out into the hinterland, touching and influencing even the land beyond the hinterland, the spacious and formless "Yonland." Urban sociologists, economists, and geographers in the United States have been and still are fascinated by this aspect of urbanism, which bureaucratizes for an entire society the social order within which these academic specialists do their daily work. Indeed, the tentacular bureaucracy of the city, whether medieval or modern, industrial or pre-industrial, provides considerable evidence for the scholarly heroism which invests the city with incredible—but unquestionably measurable —power and prestige.

Equally academic but less romantic is an entrepreneurial school of thought which argues that enterprise—any kind of collective enterprise: dynastic, ecclesiastical, military, political, industrial—is by its very nature a community-building phenomenon. The city becomes an important, indeed an essential, agent of enterprise, as we see in such familiar cases as the temple city, the fortress city, the shrine city, the capital city, the resort city, and so on. Moreover, as productive enterprise shifts from animate to inanimate sources of power, as it moves from low-energy to high-energy technology,[20] the urban aggregation of men, materials, and machines becomes ever larger, more technically subdivided, more intricately coordinated. A network of communication, control, decision-making and decision-enforcing binds these ever larger segments of humanity into a common life. Vast and complex multifunction cities mirroring the vastness and complexity of an evolving industrial technology, sometimes typifying in their uniformity the standardization of a machine technology, sometimes in their novelty and individuality the specialization and creativity of the machine—such is one perspective at least of the contemporary urbanism which is identified with a technology called industrialism.

It is not easy to maintain a balanced view of the city in the presence of these conflictive versions of the role of the city in history. A helpful moderation may perhaps be found in the ripe historical scholarship of Professor Childe in his closing comment on his survey of "man's progress through the ages":

> But just because tradition is created by societies of men and transmitted in distinctly human and rational ways, it is not fixed and immutable: it is constantly changing as society deals with ever new circumstances. Tradition makes the man, by circumscribing his behavior within certain bounds; but it is equally true that man makes the tradition. And so, we can repeat with deeper insight, "Man makes himself." [21]

Notes

1. In L. L. Bernard (ed.), *Fields and Methods of Sociology* (New York: Long and Smith, 1934), p. 328.

2. For example, compare Nels Anderson and E. C. Lindeman, *Urban Sociology* (New York: F. S. Crofts, 1930) and T. L. Smith and C. A. McMahon, *The Sociology of Urban Life* (New York: Dryden Press, 1941).

3. *American Journal of Sociology,* 44 (July 1938), pp. 1–25.

4. Reference here is to Chapters I, II in Young's volume (3rd ed.; Englewood Cliffs, New Jersey: Prentice-Hall, 1956).

5. Lewis Mumford, *The Culture of Cities* (New York: Harcourt, Brace, 1938), p. 7.

6. Cf. S. A. Queen and D. B. Carpenter, *The American City* (New York: McGraw-Hill, 1953), or W. C. Hallenbeck, *American Urban Communities* (New York: Harper, 1951).

7. For example, after a brave attempt at a global presentation, Professor Rose Hum Lee's *The City* (Philadelphia: J. B. Lippincott, 1954) settles down into familiar national grooves.

8. In this connection see the valuable paper by Gideon Sjoberg, "The Pre-Industrial City," *American Journal of Sociology,* 50 (March 1955), pp. 438–55.

9. Ralph Turner, Vol. I, *The Ancient Cities,* Vol. II, *The Classical Empires* (New York: McGraw-Hill, 1941).

10. The conceptual distinctions employed at this point are developed by the present writer in *La Tecnologia y el Orden Social,* Biblioteca de Ensayos Sociologicos, Instituto de Investigaciones Sociales, Universidad Nacional Mexico, 1956.

11. Turner, *op. cit.,* vol. I, p. 279.

12. The idea of a natural history of urbanism is not necessarily so pessimistic. Compare the following: Lewis Mumford, "The Natural History of Urbanization," 382–400, in W. L. Thomas, Jr., *Man's Role in Changing the Face of the Earth* (Chicago: University of Chicago Press, 1956) with J. H. Seward, "Cultural Evolution: A Trial Formulation of the Development of Early Civilizations," *American Anthropologist,* 51, (1949), pp. 1–27.

13. Reference here is made especially to his *Culture of Cities,* p. 235.

14. Cf. his *Technics and Civilization* (New York: Harcourt Brace, 1935).

15. A term suggested by Professor J. O. Hertzler, colleague of the present writer, in a conversation about this subject. "Urbanism" might thus refer to the intraurban society, "urbanicism" to the inter-urban society in which city is part of a system of things, interrelated, interacting, and functioning as a unity.

16. Mumford, *Culture of Cities,* p. 3.

17. Cf. *The Primitive World and Its Transformations* (Ithaca, New York: Cornell University Press, 1953).

18. *The Bias of Communication* (Toronto: University of Toronto Press, 1951).

19. George I. J. Dixon, Cultural Primitivism, unpublished doctoral dissertation in sociology, University of Nebraska, 1954.

20. On this particular theme, cf. the original and provocative work by Fred Cottrell, *Energy and Society, the Relation between Energy, Social Change, and Economic Development* (New York: McGraw-Hill, 1955).

21. *Man Makes Himself* (New York: Mentor edition, 1951), p. 188.

THE PREINDUSTRIAL CITY RECONSIDERED

Oliver C. Cox

Long before either economics or sociology assumed academic residence, practical men of affairs were cognizant of the role of manufacture and industry in developing and even modifying social systems. The mercantilists who set the stage for the industrial revolution in England were vividly conscious of the fact that manufacturing had all sorts of social and economic possibilities which were either nonexistent or relatively limited in communities dependent solely on direct production. Already it had become manifest that manufacturing and

---

Reprinted by permission of the author and publisher from *The Sociological Quarterly,* **5** (Spring, 1964), pp. 133–144.

density of population were not only associated but also desirable since the latter provided both the labor with which to carry on a teeming mercantile society and man power in times of war. The mercantilists were thus particularly interested in industrialization as it involved questions of growth in national wealth and power. As David Hume put it in 1752:

> Manufactures increase the power of the state only as they store up so much labor, and that of a kind, which the public may lay claim to without depriving any one of the necessaries of life. The more labor, therefore, is employ'd beyond mere necessaries, the more powerful is any state since the persons engag'd in that labor may easily be converted to public service. In a state without manufactures there may be the same number of hands, but there is not the same quantity of labor nor the same kind. All labor is there bestowed upon necessaries, which can admit of little or no abatement.[1]

An incidental objective of that group of nation builders was to explain what had already taken place in many localities on the continent: the simultaneous growth of commerce, industry, wealth, power and population. They were, however, never unmindful of what they considered the determining factor. Industry was clearly recognized as a dependent function of market expansion. Thus, to illustrate, in 1690, Sir William Petty, in his analysis of Dutch ascendancy, remarked typically: "I have shown . . . how foreign traffic must give them as much manufacture as they can manage themselves, and as for overplus, make the rest of the world but the workmen of their shops." [2] This conclusion, already generally accepted, was reached about seventy years before James Watt began to experiment with the steam engine.

It is possible, furthermore, to show that commerce or trade is a generic phenomenon characterized by distinct attributes in different cultural settings. Petty was not referring to "traffic" indiscriminately—many forms of which he had been aware of as "bad commerce"—but to the peculiar type of commercial relationships nurtured and institutionalized in the continental capitalist cities. The industrial revolution neither destroyed nor superseded the critical relationship between this commerce and industry; it intensified it.

Because of the advantages of industrialization, imperatively demonstrated especially in the great nations of the modern world, there seems to be a current tendency to conceive of it as something possessed of powers superior to those of the organized social system in which it had its genesis and currently operates—indeed, determinative of the social system itself.[3] It may be one thing, however, to realize that science and technology can flourish only in certain social systems and quite another to envisage them as creating peculiar social systems.

Since the period of the great depression, questions regarding industrialization—modernizing in the advanced countries and industrializing in the underdeveloped—have become increasingly urgent. This concern is presently so much a preoccupation in the United Nations that one would hardly be surprised if the motto of that assembly were restated as "peace through industrialization." Problems of economic growth now constitute the core of political economy, and sociology has entered the field through various avenues. In this critique we should like to consider entry by way of the "preindustrial city."

There seem to be, in recent literature, four principal approaches to the relevant sociology of industrialization: (a) Kingsley Davis correlates and finds a high, positive association between industrialization and urbanization in different countries and territories of the world. He derives an "index" of industrialization and upon this basis makes a demographic analysis of certain types of preindustrial countries, concluding finally that the urban milieu itself constitutes a stimulus toward economic development.[4] (b) Jean Comhaire and Werner J. Cahnman investigate the universal rise of cities emphasizing trends toward modern civilization. They observe that "the modern city viewed historically, and western civilization as we know it today, are two titles for the same thing." [5] Two types of society are here recognized: the one in which cities as independent social systems are either absent or ineffective, and the other in which cities serve as models for the larger society. (c) The present writer has sought to isolate the dominant, cultural elements of modern society, to determine their efficient origins, and to show how they function in the types of European cities which nurtured them.[6] (d) Professor Gideon Sjoberg distinguishes the modern city from "the preindustrial city" and is conscious of the value of this distinction "for anyone who hopes to understand current processes in societies now changing over from feudal to industrial modes of organization." [7] As just intimated, we are here concerned with an examination of the concept "preindustrial city" particularly as it appears in Sjoberg's analysis. Indeed, the concept preindustrial city has been justifiably associated with the extensive work of this author.[8]

Let us first consider the hypothesis. According to Professor Sjoberg there are three types of society: the folk or preliterate, the feudal or preindustrial-literate, and the industrial-urban society. Cities are found only in the feudal and the industrial-urban society.[9] The preindustrial city is thus defined as a feudal city: "a subsystem of the feudal society." [10] It has existed in different parts of the world—Europe, China, India, and elsewhere—but in all manifestations it may be characterized by "strikingly similar" social, ecological, economic, faimilial, class, political, religious, and educational "structures," which "diverge sharply from their counterparts in mature industrial cities." [11] The preindustrial city, furthermore, may be traced to its origins about 3500 B.C. in Mesopotamia, particularly at Ur, to the present day. Sjoberg suggests: "The dissolution before our very eyes of a city-type that has existed for fifty-five centuries or more is deserving of some attention." [12]

Since he defines the preindustrial city as a contrast conception,[13] it seems pertinent to observe the nature of his norm. By the very implications of the terms we should probably expect "the prime difference [between the preindustrial city and the modern industrial center to be] the absence in the former of *industrialism* which may be defined as that system of production in which inanimate sources of power are used to multiply human effort." [14] Accordingly, in the industrial city, a "subsystem of industrial society," steam, electricity, and so on supply power while the preindustrial city must depend upon that provided by human beings and animals.[15]

We should follow Professor Sjoberg's logic in reaching this conclusion. He reasons thus: "Inasmuch as preindustrial cities in numerous divergent cultural milieux display basic similarities in form, some variable other than cultural values

. . . must be operative. . . . Here technology—viz., the available *energy, tools,* and *know-how* connected with these—seems the most satisfactory explanatory variable." [16] Apparently, this comes close to saying: if it is not "cultural values," it must be technology; but not quite. Sjoberg asserts further: "Unquestionably, for cities to expand and diffuse, the level of technology had to be such as to insure the surplus of food and raw materials necessary to sustain non-agricultural specialists." [17]

The neo-Malthusian idea that food-producing technology had to develop first before cities could arise and grow seems to be a popular illusion taken as axiomatic even in textbooks on urban sociology.[18] There are certain crucial objections to this notion. A surplus may arise in response to increasing demand during a constant level of agricultural technology; the growth of cities may increase agricultural specialization and thus enhance efficiency; and improvement in distribution, which may involve quantity not quality of transportation and communication technology, can maximize the amount of food available. Indeed, it is possible for development of agricultural technology to run ahead of need; and this points to the possibility that the urban aggregation may be the cause of improved technology rather than vice-versa. In other words, an agricultural surplus for urban consumption may be derived indirectly from production in cities. Here again, then, is an instance to which correlation may not indicate causation.[19] We shall revert to this point below.

Professor Sjoberg says further: "To achieve this typology of societies [folk, feudal, and industrial], and consequently of cities, we take technology as the key independent variable; i.e., associated with varying levels of technology are distinctive types of social structure. Technology both requires and makes possible certain social forms." [20] And even still more consequential is the following: ". . . it seems clear that the transition from the preliterate to the feudal level . . . or from the latter to the industrial urban society is associated with certain crucial advances in the technological sphere." [21] No doubt this is a momentous discovery, and we should have been rewarded to have found a causal demonstration of it in Professor Sjoberg's comprehensive essay—the more so especially when we consider the universal scope, in time and place, of the conception.

The selected criterion of the "industrial city" is present-day United States; Sjoberg generalizes from social phenomena obtaining here. Such countries as Spain, Italy, France, Germany, and England will not do since there are in these too many "preindustrial" survivals; indeed, since the United States is still becoming industrialized, Professor Sjoberg explains that he had to "extrapolate for incomplete information." [22]

The "preindustrial city" is essentially an eclectic concept, a "constructed type" according to Sjoberg. Social phenomena are abstracted from a wide range of "disparate cultural settings" and identified as a type. As Professor Sjoberg points out, "although not all preindustrial cities demonstrate every structural pattern that we isolate, at least a few cities do." [23] But the few cities that do are not consistently specified. The apparent difficulty with this attempt to employ the constructed type, which Howard Becker and others elaborate, is its imprecision about concrete reality. The referent remains unstable.[24] Indeed, what the author is comparing is essentially not cities at all: "We . . . compare total systems—folk, feudal, and industrial societies." [25] In support of this procedure the following seems apposite:

> . . . recognition has been given to the theoretical distinctions between the city and a society. But empirically these fuse. . . . In practice the city is our starting point, but we have branched outward from it to encompass the total feudal order. This work is, in the end, a survey of the preindustrial civilized society with special emphasis upon the city. . . .[26]

Since, by assumption, "preindustrial civilized society" constitutes feudalism, the characteristics of the constructed type of the preindustrial city must needs be those of feudal society. The critical question here is not whether cities can be studied independently from society but whether the society of all "preindustrial cities" is feudal society.

The preindustrial city as presently conceived is a negative, not a positive construct. It is inevitably constituted by congeries of social phenomena not characteristic of contemporary metropolitan America but found to be operative inconsistently in a variety of other cultures. For this reason almost every parametric characterization of social life in the "preindustrial city" can be shown to be false for major urban areas of the world. Consider, in illustration, the following reasoning: ". . . although the Greek city was unique for its time, in its political structure it actually approximates the typical preindustrial city far more closely than it does the industrial-urban order." [27] Accordingly, a distinction from modern American society serves to identify Periclean Athens with ancient Peking, Benares, Constantinople, medieval Venice and seventeenth-century Amsterdam—not to mention the landed-estate culture of European feudalism.

One suspects that the criterial error may be seen to reside in Professor Sjoberg's assumption that all cities, at least all before the industrial revolution, were "subsystems" of feudal society. His problem thus became that of describing feudalism and partly illustrating these descriptions with a promiscuous selection of social phenomena from cities all over the world. Thus, to reiterate, his definition of feudalism includes, among other social systems, European cities of the Middle Ages, ancient Athens and Rome, and Brahmanic India. It seems necessary to call attention only to a few major distinctions. Brahmanic India was constituted by a system of villages, rigidly organized on the basis of hereditary occupational specialization, with no inherent cultural capabilities for social evolution; both ancient Athens and Rome were self-contained cities, i.e., with all major institutions, including especially their systems of power, locally resident—but, above all, they developed *citizenship,* a power structure quite incompatible with feudal society.[28] The medieval European city—Venice, Genoa, Florence, Lübeck, Antwerp, London—was not the product of feudalism. This point seems so important for an understanding of the rise of modern industrialism that we make it categorically. European feudalism created fortresses and manors, not cities of this kind. The guilds of the medieval city, defined by Sjoberg as a feudal institution, had their reasons for existence in the cities themselves, and they were undermined by the expansion of markets. There were no guilds among producers on the manor. As a corollary, it should be constantly recognized that modern, i.e., capitalistic, society did not and indeed could not have evolved directly from a feudal base.[29]

If Professor Sjoberg had appreciated the fact that the autonomous, medieval European city constituted a form of social organization distinct from feudalism, he probably would also have discerned that industrialism is not in itself a social system. In other words, industrialism and feudalism are not parallel concepts. The dichotomy industrial-preindustrial is thus a treacherous instrument for analysis of social systems. No one doubts the significance of science and technology as a dynamic force in social change. But the relationship is not a simple one. In capitalist society, industrialization seems to be principally a function of an abiding quest for efficiency, a basis of commercial competitiveness.

It was not by mere chance that early modern science became preoccupied with astronomy, and the industrial revolution with the building of cotton-spinning and weaving machinery. Neither is it inexplicable that the "revolution" should have occurred in England. In a socialist society, industrialism seems to have another function: that of achieving social goals. The point we should like to emphasize is that the role and effectiveness of science and technology tend to be determined by the social system. And, in fact, our contemporary, world-shaking debate is not about science and technology *per se* but about which social system can most successfully accommodate them.[30]

Most students who rely upon an industrial-preindustrial dichotomy in their analysis of social systems are really adopting a limited Marxian approach. They start at the same place, the industrial revolution in England; the cities of the Black Country tend to be of far more relevance than London; hence industrialism remains pivotal. Professor Sjoberg seems to be conscious of this because, in his formulations, he has occasion repeatedly to deny any affinity with Marx. And yet, consider this:

> The type of social structure required to develop and maintain a form of production utilizing inanimate sources of power is quite unlike that in the preindustrialized city. At the very least, extensive industrialization requires a rational, centralized, extra-community economic organization in which recruitment is based more upon universalism than particularism, a class system which stresses achievement rather than ascription, and a small and flexible kinship system, a system of mass education which emphasizes universalistic rather than particularistic criteria, and mass communication.[31]

Aside from questions concerning the meaning and date of appearance of these cultural traits found in Western society, the fact remains that they are presumed to have been generated by a peculiar "mode of production" in contrast to those generated by "inanimate sources of energy." [32] This hypothesis may accordingly be compared to Marx's formulation in the *Manifesto:* ". . . in every historical epoch, the prevailing mode of economic production and exchange, and the social organization necessarily following from it, form the basis upon which is built up, and from which alone can be explained, the political and intellectual history of that epoch." About four decades ago Alvin H. Hansen, in a critical analysis, referred to the approach as "the technological interpretation of history." [33] Many of Hansen's observations seem applicable to the present conceptualization of the preindustrial city.

Pertinent questions may arise. What, for example, caused "technological" production to become functional in the medieval city—Florence, Venice,

Lübeck? Why was it not similarly relied upon in earlier cities? What is the basis of its perpetuation? What were the societal conditions of the industrial revolution in England? In what sense is technology a sociological category? Valid answers to such queries may give us a better comprehension of the place of science and technology in social systems.[34]

A conception already alluded to, which seems close to the pith of Sjoberg's theory, is his observation that "the city, shaped as it is by the enfolding social-cultural system, whether preindustrial or industrial, must be taken as a *dependent* rather than independent variable." [35] Thus the assertion that "the urban community . . . is only a partial system [since] it cannot survive without the hinterland that supplies it with food and raw materials" [36] would appear to clinch the argument. It is, nevertheless, an exceedingly misleading deduction. The medieval, capitalist cities were not "closed communities," but they were essentially autonomous. They determined not only what the feudal hinterland would produce but also the production of distant lands. The cities thus gained control of far more food and raw materials than they needed for their own consumption. At length, the extractive industries of the world were made almost completely dependent upon the commercial disposition of cities. The medieval and modern city, in other words, compelled the farmer to become a dependent, specialized businessman, who produced almost as little for his own consumption as the dominant entrepreneurs of the city. Inevitably, food, in both variety and quantity, became most available in the great commercial centers, and farmers were economically powerless to withhold its flow.[37]

We are not asserting here that classification and characterization of cities should not be attempted or that such studies are not an urgent desideratum. The essential point is that the constructive typology under review seems too limited. Its significant variables deviate not merely in degree but also in kind. Some cities, like ancient Athens, Rome, and Constantinople, constituted in themselves a peculiar type of society. The autonomous medieval cities were another extremely important type of society, which became the true progenitor of the modern nation. From their very origin in the fifth century they were culturally antagonistic to feudalism; hence they can hardly be identified as dependent subsystems of feudalism. Moreover, we have no evidence to show that the medieval city was a direct descendent of earlier urban structures. The tribal aggregations or cities characteristic of very ancient times and still prevalent in some backward countries, the hierarchical community of castes constituting the Hindu village, the multitribal, multiethnic, or multiclan aggregations common in China and in Mohammedan countries are still other distinguishable types.

These latter communities were indeed subsystems of larger societies. However, the criteria of a constructed type must be of considerable generality if they are to encompass all such societies. The cities of modern nations, both capitalist and socialist, are also subsystems, but their role in this capacity can be fully understood only if it is seen in the light of the fact that the nation is a direct evolution of the autonomous medieval city.

In this discussion we have considered three basic fallacies in the postulation and analysis of "preindustrial cities": the generalization that all such cities are dependent subsystems of larger feudal societies, that technology is the "key" determinant of types of social systems, and that the industrial-preindustrial constructed types are valid heuristic devices. We make one further observation upon the latter point. The dichotomy, industrial-preindustrial, seems to have even greater potentialities for spurious deductions than some others well known to sociologists. The very term "preindustrial" may connote a logical stage of development; while the conception of industrialization in the United States as the norm of industrialized society tends to limit the attributes of that process to a peculiar social order. The preindustrial-city type lumps so many disparate societal systems that its value as an operational instrument seems nullified.

Notes

1. *Political Discourses* (Edinburgh, 1752), pp. 12–13, quoted in Oliver C. Cox, *Foundations of Capitalism* (New York, 1959), p. 376.

2. *Political Arithmetick* (London, 1690), pp. 20–21.

3. "The connection between the development of industrialism and nationalism," says Professor Talcott Parsons, "is well attested."—*The Social System* (Glencoe, Ill.: Free Press, 1951), p. 187. For an emphatic statement of a "theory of technological determination" see Leslie A. White, *The Evolution of Culture* (New York, 1959), pp. 3–32 *et passim*.

4. See particularly Kingsley Davis and Hilda Hertz Golden, "Urbanization and Development of Pre-Industrial Areas," *Economic Development and Cultural Change*, 3:6–26 (Oct., 1954), reprinted in P. K. Hatt and A. J. Reiss, Jr., *Cities and Society* (Glencoe, Ill.: Free Press, 1957), pp. 120–40. These authors define as pre-industrial all areas of the world in which more than 50 percent of occupied males engage in agriculture.—*Ibid.*, p. 122.

5. *How Cities Grew* (Madison, N. J., 1959), p. 6.

6. Cox, *Foundations of Capitalism*, pp. 25 ff.

7. *The Preindustrial City* (Glencoe, Ill., 1960), p. 333.

8. Two earlier articles, not superseded by the monograph cited are "The Preindustrial City," *American Journal of Sociology*, 60:438–45 (1955), and "Comparative Urban Sociology," in Robert K. Merton *et al.*, *Sociology Today* (New York, 1959), pp. 334–59.

9. *The Preindustrial City*, p. 7. The city is defined, "in contrast to a town or village, as having greater size, density, and heterogeneity and including a wide range of non-agricultural specialists, most significant of whom are the literati."—*Ibid.*, p. 11.

10. *Ibid.*, p. 11.

11. *Ibid.*, pp. 6 and 321.

12. *Ibid.*, pp. 335 and 27, 34.

13. He makes this explicit in saying: "The industrial urban center is the standard against which we contrast the preindustrial city; the succeeding chapters continually emphasize differences between these two types of communities."—*Ibid.*, p. 6.

14. Gideon Sjoberg, "The Preindustrial City," *American Journal of Sociology*, 60:439 (Mar., 1955). Italics mine.

15. *The Preindustrial City*, p. 8.

16. *Ibid.*, pp. 328–29.

17. *Ibid.*, p. 64. To the same effect: "The very emergence of cities is functionally related to the society's ability to produce a sizeable surplus . . ." (p. 329). Nor does the following seem sufficient: "Peasant farmers . . . rarely produce and relinquish a surplus willingly in feudal societies; thus tribute, taxation and the like must be exacted if cities are to gain the wherewithal to support their populations" (p. 68).

18. Although Lewis Mumford's orientation and purpose do not coincide with Sjoberg's, there seems to be a convergence of thought on this point. Mumford observes: "Ecologically speaking, the [medieval] city and countryside are a single unit. If one can do without the other, it is the country, not the city; the farmer not the burgher."—*The City in History* (New York, 1961), p. 338.

19. The idea is likely to be misleading in still another way. It seems to imply that cities will arise everywhere and grow almost unlimitedly if food becomes increasingly available. It should be said, however, that the earlier the urban aggregate, the greater was its tendency to depend upon the immediate hinterland for its food supply.

20. Sjoberg, *op. cit.*, p. 7.

21. *Ibid.*, p. 329.

22. *Ibid.*, pp. 342 and 335–36.

23. *Ibid.*, p. 21.

24. Cf. William J. Goode, "A Note on the Ideal Type," *American Sociological Review*, 12:473–75 (Aug., 1947); and Howard Becker, "Constructive Typology in the Social Sciences," in Harry E. Barnes, Howard Becker, and Frances B. Becker, *Contemporary Social Theory* (New York, 1940), pp. 17–46.

25. *The Preindustrial City*, p. 24.

26. *Ibid.*, p. 332.

27. *Ibid.*, p. 236. Again, in a similar observation: "Even though Athens and Rome and the large commercial centers of Europe prior to the industrial revolution displayed certain unique features, they fit the preindustrial quite well."—*American Journal of Sociology*, 60:444.

28. Max Weber, *The City*, trans. by D. Martindale and G. Neuwirth (Glencoe, Ill., 1958), pp. 83 ff.

29. On this vital subject Professor Sjoberg repeatedly confronts Henri Pirenne, but in each case his argument seems to be extremely weak. Consider in illustration the following: "Henri Pirenne, in *Medieval Cities* . . . and others have noted that European cities grew up in opposition to and were separate from the greater society. But this thesis has been overstated for Medieval Europe. Most preindustrial cities are integral parts of broader social structures."—Sjoberg, in *American Journal of Sociology*, 60:444, n. 15.

The eminent medievalist, Marc Bloch, confirms Pirenne in saying: ". . . the dominant characteristic of the town was that it was inhabited by a special type of human being. . . . With franchises won by violence or purchased with hard cash . . . the town which it was [the burgers'] ambition to build would be as it were a foreign body in feudal society. . . . It was there, in the commune, that the really revolutionary ferment was to be seen, with its violent hostility to a stratified society. . . . By substituting for the promise of obedience . . . the promise of mutual aid, [the burgesses] contributed to the social life of Europe a new element, profoundly alien to the feudal spirit, properly so called."—*Feudal Society* (Chicago, 1961), pp. 353–55.

30. If Professor Sjoberg had regarded modern science and technology as having their critical beginnings and continuous development in medieval cities—Venice, Bologna, Florence, Milan, Mainz, Nuremberg, Paris, Amsterdam—he probably would not have written the following: "Modern science . . . is practically non-existent in the non-industrial city. The emphasis is upon ethical and religious matters as one is concerned with adjusting to, not overcoming, the order of things. In contrast, industrial man is bent upon revising nature for his own purpose."—*The Preindustrial City*, p. 328.

31. *American Journal of Sociology*, 60:444. The similarity of this conclusion to Bert F. Hoselitz's analysis in his "Social Structure and Economic Growth" (*Economia Internazionale*, vol. 6, no. 3, Aug., 1953, pp. 52–72), a source admittedly influencing Sjoberg's thinking (see *Preindustrial City*, p. 23, note 20), seems manifest. Hoselitz's approach, however, appears to suffer from similar weaknesses. In his essay to derive a theory of social change relative to economic development he, in turn, relies directly upon Talcott Parsons' *Social System* for a well-known series of dichotomized social attributes, "pattern variables," assumed to be definitive of both advanced and underdeveloped countries: achievement—ascription, universalism—particularism, specificity—diffuseness, self-orientation *vs.* community orientation, neutrality—affectivity. Professor Hoselitz anticipates criticism of his use of these "value pattern variables" on grounds that they are "simply descriptive symbols." He thus strives to show—with questionable success, we think—that they are "part of a functionally related framework" (p. 61). Perhaps the besetting fault of this analysis is its failure to recognize that such attributes not only universalize too much but also centralize derived social phenomena.

32. Professor Sjoberg recognizes political power and values as significant but not determinative of type. Thus, "we make frequent reference to social power in accounting for the fluctuating fortunes of cities and the faith of technology and give due recognition to its role in producing organization in society. Nor do we ignore values. These, we have remarked in a number of contexts, account for certain divergencies from our constructed type . . ."—*The Preindustrial City*, p. 329.

33. Alvin H. Hansen, "The Technological Interpretation of History," *Quarterly Journal of Economics*. 36:72–83 (1921–22).

34. Cf. Oliver C. Cox, comments on William F. Ogburn, "Population, Private Ownership, Technology, and the Standard of Living," *American Journal of*

Sociology, 56:314–19 (Jan., 1951), *ibid.,* pp. 484 f.; and on Ogburn, "Technology and the Standard of Living in the United States," *ibid.,* 60:380–86 (Jan., 1955), *ibid.,* 61:51 f. (July, 1955), where some of these questions were raised.

35. *The Preindustrial City,* p. 15. See also "Comparative Urban Sociology," in Merton *et al., op. cit.,* p. 343.

36. *Ibid.,* p. 342.

37. This point does not refer to the role of agriculture in all social systems—in contemporary planned economies, for example.

THE WORLD'S GREAT CITIES: EVOLUTION OR DEVOLUTION?

Robert C. Cook

A major side-effect of the unprecedented speed-up in world population growth today is the ever-increasing concentration of people in cities the world over.

The rate of city growth will continue to vary in different areas of the world, decelerating in the older, industrial countries and accelerating in the agrarian, underdeveloped countries which hold two-thirds of the world's people.

Urbanization is a vastly different process in those countries than it was in the West where the Industrial Revolution generated the capital needed to build the economies which could provide for the growing populations. Jobs were plentiful in the industrial cities of the West, and this provided the "pull" for the countless millions who migrated, and still do, from country to city.

The situation is often the reverse in the underdeveloped countries today. There, the "push" is the gross overcrowding of the rural population living at or near the bare subsistence level. More often than not, the migrant goes to an even more precarious urban situation where he cannot find work readily and must spend his limited savings. From the socio-economic and humanitarian points of view, the trek to the cities in the underdeveloped countries will continue to be more of a curse than a blessing as it absorbs limited capital and generates tension.

Today, there are 61 cities with a million people or more in the world, compared with only ten in 1900.

Now, two people out of every ten live in cities of 20,000 or more population. If the present trend continues—and there is every indication that it will for some time—almost half the world's population will live in cities that size by 2000; and by 2050, nine people out of every ten.

The giant of all time, the New York-northeastern New Jersey metropolitan agglomeration, has a population of over 14.5 million, according to preliminary tabulations from the 1960 census. That is more than the combined population of Australia and New Zealand; and it is almost half the entire population of Mexico!

Reprinted by permission of the author and published from *Population Bulletin,* **16** (September, 1960), pp. 109–130.

New York's borough of Manhattan shows a 15 percent decline in population since the 1950 census. But with 1.7 million people Manhattan's population density is 75,900 per square mile.

On the other side of the world, Calcutta's population of 5.7 million is small in comparison. But projections based on current trends would give Calcutta a population of between 35 and 66 million by the year 2000! At Manhattan's density, Calcutta would sprawl over an area about as large as Rhode Island.

Obviously, such a projection is merely a *reductio ad absurdum.* The problems of food distribution and sanitation in the absence of very rapid economic development, are only two of many factors which would cause death rates to rise and check such multiplication of people long before standing-room-only develops.

Few people seem to understand that the pattern of tomorrow's city is being formed by today's rapid population growth. Will the city remain the traditional center of culture or will it degenerate into a socio-economic sinkhole for mankind?

Can the sprawling shantytowns which make up the cities of Asia, Africa and Latin America evolve into habitable places which provide adequate services so necessary to urban life?

Will the shabby, decaying, smog-ridden central cities of the industrial West be cleansed of the blight which has been accumulating since the Industrial Revolution began? Or, will the deteriorating central cities continue to sprawl out at an even faster rate, consuming untold acres of prime farm land with their insatiable appetite for space? Will these cities be able to win back the fleeing, more prosperous residents and the industries whose tax revenue is essential to their financial stability?

As man increasingly becomes a city-born and city-bred creature, the problems of city living and city organization will intensify in complexity and embrace the planet. Drift and improvisation cannot solve them. Dynamic global action is essential now if the cities of tomorrow are to have a true, not imagined, relationship to the needs and enduring values of the people who will live in them.

From the Beginning

Today's cities trace their origin to the villages of pre-history where a few hundred people lived and walked each day to their fields to produce the food necessary for survival. As animal domestication and the development of agriculture increased the efficiency of food production, those people who were no longer needed to tend the land became potters, spinners, weavers and other artisans.

The great cities of ancient time rose in India's rich alluvial Indus valley, in the lands adjacent to the Mediterranean, the Red Sea, and the Persian Gulf and in China. They were relatively small places covering a few square miles. Little is known about the size of the population of these ancient cities. Obviously, that was controlled by the agricultural economies which supported them, and the agricultural surpluses which made urban societies possible were never very large. Until about 1000 B.C., it is believed that no more than 1 or 2 percent of the world's population were city dwellers, and that these pre-historic metropolises did not exceed 100,000 people. Until very recently, urban communities have been dangerous places to live because, with primitive amenities, and no knowledge of the cause and control of disease, even low degrees of congestion invited epidemics. Brutally high death rates appear to have held life expectancy at birth to no more than about 20 years.

With the growth of population, the city grew in size. As its population pressed ever-more severely on the food supply, the city had to absorb more land. According to Harrison Brown, Professor of Geochemistry, California Institute of Technology, land seizure and the right to water were frequent causes of war; and many wars were started by "half-starved barbarians who cast envious eyes upon urban wealth and decided to attempt to take it for their own." Often they succeeded. Discussing the rise and fall of those early cities, Dr. Brown states:

> The populations of the ancient oriental empires were eventually limited by deaths resulting from starvation, disease, and war, and, to a lesser extent, by conscious control of conception, by abortion, and by infanticide. Sanitation measures were seldom taken, except in the homes of the higher classes. Famine surged over the ancient lands at frequent intervals. As the crowded conditions, the filth, and the food situation in the ancient cities worsened, contagious diseases, and with them high rates of infant mortality, prevailed.
>
> * * * *
>
> Thus increased mortality and, to a lesser extent, conscious family limitation continuously lowered the rate of population growth in the ancient oriental empires. But in the new regions where urban culture was surging upward, populations grew rapidly. The changes resulted in the destruction of old civilizations and the creation of new ones.

The fascinating history of the world's great cities cannot be told in limited space. Only the briefest discussion of the urbanization of Europe is possible here.

Many of the world's ancient cities were already in ruins by the time the Greco-Roman civilization (600 B.C. to 400 A.D.) arose and created the first great cities of the west. New civilizations in the Orient were also building proud and beautiful new cities, and many of these flourished along the great trade routes of Europe and Asia.

Athens and Rome were among the first great cities on the European continent. Rome, Alexandria and Byzantium (Constantinople, and now called Istanbul) became the giants of the period, with estimated peak populations of 350,000, 216,000 and 190,000, respectively. Some historians allege that Rome had over a million people at her zenith. Athens, Syracuse and Carthage had populations of 120,000 to 200,000.

During the early days of the Greek and Roman Empires, population growth remained in balance with the food supply. But the rapid growth of the cities soon put heavy pressure on the productive capacity of the land. Unfortunately, Greek civilization evolved in a region where only 20 percent of the land area could be cultivated, and this placed severe limits on food production. As the cities grew, their populations became increasingly dependent upon imports of grain from outlying districts and provinces. As the demand for food grew, hills and mountains were laid bare of their forests. Few of those areas have recovered from the exploitative land practices prevalent during the golden years of the Greek Empire.

The Roman Empire repeated this pattern but destruction extended over a vastly greater area. The insatiable appetite of the rapidly growing population denuded Italy's hills and mountains and made deserts of untold millions of acres along the Mediterranean. Again, as the population of the Italian peninsula grew rapidly, grain imports from adjacent regions and then from Africa became necessary to feed the multitudes. As the center of the empire continued to pile up population, the desperate need for food spurred Roman conquest. According to the historian, V. G. Simkovitch:

> Province after province was turned by Rome into a desert, for Rome's exactions naturally compelled greater exploitation of the conquered soil and its more rapid exhaustion. Province after province was conquered by Rome to feed the growing proletariat with its corn and enrich the prosperous with its loot. The only exception was Egypt, because of the overflow of the Nile . . . Latium, Campania, Sardinia, Sicily, Spain, Northern Africa, as Roman granaries, were successively reduced to exhaustion. Abandoned land in Latium and Campania turned into swamps, in Northern Africa into a desert. The forest-clad hills were denuded.

With the fall of the Roman Empire, Europe entered a period of population ebb which lasted from about 450 to 950 A.D. Italy, Gaul, Iberia, North Africa, Greece and Egypt were especially affected, and so were their cities. It has been estimated that Rome had about 350,000 people at the time of Augustus, 241,000 around 200 A.D., 172,600 about 350 A.D., 36,000–48,000 about 500 A.D., and only 30,000 in the 10th century. Cities of fairly considerable size had grown up elsewhere. Baghdad with an estimated population of 300,000 was the capital of the Caliphate Empire. Cordoba with 90,000, and Seville with 52,000 had risen in Moorish Spain. Constantinople with its 160,000 to 200,000 inhabitants was the pride of the Byzantine Empire.

Usually new cities of the period arose around an old Roman armed camp, at a crossing of a river, around a church, an abbey or a fortified chateau. Frequent wars made high places desirable locations for cities of the Middle Ages because they were easily defended. Many of these cities had two settlements, one on the heights and another nearby on a plain which provided water and fields for cultivation. A relatively small population lived within a walled area, and as population grew the walls were extended.

When Europe's population began to increase again during the 10th century, cities began to grow and the number of villages also increased. This period of growth came to an abrupt halt in 1348 when the bubonic plague swept across Europe. It has been estimated that 20 to 25 percent of the people died in two disastrous years, and that by 1400 this and other epidemics had reduced the continent's population to about 60 percent of the pre-plague level.

From the Renaissance to the Industrial Revolution, 1400–1800

Population grew slowly during the first part of the Renaissance and accelerated toward the end of the period. City population followed the general pattern. In Italy, the cradle of the Renaissance, the population of Florence shifted up and down while that of Venice and Rome about doubled.

Two of the giants of modern times, London and Paris, were testing their growth during this period. Estimates of the population of Paris by 1550 range from 130,000 to 500,000.

The impact of technology on population growth was even more abundantly demonstrated during the period 1600–1800. Technological advances in transportation gave great impetus to commerce and exploration. The people of northern Europe began the colonization of the New World, and this siphoned off some of the surplus population. Cities were established along the Atlantic coast of North America and many maritime cities of Europe grew rapidly. As the empty lands of America were filled up by the descendants of immigrants from Europe, the frontier pushed westward.

The vast breadbaskets of North America made food more plentiful in Europe. Prior to the American Revolution, Edmund Burke noted that England's annual import of grain from America exceeded a million pounds in value. The population of the North American continent grew at a rate of from 20 to 30 percent a decade after the initial settlement, but not all of this growth was due to natural increase. Immigration had been an important factor in the population growth of the United States from 1620 until World War I.

During the 17th and 18th centuries, the foundations were laid for many of the great European fortunes which later supplied the capital needed to spark the Industrial Revolution. In England, technological advances in mining, manufacturing and agriculture were setting the stage for that revolution which ushered in the most rapid population growth the world and many of its cities had ever known. The conversion of two million acres of waste land and forest to farming during the 18th century greatly increased agricultural productivity and the food surplus available for the urban population.

The discovery which possibly had a greater impact on population growth than any other was made by the British physician, Edward Jenner, whose vaccination against smallpox was introduced in 1792. This initial step in man's ability to defer death opened the way for controlling the diseases and epidemics which had flourished in villages and cities since the beginning of time. To Pasteur and an army of microbe and virus hunters who have followed Jenner goes the credit for making the city a relatively safe place in which to live.

The Industrial-Urban Revolution, 1800–1900

Throughout history, cities have often experienced rapid spurts of growth, but the tremendous growth potential they now display could not have developed without the techniques of modern medicine, public health and sanitation. These made cities safe havens for the rapidly increasing working class of the Industrial Revolution. In England, the death rate began to fall about 1730 and it continued a leisurely downward trend for more than two centuries. The slow pace of that decline allowed another important phenomenon to develop—a slow decline in the birth rate. This appears to have occurred first in France about the middle of the 17th century, in Ireland during the 1820's, in the United States after 1830 and in England during the 1870's.

TABLE 1. TOTAL WORLD POPULATION AND WORLD URBAN POPULATION: 1800–1950

Year	World population	Population (in millions) living in localities of: 20,000 to 100,000	100,000 and over	Total	Percent of world population living in localities of: 20,000 to 100,000	100,000 and over	Total
1800	906	6.1	15.6	21.7	0.7	1.7	2.4
1850	1,171	22.9	27.5	50.4	2.0	2.3	4.3
1900	1,608	59.3	88.6	147.9	3.7	5.5	9.2
1950	2,400	188.5	313.7	502.2	7.8	13.1	20.9

Source: United Nations, *Report on the World Social Situation,* New York, 1957, p. 114. (Based on data from Kingsley Davis and Hilda Hertz.)

In 1798, Thomas Robert Malthus, a 32-year-old curate who was astounded by the rabbit-like proliferation of the working people living in misery and squalor, published his famous critical analysis on the problem of poverty in England. He insisted that to effect a cure of the "unspeakable ills of society" it would be necessary to get to the root of the matter. As Malthus viewed the problem, "the poverty and misery arising from a too rapid increase of population had been distinctly seen, and the most violent remedies proposed, so long ago as the times of Plato and Aristotle." Malthus defined the problem in these terms: *How to provide for those who are in want in such a manner as to prevent a continual increase in their numbers and of the proportion which they bear to the whole society.*

Malthus was followed by a succession of "pamphleteers"—one was Francis Place, a working man himself—who denounced the congestion and miserable living conditions and urged the working people to have fewer children. Finally, in 1876, the right to discuss fertility control was established in the British Isles when the government lost the case of "Regina *vs* Charles Bradlaugh and Annie Besant." This decision established the right to distribute a pamphlet concerning birth control which had been widely circulated throughout England for 40 years and it opened the way to free dissemination of fertility control information.

Kingsley Davis, one of this country's leading students of urbanization, points to several factors which helped the cities of western Europe achieve a much higher degree of urbanization than the ancient cities:

> Yet it was precisely in western Europe, where cities and urbanization had reached a nadir during the Dark Ages, that the limitations that had characterized the ancient world were finally to be overcome. The cities of Mesopotamia, India, and Egypt, of Persia, Greece, and Rome, had all been tied to an economy that was primarily agricultural, where handicraft played at best a secondary role and where the city was still attempting to supplement its economic weakness with military strength, to command its sustenance rather than to buy it honestly. In western Europe, starting at the zero point, the development of cities not only reached the stage that the ancient world had achieved but kept going after that. It kept going on the basis of improvements in agriculture and transport, the opening of new lands and new trade routes,

and, above all, the rise in productive activity, first in highly organized handicraft and eventually in a revolutionary new form of production—the factory run by machinery and fossil fuel. The transformation thus achieved in the nineteenth century was the true urban revolution, for it meant not only the rise of a few scattered towns and cities but the appearance of genuine urbanization, in the sense that a substantial portion of the population lived in towns and cities.

England, the world's most highly urbanized country today, is the classical example of the processes of industrialization and urbanization because she led the world in both. By 1801, 26 percent of the population of England and Wales lived in cities of 5,000 or more; and 21 percent in cities of 10,000 or more. The United States did not reach this degree of urbanization until 1880 when 25 percent of the population lived in cities of 5,000 or more. In contrast, only about 20 percent of India's population live in cities of that size today.

By 1861, 55 percent of the total population of England lived in urban areas; and by 1891, 72 percent, with only 1.3 percent of the population living in urban districts smaller than 3,000 population. Until 1861, the rural population suffered a relative decline in numbers as cities grew more rapidly. The numerical peak of the rural population, 9.1 million, was reached in 1861. It declined 11 percent, to 8.1 million by 1891.

London, a mud flat on the banks of the Thames when Caesar arrived, grew from 864,800 to 4,232,000 between 1801 and 1891—an increase of almost 400 percent. In 1891, Greater London with 5.6 million people, three fourths of whom lived in the city proper and the remainder in the "outer-ring," had the distinction of being the world's largest city. It covered an area of 690 square miles and included every parish of which any part was within 12 miles of Charing Cross. Today, it has an area of 722 square miles, and includes the Administrative County of London (London AC) also Middlesex County, and parts of Surrey, Hertfordshire, Essex and Kent Counties. The population of Greater London is slightly over 8.2 million. London AC which includes the City of London and 28 metropolitan boroughs is identical with the 1891 area. It comprises 117 square miles and has a population of 3.2 million that represents a 28 percent decline from its 1901 peak.

Between 1811 and 1891, England's large cities with 100,000 population increased from 1.2 million to more than 9.2 million. Although London absorbed a lesser share of this growth, 14.6 percent of Britain's population lived in the capital city of 1891 and 17.3 percent lived in the other large cities. In terms of the aggregate urban population, 44 percent resided in London and the 23 large cities.

USA during the 1800's

The first census was taken in 1790, soon after the Republic was born. It reported a population of 3,929,214. Only 5 percent lived in the 24 "urban" places of 2,500 population or more. Obviously, the rural-urban distinction was not clear-cut, and most of the people lived under essentially rural conditions. The largest cities were port cities: Philadelphia, New York, Boston, Charleston and Baltimore.

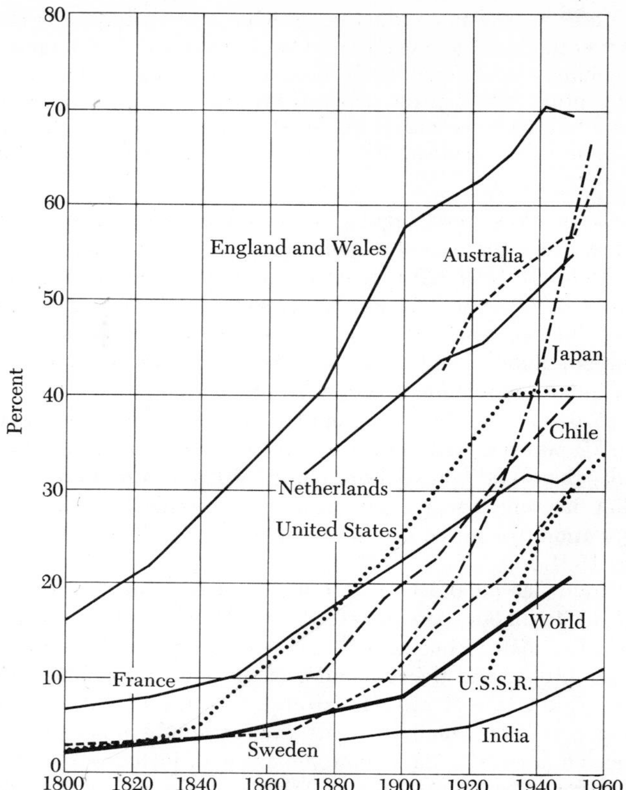

FIG. 1. THE GROWTH OF URBAN POPULATION SINCE 1800

Here is shown the percent of the total population of various countries living in localities of 20,000 or more. (The unit is 25 or more for the United States and Sweden.) For the world as a whole the proportion of dwellers in medium-size and large cities has quadrupled, from under 5 percent to over 20 percent. In the United States the proportion has increased tenfold as the nation has shifted from predominantly rural to one of the most highly urbanized countries. (Data from United Nations *Report on the World Social Situation* and other sources.)

According to Conrad and Irene B. Taeuber who are leading authorities on the growth of population in the United States:

> The clustering of settlers in small compact groupings began early, but the leading places of the colonial period were small. Boston, the largest place in the American colonies, had about 4,500 inhabitants in 1680. Ten years later the number had climbed to 7,000, but it required nearly 50 years to double this number. A decline of some 1,500 persons in the 10 years after 1740 is attributed to smallpox and war. Before recovery to the 1740 figure had occurred, the Revolutionary War had begun, and with it came a further reduction. The estimates for 1780 place Boston's numbers at only 10,000. After

that war, the city recovered rapidly, and by the time of the first census in 1790, its total population was reported as 18,000. But by then both Philadelphia and New York had overtaken Boston, with Philadelphia in the lead. In 1790, the leading cities were Philadelphia, New York, Boston, Charleston (South Carolina), and Baltimore.

As in the Old World, urban growth in the United States was stimulated by the rapid rate of population growth and the accelerating pace of technology. The abundance of fertile land could sustain an ever-growing urban population. Land was easy to own. People married early, had children early and had many of them.

The port cities were the first to grow, then as traffic on rivers and canals pushed industrialization beyond the coastal areas, new cities began to rise. After 1840, the railroads became the most important single factor in the formation of new cities and their growth.

Every decade since the first census in 1790, with the exception of that of 1870, urban population grew faster than rural. The decade of 1840 recorded the most rapid urban growth when the population in urban places almost doubled. But the urban increase was not numerically larger than the rural until the Civil War. Since 1860, with the single exception of the 1870's, every decade has shown greater urban than rural numerical growth. From 1880 until 1940, urban growth has accounted for from 60 to 90 percent of total growth. Between 1940 and 1950, United States population increased by 19 million, rural population declined 3 million while urban population grew by 22 million!

By 1900, the nation's population had grown to nearly 76 million. Almost 40 percent lived in urban areas—ten times as many people as in 1800. The number of urban areas with 2,500 population or more had increased to 1,737 by 1900. There were 38 places of 100,000 or more in the United States and, collectively, they claimed 19 percent of the country's population.

The first great city of over 100,000, New York, reached that mark in 1820. In 1790, New York City had only 33,131 people. By 1960, it had over 7.7 million, and that represents a 23,172 percent increase in 170 years.

The total population of the five largest cities has grown from 7.6 million in 1900 to 17.3 million in 1960. Now, one out of every ten United States citizens lives in these five cities.

While urban agglomeration and the growth of suburbs were well advanced by 1900, the nation had experienced nothing comparable to the rapid urban growth which was to take place during the next 60 years. By 1900, there were already 50 urban areas which would have qualified as "principal standard metropolitan areas" under the 1950 census definition, i.e., having a population of 100,000 or over. These contained 24 million people, almost one third of the total U. S. population.

World-Wide Urbanization, 1900–1960

World population is growing at an unprecedented rate today. The world still is far from a city world, even though it has been moving in that direction at an ever-accelerating rate since 1800. However, urbanization will continue to spread

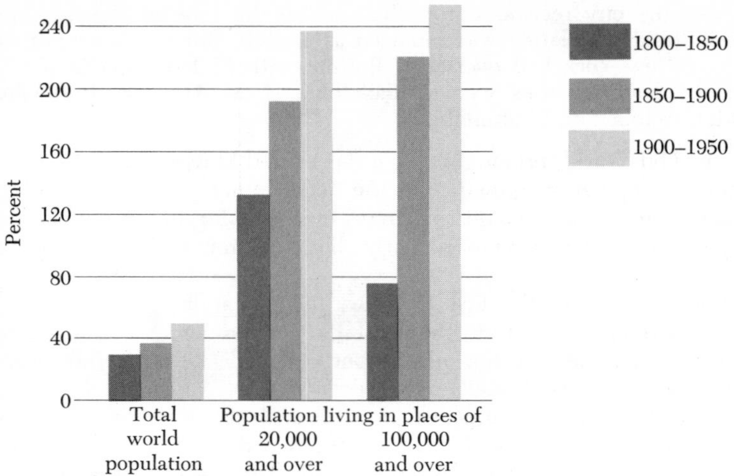

FIG. 2. THE INCREASE IN WORLD AND URBAN POPULATION

This graph shows the percentage increase in the total population of the world and of the population living in medium-size and large cities since the early part of the Industrial Revolution. During this time, world population increased at a rate unprecedented in previous history, but the movement into cities was far more rapid. In these explosive growing urban areas will be found some of the most serious political, social and economic problems in the next fifty years.

for some time to come as the underdeveloped areas strive for economic development.

Today, over 20 percent of the world's people, or more than 500 million, live in urban areas of 20,000 or more, compared with only about 2 percent in 1800. Over three fifths of today's urbanites live in large cities of 100,000 or more, and they represent 13 percent of total world population.

In 1900, there were ten cities with one million or more population in the world: five in Europe, three in North America and only one in Asia and in Russia. In 1955, there were 61 cities of that size. Of the 28 in Asia, nine were in China and six in India. Europe had 16 cities of a million or more and the United States had five.

Urban growth rates reached their peak in Europe and America during the latter part of the 19th century and tapered off after that. They have been most rapid in Asia and Africa during the first half of the 20th century. The United Nations *Report on the World Social Situation,* published in 1957, carries a detailed discussion of world urbanization which includes chapters on "Social Problems of Urbanization in Economically Underdeveloped Areas," "Urbanization in Africa South of the Sahara" and "Urbanization in Latin America." The Report utilizes the research of many leading students of urbanization, and its tables and graphs summarize historical and present growth trends. This issue of the *Bulletin* draws heavily on that important document.

TABLE 2. POPULATION IN LARGE CITIES (100,000 AND OVER) BY MAJOR CONTINENTAL REGIONS

	Population (in millions) in large cities				As percent of total population			
Area	1800	1850	1900	1950	1800	1850	1900	1950
World	15.6	27.5	88.6	313.7	1.7	2.3	5.5	13.1
Asia	9.8	12.2	19.4	105.6	1.6	1.7	2.1	7.5
Europe *	5.4	13.2	48.0	118.2	2.9	4.9	11.9	19.9
Africa	0.30	0.25	1.4	10.2	0.3	0.2	1.1	5.2
America	0.13	1.8	18.6	74.6	0.4	3.0	12.8	22.6
Oceania	—	—	1.3	5.1	—	—	21.7	39.2

* Including USSR.
Source: United Nations, *Report on the World Social Situation,* New York, 1957, p. 114. (Based on data from Kingsley Davis and Hilda Hertz.)

The speed-up in population growth in the economically underdeveloped areas of the world is accompanied by the traditional acceleration in the growth of cities in those areas. Discussing present and future trends, the Report states:

> A major factor in the present and the anticipated future acceleration is the sudden spurt of urban growth in economically under-developed countries. Between 1900 and 1950, the population living in cities of 100,000 or more in Asia mounted from an estimated 19.4 million to 105.6 million (a gain of 444 percent), and in Africa from 1.4 million to 10.2 million (a gain of 629 percent).
>
> . . . the large-city population of Asia and Africa has increased much more rapidly during the twentieth century than it did during the nineteenth century while in Europe and America, urban growth reached its peak in the latter part of the nineteenth century and slowed down thereafter. These shifting rates of growth have meant that Asia, which contained nearly two-thirds of the world's population in large cities in 1800, had less than a fourth by 1900; but then the trend started to reverse, and by 1950 Asia had one-third of the world's large-city population.

The Report compares the differences between the present trend of urban growth and urbanization in Asia and Africa with the trends in Europe during the first half of this century:

> In spite of rapid urban growth, the increase in degree of urbanization in Asia and Africa still did not equal the increase in Europe during 1900–1950. The reason for this paradox lies in the distinction . . . between urban growth and urbanization. While the population of Asia living in cities of 100,000 or more increased prodigiously from 19.4 million in 1900 to 105.6 million in 1950, the percentage of the total population living in such cities increased only from 2.1 per cent to 7.5 percent; in other words, there was only a 5.4 percent shift in the structure of the total population, while in Europe there was an 8 percent shift in the same period. Because the urban population still represents only a small proportion of the total population in Asia (and other less developed regions), a small change in the degree of urbanization will produce a large

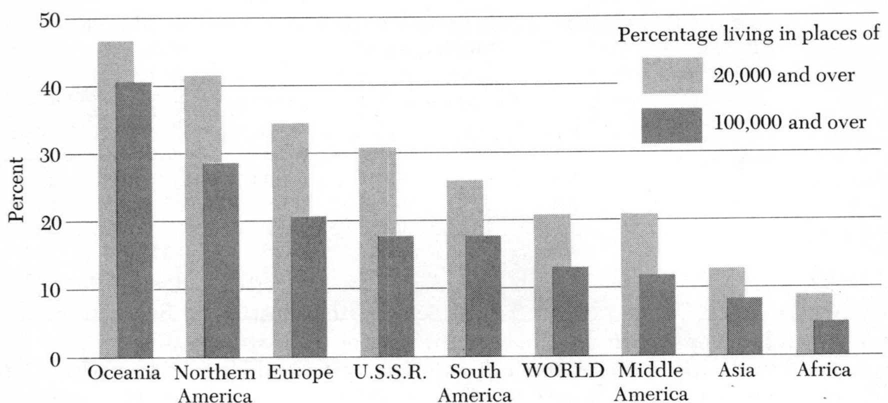

FIG. 3. PERCENTAGE OF POPULATION LIVING IN BIG CITIES

The trek to the city has gone on for centuries. Yet today, even with the enormous increase in urban population in recent decades, man remains predominantly a country dweller. If present trends continue for a century, he will become predominantly a city dweller.

amount of urban growth; or conversely stated, a large amount of urban growth is required to make a significant impact upon the population structure.

In the majority of the less developed countries, the rural population has continued to grow along with the urban population, although at a slower pace, but in many of the developed countries the absolute size of the rural population has remained constant or even declined in recent decades, so that the national population increase has been absorbed by the already heavy urban population.

Noting that there are important differences in the levels and trends of urbanization among the industrially more advanced countries and among the less developed countries, the Report states:

. . . Several of the economically less-developed countries, particularly in Latin America, have higher levels of urbanization—as measured by this particular criterion—than certain European countries.

. . . Some of the more urbanized and industrialized countries experienced a marked slowing-down of their urbanization rate during the period between 1930 and 1950 . . . France, the United States and (between 1940 and 1950) Japan; England and Wales actually experienced a slight drop between 1941 and 1951. Such a slowing-down or regression may be due to several possible factors: the reaching or approaching of a natural limit of urbanization, depending upon the economy of the country; the effects of the depression of the 1930's and of the Second World War; a shift from city growth to suburban growth—with the improvement of transportation and the overcrowding of cities, suburban localities are growing much more rapidly than cities proper in a number of countries (the United States is an outstanding example). The relative weight of these different factors is not known.

Other countries have shown a remarkable increase in degree of urbanization since 1930. This includes Puerto Rico and the USSR. In the latter country, between 1926 and 1955, while the total population increased only 34 percent, the population in cities of 100,000 or more increased more than four times.

. . . Ceylon on the other hand, is remaining relatively stable at a low level of urbanization.

Differences in the Pattern of Urbanization

In 1950, the world's major regions of industrial urban settlement were Australasia, Northwestern Europe, Northern America, Northeast Asia and Southern South America. These areas included about 25 percent of total world population, but 52 percent living in cities of 100,000 or more. By major world areas, Africa was the least urbanized, with only 9 percent of the population in cities of 20,000 or more. Australasia was the most heavily urbanized, with 47 percent in cities of that size.

During the past 25 years, the two largest countries of the communist world, USSR and China, have experienced very rapid urbanization. In the USSR in 1959, 48 percent of the total population was living in cities, compared with only 32 percent in 1939. In 20 years, the urban population grew by almost 40 million, an increase of two thirds. In 1959, 23 percent of the total population and almost 50 percent of the urban population lived in cities of 100,000 or more. Since 1939, many new cities have risen in the USSR. The seven largest are: Kaliningrad, 202,000; Angarsk, 134,000; Klaypeda, 89,000; Yuzhno-Sakhalinsk, 86,000; Volzhskiy, 67,000; Vorkuta, 65,000; Oktyabrskiy, 65,000.

It has been estimated that 20 million Chinese migrated from rural to urban areas between 1949 and 1956. This almost equals the total population of the three Benelux countries and "undoubtedly constitutes one of history's largest population shifts in so short a time . . ." China's inland cities have experienced fantastic growth. Estimates indicate that in the western provinces alone, Lanchow grew from 200,000 in 1950 to 680,000 in 1956; Paotow from 90,000 in 1949 to 430,000 in 1957; Kalgan from 270,000 in 1949 to over 630,000 in 1958; Sian from less than one-half million in 1949 to 1,050,000 in 1957.

Furthermore, there is a heavy concentration of China's urban population in her large cities. In 1953, 103 cities of 100,000 or more accounted for 49 million people, or 63 percent of the total urban population. However, only 13 percent of the total population lived in cities. In contrast, about 46 percent of the United States urban population lived in cities of 100,000 or more in 1950, and 64 percent of our total population lived in urban localities.

The growth rate of the urban population of the USSR between 1950 and 1959 was 4 percent per annum. In China between 1949 and 1956 the urban growth rate appears to have been at the rate of 6.5 percent per annum.

Within countries, there are great variations in extent and rate of urbanization. For example, in 1950, the northeastern part of the United States had one quarter of the total population and one third of its urban population. Within this region, Vermont has the lowest degree of urbanization (36 percent), while New Jersey had the highest (87 percent).

TABLE 3. ESTIMATED POPULATION OF WORLD'S 20 GREATEST METROPOLITAN AGGLOMERATIONS

Metropolitan Area	Year	Population (in thousands)	Principal City	Year	Population (in thousands)
New York—Northeastern New Jersey	1960 *	14,577	New York City	1960 *	7,710
Tokyo—Yokohama	1955	11,349	Tokyo	1955	6,969
London	1956	10,491	London	1956	3,273
Moscow	1956	7,300	Moscow	1959	5,032
Paris	1954	6,737	Paris	1954	2,850
Osaka—Kobe	1955	6,405	Osaka	1955	2,547
Shanghai	1953	—	Shanghai	1953	6,204
Chicago—Northwestern Indiana	1960 *	6,726	Chicago	1960 *	3,493
Buenos Aires	1955	5,750	Buenos Aires	1955	3,575
Calcutta	1955	5,700	Calcutta	1955	2,750
Los Angeles—Long Beach	1960 *	6,690	Los Angeles	1960 *	2,448
Essen—Dortmund—Duisburg (Inner Ruhr)	1955	5,353	Essen	1955	691
Bombay	1955	4,400	Bombay	1955	3,600
East & West Berlin	1955	4,245	East Berlin	1955	1,140
			West Berlin	1955	2,195
Philadelphia—New Jersey	1960 *	4,289	Philadelphia	1960 *	1,960
Mexico City	1955	3,900	Mexico City	1955	2,800
Rio de Janeiro	1955	3,750	Rio de Janeiro	1955	2,900
Detroit	1960 *	3,761	Detroit	1960 *	1,672
Leningrad	1955	3,500	Leningrad	1959 †	2,888
Sao Paulo	1955	3,300	Sao Paulo	1955	2,600

Source: International Urban Research, *The World's Metropolitan Areas,* Berkeley, University of California Press, 1959, unless otherwise indicated.
* U. S. Bureau of the Census; 1960 data are preliminary.
† USSR All-Union Population Census of 1959.

In some regions of the world, a single large city—usually the capital city—contains a high proportion of a nation's total population and its urban population. In many countries, well over 50 percent of all the urban population is concentrated in the capital city. This is especially true of several Latin American countries, and the trend there was discussed in an earlier *Population Bulletin,* August 1958:

> The unique feature in Latin America's urbanization is the high concentration of people in relatively few metropolitan areas, usually the national capitals. Except in Brazil and Colombia, the largest city has more inhabitants than all the other cities of 100,000 and more combined. In 13 of the 20 countries, at least 10 percent of the people live in the largest city or metropolitan area, usually the capital city. In six of these countries the largest city contains one-fifth or more of the national population: 33 percent in Uruguay, 29 percent in Argentina, 23 percent in Chile and Panama and 21 percent in Cuba and Costa Rica. One out of six Venezuelans lives in Caracas.
>
> If 20 percent of the United States' population lived in the capital city, Washington, D. C. would have 34 million people!

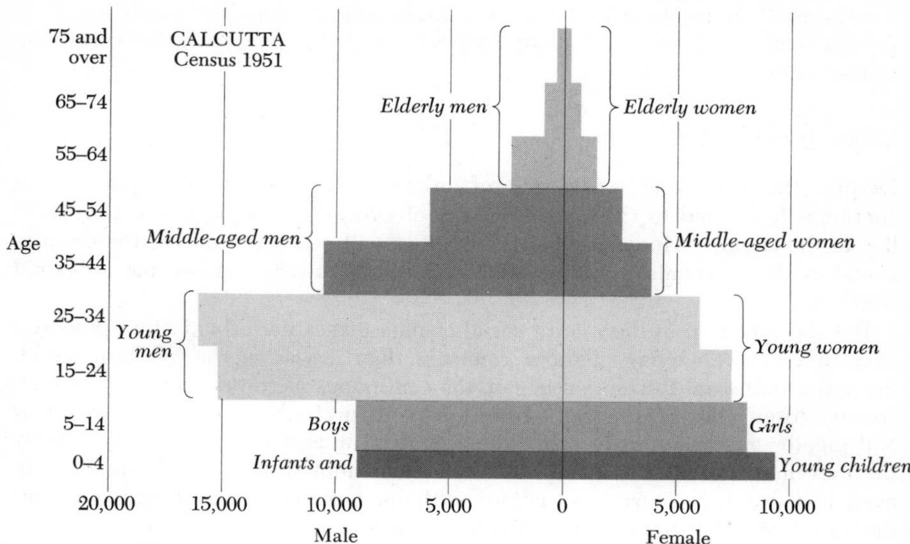

FIG. 4. AGE-SEX DISTRIBUTION OF THE POPULATION OF CALCUTTA

This graph from the 1951 census of India shows the enormous preponderance of males between 20 and 40 in a great Asian city. The excess of males is found in all ages except among those under five and 75 and over. Multitudes of men in the prime of life, separated from their families and living under primitive conditions, pose a most serious problem of urban adjustment in the underdeveloped countries.

In 1955, the world had 1,107 metropolitan areas of 100,000 or more. Asia contained almost one third of these or 341 and Europe over one fourth or 279. Northern America had 202, Latin America 78 and Oceania only 11. The nations with the largest number were the United States, 189; USSR, 148; and China, 103. Of the world's 108 metropolitan areas with one million or more, 34 were in Europe, excluding USSR, 32 were in Asia, and 26 were in North America.

The four largest metropolitan areas in the world have a total population of almost 44 million people. The Tokyo-Yokohama urban agglomeration with 11.3 million people in 1955 (almost 7 million of them in Tokyo) by now may be almost as large as the New York-New Jersey metropolitan area (over 14 million people in 1960). London's metropolitan area had 10.5 million people in 1956, 3.2 million of them in London proper. Suburbia has not reached the USSR, for in 1955, Moscow's metropolitan area, although the fourth largest in the world, was considerably smaller than the three other giants. It had 7.3 million people; and slightly over 5 million of them lived in Moscow itself.

New York City's five boroughs have a population of 7.7 million. The borough of Manhattan with 1.7 million in 1960 records a decline of 15 percent from the 1950 census. Its population density is 75,900 people per square mile!

Japan, with 92 million people and a land area about the size of Montana, is one of the most highly urbanized nations. She has 64 cities of 100,000 population or more, and their combined total is over 21.3 million. That is about a fourth of Japan's total population, and about 7 percent of all the people in the world who reside in cities of that size.

Contrasts in City Life

Despite the ever-accelerating rate of urbanization since 1800, modern man continues to be tied to the land. Four out of every five people in the world still live in the country. However, the trek to cities will accelerate during the decades ahead as the economically underdeveloped countries strive to become industrial societies.

But the speed-up in the rate of social change makes the urbanization process a very different one today in those countries than it was in the Western world. Since the Industrial Revolution began, the continuous migration in the West from country to city has been a flight from low-paid rural jobs to more lucrative jobs and greater opportunities in urban areas. But in underdeveloped countries today the movement to cities is more of a shift from unproductive rural situations to even less productive urban situations with no income gain and with grievous drain on limited savings due to higher living costs.

Because there is such a vast gulf between life in the traditional village and life in a large city, the rural-urban transition can be a painful experience. More often than not, the migrant ends up in a flimsy shantytown shelter, with no means of transportation and no job. Thus, in this pattern of urbanization, rural poverty is transferred to the cities where it becomes more concentrated and conspicuous. Observing that "the overflow of rural distress into urban districts is an outstanding characteristic of economically underdeveloped countries today," the United Nations Report states:

> The rapidly growing cities of the less developed regions of the world generally have several districts or zones which are imperfectly integrated: (1) A modern commercial, administrative, and upper-class residential centre; (2) An "old city" of narrow streets and densely occupied buildings; (3) A zone of huts or shacks, within or without the city limits proper, lacking most urban features except density of settlement and urban types of employment among the residents.
>
> This pattern has many variations. In some cases, particularly in Asia and North Africa, the modern city is completely separate from the old, and the latter has retained its traditional artisan industries, commercial activities (e.g. bazaars) and social organization, often being divided into sharply defined quarters along ethnic or religious lines. A few of the old cities (e.g. Damascus) have grown to considerable size with only a minor admixture of modern elements. In other cases, particularly in Latin America, the modern city and the old are intermingled, with the recent expansion of the former sometimes almost obliterating the latter, or reducing it to a zone of deteriorating tenement houses. In most of Africa south of the Sahara, and in various industrial, mining, and oil-producing centres in other regions, the old city has never existed.
>
> The zone of huts or shacks is usually on the periphery of the city. In some cases it is made up of coherent villages maintaining traditional values and social controls similar to those of the rural villages; more frequently however,

TABLE 4. LEVELS OF URBANIZATION

Country	Year	Percent of Population in Localities of 20,000 and Over
Europe, Northern America and Oceania		
England and Wales	1951	69
Australia	1958	64
Netherlands	1950	56
Germany (West)	1950	45
United States	1950	43
Belgium	1950	42
Denmark	1955	42
Italy	1951	41
Austria	1951	40
Hungary	1954	36
USSR	1959	36
Sweden	1950	35
Canada	1951	35
France	1954	33
Switzerland	1950	31
Finland	1950	24
Czechoslovakia	1947	21
Poland	1946	18
Yugoslavia	1948	13
Africa, Asia and Latin America		
Japan	1955	66
Argentina	1947	48
Israel	1950	46
Chile	1952	41
Uruguay	1950	36
Cuba	1953	36
Venezuela	1950	31
Egypt	1947	29
Mexico	1950	24
Iran	1950	21
Brazil	1950	20
Ecuador	1950	18
Turkey	1950	15
India	1951	12
Guatemala	1950	11
Ceylon	1953	10
Pakistan	1951	8
Haiti	1950	5
Afghanistan	1951	4

Sources: United Nations and U. S. Bureau of the Census.

this zone consists largely of amorphous mushrooming shantytowns, lacking any formal administration or any apparent informal social organization. Such shantytowns may be outside the administrative boundary of the city, so that no authority is responsible for providing urban services and enforcing housing regulations; even when the shantytown is within the city limits, however, the municipal authorities may pay little attention to its needs, particularly if, as is often true, the residents are "squatters" with no legal right to the land on which they build their shacks.

The pattern of urban growth is also complicated by the location of factories, usually around the periphery of the cities; their workers may come from neighbouring shantytowns or from more substantial workers' housing built by the employers or the state.

The Report states that the limited evidence available indicates that the housing situation in many cities, particularly in Asia, has deteriorated in recent years "since new building has not kept up with the natural increase in urban population, let alone the flood of migrants." The shantytown sprawl creates miserable living conditions:

> Under present conditions, the great majority of the urban poor are housed either in the older parts of the cities or in the peripheral villages and shantytowns. Except for housing built by employers for their own workers, there has been very little private construction with rents of purchase prices within the means of even the better-paid workers. Public low-cost housing and "aided self-help" housing, while increasingly important have in most cities thus far reached only a limited part of the low-income groups.
>
> Whether migrants to the cities move into the older tenement slums or into peripheral shantytowns depends on various factors. . . . Peripheral shantytowns spring up on land that is not being used for one reason or another. The occupant may simply set up a hut as a squatter, may pay a small rent to the owner of the land or, in the case of some better organized groups of workers, may obtain recognition from the Government of his right of occupancy. The land is often unused because it is undesirable or unsuitable for permanent buildings. It may consist of swamps (as in certain districts of Bangkok), steep hillsides (as in the favelas of Rio de Janeiro), low ground subject to flooding (as in the outskirts of Baghdad), or refuse dumps. Waste areas of these types may be found near the center of the city as well as on the outskirts. In other cases, the land is too arid for cultivation and outside the scope of the city water system. Many shantytowns also occupy land that is held vacant by urban investors in anticipation of future city growth, so that the occupants face eventual eviction; these include shacks on scattered vacant lots in the inner parts of the cities.
>
> The quality of the dwellings in the peripheral areas varies with the occupants' incomes, security of tenure, and standards of housing (the last usually derived from rural village housing). There may be a progressive change in the character of the improvised housing as the migrant stays longer in the urban area. The best of the peripheral settlements can sometimes be raised to acceptable standards by methods of aided self-help—provision of some building materials, tools and advice—plus enforcement of minimum sanitary and occupancy regulations, provision of safe water supplies, sewerage, electricity and paved streets. The lack of any community identification, however, in dwelling areas which the occupants themselves may regard as temporary and makeshift, as well as the lack of any formal or informal types of social organization, may render difficult group action for local improvement.
>
> The occupant-built peripheral zones are able to develop more freely in the cities of sparsely peopled countries in Africa and Latin America, where desert or other uninhabited land is often found at the city limits. In densely popu-

lated parts of Asia, the sudden massive movement of population to the cities, particularly the waves of refugees, has often forced the creation of shantytowns, but as a rule, the growth of peripheral shantytowns is limited in such places by the fact that land is intensively cultivated up to the edge of the city and thus too valuable for occupation by migrants. This difficulty has not prevented rapid city growth, but it has resulted in the most extreme overcrowding, both in the older parts of the cities and in the improvised slums that have sprung up on the few available pieces of vacant land—river banks, swamps, even the city streets; many also live on boats in rivers, canals and ports. It is well known that thousands of working class individuals and families in Indian cities have no shelter at all, sleeping in the streets. In the tenements of some Asian cities, families that occupy a single room may subdivide it by horizontal and vertical partitions and sublet the resulting windowless cubicles to other families. Under these conditions of extreme competition for housing, rents naturally become exhorbitant in relation to incomes.

Such overcrowding also contributes to the unstable character of urban labour in Asia. The man who migrates to the city looking for wage labour is not tempted to bring his family from his home village if they will have to sleep in the street, although he might be contented with an improvised shack. The single worker may crowd in with a family of relatives or fellow-villagers, sleep in an alley, or even sleep in the premises of a sweat shop, until he has earned enough to return home.

Life in Megalopolis—USA

Problems of urbanization are not confined to the economically underdeveloped regions of the world. As people continue to pile up in cities in the already heavily urbanized Western countries, pressures and tensions will cause unsolved social problems to grow worse and will create many new problems.

Today, population is growing very rapidly in the United States. The greatest part of this growth is, and will continue to be for some time to come, in the

TABLE 5. POPULATION OF THE TEN LARGEST CITIES IN THE U. S., 1900 and 1960

1900 City	Population	1960 City	Population
1. New York *	3,437,202	1. New York *	7,710,346
2. Chicago *	1,698,575	2. Chicago *	3,492,945
3. Philadelphia *	1,293,697	3. Los Angeles	2,448,018
4. St. Louis *	575,238	4. Philadelphia *	1,959,966
5. Boston	560,892	5. Detroit	1,672,574
6. Baltimore *	508,957	6. Houston	932,680
7. Cleveland *	381,768	7. Baltimore *	921,363
8. Buffalo	352,387	8. Cleveland *	869,867
9. San Francisco	342,782	9. Washington, D. C.	746,958
10. Cincinnati	325,902	10. St. Louis *	740,424
TOTAL	9,477,400	TOTAL	21,495,141
TOTAL U. S.	75,994,575	TOTAL U. S.	177,700,000

* Appears in both years.
Source: U. S. Bureau of the Census; 1960 data are preliminary.

metropolitan agglomerations. Furthermore, multitudes will continue to leave the farm for city and suburb each year.

Will our cities rise to the challenge of rebuilding and revitalizing which faces them? How will they cope with the even higher rates of juvenile delinquency, mental illness, alcoholism and other social ills which ever-increasing congestion in living inevitably will bring? How will they meet the numerous other problems which grow in size as cities grow: traffic congestion, air pollution, city blight, congested slums, inadequate housing and dwindling water supplies?

Luther H. Gulick, President of the Institute of Public Administration, New York, and of the Governmental Affairs Institute, Washington, D. C., states the problem in these words:

> It may well be a generation before we have a satisfactory description and analysis of what is happening to us in and around the great cities, as America becomes urbanized and a new metropolitan culture comes to dominate our life.
>
> * * * *
>
> From now on, most Americans will be born, grow up, live, work and die in great metropolitan complexes; some in the cities, some in the expanding suburbs, but mostly in urban surroundings. From now on we are an urbanized civilization.
>
> Characteristic of this development is a fluidity of population and of economic life. This flow changes and basic structure of the family, the community, social relations, employment choices, shopping, education, communication and political associations. The new metropolitanism profoundly disturbs most of our social institutions such as churches, clubs, societies, voluntary hospitals and charities, cultural and recreational establishments, political parties and even governmental operations. Traffic is suddenly snarled, transportation systems are in trouble, schools are overburdened, slums outrun modernization and renewal, water is short, pollution increases, and crime breaks out all over. While this looks pretty bad, don't forget, you and I are doing this. We are producing the metropolis. In all this mankind is reaching for some great individual and social values; but the price at this stage is terrific.

Morton Hoffman, Director of Research and Analysis, Baltimore Urban Renewal and Housing Agency, discusses the economics of the nation's urban sprawl:

> Population growth and suburban expansion have created and will continue to create unprecedented demands for new schools, roads, hospitals, water and sewerage systems and other essential facilities. As state and local authorities fall behind the necessary construction and financial pace in fulfilling the needs of families and businesses, all are touched by physical problems such as water supply, sanitation, traffic congestion, proper land use and zoning, homebuilding, and dispersal of trade and industry. Problems of governmental concern such as water pollution, smog, and other public health problems, civil defense, traffic control, fire and police protection and airport development spill over the bounds of existing governmental units.
>
> Simultaneously there has been extraordinarily high mobility within our older cities. New neighborhoods composed entirely of homeowners are created in outlying areas, while older sections of the city lose population or undergo little net change. But the latter is often the net result of the replacement of middle-class families by lower-income families. Not only is there a disturbing

TABLE 6. THE WORLD'S METROPOLITAN AREAS (*circa* 1955)

Area	Number of Metropolitan Areas with population of: 100,000 and over	1,000,000 and over
Africa	48	3
Northern America *	202	26
Middle America †	28	2
South America	50	6
Asia	341	32
Europe	279	34
Oceania	11	2
USSR	148	3
TOTAL	1107	108

* U. S. and Canada.
† Central America, Mexico and the Caribbean.
Compiled from: International Urban Research, *The World's Metropolitan Areas*, Berkeley, University of California Press, 1959. United States: 1960 data from U. S. Bureau of the Census. USSR: 1959 data from All-Union Population Census of 1959. (See *Population Bulletin*, "USSR Census," July 1959.)

The following are the metropolitan areas with populations of one million or more:
AFRICA
Egypt: Alexandria, Cairo. *So. Africa:* Johannesburg.
NORTH AMERICA
Canada: Montreal, Toronto. *United States:* Atlanta, Baltimore, Boston, Buffalo, Chicago, Cincinnati, Cleveland, Dallas, Detroit, Houston, Kansas City, Los Angeles, Milwaukee, Minneapolis, Newark, New York, Paterson, Philadelphia, Pittsburgh, St. Louis, San Diego, San Francisco, Seattle, Washington.
MIDDLE AMERICA
Cuba: Havana. *Mexico:* Mexico City.
SOUTH AMERICA
Argentina: Buenos Aires. *Brazil:* Rio de Janiero, Sao Paulo. *Chile:* Santiago. *Peru:* Lima. *Venezuela:* Caracas.
ASIA
China: Canton, Chungking, Harbin, Mukden, Nanking, Peking, Shanghai, Tientsin, Wuham. *Hong Kong. India:* Ahmedabad, Bangalore, Bombay, Calcutta, Delhi, Hyderabad, Madras. *Indonesia:* Djakarta. *Iran:* Teheran. *Japan:* Kyoto, Nagoya, Osaka-Kobe, Tokyo-Yokohama, Yahata-Shimonoseki-Kokura. *South Korea:* Pusan, Seoul. *Pakistan:* Karachi. *Philippines:* Manila. *Singapore. Thailand:* Bangkok. *Turkey:* Istanbul. *South Vietnam:* Saigon-Cholon.
EUROPE
Austria: Vienna. *Belgium:* Brussels. *Denmark:* Copenhagen. *France:* Paris. *East Germany:* East Berlin. *West Germany:* West Berlin, Cologne, Essen-Dortmund-Duisburg, Frankfort am Main, Hamburg, Mannheim-Ludwigshafen-Heidelberg, Munich, Stuttgart. *Greece:* Athens. *Hungary:* Budapest. *Italy:* Milan, Naples, Rome, Turin. *Netherlands:* Amsterdam. *Poland:* Katowice-Zabrze-Bytom, Warsaw. *Portugal:* Lisbon. *Rumania:* Bucharest. *Spain:* Barcelona, Madrid. *Sweden:* Stockholm. *United Kingdom:* Birmingham, Leeds-Bradford, Liverpool, London, Manchester, Newcastle-upon-Tyne, Glasgow.
OCEANIA
Australia: Melbourne, Sydney.
USSR
Leningrad, Moscow, Kiev.

loss of tax revenue, but the replacement of whites by nonwhites can lead to an enormous increase in the need for schools and other new public improvements. From the public finance viewpoint, one problem resulting from the combined effect of suburbanization and intra-city movement has been to increase the demand for capital outlays far beyond the available supply of capital. Another is the depletion of tax resources for the payment of normal operating expense.

Fortunately, many people are becoming aware of the dire implications in this trend toward the monstrous-sized city. Regional, state and city planning groups, and in some cities citizen groups, are being formed in an effort to correct disastrous trends and to alert public opinion to their implications.

The City of Tomorrow

When the city of antiquity first began to emerge, transportation was by foot, communication by word of mouth, and space—that playground of 20th-century man—was thought to be an inverted bowl with holes punched in it. In the field of transportation and communication, invention and technology have moved farther in one century than in the preceding two thousand centuries.

Generations of scientific research and highly sophisticated planning have brought man to the stage where he can bounce messages off a balloon orbiting in space. By jet plane he can reach any spot on the planet in less than a day. But in the area of social invention man's approach to many urgent problems, among them population control and city planning, still smacks of the Dark Ages rather than the technological age of invention and creative improvization. A do-nothing, know-nothing approach or a Micawberish hope that "something will turn up" does not resolve crises.

It is very likely that in the city man first will have to face the fact that space is the finite factor in the multiplication of people. In all probability, projections which indicate that a century hence Calcutta's population could increase by 35 to 66 million, or that New York City could be half or two thirds that size will never materialize. However, they serve to warn of nightmares to come unless man begins to apply his foresight and his great inventive skills to check his unprecedented population growth and to solve the problems which that growth has created.

—Robert C. Cook, *Editor*

Notes

In the preparation of this *Bulletin,* the following sources were consulted. The reader is referred to them for additional information.

1. Brown, Harrison. *The Challenge of Man's Future.* New York: The Viking Press, 1954.

2. Cook, Robert C. *Human Fertility: The Modern Dilemma.* New York: William Sloane Associates, 1951.

3. Davis, Kingsley. "The Origin and Growth of Urbanization in the World." *The American Journal of Sociology,* 60(5): 429–437, March 1955.

4. Davis, Kingsley and Hertz, Hilda. "The World Distribution of Urbanization." *Bulletin of the International Statistical Institute,* 33 (Pt. 4): 227–242, Dec. 1951.

5. Gulick, Luther H. "We Have Exploded into a New Era." *Urban Sprawl and Health* (Report of the 1958 National Health Forum). New York: National Health Council January 1959.

6. Hoffman, Morton. "The Economic Implications of Increasing Urbanization in the Next 20 Years." *Problems of United States Economic Development. Vol. 2.* New York: Committee for Economic Development, May 1958.

7. International Urban Research. *The World's Metropolitan Areas.* Berkeley: University of California Press, 1959.

8. Milbank Memorial Fund, *Population Trends in Eastern Europe, The USSR and Mainland China.* New York, 1960.

9. Orleans, Leo A. "The Recent Growth of China's Urban Population." *Geographical Review,* 49(1):43–57, January 1959.

10. *Population Bulletin.* "USSR Census." 15(4):61–78, July 1959.

11. Russell, J. C. "Late Ancient and Medieval Population." *Transactions of the American Philosophical Society,* New Series 48 (Pt. 3), June 1958.

12. Shabad, Theodore. "The Population of China's Cities." *Geographical Review,* 49(1):32–42, January 1959.

13. Taeuber, Conrad and Taeuber, Irene B. *The Changing Population of the United States.* New York: John Wiley & Sons, Inc., 1958.

14. United Nations. Bureau of Social Affairs. *Report on the World Social Situation.* New York, 1957.

15. United States Bureau of the Census.
   A. 1950 *Census of Population.* Vol. I, Chapter 1, "U. S. Summary: Number of Inhabitants."
   B. 1960 *Census of Population.* "Preliminary Reports: Population Counts for Standard Metropolitan Statistical Areas." Series PC (P_2).
   C. *Rank by Population Size of 50 Largest U. S. Cities.* Release dated July 25, 1960.

16. Weber, Adna F. *The Growth of Cities in the Nineteenth Century.* New York: The Macmillian Company, 1899.

SOME TENTATIVE MODIFICATIONS OF WEBER'S TYPOLOGY: OCCIDENTAL VERSUS ORIENTAL CITY

Vatro Murvar

Max Weber's typological dichotomy of urban behavior occupies a highly respectable place today in sociological theory. In this area, similarly to some other areas of Weber's research, there are certain more or less apparent difficulties which require the attention of the specialist and perhaps further clarification of several ambiguities. The rationale for this is well known. Max Weber did not finish his great opus and several parts were written at different stages of his intellectual growth. Some of the translators were without sociological training and in their hands the usage of various terminology became an additional source of confusion. The other translators, the professionally trained sociologists, were at times very much in a hurry (perhaps justifiably so) to satisfy the need for Weber's works in English. Stating it most charitably, some of them did not have a chance to measure up to the expectations of Weber's scholarship. Of course, certain

Reprinted by permission of the author and publisher from *Social Forces,* **44** (March, 1966), pp. 381–389.

German terms are untranslatable and the choice of English approximation was necessarily an individual decision. The purpose of this paper is to offer some tentative modifications in the dichotomy of urban behavior and render it more usable for sociological research and teaching. The paper will also account for a number of recent studies on ancient and Islamic medieval cities in order to test the validity of Weber's basic typology.

In his extensive studies of the great Oriental cultures, in which he particularly searched for the interdependence of religious and economic behavioral patterns, Max Weber offered among other sets of constructed types,[1] a dichotomy of the two types of urban behavior: the Oriental and Occidental city. In the Occidental type Weber included the ancient and the early as well as the late medieval Western European city. In spite of this typological decision Weber was aware of the fundamental distinction between the ancient (Greco-Roman) and the late medieval city and this awareness seems to support the need for the modification of his original formulation of the Occidental type. In the introduction to one of his earlier works written just before his death, Weber noticed that the "concept of the citizen has not existed outside the Occident, and that of the bourgeoisie outside of the modern Occident." [2] The absence of the special type of policy called town-economy and policy-making guilds from the ancient city was contrasted in his later works to the presence of the guilds with the function of ruling and policy-making in the medieval city.[3] Concerning the presence or absence of magical-animistic tribal ties in the structure of the ancient cities, Weber in later works modified his original position without changing his earlier typological formulation.[4] Finally, according to Weber, "the emergence of the autonomous and autocephalous medieval city with their own administrative council and their Consul, Mayor or Burgomaster on the top was a process of development essentially different not only from the growth of Asiatic cities but the ancient cities as well." [5] Consequently, Weber was incorrect when he spoke of the burgher in antiquity in the same sense as of the burgher in the late medieval city.[6]

A. Leo Oppenheim has recently developed a hypothesis concerning the ancient Mesopotamian cities which in his own words "relies heavily on parallels offered by the known history of the Greek cities of the fifth and fourth centuries B.C., and on certain aspects in the development of Italian cities of the early Renaissance." [7] The cuneiform documents in the transitional period from the end of the second millenium to the first millenium B.C. in Mesopotamia contain "a number of isolated indications which, taken together, reveal that a small number of old and important cities enjoyed certain privileges and exemptions with respect to the king and his power." [8] He quotes three cities in Babylonia and two in different periods in Assyria including capital cities in which, not the whole body of citizens, but only a few more influential, richer and older citizens "claimed with more or less success depending on the political situation," certain exemptions in *corvée* work, military and tax obligations. Oppenheim admits that these exemptions were not uniquely urban, but that "the granting of tax exemptions and preferential treatment with regard to *corvée* work and military service to certain landed owners and tribal chieftains or to sanctuaries had become common practice for the Babylonian kings. . . ." [9] Oppenheim also notes that

there is meager evidence on the assemblies of the citizens, who were again oligarchically dominated and whose main function was to write letters to the king. In a cultural context in which there existed, according to Oppenheim himself, only one institution—the kingship of divine origin and substance—there was simply no opportunity for the growth of autonomous bodies. The king's court within the city easily dominated the other social structures if any existed.[10] "In such a system . . . the distinction between the divine and human tends to disappear; the god is paralleled by the king or *ensi,* his family by the *ensi's* wife and her children, and the needs of both are supplied by the temple organization. . . ."[11] In contrast to Oppenheim, Adams seems correct when he states that the Mesopotamian cities lacked some of the basic characteristics of the Greco-Roman cities[12] and Weber was right when he recognized only traces of the citizens' political rights in the Babylonian patriciate.[13]

In view of these considerations it appears to be a contribution to the typological refinement of Weber's conceptual dichotomy if the Ancient City (Greco-Roman as well as Mesopotamian) is excluded from the Occidental type of urban behavior. An outstanding German social scientist, Otto Brunner considers the late ancient city and the early medieval city as belonging to the older universal type which corresponds to Weber's Oriental type, while the late medieval city represents an entirely different and basically new type.[14]

The basic change in the universal patterns of urban life (Oriental and Ancient) first appeared in the eleventh century in Western Europe where a new independent socio-politico-economic structure emerged: the community or sodality of burghers. A number of economic factors cannot be separated from the simultaneous emergence of the sodalian community of the burghers in the West, however the economic factors were not the only decisive ones. For the first time in human history, here in the West, a peculiar configuration of various elements was responsible for the formation of the unique social organization in which the burgherdom played an increasingly significant role as one of the three *Staende*[15] (in addition to the older *Staende:* independent clergy and feudal aristocracy).

The characteristics of the Oriental type are totally contradictory to the characteristics of the Occidental type of urban behavior and this totality of contrast warrants Weber's typological dichotomy which places both types at the opposing ends of a conceptual scale. Here are some, not all, of the major areas of contrast between the Oriental and Occidental types of urban behavior.

1. The Oriental city is juridically, constitutionally and materially (in the sense of legal contents) indistinguishable from the village. The residence of the ruler or of any administrative body being the focal point for the whole country or region is the most important feature in the structure and functioning of the Oriental city. As Wittfogel pointed out, the Oriental cities "were administrative and military footholds of the government; and the artisans and the merchants had no opportunity to become serious political rivals."[16] Or as Grunebaum put it concerning the Islamic medieval cities, "they were legally on the same footing with the surrounding territories (and not marked out by any special privilege), even though

in actual fact they would often constitute the most important sections of a given state." [17] Without the ruler's court or administrative headquarters the locality would remain a village. Only the presence of political power attributed to a particular aggregate of people urban distinction. The Western city is a special legal entity in the feudal world of the middle ages. It is sharply differentiated in juridical terms from all other forms of social organization (political, religious, economic). This differentiation is one of the most important elements responsible for the multiplicity and versatility of organizational forms of older Europe and is entirely lacking in all other cultures (including the ancient city which was a city-state). The separateness (*Scheidung*) between the feudal landlord-peasant sphere and the autonomous-autocephalous sphere of the city burghers, between the countryside and the city which is legally and administratively exempt from the control of the power dominating the countryside is something specifically Western European.[18] Only in the West, "the feudal-peasant and city-burgher spheres are clearly separated from each other social-organizationally, politically, legally and economically." [19]

2. Heteronomy and heterocephaly do not appear in the Oriental city, since the city is legally and constitutionally indistinguishable from the rest of the country. This characteristic fully applies to the Islamic city and here it is necessary to report on some recent research. Claude Cahen firmly emphasized that none of the elements in the Islamic city would constitute the western bourgeois "commune," not even the Ancient city. There is no "auto-administration" even in a limited sense. The great majority of Islamic cities were integrated in the Islamic state with the garrisons located in the city, all in all completely dependent on the will of the provincial governor who sends his agents, including the fiscal, to apply the common Islamic law to all the people. Taxes were naturally state taxes and the Islamic fiscal organization, similarly to the Byzantine and the Sassanide, was rooted in a common fiscal responsibility of all the inhabitants for each locality or fiscal unit.[20] G. E. Grunebaum also underlines that the Islamic city is not an autonomous association of citizens, but merely a functionally unified administrative entity. "There were no qualifications to be met to obtain admission to citizenship in the Muslim town for the simple reason that there was no body of town dwellers in whom political or civic authority was seen to reside." [21] The residents did not develop their own administrative machinery, but it was the personal will of the ruler or of the governor, appointed by the ruler, that created the machinery for them.[22] Thus the fundamental differentiation between the Occidental and the Oriental (including the Ancient) types of city is the sodalian or corporate autonomy and autocephaly of the community of the burgher-citizens in the West and the absence of the same—to use Weber's phrase—"everywhere outside the West." The city in the medieval West displayed a varying degree of autonomy and autocephaly, of course, but there was an unmistaken generalized tendency of growth in the direction of increased strengthening of the city's own political power, independence from the outside and equality within the city limits. The Western burgherdom's usurpation of ruler's rights and the breakthrough of the monolithic power of the ruler by a great number of Western cities

were considered by Weber to be truly great revolutionary innovations in contrast to cities in all other cultures.[23]

3. Merchants and artisans who happened to live in the Oriental city, and in the Orient most of them live in villages, live there to serve the ruler or the administrative body. The merchant in the Oriental city is usually an agent of the ruler,[24] otherwise he pays a heavy price for his trade privileges, and as such he is basically different from the merchant who acts in his own name and in his own right. In general, all merchants and artisans in the Oriental city depend substantially in all their activities on the good graces, tolerance and purchased license from the political power. They are actually subjects, indiscernible from any other in the realm, without opportunities to develop any traces of corporate autonomy for their trade organizations, if such would appear. The burghers in the West being predominantly merchants and artisans were never serving men of a monistic ruler. "In sharp contrast to the Asiatic situation, the citizens, as urban dwellers, owed no allegiance to any clan, caste or village association." [25] In the Western medieval city the burgherdom achieved an egalitarian political community of their own bound in religious brotherhood. Within the Western city the universal two-fold political-socio-economic stratification which one finds in all other cultures disappeared completely.

4. In the Oriental city the principle of residence never superseded the significance of the kinship ties as a basis for social organization. Consequently, the Oriental city represented a more or less loose collection of kinship and tribal groups, who monopolized particular skills and trades for themselves excluding all out-group members. Under these conditions of tribal ethnocentrism and magic which "rationalized" clan and tribal exclusiveness there was no opportunity whatsoever to develop any traces of a common solidarity binding all urban dwellers.[26] The "ideas and institutions connected with magic," [27] prevented the growth of the Western type of city in the Orient. Only in the Western medieval city the magic-animistic tribal and caste exclusiveness and connections disappeared [28] from the political, economic, religious, educational patterns of behavior and the corresponding social structures. Weber credits the prophecy among the Jews and the event of Christianity with this important contribution. [29] Paul's "historically significant" letter was quoted by Weber as having consequences directly correlated to the destruction of sacral exclusivity of any tribe or nation concerning the new religion.[30] As Weber commented, Christianity has deprived kinship and tribal ties, usually based on magic, from all ritual meaning and significance. The Christian community was, according to its most inner being, a religious brotherhood of individual believers, not a ritual kinship unit,[31] whether familial, tribal or even national. The quality of tribal and family membership based on mythical origin from the same divine progenitor or the membership conferred through magical ceremonies of adoption totally and absolutely disappeared from the Western city. The religious brotherhood of the burghers, to which an individual is admitted as an individual, not as a member of a tribe or caste, after making a personal civic oath of loyalty to his new brotherhood, is the foundation of the burghers' sodalian or corporate autonomy and autocephaly. At

the same time this religious brotherhood is the source of his individual rights. It is extremely significant that the privileged position of the burghers is a right of an individual burgher in relation to other burghers as well as to any outside third person.[32]

5. In the Orient and "everywhere outside the West," the army of the ruler is an older institution than the city. The ruler's monopoly of military power was to Weber "the basis of the distinction between the military organization of Asia and that of the West." [33] Military power of the Western city, and with it a considerable degree of political power since there was an enormous number of interdependent cities of various sizes with similar political and defense needs, was in the hands of a religiously inspired brotherhood of burghers, sodality, *Eidgenossenschaft, coniuratio,* or *universitas civium.* It was a "brotherhood in arms for mutual aid and protection, involving the usurpation of political power." [34] Every citizen, as a member of this sodality, was obligated not only to serve personally, but also to equip himself with military hardware from his own pocket. His serious commitment was dramatized by the religious oath when initiated into the sodality. The exceptional quality of military potential of the city made it possible for the citizens to strive more or less successfully for an ever increasing degree of their own sodalian or corporate autonomy and autocephaly. No ruler in the West was able to destroy the city's military power or the city itself for exemplary purposes, as the Russian and Oriental rulers did rather frequently, simply because in the West there were too many cities and they were interdependent and solidary.

6. A reference to the monistic power of the Oriental ruler seems to be necessary in this context. It is not only the monopoly of the military, but in many instances the monopoly of the economic, religious and political power, concentrated in the hands of one omnipotent and god-like ruler which is the basic configuration in the Orient. In contrast to it, the Western social structure offers an entirely different configuration: quantitative diffusion of power among kings, feudal lords, vassals, subvassals (not functional-qualitative distribution in Montesquieu's sense,[35] which is, of course, a later development); the differentiation of religious from political power; [36] and particularly in the Western city "the forms of religious brotherhood and self-equipment for war made possible the origin and existence of the [Western] city." [37]

7. The Oriental city was unable to create or foster any conditions necessary for the growth of the bourgeoisie. The absence of the bourgeoisie was one of the most conspicuous characteristics in the Oriental cultures [38] and in turn was responsible for a number of non-pluralistic and non-democratic patterns of behavior of the future. The bourgeoisie remained an exclusively Western phenomenon. In the West the bourgeoisie was a *Stand,* a privileged group, constantly bent toward achieving an ever increasing number of exemptions from the ruler's power exclusively for themselves, for their city and *Stand.* Freedom as the burghers understood it was a monopoly jealously guarded from any out-group. In spite of their refusal to share their freedom with non-city groups, the burghers were instrumental in diffusing the ideology of liberty and democratic pluralism.

The interdependence of groups and structures responsible for the development of the Western city was supported by additional social structures emerging only in the West. Three of these seem to justify special attention in this context: the free universities, the mendicant and reform-minded religious orders and the sodalities of university trained legal experts.

A. The phenomenal growth of the free universities from the twelfth century on in Italy, England, France, Spain, Portugal and Germany offered a permanent opportunity for relatively unrestrained discussion and criticism of existing institutions. Both faculty and students were of extremely colorful versatility in the sense that they came from many Western-European countries (using Latin as the language of communication). Since they also belonged to various religious orders, secular clergy and laity, this multiplicity of national origins and status orientations facilitated the appreciation of the unavoidable conflict of opinions leading toward a rationality of consensus.

The early trend within the Church to separate church law from secular law was strengthened by the existence of the early medieval universities. Their structure necessitated the need for theology to be taught as a separate entity distinct from Canon law instruction; it was already accepted that secular law should be distinguished from Canon law as well as theology. In Weber's opinion this separation was instrumental in bringing about greater institutional rationality and an ever increasing rationalization in all the academic fields and "prevented the growth of such theocratic hybrid structures as developed elsewhere." [39] In contrast to the West, "in almost all the Asiatic civilizations . . . the religious prescriptions were never differentiated from secular rules and . . . the characteristically theocratic combination of religious and ritualistic prescriptions with legal rules remained unchanged." Concerning the Orient, Weber also speaks of "an inextricable conglomeration of ethical and legal duties, moral exhortations and legal commandments without formalized explicitness. . . ." [40]

B. The mendicant and reform-minded religious orders were conceived and organized in direct conflict with the regular (secular) clergy. The preachers and professors of these religious orders repeatedly generated a moral crusade in which they bluntly accused the secular clergy of corruption, bribery, enjoyment of excessive luxury, keeping of wives and in general of betraying the ideals of the early Church. The charismatic leaders of the reform-demanding religious orders found frequently an enthusiastic moral and financial support for their reforms in the communities of burghers. The burghers were most generous in helping them to build the monasteries within the city walls or adjacent to the walls and they increasingly turned to the monks in their spiritual and religious needs rather than to the secular clergymen, who in the burghers' opinion were involved in "corruption" and politics contrary to the burghers' interests. Once successful in achieving their autonomy and autocephaly, the burghers were unwilling to continue tolerating the clergy's freedom from taxation, immunity from the city's courts and from the city's military duties as originally provided in the Canon law. In addition, the significant labor force on the clergy's land possessions outside the city walls produced surplus merchandises which competed with the city's products. Also the burghers never appreciated the clergy's insistence that interest on loans is always sinful and ought to be prohibited. It is well known that the alliance of the burghers and the religious orders helped the Papacy against the ruler, the politically involved hierarchy and the bishops who were feudal lords at the same time. However sometimes such an alliance with the ruler's support in the form of city charters or extension of the bourgeoisie's legal privileges was directed against the feudal lords, bishops and church hierarchy when endangering the city's rights. The ruler-bourgeoisie alliances were "one of the major factors which led towards formal legal rationalization." [41]

The important conclusion here is the flexibility of relationships and the opportunity for every social group or structure of the medieval polity to find a more or less temporary partner for the achievement of common goals, and the obvious probability that any combination could be dissolved in the future and a new more promising alliance with other groups created. Some bargaining in the direction of creating a consensus out of conflicting interests was always necessary before a new alliance could be established.

C. The new professional sodality of university trained jurists or legal experts was independent from existing *Staende*, but interdependent with the community of burghers, the religious orders and the universities. As Max Weber put it very forcefully, the veritable revolutionalization of political structures steadily pushing toward the development of the Western legal-rational state was carried everywhere in the West by these formally trained legal professionals. They have modified the Roman legacy by adopting in the secular and Canon law the theories and concepts of the natural law. The natural law theories were originally conceived in juristic, Stoic and early Christian thought and later secularized. The specific product of Western culture, the full rationalization of procedural law, or in Weber's terms "logically formed rationality" in law, was made possible through the reception of Roman jurisprudence, first by the Italian legal professionals (notaries), and later in the North by the learned judges. This logical formalism of legal procedure cannot be found in the legal system of any other culture of the time. In Weber's words, "there is no analogy to this on the whole earth." The rudiments of rational juristic thought in certain periods of Hindu and Islamic legal scholarship were smothered by the theological forms of thought.[42] The Western phenomenon of the Canon law, absent everywhere else, was to Weber one of the powerful influences in the development of the Western rationalization of procedural law.[43] In the hands of university trained legal professionals the Roman law was and remained a successful competitor to the Canon law. The Canon law is a sacred law and there is a normative prediction that like any other sacred law, the Canon law would sooner or later claim the absolute right to legislate on all the aspects of human behavior. The legal experts cherished the cultural value of political dualism as inherited from the time of the underground existence of the Church in the Roman catacombs. This was a period of almost absolute isolation and absence of any cooperative contact in the church-state relationship. To conserve the political as well as legal dualism there was a need for some institutional support and the Western burgherdom was sufficiently motivated to defend the continuity of legal and political dualism. "And where the

Canon law tried to extend its dominion it met with the vigorous and successful opposition of the economic interests of the bourgeoisie, including that of the Italian cities, with which the Papacy had to ally itself." [44] Similarly the burghers everywhere in the West:

> have generally tended to be intensely interested in a rational procedural system and therefore in a systematized and unambiguously formal and purposefully constructed substantive law which eliminates both obsolete traditions and arbitrariness and in which rights can have their source exclusively in general objective norms.[45]

Max Weber summarized the final product of the Western institutional configuration:

> Only the occident knows the state in the modern sense, with a professional administration, specialized officialdom and law based on the concept of citizenship. Beginnings of this institution in antiquity and in the orient were never able to develop. Only the occident knows rational law, made by jurists and rationally interpreted and applied, and only in the occident is found the concept of citizen (*civis Romanus, citoyen, bourgeois*) because only in the occident again are there cities in the specific sense.[46]

In conclusion, a final word of caution is necessary: The sociologist must insist on recognition and acceptance of the functional configuration of the Western city, Western feudalism and Western church, or in terms of social organization the functional interdependence of the entrepreneurial bourgeoisie, feudal aristocracy and politically-economically independent clergy. The free universities, mendicant orders and sodalities of legal experts basically contributed toward the stability of the whole societal system by their participation in this institutional configuration. This was the specific Western European social organization in which all three *Staende* with all the characteristics of each individual *Stand*, particularly with their own ideology and solidarity, functionally interacted. Otto Brunner warned that the phenomenon of the Western city cannot be studied as an isolated phenomenon.[47] If the total structure is neglected and only isolated groups or structural segments drawn out and then compared to the non-Western groups, one is necessarily led to external and superficial analogies and from there to the source of the most serious errors.

Notes

1. John C. McKinney, "Constructive Typology and Social Research," in *An Introduction to Social Research*, (ed.) John T. Doby (Harrisburg, Pa.: The Stackpole Co., 1954), pp. 150–155; Vatro Murvar, "Some Reflections on Weber's typology of *Herrschaft*," *The Sociological Quarterly* (Autumn 1964), pp. 374–384.

2. Max Weber, *The Protestant Ethic and the Spirit of Capitalism*, (trans.) Talcott Parsons (London: Allen & Unwin, 1930), p. 23.

3. Max Weber, *General Economic History*, (trans.) F. H. Knight (1927), pp. 326 ff. "The typical citizen of the medieval city is a merchant or craftsman; he is

a full citizen if he is also a householder. In antiquity, on the contrary, the full citizen is the landholder." In spite of some legal disadvantages for the nonlandholders, which were gradually eliminated, in his "personal relations, however, the citizen of the medieval city is free. The principle 'town air makes free' asserted that after a year and a day the lord no longer had a right to recall his runaway serf. . . . Hence the equalization of classes and removal of unfreedom became a dominant tendency in the development of the medieval city." *Ibid.*, pp. 329–330. Also Max Weber, *Wirtschaft und Gesellschaft,* (ed.) Winckelman, (trans.) Vatro Murvar (2 vols., 4th ed.; Tuebingen: J. C. B. Mohr, 1956), p. 750. In antiquity the full citizen, the owner of political rights based on his landownership and military service, was separated by a deep gap from the rest of the population without political rights, *Metics* and slaves. While slaves took care of agricultural needs, commerce and artisan trade were almost entirely in the hands of *Metics* (foreigners), who were denied landownership and military service, thus deprived of citizenship. The familiar and universal two-fold economic stratification did not disappear from the ancient city. Frequently, *Metics* and slaves, strata without any rights, were the majority of the population in the ancient city. Howard Becker and Harry Elmer Barnes, *Social Thought from Lore to Science* (Washington, D. C.: Harren Press, 1952), pp. 147–148.

4. Weber appears to argue for the absence of magical power in the ancient city by emphasizing the fact that the priestly offices were filled by auction, "since no magical limitations stood in the way as in India and elsewhere." He probably was thinking of the city of Rome, but the above practice was not universal. The present writer could point out many magical-animistic practices in other ancient cities. It appears, however, that Weber himself was aware of the weakness of his original formulation of the Occidental type when he emphasized that only in the later periods of Western institutional development was magic completely eliminated through certain specific events which occurred in the West. "The magical barriers between clans, tribes, and peoples, which were still known in the ancient *polis* to a considerable degree, were thus set aside and the establishment of the Occidental city was made possible." Weber, *General Economic History,* pp. 322–323. This statement seems to be supported by another in which Weber emphasized that the absence of magic-animistic caste and tribal ties in the western medieval city was of highest significance, "while in the ancient city there was still a residual of sacral exclusivity of one tribe against the other and against outsiders." Weber, *Wirtschaft und Gesellschaft,* p. 753.

5. *Ibid.*, p. 757.

6. Otto Brunner, *Neue Wege der Sozialgeschichte* (Goettingen: Vandenhoeck & Ruprecht, 1956), p. 83.

7. A. Leo Oppenheim, *Ancient Mesopotamia: Portrait of a Dead Civilization* (Chicago: University of Chicago Press, 1964), p. 114.

8. *Ibid.*, p. 120.

9. *Ibid.*, pp. 122–123.

10. *Ibid.*, pp. 105, 117. "Apparently the temple organization was on a steady decline after the Sumerian period, and the palace organization, grown rich and complex in a territorial state, overshadowed it increasingly as time progressed."

"While the typical city enjoyed a modicum of prosperity slightly above the subsistence level, real prosperity came to a Mesopotamian city only when it had in its midst the palace of a victorious king. . . . Only a few of the Babylonian cities had more than one or two short periods—and many none at all—of such intense flowering. From this affluence they relapsed into a drab and wretched existence, the people living among ruins, the sanctuaries dilapidated, and the city walls crumbling."

11. C. J. Gadd, "The Cities of Babylonia," *The Cambridge Ancient History* (Cambridge: Cambridge University Press 1962), fascicle of Vol. 1, chap. 13, p. 37.

12. Robert M. Adams, "The Origin of Cities," *Scientific American* (September 1960). "In particular, the development of municipal politics, of a self-conscious corporate body with at least partially autonomous, secular institutions for its own administration, was not consummated until classical times."

13. Weber, *General Economic History*, p. 315.

14. Oliver C. Cox commented on Comhaire and Cahnman's contribution in this field. "Two types of society are here recognized: the one in which cities as independent social systems are either absent or ineffective, and the other in which cities serve as models for the larger society." Oliver C. Cox, "The Preindustrial City Reconsidered," *The Sociological Quarterly* (Spring 1964), p. 135.

15. Talcott Parsons offered the best approximation of the concept *Stand,* one of the untranslatable German terms, when he interpreted it as "a social group the members of which occupy a relatively well-defined *common status,* particularly with reference to *social stratification,* though this reference is not always important. In addition . . . the members of a *Stand* have a *common mode of life* and usually more or less well-defined *code of behavior*. . . . In the present case it is the *appropriation of authority* on the part of the members . . . in such a way that their position becomes *independent of the arbitrary will of their chief,* which is decisive." Parsons, in his ed. comment in Max Weber, *The Theory of Social and Economic Organization* (New York: Oxford University Press, 1947), pp. 347–348, fn. 27. [Italics by V. M.]

16. Karl Wittfogel, *Oriental Despotism* (New Haven: Yale University Press, 1957), p. 85.

17. G. E. Grunebaum, *Islam: Essays in Nature and Growth of a Cultural Tradition* (London: Routledge, 1955), p. 143. Claude Cahen, "Zur Geschichte der staedtischen Gesellschaft im islamischen Orient des Mittelalters," *Saeculum,* 9 (1958), p. 66: In contrast to the Occident, the holders of state power reside in the city and they rule the city in the first place as well as the province as a whole, and display nothing specifically urban in their fundamental structures and functions. Cahen adds that the Islamic law does not distinguish between the urban and nonurban populations and does not recognize differentiation between social classes. [Trans. by V. M.]

18. Brunner, *op. cit.,* p. 21.

19. Brunner, *op. cit.,* p. 91.

20. Claude Cahen, *Mouvements populaires et autonomisme urbain dans l'Asie musulmane du Moyen Âge* (Leiden: E. J. Brill, 1959), pp. 81, 80, and 79. Cahen discusses some traces of factual absence of centralized control due to general political breakdown: 1. *Cadi,* normally appointed by the ruler, tends to become an hereditary office. 2. *Šutra* (police) only in small and isolated towns, never in large and capital cities, in times of crisis becomes more dependent on the local population through the fact that recruitment is locally limited. 3. Two popular movements, *fityān* and *ayyārūn,* can hardly have anything in common. One is the group of religious mystics, the other is the lowest stratum including beggars, escapees from prison, etc. Their activities do not cover the whole city, since they constitute only a segment of the urban population. Cahen adds that there is no trace of such movements in times of domestic tranquility, but only during power collapse or transition. Plundering, selling protection to the merchants or asking for jobs in police or army is their only activity. They do not appear in all Islamic cities, but are *very* marginal in terms of space and time. All three isolated phenomena are most frequently motivated by the presence of conquerors, dynasties or governors, who are newly imposed ethnic or geographic strangers. Obviously then the national or dynastic struggle is the chief motivating source of any potential autonomism or factual rebellion, and most certainly not the bourgeois-like need to institutionalize his exemptions and liberties. Cahen speaks of the uncertain and diffuse character of their leadership's function, which is visible in their title applicable to any group (tribal, ethnic, religious or vocational), the appointment by the ruler and the sphere of influence not limited to a single city but to the whole province. [Trans. by V. M.]

21. Grunebaum, *op. cit.,* p. 142.

22. *Ibid.,* pp. 149 and 151.

23. Weber, *Wirtschaft und Gesellschaft,* p. 750.

24. Even for the Mesopotamian ancient cities Oppenheim admits: "It is certainly no accident that the *rab tamkari,* 'chief trader,' was a high official at the court of the Babylonian kings." Oppenheim, *op. cit.,* p. 94. Concerning the Islamic urban vocational or professional organizations both Cahen and Grunebaum agree that these follow the Byzantine tradition: they are established and regimented by the state, without autonomy. Cahen, *op. cit.,* pp. 28–29 and Grunebaum, *op. cit.,* p. 150.

25. Jean Comhaire and Werner J. Cahnman, *How Cities Grew: The Historical Sociology of Cities* (Madison, New Jersey: The Florham Park Press, 1959), p. 8.

26. For an excellent discussion of a typical Oriental city, particularly in this respect, see Max Weber, *The Religion of China: Confucianism and Taoism,* (trans., and ed.) H. H. Gerth (Glencoe, Illinois: The Free Press, 1951), pp. 13–16.

27. Weber, *General Economic History,* p. 322.

28. Weber, *Wirtschaft und Gesellschaft,* p. 752.

29. Weber, *General Economic History,* p. 322. "For the later period in the West three great facts were crucial. The first was prophecy among the Jews, which destroyed magic within the confines of Judaism; magical procedure re-

mained real but was devilish instead of divine. The second fact was the pentecostal miracle. . . . The final factor was the day in Antioch (Gal. 2; 11 ff.) when Paul, in opposition to Peter, espoused fellowship with the uncircumcised." Comhaire and Cahnman, *op. cit.*, p. 6: "In its missionary work, Christianity obliterated all distinctions between Jew and Greek, rich and poor, local people and strangers, even between masters and slaves. . . . Sociologically speaking, Christianity emerged as the creed of the Roman proletariat, the all-encompassing religion of urbanism."

30. Weber, *Wirtschaft und Gesellschaft*, p. 753.

31. *Ibid.*, p. 755.

32. *Ibid.*, p. 756.

33. Weber, *General Economic History*, pp. 320–321.

34. *Ibid.*, p. 319.

35. Weber, *Wirtschaft und Gesellschaft*, p. 642.

36. *Ibid.*, p. 803. Actually Weber speaks here of separation of church and state since the Investiture struggle. "Separation" is perhaps too strong an expression to use for the church-state relationship of the eleventh century and after.

37. Weber, *General Economic History*, p. 321.

38. There seems to be support for this even from students of the Islamic city, who do not use the term bourgeoisie in a precise Weberian sense, but loosely to label any significant merchants' class. S. D. Goitein credits the merchants with the development of the Islamic religious law, however, they "never became an organized body and, as a class, never obtained political power. . . ." S. D. Goitein, "The Rise of the Near-Eastern Bourgeoisie in Early Islamic Times," *Cahiers d'histoire mondiale*, 3 (1957), p. 584.

39. Max Weber, *On Law in Economy and Society*, (ed.) M. Rheinstein (Cambridge: Harvard University Press 1954), p. 251.

40. *Ibid.*, p. 226.

41. *Ibid.*, p. 267.

42. Weber, *Wirtschaft und Gesellschaft*, p. 836.

43. Weber, *On Law in Economy and Society*, pp. 250 ff.

44. *Ibid.*, p. 253.

45. *Ibid.*, p. 231.

46. Weber, *General Economic History*, p. 313.

47. Brunner, *op. cit.*, p. 115.

ON THE MEANING OF "URBAN" IN URBAN STUDIES

David Popenoe

Readers of this new *Quarterly* may well wonder what "urban affairs" are, or more pointedly, what they are *not*. In a society mostly urban, aren't most affairs urban? Though the use of the term "urban" may present an unresolved problem of definition, this has not prevented it from becoming one of the more widely used terms in the current American scene. During the past several years, for example, the following events have taken place:

1) A proliferation of social science literature with the term "urban" (sometimes inappropriately) in the title.

2) The first message on "urban affairs" to the Congress by a President of the United States.

3) The establishment of this *Urban Affairs Quarterly*, representing the consummation of ten or more years of discussion about the need for such a new journal.

4) The establishment of a "Library of Urban Affairs" which provides new books in the field at discount to its members.

5) Further progress toward the imminent establishment of a cabinet level Department of Housing and Urban Affairs, and the actual establishing in a number of states of agencies concerned primarily with urban affairs.

6) The creation and growth of "urban" units within various national and local organizations (such as "Departments of Urban Life" within church bodies), and

7) The development of a number of new "urban studies" programs of many sizes and shapes within universities and colleges.

Each of these is focused, *more or less*, on the same phenomena, *viz.*, urban problems. But the term "urban problems" is no less ambiguous (but possibly more specific) than "urban affairs." We shall leave the resolution of a great bulk of this ambiguity to this *Quarterly* and its readers. The purpose of this article, however, is briefly to describe and hopefully to clarify the use of the term "urban" in connection with the seventh event listed above—"urban studies," which, as the reader might infer from the word "studies," is the academic aspect of the urban affairs syndrome. A basic question in urban studies (indeed a *very* basic question) is the meaning of the term "urban" which, because it is asked under academic auspices, takes the form, "What is the focus of the field of urban studies and what are its boundaries (or which phenomena are inside, which outside, the field's purview, and of those which are inside, which are most central)"? This, of course, is not too dissimilar to the question, "Which articles should be published by this *Quarterly*, and which left for other journals?"

Several years ago this author, together with his colleague Robert Gutman, edited a special issue of *The American Behavioral Scientist* on the theme: "Urban Studies: Present Trends and Future Prospects in an Emerging Academic

Reprinted by permission of the author and publisher from *Urban Affairs Quarterly*, 6 (February, 1963).

Field." We stated at that time that urban studies had become an academic enterprise at numerous universities across the nation (and in many other parts of the world) which seemed to have many of the characteristics of a new and distinct academic field. We further noted that the emerging field had somewhat different characteristics depending upon whether the main thrust was research, education, or extension (direct university service to the urban community), or some combination of these. This article represents, to some degree, a continuation of the same theme, but specifically concerned with urban studies as a field of *research.* Within that concern, we shall concentrate primarily on the conceptual problems of establishing definitions and boundaries.

To put the field in perspective, several general comments might be made about it at the outset. While the study of urban phenomena and urban areas is almost as old as cities themselves, it has emerged within the past few decades as a major aspect of the university scene. Because it is so new, its precise definitions and boundaries have yet to be fully agreed upon—and it could even be stated that its future as an organized academic field is somewhat in doubt. The field first developed in its modern academic form as the outcome of the research and professional interests of city planners, social scientists, and others who felt the need for an interdisciplinary approach to phenomena which each discipline or field had previously been studying in a piecemeal fashion. City planners, who most consciously felt the need for better organized and integrated knowledge of urban areas arising from the demands of their work activities, played perhaps a major role in bringing together the academic pursuits around a common focus.

The field has come to be rooted primarily in the social science disciplines, particularly economics, political science, geography, and sociology, and in certain allied professional fields, most notably city planning (together with architecture and "environmental design") and public administration, and, to a lesser degree, engineering, education, social work, law, and public health. It is also sometimes closely allied with certain hybrid disciplines or fields such as regional science, operations research and transportation. Each urban studies program has been developed with some unique combination of these various interests, usually dictated by pre-existing academic strengths within the university, the major discipline of the program's director, or the discipline or field which served as the initiator of the program. Certain academic areas seem to fit together more easily than others; thus it is common to find city planning with economics, but without much sociology, and educational and social work with sociology, but without much economics. Political science seems to get along better with all the other areas, for various reasons, than does any other discipline or field, and this explains, in part, why political scientists predominate as program directors (and possibly why, incidentally, this *Urban Affairs Quarterly* is based in a political science department)!

The field of urban studies is thus quite interdisciplinary in character, but each program has developed a somewhat distinct specialization depending upon the particular disciplines which are involved. In addition it is, like most other academic *fields,* markedly policy-oriented rather than being motivated primarily or entirely in terms of pure research and the advancement of basic knowledge.

When we speak of the characteristics of this field, we are speaking primarily of the characteristics of the activities and thinking in the variety of academic programs around the nation which are designated "urban studies," or some term closely akin to it. Among the major programs of this type at the present time, most of which are organized as separate centers or institutes, are the Joint Center for Urban Studies at Harvard–M.I.T., The Center for Metropolitan Studies at Northwestern, the Institute for Urban Studies at Pennsylvania, the Center for Urban and Regional Studies at North Carolina, the Division of Urban Affairs at Delaware, the Division of Urban Studies at Cornell, the Center for Metropolitan Studies in Washington, D. C., the Institute of Urban and Regional Development at the University of California–Berkeley, the Center for Urban Studies at Chicago, the Urban Program at Wisconsin, the Institute for Urban Studies at Columbia Teachers College, and the Urban Studies Center at Rutgers. Experiences at Rutgers will be relied on most heavily in this discussion, of course, since we know most about them. (As a matter of fact, the communication among these various programs is not great—one mark of a new field.)

That the Rutgers program is unique in several respects should be noted, since this will undoubtedly affect the orientation of this article. First, the program specializes in the social aspects of urban studies, and is rooted most firmly in the discipline of sociology. Second, it has tried to combine, in roughly equal amounts, research and extension. Third, it does not conduct any academic education programs in the urban studies field. Fourth, it is set up independently at the Provost level and does not have formal ties to any other existing department or division within the University, except through joint-appointments.

To the degree that urban studies can be academically classified it must be considered an academic *field* (not a *discipline,* and probably not a potential discipline). The primary task of a discipline is to analyze a variety of concrete phenomena by abstracting certain aspects from them (thus economics is theoretically concerned with the "allocation of scarce resources" aspect of all concrete phenomena, whether a firm, a city, or the world; sociology is theoretically concerned with the "normative" aspect of all phenomena—a family, a city, or society). The primary task of a field, on the other hand, is to focus a variety of such analytic disciplines on one set of concrete phenomena (thus medicine is concerned with the human body, education with the institution of education, international relations with the relations among national states—and each of these fields consists, essentially, of a variety of the basic disciplines working together). The field of urban studies, therefore, can be considered as analogous to the fields just mentioned plus business and a number of others, including agriculture, in that it is an interdisciplinary focus on a set of concrete phenomena to which has been given the label "urban." There is an increasing agreement in the field on this point. The principal issue, therefore, is the definition of the term "urban."

The term "urban" may not have to be carefully defined in connection with a variety of activities, but these do not include urban studies. In the academic establishment, organized intellectual pursuits must be defined with a great degree of rigor and they must tread to a minimum on other organized pursuits. A common notion has it that "urban studies are studies of the city as an entity in all its aspects." While this is a quite alluring notion, it fails to define "the city," it does not take cognizance of the fact that almost every discipline and field is studying some aspect of the city, many in a very major way, and it assumes a degree of integration in the organized pursuit of knowledge that is far beyond the capabilities of a single field, to say nothing of a single research center. Some might suggest that this lack of the capacity to be integrative is a major failing of contemporary academic institutions. But from such reasoning one would probably have to conclude that entire universities should become centers for urban studies —an intriguing idea, but one which takes us somewhat afield from the major concerns of this article.

How is the term urban used in most urban studies research programs today? Most such programs have not attempted to develop, or at least have not succeeded in developing, a *single* theoretical scheme with which to define the boundaries, foci, and organization of their research activities. They are in much the same position as the Joint Center for Urban Studies at Harvard–M.I.T., which reports that:

> . . . at the outset [it] was convinced that it ought not to commit its resources to a single research area or problem, despite the apparent advantages of a concentrated effort . . . Furthermore, it was by no means clear what the focus —if any—should have been . . . [it] decided to allocate some resources during the first few years to exploratory efforts in a wide range of disciplines to determine the kinds of research which would prove most rewarding . . . [it has been] difficult for the Joint Center in its formative years to establish a clear view of easily defined purposes and programs.[1]

A principal function of the Joint Center is "to improve fundamental knowledge about cities and regions," and its major areas of interest at present are: 1) urban transportation and communication; 2) urban design; 3) urban government and politics; 4) history, structure and growth of cities; and 5) urban and regional problems of developing nations.

It is probably fair to say that most urban studies research programs, like the Joint Center's, consist essentially of a variety of minimally interconnected research activities which for one reason or another can be labeled urban, and the term urban is used differently in different research projects, the meaning in a specific case stemming primarily from the principal discipline or disciplines involved. We will not review here the many meanings which have been given to the term urban by these various disciplines. We will suggest, however, that to the degree that urban studies research programs have developed some kind of unifying conceptual scheme, most such schemes have tended to use the term urban as signifying either "urban physical development" or "metropolitan organization and functioning," or both.

We indicated above that contemporary urban studies *as an interdisciplinary endeavor* emerged in large part from the leadership of city planners (where the physical city was the major referent for the term urban—"land uses and land occupancy in the city"). To some extent it pulled together existing urban emphases in the established disciplines, the most important being the local government area in political science (together with local public finance, which shades into economics), an urban and regional "local economies" focus in economics (a more recent development), and urban land use tradition in geography, and the urban ecology and local community foci in sociology (which stem from the 1920's and 30's). These emphases nicely coalesced around the planners' principal interest in the use of space in urban areas as a kind of output of political, economic, social, physical, and other factors. The term *urban development* is often used to denote this particular orientation, and it predominates in research programs in which the field of city planning has a major leadership role.

A distinct but related emphasis, and one which is possibly more closely associated with social science leadership, is the metropolis or *metropolitan region*. The metropolis emerged to prominance not only because it is the predominant form of urban community in contemporary society but because it also served as a rough conceptual scheme around which the particular emphases listed above could relate to one another. The metropolis is best described as a physical entity (the cluster of human settlement seen from an airplane) and as an economic entity (e.g., a labor market area). It is perhaps the most meaningful physical planning unit, and it had long caught the favor of urban geographers and ecologists. In addition, most of the major problems of the metropolis relate in a direct way to the problems of governing it with a completely fractionated political structure. While the metropolitan orientation has enabled a somewhat broader focus than "spatial output," it has also proved to be a useful system within which to interrelate the various factors which affect the use of space.

The prototypical urban problem, from the perspective of these orientations, is a metropolitan (and usually a land use) problem, as for example a problem of housing with reference to the metropolitan housing market, urban renewal with reference to the changing distribution of people and activities in metropolitan areas, the metropolitan transportation problem, metropolitan sprawl, and the lack of adequate metropolitan governmental structures. These orientations unquestionably are useful approaches to urban studies. The metropolitan orientation was, in fact, the approach promulgated in the special issue of the *American Behavioral Scientist* mentioned above, though in that presentation it was somewhat elaborated through a conception of the metropolis as a social system. But as conceptions which provide clear boundaries and foci for urban studies, they have major failings. For example, so far they have generally failed to provide fully satisfactory answers to the following kinds of questions which continue to plague the field:

1) What is the distinction between urban and industrial, as for example in the phrase "urban-industrial society?"

2) To what degree should urban studies have a "societal" as well as a "local community" or metropolitan focus?

3) Is any problem which exists in an urban area, an urban problem?

4) Should spatial relationships be the main focus of urban studies?

5) Aren't most small towns in modern society urban by virtue of the fact that they share a mostly urban culture?

6) What range of phenomena are *non*-urban?

7) How can "urban" best be conceptualized for international and comparative urban analysis?

We believe that the failure to provide satisfactory answers to these and related questions stems, in part, from the fact that the metropolitan region and urban development conceptions for urban studies are not always relevant, or at least the most relevant, perspectives from which to analyze a variety of *social* phenomena associated with the term "urban." These social phenomena increasingly command the attention of many persons in the urban field. Persons with metropolitan and urban development orientations are much concerned about "human renewal" and the fact that "planning is for people," about poverty and delinquency, etc., but at the same time they are extremely uneasy about opening the flood gates of urban studies to the frankly social and cultural realm. A leading scholar in this field was overheard proclaiming, just the other day, "by urban studies we mean a focus on urban development (from the point of view given above)—we shouldn't get caught in the trap of studying urban life and culture, and things like that, because then you end up studying almost everything in society under the term urban." His main reference was to the fact that urban life and culture are as much societal as specifically urban phenomena, and in any event they often have little to do with a metropolitan and spatial orientation.

Yet, social problems are just as important in cities these days as physical problems, and possibly more so, and the various problems of the city are inextricably related to one another. If urban studies were in the nature of a discipline it could perhaps decide that its exclusive concern was with various factors having to do with the use of urban space or metropolitan organization. But it is a problem-oriented field, and because of this fact it must develop the conceptual apparatus necessary for analyzing and finding solutions to these problems. The conceptual apparatus it now has is not up to the job of dealing with urban social problems, by almost everyone's common agreement.

Should urban studies be concerned, therefore, with *all* aspects of the culture and social process of urban areas? It must be fairly obvious that *urban* culture and social processes make up the great bulk of such phenomena in contemporary society. For this reason they are the concern of all culturally and socially oriented disciplines and fields, and not just a single field. A dilemma of urban studies is that the term urban ranges in meaning from the very specific to the very general, and the field can not afford to embrace either extreme. On the one extreme it would get caught as a limited concern not up to the demands made on it, and on the other it would be a presumptuous and untenable academic enterprise.

The most desirable conception of the field would consist of a focus on urban phenomena with the later defined in a meaningful yet not too limited way, and a scope which includes the social and cultural but does not embrace every aspect of the social sciences. Such a conception, and the urban theories and research which would be derived from it, should also be able to provide answers to the kinds of questions raised above, and be of some assistance in solving the range of problems (physical, economic, political, and social) found in urban areas.

What would such a conception look like, and would a field based on it be manageable and defensible in the academic system? In the remainder of this paper we shall try to answer both of these questions, first by putting forth *tentatively* and *briefly* the outlines of a conceptual scheme for urban studies, and second by discussing the implications of the scheme for urban studies as an academic field. In the process, we shall hope to clarify the meaning of the term urban as it seems most appropriately used in an integrated and interdisciplinary academic research enterprise.

In our judgment, the academic field of urban studies should be focused primarily on two things: [2]

a) the structure and function of communities which are *relatively urban* in character; and

b) the causes, conditions, and consequences of the *urban process* as it manifests itself within communities and societies.

Thus the field is concerned with both a structural-functional and a process approach. In regard to the first approach, the term urban is used to refer to communities which are substantially *affected by the urban process* in comparison with other communities (usually within the same society). There can be no hard and fast rule as to what is urban and what is non-urban in this sense—it is always a matter of degree. A *society* is urbanized (affected by the urban process) to the degree that its constituent communities are urbanized (internally and interdependently). One can therefore speak of an urban society, but only with reference to the aggregated characteristics of its constituent communities and community interdependencies, (and one can speak of an urban community, but only with the inclusion of reference—as we shall explain more fully below—to its relationships to other communities and the parent society).

The second approach (process) concerns certain general processes of social organization which affect all units of a society but which, when they are manifest in community units, can collectively be called the urban process.

The basic questions to which we must address ourselves, therefore, are: a) What is a community, b) How does it relate to other communities and to the larger society, c) What is the urban process, and, d) How does the urban process affect communities?

1. The Nature of Communities

The term "community" is one of the most ambiguous in the literature of the social sciences, but it is nonetheless a term which is difficult to dispense with. We use the term to mean *local community,* having to do with a locality or spatial grouping rather than "sense of community" as in "a community of scholars," though the latter meaning of the term is related.

For purposes of this paper, let us define community as a sub-societal social unit which consists of persons who share a common geographic area interacting in terms of a common culture and which incorporates a range of social structures which function to meet a relatively broad range of needs of all persons who make up the social unit. Thus it is a kind of locality group (which is composed of all persons who reside within a bounded territory) as opposed to a *functional* group (which is composed of persons who are bound together in order to perform a specific set of functions). The latter class of groups includes schools, banks, governments, churches, etc., which can be considered for certain purposes as the primary units of communities (as well as of nations as a particular kind of locality grouping).

There are three principal types of communities:

a) *neighborhoods,* which are socially bounded spatial units (i.e., the boundary is primarily as perceived by its occupants);

b) *municipalities*—politically bounded spatial units, (e.g., cities); and,

c) *ecological areas*—physically bounded spatial units (e.g., metropolitan regions).

These communities have different hierarchical positions (though not necessarily with reference to political authority), they have somewhat different functions, and each presents a useful orientation with which to view *certain classes* of phenomena. All three are "affected by the urban process," though they are not defined in relation to that process.

Strictly speaking, community phenomena are not all the phenomena which take place within communities (i.e., within a spatially bounded area). Rather, community phenomena consist of those ways in which the functions of community units (schools, families, governments, stores, etc.) are integrated with one another so as to maintain community order and cohesion. The community focus, therefore, is on inter-organizational and inter-institutional relationships and integrative mechanisms at the level of "localized" social interaction within a society. This is sometimes referred to as the "residual" notion of community, or what is left when the primary functions and activities of functional and (sub) locality groups are analytically factored out. Community integrative mechanisms include the market, the political process (as distinct from the government), communication and transportation, class stratification and the distribution of power and prestige, symbolic integration and "expressive" integration (sense-of-community).

Finally, space is a relatively more important phenomenon for locality than for functional groups, as a behavioral cause, condition, and facility; but it is by no means the only important phenomenon associated with the community concept.

2. How Do Communities Relate to One Another and to the Larger Society?

First, the units (groups) of a community are related outside the community:

a) as part of an organizational hierarchy (local-national government, local unit of General Motors to the national corporation, local church to the national body, etc.); and,

b) to the larger culture usually in an institutionalized way (schools to the institution of education, churches to the institution of religion, etc.) Note that most academic fields are focused on such institutional complexes, *viz.,* business, education, social welfare, agriculture, and so on.

Second, inter-organizational and inter-institutional integrative phenomena at the community level are related to the same phenomena in other communities and at the societal level. The local market is a specialized part of regional and national markets, local transportation and communication are parts of societal systems, local class allocations are closely tied to a societal network, and so on.

3. What Is the Urban Process?

Communities are affected by many different forces or processes, such as the natural environment (climate, natural resources, etc.), demographic trends, cultural values, norms, and definitions, social organizational processes, and technological developments. It has never been clearly resolved which of these factors cause communities to manifest attributes which can be labeled urban, a difficulty which is increased by the fact that they are interrelated in a very complex way.

We feel that it is most useful to use the term urban to refer to processes of *social organization,* which however affect and are affected by the various other factors. Very briefly, the urban process consists essentially of the community application of the process through which units of organization become more *specialized* (division of labor) and hence more *interdependent,* and the sum of units becomes more *complex.* Thus urban communities, relative to non-urban communities, are invariably more complex due to the fact that urban community units are more specialized (both functionally and spatially) and more interdependent.

While this organizational *condition* is the principal mark of the urban process, a variant of the process which is both a response to the condition and to some degree a cause of it (and which may or may not usefully be included under the term "urban process") is the rationalized coordination of social units which is made necessary by the facts of specialization and interdependence. The process of rationalizing organization in society leads to further "conditions" which are often called urban, e.g., an increased scale of organization (and span of organizational control), a greater amount of prescribed behavior and centralized decision making, and still further specialization and complexity. The dominant mode of the rationalizing process is *bureaucratization.*

Urbanization (the aggregation of people into relatively large, dense, and heterogeneous settlements) is not the same thing as the urban process. Rather, it is a *spatial* manifestation of that process. People and activities cluster in larger and denser spatial aggregates as a concomitant of the broader urban process. This distinction is critical because, among other reasons, "urbanism" (a term which generally refers to the culture of urbanized communities) so often is discussed as a *result* of urbanization; whereas it is in fact a result of the broader urban process (together with related processes).

Another critical distinction is between the urban process and the *industrial-automative* process. The latter refers primarily to technological rather than organizational phenomena, though these phenomena are often two sides of the same coin. Technology is advanced through processes of rationalized (industrial) organization (but also through invention, cultural assimilation, etc.), and organizational forms are greatly affected by technological developments (witness the automobile). But strictly speaking, industrialization refers to the substitution of non-human for human sources of energy, and automation refers to the substitution of sources of control (in the one case muscle, and in the other, mind). Comparisons of urban-industrial with urban-pre-industrial communities point up the distinctions between the two processes, although much more knowledge in this area is needed.

Cultural phenomena of course overlay these processes, in part cause and in part effect. Certainly the role of ethnicity and religion in cities, and the effect on community forms of a "capitalist" rather than a "socialist" economy, have to be treated as somewhat independent of the urban process. In the same sense, the effects of the natural environment must be considered as independent, e.g., a port city vs. an inland city, or a tropical city vs. an arctic city.

4. How Does the Urban Process Affect Communities?

All social units may be studied in terms of the degree to which they are affected by the above forces and processes. For example, schools in our society are becoming increasingly specialized and complex, and their organization is becoming more rationalized, etc. This in fact is one of the main interests of the academic field of education. The effect of the urban process on communities is the aggregate of such urbanizing effects on community units, and in particular the effects on *community integration* of increasing specialization and of the increasing loss of community *autonomy* due to the fact that community units at the same time become more interdependent with *extra-community* units. The pre-eminent urban problem, therefore, is the lack of coordination and integration of community units in the face of interdependence, from both an intra- and extra-community point of view.

Thus community market mechanisms cannot cope with urban sprawl and with the whole gamut of needs for housing and open space; culture patterns are poorly adapted to demands for desegregation and equal opportunity; socialization mechanisms are inadequate for the culturally deprived child; health and welfare mechanisms are inadequate for multi-problem families; transportation mechanisms have not adequately adapted to new spatial relationships; governmental boundaries and departmental separation hinder comprehensive urban planning, and so on, and local community processes in general are less able to cope with these integrative needs because the need for coordination spans ever larger areas of society.

It is important to note that urban problems and the solutions to these problems refer to the same phenomena, i.e., inter-organizational and inter-institutional relationships. An urban problem results from a lack of coordination in the face of the need for it, and the solution to that problem is better coordination. Usually this coordination is improved through the processes of rationalized organization mentioned above.

Implications for the Field of Urban Studies

We have presented little more than what we hope is a useful set of concepts, at a fairly high level of abstraction, with which to clarify the meaning of the term urban and the foci and boundaries of the field of urban studies. Time and space do not permit the elaboration of these concepts into an urban theory, but such an elaboration will be presented in future papers. At this point, however, a number of implications of this approach for the field of urban studies might be noted.

We have suggested, in summary, that the proper foci of urban studies are the urban process and community phenomena as they are affected by this process, and that by community phenomena we mean inter-organizational integrative relationships and mechanisms associated with neighborhoods, municipalities, and ecological areas. We have indicated that urban studies is an interdisciplinary academic field (and have distinguished a field from a discipline), and that because of the nature of a field urban studies has a primary interest in urban problems and their solution (as defined above).

How is urban studies differentiated from other academic fields? Most academic fields are concerned as we suggested, with institutional complexes—education, religion, business, law, medicine, etc. (and very often a *profession* with the same name is the action side of these fields). Urban studies is focused on the way in which these institutions (and their organizational manifestations) are integrated at the level of the urban community or locality group.

A case is sometimes made that, to be realistic, urban studies must be concerned with inter-institutional relationships at *all* levels of society. Among the reasons given for this are that as communities become more urban, they become more intertwined with the larger society, and that the solution to urban community problems almost always involves improved societal coordination in addition to community coordination. A case can probably be made for *every* field of knowledge that it is impossible properly to study something without studying everything. In the case of urban studies, however, it is extremely important that urban community integration be studied with explicit reference to its interdependence with the larger society and culture. Urban studies is not interested in the larger society and culture (e.g., all inter-institutional relationships) *per se*, but rather as they affect and are affected by intergration at the locality group level. This does not mean, however, that local community integration is not analytically a more or less independent set of variables, for it is this *analytic* independence which gives the field its primary boundary. To deny this is to suggest that what already must be considered as *a* "master" field should be *the* master field.

Incidentally, the professional counterpart of the urban studies field is not at all clear, but because it is something of a master field there may have to be more than one specialized professional off-shoot of it. Undoubtedly, in view of what we have said above, these specialized professions will center around the process of planning—the rationalization of social organization so as purposefully to guide social change. Contemporary "city" planning, with its spatial orientation, is one such specialized profession.

It is possible, as we hinted at the outset of this paper, that urban studies, particularly as we have defined it, is of such a nature that it will face some real obstacles in its pursuit of solid academic status. Surely an integrative field like urban studies is somewhat out of keeping with the long-run trend toward the specialization of knowledge; and while urban studies is riding on a current wave of interdisciplinary endeavor in academia, the latter may be no more than a passing fad—though we suspect and certainly hope that it is not. Just as specialization causes the need for coordination in urban areas, the same is true in regard to the pursuit of knowledge, and urban studies may usefully fill such a coordinative role. But to fill such a role, a unified conceptual scheme will doubtless be necessary. Urban research can clearly proceed without it, as is the case at present, but an integrated field of urban studies probably can not. The development of such a scheme is not without its difficulties, as the reader of this paper by now must be aware.

This new *Urban Affairs Quarterly,* insofar as it is academically oriented, could contribute substantially toward the clarification of many of these and other issues discussed in this paper. As for non-academics (and we hope it will be oriented to both audiences), they can often slice through academic roadblocks merely by bringing reality into the picture! Finally, and in spite of the complex conceptual issues raised in this paper, some satisfaction can be drawn from the fact that in the time it takes for this paper to go to press at least one new urban studies program will probably have been established at some university or college in the United States.

Notes

1. *The First Five Years—1959 to 1964,* Cambridge, Mass.: Joint Center for Urban Studies of M.I.T. and Harvard, April, 1964, pp. 8–11.

2. This scheme is an outgrowth of a good many theoretical developments, mostly within the discipline of sociology, particularly community studies and ecological theories (see especially: Warren, Roland, *The Community in America.* Chicago: Rand McNally and Company, 1963), theories of urbanization and the urban process, most notably the work of the Center for Metropolitan Studies at Northwestern University (see especially: Greer, Scott, *The Emerging City; Myth and Reality,* Glencoe: Free Press, 1962, and Mack, Raymond W. and Dennis C. McElrath, "Urban Social Differentiation and the Allocation of Resources," *The Annals,* Vol. 352, March, 1964, pp. 26–32), and theories of social integration (e.g., Bredemeier, Harry C., *Urban Problems and Social Integration,* unpublished manuscript, Urban Studies Center, Rutgers—The State University, 1962.

CHAPTER TWO

ECOLOGICAL AND DEMOGRAPHIC ASPECTS OF URBAN LIFE

INTRODUCTION

Among urban theorists and researchers there is a strong temptation not only to fashion theory in terms of available empirical data, but also to form popular explanatory models derived from a limited range of data. The study of the city as a type as well as a level of human settlement is a case in point. For a long time in this country the ecology and demography of the city were presented largely in terms of the American (that is, North American) scene. No less dominant was the conviction that urban sociology is indeed really urban ecology.

That picture has changed, thanks in great measure to the prodigious labors of geographers, historians, and anthropologists who have set forth the historical, geographical, and ecological processes, forms, and factors of cities in all parts of the world; that work is still going on. In addition, it became increasingly clear to many social theorists that the more limited ecological model, for the most part associated with the work of the "Chicago school"—one thinks of the outstanding work of Park, Burgess, McKenzie, and Wirth during the twenties and thirties—seriously needed restatement. Currently an ecological revisionism is under way, as the following selections make clear: the reference here is mainly to the articles by Orleans, Duncan, and Willhelm, although Schnore is by no means uncritical of the fashionable (but also, it must be remembered, pioneering) work of the interwar period. The remaining articles in this chapter suggest not only the continuing importance and utility of the ecological approach to the study of urbanism and urbanization, but also demonstrate the various analytical interests motivating the investigations of the urban ecologists: their interests in social interaction, in social structure, and in demography of the city.

Far from being a closed book, the ecology of the city remains to be established on a solid cross-cultural and historically comparative basis. Cognizance must be taken of the inherent variability between "primordial," "classic," and "industrial" urbanisms, to use Lampard's distinctions. Urban ecological theory, particularly if guided and not dominated by prevailing ecological models, is surely on the threshold of a great new volume of impressive contributions to our knowledge of the city.

THE MYTH OF HUMAN ECOLOGY

Leo F. Schnore

I have been motivated to give some thought to the matter of ecology's place in sociology by Kingsley Davis's recent discussion of "The Myth of Functional Analysis." I was struck for example, by his reference to the fact that "Characteristics that the functionalists themselves regard as either accidental faults or as totally alien to their point of view . . . critics often regard as the essence of the approach." [1] Davis also observes that "so-called functionalists and professed enemies of functionalism are often *doing* the same kind of analysis." [2] Both of these remarks, of course, could be applied to human ecology and ecologists with some justification, and one could list examples at some length. An ecologist is not inclined to claim that his approach is the only mode of analysis that deserves recognition as distinctively sociological, but if we agree from the start that human ecology does not represent the sum and substance of sociology, where does it fit? How does it articulate with the main body of sociological analysis? In my opinion, the prevailing *"myth"* of human ecology is that ecology is somehow *"marginal"* to sociology.

One finds ecology represented as marginal, for example, in introductory textbooks, as when Arnold Rose states that sociology, as a discipline, "has historically come to include the study of two sets of phenomena which are not logically part of their central subject matter, any more than economics and political science are part of sociology. These two sub-disciplines are demography . . . and human ecology." [3] A more extreme version is to be found in Boskoff's assertion that "In seeking a distinctive set of phenomena, orthodox human ecology has not only seceded from modern sociology—it has largely withdrawn from science." [4] But advocates as well as critics are numbered among those who regard ecology as marginal to sociology. Thus we find one of the acknowledged founders of human ecology—Ernest W. Burgess—contending that "human ecology, strictly speaking, falls outside of sociology . . . Human ecology, logically, is a separate discipline from sociology. Like population studies, it has become attached to sociology because it provides the substructure for the study of social factors in human behavior." [5]

In the following sections, I intend to argue that human ecology—rather than being marginal to sociology—represents one effort to deal with *the central problem of sociological analysis*. Further, I shall argue that the ecologist's efforts appear to be marginal only in the light of certain *tendencies within American sociology*—tendencies which are themselves to be explained in large part by methodological developments. Finally, I shall argue that ecology's real potential lies in its *contributions to a macro- as over against a micro-sociology*. I shall take up these points in somewhat different order, and then proceed to identify ecology's distinctive attack upon the central problem of sociology.

Reprinted from *Sociological Inquiry,* Vol. XXXI, No. 2, 1961.

The Need

One key task confronting anyone who advocates a particular approach is the obligation to demonstrate that it has emerged naturally as an extension of prior work. In any essay concerned with Durkheim's "social morphology," I tried to show that ecology has a legitimate *sociological* ancestry, and that it is something more than a simple attempt to "apply" some rudimentary biological concepts to social phenomena; the latter is one of the older and lesser myths of human ecology.[6] A more critical task is to show that the approach one advocates is fruitful, i.e., that it yields distinctive hypotheses for research. This stipulation amounts to saying that one must demonstrate the existence of a genuine *need*. While I do not pretend that there is a great popular clamor on behalf of the ecological perspective, I am convinced that there is a widespread and barely hidden dissatisfaction with certain salient features of contemporary American sociology.

First of all, several writers, including representatives of radically different schools of thought, have commented upon the micro-sociological—and even psychological—drift of American sociology in recent decades. Some of these writers adopt a neutral stance, expressing no explicit preference for the macroscopic as over against the microscopic approach. Others, however, have expressed varying degrees of dissatisfaction with the current state of the field. Thus Bellah has observed that "Since the generation of Weber and Durkheim macroscopic problems involving comparative and historical research have been somewhat slighted as microscopic research based on new methods and instruments has come to the fore. Not only general sociology, but micro-sociology itself, would suffer if this imbalance were to go too far."[7]

The technical-methodological basis of this drift toward the microscopic has been noted elsewhere. Perhaps the most sweeping indictment of all is to be found in the charges levelled by James Coleman: "Social theory has, I think, allowed itself to be sidetracked off its main task, which is to develop theories for social systems—whether they be total social systems or systems of behavior in small groups. Our attention is too often drawn away from the system itself to the individuals within it, so that we construct theories to account for some individual's behavior."[8] Coleman agrees that our techniques have led us in the direction of micro-sociology:

> Two things have happened: the complexity of these [data-gathering] techniques has shifted our focus from substantive problems to the techniques themselves; and secondly, this very move down to the individual level has kept us fascinated there, unable to get back up to the social level. Survey research has continued to be a kind of aggregate psychology, rather than sociology; it has continued to study the opinions of a population sample rather than public opinion, to study buyers rather than the market, so study individuals rather than the community . . .
>
> The second problem, the psychologizing of sociology through survey research, has already shown signs of solution. Techniques are being devised, and studies are being designed and carried out, which pervert the survey into a truly sociological instrument. Structural effects analysis, comparing several social contexts, relational analysis, using sociometric techniques, and more traditional survey methods, using variables like social class and sibling position in the

> family, or status in an organization, and so on, are beginning to allow the study of sociological problems rather than purely psychological ones . . . Yet in most of these techniques, the individual behavior or attitude is still the dependent variable, though social structure or norms are the independent variables. The functioning of a social system is seldom analyzed by quantitative techniques—as it has been by qualitative observational studies.[9]

With respect to the difficulties attending the microscopic interpretation of macroscopic problems, C. Wright Mills has presented an equally forceful statement:

> The idea of social structure cannot be built up only from ideas or facts about a specific series of individuals and their reactions to their milieux. Attempts to explain social and historical events on the basis of psychological theories about "the individual" often rest upon the assumption that society is nothing but a great scatter of individuals and that, accordingly, if we know all about these 'atoms' we can in some way add up the information and thus know about society. It is not a fruitful assumption.[10]

But enough of appeals to authority. Each of these eminent writers would very probably prescribe different solutions to the same problem. I am not trying to persuade anyone that these anti-microscopic views have suddenly become dominant; far from it, for these are the words of "critics of the existing order." Nor am I advocating an ecological approach as the sole solution—or even the "best" solution—to the problems they have raised. Certainly human ecology is not widely regarded as a strong intellectual force in contemporary American sociology, if one may judge (1) from the fact that only 100 out of 4200 members of our professional association select it as a major interest, and (2) from the extremely limited attention given it in three recent evaluations of the current status and future prospects of the field as a whole. Ecology receives only brief treatment in the chapters devoted to urban sociology in the volumes entitled *Sociology in the United States of America, Review of Sociology: Analysis of a Decade,* and *Sociology Today: Problems and Prospects.*[11] In the last two, in fact, emphasis is placed upon the rash of criticisms of the ecological approach that appeared in the late 'forties and early 'fifties. But some of us are persuaded that human ecology —despite its possible defects and imperfections—has a great deal to offer contemporary sociology, and that its signal contribution might be toward a genuine *macro-sociology.*

We can start with the proposition that the study of *social organization* is the central focus of the entire sociological enterprise.[12] In Rossi's words, "The proper study of sociology is social organization. On this perspective there is probably the greatest degree of agreement in our discipline." [13] But the logical status of the concept "organization" varies significantly according to its *analytical position* in the frame of reference that is employed. At risk of oversimplification, it can be said that aspects of organization—or, more generally, structural properties of whole populations—appear in two quite separate guises in sociological analysis: as *independent* and as *dependent* variables. Similarly, properties of individual organisms have these dual analytical positions. The logically possible frames of reference are four in number, and we may first of all distinguish two general modes of analysis directed to the explanation of the behavior of the individual organism: *individual* psychology and *social* psychology.

Individual Psychology

"Individual psychology" largely seeks its explanatory variables among properties of individual organisms other than that which is the *explanandum* at the moment. Thus a psychologist setting out to account for variations in learning or perception tends to confine himself to properties of the organism in his search for independent variables. Because sociology is our subject, a universally acceptable definition of individual psychology is not essential to my purposes, but we might pause to consider the following statement by Tolman: "The final dependent variable in which, as a psychologist, I am interested is behavior. It is the behavior of organisms, human and sub-human, which I wish to predict and control." He goes on to identify "the five independent variables of 1) *environmental stimuli,* 2) *physiological drive,* 3) *heredity,* 4) *previous training, and* 5) *maturity.*"[14]

The last four of these are clearly properties of individual organisms, but "environmental stimuli" are clearly external to the organism. However, it seems to be commonly accepted as axiomatic that it is only as these stimuli are experienced by the organism that behavioral reactions ensue. Thus there is justification for asserting that individual psychologists tend generally to predict from one property of an individual organism to another, or to another set of behaviors. If this effort is pursued self-consciously and consistently at the individual level of analysis, the result is a kind of biological or physiological inquiry; it seeks a universalistic explanation of a particular psychological process, an account that holds for all men everywhere, without respect to social position, group membership, allegiance to particular norms, etc.

Social Psychology

As soon as these last-named variables enter the analysis, however, the analyst leaves the domain of individual psychology *per se*—psychology unadorned by qualifying adjectives—and enters the realm of "social psychology."

This view is distinctive in that it seems to represent an attempt to move between two levels of analysis, with certain group properties (e.g., size) serving as independent variables, and certain individual properties (e.g., cognitive processes) taken as dependent variables. Much of the work in "small group" research is of this nature, but this mode of analysis is by no means confined to situations in which face-to-face interaction is possible. (In addition, we shall see that not all small-group research is social psychological in orientation.) The use of "social" explanations of "psychological" processes can also be found in analyses of society in the large, especially within that portion of the literature that focusses upon "cultural" differences in behavior.

In general, it may be said that any effort to explain individual behavior by reference to group membership or position, real or imagined, makes use of a social-psychological hypothesis. Social psychology tends to ignore what is common to all men (this is left to individual psychology) and to ignore what is unique to particular individuals (this is left to the biographer); it deals with what is common to classes of individuals in a particular culture, a particular stratum, a particular role. (This point sometimes leads to needless confusion. Some social psychologists firmly deny that they deal with "individual behavior." What they mean is that they eschew any concern with the actions of particular, named individuals. However, the conduct of classes of individuals or "actors"—or classes of individual behavior—is precisely central to their interests.)

Now the treatment of "social organization" is not inevitably the same in all social-psychological inquiries. The explanation ordinarily proceeds by predicting from population to individual properties. An example is Wirth's famous analysis of "urbanism as a way of life," in which variations in population size, density, and heterogeneity are employed in an attempt to account for variations in individual behavior and outlook in the urban setting.[15] In addition to appearing as attributes of populations, however, certain aspects of social organization may be transmuted into individual properties for analytical purposes. Examples of social-psychological analyses strictly confined to the individual level are to be found in most of the work subsumed under "role analysis," almost all of contemporary survey research, and in the analysis of "reference groups." Here the individual's position in the social structure is essentially regarded as a *personal* attribute, analytically speaking, and it is employed to explain his behavior *vis-a-vis* other persons playing complementary roles, or in particular areas of conduct that are amenable to a survey approach, such as voting or fertility. The "reference group" too is an individual attribute, in that it designates an individual's sense of allegiance to or affiliation with a group or category, without respect to actual membership; in some instances, in fact, it refers to little more than a stereotype in the mind of an individual, while in others it specifies a specific position or a broad social category to which he aspires.

Organization has a different meaning in these various inquiries, sometimes appearing as the "social environment" which is perceived by the actor, sometimes as a set of normative constraints, sometimes as a congeries of cultural values. In all of them, however, the common stamp is an effort to explain individual behavior by reference to organizational attributes of populations or to real or imagined positions within the social structure. In summary, we may identify the major mode of social-psychological inquiry as a broad-scale research strategy that attempts to predict—if only contextually—from some aspect of social organization to some individual behavior or conduct. Thus Newcomb has specified "the characteristic point of view of social psychology" as follows:

> We may say that social psychology deals with the association of variations in the behavior of one or more individuals with variations in social environment . . . Secondly, differences in social environment and the way in which they are experienced are very largely determined by the way in which the individual's society is organized.[16]

Psychological Sociology

In contrast to "social psychology" is an approach that I prefer to call "psychological sociology." The positions of the adjective and the noun designate the independent and dependent variables respectively. "Psychological sociology" subsumes all efforts to explain properties of populations by reference to the properties of the individuals who—from one perspective—may be said to compose these populations. One of the most succinct expressions of this point of view is to be found in a plea by Swanson, who asks

> that we take seriously the dictum of Thomas, Znaniecki, and a host of others that, in theorizing about the causes of *any* behavior, *individual or collective,* we conceive of our independent variables in terms of the environment as experienced by those behaving, and that we assume that their acts are efforts to deal with the world as they perceive it. This has many implications. The only one stressed here is the suggestion that, assuming human biology to be constant for purposes of theory-building, *one may predict variations in the organization of a group* from variations in environmental problems as its members experience them.[17]

Many other examples are to be found in the literature on "culture and personality," at least in that phase of this work which attempts to account for such macroscopic features as forms of political organization in terms of individual experience with child-rearing practices, etc. Particular analyses, of course, are likely to slip into the social-psychological mode of reasoning from time to time. Moreover, certain population attributes appear sometimes as no more than "intervening variables," where individual properties are said to give rise to certain group properties, and the latter—in their turn—are viewed as influencing individual behavior. One of the best-known examples is to be found in Kardiner's discussion of "primary" and "secondary" institutions and their mutual relations to individual behavior.[18]

In any event, most efforts to explain macroscopic social phenomena in terms of "basic personality structure" or "national character" partake of the assumptions identified here as those of psychological sociology. To a strict and doctrinaire Durkheimian, these efforts are almost doomed to defeat, since they patently violate his famous methodological stricture: "The determining cause of a social fact should be sought among the social facts preceding it and not among the states of the individual consciousness."[19] However, to the extent that these efforts are ultimately directed, no matter how circuitously, toward the explanation of individual behavior they may be regarded as entirely legitimate, even from the standpoint of one who insists upon viewing society as a phenomenon *sui generis.*

It is evident here that one's assumptions concerning levels of "emergence" are crucial to the development of his position on these matters. Some writers assume that "only the individual is real," and that social structure is either a kind of convenient fiction or a shorthand designation for summarizing individual behavior in aggregative terms; these "social nominalists" are inclined to the view here labelled "psychological sociology," although they eclectically adopt certain aspects of social-psychological thought as it suits their analytical needs. In contrast, "social realists" assert that social structure represents something other than the simple sum of individual actions, and they are much more likely to confine themselves to social psychology, as defined here, or else to adopt an ecological perspective.[20] They tend to be Durkheimian in orientation, rejecting the easy reductionism that underlies psychological sociology. Needless to say, it is difficult to place individual writers in one or another of these convenient categories;

different portions of the work of particular authors, however, can be readily identified in these terms. One might even say that a sure index of an analyst's theoretical sophistication is the extent to which he gives evidence that he is aware of a shift in the direction of his analysis when it does occur.

Macro-Sociology

The first of the two modes of analysis identified here as "macro-sociological" has one feature in common with "psychological sociology" as defined above. Both approaches take organization, or some particular aspect of it, as the *explanandum*. Aside from a common interest in the same type of dependent variable, however, there are few other similarities. This is most clear with respect to human ecology, especially as it has been developed by Amos H. Hawley.[21] For one thing, the ecological mode of analysis remains at one level with respect to the variables it employs; it seeks its independent variables among other "attributes of organized populations," such as their demographic features. (It should be added, of course, that there is nothing to prevent the use of other organizational features in the effort to explain a given facet of organization. Durkheim's use of increasing "dynamic density" and competition to explain mounting structural differentiation is a case in point. In fact, this is the only one of the perspectives discussed so far that conforms strictly to Durkheim's rule regarding the explanation of "social facts.")

There is, however, another macro-sociological mode of analysis that can be identified, and it is one that ecologists are inclined to use from time to time. Here organization appears—not as the dependent variable—but as one of the *independent* variables. In point of fact, human ecology represents a broad *type* of analysis, within which more specific types can be identified, with their designation depending upon the nature of the dependent variable. Within the ecological framework, effort can be directed to the explanation of technological, environmental, or demographic features, so that several "ecologies" might be identified. Just as different varieties of individual psychology are designated by subclassification according to the analytical purposes at hand (e.g., the various "psychologies" of perception, learning, memory, etc.) one can similarly identify "population ecology" and "organizational ecology." [22]

Now both of the "macro-sociological" approaches I have identified can be applied to populations of any size and degree of complexity; that is why I label them "macro-sociological" rather than "ecological." Human ecology is only one of a *variety* of conceivable macro-sociological modes of analysis. In fact, one of the major themes in "small group" research and theory is directed toward the analysis of group properties *per se*. For example, the analysis of the interrelations of group size and patterns of internal communication can be conducted from either of these last two perspectives. In addition, of course, sociometric techniques are adaptable to these modes of inquiry; rather than utilizing sociometric observations to identify individuals (as "stars," "isolates," etc.), one simply characterizes whole networks of interaction according to patterns, and then proceeds to deal with these patterns *as properties of aggregates*.[23]

Conclusions

The four modes of analysis identified here are broad indeed; they crosscut much of social science. For one thing, a single "discipline" may employ all of them at one point or another. And I have already noted that a particular investigator may use all of them in different parts of his work. Even a single study—particularly a comprehensive effort—may employ these different approaches in rapid succession; an outstanding example is the recent study of *Union Democracy* by Lipset, Trow and Coleman.[24] Community studies are particularly prone to make use of all of these devices at one point or another in the analysis. Perhaps there is danger in undisciplined eclecticism, for the analyst may not be aware that he is shifting perspectives, or moving to another level of analysis. Burgess has sounded a clear warning against this hazard:

> It is possible to inquire how ecological processes work, without the necessity of doing research on the social psychological processes. It is also possible to inquire about the social psychological processes, without doing research on the ecological aspects. These are two different ways of looking at human behavior . . . While it is true that both approaches can be brought together to produce significant findings on particular problems, their joint use should be conscious and deliberate. Many research workers unwittingly mix the two; as a consequence, they make a mess of their studies.[25]

Despite these reservations, however, a single "subject matter" may be greatly illuminated by the use of all four perspectives. To take an area with which I have some acquaintance—population analysis—valuable examples of each type of inquiry can be readily cited. First, there is a substantial literature dealing with the individual physiology and psychology of reproduction, aging, and death; contributions can be found in disciplines located throughout the full range of biology. Secondly, the social-psychological approach is employed with increasing frequency, particularly by students of migration and fertility. There is even an occasional effort to apply the approach that I have labelled "psychological sociology," for some writers have tried to explain certain aspects of the reorganization and redistribution of metropolitan populations by reference to assumed individual propensities.[26] Lastly, there are numerous instances of the "macro-sociological"—and particularly the ecological—modes of analysis. For example, a substantial literature has accumulated in which the organizational consequences of variations in population size are examined; a recent and detailed illustration may be found in the work of Duncan and Reiss.[27] Organizational variables are also frequently utilized as explanatory factors in demographic analysis, as in various efforts to account for variations in population composition in terms of the economic base and functional organization of communities.

In summary, I have attempted to identify four more-or-less distinctive modes of analysis to be found in social science, one of which is the "macro-sociological." I have indicated some of the ways in which I see this mode as different from two other major types of inquiry within sociology, and I have suggested that *"human ecology" might be best regarded as a type of "macro-sociology."* Its most distinctive feature can perhaps be seen in its adherence to a single level of analysis, in which properties of whole populations are at issue. Although other approaches also take social organization as an independent or dependent variable, this adherence to a consistent level of analysis makes the perspective of human ecology somewhat unusual in the analytical *armamentarium* of the discipline. At the same time, the central role given to organization—as dependent or independent variable—places ecology clearly within the sphere of activities in which sociologists claim distinctive competence, i.e., the analysis of social organization. If human ecology is "marginal" to sociology, what is central?

Notes

1. Kingsley Davis, "The Myth of Functional Analysis as a Special Method in Sociology and Anthropology," *American Sociological Review,* 24 (1959), p. 758.

2. *Ibid.,* p. 771.

3. Arnold M. Rose, *Sociology: The Study of Human Relations* (New York: Alfred A. Knopf, 1956), p. 366.

4. Alvin Boskoff, "An Ecological Approach to Rural Society," *Rural Sociology,* 14 (1949), p. 308.

5. Quoted in Howard W. Odum, *American Sociology* (New York: Longmans, Green & Co., 1951), p. 353.

6. Leo F. Schnore, "Social Morphology and Human Ecology," *American Journal of Sociology,* 63 (1958), pp. 620–634.

7. Robert N. Bellah, "Durkheim and History," *American Sociological Review,* 24 (1959), p. 461.

8. James S. Coleman, "The Future of Sociology," a paper presented at the 36th Annual Institute of the Society for Social Research, University of Chicago, May 23, 1959, p. 10.

9. *Ibid.,* pp. 19–20.

10. C. Wright Mills, *The Sociological Imagination* (New York: Oxford University Press, 1959), p. 163.

11. Hans H. Zetterberg (editor), *Sociology in the United States of America* (Paris: UNESCO, 1956); Joseph B. Gittler (editor), *Review of Sociology: Analysis of a Decade* (New York: John Wiley and Sons, 1957); Robert K. Merton, Leonard Broom, and Leonard S. Cottrell (editors), *Sociology Today: Problems and Prospects* (New York: Basic Books, 1959).

12. Jack P. Gibbs and Walter T. Martin, "Toward a Theoretical System of Human Ecology," *Pacific Sociological Review,* 2 (1959), pp. 29–36.

13. Peter H. Rossi, "Comment," *American Journal of Sociology,* 65 (1959), p. 146.

14. Edward C. Tolman, "The Intervening Variable," in Melvin N. Marx (editor), *Psychological Theory* (New York: Macmillan Co., 1951), pp. 88–89.

15. Louis Wirth, "Urbanism as a Way of Life," *American Journal of Sociology,* 44 (1938), pp. 1–24.

16. Theodore Newcomb, *Social Psychology* (New York: Dryden Press, 1950), p. 25.

17. G. E. Swanson, "A Preliminary Laboratory Study of the Acting Crowd," *American Sociological Review,* 18 (1953), p. 522; italics added.

18. Abram Kardiner, *The Individual and His Society* (New York: Columbia University Press, 1939).

19. Émile Durkheim, *The Rules of Sociological Method* (Glencoe: Free Press, 1950), p. 110.

20. For a recent use of the distinction between realism and nominalism, see Kurt H. Wolff, "The Sociology of Knowledge and Sociological Theory," in Llewellyn Gross (editor), *Symposium on Sociological Theory* (Evanston: Row, Peterson, 1959), pp. 557–602.

21. Amos H. Hawley, *Human Ecology: A Theory of Community Structure* (New York: Ronald Press, 1950).

22. Jack P. Gibbs and Walter T. Martin, "Urbanization and Natural Resources: A Study in Organizational Ecology," *American Sociological Review,* 23 (1958), pp. 266–277.

23. One would hesitate to call such sociometric inquiries "ecological," and to regard small-group interests as "macrosociological," but the fundamental similarity in approach is noteworthy, despite the strain placed on the language. Perhaps "holistic" versus "atomistic" would provide a more clearcut set of alternatives; this possibility was suggested by Professor Duncan in a private communication. With him, I am inclined to reserve the term "human ecology" for efforts to understand the interconnections between variations in population, organization, environment and technology in the context of such macroscopic *units* as communities, regions and societies. See Otis Dudley Duncan, "Human Ecology and Population Studies," in Philip M. Hauser and Otis Dudley Duncan (editors), *The Study of Population* (Chicago: University of Chicago Press, 1959), pp. 678–716; and Otis Dudley Duncan and Leo F. Schnore, "Cultural, Behavioral, and Ecological Perspectives in the Study of Social Organization," *American Journal of Sociology,* 65 (1959), pp. 132–146.

24. S. M. Lipset, Martin A. Trow, and James S. Coleman, *Union Democracy* (Glencoe: Free Press, 1957).

25. Ernest W. Burgess, "The Ecology and Social Psychology of the City," in Donald J. Bogue (editor), *Needed Urban and Metropolitan Research* (Oxford, Ohio and Chicago: Spripps Foundation for Research in Population Problems, and Population Research and Training Center, University of Chicago, 1953), p. 80.

26. Wendell Bell, "Familism and Suburbanization: One Test of the Social Choice Hypothesis," *Rural Sociology,* 21 (1956), pp. 276–283; Sylvia Fleis Fava,

"Suburbanism as a Way of Life," *American Sociological Review,* 21 (1956), pp. 34–37.

27. Otis Dudley Duncan and Albert J. Reiss, Jr., *Social Characteristics of Urban and Rural Communities,* 1950 (New York: John Wiley and Sons, 1956).

FROM SOCIAL SYSTEM TO ECOSYSTEM

Otis Dudley Duncan

Levels and Systems

All science proceeds by a selective ordering of data by means of conceptual schemes. Although the formulation and application of conceptual schemes are recognized to entail, at some stage of inquiry, more or less arbitrary choices on the part of the theorist or investigator, we all acknowledge, or at least feel, that the nature of the "real world" exercises strong constraints on the development of schemes in science. Some schemes, used fruitfully over long periods of time, come to seem so natural that we find it difficult to imagine their being superseded. One type of scheme is deeply ingrained by our training as social scientists, to wit, the organization of data by *levels.* Kroeber is only voicing the consensus of a majority of scientists when he writes: [1]

> The subjects or materials of science . . . fall into four main classes or levels: the inorganic, organic, psychic, and sociocultural. . . . There is no intention to assert that the levels are absolutely separate, or separable by unassailable definitions. They are substantially distinct in the experience of the totality of science, and that is enough.

MacIver gives substantially the same classification, but instead of using the relatively colorless term "levels," he chooses to segregate the several "nexus of causation" into "great dynamic realms." [2]

It is significant that scientists, insofar as they do accept the doctrine of levels, tend to work *within* a level, not *with* it. The scheme of levels does not itself produce hypotheses; it can scarcely even be said to be heuristic. Its major contribution to the history of ideas has been to confer legitimacy upon the newer scientific approaches to the empirical world that, when they were emerging, had good use for any kind of ideological support.

Quite another type of conceptual scheme, the notion of *system,* is employed by the scientist in his day-to-day work. Conceptions of interdependent variation, of cause and effect, or even of mere patterning of sequence, derive from the idea that nature (using the term broadly for whatever can be studied naturalistically) manifests itself in collections of elements with more than nominal properties of unity.

No doubt there are many kinds of system, reflecting the kinds of elements comprising them and the modes of relationship conceived to hold among these elements. The point about this diversity that is critical to my argument is this.

Reprinted by permission of the author and publisher from *Sociological Inquiry,* Vol. 31, No. 2 (Spring, 1961), pp. 140–149.

When we elect, wittingly or unwittingly, to work *within* a level (as this term was illustrated above) we tend to discern or construct—whichever emphasis you prefer—only those kinds of system whose elements are confined to that level. From this standpoint, the doctrine of levels may not only fail to be heuristic, it may actually become anti-heuristic, if it blinds us to fruitful results obtainable by recognizing *systems that cut across levels.*

One such system, probably because it is virtually a datum of immediate experience, is rather readily accepted by social scientists: personality. Manifestly and phenomenologically an integration of nonrandomly selected genetic, physiologic, social, and psycho-cultural elements, personality has a kind of hard reality that coerces recognition, even when it can be related to other systems only with difficulty or embarrassment. If I am not mistaken, however, the concept of personality system enjoys a sort of privileged status. We do not so readily accede to the introduction into scientific discourse of other sorts of system concept entailing integration of elements from diverse levels. The resistance to such concepts is likely to be disguised in charges of "environmental determinism" or "reductionism." An example: The working assumption of some human ecologists that the human community is, among other things, an organization of activities in physical space is criticized (though hardly refuted!) by the contention that such a conceptual scheme is contrary to "'essentially and profoundly social" facts, i.e., "conscious choice of actors who vary in their ends and values." [3] We must resist the temptation to comment here on the curious assumption that the "essentially and profoundly social" has to do with such personal and subjective states as "ends and values," rather than with objective relations among interdependent living units. (Surely the latter is the prior significance of the "social," in an evolutionary if not an etymological sense.) The point to emphasize at present is, rather, that such a reaction to ecological formulations is tantamount to a denial of the crucial possibility that one can at least conceive of systems encompassing both human and physical elements. The "dynamic realm" of the psycho-social has indeed become a "realm," one ruled by an intellectual tyrant, when this possibility is willfully neglected or denied.

The Ecosystem

Acknowledged dangers of premature synthesis and superficial generalization notwithstanding, ecologists have been forced by the complexity of relationships manifested in their data to devise quite embracing conceptual schemes. The concept of ecosystem, a case in point, has become increasingly prominent in ecological study since the introduction of the term a quarter-century ago by the botanist, A. G. Tansley. "The *ecosystem,*" according to Allee and collaborators, "may be defined as the interacting environmental and biotic system." [4] Odum characterizes the ecosystem as a "natural unit . . . in which the exchange of materials between the living and nonliving parts follows circular paths." [5] The first quotation comes from an enlightening synthesis of information now available on the evolution of ecosystems; the second prefaces an exposition of principles concerning the operation of "biogeochemical cycles" in ecosystems. Social scientists whose acquaintance with general ecology is limited to gleanings from the essays of Park [6] or the polemic by Alihan [7] might do well to inform themselves concerning current developments in ecological theory by consulting such sources as these. Even more readily accessible is the statement of Dice: [8]

> Ecologists use the term ecosystem to refer to a community together with its habitat. An ecosystem, then, is an aggregation of associated species of plants and animals, together with the physical features of their habitat. Ecosystems . . . can be of any size or ecologic rank. . . . At the extreme, the whole earth and all its plant and animal inhabitants together constitute a world ecosystem.

Later in his text (ch. xv) the same author undertakes a classification of "human ecosystems." This classification presents in elementary fashion much material familiar to social scientists; but it also conveys an unaccustomed emphasis on the "diverse relationships" of human societies "to their associated species of plants and animals, their physical habitats, and other human societies." [9]

Popularization of the ecosystem concept is threatened by the felicitous exposition by the economist, K. E. Boulding,[10] of "society as an ecosystem." The word "threatened" is well advised, for Boulding uses "ecosystem" only as an analogy, illustrating how human society is "something like" an ecosystem. His ecosystem analogy is, to be sure, quite an improvement over the old organismic analogy. But ecosystem is much too valuable a conceptual scheme to be sacrificed on the altar of metaphor. Human ecology has already inspired a generation of critics too easily irritated by figures of speech.

If the foregoing remarks suggest that general ecologists have come up with cogent principles concerning the role of human society in the ecosystem, then the discussion has been misleading. Actually, the writing of Dice is exception as a responsible attempt to extend general ecology into the human field. Most biological scientists would probably still hold with the caution of Clements and Shelford, that "ecology will come to be applied to the fields that touch man immediately only as the feeling for synthesis grows." [11] There is abundant evidence in their own writing of the inadvisability of leaving to biological scientists the whole task of investigating the ecosystem and its human phases in particular. As a discipline, they clearly have not heeded the plea of the pioneer ecologist, S. A. Forbes, for a "humanized ecology": [12]

> I would humanize ecology . . . first by taking the actions and relations of civilized man as fully into account in its definitions, divisions, and coordinations as those of any other kind of organism. The ecological system of the existing twentieth-century world must include the twentieth-century man as its dominant species—dominant, that is, in the sense of dynamic ecology as the most influential, the controlling member of his associate group.

Symptomatically, even when discussing the "ecology of man," the biologist's tendency is to deplore and to exhort, not to analyze and explain. The shibboleths include such phrasings as "disruption," "tampering," "interference," "damage," and "blunder," applied to the transformations of ecosystems wrought by human activities. Such authorities as Elton, Darling, and Sears state very well some of the dilemmas and problems of human life in the ecosystem.[13] They evidently need the help of social scientists in order to make intelligible those human behaviors that seem from an Olympian vantage point to be merely irrational and shortsighted. Insofar as they recommend reforms—and surely some of their suggestions should be heeded—they need to be instructed, if indeed social science now or ultimately can instruct them, in "The Unanticipated Consequences of Purposive Social Action."[14] If social science falls down on its job, a statement like the following will remain empty rhetoric: "Humanity now has, as never before, the means of knowing the consequences of its actions and the dreadful responsibility for those consequences."[15]

Illustration

Now, it is all very well to assert the possibility of conceptual schemes, like ecosystem, ascribing system properties to associations of physical, biological, and social elements. But can such a scheme lead to anything more than a disorderly collection of arbitrarily concatenated data? I think the proof of the ecosystem concept could be exemplified by a number of studies, ranging from particularistic to global scope, in which some such scheme, if implicit, is nevertheless essential to the analysis.[16] Instead of reviewing a sample of these studies, however, I would like to sketch a problematic situation that has yet to be analyzed adequately in ecosystem terms. This example, since it is deliberately "open-ended," will, I hope, convey the challenge of the concept.

The framework for the discussion is the set of categories suggested elsewhere[17] under the heading, "the ecological complex." These categories, population, organization, environment, and technology (P, O, E, T), provide a somewhat arbitrarily simplified way of identifying clusters of relationships in a preliminary description of ecosystem processes. The description is, by design, so biased as to indicate how the human elements in the ecosystem appear as foci of these processes. Such an anthropo-centric description, though perfectly appropriate for a *human* ecology, has no intrinsic scientific priority over any other useful strategy for initiating study of an ecosystem.

The example is the problem of air pollution, more particularly that of "smog," as experienced during the last two decades in the community of Los Angeles. Southern California has no monopoly on this problem, as other communities are learning to their chagrin. But the somewhat special situation there seems to present a configuration in which the role of each of the four aspects of the ecological complex, including its relation to the others, is salient. I have made no technical investigation of the Los Angeles situation and have at hand only a haphazard collection of materials dealing with it, most of them designed for popular rather than scientific consumption. (The personal experience of living through a summer of Los Angeles smog is of value here only in that it permits sincere testimony to the effect that the problem is real.) The merit of the illustration, however, is that ramifying influences like those postulated by the ecosystem concept are superficially evident even when their nature is poorly understood and inadequately described. I am quite prepared to be corrected on the facts of the case, many of which have yet to come to light. I shall be greatly surprised, however, if anyone is able to produce an account of the smog problem in terms of a conceptual scheme materially *less* elaborate than the ecological complex.

During World War II residents of Los Angeles began to experience episodes of a bluish-gray haze in the atmosphere that reduced visibility and produced irritation of the eyes and respiratory tract (E→P); it was also found to damage growing plants (E→E), including some of considerable economic importance, and to crack rubber, accelerating the rate of deterioration of automobile tires, for example (E→T). In response to the episodes of smog, various civic movements were launched, abatement officers were designated in the city and county health departments, and a model control ordinance was promulgated (E→O). All these measures were without noticeable effect on the smog. At the time, little was known about the sources of pollution, although various industrial operations were suspected. By 1947, a comprehensive authority, the Los Angeles County Air Pollution Control District, was established by action of the California State Assembly and authorized to conduct research and to exercise broad powers of regulation. Various known and newly developed abatement devices were installed in industrial plants at the insistence of the APCD, at a cost of millions of dollars (O→T).

Meanwhile, research by chemists and engineers was developing and confirming the "factory in the sky" theory of smog formation. Combustion and certain other processes release unburned hydrocarbons and oxides of nitrogen into the atmosphere (T→E). As these reach a sufficiently high concentration and are subjected to strong sunlight, chemical reactions occur that liberate large amounts of ozone and form smog. In particular, it was discovered that automobile exhaust contains the essential ingredients in nearly ideal proportions and that this exhaust is the major source of the contaminants implicated in smog formation. It became all the more important as a source when industrial control measures and the prohibition of household open incinerators (O→T) reduced these sources (T→E). Also implicated in the problem was the meteorological situation of the Los Angeles Basin. Ringed by mountains and enjoying only a very low average wind velocity, the basin frequently is blanketed by a layer of warm air moving in from the Pacific. This temperature inversion prevents the polluted air from rising very far above ground level; the still air hovering over the area is then subject to the afore-mentioned smog-inducing action of Southern California's famous sunshine (E→E).

The problem, severe enough at onset, was hardly alleviated by the rapid growth of population in the Los Angeles area, spreading out as it did over a wide territory (P→E), and thereby heightening its dependence on the already ubiquitous automobile as the primary means of local movement (T↔O). Where could one find a more poignant instance of the principle of circular causation, so central to ecological theory, than that of the Los Angelenos speeding down their freeways in a rush to escape the smog produced by emissions from the very vehicles conveying them?

A number of diverse organizational responses (E→O) to the smog problem have occurred. In 1953 a "nonprofit, privately supported, scientific research organization, dedicated to the solution of the smog problem," the Air Pollution Foundation, was set up under the sponsorship of some 200 business enterprises, many of them in industries subject to actual or prospective regulatory measures. The complex interplay of interests and pressures among such private organizations and the several levels and branches of government that were involved (O→O) has not, to my knowledge, been the subject of an adequate investigation by a student of the political process. Two noteworthy outcomes of this process merit attention in particular. The first is the development of large-scale programs of public health research and action (O→P, E) concerned with air pollution effects (E→P). Comparatively little is known in this field of epidemiology (or as some research workers would say nowadays, medical ecology), but major programs have been set up within the last five years in the U. S. Public Health Service (whose interest, of course, is not confined to Los Angeles) as well as such agencies as the California State Department of Public Health. Here is a striking instance of interrelations between medical ecology and the ecology of medicine illustrating not merely "organizational growth," as studied in conventional sociology, but also an organizational response to environmental-demographic changes. Second, there has been a channeling of both public and private research effort into the search for a "workable device," such as an automatic fuel cutoff, a catalytic muffler, or an afterburner, which will eliminate or reduce the noxious properties of automobile exhaust. California now has on its statute books a law requiring manufacturers to equip automobiles with such a device if and when its workability is demonstrated (O→T).

Some engineers are confident that workable devices will soon be forthcoming. The Air Pollution Foundation has gone so far as to declare that the day is "near when Los Angeles' smog will be only a memory." Should the problem be thus happily resolved, with reduction of pollution to tolerable levels, the resolution will surely have to be interpreted as the net result of an intricate interaction of factors in the ecological complex (P, O, T→E). But if the condition is only partially alleviated, how much more growth of population and increase in automobile use will have to occur before even more drastic technological and organizational changes will be required: redevelopment of mass transit, introduction of private electric automobiles, rationing of travel, limitation of population expansion, or whatever they may be? What will be the outcome of experience with increasing air pollution in other communities, whose problems differ in various ways from that of Los Angeles? And the question of questions—Is the convulsion of the ecosystem occasioned by smog merely a small-scale prototype of what we must expect in a world seemingly destined to become ever more dependent upon nuclear energy and subject to its hazards of ionizing radiation?

Conclusion

I must assume that the reader will be kind enough to pass lightly over the defects of the foregoing exposition. In particular, he must credit the author with being aware of the many complications concealed by the use of arrows linking the broad and heterogeneous categories of the ecological complex. The arrows are meant only to suggest the existence of problems for research concerning the mechanisms of cause, influence, or response at work in the situation so sketchily portrayed. Even the barest account of that situation, however, can leave no doubt that social change and environmental modification occurred in the closest interdependence—so close, in fact, that the two "levels" of change were *systematically* interrelated. Change on either level can be comprehended only by application of a conceptual scheme at least as encompassing as that of ecosystem.

The reader's imagination, again, must substitute for documentation of the point that smog, though a spectacular case and full of human interest, is no isolated example of how problems of human collective existence require an ecosystem framework for adequate conceptualization. I do not intend to argue, of course, that sociologists must somehow shoulder the entire burden of research suggested by such a conceptualization. Science, after all, is one of our finest examples of the advantages of a division of labor. But labor can be effectively divided only if there is articulation of the several sub-tasks; in scientific work, such articulation is achieved by employment of a common conceptual framework.

Sociologists may or may not—I am not especially optimistic on this score—take up the challenge to investigate the social life of man as a phase of the ecosystem, with all the revisions in their thought patterns that this kind of formulation will demand. If they shirk this responsibility, however, other disciplines are not unprepared to take the leadership. Anthropology of late has demonstrated its hospitality to ecological concepts.[18] Geography, for its part, cannot forget that it laid claim to human ecology as early as did sociology.[19]

Of even greater ultimate significance may be the impending reorientation of much of what we now call social science to such concepts as welfare, level of living, and public health. Programs to achieve such "national goals" (to use the former President's language), like the studies on which such programs are based, are finding and will find two things: first, each of these concepts is capable of almost indefinite expansion to comprehend virtually any problem of human collective life; and, second, measures or indicators of status or progress in respect to them must be multi-faceted and relational. Public health, to take that example, is surely some sort of function of all elements in the ecological complex; it is observable in any sufficiently comprehensive sense only in terms of interrelations of variables located at all levels of the ecosystem. Extrapolation of current trends over even a short projection period is sufficient to suggest the future preoccupation of the sciences touching on man with much more macroscopic problems than they now dare to set for themselves. It is perhaps symptomatic that spokesmen for the nation's health programs now declare that the "science of health is a branch of the wider science of human ecology," [20] and that expositions of the problem of economic development have come to emphasize the necessary shift "From Political Economy to Political Ecology." [21] Even the literati proclaim that the "fundamental human problem is ecological." [22] (Cf. the similar remark of Kenneth Burke: "Among the sciences, there is one little fellow named Ecology, and in time we shall pay him more attention." [23]) If one holds with Durkheim that the basic categories of science, as well as the interpretive schemes of everyday life, arise from the nature and exigencies of human collective existence, it cannot be long before we are forced to conjure with some version of the ecosystem concept. The question is whether sociology will lead or lag behind in this intellectual movement.

Notes

1. A. L. Kroeber, "So-Called Social Science," ch. vii in *The Nature of Culture* (Chicago: University of Chicago Press, 1952), pp. 66–67.

2. R. M. MacIver, *Social Causation* (Boston: Ginn & Co., 1942), pp. 271–72.

3. Arnold S. Feldman and Charles Tilly, "The Interaction of Social and Physical Space," *American Sociological Review,* 25 (December, 1960), p. 878.

4. W. C. Allee, Alfred E. Emerson, Orlando Park, Thomas Park, and Karl P. Schmidt, *Principles of Animal Ecology* (Philadelphia: W. B. Saunders Co., 1949), p. 695.

5. Eugene P. Odum, *Fundamentals of Ecology* (Philadelphia: W. B. Saunders Co., 1953), p. 9.

6. Robert E. Park, *Human Communities: The City and Human Ecology* (Glencoe, Ill.: The Free Press, 1952).

7. Milla Aïssa Alihan, *Social Ecology: A Critical Analysis* (New York: Columbia University Press, 1938).

8. Lee R. Dice, *Man's Nature and Nature's Man: The Ecology of Human Communities* (Ann Arbor: University of Michigan Press, 1955), pp. 2–3.

9. *Ibid.,* pp. 252–53.

10. Kenneth E. Boulding, *Principles of Economic Policy* (Englewood Cliffs, N. J.: Prentice-Hall, Inc., 1958), pp. 14–16.

11. Frederic E. Clements and Victor E. Shelford, *Bio-ecology* (New York: John Wiley & Sons, 1939), p. 1. Cf. F. Fraser Darling, "Pastoralism in Relation to Populations of Men and Animals," in *The Numbers of Man and Animals,* edited by J. B. Cragg and N. W. Pirie (Edinburgh: Oliver & Boyd, 1955).

12. Stephen A. Forbes, "The Humanizing of Ecology," *Ecology,* 3 (April, 1922), p. 90.

13. Charles S. Elton, *The Ecology of Invasions by Animals and Plants* (London: Methuen & Co., Ltd., 1958); F. Fraser Darling, *West Highland Survey: An Essay in Human Ecology* (Oxford: Oxford University Press, 1955); Paul B. Sears, *The Ecology of Man,* "Condon Lectures" (Eugene: Oregon State System of Higher Education, 1957). See also, F. Fraser Darling, "The Ecology of Man," *The American Scholar,* 25 (Winter, 1955–56), pp. 38–46; Donald F. Chapp, "Ecology —A Science Going to Waste," *Chicago Review,* 9 (Summer, 1955), pp. 15–26.

14. Title of an early essay by Robert K. Merton, *American Sociological Review,* 1 (December, 1936), pp. 894–904; a recent statement, pertinent to ecology, is Walter Firey's *Man, Mind and Land: A Theory of Resource Use* (Glencoe, Ill.: The Free Press, 1960).

15. Sears, *op. cit.,* p. 50.

16. The following are merely illustrative: A. Irving Hallowell, "The Size of Algonkian Hunting Territories: A Function of Ecological Adjustment," *American Anthropologist,* 51 (January-March, 1949), pp. 34–45; Laura Thompson, "The Relations of Men, Animals, and Plants in an Island Community (Fiji)," *American Anthropologist,* 51 (April-June, 1949), pp. 253–76; Edgar Anderson, *Plants, Man and Life* (Boston: Little, Brown & Co., 1952); Fred Cottrell, *Energy and Society* (New York: McGraw-Hill Book Co., 1955); Harrison Brown, *The Challenge of Man's Future* (New York: Viking Press, 1954).

17. Otis Dudley Duncan, "Human Ecology and Population Studies," ch. xxviii in *The Study of Population,* edited by Philip M. Hauser and Otis Dudley Duncan (Chicago: University of Chicago Press, 1959).

18. Marston Bates, "Human Ecology," in *Anthropology Today,* edited by A. L. Kroeber (Chicago: University of Chicago Press, 1953); J. G. D. Clark, *Prehistoric Europe: The Economic Basis* (New York: Philosophical Library, 1952); Julian H. Steward, *Theory of Culture Change* (Urbana: University of Illinois Press, 1955).

19. H. H. Barrows, "Geography as Human Ecology," *Annals of the Association of American Geographers,* 13 (March, 1923), pp. 1–14; William L. Thomas, Jr., editor, *Man's Role in Changing the Face of the Earth* (Chicago: University of Chicago Press, 1956).

20. President's Commission on the Health Needs of the Nation, *America's Health Status, Needs and Resources. Building America's Health,* vol. 2 (Washington: Government Printing Office, 1953), p. 13.

21. Title of an essay by Bertrand de Jouvenel, *Bulletin of the Atomic Scientists,* 8 (October, 1957), pp. 287–91.

22. Aldous Huxley, *The Devils of Loudon,* "Torchbook edition" (New York: Harper & Bros., 1959), p. 302.

23. Kenneth Burke, *Attitudes toward History,* Vol. I (New York: The New Republic, 1937), p. 192.

ROBERT PARK AND SOCIAL AREA ANALYSIS: A CONVERGENCE IN URBAN SOCIOLOGY

Peter Orleans

In 1915, Robert Park published "The City: Suggestions for the Investigation of Human Behavior in the Urban Environment." [1] That essay served as a prolegomenon for the research which occupied students of the Chicago school of urban studies for more than a quarter of a century. Thirty-four years later, in 1949, Eshref Shevky introduced an alternative approach to the study of urban phenomena in his volume on the social areas of Los Angeles.[2] Following in the tradition encompassed by social area analysis, Scott Greer, in 1962 with the publication of *The Emerging City: Myth and Reality,* addressed himself to questions similar to those broached by Park.[3] This paper will examine several aspects of the work represented by these two approaches in American urban sociology in an attempt to indicate the contributions each has made and can make to the elaboration of a coherent theory of urban life.

The study of urban life has been concerned with the analysis of ecological space and social differentiation, the interaction of both, and the bearing of each upon the development and maintenance of order within the urban milieu. The apparent discrepancy between the two traditions of urban study to be examined in this paper stems in large measure from the extent to which they emphasize one of these concerns (ecological space or social differentiation) to the relative exclusion of the other. It will be argued that this difference in emphasis is based on different views of the structure and quality of urban life. Each, in turn, has influenced the way in which the problem of order in the urban milieu has been stated and treated.

A preliminary note of caution is required. The discussion to follow is concerned largely with the work of three scholars. It is not the writer's intention to deprecate or to caricature the work of any of them. Park is unquestionably a seminal figure in the field of urban sociology and his essay, "The City," has had a considerable impact on the direction and organization of urban studies in the United States over the last half-century. It cannot and should not be lightly dismissed; but it must be considered in the light of parallel as well as subsequent developments if advances in the field of urban studies are to be made and are to be cumulative.

It is clear that the work of Shevky and his students has been informed by Park's contributions, even though it represents both a departure from and an extension of Park's work. Only time and newly accumulated research can determine its significance. But, a comparison of the two approaches—a comparison which delineates the points of contrast and emphasizes the areas of convergence, and a comparison which attempts to analyze the reasons for both—might assist in furthering the art.

Reprinted by permission of the publisher and the author from *Urban Affairs Quarterly,* 1 (June 1966), 5–19.

Ecological Space and Social Differentiation

Although Park's analysis of urban life emphasized the significance of ecological factors, his work clearly indicates a recognition of the importance of social differentiation. This communality with social area analysis is often overlooked by students working in both traditions. Social area analysis has been criticized for its inadequate conceptualization of ecological factors and its almost exclusive concern with social differentiation. The discrepant aspects of these two approaches, as well as the areas of convergence between them, the reasons for both, and the implications of each will be explored below.

In the portion of his essay entitled "Industrialization and the Moral Order," Park notes that the disposition to barter or exchange goods and services gives rise to the division of labor and that the proliferation of tasks is a function of the extent of the market. "The outcome of this process is to break down or modify the older economic and social organization of society, which was based on family ties, local associations, on culture, caste, and status, and to substitute for it an organization based on occupational and vocational interests."[4] The result is the development of occupational types and vocationally oriented interest-based organizations.

Here, then, Park focuses on the conditions which produce the communality of interests that give rise to association. In recognizing these conditions, he shares a common concern with students in the social area analysis tradition, notably Greer.[5] However, whereas social area analysts are concerned with explicating the significance of the occupational form of differentiation (as well as others) for the development of a normative order, Park devalues the role played by occupationally based secondary organizations in generating and sustaining the moral order.

> The effect of the vocations and the division of labor is to produce . . . not social groups but vocational types: the actor, the plumber and the lumber-jack. The organizations like the trade and labor unions which men of the same trade or profession form are based on common interests. In this respect they differ from forms of association like the neighborhood which are based on contiguity, personal association, and the common ties of humanity . . . The effects of the division of labor as a discipline, i.e., as a means of molding character, may therefore be best studied in the vocational types produced.[6]

Accordingly, Park chooses to emphasize individual predilections, attitudes, natural abilities, and the like and to focus on recruitment and mobility within and between occupations instead of the changing structure of occupations and its implications for the organization of occupationally based secondary associations in the urban community.

That Park does not see interest-based associations as generators of a moral order is, perhaps, due to the fact that he relies on spatial contiguity for this purpose. This is made clear by his discussion in the section of his essay entitled "The City Plan and Local Organization." His thesis is that natural geographic advantages and disadvantages determine in advance the outline of the urban plan, the location, and the character of the city's constructions. Eventually, however, subtler influences of rivalry and economic necessity tend to control the distribution of the population.

> Within the limitations prescribed . . . personal tastes and conveniences, vocational and economic interests, infallibly tend to classify the population of big cities. In this way the city acquires an organization and distribution of the population which is neither designed nor controlled.[7]

Each section of the city takes on the character and the quality of its inhabitants, its differentiated and relatively segregated populations. Thus, what was initially a mere geographic expression is transformed into a congeries of neighborhoods with sentiments, traditions, and local histories, and the past imposes itself upon the present in each of these semiautonomous areas—that mosaic of social worlds that touch but do not interpenetrate.

In this view the geographic contiguity of people serves as a basis for social contact and association out of which a normative order eventually develops. Thus, in this portion of his essay, Park indicates a concern for *both* the spatial distribution and the social differentiation of the population, the implications of each for the other, and of both for the total urban complex. Natural forces are seen as responsible for the initial distribution, concentration, and segregation of urban populations. Social organization derives after the fact from proximity and neighborly contact as well as the relative homogeneity of the spatially contiguous populations. "Local interests and associations breed local sentiment, and under a system which makes residence the basis for participation in government, the neighborhood becomes the basis for political control." [8] In other words, neighborhood provides the site for a developing normative order.

It is Park's recognition of the important role played by spatial contiguity in the development of normative order that leads him to pose the following kinds of questions:

> What are the outstanding "natural" areas, i.e., areas of population segregation?
>
> How is the distribution of population within the city affected by (a) economic interests, i.e., land values? (b) sentimental interest, race? vocation, etc.?
>
> What are the elements of which (neighborhoods) are composed? To what extent are (neighborhoods) the product of a selective process?
>
> What are the relative permanence and stability of (neighborhood) populations?
>
> What about the age, sex, and social condition of the people? [9]

In effect, Park is asking what characteristics of a population distributed in distinctive spatial enclaves have what kinds of effect on the development of the normative order. The strong implication is that the organization of urban populations is largely a function of the interaction of the differentiated attributes of such populations and their spatial distribution (concentration and segregation).

In short, as he sought to delineate appropriate research topics in the sections of his essay discussed above, Park relied on conceptions of a naturalistic ecology and *laissez faire* economics (both of which emphasize the fortuitous and problematic organization and the normative dislocation of the population) to adduce two aspects of urban society. According to one view, the basis of association rests with the congruence of occupational and/or economic interests. According to the other view, the basis of association rests with the exigencies of the spatial configuration of distinct populations. Each of the two bases of association discussed by Park may be seen as establishing preconditions for a normative order.

Park's conceptualization of the problem is distinguished from that of the social area analysts by its emphasis on the ecological community (the "natural" area) and its concern with the spatial basis of association rather than association growing out of a communality of interest. The implications of this difference for the formulation and treatment of the problem of order in the urban milieu will be considered below. First, however, it is necessary to examine the social area analysis approach offered by Shevky and his students.

In contrast to Park, Shevky neglects ecological space and focuses almost entirely upon social differentiation. His work has often been treated as though it represented a revision or extension of the traditional ecological approach to urban studies; but such an interpretation derives, in this writer's estimation, from a misreading of his efforts.[10] Shevky has never purported to have offered an ecological analysis. Rather he emphasized the significance of what he refers to as *social space*.

Social space refers to an attribute space representing a conceptual typology of positional differences which are denoted by measures of a series of characteristics of population aggregates. While there is no denying that these population aggregates are located in ecological space and that their location may have consequences for their internal organization as well as their interdependence with the encompassing milieu, the aggregated characteristics of such populations are seen by Shevky and his students as more significant than their spatial *location*. Hence, social area analysts are led to a formulation in which ecological space *per se* is of minor importance.[11]

A weakness of the social area analysis formulation has not been its disregard of ecological factors but rather its lack of any systematic specification of the relationship that social space bears to physical space. It is undoubtedly the failure to delineate this relationship that has elicited much of the confusion over its status *vis-à-vis* ecological theory and research.

Shevky's neglect of ecological space constitutes a radical departure from the Chicago school of urban studies as represented in the work of Park and his students. Social area analysis facilitates the study of forms of social differentiation apart from considerations of spatial location. The assumption upon which this mode of analysis rests is that positional similarity, with respect to a limited number of significant social attributes (e.g., skills, ethnicity, life style, migrant status), reflects common situations. For example, the specific attributes of population aggregates, which denote various forms of social differentiation, are presumed to indicate differences in access to limited sets of opportunities as well as subjugation to particular sets of constraints. Accordingly, positional similarity is considered to be indicative of a communality of interests. This, in turn, provides a basis for the social contact and association which generate and support a normative order.[12]

Approaching the analysis of urban life through the study of significant forms of social differentiation permits one to locate and examine normative orders independent of spatial considerations. Some forms of differentiation, such as life style or ethnicity, may locate spatially distinct enclaves—the fertile valleys of suburbia or the ethnic ghettos in the central city. Others, such as skill or migration distinctions, may locate spatially unbounded communities of interest—occupational communities or regional associations.

Under most circumstances, the nexus of several forms of differentiation will locate ecologically undefined population aggregates (social spaces or social areas). These exhibit varying propensities to become engaged in different kinds of spatially unbounded communities of interest often represented in secondary organizations (e.g., the League of Women Voters, industrial and craft unions, religious cults, athletic associations, professional societies, philanthropic clubs).

Each secondary organization, with its own distinctive normative order, may generate primary ties which do not depend upon spatial contiguity for their sustenance. These primary ties may provide a satisfactory alternative to the amenities generally associated with spatially contained communities and ecologically distinct natural areas. In general, social area analysts are concerned initially with locating organizationally distinctive, but ecologically indeterminate, communities of interest, and ultimately with exploring their implications for the normative organization of diverse populations in the urban environment.

To recapitulate briefly what has been stated above, both Park and Shevky in their efforts to develop an approach to the study of urban life have emphasized the importance of various forms of social differentiation and their potential consequences for the development of a normative order. Park was much more explicit in his recognition of the role played by spatial contiguity in the development of such a normative order, tending to neglect the essentially nonspatial alternative of normative orders deriving from communities of interest. Shevky, by contrast, neglected the effects of ecological space and thereby failed to specify the significance of spatial contiguity for the development of a normative order.

In the absence of an explicit recognition and acknowledgment of the significance of ecological space, Shevky is restricted to a consideration of communities of interest alone as the generators of a normative order. For Shevky, spatial contiguity is, in effect, an unexplicated concept. Of the students in the social area analysis tradition, Greer alone has attempted to deal with the role played by ecological space in setting the conditions for the development of a normative order. Accordingly, Greer's extension of Shevky's formulation (as it is presented in his book *The Emerging City: Myth and Reality*) serves as a basis for the discussion of the social area analysis formulation in the balance of this paper.[13]

The Antiurban Bias and the Problem of Order

It is one thing to suggest that two schools of thought differ in the emphasis they ascribe to different mechanisms—association based on spatial contiguity as opposed to association predicated on a communality of interests—seen to be generators and maintainers of normative order. It is something else to attempt to understand the reasoning which underlies and supports the differing emphases and to recognize the implications that these alternative conceptualizations bear to the statement and treatment of the problem of order in the urban milieu. Our contention here is that the romantic attachment to the preurban community is largely responsible for the ecologically and pathogically oriented studies of urban life, and further that the concern with the pathological conditions of life in the city grew out of the assumption that the normative efficacy of the spatially inclusive community declined in proportion to the urbanization of society.[14]

Prior to the advent of the extreme aggregation of populations at fixed locations and the accompanying proliferation of specialized tasks required to coordinate and control human activities under such circumstances, there existed neither the need for nor the possibility of developing and sustaining interaction patterns contingent upon the communalities of differentiated interests. However, the urban-industrial revolution made possible—indeed required—the development of new forms of association growing out of newly created and elaborated types of collectives, which may have supplemented rather than replaced their predecessors.

The radical transformation of the human condition brought about by the urban-industrial revolution was initially disruptive of traditional values and institutions. And it was not uncommon for perceptive analysts to decry the loss of the significance of the spatially inclusive community—the traditional ecological community—that had been so familiar. But, in our view, the theoretical bankruptcy of much contemporary urban analysis is attributable largely to the failure to overcome traditional biases and to replace outmoded notions about the conditions which sustain and nurture a normative order with conceptions which are more appropriate to current conditions.

Both Park and Greer emphasize the contrast between the urban milieu and preurban or nonurban settlements. Because the urban community is different, it poses new problems with respect to the maintenance or order. Accordingly, both men are centrally concerned with the problem of order. But the concern of each is affected by his assumptions regarding how and why the urban community differs from other kinds of settlements.

Most students of urban life assume, at least implicitly, that urbanization entails change. However, they differ in their assessment of the implications of this change. To a large extent the difference is a function of the extent to which the change is seen as evolutionary in character (i.e., from a noncomplex to a complex communal form; from a spatially inclusive locality group to a community consisting of spatially indistinct exclusive membership groups).

Some students, including Shevky and Greer, assume that urbanization involves an organizational transformation. Others, Park among them, assume that urbanization involves an organizational disruption or dislocation. The difference in these assumptions is critical because it ultimately affects the kinds of theoretical issues addressed—the kind of urban theory to be constructed.

The pathological view of urban life that has dominated American urban sociology stems largely from the conception that the evolutionary development of the communal form involves a dislocation of traditional and valued institutions and that this has deleterious effects on the individuals involved. The characterization of the urban community as seen from this perspective is usually based on the enumeration of interactional qualities which are presumed to be distinctive. Simmel's view that urban life is abstracted, segmentalized, pecuniary, sophisticated, predatory, and impersonal is a case in point.[15] To the extent that Park, a student of Simmel's, accepted such a characterization of urban life, his concern with the problem of order in the urban community came to be focused on the study of the personal consequences of and reactions to life in a socially disruptive and disorganized environment—an environment in which the opportunities and constraints circumscribed by the spatially inclusive community are devalued, modified, or replaced.

If Park attempts to draw attention to the changing conditions of an urbanizing economic organization in his discussion of "Industrialization and the Moral Order," he also discusses some of the implications of such changes for the maintenance of order in the urban community. The last two sections of his essay, which deal with "Secondary Relations and Social Control" and "Temperament and the Urban Environment," constitute an elaboration of this concern. It is in these two sections of the essay that Park betrays, or portrays, his ambivalence about urbanism as a way of life.

In these sections of the essay, Park reiterates a point made earlier—that changes in the economic organization of the city ultimately require a modification of the mechanisms of social control. The reasoning here is that changes in the economic order, because they are destructive of the traditional spatially inclusive community, modify the nature of social relations and therefore alter interpersonal expectations and obligations. He suggests that:

> The interactions which take place among the members of (the urban community) are immediate and unreflecting. Intercourse is carried on largely within the region of instinct and feeling. Social control arises, for the most part spontaneously, in direct response to personal influences and public sentiment. It is the result of a personal accommodation, rather than the formulation of a rational and abstract principle.[16]

Given such a world view it is possible to invoke value judgments in developing comparative appraisals of the urban and the nonurban community. And given the difficult adjustments required of individual men under the conditions of rapid change associated with the urbanization of society, as well as the existence of pervasive traditional values which are likely to be in conflict with those that support and sustain urban life, it is not surprising that the study of pathology becomes a focal point for the analyses of urban life.

Accordingly, Park devotes his attention to the "disintegrating influences of city life" attributable in large measure to the proliferation of secondary relations which have affected and presumably infected "most of our traditional institutions, the church, the school, and the family." Along these lines, he chooses to pose the following kinds of questions in outlining appropriate lines of research for the urban sociologist:

> To what extent are the moral qualities of individuals based on native character? To what extent are they conventionalized habits imposed upon them or taken over by them from the group?
>
> What are the native qualities and characteristics upon which the moral and immoral character accepted and conventionalized by the group are based?

What connection or what divorce appears to exist between mental and moral qualities in the groups and in the individuals composing them?

What are the external facts in regard to the life in Bohemia, the half-world, the red-light district, and other "moral regions" less pronounced in character? To what extent are the regions referred to the product of the license; to what extent are they due to the restrictions imposed by city life on the natural man? [17]

For the most part American urban sociology, responding to the Parkian heritage and abetted by the enigmatic nature of the complex urban environment, has attended to the collective behavior, institutional dislocation, and psychodynamic aspects of urban life.

In contrast to this approach, Greer's attention to the problem of order in the urban community has focused on newly innovated mechanisms of social control or on the revision of old mechanisms of social control. This orientation stems from a position that takes as its point of departure the idea that the city represents a different communal form from that to be found in the nonurban settlement because it constitutes a distinctive set of problems related to the coordination and control of human activities.

While he does not deny that individuals may confront difficult problems of personal adjustment and that they vary in the extent of their involvement in the urban community, Greer is more concerned with the organizational aspects of life in the metropolis. Accordingly, the significance of the pathology of the urban condition, at least at the individual level, is minimized and muted in his analyses. Greer's concern with pathology is generally restricted to the organizational problems of urban life engendered by the diversity of values to be found in various segments of the metropolitan population.[18]

Greer succeeds in extricating himself from the ecological considerations which held Park in check. Influenced by Shevky's concern with the positional implications of various social attributes and using the social area analysis schema to locate urban populations which share distinctive qualities along several dimensions of social differentiation, Greer is able to emphasize the normative significance of spatially unrestricted communities of interest which derive from the elaboration of functional activities in the urban setting. This is indicated by his statement that "the highly differentiated set of activities necessary for [the persistence of the city] requires complex and effective integrative mechanisms in order to produce predictability and structural stability through time." [19] The city, as an organizational unit, displays massive uniformities, orderly change, remarkable stability. Accordingly, "much of the behavior of the urban population can be understood and predicted through a knowledge of the group structures that absorb the energy of individuals and coordinate their behavior in time." [20]

To give substance to this assertion Greer relies on two mechanisms that bear a remarkable resemblance to the forms of association based on space and specialty described by Park in the first two sections of his essay. He develops the notions of the inclusive locality group and the exclusive membership group.[21] The latter can be broader in content than the occupational community; but it is definitely a collectivity, nonspatially defined, based upon a communality of interests and the generator of a normative order. The former is analogous to the traditional ecological community, the natural area, the neighborhood.

These two types of collectivities cross-cut one another and between them they account, in large measure, for the development and the maintenance of normative order in the urban setting. And, they amount to an attempt, on Greer's part, to interrelate as well as to distinguish between spatially distinct and spatially unbounded forms of association—an attempt to tie Shevky's notion of social space to what in the social area analysis schema is the unexplicated concept of ecological space.

There are undoubtedly spatially distinct and socially differentiated population aggregates in the urban milieu which fail to generate either associations based upon spatial contiguity or associations predicated upon communalities of interest. Although such segments of the urban population are undoubtedly not representative of the urban condition, they represent a significant social (or, perhaps more correctly, asocial) form. For such populations, Park's concern with the problem of order is critical. But, it would be a serious error to focus attention primarily upon such populations, considering them representative of urban conditions as a whole, and thereby obscuring a conception of urban social organization.

The point to be stressed, then, is essentially this: Diversity and complexity are not necessarily productive of social disorganization. To restrict one's concerns to the pathology of urban life is to leave unaccounted for the most distinctive, if more subtle, fact of urbanism as a way of life, indeed of all collective life, namely, its organization.

The main thrust of the argument in this paper has been to urge that students of urban life consider the existence and importance of inclusive locality groups in the city to be problematic, and further to recognize that the lack of a spatially based normative order may be supplanted or supplemented by the kind of spatially unrestricted normative order generally associated with exclusive membership groups. Moreover, it has been suggested that the rudiments of each are embodied in the two approaches to the study of urban life offered by Park and the social area analysts. This represents a significant point of convergence between these two traditions in urban sociology. Once this convergence has been recognized, the next step is to explicitly and systematically make the conceptual connection between the socially differentiated community and the spatially distinct community and to begin to determine empirically the relationship spatially unrestricted communities of interest bear to those communities in which association is a function of spatial contiguity.

Notes

1. Robert Park, "The City: Suggestions for the Investigation of Human Behavior in the Urban Environment," originally published in the *American Journal of Sociology,* XX (March, 1916), pp. 577–613; reprinted with the corpus of his work in urban sociology in Robert Park, *Human Communities: The City and Human Ecology* (New York: The Free Press, 1952).

2. Eshref Shevky and Marilyn Williams, *The Social Areas of Los Angeles* (Berkeley and Los Angeles: The University of California Press, 1949). This publication was followed in 1955 by the publication of Eshref Shevky and Wendell Bell, *Social Area Analysis: Theory, Illustrative Application and Computational Procedures* (Stanford: Stanford University Press, 1955). Further amplification of the approach is to be found in Wendell Bell, "Social Areas: Typology of Neighborhoods," and an example of research in this tradition is to be found in Scott Greer and Ella Kube, "Urbanism and Social Structure: A Los Angeles Study." Both of these papers were originally published as Chapters 3 and 4 in Marvin Sussman (ed.), *Community Structure and Analysis* (New York: Thomas Y. Crowell, 1959).

3. Scott Greer, *The Emerging City: Myth and Reality* (New York: The Free Press, 1962), especially Chapters 2 and 3.

4. Robert Park, *op. cit.*, p. 24.

5. Scott Greer, *op. cit.*, passim.

6. Robert Park, *op. cit.*, p. 24.

7. Robert Park, *ibid.*, p. 16.

8. Robert Park, *ibid.*, p. 18.

9. Robert Park, *ibid.*, pp. 18, 22.

10. A. Hawley and O. D. Duncan, "Social Area Analysis: A Critical Appraisal," *Land Economics*, 1957, 33, 337–345. See also George Theodorson (ed.), *Studies in Human Ecology* (New York: Harper and Row, 1961), especially the introduction to Part II, pp. 129–134.

11. Such a position should not seem strange to sociologists who have a long and revered tradition of attributing behavioral variation to variables such as class and race, etc., treated as though they are ecologically unbounded.

12. Scott Greer and Peter Orleans, "The Mass Society and the Para-Political Structure," *American Sociological Review*, 27 (October, 1962), pp. 634–646. A similar thesis is advanced by James Beshers in his book *Urban Social Structure* (New York: The Free Press, 1962).

13. For an attempt to relate gross variations in population type to a theory of spatially based social organization, see Scott Greer, "The Social Structure and Political Process of Suburbia," *American Sociological Review*, 25 (August, 1960), pp. 514–526.

14. The antiurban bias in American letters and science has been aptly described by Morton and Lucia White in their book, *The Intellectual Versus the City* (Cambridge: Harvard University Press and The M.I.T. Press, 1962). Chapter 10, which takes up Park's work, is especially relevant.

15. Georg Simmel, "The Metropolis and Mental Life," in Kurt Wolff (trans.), *The Sociology of Georg Simmel* (New York: The Fress Press, 1950).

16. Robert Park, *op. cit.*, p. 33.

17. Robert Park, *op. cit.*, pp. 48, 50.

18. For an example of his treatment of an organizational problem of urban life see Scott Greer, "Traffic, Transportation, and the Problems of the Metropolis," in Robert Merton and Robert Nisbet (eds.), *Contemporary Social Problems* (New York: Harcourt, Brace & World, 1961).

19. Scott Greer, *op. cit.*, p. 54.

20. Scott Greer, *op. cit.*, p. 56.

21. Scott Greer, *op. cit.*, Chapter 2.

THE CONCEPT OF THE 'ECOLOGICAL COMPLEX': A CRITIQUE

Sidney M. Willhelm

The writings dealing with human ecology reflect two schools of thought. There is what we can refer to as the materialistic orientation on the one hand and the voluntaristic approach on the other.

Materialistic writers seek explanation for ecological developments in non-social conditions by arguing that specific forces determine ecological phenomena apart from man's efforts to intervene through the imposition of social choice. In defending their case, materialists implicitly or specifically deny the relevance of social values and/or culture. A schism, however, prevails among materialistic ecologists: one group holds to a biotic interpretation of ecological developments, while another advocates a physical viewpoint. We shall label the biotic position "traditional materialism" and the physical orientation "neoclassical materialism."

The biotic ecological approach of traditional materialists, stemming out of Social Darwinism, generally defines man's distribution over space resulting from biotic competition as the subject matter for human ecology. Traditional materialists then proceed to study biotic competition as a subsocial process through such concepts as dominance, succession, invasion, natural areas, concentric zones, sectors, etc. Sociologists such as Robert Park, Ernest Burgess, Roderick McKenzie, Robert Faris, among others, founded the now passé biotic perspective.[1]

In 1938, the biotic framework came under severe criticism with the publication of Milla Aissa Alihan's critique, *Social Ecology,* and Warner Gettys' significant article.[2] In 1947, two other works questioning traditional materialism appeared: Walter Firey's *Land Use in Central Boston* and an article by A. B. Hollingshead.[3] These writers launched a new perspective for human ecology which we can call the "voluntaristic" approach. Writers voicing the voluntaristic orientation vigorously attack as unrealistic the biological premises of traditional materialism and demand instead that ecologists seek explanation solely in man's social organization. We might also mention the names of William Form, Christen Jonassen and Gideon Sjoberg, who, among others, persist in writing as voluntarists.[4]

Reprinted by permission of the author and publisher from *The American Journal of Economics and Sociology,* **23** (July, 1964) 241–248.

However, for purposes of this paper, we shall focus our attention upon the most recent ecological argument, namely, the "neoclassical" materialistic position. We may identify writers of this type by their reliance upon *physical* factors. The neoclassical ecologists, while relinquishing the biotic inclinations of their materialistic predecessors, nonetheless hold to impersonal notions to justify the "neoclassical" label. The most outstanding representatives of neoclassical materialism are Amos Hawley, Otis Duncan, Leo Schnore, Jack Gibbs and Walter Martin.[5]

Neoclassical materialists generally define the responses of man's sustenance and/or social organization [6] to certain "objectified" elements as the domain for ecological investigation; they firmly reject notions of subjectivity. These writers examine what is commonly called the "ecological complex"—consisting of population, social organization, environment and technology.

These four factors, according to neoclassical materialists, are external, physical—hence impersonal—conditions that absolutely determine ecological phenomena regardless of cultural or social efforts to interject direction and choice. Man's behavior—irrespective of his culture and social values and his social activities and irrespective of volition—must comply with certain impersonal physical conditions to be ecologically relevant from this materialistic perspective.

A methodological evaluation of the neoclassical argument indicates, however, that, like its biotic predecessors, this contemporary attempt to establish the field of human ecology on an impersonal basis simply cannot be sustained. The non-social contentions of neoclassical materialism fail to meet valid standards of performance owing to the several errors arising from the attention ecological materialists give to false analytical premises.

First, materialists resort to tautological reasoning when they lay claim to the ecological complex in formulating a problem for investigation. According to this orientation, ecologists should examine "the precise technological, demographic, and environmental conditions under which various urban forms of organization may be expected to appear." [7] Hawley, Duncan, Schnore, Gibbs and Martin, among others, insist, then, that they seek to investigate the interrelationships between the variables constituting the ecological complex. After positing data relevant only to the ecological complex as "analytically distinguishable elements," [8] neoclassical materialists then proceed to explain their ecological data by the identical "ecological complex." Thereby they become tautological.

In short, the neoclassical materialist relies upon the ecological complex not only to furnish his data but also to analyze his data. Thus the subject matter and explanation are identical for the neoclassical materialist: population, organization, environment and technology provide the data for analysis in terms of population, organization, environment and technology.[9] Because it remains to be demonstrated that a tautological proposition can be empirically tested, the neoclassical orientation offers little in the way of scientific comprehension.

A second error committed by neoclassical materialists results from the mixed order of data that resides in the ecological complex. In this complex, we find the neoclassical materialists indiscriminately blending the non-material element of social organization with the material components of technology, geography and population. While these writers define all ecological variables external to the acting individuals, this cannot provide a rational basis for their insistence that material elements, such as the environment, determine the modes and/or content of social organizations. In no instance do we find an ecological materialist offering a *common* basis for the possibility of *interaction* between physical and social data. In short, where is the level of analysis that includes both orders of data? Stuart Chase, among others, notes the lack of logical premises for this type of neoclassical argument by exclaiming:

> The scientific method demands that when facts are compared, they must be of the same order. Do not add cabbages to electrons and expect to get a total which means anything.[10]

Sorokin's many works reflect his insistence that the two orders cannot be mixed in such a way that analyses "derive the conclusion that the material variable . . . determines the immaterial variable." [11] On the basis of similar reasoning, it can be shown that the neoclassical's "ecosystem" [12] has no empirical referent and hence cannot prevail even on a conceptual level.

A third shortcoming in this position stems from its firm belief that social values are psychological and therefore must be excluded from an ecological inquiry. The justification for this neoclassical statement rests upon the contention that ecologists must assume a collective perspective rather than an individualistic framework supposedly intrinsic to the social-value concept. This logic, however, necessitates the omission of problems that simply cannot be separated by analytical finesse. Furthermore, we shall note that the neoclassical materialist fails to present a collective perspective since he relies upon data that are entirely individualistic. But let us first consider the error of data-omission that results from the attempt by neoclassical ecologists to separate the inseparable.

Complete trust in external determinants precludes the possibility of choice. Yet there are many instances of choice situations within the very subjects presented by neoclassical materialists. Duncan, for example, deals with the smog situation in Los Angeles as though a population *automatically* reflects the changing physical setting through a social organization's implementation of technological devices in a *unidirectional* fashion, when in fact serious alternative responses have been and are now being discussed by governmental agencies as well as other social organizations.[13] Disputes involving *populations* with regard to establishing the form and/or content of *social organizations* within Los Angeles for *technological* control of the *environmental* smog are taking place. But Duncan presents his analysis as though a social organization merely mirrors environmental alterations in a rigor mortis fashion.

Schnore continually acknowledges the possibility of choice in dealing with social problems of underdeveloped countries from an ecological perspective—*e.g.*, the on-and-off-again birth-control policy in Communist China, the alternatives of capitalism and Marxism for industrialization, the possibility of choosing the "correct" course of action in contradistinction to "failure." [14] He goes so far as to claim: "The harsh truth is that there are *alternative* forms of government, and the main organizational question facing us is which of the various directions will be taken by the new nations of the world." [15]

Yet such writers do not introduce concepts in their ecological framework to deal with choice situations. Instead, they perceive fixed relationships between the forces composing the ecological complex which operate outside any individual and which dictate the course of ecological developments.[16] Neoclassical materialists insist that the social structure, population, technology and environment *preordain* the course of ecological events. Even in their analyses of social organization they perceive external determinism by relying solely upon what we might call the "normative argument"—the implicit contention that the mere presence of a norm and recognition of it by actors result in conformity to the requirements of the norm. If this proposition be true, rather than social action we have reflex in human behavior; rather than decision-making processes, we have structural edict; rather than actors choosing between alternatives, we have the structure "making" decisions. Social action becomes irrelevant and is, at most, a mere revelation of the social structure rather than the establishment of a social structure.

But the normative argument fails to account for social behavior and an existing social organization because it cannot explain (1) the selection from alternative normative courses of action and (2) conformity or nonconformity to the normative pattern itself.[17] To insist that a social structure chooses from its own alternative structural possibilities and that it is the very nature of a social structure to generate conformity or nonconformity to its own structural features as implied by neoclassical ecologists—all this is only to argue from a tautological perspective of structure determining structure. There can be no empirical testing of this tautological position.

The elimination of the concept of social values by neoclassical materialists inadvertently leaves only a theory that makes both social action and social organization preordained, inevitable and unalterable; man himself is only a passive creature manipulated by forces of change that the neoclassical ecologists define as "external," "physical" conditions; man is simply a physical particle performing in limbo to the dictates of the ecological complex.

The concept of social values is not, as claimed by neoclassical ecologists, a psychological analytical tool; the concept is as sociologically relevant as the notion of social organization. Social values involve the conceptual characteristics of any other sociological construct in that they have references to aspects of social life that are shared, acquired, transmitted from one generation to another as well as from one society to another, etc.

The rejection of the social-value concept, however, has not meant that the neoclassical materialists have rid themselves of individualistic notions in favor of a collective emphasis. The overwhelming preference for employing census material as a basic source for ecological data [18] commits the neoclassical ecologists not to a collective orientation at all, but rather to the notion that the mere summation of discrete units yields the whole. Census data do not form a collective representation; such information is strictly individualistic and is collected from that point of view to contradict the neoclassical collective perspective. Moreover, neoclassical materialists do not fully appreciate the apparent fact that census data represent the collection of characteristics selected according to specific governmental requirements which are not necessarily conducive to proper scientific inquiry.[19] To permit a formal agency the opportunity to gather data according to the needs of a certain organization rather than by the scientist for scientific investigation prevents the intrusion of data which could be relevant for ecology. In short, the ecologist must not come to rely, as do the neoclassical ones, upon others for data that involve obvious nonscientific criteria for collection.

A final aspect concerning values includes both traditional and neoclassical ecology. In each perspective we find a rejection of the social-value concept on the ground that explanations must be established in terms of non-social and impersonal forces. By stressing biotic and physical factors that "demand" compliance, ecological materialism offers a positivistic approach which denies the relevance of volition. However, materialism is not value-free simply because there is ample empirical evidence to demonstrate that it merely expresses a particular value system existing within the American culture at the present time. Several studies of zoning activities clearly sustain this contention.[20] The empirical data reveal that the theoretical approach of ecological materialism reflects what has been called the "economic-value orientation"—a social-value perspective voiced by certain decision-makers who contribute to the zoning process.[21] Both materialists and economically oriented decision-makers perceive identical physical conditions as determining the forms of social organization in the adaptation to space.

The competitive process which ecological materialists contend takes place in accordance with efficiency [22] is merely a reflection of the profit-motive orientation of some decision-makers in the zoning process and, more broadly, of many individuals in the American culture. The zoning data show that man's efforts to accommodate to cost [23] simply express a desire on the part of certain individuals to adjust in this manner. The facts of existing land usages and geographical conditions which ecological materialists label "impersonal" forces dictating the distribution of ecological phenomena [24] are essential aspects of the economic-value orientation to be found in the zoning process. And, finally, the notion of "functional organization" [25] in terms of an "ecological complex," espoused by certain ecological materialists, restricts ecological investigation to those very aspects of social life considered to be the *only* relevant data by the persons in the community who advocate the economic-value orientation in the zoning of property.

Consequently, in the light of empirical testing, it is most difficult for materialists to argue a value-free exposition when in fact they voice a prevailing American value system.

A final limiting consideration we shall note in our evaluation of neoclassical materialism is the inability of the orientation to delineate a field of study. That is, the ecological complex simply does not specify the subject matter for the human ecologist in a discriminating fashion. If human ecology is the study of data involved in the ecological complex advanced by the neoclassical proponents, then there is no aspect of modern society that lies beyond the ecological orbit. In other words, there are no sociological phenomena aside from ecological considerations in coping with industrialized societies. What social activity, for example, can take place within the American society that does not involve a population, an environment, an organization and a technology? The ecological complex presents a distinction without a difference.

In sum, the ecological position now so much in vogue cannot persist without basic modification. The tautological reasoning, the physical orientation, the mixed order of data, the indifference toward the social-value concept, the reliance upon individualistic census data in lieu of a collective approach, and a non-delineated subject are outstanding fallacies inherent in the present neoclassical position. An ecological perspective that contains these limitations cannot lead to a fruitful examination of sociological or ecological phenomena.

Notes

1. Robert E. Park, *Human Communities: The City and Human Ecology* (Glencoe, Ill.: Free Press, 1952); Ernest W. Burgess, *The Urban Community* (Chicago: University of Chicago Press, 1926); R. D. McKenzie, *The Metropolitan Community* (New York: McGraw-Hill, 1933); Robert E. L. Faris, "Ecological Factors in Human Behavior," in J. McV. Hunt (ed.), *Personality and the Behavior Disorder* (New York: Ronald Press Co., 1944), pp. 736–57.

2. Milla Aissa Alihan, *Social Ecology* (New York: Columbia University Press, 1938); Warner E. Gettys, "Human Ecology and Social Theory," *Social Forces,* 18 (May, 1940), pp. 469–76.

3. Walter Firey, *Land Use in Central Boston* (Cambridge: Harvard University Press, 1947); A. B. Hollingshead, "A Re-Examination of Ecological Theory," *Sociology and Social Research,* 31 (January–February, 1947), pp. 194–204.

4. William Form, "The Place of Social Structure in the Determination of Land Use: Some Implications for a Theory of Urban Ecology," *Social Forces,* 32 (May, 1954), pp. 317–23; Christen Jonassen, "Cultural Variables in the Ecology of an Ethnic Group," *American Sociological Review,* 19 (February, 1954), pp. 3–10; Gideon Sjoberg, *The Preindustrial City* (Glencoe, Ill.: Free Press, 1960), Chap. IV.

5. Amos Hawley, *Human Ecology* (New York: Ronald Press, 1950); Otis Dudley Duncan and Leo Schnore, "Cultural, Behavioral, and Ecological Perspectives in the Study of Social Organization," *American Journal of Sociology,* 65 (September, 1959), pp. 132–49; Leo F. Schnore, "Social Morphology and Human Ecology," *American Journal of Sociology,* 63 (May, 1958), pp. 620–34; Jack P. Gibbs and Walter T. Martin, "Toward a Theoretical System of Human Ecology," *Pacific Sociological Review,* 2 (Spring, 1959), pp. 29–36.

6. For purposes of our summary and analysis of the writings by neoclassical materialists, we shall equate "sustenance activities" and "social organization."

7. Duncan and Schnore, *op. cit.*, p. 138.

8. Otis Dudley Duncan, "Human Ecology and Population Studies," in Philip M. Hauser and Otis Dudley Duncan (eds.), *The Study of Population* (Chicago: University of Chicago Press, 1959), pp. 683–84.

9. Substantiation for this contention can be found in the many articles in which the neoclassical concept is applied. For example: Leo F. Schnore, "Social Problems in the Underdeveloped Areas: An Ecological View," *Social Problems,* 8 (Winter, 1961), pp. 182–201; Otis Dudley Duncan, "From Social System to Ecosystem," *Sociological Inquiry,* 31 (Spring, 1961), pp. 140–9.

10. Stuart Chase, *The Proper Study of Mankind* (New York: Harper, 1948), p. 21.

11. Pitirim A. Sorokin, *Sociocultural Causality, Space, Time* (Durham: Duke University Press, 1943), p. 61.

12. Duncan, "From Social System to Ecosystem," *op. cit.*

13. *Ibid.*

14. Schnore, "Social Problems in the Underdeveloped Areas," *op. cit.*

15. *Ibid.*, p. 191. Emphasis in the original.

16. The ecological studies by other neoclassical writers also contain this fixation notion. For example: Jack P. Gibbs and Walter T. Martin, "Urbanization and Natural Resources: A Study in Organizational Ecology," *American Sociological Review*, 23 (June, 1958), pp. 266–77.

17. The normative argument is suggested by Emile Durkheim's observation that the very existence of norms infers that social behavior is or could be contrary to normative stipulations.

18. For example: Hawley, *op. cit.*, Part II; Otis Dudley Duncan, "Population Distribution and Community Structure," *Cold Spring Harbor Symposia on Quantitative Biology*, 22 (1957), pp. 357–71. The strongest statement on this facet of neoclassical materialism has been expressed by Leo Schnore in a paper delivered at the national meetings of the American Sociological Association, St. Louis, September, 1961.

19. See Henry S. Shryock, Jr., "The Natural History of Standard Metropolitan Areas," *American Journal of Sociology*, 63 (September, 1957), pp. 163–70.

20. Sidney Willhelm and Gideon Sjoberg, "Economic vs. Protective Values in Urban Land Use Change," *American Journal of Economics and Sociology*, 19 (January, 1960), pp. 151–60; Form, *op. cit.* An extensive discussion of this point is to be found in Sidney M. Willhelm, *Urban Zoning and Land-Use Theory* (New York: Free Press of Glencoe, 1962), Chap. VII.

21. Willhelm and Sjoberg, *op. cit.*

22. For example: George Kingsley Zipf, *Human Behavior and the Principle of Least Effort* (Cambridge: Addison-Wesley Press, 1949), p. 350; Robert E. L. Faris, *op. cit.*, p. 373; and Amos Hawley, *op. cit.*, pp. 178 and 215.

23. Robert Murray Haig, "Toward an Understanding of the Metropolis," *Quarterly Journal of Economics*, 40 (May, 1926), pp. 420–4; Richard U. Ratcliff, "Efficiency and the Location of Urban Activities," in Robert Moore Fisher (ed.), *The Metropolis in Modern Life* (New York: Doubleday, 1955), pp. 125–48; Richard U. Ratcliff, *Real Estate Analysis* (New York: McGraw-Hill, 1961), p. 36.

24. McKenzie, *op. cit.*, p. 247; Hawley, *op. cit.*, p. 385; Duncan and Schnore, *op. cit.*, p. 144; Duncan, "Human Ecology and Population Studies," *op. cit.*, p. 683.

25. Duncan and Schnore, *op. cit.*, p. 145.

A FLIGHT FROM SUBURBIA: A DEMOGRAPHIC ANALYSIS

Alan B. Kirschenbaum

The metropolitan area is composed of two principal parts: the central city and the surrounding area, or ring.[1] The population structure of any segment of a metropolitan area is dependent upon the movement of persons into and out of that area.[2] It is the aim of this paper (1) to ascertain the characteristics of ring to central city migrants, and (2) to determine the impact of ring to central city migration upon the population structure of the ring area.

Before pursuing these questions, it is important to describe the traditional pattern of metropolitan population movements. Historically, the growth of urban areas began with a concentration of population within certain geographic limits. Urban areas were based on complex interactions of human behavior supported and circumscribed by the contemporary technology. The population growth of these core areas pushed the residents of their fringe regions outward. But, due to technologically determined time-cost factors, the boundaries of these areas remained relatively small. When technological change allowed limiting time-cost factors to expand (through rail transport, the automobile, and the like), a further widening of the physical boundaries of metropolitan areas occurred. Thus, in the past, studies have concluded or implied that urban areal growth was due mainly to expansion from the city core into the fringe of the metropolitan region.[3] Several theoretical views of this expansion process are in current use,[4] and the "expansion" frame of reference has been used in several studies of the decentralization of both industry and population.[5]

Today, however, there are several reasons to suspect that the push outward into the suburban areas from the central city is slowing down considerably. Nearly 70 percent of the nation's population already resides within metropolitan areas, and the vast influx into the central city from both rural areas and foreign shores has declined sharply. Furthermore, within the metropolitan area, the great population growth of the central city has come to an end. In addition, the selective rebuilding of the central city area may attract some population groups from surrounding areas into the city. It is the contention of this paper that the traditional "expansion" model no longer applies to urban growth. This conclusion is suggested by a large counter-migration from the ring area to the central city. An analysis of the social and demographic characteristics of the ring to city migrants illustrates the size and impact of this population movement.

Research Design

By supplementing the usual census migration categories with the one-in-a-thousand sample census data,[6] the total population in the ring in 1955 (before migration) and the total population in 1960 (after migration) may be determined. The sample was limited to persons residing within an SMSA between 1955 and 1960. A homogeneous population was selected, restricted to white,

Reprinted by permission of the author and publisher from *The Maxwell Review*, The Maxwell Graduate School, Syracuse University, 4 (October, 1967), 17–26.

employed, male, household heads between 14 and 64 years of age. These restrictions permitted a detailed analysis of the characteristics of migration streams while directly controlling for other variables.[7] However, the restrictions also introduced limitations into the analysis. The generalizations from this sample may not be applicable to other population groups. Also, no attention has been given to rural-to-urban migration or to the important population movements within the central city and within the ring.

Cross-tabulations were used to obtain data for non-movers as well as migrants. The categories set up for age, education, occupation, and family composition are presented below.

1. Age: The categories roughly follow the stages of the family life cycle with particular emphasis on differentiating the younger and older groups. Age differences are those of the male household head only.
2. Education: Degree attainment played an important role in defining the education categories. High school educated individuals are further divided into 1–3 years of high school and 4 years of high school. This division was applied to the college educated as well.
3. Occupation: Two categories are set up: white-collar and blue-collar workers. Both encompass several occupational levels.[8]
4. Family Composition: Each household is defined as having a male head with married spouse present. The composition of the household is defined by the number of resident children.

The actual migration data were obtained by cross-tabulating residence in 1955 with that in 1960. The 1955 classification refers to the initial place of residence before a move was made. Residence in 1960 refers to the destination point in 1960. Non-mover household heads were tabulated as living in the same house over the five-year period. Because the focus of this study is primarily on migration between the ring and city, and in order to obtain the total population in the ring before and after movement has occurred, an additive process was necessary.[9]

The 1955 population of the ring was calculated by adding the non-movers in the ring, the within-ring movers, and the ring-to-central-city movers. The population of the ring after a move has taken place was obtained by adding the non-movers in the ring, the within-ring movers, and the central-city-to-ring migrants. This provided the 1960 population in the ring.

This additive process gives information about population size and characteristics before and after a move was made, permitting comparisons between 1955 and 1960. By determining the characteristics of those who are moving, it is possible to examine the impact of their loss upon the ring population.

The Move Inward

An outward expansion of the population, for the sample used in this study, does not materialize. The rate of ring-to-city migrations per 1000 population in the ring is 161.4, in sharp contrast to the rate of 46.9 per 1000 population in the central city for city to ring migrants.[10] This indicates that the large outward

TABLE 1. RATES OF OUT-MIGRATION FOR HOUSEHOLD HEAD BASED ON SPECIFIC CHARACTERISTICS OF THE HEAD. RATES BASED ON TOTAL POPULATION FOR EACH SEGMENT PER 1000 POPULATION

Characteristics	City to Ring	Ring to City
Age		
14–19	0.3	0.2
20–24	6.4	9.0
25–34	15.0	59.3
35–44	12.3	53.2
45–54	8.9	26.8
55–64	4.0	12.8
Total	46.9	161.4
Education		
Elementary	8.3	27.6
1–3 High School	11.2	36.8
4 High School	14.0	47.7
1–3 College	8.3	23.0
4+ College	5.2	26.2
Total	46.9	161.4
Occupation		
Blue-Collar	25.9	84.4
White-Collar	21.0	77.0
Total	46.9	161.4

migration of household heads has ceased. Nearly four times as many ring migrants (including their families) moved into the central city as city migrants moved outward into the ring. Table 1 indicates the rates of out-migration from the two segments of the metropolitan area by specific characteristics of the household head.

From Table 1, certain disproportionate rates of migration emerge. In all age groups except the youngest, ring-to-city migrants have rates that are higher than city-to-ring migrants. Those 20–24 years of age have slightly higher rates, while those in the middle-aged groups (25–44) show the most marked differences. The rate of ring-to-central-city migration among the oldest age group is three times the rate of central-city-to-ring migration among the same group.

In all educational groups, ring-to-city migrants have much higher rates than those of city-to-ring migrants. The college educated migrants (those with 4 years of college or more) leaving the ring have a rate five times that of their counterparts moving from the city into the ring area. While blue-collar workers are slightly more mobile than white-collar workers, a comparison of the two streams of movement indicates that ring-to-city migrants have over three times the rate of migration as do city-to-ring migrants. We also find that central-city and ring families with large numbers of children have about equal rates of migration, while among the smaller families, ring-to-city migrants have markedly higher rates.

Characteristics of Ring-to-City Migrants

The social and demographic characteristics of ring-to-city migrants are displayed in Table 2, which presents a percentage distribution of the migrants by characteristics of the household head. The results are outlined below.

Age. Several studies have indicated that it is the young migrant, either single or newly married, who is coming into the central city from the suburban areas surrounding it.[11] The data provided here are in contradiction to these findings. They indicate that most of the migrants fall within the age bracket 25–44 years. Migrant household heads below 25 years of age comprise only 5.8 percent of the total migrating population from the ring. At the other extreme, one-quarter (24.5 percent) of ring-to-city migrants are between 45 and 64 years, while the bulk of the migrants are between 25 and 44 years (69.8 percent). The data indicate that it is not the young who are moving into the city from the ring, but middle and older age groups.

TABLE 2. PERCENTAGE DISTRIBUTION OF RING-TO-CITY MIGRANT HEADS-OF-FAMILY BY SPECIFIC CHARACTERISTICS

Characteristics	Ring-to-City Migrants (N = 1325)	Characteristics	Ring-to-City Migrants (N = 1325)
Age		*Occupation*	
14–19	0.2	White-Collar	47.7
20–24	5.6	Blue-Collar	52.3
25–34	36.8	Total	100.0
35–44	33.0		
45–54	16.6	*Family Composition*	
55–64	7.9	No Children	26.9
Total	100.0	One Child	20.2
		Two Children	24.8
Education		Three Children	18.4
Elementary	17.1	Four Children	6.0
1–3 High School	22.8	5+ Children	3.5
4 High School	29.6	Total	100.0
1–3 College	14.3		
4+ College	16.2		
Total	100.0		

Education. More than 50 percent of the migrants from the ring into the city have between 1–3 years of high school or have completed high school. College graduates migrated from the ring to the city at the same rate as persons with only an elementary education. If education can serve as a rough indicator of socio-economic status, this suggests that migrants from the ring to the city are not concentrated in lower socio-economic groups, but rather are distributed more or less evenly among all groups.

Occupation. The distribution by occupation indicates that blue-collar and white-collar workers migrated into the central city from the ring at about equal rates. This fact tends to validate the earlier contention that migrants from the ring to the central city are not predominantly from lower socio-economic groups. The relatively low socio-economic level of the central city is due not to ring-to-city migration of persons of lower socio-economic status but rather to the large influx of rural migrants (the majority of whom are Negro).[12]

Family Composition. In general, the proportion of ring-to-city migrants decreases as family size increases. Family size structure serves as a good indicator of probable movement in a population.

Impact of Migration upon the Ring

In order to determine the impact of ring-to-city and city-to-ring migration on the population structure of the ring it was necessary to reconstruct the population structure before migration took place and after it occurred. The problem was complicated by the fact that city-to-ring migrants had to be taken into account. The results of this reconstruction are seen in Table 3.

The net change between 1955 and 1960 in the population structure of the ring was very slight. This small change, however, is in terms of differing proportions and does not indicate the large loss in absolute numbers of families in the ring (even with replacement due to city-to-ring migrants). This net change may be the result of (1) an out-migration from each category in proportion to its share of total ring population, or (2) an in-migration of persons with the same characteristics as those who left. In any case, little change occurred over the five-year period in the proportions of ring inhabitants displaying the social and demographic characteristics under study.

The results indicate that the only sizable changes occurred in the age and occupational categories. There were gains in the younger and oldest age groupings, with losses in the middle-age categories. The proportion of blue-collar workers among heads of households in the ring increased by an amount equal to the decrease in the proportion of white-collar workers. There was a slight gain in the elementary educated category, and losses in the high school and college educated categories. Gains also occurred among those families with one or no children, while losses occurred among families with two or three children. The proportions of large families remained the same.

Summary

The data, based on a sample of white, male, employed heads of households, indicate that the "expansion" model of urban population growth may no longer be applicable. The rate of ring-to-city migration is nearly four times as great as the rate of migration from the central city to the ring. When divided into specific characteristics, ring-to-city migrants, with slight exceptions, continue to have rates of migration within each category at least three times those of city-to-ring migrants.

TABLE 3. PERCENTAGE POPULATION STRUCTURE OF RING BEFORE AND AFTER MIGRATION, BY SPECIFIC CHARACTERISTICS OF HOUSEHOLD HEAD FOR 1955 AND 1960

Characteristics	Percent of Population in 1955	Percent of Population in 1960	Net Change
Age			
14–19	0.2	0.3	+0.1
20–24	3.4	3.5	+0.1
25–34	22.0	19.7	−2.3
35–44	33.5	33.3	−0.2
45–54	25.6	26.9	+1.3
55–65	15.3	16.3	+1.0
Total	100.0	100.0	0.0
Education			
Elementary	24.7	25.8	+1.1
1–3 High School	22.8	22.8	0.0
4 High School	28.0	27.8	−0.2
1–3 College	11.7	11.4	−0.3
4+ College	12.8	12.1	−0.7
Total	100.0	100.0	−0.1
Occupation			
White-Collar	44.0	43.3	−0.7
Blue-Collar	56.0	56.7	+0.7
Total	100.0	100.0	0.0
Family Composition			
No Children	30.3	31.2	+0.9
One Child	21.0	21.3	+0.3
Two Children	23.7	23.4	−0.3
Three Children	14.6	13.8	−0.8
Four Children	6.3	6.3	0.0
5+ Children	4.0	4.0	0.0
Total	100.0	100.0	+0.1

The characteristics of ring-to-city migrants indicate that persons migrating from the ring to the central city tend to be of middle rather than low socio-economic status. Most ring-to-city migrants are between 25 and 44 years of age, have some high school education, tend to have small families, and are proportionally distributed between white- and blue-collar workers.

The impact of migration out of the ring on the ring's population structure is small in terms of changes in the proportions of persons with the social and demographic characteristics examined here. The ring suffers an absolute loss of population even after replacement by migrants from the central city.[13] The most noticeable change took place in age and occupational structures. Young and old age groups gained in proportion to the 1955 population in the ring while middle age groups lost. There was a gain in the proportion of blue-collar workers and a loss in the proportion of white-collar workers. Likewise, there appeared a decrease in the proportion of high school and college educated individuals and an increase in the proportion of families with few children.

Thus, an analysis of ring-to-city migration shows that a reverse trend is occurring. The main stream of migration is no longer outward from the core of the metropolitan area, but rather inward from the ring to the central city. The earlier expansion of its physical boundaries due to the population explosion within the core and the concomitant movement of individuals outward into the suburbs appears to be slackening. The analysis suggests that the theoretical designs postulated in the expansion model may no longer be applicable.

Notes

1. The ring, or outside central city region, of a Standard Metropolitan Statistical Area (SMSA) includes all metropolitan population not residing within the political boundaries of the central city of the SMSA. The ring encompasses a broad area of suburban living which includes industrial and dormitory suburbs as well as a variety of fringe communities.

2. Migration is only one factor in population change: fertility and mortality are also important. However, only migration is considered here.

3. Donald J. Bogue, *Metropolitan Decentralization: A Study of Differential Growth,* Scripps Foundation Studies in Population Distribution, No. 2 (Oxford, Ohio: Scripps Foundation, 1950). See also: Amos Hawley, *The Changing Shape of Metropolitan America: Decentralization Since 1920* (Glencoe, Ill.: Free Press, 1956).

4. Ernest W. Burgess, "The Growth of the City: An Introduction to a Research Project," *The City,* ed. R. E. Park, E. W. Burgess and R. D. McKenzie (Chicago: Chicago University Press, 1925), pp. 47–62. See also: Homer Hoyt, "Forces of Urban Centralization and Decentralization," *American Journal of Sociology* (May, 1941), 843–52.

5. United Nations, *The Determinants and Consequences of Population Trends* (New York, 1953); National Resources Committee, "The Process of Urbanization: Underlying Forces and Emerging Trends," *Cities and Society,* ed. P. H. Hatt and A. J. Reiss (New York: Free Press, 1964).

6. U. S. Department of Commerce: Bureau of the Census, *U. S. Census of Population: 1960. One-In-A-Thousand Sample Technical Documentation.*

7. The sample census cross-tabulation program (IBM 7070) allowed a maximum of only four controls. The total number of cells was limited to 1000, thereby limiting the number of categories that could be used. If additional variables were introduced, the programs that were executed would have become impossible.

8. White collar: Professional, Technical and Kindred, Managers, Officials, Proprietors (except Farm), Clerical and Kindred, and Sales Workers. Blue collar: Craftsmen, Foremen and Kindred, Operatives and Kindred, Private Household Workers, Service Workers, and Laborers (except Farm and Mine).

9. The additive process of obtaining the total populations refers specifically to the total sample population. It does not take into account changes in fertility or mortality. Specifically, it takes into account family unit migration as opposed to individual migration. See P. H. Rossi, *Why Families Move: A Study in the Social Psychology of Urban Residential Mobility* (Glencoe, Ill.: Free Press, 1955); A. H. Hobbs, "Specificity and Selective Migration," *American Sociological Review* (December, 1942), 776.

10. The migration rate is based on the total number of household heads who left their area of origin (i.e., central city or ring) per 1000 population of that area in 1955, before the migration took place.

11. Leslie Kish, "Differentiation in Metropolitan Areas," *American Sociological Review* (August, 1954), 388–98. See also: Sidney Goldstein, "Some Economic Consequences of Suburbanization in the Copenhagen Metropolitan Area," *American Journal of Sociology* (March, 1963), pp. 551–564.

12. H. Sharp and L. F. Schnore, "The Changing Color Composition of Metropolitan Areas," *Land Economics* (May, 1962), 169–85.

13. This does not take into account inter-metropolitan or urban-to-rural movement, or changes due to fertility and mortality.

URBAN NEIGHBORHOODS AND INDIVIDUAL BEHAVIOR

Wendell Bell

It is a matter of everyday observation that metropolitan areas are subdivided into different sections, each exhibiting certain distinctive features. There are manufacturing, warehouse, theater, financial, department store, used car lot, residential, and many other districts in most modern American cities. The residential areas themselves are further differentiated with respect to many additional characteristics. Some are inhabited predominantly by Negroes, Chinese, Japanese, Puerto Ricans, Italians, Germans, Poles, Swedes, Mexicans, or some other racial or nationality group. Some districts are set apart from others because Jews, Catholics, or the members of a particular Protestant denomination live there in relatively large numbers.

Some districts are characterized by old, dilapidated dwellings, or by large apartment houses, or by access to such desirable places as lake fronts, beaches, or river views, and still others by prominence of concrete, steel, asphalt, or general neglect. All urban areas have sections where the "rich people" live; others where the "poor people" live; and most urban subcommunities contain residents representing the many gradations in amount of wealth or income between these two extremes. Some neighborhood communities are marked by the presence of older

---

I am indebted to the Center for Advanced Study in the Behavioral Sciences for a fellowship during 1963–64 which enabled me to prepare this review of research, bringing up to date an earlier review published under the title "Social Areas: Typology of Urban Neighborhoods" (Bell, 1959) with permission of the publisher.

persons, renters instead of home owners, more women than men, or certain occupations such as proprietors, professionals, managers, and officials. Others contain unskilled or semiskilled workers, or many unrelated individuals, or many persons living together in family units.

Recognizing this diversity in the social characters of urban subcommunities, Louis Wirth (1938) described the city as "a mosaic of social worlds" and emphasized that the different sections of the city can be thought of as separate worlds, with the transition between them often very abrupt, reflecting their different populations, subcultures, ways of life, and social organizations.

The casual observer usually is aware of these neighborhood community differences; yet he may consider them more as a crazy quilt than as a neat, orderly, and systematic pattern. On a superficial level, he is often correct, since the various neighborhoods are of miscellaneous sizes and shapes. But various economists, geographers, sociologists, and other social scientists studying the city have located and traced various kinds of orderly patterns underlying the apparently unsystematic nature, growth, and change of neighborhoods. The study of human ecology, for example, has resulted in many generalizations concerning the spatial distribution of different kinds of people and of various functions and activities. Such works as those of Hawley (1950) and Quinn (1950) attest that the body of knowledge created with ecological concepts and techniques of analysis has been productive and fruitful. Generalizations concerning the orderly patterns of city growth and spatial structure include the concentric zone theory of Burgess (1929), Hoyt's sector theory (1939), and Harris and Ullman's multiple nuclei theory (1945). These generalizations are to be found in most recent textbooks in introductory sociology and urban sociology published in this country.

Recently, new methods for the systematic analysis of population differences between urban subcommunities have been proposed; and sufficient work has been done with the methods by enough different research workers that a sizable body of information is beginning to emerge. One of these methods, first presented by Shevky and Williams (1949) and later modified by Shevky and Bell (1955), will be discussed in some detail in this chapter along with some of the work of other persons within the Shevky framework. Occasional reference will be made to a similar method constructed by Tryon (1955). In general, these methods can be referred to as *social area analysis,* although the particular techniques by which neighborhoods are combined into social areas differ somewhat in each case.

The purposes of this chapter are to review the method of social area analysis and some of the research that has resulted from its use, and to evaluate the method in the light of recent work. In particular, the utility of the social area method for the design and analysis of urban subarea field studies will be explored: Specifically, does social area analysis of census tract statistics for a metropolitan area provide a useful frame in which to design and execute detailed investigations of the behavior of individuals and groups in different subcommunities? If so, what is the function of social area analysis for such studies?

Since a logical place to begin is with the basic data that the method utilizes, a discussion of the nature of census tract statistics precedes a description of the social area typology.

Census Tract Statistics

The basic unit of analysis used in the construction of social areas is the census tract.[1] Census tracts are relatively small geographical areas into which certain cities and often their adjacent areas have been subdivided. They are larger than blocks and usually contain between 3,000 and 6,000 persons. In 1950, a metropolitan area the size of Chicago was divided into approximately 1,000 of these small units; the San Francisco-Oakland area about 244; San Jose, California, as few as 59; and smaller areas into even fewer tracts. Data collected in connection with the regular decennial census of the United States are published in a form that allows study of population and housing characteristics of these tracts or subareas.

The census tract program is a relatively recent development. New York City and seven other cities having populations over 500,000 were divided into census tracts in 1910, and census data were tabulated by tracts within these cities for the first time. The purpose was to obtain detailed population data for sufficiently small areas within the city so that neighborhood communities could be studied. In 1920, tract data were again tabulated for the same eight cities, and in 1930 this number was increased to 18. By 1940 tract data were available for 60 urban places. By 1950 as many as 69 urban places in the United States and its territories had been divided into census tracts. By 1960, the program had expanded to include published reports for 180 tracted areas, three of which were in Puerto Rico (see U. S. Bureau of Census, 1958, 1960). Comparative studies of urban neighborhoods with a scope and adequacy never before possible can now be made.

Some of the information contained in the census tract bulletins represented a complete count of all the persons in the census tracts. Additional information was presented which was obtained from a 20 percent sample of persons in the tracts. The information given for each census tract for 1950 is listed below:

Total population
Race
Sex
Nativity
Married couples
Families or unrelated individuals
Number of dwelling units
Owner- or renter-occupied dwelling units
Institutional population
Years of school completed
Residence in 1949
Income in 1949
Age
Marital status
Employment status
Major occupational group
Type of structure
Condition and plumbing facilities
Year structure was built
Number of all occupied dwelling units
Number of persons in dwelling unit
Number of households
Population per household
Population in households
Women in the labor force
Persons per room
Type of heating fuel
Refrigeration equipment
Television
Contract monthly rent
Value of one-dwelling-unit structures
Spanish surnames (for certain areas only)

The above list, of course, greatly underestimates the total number of useful measures contained in the tract bulletins, since many combinations and permutations are possible. For example, an investigator can use data on age and sex to compute a fertility ratio for a tract by taking the number of women from age 15 to age 44, dividing that sum into the number of children under age 5, and then multiplying by 1,000. Thus, the fertility ratios of tract populations can be compared. Many other such permutations of the above variables giving important information about a tract population can be made.

If one wishes to get a coherent and easily understandable picture of the character of a tract population, however, it is cumbersome and inefficient to deal separately with as many different variables (and their permutations) as are contained in the census bulletins. For example, if one tried to compare and contrast the 244 tracts in the San Francisco Bay area with respect to thirty or more variables simultaneously, each handled individually, the task would be exceedingly tedious and would result in complex patterns difficult to comprehend. Thus, some ordering or clustering of the variables should be made as a prior step in constructing a composite of a tract's social characteristics.

Ordering of Census Variables

Apart from the variables reflecting sheer size of the census tract, there appear to be three sets of general characteristics in the census tract bulletins: *socioeconomic*, *family*, and *ethnic* characteristics. There are, no doubt, other ways in which the census variables can be ordered. For example, there are variables which refer to housing and other variables which refer to population. But for the purposes of systematically analyzing the social features of urban neighborhood communities, the division of the variables into those which are socioeconomic or socioeconomic-related, those which indicate the presence or lack of families, and those which reflect the presence or absence of certain racial and nationality groups seemed most revealing to those of us engaged in the early work using the social area typology. Looking back over the census variables given above, one can easily group most of them into one of these three categories. This has been done below:

Socioeconomic Characteristics	Family Characteristics	Ethnic Characteristics
Condition and plumbing facilities	Sex	Race
Persons per room	Married couples	Nativity
Years of school completed	Families or unrelated individuals	Spanish surnames
Income in 1949	Owner- or renter-occupied dwelling units	
Employment status	Type of structure	
Major occupational group	Age	
Type of heating fuel	Marital status	
Refrigeration equipment	Women in the labor force	
Contract monthly rent	Lack of institutional population	
Value of one-dwelling-unit structures		

The census variables were first grouped this way in the development of social area analysis by Shevky and Williams (1949). The author verified the classification by using 1940 census data for the Los Angeles area and the San Francisco Bay area (Bell, 1955a). Tryon (1955), working independently, analyzed all the census variables for the San Francisco Bay area as of 1940 and reached practically the same classification. In addition, Walter C. Kaufman (1961) has found that this grouping of variables is, in general, valid for the San Francisco Bay and Chicago areas as of 1950 as well.

Some of the work of Van Arsdol, Camilleri, and Schmid (1957, 1958a) is important in this connection. They performed a factor analysis of selected variables from the 1950 census tract data for ten American cities—Akron, Ohio; Atlanta, Georgia; Birmingham, Alabama; Kansas City, Missouri; Louisville, Kentucky; Minneapolis, Minnesota; Portland, Oregon; Providence, Rhode Island; Rochester, New York; and Seattle, Washington. They concluded that this grouping of census variables is an adequate measure of socioeconomic, family, and ethnic characteristics in eight of these cities.

In general, the ordering of the census variables into three basic types has been strongly confirmed by much of the research designed to test it. But Van Arsdol, Camilleri, and Schmid's deviant cases, along with the recent research results of Anderson and Bean (1961), suggest that additional attention should be paid to the possibility of some alternative—perhaps more complicated—clustering of the basic census variables.

For example, Anderson and Bean conclude from a factorial analysis of 1950 census tract statistics for Toledo (Ohio) that two factors, rather than one, constitute a more adequate representation of the second set of variables listed above. They divide the variables into *housing characteristics* (which they are willing to call *urbanization* after Shevky's original label for this index) and *family characteristics,* which is consistent with the suggested re-interpretation of this same index, *familism,* made by the present writer (Shevky and Bell, 1955, p. 68). More will be said of this later.

Indexes of Socioeconomic Status, Familism, and Ethnicity

All the census variables can be reduced to three more basic factors, although more different factors may prove necessary in the long run. Using these three basic factors, it is possible to construct a picture of the smaller social worlds into which an urban area is subdivided in terms of the socioeconomic, family, and ethnic characteristics of the tract populations. It is neither necessary nor efficient to include all the possible measures of the three factors in indexes for them. A few indicators of a factor are sufficient.

Of course, some census variables are better measures of their particular factor than others. Thus, certain census variables were selected, and their average value used as an index of the socioeconomic characteristics of a census tract. The index was named the *index of socioeconomic status.* Other variables were selected to be averaged as an indicator of the family characteristics of a tract population, and this was named the *index of familism.* Finally, the average of still other variables was made an indicator of the racial and nationality characteristics of a tract population and was named the *index of ethnicity*. The variables selected to measure the three factors were as follows:

Index of Socioeconomic Status	Index of Familism	Index of Ethnicity
Rent Education Occupation	Fertility ratio Women not in the labor force Single-family detached dwellings	Race Nativity Spanish surnames (when available)

The specific procedures for the computation of the indexes are given in the appendix to this chapter. There have been some changes in composition, and there may be more, as indicated above. For example, for technical reasons the measure of rent was dropped in computing the socioeconomic index after 1940. It suffices to say here that each census tract can be given three scores—for the indexes of socioeconomic status, familism, and ethnicity. These scores have been standardized to range from zero to 100 according to the extremes on each measure in the Los Angeles area as of 1940. Therefore, it is possible for tracts in other urban areas (or in Los Angeles in other years) to receive scores less than zero or somewhat greater than 100. Ideally, of course, the scores should be standardized to the range of all the census tracts in the entire United States—or even throughout the world, when small area statistics become available for the metropolitan areas in other countries—or to some extreme lower and upper limits which cannot in fact be quickly transcended by the data for any particular time and place.

In tracts with high scores on the index of socioeconomic status there are many persons with white-collar occupations, such as professionals, proprietors, managers, officials, salesmen, clerks; many persons have a higher education; and rents are high. In tracts with low scores, there are many persons with blue-collar occupations, such as craftsmen, foremen, operatives, and laborers; many persons have no more than a grade school education; and rents are low.

This index was originally labeled *social rank* by Shevky, and is so designated by some other researchers using the social area typology. Although I have been using the term *economic status,* for reasons which do not seem too important in hindsight, perhaps a good compromise would be *socioeconomic status* or *level.* No significant alteration in the conceptual interpretation was intended in any event. On the other hand, Anderson and Bean (1961, p. 123) argue that to call this dimension *social rank* (or *economic status* either, apparently) is inappropriate. They suggest that the underlying factor measured by the index be "classed a measure of the *prestige value* of the neighborhood." Only additional data, along with conceptual and theoretical analysis, can lead to an adequate resolution of their difference of opinion.

It is possible for tracts to vary in family characteristics regardless of their scores on the index of socioeconomic status. Tracts having high scores on the index of familism contain populations which have high fertility ratios (that is, many children under age 5 in relation to the number of women between the ages of 15 and 44); many women not in the labor force, but at home in the roles of housewives and mothers; and many single-family detached dwellings. Tracts with low fertility ratios, many women in the labor force, and many multiple dwellings achieve low scores on the index of familism.

Originally, Shevky called this index *urbanization* (high urbanization being equivalent in operational terms to low familism), but his designation contains conceptual elements inadequately measured by the items comprising the index. It is also true that additional marital and family characteristics probably should be added to the index if a better indicator of the *family life characteristics* of census tract populations is desired. Scott Greer (1956, 1960, 1962a, 1962b), Greer and Kube (1959), Greer and Orleans (1962), and Kaufman and Greer (1960), among others, have compromised, while creatively elaborating the concept and stressing the underlying agreement and similarity of the two designations as referring to differential life styles or choice patterns of urban residents. They prominently use *urbanism-familism,* which seems to be a good solution to this terminological problem at the present time. The factor analysis of Anderson and Bean, mentioned above, which located two factors within the *urbanism-familism* index, as well as some recent work of the Sherifs (1964), should stimulate additional work on this question. The latter researchers have decided that low *urbanization,* rather than high *familism,* is a better term to describe the family characteristics of a sample of low socioeconomic, largely Spanish-speaking populations, since almost a quarter of the large families lacked a male breadwinner. These facts seemed congenial to the idea that these populations were low in their acculturation to an urban way of life, a notion better conveyed by *urbanization* than by *familism.* The low socioeconomic level of these tracts may modify the nature of the family life in them and explain the absence of male breadwinners, while the concentration of Spanish-speaking persons may explain the low level of acculturation. Nonetheless, one can agree that more experimentation with this and alternative indexes needs to be done.

One additional problem has arisen with the designation *index of family status,* which I have suggested before for the urbanism-familism dimension. Fortunately, it is merely a terminological and not a conceptual problem. The use of *status* in the label led some readers to believe that the referent was the economic status, the social rank, or the prestige of the families in the census tracts. Such is not the case. Thus, *familism* or *urbanism-familism* may be superior as labels on the simple grounds that they more clearly convey the meaning intended.

Tracts which contain many Negroes, persons of other non-white races, persons with Spanish surnames, and foreign-born whites from certain countries receive high scores; and tracts which contain mostly native-born whites receive low scores on the index of ethnicity. This index, of course, is negatively related to the index of socioeconomic status, since Negroes and many other Amercan minority groups are most often located in urban neighborhoods of low socioeconomic status. However, it is possible to find some neighborhood communities in which generally subordinate minority groups have high socioeconomic status and to find others inhabited by native-born whites of low socioeconomic status. Moreover, socioeconomic status is not the same thing as race and nationality; that is, the social significance of these two types of variables is different even though they have often been confused. Consequently, in spite of the empirical relationship between the indexes of socioeconomic status and ethnicity, they should be kept conceptually distinct in any sociological analysis, including one of urban communities.

Construction of the Social Area Typology

Since the three indexes are to be utilized as *distinct* properties of urban subcommunities, they cannot be simply added together. Some method must be devised to use them simultaneously in the analysis. To do this, types or a typology must be constructed. The use of the concept of type here follows Lazarsfeld (1937) who said:

> One is safe in saying that the concept of type is always used in referring to special compounds of attributes. In speaking of the Middle-western type of American, one may have in mind certain physical features, certain attitudes and habits, certain affiliations and talents attributed to the inhabitants of this region. In speaking of types of books or of types of governments, a special combination of attributes is thrown into relief.

The special "compound of attributes" used in social area analysis is that composed of economic, family, and ethnic characteristics. Instead of a "Middle-western type of American," "types of books," or "types of governments," the types are composed of urban neighborhoods. As shown in Figure 10, a social attribute space is constructed which is bounded by the indexes of socioeconomic status and familism. Census tract populations near to each other in the social area diagram would necessarily have similar configurations of scores on the two indexes. Such tracts are grouped together by the divisions which are made in the indexes, segmenting each into four parts.

The social space has been segmented by divisions passing through socioeconomic status scores of 25, 50, and 75, and through familism scores also of 25, 50, and 75. Thus, potentially, sixteen groupings of census tract populations are made, and these represent different social types of tract populations. These *types* are also called social areas.

Social areas so far, then, are composed of a tract or tracts with particular patterns of scores on the indexes of socioeconomic status and familism. They are called *social* in that the properties of neighborhood communities dealt with are

Familism				
High	1A	2A	3A	4A
	1B	2B	3B	4B
	1C	2C	3C	4C
Low	1D	2D	3D	4D
	Low			High
	Socioeconomic status			

Fig. 10. Social Area Key Based on Socioeconomic Status and Familism.

social properties. The term *area* is employed because a geometric space frame is utilized. By similar reasoning the diagram shown in Figures 10 and 11 can be referred to as a "social space diagram."

A number and letter designation are given to each of the types as shown in Figure 10. Social area 1D, for example, contains tract populations with low socioeconomic status and low familism. Tract populations in social area 1A would have the same socioeconomic status as those contained in 1D, but the familism of tracts in 1A would be high instead of low. Likewise, social area 4D varies systematically from 1D, but in this case the familism (or conversely urbanism) of the two groups of census tracts is the same, while the socioeconomic status differs, social area 4D containing tract populations low on familism (or high on urbanism) but high on socioeconomic status. Thus, each type of social area delimits census tracts which have a particular configuration of scores with respect to economic and family characteristics (see Figure 10 for positions and designations of other social areas).

The third factor, ethnicity, adds to the typology so far constructed by distinguishing those census tracts which contain relatively many members of American racial and nationality minority groups. Tract populations having high indexes of ethnicity are given an "S" along with their social area designations as given in Figure 10. Tracts which have low indexes of ethnicity remain with only the designation as shown in Figure 10. Thus, there are thirty-two possible social areas or types of urban subcommunities: 1A, 1B . . . 4D and 1AS, 1BS . . . 4DS.[2]

Shevky called this index *segregation*, considering those tract populations which contained relatively more than average percentages of subordinate ethnic groups as segregated; and those which contained less than average as not segregated. This label created some confusion with another meaning of segregation used by Shevky as well as others (*e.g.*, Bell, 1954; Bell and Willis, 1957), namely the degree of residential segregation of a particular *group* summing across neighborhoods. Therefore, some of us began using the label *ethnic status* to refer to the racial and nationality composition of particular neighborhoods. This label, however, led to further lack of clarity, since *high* ethnic status designated tract populations with higher than average percentages of *subordinate* ethnic groups, groups generally having low rather than high status in the larger society. Thus, using *ethnic status* in this way flies in the face of common parlance by reversing general meaning. Again, this is simply a terminological problem, which several writers have solved by using the term *ethnicity* to refer to the ethnic composition of a census tract population, *high ethnicity* referring to a tract with relatively many members of subordinate ethnic groups.

Some Illustrations of the Use of Social Area Analysis

Since this chapter cannot discuss completely all the work using social area analysis, a selection of research executed in this framework will illustrate some of the uses and the nature of the findings. The census tracts of the San Francisco Bay area are plotted in the social space diagram in Figure 11 according to their scores on the three indexes for 1950. Included are 244 tracts with a total population of 1,509,678. The social position of each tract population can be seen in relation to all other tracts in the Bay area.

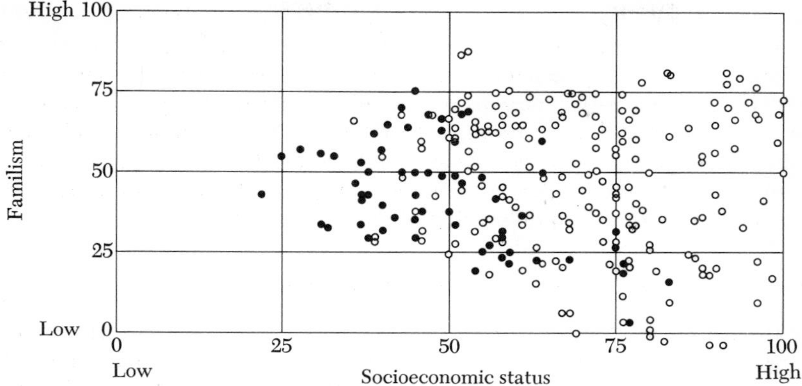

FIG. 11. DISTRIBUTION OF THE CENSUS TRACTS IN THE SOCIAL AREAS OF THE SAN FRANCISCO BAY REGION, 1950.

Notice on Figure 11 that there is little relationship between the indexes of familism and socioeconomic status, the correlation being −.13 between them. The correlation between the indexes of socioeconomic status and ethnicity is −.50, reflecting the fact that Negroes, Orientals, other non-whites, Mexican-Americans, and members of certain other foreign-born groups are most likely to live in neighborhoods characterized by low socioeconomic status. These groups are also increasingly likely to live in areas having little family life, as the socioeconomic levels of their neighborhoods increase.

Similar patterns of relationships have been noted for Los Angeles (Bell, 1955a) and Chicago (Kaufman, 1961). Whether the relations between the factors will vary markedly for other cities, or whether the stability of these patterns represents a generalization about the social structure of American cities at least for a particular time is a matter for future research. The Van Arsdol, Camilleri, and Schmid (1958a) research on the ten cities, which was mentioned earlier, suggests that this pattern of intercorrelations may be fairly general. But variation was reported for some of the cities, which may indicate the existence of differential patterns of social area distributions in cities of different regions, ages, economic bases, etc.

Orderly patterns have been found in the relationship between the sex ratio and the social areas in both Los Angeles and San Francisco. The sex ratio varies inversely with familism at low levels of socioeconomic status, and directly with familism at high levels of socioeconomic status; it varies inversely with socioeconomic status at all levels of familism. Thus, realtively more women than men are located in higher socioeconomic status neighborhoods, with the greatest concentration of women in relation to men occurring in areas of expensive apartment houses, and the greatest concentration of men in relation to women cccurring in the cheap rooming-house areas (Shevky and Williams, 1949; Bell, 1953; Shevky and Bell, 1955).

The age distributions of the persons in social areas also show systematic differences. In Los Angeles and San Francisco, the percentage of older persons increases with the socioeconomic status and decreases with the familism of a tract. The percentage of persons under fifteen years of age decreases with socioeconomic status and increases with familism. For example, social area 4D contains the largest percentage of older and the smallest percentage of younger persons. Although the pattern is less clear, the social area distribution of the middle-aged group tends to follow that of the older group.

Studies of the Nature and Pattern of Subcommunities

Once the census tracts of a metropolitan area have been given scores according to their socioeconomic, family, and ethnic characteristics, it becomes possible to execute systematically a variety of investigations into the nature of different urban subcommunities within the social area framework. For example, an examination of neighborhood place names used by the residents of a city allows a study of the relationship between subjective evaluations of urban neighborhoods and the social characteristics of the neighborhoods as determined by an analysis of census variables. Some named places in San Francisco are given below with their scores on the three indexes for 1950 (Shevky and Bell, 1955, pp. 61–63).

Identifying Place Name	Index of Socioeconomic Status	Index of Familism	Index of Ethnicity	Social Area
Nob Hill (A-12)	91	−4	9	4D
Chinatown (A-15)	46	37	92	2CS
Sea Cliff (E-1)	93	58	10	4B
Potrero (L-1)	38	52	29	2BS
Diamond Heights (N-13)	52	71	11	3B

Studies could be designed to determine subjective evaluations of the social images of these named places. These evaluations could then be analyzed with respect to both the social characteristics of the named places and the social characteristics of the persons doing the evaluating.

Land use and topography, as might be expected, are related to social areas. Generally, in the San Francisco Bay area, neighborhoods of low socioeconomic status are located adjacent to the industrially occupied, low elevation areas of the inner Bay, while neighborhoods of high socioeconomic status are usually in areas of high elevation, farther from industrially occupied land. Neighborhoods of low familism are near commercial areas, especially near the downtown business district, while neighborhoods of high familism are located farther from the downtown commercial area, nearer to parks, lakes, or ocean beaches. The census tracts composing a social area, however, are not necessarily contiguous and continuous.

Additional studies of the spatial aspects of social area analysis have been made by Anderson and Egeland (1961) for four American cities between 200,000 and

500,000 population in 1950: Akron and Dayton, Ohio, Indianapolis, Indiana, and Syracuse, New York; by McElrath (1962) for Rome (Italy) using 1951 census data; and by McElrath and Barkey (no date) for Chicago in 1960.[3] These studies are of particular significance because they relate social areas to the well-known concentric zonal theory of Burgess and the sector theory of Hoyt.

Consistently, in every city, the familism-urbanism dimension is zonally distributed; it is also distributed sectorially in Rome and Chicago, but not in the four cities studied by Anderson and Egeland. Socioeconomic status (or social rank) is distributed differentially by zones in Chicago, Indianapolis, and Rome, but not in the three smallest U. S. cities studied. *However, in Chicago the high socioeconomic neighborhoods were located near the periphery of the metropolitan area, while in Rome they were located in the central districts.* Socioeconomic levels of neighborhood populations were clearly sectorial in all the cities except Chicago. Ethnicity was included in the analysis only in Chicago. There it was not distributed zonally, although there was a tendency for it to be distributed sectorially.

Studies of Prevalent Attitudes and Actions in Different Areas

The social area typology has now been used in numerous studies as an analytic frame for the study of individual beliefs, attitudes, and behaviors. A review of a few of these studies will serve to further illustrate the analytic utility of the method.

Bell, Boat, and Force (1954) examined the Shevky social space diagram (see Figure 11) and selected four census tracts in San Francisco which had low scores on the index of ethnicity, but widely different scores in the indexes of socioeconomic status and familism. In these tracts, an investigation was made of the social isolation and participation of urbanites. The social space positions of the four subpopulations are shown in Figure 12 along with their census tract designations and their identifying neighborhood community names. From Figure 12 it can be noted that Mission, a low-rent rooming-house area, is characterized by low socioeconomic status and low familism. Pacific Heights, a high-rent apartment-house area, is high on socioeconomic status, but low on familism. Outer Mission,

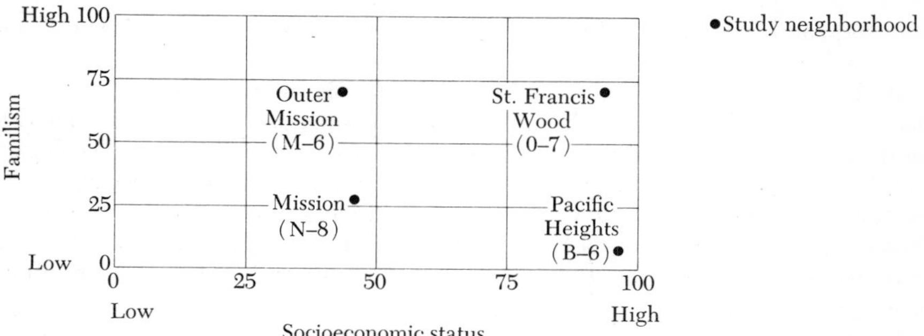

FIG. 12. THE FOUR FRANCISCO STUDY TRACTS LOCATED IN THE SOCIAL SPACE DIAGRAM, 1950.

characterized by small single-family detached houses and residents of modest means, is low on socioeconomic status and high on familism. St. Francis Wood, an area of large single-family detached houses with residents who are fairly well off financially, is high in both economic and family characteristics.

After the selection of the study tracts, as described above, probability samples were drawn from a complete list of all the dwelling units within each tract. A total of 701 interviews was obtained with a response rate of more than 85 percent, one randomly selected male over age 21 in each sample dwelling being interviewed.

The results of this study show different patterns of social participation in the different neighborhoods. Men living in high socioeconomic status neighborhoods (Pacific Heights and St. Francis Wood), when compared to those living in low socioeconomic status neighborhoods (Mission and Outer Mission), belong to a greater number of formal associations, attend formal association meetings more frequently, and are more likely to hold offices in formal associations (Bell and Force, 1956a). A greater percentage of their memberships are in general-interest types of associations (Bell and Force, 1956b); they interact with their co-workers away from work more frequently, have more informal contacts with friends who are not neighbors or relatives, rely more on their co-workers, are less likely to be calculating in their relationships with their neighbors (Bell and Boat, 1957), and are much more likely to achieve low anomia scores on the Srole Scale (Bell, 1957). Jews and, to a lesser extent, Protestants, are more likely to live in the areas of high socioeconomic status than in neighborhoods of low socioeconomic status. The reverse is true of Catholics (Bell and Force, 1957).

Men who live in high familism neighborhoods (St. Francis Wood and Outer Mission), when compared with those in neighborhoods low on familism (Pacific Heights and Mission), are somewhat less socially isolated from informal group participation, have more social contacts with neighbors and kin, and are more likely to have met their close personal friends in their neighborhoods (Bell and Boat, 1957). Of the men in the two high socioeconomic status neighborhoods, those in Pacific Heights belong to fewer formal associations, attend meetings less often, are less likely to hold office, and are more likely to belong to special individual-interest types of formal associations than the men living in St. Francis Wood. Catholics are relatively more numerous in neighborhoods high in familism than they are in neighborhoods low in familism. "Independents," "agnostics," and "atheists" are most likely to live in areas low in familism.

It should be noted that the method and analysis in these studies were such that we can conclude that social participation or isolation variables are related to residency in these areas. Some work in social area analysis has used "ecological correlations," which contain pitfalls of incorrect interpretation made well known by Robinson (1950) in a now classic article. Such studies must be interpreted accordingly. The emphasis here is upon the research value of social areas as "independent variables" for studying attitudes and life styles of particular subsets of the populations.

Using the social areas of Los Angeles, Scott Greer (1956; Greer and Kube, 1955, 1959) also selected four local areas in which to conduct a study of social participation in urban neighborhoods. His strategy, however was to hold both economic and ethnic characteristics constant in his study tracts and to vary family characteristics widely. For 1950, Temple City had a score of 74 on the index of familism, Eagle Rock, 64, Silver Lake, 45, and Central Hollywood, 20. Each of these subcommunities had scores of about 70 on the index of socioeconomic status and scores of 6 or less on the index of ethnicity. From his interviews with persons in these four neighborhood communities, Greer concludes that the greater the amount of family life in a neighborhood, the more "neighboring," the more persons who have friends in their neighborhood, the more likely a person is to attend a cultural event in his neighborhood, the larger the percentage of persons who belong to formal organizations meeting in the local area, and the the more husbands who belong to organizations meeting in the local area, and the more persons who could name at least one local leader.

Greer also found that persons living in high familism neighborhoods, as compared with residents of neighborhoods low on familism, are more likely to think of their local area as a "little community," like a "small town," where "people are friendly and neighborly." They are less likely to mention the convenience of their location in terms of its nearness to "downtown and everything." They are less likely to speak of their neighbors as "nice people who leave you alone and mind their own business"; but they are more committed to remaining in their neighborhoods, and more apt to have their friends (other than friends who are neighbors) in other high familism tracts.

McElrath (1955) and Williamson (1953, 1954) have used social area analysis in the design and analysis of sample surveys. Using the typology, they selected samples within neighborhoods in the Los Angeles metropolitan area. They reported, respectively, that the social areas were predictive of the prestige and esteem ratings for individuals and the degree of their marital adjustment (see also Sussman, 1959). Curtis (1957) has used the method as a sampling device in his study of the employability of aging workers in Buffalo, New York.

There are many other uses to which social area analysis has been put. Studying 1,107 petitioners for change of name in Los Angeles County, Broom, Beem, and Harris (1955) find that name changers were more likely than the general population to live in areas rated high in socioeconomic status, low in familism, and low in ethnicity. This suggests that name changers may be upwardly mobile persons, who have broken away from family ties and have been, or are being, assimilated into the larger society, and are moving away from membership in and identification with some particular ethnic group.

In another study Broom and Shevky (1949) demonstrated the utility of the typological framework for the differentiation of an ethnic group. They found Jewish neighborhoods in Los Angeles in the lower ranges of familism and in the full range of socioeconomic status. Tracts lacking Russian-born persons (which indicator was used for one segment of the Jewish population) tended to fall in the high ranges of familism, with a noticeable cluster at the lowest levels of socioeconomic status. Taking the members of four Jewish fraternities on the Los Angeles campus of the University of California, they found that the two rated by campus consensus as having high prestige had members from tract locations with significantly higher socioeconomic status than members of the two lower-prestige fraternities.

Studies of the incidence of suicide and juvenile delinquency have been made by Wendling (1954) and Polk (1958). Polk (1957, 1957–58), for example, found juvenile delinquency rates highest in those areas of San Diego in which minority group members live, and lowest in areas inhabited by native whites. Smaller correlations are reported for the other two indexes, but juvenile delinquency was negatively related to socioeconomic status and familism. The highest rates of juvenile delinquency occurred in neighborhoods with high indexes of ethnicity, with low levels of income, occupation, and education, and with little family life. The only significant correlation between suicide and any of the three indexes in Polk's San Diego study is a negative correlation between familism and suicide.

In his study of the social areas of Portland in 1960, Polk empirically demonstrates the need for a typological approach in relating delinquency rates to urban neighborhoods. He notes among other things that delinquency rates increase with socioeconomic status of the neighborhood at the lowest level of familism, but decrease with socioeconomic status generally.

The typology has been used to facilitate adequate social welfare planning for local areas in the San Francisco Bay area (Bange, *et al.*, 1953). The hypothesis was that each of the social areas had certain distinctive social welfare problems related to their differences in economic, family, and ethnic characteristics. This work does a great deal in suggesting one of the many possible practical applications of the social area typology.

Robert L. Wilson (1958) has used the social area typology for a comparative study of Episcopal, Methodist, Presbyterian, and United Lutheran churches in selected cities throughout the United States. He indicates that generalizations can be made regarding the relation of churches to social areas. Curtis, Avesing, and Klosek (1957) and Sullivan (1961) have related social areas to Catholic parishes.

Tryon and his associates have related social areas to additional variables such as political preference, voting participation, psychiatric hospitalization, and the probability of an individual's attending a university. There is insufficient space to elaborate with a detailed consideration of these findings. However, Tryon's findings and interpretations on the stability of social areas deserve further comment. Tryon (1955, p. 31) argued that:

> It is difficult to believe that a social area, including a number of tracts of people having the same configuration of demographic and correlated psychosocial ways, would change much in a decade, or perhaps many decades. A change would be gradual. Individual persons may be born into the area, move out or die, but it should retain its subcultural homogeneity with considerable constancy, short of socially catastrophic events. Even those areas that undergo rapid growth through construction of new homes are likely to incorporate new groups of persons homogeneous with those already there.

Tryon (1955, p. 32) also concludes from his analysis of the homogeneity of his 1940 San Francisco social areas with respect to 1950 median rent that ". . . little change in homogeneity of the tracts composing the various areas has occurred in 10 years." He also reports a comparison between the 1940 vote for Roosevelt and the 1947 vote for the Democratic candidate for Congress, Havenner, a man identified with the Roosevelt-Truman program. The census tracts show practically the same rank order for Roosevelt as for Havenner, the correlation coefficient being .94.

Other evidence that social areas remain relatively constant is found in McElrath's Los Angeles study (1955). He reports that thirteen years after the collection of the data on which the social area scores were based, he achieved the anticipated results in his sample survey with respect to differences in economic, family, and ethnic characteristics in his study areas.

This is not to say that tracts never change their social area positions, but rather that most of them, short of catastrophe, can be expected to maintain consistent social patterns for relatively long periods of time. Still, the social area approach is most useful for analysis of current conditions when census data are up to date, close to census years. There is a need for techniques to keep social area analysis current due to the high rates of change in certain parts of most American cities.

Tryon's comments are not to be construed to mean that the census tract populations need be homogeneous for the method to be valid. It is not inconsistent with the typology to find some urban neighborhoods that are typically characterized by heterogeneity in certain variables. Census tracts classified together in a social area, however, should have *about the same degree of heterogeneity* with respect to *the same set of variables.*

Studies of Social Organization in Different Areas

Scott Greer and his associates (Greer, 1960, 1962a, 1962b; Kaufman and Greer, 1960; Greer and Orleans, 1962), in a 1957 study of the St. Louis metropolitan area, raise some serious doubts about the pessimistic view of the modern urban world which sees no structured force interposed between the massive power of large-scale organizations and the isolated (and therefore vulnerable) individual. (See Bollens, 1961, for a comprehensive report on the St. Louis survey.) In so doing, they both demonstrate the analytic utility of the social area typology and contribute to increasing confidence in the typology by showing its essential isomorphism with the realities of urban life. The city is not a single way of life, but many ways of life. The different ways are, for the most part, patterned and systematically variable. Greer and Orleans (1962, p. 645) wrote:

> The theory of the mass society postulates an administrative state, a massified citizenry, and no mediating organizations between. We have discovered, in metropolitan St. Louis, that a widespread network of parapolitical organizations has consequences for the involvement and the competence of the citizenry with respect to local government.

In the St. Louis study, the strength of the parapolitical structure, the direction of the vote in presidential and local elections, a typology of local social participators, the amount of an individual's political participation, and the degree of individual political competence vary widely from one type of social area to another. In the discussion of their findings, Greer et al. make important elaborations of the theoretical bases of the social area types in terms of the *differential opportunity structures* they offer.

Studies of Areas as Variables in Reference Groups of Residents

There is yet another way in which social area analysis can be utilized in connection with urban subcommunity field studies. This is in the analysis of the combined or independent effect of personal and unit characteristics on variables dependent on them. Lazarsfeld and Barton (1951) have discussed the difference between personal characteristics and unit characteristics:

> Personal data characterize individuals. . . . Unit data characterize some aggregation of people. . . . Of course, people can be aggregated in many different ways, some of which imply social interaction and others only categorization by the observer. A "unit" in our sense will be any aggregation—an Army company, a neighborhood, an occupational category, a political party.

In the San Francisco study two subcommunities with high socioeconomic status and two with low were selected as study areas. In general, the men living in the high socioeconomic status neighborhoods had, as expected, higher educational levels than those in the low socioeconomic status neighborhoods; the median educational level for Pacific Heights and St. Francis Wood combined being "some college or more," and for men in Mission and Outer Mission being in the "some high school or less" category. This is a *neighborhood* or, as defined above, a *unit* characteristic, and can be assigned to all the men living in a particular neighborhood community as an attribute of their residence area. However, there are men living in Pacific Heights and St. Francis Wood who can be classified on the basis of their own educational level (a *personal* characteristic) as having only a grade school education or less (10.9 percent so report). Likewise, some men in Mission and Outer Mission (9.6 percent) report having some college or more. This raises an interesting question: Does the educational level of the neighborhood in which a person lives affect his attitudes and behavior, even when his individaul educational level is controlled? The answer seems to be "yes" in many of the cases so far tested!

Table 7, for example, shows the percentage of men who attend formal association meetings frequently according to both the average educational level of the neighborhood and the respondent's own education. Comparing the percentages *within each neighborhood,* the general tendency is for the more frequent attenders to have completed more years of schooling. However, of particular interest here is the comparison of amount of formal association participation *between* neighborhoods for individuals with comparable personal education. In each of the individual education categories, men living in the neighborhoods with higher educational levels are more likely to be frequent attenders than the men in neighborhoods of lower educational levels. Considering that similar differences are found when personal measures of occupation and income are taken into account, it is suggested that the socioeconomic characteristics of a neighborhood population *as a unit* may be important indicators of the economic *reference group* of those living in the neighborhood; and that this reference group provides a set of expectations for the associational behavior of the residents.

More recently, the Sherifs (1964), in a multi-faceted approach to the study of adolescent behavior in selected cities in the Southwest, have linked the study

TABLE 7. PERCENTAGE OF MEN WHO ATTEND FORMAL ASSOCIATION MEETINGS FREQUENTLY BY NEIGHBORHOOD AND INDIVIDUAL EDUCATIONAL LEVELS *

	Neighborhood Education	
Individual Education	Low (Mission and Outer Mission) (percentage)	High (Pacific Heights and St. Francis Wood) (percentage)
Some college or more	27.3 (33) †	46.4 (181)
Completed high school only	14.5 (83)	28.3 (92)
Some high school	17.3 (81)	30.4 (46)
Grade school or less	7.6 (144)	23.1 (39)

* Men were classified as "frequent attenders" if they attended meetings 37 or more times per year.
† The total number of cases on which the percentage is based is given in parentheses in each case.
Source: Adapted from Bell and Force (1956a, p. 31).

of behavior in small groups with the sociocultural settings in which such groups actually function. Oversimplifying, one can summarize their first report as including three major steps:

1. The selection of particular urban neighborhoods as study areas using social area analysis.

2. The assessment of the values and goals prevailing among representative adolescents in the study areas.

3. The intensive field observation of attitudes and behaviors of adolescents belonging to groups of their own choosing—that is, to "naturally-formed" groups whose members do not realize they are being studied—within the study areas.

The Sherifs' work is noteworthy in several ways—not the least of which is their determination to study *real* groups as they *actually* perform and function. Of particular significance here is their methodological strategy of simultaneous, multi-level analysis in their focus on the *individual behavior—small group—neighborhood* (*i.e.*, setting) relationship. To them, the social areas are the physical, demographic, and normative settings within which the interaction process within the small groups takes place. It is clear from their major findings regarding the perceptions, social values, and goals of adolescents in different social areas that the social areas are real, not only in the sheer perceptual sense of being part of the maps of social reality carried about in individuals' heads, but also in the sense of providing individuals with significant reference groups for gauging their own behavior as well as the behavior of others. Furthermore, the sociological reality of the social areas as differential opportunity structures (cf. Greer and Orleans, 1962) is elaborated and made concrete in the detailed case histories of the lives of particular adolescents.

Summary and Conclusions

In this chapter on the nature of social area analysis and some of its uses, it has not been possible to discuss all the studies that have used this method of analysis. Nor has it been possible to discuss the underlying theory, methodological problems, and differing evaluations of its contribution to urban studies.[4]

Some of the procedural difficulties in a comparative study of American cities have been solved simply by the tracting of cities for the 1960 census. But there remain other difficulties stemming from the nature of census data, and still others from the specific techniques employed in the method. Nonetheless, as presently constructed, the typology has proved useful as an approach to the systematic study of the smaller social worlds which a city's neighborhood communities comprise.

In sum, the various uses to which social area analysis has been put are as follows:

1. *The delineation of subareas.* Through the application of these methods to data available for American cities, it is possible to delineate systematically urban neighborhood communities having different social characteristics. Such a delineation, with the precision with which it can be accomplished, has descriptive value to the social scientist and city planner alike.

2. *Comparative studies at one point in time.* Comparative studies of the social areas of different cities at one point in time can be made. The social areas of Los Angeles can be compared with the social areas of New York, Chicago, Philadelphia, San Francisco, Dallas, St. Louis, Miami, or other urban areas. Social area distribution of the neighborhoods in different cities can be compared to determine patterns differentiated by the regions in which the cities are located, the sizes of the cities, their chief economic functions, their relative ages, their topographies, their ethnic compositions, and their transportation bases.

3. *Comparative studies at two points in time.* Despite the relative stability of many social areas, some neighborhood communities within a given urban area are undergoing change. New neighborhoods appear, they grow and develop, they become old, and sometimes they change with respect to the condition of the buildings, the type of building structures, and the kinds of residents. Other neighborhood communities may maintain the same social character for generations, like Beacon Hill in Boston (Firey, 1945). The application of the social area typology can result in a systematic description and analysis of social changes in a neighborhood.

4. *A framework for the execution of other types of research.* In addition to the above uses, the social area method can also be utilized as a framework for analyzing the attitudes and behavior of individuals. As indicated by the research cited in this chapter, neighborhood populations differ not only in demographic features, but also in values and social structure, in life styles and differential opportunities. And variations *between* neighborhoods have important implications for variations in individual attitudes and behavior. Even from present formulations in sociological theory, it is possible to hypothesize many relationships between neighborhood differences and the attitudes and behavior of

individual residents, ranging from suicide, voting behavior, religious preference, mental disorder, personal morale, and type of crimes, to such things as frequency and nature of participation in formal organizations, amount of close contact with neighbors, local community identification, extent of kinship ties, child-rearing practices, and patterns of courtship.

As a tool for urban subarea field studies, the typology serves a number of functions:

a. The typology can be used in the selection of neighborhoods for intensive study. In the examples given, census tracts were selected for particular economic, family, and ethnic characteristics. As an aid to sampling, the typology allows the research worker to select urban subcommunities for intensive study on the basis of informed judgment concerning the social positions of the subcommunities in the larger urban area.

b. The typology provides an integrative frame for urban subcommunity field studies by codifying a large mass of ordered data. In the Bell and Greer studies, for example, relationships are specified between particular census tracts and all other tracts in the same city with respect to socioeconomic status, familism, and ethnicity. In addition, the analysis of social participation and isolation between neighborhoods becomes possible in terms of variations in, or spacific patterns of, economic, family, and ethnic characteristics of the study neighborhoods.

c. The typology permits the investigation of the combined or independent effect of personal and unit characteristics on dependent variables. The characteristics of a neighborhood may be related to the behavior and the attitudes of individuals. In one example given, men living in high socioeconomic status neighborhoods were more frequent attenders of formal association meetings than men in low socioeconomic status neighborhoods, even though their personal socioeconomic characteristics were held constant. It was suggested that the socioeconomic character of a neighborhood population as a unit may be an important indicator of the socioeconomic group with which those living in the neighborhood identify themselves, and this may provide a set of expectations for the associational behavior of the residents. In another example, social areas were shown to constitute reference groups for adolescents in a multi-level analysis.

The relationship between neighborhood characteristics and individual behaviors and attitudes is clearly a promising subject for additional research.

Appendix

Computation of the Indexes of Socioeconomic Status, Familism, and Ethnicity.[5] The procedures for the computation of the three indexes are given in this section. The ratios for each variable are computed directly from census tract statistics, and the standard scores for the variables from the formulas given. All the variables composing the indexes of socioeconomic status and familism have been standardized to their respective ranges in Los Angeles as of 1940. A single scale is thus established for the direct comparison of census tract scores on the respective indexes for different cities at the same time or the same city at different times. The range, lower limit, and conversion factor are given for each variable for Los Angeles, 1940. The index of ethnicity, of course, is comparable from place to place and time to time since it is a simple percentage.

A. The formula for standardization:

$$s = x(r - o)$$

where

s = standardized score for a particular variable
o = lower limit of the census tract ratio for a particular variable
r = census tract ratio for a particular variable

$$x = \frac{100}{\text{range of the ratio for a particular variable}}$$

B. For those variables (occupation, education, and women in the labor force) which have an inverse relation to the basic indexes for which they are computed, the formula is adjusted to read as follows:

$$s = 100 - [x(r - o)]$$

C. Index of Socioeconomic Status

1. Compute the following ratios:
   a. Occupation ratio: the total number of craftsmen, operatives, and laborers per 1,000 employed persons.
   b. Education ratio: the number of persons who have completed no more than grade school per 1,000 persons 25 years old and over.
2. Compute occupation and education standard scores using the formula given in B above and the conversion factors (x) given in F below.
3. Compute a simple average of the occupation and education standard scores. The average is the Index of Socioeconomic Status for a census tract.

D. Index of Familism

1. Compute the following ratios:
   a. Fertility ratio: the number of children under 5 years per 1,000 females age 15 through 44.
   b. Women in the labor force ratio: the number of females in the labor force per 1,000 females 14 years old and over.
   c. Single-family detached dwelling units ratio: the number of single-family dwelling units per 1,000 dwelling units of all types.
2. Compute the fertility and single-family dwelling unit standard scores from the formula given in A above and the conversion factors (x) given in F below.
3. Compute the women in the labor force standard score using formula given in B above and conversion factor (x) given in F below.
4. Compute a simple average of the standard scores for fertility, women in the labor force, and single-family dwelling units. The average is the Index of Familism for a census tract.

E. Index of Ethnicity (categories for 1950 only; see Shevky and Bell, 1955)

1. Add together the number of persons designated Negro; Other Races; and foreign-born white from Poland, Czechoslovakia, Hungary, Yugoslavia, U.S.S.R., Lithuania, Finland, Rumania, Greece, Italy, Other Europe, Asia, French Canada, Mexico, and Other America. (Note: In this enumeration, include foreign-born white from Other Europe *only* if the category contains mostly foreign-born white from southern and eastern Europe. For urban areas in Arizona, California, Colorado, New Mexico, and Texas, the number of white persons with Spanish surnames can be used instead of the number of foreign-born white from Mexico and Other America. A special tabulation may have to be requested to obtain Spanish surname data for each census tract. If "white persons with Spanish surnames" is used, the figures given for *native whites* should be adjusted by subtracting the number of *native whites with Spanish surnames* from the total number of native whites in each tract.)
2. Divide the above sum by the total population in each tract.
3. Multiply the above quotient by 100 to obtain the Index of Ethnicity for each census tract. Separate the census tracts into two groups on the basis of their scores on the index of ethnicity. Select as the cutting point the per cent of the total population of the *urban area* represented by the *combined* racial and nationality groups listed. Those tracts with more than the average proportion of the combined racial and nationality groups are designated as being "high" in ethnicity; those tracts with less than the average proportion of the combined racial and nationality groups are designated as having "low" ethnicity.

F. The range, the lower limit of the range, and the conversion factor (x) for each of the ratios for the Los Angeles area, 1940, are as follows:

Ratio	Range	Lower Limit (o)	Conversion Factor (x)
Occupation	748	0	.1336898
Education	770	130	.1298701
Fertility	602	9	.1661130
Women in the labor force	458	86	.2183406
Single-family dwelling units	994	6	.1006441

Notes

1. Other units of analysis can be and, to some extent, have been used, such as the county, the state, countries as a whole, etc. The chief use of the social area typology to date, however, has been in connection with the census tract; thus, for simplicity this discussion will deal only with research related to the use of census tracts.

2. Tryon's method of constructing social areas differs somewhat from the Shevky method which is discussed here. However, the results are much the

same; for instance, the social areas of the San Francisco Bay area as of 1940 and as established by the Tryon method are for all practical purposes the same as those achieved by the Shevky method (Eta = .82).

3. Other work outside the United States includes Gagnon's study of Quebec (1960) and McElrath's study of Accra, Ghana (no date). Also, see Brody (1962) for a study of spatial aspects of social areas in ten additional American cities.

4. The interested reader can find these topics discussed in the following: Bell (1955b), Bell and Greer (1962), Bell and Moskos (1964), Beshers (1959, 1960), Buechley (1956), Carpenter (1955), Duncan (1955a, 1955b, 1956), Farber and Osoinach (1959), Hawley and Duncan (1957), Schnore (1962), Tiebout (1958), Udry (1964) and Van Arsdol, Camilleri, and Schmid (1958b, 1961, 1962).

5. For manual computation, a table of standard scores is now available (see Avesing, 1960). An IBM 709 computer program is available for machine computation (see Center for Metropolitan Studies, 1963).

References

ANDERSON, T. R., AND L. L. BEAN, 1961. The Shevky-Bell social areas: confirmation of results and a reinterpretation. *Social Forces,* 40, 119–124.

ANDERSON, T. R., AND J. A. EGELAND, 1961. Spatial aspects of social area analysis. *Amer. sociol. Rev.,* 26, 392–398.

AVESING, F., 1960. *Table of Standard Scores for Social Area Analysis.* (New York: Le Play Research, Inc.)

BANGE, E., *et al.,* 1955. A Study of Selected Population Changes and Characteristics with Special Reference to Implications for Social Welfare. A group research project submitted in partial fulfillment of requirements for the Master of Social Welfare Degree. (Berkeley: University of California.) (Mimeographed.)

BELL, W., 1953. The social areas of the San Francisco Bay Region. *Amer. soc. Rev.,* 18, 39–47.

——, 1954. A probability model for the measurement of ecological segregation. *Social Forces,* 32, 357–364.

——, 1955a. Economic, family, and ethnic status: An empirical test. *Amer. sociol. Rev.,* 20, 45–52.

——, 1955b. Comment on Duncan's review of "Social Area Analysis." *Amer. J. Sociol.,* 61, 260–261.

——, 1957. Anomie, social isolation, and the class structure. *Sociometry,* 20, 105–116.

——, 1958. The utility of the Shevky typology for the design of urban subarea field studies. *J. soc. Psychol.,* 47, 71–83.

——, 1959. Social areas: typology of urban neighborhoods. In M. Sussman (ed.), *Community Structure and Analysis* (New York: Crowell), 61–92.

Bell, W., in collaboration with M. D. Boat and M. T. Force, 1954. *People of the City.* (Mimeographed, Stanford University.)

Bell, W., and M. D. Boat, 1957. Urban neighborhoods and informal social relations. *Amer. J. Sociol.,* 62, 391–398.

Bell, W., and M. T. Force, 1956a. Urban neighborhood types and participation in formal associations. *Amer. sociol. Rev.,* 21, 25–34.

——, 1956b. Social structure and participation in different types of formal associations. *Social Forces,* 34, 345–350.

——, 1957. Religious preference, familism and the class structure. *Midwest Sociologist,* 19, 79–86.

Bell, W., and S. Greer, 1962. Social area analysis and its critics. *Pacific sociol. Rev.,* 5, 3–9.

Bell, W., and C. C. Moskos, Jr., 1964. A comment on Udry's "increasing scale and spatial differentiation." *Social Forces,* 42, 414–417.

Bell, W., and E. M. Willis, 1957. The segregation of Negroes in American cities. *Social and econ. Studies,* 6, 59–75.

Beshers, J. M., 1959. The construction of "social area" indices: an evaluation of procedures. Social Statistics Section, American Statistical Association, 65–70.

——, 1960. Statistical inferences from small area data. *Social Forces,* 38, 341–348.

Brody, S. A., 1962. Urban characteristics of centralization. *Sociol. and soc. Research,* 46, 326–331.

Broom, L., H. P. Beem, and V. Harris, 1955. *Amer. sociol. Rev.,* 20, 33–39.

Broom, L., and E. Shevky, 1949. The differentiation of an ethnic group. *Amer. sociol. Rev.,* 14, 476–481.

Bollens, J. C. (ed.), 1961. *Exploring the Metropolitan Community.* (Berkeley and Los Angeles: University of California Press.)

Buechley, R. W., 1956. Review of "Social Area Analysis." *J. Amer. statistical Assoc.,* 51, 195–197.

Burgess, E. W., 1929. Urban areas. In T. V. Smith and L. D. White (eds.), *Chicago, An Experiment in Social Science Research.* (Chicago: University of Chicago Press.)

Carpenter, D. B., 1955. Review of "Social Area Analysis." *Amer. sociol. Rev.,* 20, 497–498.

Center for Metropolitan Studies, 1963. *CENSAN: A 709 Program for the Computation of Social Area Analysis.* (Unpublished program description, Northwestern University.)

Curtis, J. H., 1957. The employability of aging workers in social areas of high urbanization and low social rank. (Unpublished paper read at the annual meetings of the American Sociological Association, Washington, D. C.)

Curtis, J. H., F. Avesing, and I. Klosek, 1957. Urban parishes as social areas. *Amer. Catholic sociol. Rev.,* 18, 1–7.

DUNCAN, O. D., 1955a. Review of "Social Area Analysis." *Amer. J. Sociol.*, 61, 84–85.

——, 1955b. Reply to Bell. *Amer. J. Sociol.*, 61, 261–262.

——, 1956. Review of "Identification of Social Areas by Cluster Analysis." *Amer. sociol. Rev.*, 21, 107–108.

FARBER, B., AND J. C. OSOINACH, 1959. An index of socio-economic rank of census tracts in urban areas. *Amer. sociol. Rev.*, 24, 630–640.

FIREY, W., 1945. Sentiment and symbolism as ecological variables. *Amer. sociol. Rev.*, 10, 140–148.

GAGNON, GABRIEL, 1960. Les zones sociales de l'agglomeration de Quebec. *Recherches Sociographiques.*

GREER, S., 1956. Urbanism reconsidered: A comparative study of local areas in a metropolis. *Amer. sociol. Rev.*, 21, 19–25.

——, 1960. The social structure and political process of suburbia. *Amer. sociol. Rev.*, 25, 514–526.

——, 1962a. The social structure and political process of suburbia: empirical test. *Rural Sociology*, 27, 438–459.

——, 1962b. *The Emerging City.* (New York: The Free Press of Glencoe.)

GREER, S., AND E. KUBE, 1955. *Urban Worlds.* Laboratory in Urban Culture, Occidental College. (Mimeographed report.)

——, 1959. Urbanism and social structure: a Los Angeles study. In M. Sussman (ed.), *Community structure and analysis.* (New York: Crowell.)

GREER, S., AND P. ORLEANS, 1962. The mass society and the parapolitical structure. *Amer. sociol. Rev.*, 27, 634–646.

HARRIS, C. D., AND E. U. ULLMAN, 1945. The nature of cities. *Annals of the Amer. Acad. pol. soc. Science*, 242, 7–17.

HAWLEY, A. H., 1950. *Human Ecology.* (New York: Ronald.)

HAWLEY, A. H., AND O. D. DUNCAN, 1957. Social area analysis: A critical appraisal. *Land Economics*, 33, 337–345.

HOYT, H., 1939. *The structure and growth of residential neighborhoods in American cities.* (Washington, D. C.: Federal Housing Administration.)

KAUFMAN, W. C., 1961. A Factor-Analytic Test of Revisions in the Shevky-Bell Typology for Chicago and San Francisco, 1950. (Unpublished Ph.D. dissertation, Northwestern University.)

KAUFMAN, W. C., AND S. GREER, 1960. Voting in a metropolitan community: an application of social area analysis. *Social Forces*, 38, 196–204.

LAZARSFELD, P. F., 1937. Some remarks on the typological procedures in social research. *Zeitschrift für Sozialforschung*, 6, 119–139.

LAZARSFELD, P. F., AND A. H. BARTON, 1951. Qualitative measurement in the social sciences: classification, typologies, and indexes. In D. Lerner and H. D. Lasswell (eds.), *Policy Sciences.* (Stanford: Stanford University Press.)

McElrath, D. C., 1955. Prestige and esteem identification in selected urban areas. *Research Studies of the State College of Washington,* 23, 130–137.

——, 1962. The social areas of Rome: A comparative analysis. *Amer. sociol. Rev.,* 27, 376–391.

——, no date. The social differentiation of migrants in Accra, Ghana. (Unpublished paper, Center for Metropolitan Studies, Northwestern University.)

McElrath, D. C., and J. W. Barkey, no date. Social and physical space: Models of metropolitan differentiation. (Unpublished paper, Center for Metropolitan Studies, Northwestern University.)

Polk, K., 1957. The social areas of San Diego. (Unpublished M. A. thesis, Northwestern University.)

——, 1957–58. Juvenile delinquency and social areas. *Social Problems,* 5, 214–217.

——, no date. Urban social areas and delinquency. (Unpublished paper, Lane County Youth Project, University of Oregon.)

Quinn, J. A., 1950. *Human Ecology.* (New York: Prentice-Hall.)

Reeks, O., 1953. The social areas of New Orleans. (Unpublished M. A. thesis, University of California, Los Angeles.)

Robinson, W. S., 1950. Ecological correlations and the behavior of individuals. *Amer. sociol. Rev.,* 15, 351–357.

Schnore, Leo F., 1962. Another comment on social area analysis. *Pacific sociol. Rev.,* 5, 13–15.

Sherif, M., and Carolyn W. Sherif, 1964. *Reference Groups.* (New York: Harper and Row.)

Shevky, E., and W. Bell, 1955. *Social Area Analysis.* (Stanford: Stanford University Press.)

Shevky, E., and M. Williams, 1949. *The Social Areas of Los Angeles: Analysis and Typology.* (Berkeley and Los Angeles: University of California Press.)

Sullivan, T., 1961. The application of Shevky-Bell indices to parish analysis. *Amer. Catholic sociol. Rev.*

Sussman, M. B., 1959. The isolated nuclear family: fact or fiction. *Social Problems,* 6, 333–340.

Tiebout, C. M., 1958. Hawley and Duncan on social area analysis: a comment. *Land Economics,* 34, 182–184.

Tryon, R. C., 1955. *Identification of Social Areas by Cluster Analysis.* (Berkeley and Los Angeles: University of California Press.)

U. S. Bureau of the Census, 1958. *Census Tract Manual* (2nd ed.). (Washington, D. C.: Government Printing Office.)

U. S. Bureau of the Census, 1960. *Census Tracts,* series PHC (1). (Washington, D. C.: Government Printing Office.)

UDRY, J. R., 1964. Increasing scale and spatial differentiation: new tests of two theories from Shevky and Bell. *Social Forces,* 42, 403–413.

VAN ARSDOL, M. D., JR., S. F. CAMILLERI, AND C. F. SCHMID, 1957. A deviant case of Shevky's dimensions of urban structure. Proceedings of the Pacific Sociological Society in *Research Studies of the State College of Washington,* 25, 171–177.

——, 1958a. The generality of the Shevky social area indexes. *Amer. sociol. Rev.,* 23, 277–284.

——, 1958b. An application of the Shevky social area indexes to a model of urban society. *Social Forces,* 37, 26–32.

——, 1961. An investigation of the utility of urban typology. *Pacific sociol. Rev.,* 4, 26–32.

——, 1962. Further comments on the utility of urban typology. *Pacific sociol. Rev.,* 5, 9–13.

WENDLING, A., 1954. Suicide in the San Francisco Bay Region 1938–1942 and 1948–1952. (Unpublished Ph.D. dissertation, University of Washington.)

WENDLING, A., AND K. POLK, 1958. Suicide and social areas. *Pacific sociol. Rev.,* 1, 50–53.

WILLIAMSON, R. C., 1953. Selected urban factors in marital adjustment. *Research Studies of the State College of Washington,* 21, 237–241.

——, 1954. Socio-economic factors and marital adjustment in an urban setting. *Amer. sociol. Rev.,* 19, 213–216.

WILSON, R. L., 1958. The association of urban social areas in four cities and the institutional characteristics of local churches in five denominations. (Unpublished Ph.D. dissertation, Northwestern University.)

WIRTH, L., 1938. Urbanism as a way of life. *Amer. J. Sociol.,* 44, 1–24.

URBANIZATION, TECHNOLOGY, AND THE DIVISION OF LABOR: INTERNATIONAL PATTERNS

Jack P. Gibbs and Walter T. Martin

In a previous paper [1] the authors advanced a theory which links the degree of urbanization in a society to the spatial dispersion of objects consumed by the population. A series of tests based on pre-World War II data yielded strong supporting evidence.[2]

The theory does not assume a simple cause and effect relationship; on the contrary, it recognizes that a high degree of urbanization depends on widely

Reprinted by permission of the authors and publishers from *American Sociological Review,* **27,** No. 5, October, 1962.

scattered materials and represents the type of spatial organization necessary for acquiring them. The present paper seeks to identify those factors which underlie both urbanization and the dispersion of objects of consumption.

It is helpful to begin by recognizing that a city, as a large population settled in a small area, cannot possibly develop, within its own limits, the materials necessary for its inhabitants to survive. Stated otherwise, a city depends on the acquisition of objects of consumption originating outside of its boundaries. However, as we shall see, it is only through the division of labor and an advanced technology that a population is able to bring material from great distances. It is in this particular connection that the relationship between urbanization and the spatial dispersion of objects of consumption can best be understood. For if large-scale urbanization requires that materials be brought from great distances, and if a high degree of division of labor and technological development are necessary for this, then the level of urbanization is contingent, at least in part, on the division of labor and technology.

Dispersion of Objects of Consumption, Division of Labor, and Level of Technology

For purposes of discussion two types of dispersion of objects of consumption are distinguished. The degree of "internal dispersion" in a society refers to the average distance between the points of origin of raw materials and the points at which the materials are consumed, with both points being within the society's boundaries. The degree of "external dispersion," on the other hand, is the average distance between the points when the origin is outside the society.

A high degree of internal dispersion immediately suggests that the society is characterized by territorial specialization and a certain minimal level of technology. As a rule, objects are not imported unless they are derived from raw materials that are not a natural resource of the area. Speaking colloquially, one does not take coal to Newcastle. It is this exchange among different geographical areas of a society that forms one dimension of the division of labor. The very fact of exchange means that different objects are being produced. This is a basic factor in occupational differentiation. Further division of labor is suggested by the fact that movement of materials necessitates the development of specialized occupations related to transportation and communication. The movement of materials also requires the establishment of commercial institutions and related occupations to facilitate the exchange. In addition, the flow of raw materials often calls for processing to reduce their bulk or to preserve them. This activity forms the basis for numerous occupations and industries. In each of these instances, the development of specialized occupations and industries goes hand in hand with technological advances.

The development of specialized occupations and industries, for whatever reason, leads to the use of greater varieties and amounts of raw materials. On a probabilistic basis, this makes for a greater dispersion of objects of consumption. Moreover, occupational specialization plays a major role in the creation of new objects of consumption. For example, unlike certain food items, rubber in its raw state is relatively useless. However, given occupational specialization and a certain type of technological system, raw rubber can be processed and put to many uses, and it is sought over the world as a consequence.

Still another consideration is the fact that different kinds of raw materials may be combined in a way that increases the demand for each. Thus, the automobile has increased the demand for both rubber and steel. As a consequence, these materials travel great distances between their raw material states and points of acceptance as parts on an automobile. Such combinations, needless to say, are not possible without an elaborate division of labor and an advanced technology.

Most of what has been said about the relationship of internal dispersion to technology and occupational specialization applies equally well to external dispersion. The establishment of trade with countries throughout the world requires, as a rule, the production and processing of a variety of different objects for exchange. Even if a country can establish extensive trade relations on the basis of one natural resource, it is still necessary to have transportation, communication, and commercial industries to process the export and handle the flow of imports.

The line of reasoning pursued in the earlier paper led to the following proposition: *The degree of urbanization in a society varies directly with the dispersion of objects of consumption.*[3] This generalization, even when strongly supported by empirical data, does not explain the relationship. However, the additional observations expressed above generate four propositions which link urbanization to dispersion. In propositions IA and IB the division of labor serves as the connecting link:

IA. *The degree of urbanization in a society varies directly with the division of labor;*

IB. *The division of labor in a society varies directly with the dispersion of objects of consumption.*

In propositions IIA and IIB the connecting link is the level of technological development:

IIA. *The degree of urbanization in a society varies directly with technological development;*

IIB. *Technological development in a society varies directly with the dispersion of objects of consumption.*

Note that if these statements are treated as postulates, the proposition advanced in the earlier paper can then be stated as a derived theorem. In addition, there is an important corollary proposition: III. *The degree of the division of labor in a society varies directly with technological development.* Thus, it can be seen that all of the propositions are logically interrelated in such a way that evidence supporting any one of the propositions can be regarded as lending credence to all of them. Specifically, propositions IA, IB, and IIA, IIB, if supported by the data, will show that the direct relationship between urbanization and dispersion of objects of consumption is neither fortuitous nor inexplicable.

The Division of Labor and Its Measurement at the Societal Level

The concept of division of labor has had a somewhat strange career in the history of sociology. On the one hand, the concept has achieved wide acceptance, particularly since Durkheim's classic treatment.[4] On the other hand, it is rarely employed in the generation of testable hypotheses. This is even true for the field of human ecology where, like competition,[5] the concept is often invoked in pure theory but remains in the background as far as research is concerned.

The empirical referents of the division of labor have yet to be specified in any rigorous fashion, but there are two general ideas associated with the concept. First, there is the suggestion of occupational differentiation. However, more is involved than individuals "doing different things." In addition to differentiation there is functional interdependence. Occupational groups do something more than produce different goods and services. They also exchange goods and services and it is this exchange which underlies occupational differentiation.

A second idea associated with the concept is often confused with the first. In the process of differentiation a person's occupational status may be determined, more or less, by biological characteristics, ethnic-caste status, or territorial location. These distinctions may be called the bases of the division of labor, but they are not to be confused with the degree of the division of labor. Occupations in a society may be closely correlated with non-occupational distinctions, but, at the same time, the number of different occupations may be small. This means a low degree of division of labor.

TABLE 1. ILLUSTRATIONS OF THE MEASUREMENT OF INDUSTRY DIVERSIFICATION

Industries	Hypothetical Society A	Hypothetical Society B	United States 1950 *	New Zealand 1951 *
Agriculture, forestry, hunting and fishing	500,000	2,000,000	7,331,353	135,889
Mining and quarrying	......	2,000,000	968,702	7,807
Manufacturing	......	2,000,000	16,113,479	177,430
Construction	......	2,000,000	3,743,183	62,314
Electricity, gas, water, and sanitary services	......	2,000,000	797,528	8,298
Commerce	......	2,000,000	11,082,470	121,681
Transport, storage, and communication	......	2,000,000	4,184,123	78,066
Services	......	2,000,000	14,221,018	143,936
Not classifiable elsewhere	......	2,000,000	1,595,591	5,075
ΣX	500,000	18,000,000	60,037,447	740,496
ΣX^2	25,000,000,000	3,600,000,000,000	674,090,085,916,761	95,603,959,708
$1-[\Sigma X^2/(\Sigma X^2)]$	0.0000	0.8889	0.8130	0.8256

* Souce of data: *Demographic Yearbook, 1956,* Table 12.

If one is concerned, as we are here, with the degree and not the basis of the division of labor, then the most relevant data pertain to occupations and industries. The distinction between occupation and industry in the analysis of the degree of the division of labor has evidently not been determined, conceptually or empirically. For present purposes, however, it makes little difference since the only data available for a large number of countries pertain to the industry composition of the labor force (i.e., the economically active population). The data consist of the number of persons in nine industry categories by countries and territories, as reported by the United Nation's Statistical Office.[6] Only autonomous countries have been considered in this study, and many of these could not be included because data on them were either not available or not reported in a way comparable to other countries.

The industry categories employed in the Statistical Office's report are shown in Table 1, with the United States and New Zealand serving as examples.

Regardless of the type of measure considered, there are certain obvious shortcomings in the industry statistics. The categories, for one thing, are far too gross, particularly manufacturing, commerce, and services. In addition, they do not directly take occupational differentiation into account. Furthermore, the data at best only indicate differentiation and not the degree of functional interdependence.

Certain technical deficiencies are also present in the data. There are reasons to believe that the industry categories are not applied in an absolutely uniform way from one country to the next. This is particularly true for the category "Not classifiable elsewhere." This category was retained only after experimentation revealed that its exclusion had no appreciable effect on the adopted measure. A more detailed discussion of limitations as to reliability and comparability is provided in the Statistical Office's report.[7]

Measurement of the degree of division of labor. The statistics at hand make possible only a measure of industry diversification, and it is used on the assumption that it would bear a close relationship to a more refined measure of the division of labor. In columns 1 and 2 of Table 1, two hypothetical societies are considered—one (Society A) in which industry diversification is at a minimum and the other (Society B) in which it is at a maximum. To measure the deviation of countries from these polar types a formula has been developed which differentiates between the two. With "X" as the number of persons in each of the nine industry categories, this formula is: $1-[\Sigma X^2/(\Sigma X)^2]$. Where all of the economically active are concentrated in one industry, the measure would be .0000; and for a population with an even distribution throughout the nine industries the measure would be .8889. Measures of industry diversification for 45 countries are shown in column 2 of Table 2.

A problem in measurement is posed with regard to one of the polar types, the society in which industry diversification is at a maximum (.8889). For a population to reach this point the number of economically active in what is usually considered a minor industry (public utilities, for example) would have to equal the number in a major industry (agriculture and manufacturing). This suggests that the polar type is unrealistic in that it is virtually impossible for a society to resemble it. The objection is made less serious by the fact that 14 of the 45 countries are within .1000 of the maximum value, while none of the countries is this close to the lowest possible value. There would appear to be little doubt, however, that numerous historical societies and non-literate peoples closely resembled the polar type in which the measure is at a minimum.

Level of Technological Development and Its Measurement at the Societal Level

Technology, like division of labor, is a concept frequently utilized in sociological discourse, especially in observations on the location, growth, development, and physical structure of individual cities.[8] Less attention has been given to the relationship between technological development and the amount or rate of urbanization, but observations and research findings do suggest that the two are closely related.[9]

Among sociologists, at least, there appears to be a general consensus as to the meaning of technology.[10] In some cases there is an emphasis on technology as material culture, a conception which is rejected by those who stress the ideational content, i.e., the application of knowledge and beliefs.[11] Despite the differing emphases, however, there is general recognition that technology involves the application of knowledge and beliefs in carrying out tasks and includes the artifacts developed to reduce the amount of labor or to accomplish what cannot be achieved by manpower alone. In societies where technical knowledge is primitive, the utilitarian artifacts are simple and operate with little or no use of inorganic energy; where technical knowledge is highly advanced there is a great complex of utilitarian artifacts that operate largely through inorganic energy. Stated otherwise, societies with primitive technologies are low-energy societies, those with advanced technologies are high-energy societies.[12] Thus, the best indicator of the level of technological development would appear to be the per capita consumption of energy.[13] In this study the data used are for the estimated consumption of commercial sources of energy expressed in metric tons of coal per capita reported in the *Statistical Yearbook*.[14] These data are shown in column 3 of Table 2 for 45 countries.

Measures of the Degree of Urbanization

Census reports and publications of the United Nation's Statistical Office make possible a variety of measures of urbanization at the national level. However, the most reliable and comparable measure is the percentage of the total population who reside in the Metropolitan Areas delimited by International Urban Research.[15] The percentage is shown for 45 countries in column 1 of Table 2.

Measurement of External Dispersion of Objects of Consumption

The measure of the external dispersion of objects of consumption (MED) used in the present research is considerably improved over the one employed in the earlier study,[16] although still necessarily far from precise. It considers the amount of materials (expressed in dollar value) imported by a given country from all other countries and the distance the materials are transported in each instance. For example, in the case of Switzerland, the dollar value of imports in 1951 was obtained for each country exporting to Switzerland. The value of each country's shipments [17] was then multiplied by the distance between the center of that country and the center of Switzerland following usual traffic lanes as closely as possible.[18] The resulting products were summed and the total divided by the 1950 population of Switzerland to give a per capita figure.[19] This per capita figure is thus a gauge of the extent to which the Swiss nation acquired globally dispersed objects. MED's for 45 countries are shown in column 4 of Table 2. There are clearly many deficiencies in this measure, e.g., (1) the weight of goods imported is not considered; (2) the measure assumes that all goods originate at the geographic center of the exporting country and are consumed at the approximate geographic center of the importing country, an assumption that obviously distorts the situation; [20] and (3) the measure necessarily assumes that

TABLE 2. PERCENTAGE OF POPULATION IN METROPOLITAN AREAS AND MEASURES OF INDUSTRIAL DIVERSIFICATION, TECHNOLOGICAL DEVELOPMENT, AND THE EXTERNAL DISPERSION OF OBJECTS OF CONSUMPTION, FOR 45 COUNTRIES, *Circa* 1950

Country	(Col. 1) Percentage of Population in Metropolitan Areas *	(Col. 2) Measure of Industrial Diversification (MID) **	(Col. 3) Measure of Technological Development (MTD) ***	(Col. 4) Measure of External Dispersion (MED) ****
Argentina, 1947	44.6	.8147	0.76	604
Australia, 1947	55.4	.8348	3.12	1457
Austria, 1951	37.7	.7911	1.54	237
Belgium, 1947	41.4	.7969	0.28	793
Canada, 1951	42.7	.8197	6.47	1373
Ceylon, 1946	9.5	.6723	0.08	197
Colombia, 1951	19.3	.6624	0.27	119
Costa Rica, 1950	19.9	.6565	0.24	224
Cuba, 1953	26.1	.7420	0.48	248
Denmark, 1950	37.3	.8007	2.09	464
Dominican Republic, 1950	11.2	.6293	0.09	100
Ecuador, 1950	14.9	.6793	0.12	81
Egypt, 1947	19.6	.6394	0.22	143
El Salvador, 1950	11.9	.5689	0.09	134
Finland, 1950	17.0	.7193	1.17	509
France, 1954	34.7	.8100	2.03	360
Greece, 1951	22.0	.7114	0.22	235
Guatemala, 1950	10.5	.5086	0.14	82

* Source: Data prepared by International Urban Research. These percentages supersede earlier provisional figures reported by Gibbs and Davis in the *American Sociological Review*, *23* (October, 1958), pp. 504–514.
** Source: *Demographic Yearbook*. See text for a description of the measure.
*** Source: *Statistical Yearbook*. Commercial consumption of energy expressed in metric tons of coal per capita.
**** Source: United Nations, *Statistical Papers*, Series T, Vol. 6, No. 10. See text for a description of the measure.

the movement of all goods between any two countries follows a single route. These deficiencies appear to influence the preciseness of the measure rather than its general ability to rank countries in terms of the external dispersion of their objects of consumption. Thus there appears to be no doubt that objects of consumption in New Zealand and Canada are much more externally dispersed than are those in Thailand, Pakistan, and even the United States. Note, however, that in no instance does MED reveal the "internal dispersion" of objects of consumption, and a truly adequate test of any theory pertaining to dispersion of objects of consumption cannot be conducted without considering both external and internal dispersion. Since international data on internal dispersion are not available, it has been necessary to assume that there is a fairly close relation between the two kinds of dispersion. However, this may not be true for certain countries (particularly the large ones), and therefore some exceptions to the predicted relationship between dispersion and other variables are not unexpected.

TABLE 2 (*Continued*)

Country	(Col. 1) Percentage of Population in Metro-politan Areas *	(Col. 2) Measure of Industrial Diversification (MID) **	(Col. 3) Measure of Technological Development (MTD) ***	(Col. 4) Measure of External Dispersion (MED) ****
Haiti, 1950	6.0	.3010	0.02	46
Honduras, 1950	7.3	.3029	0.15	73
India, 1951	7.8	.4788	0.10	34
Ireland, 1951	27.5	.7631	1.10	504
Israel, 1948–52	55.8	.8187	0.80	919
Japan, 1950	36.6	.7055	0.78	164
Malaya, 1947	12.7	.5500	0.28	846
Mexico, 1950	20.6	.6303	0.60	95
Netherlands, 1947	45.5	.8132	1.96	655
New Zealand, 1951	43.6	.8256	2.43	3310
Nicaragua, 1950	13.3	.5140	0.09	51
Norway, 1950	21.8	.8098	4.37	738
Pakistan, 1951	5.1	.4033	0.04	42
Panama, 1950	23.9	.6956	0.30	234
Paraguay, 1950	15.6	.6549	0.02	104
Peru, 1940	11.0	.5816	0.19	58
Philippines, 1948	10.3	.5418	0.09	235
Portugal, 1950	19.6	.7073	0.26	129
Spain, 1950	25.5	.7014	0.57	41
Sweden, 1950	22.4	.8007	3.22	873
Switzerland, 1950	28.9	.7762	2.15	882
Thailand, 1947	6.8	.2735	0.02	35
Turkey, 1950	9.5	.4082	0.26	82
Union of So. Africa, 1951	29.9	.7059	1.89	796
United Kingdom, 1951	71.5	.7687	4.42	1188
United States, 1950	55.9	.8130	7.74	381
Venezuela, 1950	25.2	.7597	0.77	420

Tests of the Propositions

According to proposition IA, there is a direct relationship at the societal level between the degree of urbanization and the division of labor. On this basis we should find a high positive correlation between the percentage of the population in Metropolitan Areas and the measures of industrial diversification. A rank-order correlation coefficient of +.91 between the values in columns 1 and 2 of Table 2 provides strong support for the proposition.

Proposition IB anticipates a direct relationship between the division of labor and the dispersion of objects of consumption. The two variables used to test the proposition are the measures of industrial diversification and the measures of external dispersion in columns 2 and 4 of Table 2. *Rho* in this instance is +.83 and, accordingly, consistent with the proposition.

On the basis of proposition IIA, a direct relationship should hold between the percentage of the population in Metropolitan Areas and the measures of technological development shown in column 3 of Table 2. A *rho* value of +.84 indicates that the relationship is substantially as predicted.

The prediction in the case of proposition IIB is the existence of a direct relationship between the measures of technological development and the measures of external dispersion of objects of consumption. A *rho* value of +.79 is thus consistent with the proposition.

Finally, proposition III leads to the prediction of a direct relationship between the measures of industrial diversification and the measures of technological development. A *rho* of +.85 represents supporting evidence.[21]

Another aspect of the relationships. If both the division of labor and technological development are closely linked to the dispersion of objects of consumption, then their relationship to urbanization should conform to particular pattern. The earlier study [22] revealed that dispersion of objects of consumption bears the closest relationship to large-scale urbanization,[23] the percentage of the total population in urban places of 100,000 population or more, and the least relationship to small-scale urbanization, the percentage of the total population in urban places of 5,000–9,999 inhabitants. Similar findings based on more recent data have also been reported elsewhere.[24] These differential relationships were anticipated on the grounds that large-scale urbanization makes it necessary for the inhabitants of the large cities to draw their objects of consumption from a great distance. A large proportion of the population in small urban places, however, does not necessitate a high degree of dispersion of objects of consumption, since the inhabitants of such places can live off their immediate environs. In short, the percentage in small urban places varies independently of the dispersion of objects of consumption because a high degree of dispersion is not a necessity for survival.

Just as it is necessary for the populations of large cities to draw objects of consumption from great distances so is it equally necessary for them to have a high degree of division of labor and technological development to accomplish the task. Conversely, small urban places can survive with or without a high degree of division of labor and technological development. If this is the case, then MID and MTD should be more closely associated with large-scale urbanization than with small-scale urbanization.

TABLE 3. PERCENTAGE OF POPULATION IN URBAN LOCALITIES FOR 41 COUNTRIES, *Circa* 1950 *

Countries by Type of Locality **	Percentage of Population in Localities by Size					
	(Col. 1) 2,000–4,999	(Col. 2) 5,000–9,999	(Col. 3) 10,000–19,999	(Col. 4) 20,000–49,999	(Col. 5) 50,000–99,999	(Col. 6) 100,000+
Type A						
Argentina, 1947	5.6	4.2	4.4	6.2	4.9	37.2
Australia, 1947	7.8	4.8	4.3	4.9	1.0	51.4
Cuba, 1953	5.9	4.1	4.4	8.0	6.6	21.9
Denmark, 1950	3.1	4.3	6.6	8.1	3.2	33.5
France, 1954	7.8	5.6	7.0	8.6	6.2	15.0
India, 1951	16.6	5.8	3.3	3.3	2.1	6.6
Ireland, 1951	5.0	3.3	3.9	4.6	6.1	17.6
Israel, 1949	7.4	4.3	10.6	5.7	0.0	45.6
Netherlands, 1947	9.0	7.5	6.3	8.5	8.6	32.7
Norway, 1950	3.8	1.9	5.7	6.7	6.2	19.8
Pakistan, 1951	0.2	0.9	1.1	2.1	0.8	5.1
Portugal, 1950	6.6	5.2	3.0	3.7	0.0	12.7
Sweden, 1950	6.5	5.1	7.3	7.5	6.1	19.4
United States, 1950	4.8	4.1	4.2	5.2	2.9	43.9
Type B						
Canada, 1951	5.4	5.1	5.1	7.6	4.2	23.3
Ceylon, 1946	0.4	0.8	2.6	2.7	3.3	5.4
Colombia, 1951	5.6	3.6	3.1	4.2	3.5	14.7
Costa Rica, 1950	4.9	4.9	7.9	0.0	10.9	0.0
Dominican Republic, 1950	3.0	2.5	4.9	0.0	2.6	8.5
Ecuador, 1950	3.7	2.7	3.5	3.2	0.0	14.6
El Salvador, 1950	5.9	4.4	4.4	1.4	2.8	8.7
Finland, 1950	3.5	3.4	6.0	8.0	0.0	14.2
Greece, 1951	11.4	4.4	7.1	10.8	3.3	12.7
Guatemala, 1950	7.1	4.3	1.3	1.0	0.0	10.2
Haiti, 1950	1.8	1.9	1.2	0.8	0.0	4.3
Honduras, 1950	5.4	2.0	3.0	1.5	5.3	0.0
Japan, 1950	1.6	7.3	8.6	8.9	7.6	25.6
Malaya, 1947	3.1	2.2	1.9	6.9	2.8	7.4
Mexico, 1950	10.9	5.7	4.9	5.3	3.6	15.1
New Zealand, 1951	5.5	3.2	2.8	12.6	8.8	32.8
Nicaragua, 1950	6.3	2.7	3.8	4.9	0.0	10.3
Panama, 1950	8.7	6.0	5.4	0.0	6.5	15.9
Paraguay, 1950	7.9	1.8	3.2	0.0	0.0	15.2
Peru, 1940	5.1	2.9	3.6	3.4	2.1	8.4
Philippines, 1948	7.2	4.9	2.6	2.2	0.7	3.4
Thailand, 1947	0.1	0.9	2.2	2.2	0.0	4.5
Turkey, 1950	6.3	3.7	4.2	4.4	1.9	8.2
Union of So. Africa, 1951	3.6	3.0	2.5	2.5	4.2	24.0
United Kingdom, 1951	2.1	3.6	7.1	16.1	14.7	36.1
Venezuela, 1950	7.3	5.6	4.6	7.5	4.1	20.6
Yugoslavia, 1948	0.0	1.0	3.1	4.1	1.9	6.3

* Sources: *Demographic Yearbook* and census reports.
** See text for a description of the two types of localities.

The data in Table 3 provide a basis for a test of the hypothesis stated above. They show for each of 41 countries the percentage of the population who reside in urban localities by size range of localities.[25] Variation in census practices makes it necessary to consider two types of localities. Type A localities are agglomerations delimited without regard to political boundaries. They therefore correspond to an urban area as a physical entity, in much the same sense as the Urbanized Areas delimited by the Bureau of the Census. Type B localities, in contrast, have definite administrative limits and thereby correspond to cities as political entities.

According to the hypothesis in question, we should find that the magnitude of the correlation coefficients between MID or MTD and component measures of urbanization increase directly with the size range of the urban localities. Thus, the coefficient of correlation should be at a minimum for urban localities of 2,000–4,999 inhabitants and at a maximum where the size of the localities is 100,000 or more. Tables 4 and 5 show that the correlation coefficients do vary in substantially the way predicted.

Complete conformity to the predicted pattern would prevail if each coefficient were of greater magnitude than all coefficients below it on the urbanization scale and of less magnitude than all coefficients above it on the urbanization scale. Among the Type B countries in Table 4 (which considers the relationship between MTD and component measures of urbanization) there are only six exceptions to the expected pattern in a total of 30 comparisons, and the corresponding figures for Types A and B combined are two and 30. On the basis of chance we would expect to find 30 exceptions in 60 comparisons, but there are in fact only eight.

The coefficients of correlation between MID and the component measures of urbanization in Table 5 also conform closely to the predicted pattern. There is no exception in a total of 30 comparisons for Type B countries, and only six

TABLE 4. RANK-ORDER COEFFICIENTS OF CORRELATION BY COUNTRIES BETWEEN MEASURES OF TECHNOLOGICAL DEVELOPMENT AND THE PERCENTAGE OF THE POPULATION IN URBAN LOCALITIES *

Urban Localities by Size Range	Countries Grouped by Type of Locality **	
	Type B (N = 27)	Types A and B (N = 41)
100,000+	.652	.79
50,000–99,999	.648	.56
20,000–49,999	.67	.72
10,000–19,999	.43	.55
5,000– 9,999	.51	.40
2,000– 4,999	.01	.07

* Sources of data on percentage of population in urban localities: *Demographic Yearbook* and census reports on individual countries.

** See text for a description of the locality types.

TABLE 5. RANK-ORDER COEFFICIENTS OF CORRELATION BY COUNTRIES BETWEEN MEASURES OF INDUSTRIAL DIVERSIFICATION AND THE PERCENTAGE OF THE POPULATION IN URBAN LOCALITIES *

Urban Localities by Size Range	Countries Grouped by Type of Locality: Type B (N = 27)	Types A and B (N = 41)
100,000+	.77	.87
50,000–99,999	.58	.47
20,000–49,999	.537	.66
10,000–19,999	.536	.58
5,000– 9,999	.43	.29
2,000– 4,999	−.11	.22

* See footnotes for Table 4.

exceptions in the 30 comparisons for Types A and B combined. Thus, whereas 30 exceptions in 60 comparisons would be expected on the basis of chance, there are actually only six.

These findings leave little doubt that both the division of labor and technological development are, as anticipated, more closely related to large-scale urbanization than to small-scale urbanization.

Other Considerations and Conclusions

The findings of this study and those presented in earlier papers demonstrate consistent relationships among urbanization, the division of labor, the level of technological development, and the dispersion of objects of consumption. The relationships are obviously not so close as to preclude exceptions. Exceptions do occur, and some of them are probably "real" exceptions, that is, not subject to explanation in terms of inadequate data or crude measures. We do not deny the possibility of exceptions, but we do maintain that societies can deviate only within certain limits and, in any case, there are certain identifiable consequences of deviation. For example, some societies may have a much higher degree of urbanization than would be anticipated on the basis of the present propositions. There is, however, a limit as to how high urbanization can go without increases in the division of labor, in technological efficiency, and in the dispersion of objects of consumption. And, with regard to consequences of deviation, one effect of over-urbanization is likely to be a low standard of living.

The explanation of deviant cases and the identification of the consequences of deviation must await improvements in the scope and quality of international statistics, particularly data pertaining to the degree of the internal dispersion of objects of consumption and to the division of labor. Even before this, however, we can anticipate alternative explanations of urbanization and the relationships reported here. Of the various alternative explanations, there is a certain type which particularly deserves consideration, because it is traditionally viewed in opposition to the theoretical orientation which characterizes the present paper.

One could argue that a high or low degree of urbanization and the relationship of urbanization to other variables is largely a matter of socio-cultural values and ideologies. We reject such an interpretation and emphasize that a high degree of urbanization depends on the division of labor, technology, and organization to requisition dispersed materials. The value systems of some societies may in fact favor a high degree of urbanization, but there is no particular set of values that is a sufficient condition for a high degree of urbanization. It makes no great difference whether the population professes socialism or capitalism, liberalism or conservatism, Buddhism or Free Methodism; for if a high degree of urbanization is to be maintained, widely dispersed materials must be requisitioned, and this can be accomplished only through the division of labor and technological efficiency.

Note, however, that the writers do not deny that values and ideologies may largely determine certain types of behavior. It may even be true that, *within* certain limits, socio-cultural values and ideologies influence urbanization. But we do reject these phenomena as possible explanations of the particular relationships observed in this study. This would be the case even if a spatial association between urbanization and certain types of values could be demonstrated. It is entirely possible that as urbanization occurs certain values will come to prevail. Unfortunately, this opens the door to future confusion by making it possible at some later date for observers to conclude that the presence of these values explains urbanization.

Notes

1. Jack P. Gibbs and Walter T. Martin, "Urbanization and Natural Resources: A Study in Organizational Ecology," *American Sociological Review*, 23 (June, 1958), pp. 266–277.

2. Additional tests for a larger number of countries and with improved measures of urbanization and dispersion of resources also provided strong support. See Walter T. Martin, "Urbanization and National Power to Requisition External Resources." (Scheduled for publication in *Pacific Sociological Review*, 5 [Fall, 1962]).

3. Gibbs and Martin, *op. cit.*, p. 270; Martin, *op. cit.*

4. Emile Durkheim, *The Division of Labor in Society*, translated by George Simpson, Glencoe, Illinois: The Free Press, 1949. Durkheim suggests a direct relationship between division of labor and urbanization in this work (pp. 256–260).

5. Amos H. Hawley, "Ecology and Human Ecology," *Social Forces*, 22 (May, 1944), p. 401.

6. United Nations, *Demographic Yearbook, 1956*, New York: 1956, Table 12, pp. 344–387. Some data on occupations by countries are also reported in this source (Table 13), but they are not nearly as complete and comparable as is the case for industry data.

7. *Ibid.*, p. 38.

8. See, e.g., William Fielding Ogburn, "Technology and Cities: The Dilemma of the Modern Metropolis," *The Sociological Quarterly,* 1 (July, 1960), pp. 139–153.

9. Kingsley Davis, "The Origin and Growth of Urbanization in the World," *American Journal of Sociology,* 60 (March, 1955), pp. 431–432; and Jack P. Gibbs and Leo F. Schnore, "Metropolitan Growth: An International Study," *American Journal of Sociology,* 66 (September, 1960), pp. 160–170.

10. Francis R. Allen, *et al., Technology and Social Change,* New York: Appleton-Century-Crofts, Inc., 1957, Chapter 1.

11. Kingsley Davis, *Human Society,* New York: Macmillan Company, 1949, pp. 435–436; Robin M. Williams, Jr., *American Society,* New York: Alfred A. Knopf, 1960, p. 24.

12. See Fred Cottrell, *Energy and Society,* New York: McGraw-Hill Book Company, Inc., 1955.

13. See William F. Ogburn and Francis R. Allen, "Technological Development and Per Capita Income," *American Journal of Sociology,* 65 (September, 1959), pp. 127–131; William F. Ogburn, "Technology and the Standard of Living in the United States," *American Journal of Sociology,* 60 (January, 1955), pp. 380–386; William F. Ogburn, "Population, Private Ownership, Technology, and the Standard of Living," *American Journal of Sociology,* 56 (January, 1951), pp. 314–319.

14. United Nations, *Statistical Yearbook, 1953,* New York: 1953, Table 127, pp. 276–278.

15. See Jack P. Gibbs and Kingsley Davis, "Conventional Versus Metropolitan Data in the International Study of Urbanization," *American Sociological Review,* 23 (October, 1958), pp. 505–514; and International Urban Research, *The World's Metropolitan Areas,* Berkeley and Los Angeles: University of California Press, 1959.

16. Gibbs and Martin, *op. cit.*

17. Statistical Office of the United Nations, "Direction of International Trade," in *Statistical Papers,* Series T, Vol. 6, No. 10.

18. This figure was calculated in most cases by taking sea-lane mileage between major ports and adding the approximate mileage from the two ports to the center of their respective countries.

19. The operations can be summarized as follows:

$$\frac{\sum_{i}^{n} (X_i)\ (Y_i) + (X_j)\ (Y_j) + \cdots + (X_n)\ (Y_n)}{Pa} \times 1000$$

Where: i. . .n countries from which imports are received.
X_i: $ value of imports from country i.
Y_i: estimated average miles imports from i were transported.
Pa: population of the importing country.

20. In a few extreme cases an adjustment was made to take into account the fact that the heavy concentration of population near the port of entry made it very unlikely that on the average the imported materials were transported as far as the center of the country.

21. *Rho* was used in this series of tests rather than *r* because of the existence of non-linear relationships in all cases. In each instance, an increase in one variable beyond a certain point is associated with progressively greater or smaller increase in the other variable. Although *rho* is applicable in such cases, it probably underestimates the degree of association. The relationships should eventually be expressed as a correlation ratio (*eta*).

22. Gibbs and Martin, *op. cit.*

23. Referred to in the earlier study as "metropolitanization."

24. Martin, *op. cit.*

25. Five of the countries in Table 2 (Austria, Belgium, Egypt, Spain, and Switzerland) are not included in Table 3 because their locality statistics in the *Demographic Yearbook* are based on minor civil divisions (Type C localities) rather than Type A or Type B localities. Yugoslavia is the only country in Table 3 which is not also in Table 2. It was excluded from Table 2 because data relating to Metropolitan Areas and imports could not be obtained. MID for Yugoslavia is .5250, and its MTD is 0.41.

CHAPTER THREE

THE SOCIAL ORGANIZATION OF URBAN LIFE

INTRODUCTION

The fundamental assumption underlying the sociological approach is that group behavior is organized. The sociologist seeks to describe and explain the nature of the organized activities characteristic of two or more persons in a given place and time period. What aspect of organization is selected and what sources are stressed varies with the particular perspective of the disciplined observer. In the preceding chapter, the spatial and demographic organization of urban life was stressed. The present chapter focuses on social structural aspects of social organization in urban settlements.

The several types of social stratification collectivities—including classes, castes, and estates; family groups; ethnic groups; religious organizations; clubs and associations—are all examples of social structure. All are characterized by distinctions between members and nonmembers and by organized efforts to direct and control the activities of group participants. Members are assigned roles and are expected to act in designated ways. Some of these roles are formal and traditional, and others are informal and temporal. In short, behavior in groups is not random, it is organized.

A major problem in contemporary urban life in the United States is how to attain some degree of cohesion in an urbanized, mass society. Leonard Reissman addresses himself to this question.

Several studies of organized urban activities illustrate the varieties of urban life cross-culturally. The significance of kinship activities among the Chinese in the United States has sustained the interest of urban sociologists for several decades (see the work of the late Rose Hum Lee, *The Chinese in the United States of America,* Hong Kong: Oxford U. Press, 1960). In a recent study, Milton Barnett describes how kinship affects economic adaptation among the Cantonese, probably the most significant of the Chinese subgroups in the United States.

Manfred Stanley's study of Jehovah's Witnesses, published here for the first time, challenges the image of urban life as secular and asks some fundamental questions about sociological perspectives. Theodore Caplow provides us with a succinct view of urban life in another complex society, France.

Africa is a continent whose societies and cultures are as diverse as any in the world. Some of the most interesting urban processes are unfolding in the various developing nations there and, for that reason, at least in part, we have selected a number of papers dealing with aspects of urban life in Sub-Saharan Africa. Peter Gutkind analyzes the relationship between African urban family life and the larger urban society as interdependent systems, and Robert Bogden in still another previously unpublished paper describes the various youth clubs and their functions in Ibadan, Nigeria.

The papers by Mangin, Buikhuisen, Weinberg, Howton, Carpenter, Gutkind, Mitchell, and Pioro *et al.*, in the chapters which follow deal with a variety of problems and phases of the social organization of urban life in settings that are not so familiar to American students, but which are essential for an adequate understanding of urban sociology.

CLASS, THE CITY, AND SOCIAL COHESION

Leonard Reissman

The three concepts that comprise the title of this paper might be distinguished by the volume of disagreement they have produced in the sociological literature. Each of them can easily be included as among the most reticular terms in the conceptual vocabulary of the social sciences. For that reason, I have deliberately kept the title neutral and straightforward, meant only to inventory the terms not to relate them to each other. Yet, these same concepts are among the most pivotal for a great many sociological investigations, theoretical and empirical. It would be presumptuous of me even to imply that I intend to fix their usage and meaning, definitely. Rather, I wish only to comment upon some of the scientific motives behind their use as these have appeared in the literature. Little more would be profitable, for as Weber has so aptly noted, some scientists approach the terminology of another as it were his toothbrush.

What is distinctive about each of these concepts is that the disagreement around them touches on much more than purely semantic matters; their connotations are obscure but significant. The several points of controversy represent quite different orientations, yet these are seldom made explicit even though they locate the real issue. The differences in definition and usage reveal major differences in the type of problem that is identified and in the type of solution advanced whether it be applied or theoretical. But there is more involved here than objective and scientific issues alone. If the term were not so badly misunderstood today, I would describe the difference in orientation as "political" in the broader meaning of that word. Certainly "class" has had its share of explicit and implicit political overtones. Perhaps less obviously, the conceptions of the "city" have been similarly involved; the town planners from Ebenezer Howard to Frank Lloyd Wright never really tried to hide the political implications nor the political

---

Reprinted by permission of the author and publisher from *International Review of Community Development*, 7 (1961), pp. 39–51.

requirements needed to make their plans for Garden City or Broadacre City successful. (Cohesion), more recently, has come to have some political resonance, as the discussion will show.

There is no need to belabor the point because it is not absolutely essential for the present discussion. It has been mentioned only because I believe that an awareness of this dimension can fill out the assessment of the several points of view that are considered in this paper. The reader, however, is still free to consider the argument of the paper more specifically, as a description of alternate views hovering over the three concepts involved.

Let me preface the analysis by presenting three generalizations that affect directly the subject at hand, and that define some features of the social terrain that must be traveled in the discussion.

Class and urbanism are products of industrialization. The statement is obvious although much too often is overlooked, especially by those who insist upon the historical continuity of stratification and urban development. Cities and social divisions, apparently, are not new to human societies. In one form or another both social phenomena can be traced back to the civilizations of Mesopotamia and Egypt, and perhaps beyond. Historical origins, however, do not always explain the social phenomena of the present even though all events have historical roots. A study of origins may inform an analysis, but as in the present instance, the need is for a greater specification of social dynamics, not alone an appreciation for the general timeless qualities that may be involved. Furthermore, many historical comparisons depend upon a willingness to define "city" and "class" in such a way as to make the historical instances of those two phenomena comparable. For some purposes, however, the differences and not the similarities need to be stressed.

Preindustrial cities were not as large nor as socially complex as are typical industrial cities. Preindustrial cities did not possess the basic technology that would allow the urban environment to spread, yet at the same time would be sufficiently unified into a functioning social entity. Industrial cities of today are more than large agglomerations of people, even though their size is the first impression that one gets of them. These cities are complex wholes, whose existence depends minimally upon a highly differentiated labor force, a technology for mass communication, an orderly economy with international ramifications, and a rational political bureaucracy. The cities of antiquity and of later preindustrial eras possessed some of these characteristics to a limited degree, but not developed nor integrated to the extent we have come to accept as ordinary in the industrial city.

The social divisions of preindustrial societies also differed, in crucial particulars, from those found in an industrial class system. The characteristic social rigidity that was a mark of earlier aristocracies was the opposite of the social mobility encouraged by industrial societies, whether or not that mobility is fully realized. The "middle class" that Gordon Childe, for example, described for Egypt, composed of artisans, priests, and merchants, was only a very distant cousin of the industrial middle class. I would contend that little is gained by stretching the comparison. The means for legitimating class position and the power that is regularly available to the different classes, have both been drastically altered under industrialism compared with earlier eras.

The analysis of urbanism and of class, therefore, is best aided by first recognizing the uniqueness of the present period and the effects of recognizing the uniqueness of the present period and the effects of industrialization. The social scientist is well advised to maintain an historical perspective, but I do not take this proscription to mean that historical continuity must always be the dominant concern. The study of urbanism, especially, has been hindered greatly by the attempt to consider the industrial city simply an extension of its historical precursors. The modern industrial city has added so many new dimensions of meaning to urbanism that it would seem to be essential to deal with it alone, as a specifically novel social occurrence, before putting it in historical perspective. Presumably, the social manifestations of contemporary cities have an historical genesis, but the sequence sometimes has to be turned around in scientific analysis. Historical chronology, in other words, is not always scientific chronology.

Class and urbanism have developed contrary to dominating ideologies. One way I would suggest in which the historical perspective can be useful, but not overdominant, is to understand the milieu out of which class and urbanism have developed. Both have gone counter to the existing ideologies, developing as if in spite of such values.

The industrial city emerged in opposition to a rural ideology of naturalism. The supposedly idyllic, natural, and socially integrated society of the country-side was destroyed by the city, which transformed it into a society that supposedly was artificial, impersonal, and socially disintegrating. The agrarian philosophy with roots in feudalism, encountered the concrete reality of the urban environment and found little encouragement. The "insensate industrial town," as Lewis Mumford called the city, had little to recommend it to those who were sensitive to the human condition. Slums, poverty, and an airless, dehumanizing existence were all that confronted the masses flocking to the city whether they were pushed or pulled from the land. Under the *laissez faire* economic philosophy the city was allowed to develop according to the rules of the market place, and consequently it did develop without plan and without conscience. It was against these blatent evils of urban industrialism that Marx and Engels, Ebenezer Howard, Patrick Geddes and many others reacted. And with reason. The nineteenth century industrial city had little to commend it as a human environment.

Typically, the reaction to the industrial city by intellectuals was part of a larger social protest that sought as its goal a re-establishment of the desirable conditions of the rural past precisely because they were so obviously absent in the urban present. Plans for rural Utopias were drawn and redrawn as the urban critics sought to recreate the imagined advantages of the past into a contemporary social framework. Nowhere was this more evident than in the planning movement initiated by Howard, who had hoped through the garden city to recapture the virtues of preindustrial society. City and town planners have not abandoned the dream, differing from one another principally in architectural details.

It is but recently that the city has come to be accepted in its own right; only as we have realized that the urban conditions during the early decades of industrialization were not an inevitable consequence of industry but due much more to the uncontrolled and encouraged self-interest of economic man. Make no mistake: this reorientation toward the city is important, for it allows us to view the urban community for what it is and might be, rather than for what it was not. The city is not, and cannot be, a rural paradise anymore than the industrial system could have flourished under feudal society. The city, in its own way, had to break sharply with former human environments, just as capitalism had to destroy the feudal economy. I might point out in this connection, that those who see in the suburban movement a return to ruralism are deluding themselves; the analogy might be tempting but the rurality of old is long out of reach and no social form that industrial society might create could ever duplicate it. On the contrary, everywhere in the world, the movement toward industrialism is destroying the rural locales, geographically as socially, and replacing them with an urban civilization.

Class, too, has developed in the face of ideologies contrary to it. The situation, however, had a different time perspective from that for urban development. In the case of the city, the ideology of ruralism had its roots in an earlier historical period. In the case of class, on the contrary, the ideology of equality was in a sense coterminus with the movement toward industrialism. Industrialism simultaneously depended on and developed as its legitimating social philosophy an ideology of democratic equality, economic individualism and political freedom that eschewed social divisions. This ideology was strongly anti-aristocratic, focussed as it was to support the rationale for dissolving the capricious power of the feudal order concentrated in an hereditary elite. The legitimating ideology and the social requirements for industrial development needed each other. Hence, the appearance of a class system could not be formally recognized, even though it was an inevitable consequence of industrialism. For class bespoke of inequality, of differential power, and of the narrowing of effective economic choices. Only recently has the analysis of class become more realistic among a large number of social scientists. Although its existence has long been known, only recently have we consented to appraise its role in society more objectively than before. Here too, as was the case for urban study, the reorientation has been helpful for more intelligent analysis.

Class and urbanism are identified as socially divisive. Of direct interest to the subject of this paper is the fact that both class and urbanism have been considered as prime factors creating social disunity. The dominant image of class has been one of struggle and conflict. Marx gave class its connotation: class dynamics necessarily entailed social upheaval and revolt, and by the dialectics of that process the proletariat would win its historically assured position of superiority. Hence, the class struggle was a social feature inherent in capitalism. However, even in much less radical formulations, such as those of the urban ecologists, the class system was understood as a categorizer of the urban population, dividing it into socially competitive worlds. To be sure, the ecologist looked upon competition as a "natural" process, but even so it was a process that was potentially disruptive in its effects and was a major source of urban change.

Class has also been identified as a divisive force in the city, for it created separate social worlds in the city and insulated them from one another. By so doing, class only maximized the already divisive forces of urban society itself. The city, geographically extensive and excessively populated, has been seen almost universally as the destroyer of "community"—a social habitat that still connotes a social existence which is integrated, personal, stable, and intimate. If only because of its size, the city could never duplicate that type of existence. The city, therefore, came to be defined as an anti-social and artificially created environment, for it had destroyed the "sense of belonging," or in the words of town planners, had vulgarized the "human scale" of life. Bureaucratic relationships came to be substituted for personal relationships; segmentalized business-like contracts replaced primary group involvements; and the clock and the calendar replaced the sun and the season as man's measure of time. In short, the city had encouraged an artificial and paper unity in place of the natural unity of community. It is really no wonder, then, that both class and urbanism were viewed with suspicion, mistrust, and distaste. They had destroyed the sweet images created by the popular ideologies and instead forced upon us a consciousness of a reality we were most reluctant to accept.

It was my first intention to argue for the cohesive elements that can be found in the urban class structure: the intricate social interdependence that stems from and also permits a division of labor to function, the consensus on status symbols and on the channels for social mobility, the legitimation of political forms, and the acceptance of power in its legitimate aspects. Instead I have altered the focus of the analysis so as to describe three different points of view for each of the concepts in the title of this paper. As I try to show, each point of view has its own unity that is evident in the manner in which it considers social cohesion, class, and the city.

Social Cohesion

Let us consider social cohesion first and three views of the concept that can be discerned. Given the focus of this paper, I have chosen as the major measure of distinction the estimates made of the degree of cohesion that is presumed to exist in industrial society. There is no way, of course, to measure this phenomenon directly, and it is precisely the wide range of possible interpretation with its dependence upon indirect estimates of trends that has created alternative points of view. One view, which shall be called the "psychological," holds that the extent of social cohesion in the industrial city is excessive and undesirably so. So excessive, in fact, that the integrity of the individual, *qua* individual, is seriously threatened. Perhaps unjustly, I have equated excessive cohesion with extreme conformity. Yet I do not believe that the equivalence is unfair or unjustified. "Cohesion," like "conformity" and "solidarity," implies social unity. And although we have come to use "conformity" mostly in a negative sense, (i.e. destructive of individuality) and to use "cohesion" in a positive sense, (i.e. integrative), the terms are highly comparable. Excessive cohesion, I would maintain, shares the relevant features of overconformity and hence is at the center of the psychological orientation here being considered.

For whatever reason, the demands by society for cohesion have been met at the individual's expense. The person has had to give up or to hide much of his own distinctiveness and individual uniqueness as the price for his acceptance by the group. The origin of this cohesive force is located by some in the society at large and by others within the individual himself, although it is most likely a combination of the two. The growth of bureaucratic organizations in so many sectors of social life, and their combined demands upon the individual has been identified as the major societal source for the origin of excessive cohesion. Bureaucrats, typically, impersonalize their clients even as they themselves are depersonalized by the organization. The heavy increase in the number, variety and power of such bureaucracies in industrial society has meant, the proponents of this view have contended, an equally steady squeeze towards greater social conformity. We are dangerously close to the point where we do more than cohere: we are in danger of fusing our personalities with the undifferentiated mass. Then we are individuals no more but social automatons.

The contrasting point of view maintains that social cohesion, far from being abnormally oppressive, is instead, absent. Again, for the sake of easier identification, this orientation can be called "deterministic". The argument here is that the major dynamics of industrial society have functioned centrifugally to tear individuals away from their traditional preindustrial allegiances: the home, the village community, the church, and the land. The result has been the effective destruction of integrative ties between the citizens of industrial society. They have been atomized. The forces for social cohesiveness have been neutralized. People remain but loosely attached to the large, secondary, social groups that cannot supply the cohesive ingredient. These are people suffering from anomie, as the earlier cohesive ties have loosened. Interestingly, the proponents of a deterministic view read opposite conclusions into the growth of bureaucracy and large secondary organizations compared with those who hold the psychological view just described. For the determinists, bureaucratic expansion is socially disintegrating, but for the latter it is a movement toward excessive conformity. The difference in these and similar interpretations, I have contended, can be explained principally in terms of these viewpoints. In effect, the observer interprets what he sees, but sees what he is sensitized to see.

Among those who have promulgated this point of view have been the town planners: Ebenezer Howard, Frank Lloyd Wright, Saarinen, and Gallion and to a lesser extent, Mumford. These men have traced the lack of community cohesion directly to its source in the industrial city. As the city has grown, community cohesion has been destroyed. There are others who should be placed in this category of those who see in the growth of cities the primary cause of social disunity. Some of them are considered below when the urban environment is more specifically discussed.

A third position regarding social cohesion, the "sociological" is midway between these two extreme views. This is the point of view advanced by the functionalists who view the social system as an operating mechanism. It is their basic contention that a minimum amount of social cohesion, however much that may be, is necessary to maintain any society. Therefore, any society that continues to exist must be able to satisfy that requirement by means of consensus or an "organic solidarity" in Durkheim's terms. The proponents of this view, it seems to me, are not easily stampeded into judgments of whether social cohesion is excessive or not. For example, one of the main points made by Merton in his article in the *American Sociological Review* on "Social Conformity, Deviation, and Opportunity Structures," was that conformity had to be considered at different levels: doctrinal, behavioral, and attitudinal. What may appear to be conformistic, or overly cohesive, on the first two levels as judged by what a person says or does, may in point of fact not be so at all because there is no conformity at the attitudinal level. Yet, it is at the level of attitudes that one begins to be concerned about conformity, for it is here that behavior can be said to originate. In short, social cohesion is a property of all social systems and is supported by many other elements of the system. Whether cohesion is excessive, minimal, or somewhere in between must be evaluated in terms of the system as a whole and of the responses of its members: the values and attitudes that are held and the major ideologies that are praised. At best this is a complex judgment to make, for what might appear to be excessive at the personal level might be mandatory for survival at the societal level. The sociological view, therefore, tends to be more cautious; cohesion and conformity are nebulous social characteristics, that require a standard of evaluation which does not readily exist. Durkheim, for example, in his analysis of the division of labor concluded that simpler societies dependent on "mechanical solidarity" or likeness, functioned by different rules than complex societies that relied on "organic solidarity" or interdependence. It is really not to the point to ask which type of society had the greater social cohesiveness, for the needs of each society were demonstrably different.

Class

Three different positions concerning the reality of the class system in industrial society can also be discerned. I wish to make it clear that many ramifications, variations and nuances that are usually involved in a consideration of class phenomena must be excluded from the present analysis. For present purposes we are concerned with only one facet of class: whether the class system is seen to exist or not, and associatively, what is its principal characteristic.

One point of view regarding the reality of the class system contends that *status* not *class* is the matter at issue. The argument is also alternatively phrased that a massive and continuous leveling of the class system has occurred as societies have moved into the later phase of industrialization. The industrial system, it is argued, has functioned to greatly expand the middle classes, and at the same time has disseminated middle class values and tastes throughout all class levels of society. These processes have moved us closer to a "classless" society in the sense that the class struggle has been neutralized and that the standards and values of one class more or less have become the accepted goals of all. The proponents of this view, having emphasized status rather than class differences, have thereby moved their attention away from problems of power to an almost exclusive concern with matter of prestige, consumption and social honor.

This position just described, closely duplicates the "psychological" position on the subject of social cohesion discussed previously. The combination is sociologically consistent. They argue that the status system has produced excessive social cohesion. For status striving and status achievements depend upon the judgments of the community in order to legitimize the latter and to encourage the former. Such judgments, in turn, bind persons ever more tightly into their accepted status community and commit them to its values. In the extreme, the result is overconformity. Those engaged in the pursuit of status must be cautious in their relationships; careful to respect the evaluations of others since success depends upon it. Deviations from the community's norms would be social suicide. It is not long, then, before conformity with the standard becomes a goal in its own right directing behavior totally. What was once thought to be class has now been transformed from a dynamic struggle for power into a deliberate striving for status and for acceptance in which the community is the supreme arbiter.

The "deterministic" position on class would seriously dispute the psychological image just described. On the contrary, those of a deterministic persuasion contend that class still continues to be a dynamic struggle for power, perhaps altered in some particulars from what it had been in the earlier periods of industrial growth. Essentially, this position is a restatement, brought up-to-date, of Marx's conception of class. Although Marx did not correctly foresee the heavy expansion of the middle class in the later phases of industrialism, he did correctly predict the narrowing concentration of power that would occur in the class system. The determinists hold that the status struggles of the middle class are relatively unimportant when seen against the power domination of the ruling class elites. The social processes created by industrialization, these proponents would maintain, have not been seriously altered by the apparent growth in size of the middle class or by its noisy status concerns; the combatants in the class struggle are still being primed in the arena of power and status concerns there mean relatively little.

The relationship between the deterministic positions on class and cohesion is less obvious than was the case for the psychological view. Two general features of the viewpoint make the bridge for continuity between the two concepts. The first is a continued emphasis upon social forces rather than upon individual behavior as the source of direction and change in society. The person is seen as caught in the sway of social forces beyond his control and often beyond his understanding. A second feature common to both concepts is the emphasis upon divisiveness, upon the social wedge that has been effectively driven between groups. The segregation of classes from one another is another way of viewing the decay of community, and consequently the absence of any real social cohesion. The determinist argues that people have been alienated from each other to the point that "callous self interest" is the only remaining basis for human relationships. Community cannot flourish upon such barren social ground.

The third position, the sociological, once again argues for something between the two extremes just as it did for cohesion. The best statement of this sociological orientation toward class is Weber's. It is impossible to detail fully the features of Weber's views on stratification, as I have done in *Class in American Society*. It should be sufficient here to indicate briefly the three dimensions of stratification that Weber has described. The dominant basis of social stratification for Weber was the unequal distribution of power that he analytically separated into three social sectors. Class, Weber defined, by the criteria of economic power, generally reflecting the extent of control exerted in the economic institutions. Such power was relatively independent of community recognition, relying more on the real or potential influence that individuals or groups could bring into the market, i.e., economic relationships. Status for Weber, on the other hand, was defined by the criteria of social honor and depended very much upon community recognition and consensus. For social honor could be judged and legitimated only in the community, which is to say that status qualities are not impersonal but tied to personal judgments and appraisals. Status power thus accrued to those who were able to reach the upper levels of the hierarchy as judged by the community. Those located favorably in the status hierarchy might further attempt, and it was Weber's implication that they did, to monopolize their position and to control entry into the status elite. Finally, political power was similarly dependent upon community judgments, for such power required legitimation to be effective in a regular fashion. Political power, like status, is differentially accorded to individuals depending upon the criteria of legitimation accepted within the community. For that reason, political and status power often come to reside in the same group of persons. Economic power also carries consequences for power in the other two spheres because of the close nexus of these three spheres in society.

These few remarks on the sociological view of class should be sufficient to indicate the more balanced view behind this orientation. In some particulars it draws from the two other positions. The sense of power in the Marxian sense is present, as is too, the recognition of status as a social reality in industrial societies. Like its view on social cohesion, the sociological position on class recognizes the existence of certain necessary requirements for the continued existence of any social system. A minimal degree of cohesion is functionally necessary. Similarly, these three dimensions of power are functionally interrelated with the needs of the system as a whole. Furthermore, there tends to be a strong relationship between all three dimensions, since in any society the degree of power that is held in one sector tends to carry strong consequences for the degree of power held in other sectors as well.

The City

The last concept of this trilogy that needs to be considered from the viewpoint of each orientation is that of the urban environment; the social locale in which cohesion and class are of central importance. A consideration of the city in the present context, then, can serve as a summary description, for it tends to incorporate the principal consequences of industrialization as seen by the three orientations.

The psychological view of the city is generally negative in tone, for it has been in the city that the dynamics of conformity have been spawned and nurtured. By the pressures of mass communications, the habits, tastes, and attitudes of urbanites have become standardized. Suburbanization has further heightened that trend, forcing a greater dependence on mass techniques. Additionally, the suburbs have preselected homogeneous social groups from the city and located them in the same residential area. Social differences, thereby, are less encouraged and because of proximity are more easily identified. The suburb has become, according to this view, the final extrapolation of most of the negative social influences that urbanism started. The "real" community of common interests in which individuals continue to retain their identity has been effectively destroyed.

The emphasis of this view is psychological. Therefore, one of the main problems that this orientation identified is the loss of ego identity. By losing the sense of community, we also lost our sense of identity and individuality. It is this point that Stein, for example, in *The Eclipse of Community,* stressed most heavily. He has argued for the need to regain this ego identity as one of the most pressing demands in the urban environment today. The unabated flight to the suburbs and the consequent growth of metropolitan and supermetropolitan areas has heightened this trend by increasing the emphasis on the mass at the expense of the individual himself. Wheelis, in a most intriguing book, *In Quest of Identity,* has implied a similar argument. Twentieth century man has to recognize that the loss of identity is his major psychological problem. Nineteenth century man, with whom Freud was principally concerned, faced socially enforced repression of strong ego drives as his major problem. One cannot help but feel here that the twentieth century city is at fault.

The position of the determinists concerning the city resembles the psychologist's view. The principal difference is that the determinists place the primary fault upon the social system rather than upon the individual. The destruction of community and the destruction of effective social ties between its members have been brought about by industrialization and the city which is its product. The movement toward urbanization has been everywhere accompanied by depersonalization, by a secular rather than a religious emphasis, and by the destruction of intimate primary groups. Marx was ready to credit the bourgeoisie with urban development, which he generally looked upon with favor. Urbanization, for him as for other nineteenth century social theorists, was equated with civilization: the development of technology, literature, art, and the escape from what Marx called "the idiocy of rural life." Whatever the city contained that was undesirable or evil was the fault not of the city *per se,* but only of the city under capitalism.

Redfield, specifically, and I suspect other anthropologists as well, hold a much more negative view of the city that should be included in this category. He and they appear to bemoan, scientifically, the destruction of the village and the town under the impact of urbanization and industrialization. They see in that development the loss of cultural variability as formerly isolated areas of the world are brought into the modern fold. Hence, Redfield has described the urban end of his theoretical folk-urban continuum primarily in negative terms, in the total destruction of the folk community and its values. Or again, Scott and Lynton in a UNESCO study on *The Community Factor in Modern Technology,* have listed four characteristics of "established communities," each one of which by definition would be impossible in the urban setting: "First, all aspects of life are closely integrated—work, for instance, is not something separate and distinct. Secondly, social 'belonging' is automatic. Thirdly, change is slow, and continuity is sustained by attitudes, customs and institutions. And lastly, the important social groupings are small." Such a view forever denies to the city the ability to create a community.

The demand for greater urban concentration has spelled massive consequences for the whole of any society that is so involved: its unifying values have been destroyed and replaced by more rational, and more impersonal ones. The effects upon the individual, as Simmel for example has detailed them, have been equally great: impersonality, calculability, and a blasé attitude have come to be encouraged as necessary traits of the urbanite. In short, the city has concentrated the anti-community forces of industrial society and thereby has effectively destroyed community. Nothing short of a radical recreation of the city would do for the determinists: urban concentrations must be relocated and smaller residential enclaves that could be socially self-sufficient must be built.

The sociological position toward the city and its effects is less clearly demarcated than the other two orientations. One point, however, is clear: the city is a consequence of industrialization. There can be no return to some imagined and romanticized "community" of the past. Nor can change be brought about through altering individual attitudes and desires without reference to the massive social forces that set these patterns to begin with.

The growth of cities and the development of the class structure are intimately linked to each other. Also involved is the ideology and political philosophy of nationalism, by which the primary loyalty of individuals is to the nation not to the local community. Those who see the city as the culprit in what they consider as a thoroughly undesirable development have failed to grasp the complexity and scope of the forces that are involved. The community, in its earlier appearance as a small, local, socially homogeneous, and intimate society, has been overwhelmed by the social processes set in motion by the needs of an industrializing society: the growth and expansion of the class system, its antagonisms and power differentials, as well as the development of nationalism as an ideology that has unified an urbanized society into a functioning entity.

The four variables suggested in this complex—industrialization, urban growth, class and nationalism have come to the attention of scholars from different disciplines, including economics, political science, history, and sociology. It is around these variables that the city, class, and social cohesion must be considered in the present era, for both industrially developing as well as of highly developed countries. Yet, it is only recently that we have been able to properly consider these four forces in an objective way. Until quite recently, much of urban analysis as well as of class analysis has been structured by an ideological bias rather than by scientific demands. Urban analysts suffered from a kind of rural provincialism. They saw the city as evil and were concerned with proving their bias. In rural-urban comparisons, the city always seemed to come out second best. Class analysts, on the other hand, seem to have suffered from a kind of political provincialism. So many were so occupied with disputing a rigid Marxian formulation of class struggle and proletarian victory that they failed to appreciate the more basic power dynamics of class that Marx had correctly noted and that Weber so carefully developed.

Weighted down then by these provincial biases, often unconsciously held, we have failed to identify properly what had been going on. The urban environment was not so much described as it was disputed in much of the scientific literature. The major source of new information has come from the industrial urban developments that can be observed in underdeveloped countries as they move out of an agricultural and traditional type of society toward the industrial urban society. For the first time, the social scientist interested in this subject has the opportunity to find contrasts for the highly industrialized society in which he has been immersed and for which primitive society was not adequate as a contrast. It seems to be abundantly clear that once industrialization begins, when there is an industrial "take-off" in Rostow's sense of that term, urban growth, a class system, and a nationalistic political philosophy also are evident partners in that process, thereby ending the former state of rural settlements, a feudal type of landed aristocracy, and a localistic political philosophy.

The sequence of this development, the criteria for measuring it, and the conditions that aid or hinder it are among the problems that need yet to be solved. One very suggestive beginning, for example, has been made by Kerr, Dunlop, Harbison and Myers in their recent theoretical analysis, *Industrialism and Industrial Man.* By means of a typology of industrializing elites—dynastic, middle class, revolutionary-intellectual, colonial administrators, and nationalistic leaders—they have analyzed different facets of the industrializing process and the directions of that process as dictated by the several elite types. Interestingly enough, the elites that Kerr and his co-authors have named lend some support to the four variables that have been specified in this paper.

The direction of inquiry seems right, and if it is right then the three concepts that have been the subject of this paper will have to be seen in a new perspective; one as different from the older points of view as could possibly be imagined. In effect, cohesion, class, and the city are all aspects of the same social complex. They are manifestations, in one way or another, of the complexity that is industrial urbanism, and their form at the present time is a direct consequence of the stage of industrial urban development.

KINSHIP AS A FACTOR AFFECTING CANTONESE ECONOMIC ADAPTATION IN THE UNITED STATES

Milton L. Barnett

The joint family system in Chinese society has shown remarkable survival strength among the Chinese immigrants to the United States, contrary to what might have been expected from previous studies of the impact of migration and city life upon family organization. It is generally assumed that economic change is necessarily destructive to the joint family system and that the corporate nature of the latter is antithetical to the stress given individual initiative and performance in Western commercial enterprises. Schapera has described the disruptive influence of a money economy among the Kgatla of Bechuanaland,[1] and similar instances can be readily drawn from other parts of the world. These have been sufficient in number to warrant Linton's stating:

> . . . as a theorem, valid in a very high percentage of cases, that the greater the opportunities for individual economic profit provided by any socio-cultural situation, the weaker the ties of extended kinship will become.[2]

If, indeed, the theorem has been demonstrated, there nevertheless appears to be a need for corollaries dealing with such dimensions as time and intensity of intra-familial relationships, as well as distinguishing between tribal cultures such

Reprinted by permission of the author and publisher from *Human Organization,* **19** (1960), pp. 40–46.

as the Bantu and those where both extended family organization and money economy have long been in functional dependence upon one another. The economic activities of the overseas Chinese, the *hua ch'iao,* as a reflection of the second, more complex level of socioeconomic integration, are of particular interest. Members of a subculture wherein a system of money and the joint family have been native features, the *hua ch'iao* participate in a national culture whose economic institutions should be dominant and disruptive.

First-generation Chinese should be seen as transient rather than settlers in the United States. Virtually all emigrants from South China came with the firm intention of returning home; the status of sojourner was self-defined and consistent with the expectations of kinsmen, both in China and abroad. Motivations were largely economic with the goal of earning money to allow regular remittances to family members in China and with the aim of ultimately resuming one's place in the family, the latter now perhaps improved by higher social and economic standing. Examination of correspondence written during the last century reveals financial gain as the dominant aspiration of those leaving Kwangtung; numerous interviews in the contemporary period confirm this sustained monetary interest.

Unlike many other overseas Chinese populations, in those of the New World there has been a preponderance of people coming from the Sz-Yap, the Four Districts. Lying southwest of Canton, these are contiguous, predominantly rural counties with market centers. Hakka speakers and other Kwangtung immigrants, in addition to an insignificant number of persons from other provinces, make up the remainder of the American *hua ch'iao* communities.

Rather than becoming fully integrated into the commercial and industrial life of the United States, the Cantonese were compelled to entrench themselves in those areas of trade where competition with the remainder of the population was minimal. At least since the financial crisis of the 1870's and its later effects in California, the now traditional prejudicial attitudes toward these immigrants, implemented by vested economic interests of white occupational groups were instrumental in constraining them within circumscribed economic operations. Successful exploitation of their endeavors, reinforced by a continuing minority group status, has favored the maintenance of generally narrow and segregated business pursuits. Only since World War II have exceptions become more numerous; these, in the main, are in professional and technical fields.

The major business activities have been further limited by specialization in the *Chinese* aspects of commerce. That is to say, those engaged in exporting and importing have focused upon the China trade. Curio shops handle a variety of items, but the bulk of their wares consists of porcelain and wicker-ware, soapstone carvings, and other craft material coming from China. Restaurants may have the usual American dishes on their menus, but these occupy a secondary place when compared to the traditional and Chinese-style offerings. In a similar manner, the Chinese hand laundry sign is associated with particularistic meaning and has come to symbolize specialized processing. Many of these various *Chinese* enterprises are distributed throughout urban areas and are oriented toward obtaining trade with the broader metropolitan community rather than with the Chinese population within it. The organizational center of most of these activities is the Chinatown or its associational adjuncts in smaller cities.

Economic Organization

The Chinese-Americans have tended to go into small, commercial enterprises. A laundry can be opened with a relatively small sum needed for the equipment and requisite counter and shelf space. While more ambitious undertakings, such as restaurants, obviously require greater initial capital outlay, some credit is extended by supply firms. Beyond the limits of this credit, the establishment of even the most modest enterprise does involve immediate expenditure of funds. In Chinatown, modes of accumulation of capital for initial investment tend to be somewhat more limited than elsewhere in a city's economic life. Nevertheless, the smaller amount of ready money necessary to open a business encourages the launching of commercial enterprise.

Many industrious and thrifty individuals work for years building the required capital on their own; more frequently, the process is accelerated by borrowing from family members or friends. Others, who are less successful in readying themselves for an independent venture, often will invest their own small savings in the projected undertaking of another. And, for a fortunate few, gambling provides an unexpected source of income to be used for initial capital. (To be sure, some are reduced to a penniless state after wagering a shop or shares in a firm as "ante" in a game of chance.) Whatever the means of capital accumulation, the values of "going into business" and having a business of one's own appear to be predominant when compared with the satisfactions expressed by some Cantonese concerned with obtaining steady, well-paying employment.

Two major forms of ownership prevail: First, the establishment is owned by a single entrepreneur or family, and second, the establishment is owned by a group of partners, as few as two and very often as many as eight to twelve. The impersonal corporation, with its underlying conception of limited liability, is virtually unknown. The premises on which this business form is built conflict with those linked with traditional Chinese socioeconomic structure.

Single Ownership

A general merchandise shop in a Chinatown or a laundry in an urban neighborhood may require the labor of only one person. The relatively little trade by the small-scale concern can be managed with no great difficulty. In many stores, however, an entire family may participate in running the enterprise, employing additional help only when the flow of business warrants it. The following examples serve to illustrate the range of personnel situations found in the single-owner type of operation:

Case 1

Harry Lou runs a jewelry and curio shop located in an unprepossessing building off a main shopping avenue. His store has an overhead which is not excessive in proportion to his average gross income. Trade is easily handled by Lou, who seldom has more than one or two customers at one time. To obtain an adequate financial return, the premises must be kept open during the week from nine in the morning until eight o'clock each night. Business proceeds more briskly on Saturdays and Lou's stays open until ten. The store is closed on Sunday, when virtually all activity in the locality is nonexistent. The presence of visiting friends may be used to the proprietor's advantage if a flurry of business should require it. Similarly, friends or relatives are called upon to take over when the owner, a bachelor, must leave to conduct some commercial negotiation.

The same situation obtains for the vast majority of laundries. Primarily serving a non-family clientele and those who prefer the more careful hand-ironing to the flatwork of the power laundries, Chinese laundrymen have managed to eke out a living by dint of frugality and incredibly long work hours. Most shops open at seven or eight in the morning to be available to customers en route to work. Doors often are not shut until late in the night. Not only do the laundrymen work twelve and more hours daily, but six and often seven days a week. With mechanization in the industry and a greater reliance on power-driven machinery operated by large firms, plus "shirt factories" wherein low-paid Puerto Rican and Negro labor is employed to perform tedious ironing tasks, the hand laundryman increasingly has become a middleman, participating less and less in the actual laundering processes. As a consequence of these developments, his economic position has become more precarious.

Case 2

A successful laundry in a middle-class neighborhood is operated by Mr. and Mrs. Lee. An older daughter, a college student, is able to help during evenings. Until she reached marriageable age, the girl had the sole responsibility of running the laundry on Saturdays, with two younger siblings assisting her. The parents thus carry the burden of the manual labor, yet are afforded some respite from it.

Here the nuclear family is the unit of economic activity. This is characteristic of most family-owned Cantonese business ventures operated on a small scale. The economic value of children is enhanced when their labor can replace that which would have to be hired for wages. Few children working in the establishments of their parents receive formal wages; the more common practice of parents is to provide funds voluntarily or on request. The convenience of having kin working in one's place of business frequently extends beyond the nuclear group to collateral and even more distant relatives. When this occurs, the same flexible financial arrangement often prevails although set salaries are paid in a greater number of instances than in the nuclear family. Those financially independent of the employer receive wages; those in an apprentice status (see below) receive a lesser amount, consistent with a mutual agreement establishing the relationship between the apprentice and the employer.

Case 3

A restaurant owned by a family is located in a Chinatown, serving a clientele, fifty percent of which is estimated to be Chinese. The father acts as manager and occasionally waits on table. A part-time cook, a clan "cousin," is employed on weekends; the mother carries the kitchen chores by herself during the remainder of the week. Three sons and a daughter, all attending school, follow a rather definite schedule, taking turns as waiters. When business prospers, waiters or additional kitchen help are hired and the children released from work responsibility on school days. Those employed invariably are kinsmen, having direct blood ties or sharing a common surname with that of the family.

Counter to the hiring policy which involves consideration of familial, regional, or associational ties are the less personal practices more typical of American employers. The Cantonese community is so closely knit in its interpersonal relations that such employment procedures would scarcely seem possible. Nevertheless, they have been attempted on occasion by a few establishments.

Case 4

In an Atlantic Seaboard Chinatown, a member of the Kau family owns a large, successful restaurant specializing in the non-Chinese trade. Of the twenty-odd men employed, only one is a kinsman. While many of the waiters are engaged through the usual informal channels, the owner, on occasion, contacts a not very thriving local Chinese-operated employment agency for additional personnel. The owner's three sons, all in their twenties, seldom appear at the restaurant other than to dine there or, even less frequently, to do some work to supplement allowances. The sons have shown no interest in their father's business, nor have they made any effort to participate in its management.

In such cases, the personnel structure does not have as supportive bases the ties of kinship, friendship, or common village residence in Kwangtung Province. An impersonal, "strictly business" attitude between workers and employer is encouraged by the narrow wage-and-hours basis of their relationship. Employees voice numerous dissatisfactions with their jobs and a high rate of labor turnover is to be found in the handful of business establishments which operate in this manner. Both workers and other shop proprietors are equally denunciatory of this policy disregarding traditional obligations as it does. Criticism often becomes transformed into malicious gossip and its targets are forced to be somewhat judicious and politic with the local population, not proceeding entirely along so-called "American" or individualistic lines. In the present structure of Cantonese-American economic life, business interests do not override personal considerations. Priority is given to relatives and kinsmen when a proprietor engages a staff of employees. Intimate family friendships provide secondary reinforcement of this general personnel policy.

The Partnership

A young second generation writer complained:

> Everybody in Chinatown wants to be a partner. I know a couple that has a fifty dollar share of Yee's grocery. They get a one dollar bill as a dividend once a year, but they can say that they own the place.

Prestige as a motive for investment is undoubtedly an adjunct of the entrepreneurial orientation so widespread in the Cantonese-American population. With the group, especially the China-born, so nearly completely dependent upon commercial activity, successful businesses bring not only rewards of an economic nature, but those of prestige value as well. Even before practical difficulties in remitting money to families in China existed, small dispersed investments were preferred by those with meager savings who saw no more advantageous manner of using their funds.

Whatever the motivations of the secondary investors, the purpose of the major investors is twofold: monetary gain and, if necessary, self-employment. The partnership—the pooling of funds—is the solution for those who wish to start a business but lack the necessary capital. A family member, a close friend, or a fellow-villager generally is preferred as an associate but sometimes individuals seeking a partner may be brought together by a third party. Collaboration in such cases may be arranged after cautious indirect investigation by each of the prospective investors. The individual promoting the partnership may be given a monetary commission or a minor share in the venture. The latter alternative is more usual; in that way, the go-between assumes some risk, gaining only if his introductions have a successful conclusion.

Case 5

In 1947, three casual acquaintances were brought together by a fellow-member of a regional association to discuss investment in a restaurant in a Southern city. The three finally formed a "company" (*kongsi*) and bought the establishment for $17,000. One of them, with some restaurant experience, moved his family from New York so that he might manage the business. The other two, a waiter and a sometime cook on a coastal steamer, received monthly reports, offered advice, but otherwise played passive roles. Two years later, the trio sold their holding for $26,000, with some of the profit going to minor investors whose support had been enlisted in raising the initial capital. The short-lived partnership was consistent with the original plan of the trio who hoped from the onset to improve the place for resale.[3]

Partnerships may involve more than merger of funds for capital investment. In most enterprises, the major shareholders engage in direct operation of the business. Thus, in a simple partnership, two Cantonese pharmacists share work and hours in running their thriving Chinatown drugstore. Each receives a monthly salary agreed upon by both, and, at the year's end, division of the pharmacy's net gains is made.

Depending upon the nature of the undertaking, division of labor among partners varies. Individual differences and abilities are considered in apportioning responsibility. In a restaurant or laundry, the individual more articulate in English will very likely act as contact with the non-Chinese clientele, e.g., as cashier. Experience and "know-how," as practical assets, tend to supplant other criteria in defining job status. In two partnerships with which the writer is familiar, the largest stockholder of each acts as a mere waiter. A headwaiter of one restaurant and the cashier of the other are minor partners in the financial arrangements. Occupational statuses, therefore, become functional rather than prestige-providing. It should be pointed out, however, that this pattern does not pertain to the larger, wealthier establishments where major stockholders often assume clearly distinguishable managerial roles.

When a large number of partners is associated, leadership and responsibility may be conferred by the group on one or two individuals. The other shareholders remain inactive with the exception of those actually holding jobs in the enterprise. In such cases, the latter receive wages commensurate with their positions.

Investors are usually apprised of the financial state of the firm by the preparation and distribution of a *üt kit,* monthly statement. An annual or semi-annual declaration of profits and dividends is made and, sometimes, business permitting, the dividends are apportioned more frequently. The reinvestment of profits into the working capital of the company and the determination of dividends is decided by the shareholders in meeting, with long-range policy and other business considerations also being resolved. At such meetings, disagreements concerning operating procedures are thrashed over and conclusions reached.

Apprentices

Irrespective of mode of ownership, a master-apprentice relationship is found in some Chinese-owned businesses. The apprentice of recent times is seldom of the second generation except insofar as a father-son or similar bond is concerned. The practice, which has been extremely common, appears to be on the wane. For example, apprentices had been fairly common in the laundries. With modernization of equipment and the utilization of mass-production methods and facilities, the desirability of expending funds for apprentice labor has dwindled considerably. In the long run, Negro and Puerto Rican labor can be obtained more cheaply with no initial investment required. Moreover, marriage and the growth of families in the United States as more Chinese change their status of "sojourner" have made the apprentice system less advantageous or unnecessary. Some individuals who are unmarried, or whose immediate families reside in Kwangtung, still prefer having an apprentice since it affords some degree of companionship.

Case 6

A restaurant owner living in a small city some distance from the nearest metropolitan center containing a Chinese community arranged to have his younger brother's son, aged fifteen, sent from T'oi San. He estimated that more than $4,000 had been spent by him in making the necessary arrangements—American birth certificate, ship passage, lawyer's fees, etc. The boy had worked in the restaurant for five years, receiving training as a cook. At some point during this period (the date could not be established), the boy ceased to use the term of address, *A Pak,* father's elder brother. In its stead and at the older man's urging, he would address the latter as *A Te* or *A Ye,* father, and referred to him in this newly adopted category. The financial obligation incurred by the boy as a result of his entry into the country was nearly fully repaid and a partnership was in the offing.

Generally speaking, enterprises whose function it is to serve the needs of the Chinese population, e.g., native groceries and herb shops, are more likely today to have apprentices than are those establishments dealing directly with a non-Chinese set of customers.

Conflict and Dispute

In Cantonese-American economic activities, as well as in other affairs, there is a marked tendency not to rely upon or follow American legal procedures. Thus, formal articles of partnership may or may not be prepared, depending upon the relationship between the participants. In either event, should disagreement occur which cannot be settled amicably within the firm, recourse may be made to the elders of the family association, regional, or occupational groups or, if necessary, to the *Chung Wah Kung Sho,* the Chinese Benevolent Association. In the councils of these quasi-governmental organs of the community, arbitration will take place when efforts at mediation have failed at lower levels.

Composed of some sixty-odd organizations, the Association's functions include

> . . . officiating any major transactions of business in Chinatown, especially those of transfer of property or of ownership of business firms; settling disputes among people or among associations.[4]

Leong's less formalistic interpretation of its activities suggests a considerably broader scope of influence, including legislative and executive prerogatives affecting the entire Cantonese population of the eastern seaboard of the United States.[5] He writes of its arbitrary methods and of its self-imposed authority to levy fees and to fine Chinese who violate its codes.

Thirty years after publication of Leong's book, the organization still occupies a superordinate position in the pyramidal structure of Cantonese-American associational life, but its influence appears to be in decline. Its support of economically obstructive practices such as *po-tai*[6] has irritated those who were victims of the system. Nepotism, rumored financial unreliability of some of its officials, and ineffectual leadership have disillusioned many persons in the past. The Association's close ties with right-wing politics have alienated those who are in other political camps as well as those opposed to any partisanship in the affairs of China. Policies impeding economic incentive and enterprise have created impatience and resentment. Finally, its constituent organizations have themselves suffered from inactivity and a waning membership, thus seriously weakening the influence, strength, and prestige of the supreme body.

Familial, territorial, and other bonds may foster the creation of a smoothly functioning relationship, but not all partnerships are harmonious ones. Nevertheless, many continue to exist despite acrimony. Fear of ridicule, gossip in the neighborhood, intrafamilial censure, and similar negative sanctions often deter partners from airing their grievances or from seeking the advice of others. Rather than jeopardize important personal relations or subject one's self to social discomfort, the aggrieved individuals may take no action; while socially approved channels for mediation are available, the danger of loss of face inhibits their use.

Inaction on the part of a stockholder may be seen in the following situation: A grocer, in partnership with his wife's brother, viewed with dismay the decline of trade undoubtedly due to the commercial ineptitude of the latter. The grocer had built a successful business and, after his marriage, had been persuaded to accept the partner. Some tactful suggestions made by him to his brother-in-law had been ignored, after an ungracious reception; since that time, he had been silent, taking no steps to prevent the inescapable collapse of his business. He had rejected the possibility of making an appeal for aid and advice from his own family. To voice criticism of his brother-in-law, he maintained, would mean to cast a poor light on his marriage. It would disgrace not only his mother, who had arranged it, but also his wife's father, whom he deeply respected. Furthermore, any critical attitude displayed by him would distress his wife. Last, but not least, what would people think of the way he had allowed himself to get involved in such a situation?

A somewhat different dilemma was faced by five men when another partner embezzled money from the firm. The six had been schoolmates and fellow-villagers. They had pooled their funds and skills in establishing a commercial house exporting technical supplies to the Far East. In a series of meetings with and without the presence of the culprit, efforts were made to rectify the situation. When the partners gathered (there are branch offices in two other cities), a regular notice would be sent the malefactor. On occasions when he attended, nothing was said about the missing money; circumlocution took the form of discussing an unexplained deficit. Taking legal measures was automatically dismissed as undesirable. The group was also unwilling to go beyond its own circle to seek redress. "Gwan is very sensitive. He would be terribly embarrassed if we told his family," one partner said. Another remarked one day, "After all, Gwan is a friend of mine. What he did was pretty bad, but what can we do? You wouldn't think we were very good friends if we got rough with him. Which is more valuable, money or friendship?"

The political turnover in China, the closing of the port of Shanghai, and the breakdown of exports to Canton proved calamitous to the firm. In order to maintain their offices and warehouse in the face of limited incoming revenue, the partners began to draw on individual funds. Notwithstanding the financial crisis, no direct request for reimbursement was made of the sixth partner. He finally was excluded from plans involving a reorientation of the firm's activities.

To accept the statements made by the plaintiffs in both cases as adequate and complete explanations of their behavior would be misleading over-simplification. Overtones are apparent of more complex psychosocial factors influencing the motivations of those concerned. Nevertheless, the averred doubts and hesitations are indicative of some of the direct social pressures felt by these individuals under situational stress. No matter how justified their complaints, nor how unscrupulous the errant partners, even the wronged individuals have experienced misgivings sufficiently powerful to prevent retaliation or redress.

Rarely are steps taken which involve civil suits or, in more drastic cases, criminal charges. The former type of legal procedure has some incidence although it is still comparatively uncommon. The willingness to go to the American courts is to be found more frequently among the second-generation than among the China-born.

Whispers are still to be heard of a court trial in the 1940's which involved a well-known, highly respected member of a Cantonese-American community. He had been accused of embezzlement by the firm in which he was employed, a publicly registered limited liability company. The defendant was found guilty and served a prison term in a federal penitentiary. The very publicity given the case by the Chinese language press at the time of the trial, let alone the actual prosecution, may be regarded as atypical action in Chinatown. In discussion of the case, native-born as well as those coming from China deplored the public action involving the courts. Conviction of the embezzler, it was contended, brought not only shame upon his family but upon the entire community. A school teacher said in disapproval,

> It was bad enough when the story came out in the Chinatown papers, but when we read about it in the American papers, that was too much. Everybody in New York knew about it then. We were disgraced.

Punitive or protective measures employing extra-legal organizations have been popular in the past and still are reported. When two middle-aged, China-born brothers quarreled over the division of their restaurant's profits, conciliatory efforts by their father were of no avail. After a threat to his life, the elder brother sought the protection of the *Ih T'ien* Association by joining it. The *Ih T'ien* is one of the larger "tongs" with a territory in the mid-West and East. Two of its members visited the offending brother to "reason" with him. Taking warning, he fled to Chicago where he remained for ten months. Upon the younger man's return, he failed to establish contact with his brother, who had continued to operate the restaurant. A settlement involving the dissolution of the partnership was finally arranged, with the father acting as intermediary.[7] The settlement was by no means disadvantageous to the younger brother. The break, however, became complete in all respects—even to the point of contacts between the men's wives and children. Up to the time of the settlement, none but the closest friends on both sides of the controversy had been aware that dissension existed. Casual responses had been made to explain the brother's protracted absence. Later, a contrived story was circulated to account for his withdrawal from business association with his brother.

Even when a Chinese prefers to resort to the more direct, and perhaps more satisfying, governmental apparatus such as the police or the courts, dissuasion and constraints will be encountered, coming from those who follow the conventional channels of mediation. *Lo fan* ("foreign" or "barbarian") agencies, it is widely held, should be respected, but shunned.

A few intrepid individuals may take the initial steps, but few go beyond them to the ultimate conclusion of lawsuit and litigation. Such was the case in a quarrel involving a member of the Ng family who had disposed of his share in a Chinatown grocery. Although his ties with the store were formally broken, he still used it as a *ch'ut yap*, a "hang-out." One afternoon, the ex-partner, a man in his late fifties, entered the office of the establishment. Loudly he accused those present of having mulcted him of his holdings in the company. In anger, he pounded on the counter with his fists, directing most of his uncomplimentary remarks at the octogenarian major stockholder, main target of his vehemence. The latter's son approached the accuser from the rear, twisted the man's arm behind his back and forced him out of the grocery. Drawn by the shouting within, a crowd had collected and increased in number as the son moved the abusive man away from the store-front. Onlookers from the opposite side of the street watched with interest as the group of about thirty persons clustered around the two. The ex-partner shouted his grievances with triumphant indignation to all within earshot, interspersing his tirade with warnings to his captor to be careful lest his arm be broken.

A policeman was attracted by the commotion and approached the crowd. After some discussion, he led the two men off to the precinct headquarters, located a few hundred yards away from the scene. There, the ex-partner was booked on a charge of assault, with the complaint being made in the name of the grocery's bookkeeper, a man who had been present during the dispute. (The policeman later expressed surprise that a formal complaint had actually been filed:

> They don't usually go through with it. Usually it's enough when we tell them to keep quiet and take it easy or we'll run them all in.)

In the days intervening between the incident and the forthcoming court hearing, meetings took place among the leaders of the *fong*, sub-section of the family association, and those involved in the altercation. Elders of the association were also drawn into the discussions. All of the shareholders in the firm, including the ex-partner, bear the same surname and hence the use of the association as a mechanism for mediation was quite practical.

Association pressures were sufficiently strong to induce the bookkeeper not to press charges against his kinsman. The major contention of those who felt that court proceedings should be abandoned was that the family name had already been seriously injured. They insisted that court action could only result in additional undesirable publicity and damaging gossip. Disputes ought not to occur between relatives, it was maintained, but, if they should take place, their settlement should be made within the family group. One participant in these discussions later remarked that both parties in the quarrel had gained some face. The man who felt wronged had let the community know of his adversity and thus publicly disgraced his opponents. The opposite side was able at least to salvage recognition of the son as the defender of the aged and as a courageous avenger of unjustified insults to his father. Had he not humiliated his parent's attacker by parading the man through the community's main streets?

A close friend of the family was asked to account for the bookkeeper's seeming defiance of the majority stockholder in refusing to appear at the trial. Asked whether the bookkeeper had thus endangered his job, he responded, "Of course not. He's a shareholder, too. . . All of the Ngs lost," the family friend observed. "Only *Mut Kai* [8] came out winning. Lots to talk about now; lots to gloat over."

The settling of quarrels and disagreements between partners is not always complicated. Often the problem is handled in a direct, conclusive manner. Two partners with equal shares in a small business could not agree on its conduct. A stormy scene finally ensued and a few days were spent with scant conversation between them. It was at last decided to dissolve the partnership, with one man buying the share of the other. The full owner would have to assume complete responsibility for the policies he advocated. The ex-partner continued to work at his job, but now as a salaried employee. Both were obviously satisfied with the new arrangement which erased the discord that had threatened to disturb a close friendship.

Working Conditions

It has already been suggested that personnel practices in Chinatown are based, in large measure, upon familial and personal relations. Priority is given to relatives and fellow-villagers when a proprietor engages a staff of employees. Whatever the nature of the ties, they are frequently strengthened by the provision of room and board to one's workers. Most large shops have a cook whose task it is to provide meals for the entire work staff; when this arrangement is unfeasible, a restaurant may be used as a catering agent. A number of advantages are derived from this practice:

1. Employees, single men in particular, obtain some degree of regularity and convenience in eating arrangements.

2. Although a somewhat lower wage results when meals are supplied, there still remains some economic gain for the worker who otherwise would have to patronize restaurants.
3. The social nature of the meal is enhanced by the occasional visits of friends who dine with the entire group.
4. Since many proprietors prefer to dine in their shops rather than eat at home, their presence serves to emphasize personal ties within the group as a whole.[9] Solidarity and morale are more easily maintained, and work problems or differences of opinion may be aired, discussed, and resolved.
5. Eating on the premises obviates the need of regular lunch hours for the staff and makes them constantly available.

Personal life and economic activity become even more closely integrated when workers buy shares in the establishment where they are employed. This is encouraged by many owners who consider such transactions advantageous to themselves. Working capital for the enterprise is increased by the new investment. Obligations of the ownership under state workmen's compensation legislation may be decreased; payments made by the employer for other worker benefits will no longer be required. In addition to these perceived gains are a number of others which tend to be less overt.

The psychological conclusion of purchasing shares is the identification of employee with ownership. As a shareholder who will gain from the concern's profits, the incentive of the employee to work longer hours may be increased. Prestige as an "owner" and the newly acquired ideology of the entrepreneur tend to obscure those needs and attitudes emanating from the status of wage earner. This ambivalence is supported by the minimizing of rank distinction between employer and employee which pervades the varied work relationships in the *hua ch'iao* economy.

If economic position were separable from the other facets of societal life, it might be expected, in view of the predominantly pecuniary interests of the migrants, that upward social mobility in the overseas community would be an event of no great significance. Honors bestowed for social achievement abroad undoubtedly help build the prestige of the individual's family in Kwangtung; but such rewards, while satisfying to the other person and impressive to the group, are at best secondary, unanticipated, and unsought for features of the overseas venture. Modesty in aspiration notwithstanding, in the Cantonese-American community business accomplishment and increasing social influence are linked, and have their consequences not only for the prospering man but for those who work for him.

Men who achieve economic success, either in Chinatown or elsewhere in a city's environs, reach prominence in the *hua ch'iao* community, becoming active in the councils of the surname and regional associations and in the occupational guilds. With the increased participation of an employer in these groups, the worker's dependence upon him for social approval is intensified. The social necessity of conforming to local *Chinese* modes of economic behavior becomes all the more crucial as the employer acquires the status of lineage elder or quasi-governmental official. The process of upward social mobility for some thus has its effect upon those in the lower socioeconomic levels; clerks and other mercantile employees become enmeshed in job situations which discourage their joining unions. It is striking to note that, the existence of a highly developed American trade union movement notwithstanding, the traditional Chinese guild, comprised of employers and employees, still plays a decisive role with respect to wages, hours, and conditions of work. The social bonds of genealogical relationship and locality ties, rather than class identification, provide the framework for the *hua ch'iao* economy.

Conclusion

In a contact situation which has not been conducive to total "assimilation," the orientation of Cantonese-American economic life has been constrictive, channeling activity along lines approaching ethnic occupational specialization. A question raised elsewhere by Ralph Beals, "Does kinship sink into insignificance in the Chinese city?"[10] obtains here a negative response. At least insofar as North American urban situations are concerned, Chinese economic adaptation has been accompanied by a persistent adherence to many Kwangtung behavioral norms, especially those related to kinship.

In the still evolving Chinese-American subculture, retention and reconstruction of aspects of Kwangtung social structure have been major accommodating devices whereby the enclave community has exercised some degree of control over its immigrant and native-born population. Distinctive cultural characteristics have been perpetuated, others have been reinterpreted; some traits of the dominant culture have been adopted and others resisted. Kinship and quasi-kinship relations have played an important part in all of these cultural processes.

Notes

1. I. Schapera, *Married Life in an African Tribe,* Sheridan, New York, 1941.

2. Ralph Linton, "Cultural and Personality Factors Affecting Economic Growth" in B. F. Hoselitz, *The Progress of Underdeveloped Areas,* University of Chicago Press, Chicago, Illinois, 1952, p. 84.

3. Long-term investment plays a lesser role in Chinese economic history than the preference for ventures with rapid returns.

4. Richard P. Wang, "A Study of Chinatown Associations." A paper presented at the annual meeting of the American Anthropological Association at Toronto on December 30, 1948.

5. Gor Yun Leong, *Chinatown Inside Out,* Mussey, New York, 1936, pp. 26–52.

6. A prospective Chinese tenant of business space must pay the former Chinese lessee a fee. Even though the latter may not have occupied the place for some time and non-Chinese might have rented it in the intervening period, his rights of payment are still recognized. As each occupant vacates the site, the *po-tai* or "basic property right" is usually increased with the justification that goodwill has been augmented. Eventually the sum of money expected from a

new tenant becomes prohibitive, in some cases exceeding the annual rental. These transactions are made exclusive of the landlord, who usually is unaware of the demands being made on the prospective tenant.

7. The father later renounced this neutral position and also joined the *Ih T'ien* group. The younger brother then took to wearing black mourning bands. To solicitious friends and acquaintances who inquired of his grief, he would confide that he had lost a father. This was the first overt and decisive sign of a break in the partnership and family.

8. The Cantonese transliteration of Mott Street.

9. On the other hand, this practice also has a negative effect on family relationships. *Cf.* M. L. Barnett, "Some Cantonese-American Problems of Status Adjustment," *Phylon,* XVIII (January, 1958), 420–427.

10. Ralph Beals, "Urbanism, Urbanization and Acculturation," *American Anthropologist,* LIII (January–March, 1951), 9.

JEHOVAH IN THE CITY OF MAMMON: ON THE SOCIOLOGY OF ANTITHETICAL WORLDS

Manfred Stanley

During the 1880's, in urban America, there appeared a movement dedicated to a realm of meaning very different from that of the world of industrial secular modernism then in process of emerging. Since that time, these two worlds have gone their separate ways, each prospering, each utilizing the instrumentalities of secular technique to maintain the integrity of values almost totally antithetical to one another. Today the average men of industrial society stand before nature in the secular context of the will-to-power. Within their midst are men who believe this world doomed in a coming cataclysm of divine vengeance and who stand before a deity which has charged them with the mission of preaching his wrath and mercy to the people of a world hopelessly suffused with evil. How has it come to be that in the heart of an urban industrial society there can flourish two antithetical worlds of faith: one in machines, bureaucracies, weapons and secular progress, and the other in divine love and hate, sin and redemption, satanic greed and the cosmic justice of divine sovereignty? The movement referred to has come to be known as the Jehovah's Witnesses, and to account for their survival in urban America is the task of this paper.

The issue is of far more than simply esoteric interest. A crucial problem in social change theory is involved. Sociology itself was born amid speculation about recent social change as a seemingly unilinear movement from some traditional point of reference to a modern point of reference (e.g., Comte, Maine, Durkheim, Spencer, Toennies, Weber, Redfield). It is not clear in the case of most of these writers whether they felt that the process was in some way inevitable or irreversible. Durkheim sometimes wrote in his early period as if he believed it was, but in what sense was never clear. Subsequent to his work on suicide,

Written for this volume.

however, with its formulation of anomie, the problem of social unity and integration emerged as his central theoretical and policy focus. By the time of his work on religion, the realm of the sacred stands forth as a functional requisite of society itself, and Durkheim died with the conviction with which he began, namely that contemporary society is a stage of transition. Weber, whose notions of modernism as the intellectualization of nature and the rationalization of social relations form the most common basis for contemporary discussions, was far too astute a methodologist to arrive at any final explicit conclusion. But scattered throughout his writing are hints of a fear of historical closure to new sources of charismatic inspiration and, indeed, against human spontaneity itself.

In theories of urbanization one could find implications that modernization as urbanization was a unidirectional process, and in some quarters "urban" became virtually a synonym for "mass" in the modern industrial context. Within the last decade and a half there has arisen a counter-literature stressing the communal features of modern urban life,[1] but it is not yet altogether clear from these studies what is being asserted regarding the main theoretical problem of historical directionality as far as "modernization" is concerned.

Furthermore, because of the pragmatic and somewhat historically short-range orientations imposed by current interest in economic development, the term modernization has often come to be used in such a way as to imply that it is a single dimension of change or a set of dimensions which vary together. This implication has been strong enough to carry over into religious thought, so that many people assume that there is also a general movement from "orthodoxies," often thought of as pre-modern world-views, to "liberalism," usually defined as accommodation with "secular" (variously meaning urban, industrial, scientific, individualistic) world-views. Yet, a broader historical perspective serves to warn us that such extrapolation may be premature.[2]

It is problems such as these which lend theoretical importance to case studies of movements like the Jehovah's Witnesses. For this movement presents the interesting paradox of people animated by a radically anti-modernist theology utilizing some dimensions of modernist techniques and symbolism to protect the integrity of their world outlook and facilitate its use as a tool of conversion in the secular environment. Other movements of equal success are interesting for the same reasons, of course,[3] but it is difficult to find a theology as starkly anti-modern in its commitment and its logic as the dualistic perspective of the Jehovah's Witnesses. For them, despite all casuistic intricacies, there have always remained but two clearly identifiable realms: good and evil. And this has been sustained for more than eighty years as their primary message to the world. It is evident that the success of this movement poses some profound theoretical questions for sociology and for all those interested in social change and in the significance of consistency as a factor in cultural existence.

Method

It is obviously necessary and appropriate in an investigation of an organized social movement to speak of system problems, boundary maintenance and system survival. But unlike those in the mainstream of structural-functional theory, we wonder about the validity of beginning with the content of such "problems" assumed as theoretically given in the sense of the "functional prerequisities" argument. Without entering here into the wider ramifications of this controversy,[4] we note, however, that the sociology of religion has suffered from a lack of focus upon that which it presumably studies, namely the social distribution of religious meanings and modes of existential encounter with such meanings.[5] It seems to us advisable to approach problems such as norms, role definitions, allocation of facilities and the like only in the light, first, of meaning-contexts which form the justificatory frameworks for patterns of behavior and, second, the clashes of interests and credibilities between alternate contexts which form the basis for the problem of power.[6]

Accordingly, the social system problems of the Jehovah's Witnesses to be discussed below are deduced from the basic implications of their primary message to which they were and remain committed. These implications can be derived from viewing this message in the context of a modernist industrial-urban environment,[7] an exercise which leads to the conclusion that the major axis of relatedness between this movement and its environment must inevitably be one of mutual hostility.

Our data sources fall into four categories. The first and most useful is the literature of the Witnesses, including theological works, autobiographies by Witness members,[8] tracts and, most valuable for our purpose, the *Watchtower* magazine every single issue of which the writer has read from the first in 1879 up to 1960.[9] The second source was an unpublished undergraduate honors thesis by a student who carried out a participant-observation study incognito of a Kingdom Hall (local congregation) in New York City.[10] The third was a small number of individual interviews carried out by the writer with Witnesses in the Brooklyn headquarters some years ago and with assorted Witness proseletyzers over a long period of time. Finally, there are the few secondary works on the Witness movement by other observers.[11]

General History and Primary Message of the Witness Movement

The movement was founded largely by one man, Charles Taze Russell (known to his followers as Pastor Russell). He was of independent means and possessed by a desire for the "true" Christianity, having early rejected the traditional Christian dogmas on the basis of his claim that careful etymological study of the Bible indicated radical inaccuracies in translation. Originally he and his followers see themselves as a Bible study group devoted to objective investigation of the Greek and Hebrew sources of modern translations with a view toward systematically resolving perplexing problems which they claimed most Christians falsely assumed were answered for them by their churches. Russell personally was inspired by some of the doctrines of the Second Adventists and felt that they had grasped part of the truth.

He organized the *Watchtower* magazine (originally called *Watchtower and Herald of Christ's Presence*) of which the first issue appeared in July 1879, and set about writing down his ideas. His works, both articles and books, were to be voluminous and in them he worked out what he considered to be revelation concerning the future of mankind. Russell was a man of powerful charismatic force who enjoyed being with people and was possessed of strong convictions and abilities. In 1884 the Watchtower Bible and Tract Society of Pennsylvania was organized and this is a convenient founding date for the movement in a more formal sense.

Russell died in 1916, and since nothing is really known to outsiders of the internal political processes of the movement, all that we do know is that J. F. Rutherford, former legal counsel to the Witnesses, succeeded Russell as president of the board of directors of the Pennsylvania organization. He was a different type of personality than Russell, being rather quiet and withdrawn. In 1918 the main leaders of the organization were arrested and convicted by the United States government for sedition, although they were released from prison in 1919. The basis of the charge was the opposition of the Witness movement to World War I expressed in various forms of activity.[12] This was the lowest point in the history of the movement, and under Rutherford (who died in 1942), its development henceforth was toward reorganization, centralization and recovery.

Witness theology is intricate and worked out in voluminous detail. For our purpose, which is briefly to set forth their version of their primary message to the world, it is instructive to sketch in the main themes in two parts: pre-1914 and post-1914.

Russell and his followers identified themselves with the apocalyptic tradition of Christianity and predicted the year 1914 as the end of the "time of the gentiles" when Christ would descend again and Armaggedon would be upon the world. Jehovah, in his goodness, had sent Jesus to Man to pay the ransom price through his death by means of which Man might be redeemed. Thanks to this ransom, every man had the right restored to him of a chance for eternal life. Russell held that the "dead" were not really dead but asleep, and would be restored to life after Armageddon in 1914. After this event, the newly revived together with the living were to receive a second testing during a thousand-year rule of Christ on earth. Those who failed again would not be relegated to hell. The Witnesses, from the beginning, have vigorously rejected the doctrine of hell. Rather, the failed would truly die, never to live again. Man cannot be said to have an immortal soul; rather he himself is a soul, and under the judgment of Jehovah, he can die forever. Thus, for the Witnesses, no eternal life follows what they define as death.

Further, the time between the first and the second coming of Christ was one devoted to the gathering of the Remnant class of 144,000 (a biblical figure) who are to rule with Christ in heaven. Not all who accept and believe are members of this category, for salvation basically means immortality on the 'new earth' (a restored Eden). A close reading of Russell's writings and of the *Watchtower* suggests that in this period the distinction between the Remnant and the other saved categories was not of structural significance in the sociology of the movement itself. This was to change after Russell's death.

Finally, all secular life including the great religions are agents of Satan. Acceptance of Russell's doctrines meant total sectarian withdrawal from the world as we know it save preaching the dawn of a new paradise on earth. Indeed, the first call to mission appeared in the *Watchtower* in 1881.

Significant changes took place in Witness theology after 1914 in obvious response to the three severe crises which shook the movement: the failure of the prediction of Armageddon in 1914, the death of the charismatic founder in 1916, and the arrest and conviction for sedition of the leadership in 1918. Our summary of the Witness message as it evolved subsequent to these years is a composite of continuities from Russell's time, and innovations which emerged over a period of approximately two to three decades, with some of the major ones occurring in the 1930's. What follows is also, therefore, a summary of what contemporary Witnesses are encouraged to believe about the nature of the crises which beset the movement during the second decade of this century.

Man's fall through the sin of Adam was a direct result of a challenge by Satan (a fallen angel) against Jehovah for a cosmic duel. At stake was the loyalty of man and control of the universe. Satan built, for this purpose, an organization to combat that of Jehovah, and his Satanic social organization consists of the great institutions of secular society: political, social and also religious. The issue at hand is no less than supreme sovereignty over all reality. The purpose of History is the vindication of the challenged sovereignty of Jehovah over man and cosmos, for if Jehovah cannot command the voluntary loyalty of men, then it is Satan and not Jehovah who is Lord.

Jehovah has utilized History and the Bible as vehicles for the gradual revelation of his purposes. Christ was sent to earth within the context of this revelation, but Satan succeeded in corrupting the later Christians, and a mighty Satanic church was formed on the roots of Jehovah's revelation to the apostles—the Roman Catholic. However, the witness to Jehovah's purpose and vindication begun by Christ as the first perfect being has been continued through History by the enumerable sects which arose during the medieval ages and later.

In the nineteenth century a man named Charles Taze Russell was chosen to carry on the witness. The rule of the gentiles was drawing to a close and Jehovah's organization had to be constituted on a world scale if humanity was to be given a chance of survival. But Russell partially misunderstood the revelation concerning 1914, as did many of the early Witnesses. Jehovah's mercy was too great to allow Armageddon to come before all the peoples of the world had a chance to freely choose their destinies. What really occurred in 1914 was that Christ hurled Satan out of heaven and assumed the throne of heaven and earth in spiritual form. This great battle was marked "below" by the terrible upheavals associated with and deriving from World War I and which will never come to an end until Armageddon itself. The world is destined for cataclysm, destruction, war and persecution until the great apocalypse, when Christ will come to earth with all the hosts of Jehovah's kingdom to wage cosmic war against the legions of the damned.

The time between 1914 and Armageddon, for which there is now no announced date but which Witnesses believe is by no means far off, has been set aside through the mercy of Jehovah as a time of mission during which the Witnesses must wander over the earth proclaiming the fate of the world and the vindication of their Lord. Those that hear and believe, the "other sheep," may take shelter under the wings of the organization and will receive a new chance for eternal life. Those who hear and scorn will die never to be revived. With the apocalypse, the great cosmic duel between Satan's and Jehovah's organization will come to a final end. Satan will be vanquished, and those who survive through grace will inherit a perfect earth as originally intended for Adam. The Remnant 144,000 who will have been gathered gradually all through recorded History will ascend to heaven with Christ to rule.

Meanwhile Satan seeks to deceive the world by appearing to organize political means for the salvation of humanity such as first the League of Nations and now the United Nations. He seeks to corrupt the yearnings of people for Jehovah through false religions. Jehovah's Witnesses (the actual title was chosen by Rutherford in 1931) are endowed with just one mission, to preach Jehovah's vindication. They are not to pledge loyalty to any of Satan's institutions, neither are they to take up arms against them. For they are members of a new "nation," indeed a new world. They are to study their Bible (there is a special Witness version) and never to forget their primary mission despite all temptations. Theirs is a sacred trust, the greatest in the history of the universe.

This, then, is the primary message which the Witness movement has to deliver to the modernist environment in which it functions. It is, of course, a message of the movement, not of the individuals within it.[13] Not only has the movement survived into its second generation, but there have been massive upheavals during which struggles for power, mutual "excommunications," purges and other signs of conflict emerged.[14] Further, the defeat by 1938 of the "elective elder spirit" (congregational democracy) by the principle of theocracy means that the message is one formulated by an associational elite. Nonetheless there are many who appear to accept it throughout the world sufficiently to function as its agents (membership status demands a degree of active participation in mission work matched by few large-scale voluntary associations). And since the movement rather than the individuals within it is our unit of analysis, the manner in which the message is fashioned and articulated is not really a very relevant consideration so far as judging its potency in the environment is concerned. What is relevant is the manner in which its proponents, whoever they were at a given time, preserved the integrity and influence of the message in face of the multiple crises generated by the contradictions born of the dialectic between its inner logic and the history of the secular world. To this question we must now turn.

The Witness Movement as Social Meaning and Social System

To approach social systems from the standpoint of a fixed notion of system-problems seems to us to do justice neither to the complex empirical variability of human groupings and their circumstances, nor the intimate connections between goals and other meanings by which people live, and the fate of the associations created by people to express such meanings in the world. It is, of course, true that system "survival" can mean in some cases the attempt to perpetuate the association as a kind of community in the environment even after the original reasons for its existence have been nullified.[15] It is quite another matter to limit the definition of survival as a problem to this sense.

Indeed, one of the serious drawbacks of the sect-church typology in the sociology of religion has been that it obscures to some degree the connections between meanings and functional problems of social organization. The notion of sect-to-church transformation is sometimes regarded as simply a problem of organizational survival through "compromise," whereas the word "compromise" may be quite misleading for the interpretation of what is going on from the standpoint of participants in the movement at issue. Whenever a word like "compromise" is used, it is necessary to make clear whether it is an observer and/or a participant definition, and to what specific types of behavior or meanings the word is being applied. Had this always been done, one suspects that the radical doubt recently cast upon the utility of this typology [16] would have occurred much earlier. In the case of the Witness movement, it appears to us that the typology is misleading and therefore useless. More to the point is the question of how the primary message of the Jehovah's Witnesses, in the context of a modernist environment, created paradoxes which threatened both the plausibility of the message and the functioning of the association dedicated to its dissemination. Only from a consideration of such paradoxes (which should never be seen as constants but always as varying according to the message and the environment), can relevant social system problems be validly deduced. This exercise is set forth diagramatically in Fig. 1.

PARADOXES OF THE PRIMARY WITNESS MESSAGE

REJECTION OF THE ENVIRONMENT (HISTORICAL PESSIMISM)		MISSION TO THE ENVIRONMENT (ESCHATOLOGICAL OPTIMISM)
	SOCIAL SYSTEM PROBLEMS	
Aggression-against-environment		*Justification-in-environment*
	"Survival"	
Persecution-by-environment		*Defense-against-environment*
	"Integration"	
Symbolic-antithesis-of-environment		*Communication-with-environment*
	"Credibility"	
Segregation-from-environment		*Diffusion-in-environment*
	"Goal Achievement"	

FIGURE 1.

As is noted in Fig. 1, it is the combination of rejection-of-environment and mission-to-environment which generates the paradoxes that underlie the social system problems of the Witness movement. There are four such problems and the Witness solutions will be discussed separately for each.

Survival. In the present context, survival has reference to attempts on the part of agents of the larger environment to coerce the dissolution of the organization. The Witness message quite obviously constitutes an aggression upon the environment, branding it as the manifestation of evil and totally to be rejected. Yet the organization must somehow justify its existence within the environment against coercion defined within the Witness framework as Satanic retaliation. Cole lists 38 Supreme Court cases involving the movement between 1938 and 1955, states that from 1946 to 1953 members in Canada were involved in 1,665 prosecutions in Quebec, and cites examples of official persecution since World War II in seven countries of Eastern Europe.[17] Such examples of survival problems can be duplicated in the non-Western world as well wherever Witness mission activity existed.[18]

The predominant mode of survival technique exercised by the movement has been legalistic justification. Two of the major figures in the Witness elite pantheon have been legal counsels to the organization, one being Joseph Franklin Rutherford who succeeded Russell in 1917 as President of the Watchtower Bible and Tract Society until his death in 1942 and under whom the movement survived its crisis years. The other almost equally important individual was Hayden Cooper Covington who followed Rutherford as legal counsel in 1942. As of the year 1953, Covington had personally argued 41 major cases for his organization before the U. S. Supreme Court alone and had twice persuaded it to reverse its own previous decisions.

Further, although the members as individuals are not incorporated, all representation in North America occurs through legal corporate agents. These corporations are distinct although direction of the movement on the world level is coordinated by the leadership operating from the Watch Tower Bible and Tract Society with headquarters in Brooklyn, New York City. (This was the original Zion's Watch Tower Tract Society of Pennsylvania founded by Russell in Pittsburgh in 1884; it moved to New York in 1909. Members are encouraged to refer to their organization as the New World Society.) The movement is represented in England by the International Bible Students Association of Great Britain founded in 1914.[19] Control is effected, via the principle of theocracy, through a structure of branches in foreign areas and, in North America, through regional, zonal and local (Kingdom Hall) administrative divisions. The efficacy of this control apparatus varies in different parts of the world, being apparently most effective closest to home.[20]

Integration. The problems of integration for a movement bearing a message like that of the Witnesses are self-evident. However the major crises of integration did not really beset the movement until the second decade of this century. In the early stages, authority was firmly resident in a single charismatic figure,[21] and membership was often defined only in terms of a subscription to the early version of the *Watchtower,* all of which meant that the personnel of the movement were almost "invisible" to the surrounding environment, major doctrinal predictions had not yet failed, and membership was sufficiently limited to facilitate effective ceremonial occasions in which all could come together for mutual reinforcement.

But by 1919, the year the leaders were released from prison, the situation was desperate: the ranks of the organization were decimated, the charismatic founder was gone, finances and physical facilities seemed depleted, and the general mood of secular society at the end of the most destructive war in history to that time was hardly conducive to an apocalyptic interpretation of history. The response to these integrative crises can be summarized in two related categories of development: Formal reorganization of the movement rooted in a sacralization of the bureaucracy; and reconstitution of communication, ritual and doctrine to accommodate a widely dispersed membership in such a way as to both reinforce membership as pattern of behavior and protect personnel against erosive counter-stimuli from the surrounding environment.

Almost immediately following his succession to leadership, but especially after his release from imprisonment, Rutherford began to launch a vigorous attack against "creature worship" (the Witness version of Krushchev's "personality cult"). It appears that Rutherford always had a clear understanding of the charismatic sources of Russell's authority and recognized that he would have to substitute something in its place if the movement were to survive. A hint of what was to come appeared as early as 1923 in the Watchtower with the warning that officers are not to be considered *the* Society but servants *of* it.[22] The problem of the individual versus central authority had been brought home early to Rutherford by the Johnson affair. Rutherford had sent P. S. L. Johnson as a representative to England in 1916 to preach to the troops. While there, he allegedly attempted to usurp authority and, taking advantage of the confusion engendered by Russell's death, sought to enlist various English Witnesses to his own banner. There ensued a severe conflict over who were legally members of the board of directors of the corporation and hence had the authority to formulate policy in the eyes of secular society.

The details of the victory of Rutherford over his opposition are not, of course, publicly known. Suffice it to say that after Rutherford's authority was legally consolidated, increasing references began to appear in the *Watchtower* and other sources such as Rutherford's own voluminous writings, referring to the Society as the agent of Jehovah's purpose. Numerous letters from members expressing loyalty to the organization began to appear; their theme was renunciation of local decision-making and affirmation of the *Watchtower* as the legitimate source of doctrine.[23] Almost all these letters are addressed to the Society, and not to Rutherford which had not been the case during Russell's tenure as leader. During this period, however, the movement on the grass roots level was still organized somewhat democratically in that the local congregational officers were elected through voting.

But in 1938 there suddenly appeared a letter from London requesting reorganization of the movement as a theocracy,[24] and in the very next issue of the *Watchtower* the statement officially establishing the theocracy can be found. That this move, however, was not as spontaneously unanimous as the *Watchtower* would have had it appear is suggested by a long letter signed by Rutherford in a later issue of the same year, apparently in reply to an anxious inquiry from one of the faithful.[25] This letter contains the henceforth authoritative interpretation of the necessity of theocracy in light of the primary message of the movement. The exclamation point to this new policy appeared in the following issue of the *Watchtower* which set forth in detail the official role of the congregation-leader, including the warning that members are not to allow him too much time for summation of *Watchtower* doctrine.[26] The latter is instructive once it is recognized that it is in the process of commentary upon a doctrinal presentation that the greatest chance for individual and hence potentially schismatic interpretation occurs. The elapsed time between the first published proposal from England concerning reorganization and the final authoritative announcement was only four months. It would thus not be difficult to conclude that this was a campaign carefully planned in advance by an astute organizational elite. Thus the present theocratic structure can be officially dated from 1938.

Additional evidence of the social engineering involved in this reorganization lies in the transformation not only of the authority structure but of the entire sacred status system. It is a sociological truism that elites stand and fall according to the support they receive from the social structure they aspire to command. Thus, to some extent, elites try to adjust a social structure in their image, so to speak. That is, they aim at a structure that both consolidates elite power and makes it appear functionally necessary and hence legitimate. Such efforts are always circumscribed by the social system problems which set limits to what can be attempted. Thus, in the case of the Witnesses, these attempts had to be legal in the view of the environment, could not threaten the internal integration of the total movement, had to remain credible in justificatory ideology, and had to prove functional to the performance of the movement in the environment. There is evidence that the organizational elite carried out such a transformation within these limits by refining and operationalizing status distinctions inherent in the sacral world-view of Charles Taze Russell.

In Russell's early work there can be found the basis of a sacred status order applicable to the entire world.[27] There were apparently four approximate categories. Highest was the Sanctuary class, or those who knew themselves true believers and "dead with Christ," part of the 144,000. Second came the far larger group who were spirit "begotten" and "covenanted," the "Sheep." Third came those who were "justified but not sanctified," i.e., the true believers but definitely not part of the 144,000. Last came the "wolves in sheep's clothing" or those who had heard the message of Jehovah but rejected it. There is little evidence that these categories were operative in any social engineering sense since the movement was rather limited in size and integrated by the sense of the priesthood of all believers plus the common loyalty to a charismatic founder.

Subsequent to the years of crises, however, one begins to notice an increasing number of references to the status structure of the movement. The Remnant especially began to take on increased importance as a new elite. With the crystallized theology of mission of the New World Society, great emphasis came to be placed upon the role of those who had allegedly remained faithful through the period of doubt and dissension as against those who had faltered and failed. Already in 1919 the Society had begun to appoint one person in each congregation to represent it directly in organizing the work of "witnessing." This received divine justification from the doctrine of the coming of Christ as Jehovah's messenger to the "temple" in the spring of 1918 to separate the "faithful and discreet slave class from the evil slave group." [28]

The following, in general terms, appears to be the overall status structure which emerged during these later years.

The Remnant: a concept derived from scripture and referring to 144,000 persons who are to rule with Christ in heaven according to Witness interpretation.

The Jonadebs: those who have heard and accepted the message of Jehovah but are not to die with Christ but to remain on earth to live forever. They lack the special inner signs of revelation which distinguish the Remnant.

The Other Sheep: those of the world who have not heard the message but would accept it if they could. It is the mission of the Witnesses to reach this class.

The Damned: those who have heard and not believed. They shall be forever dead after Armageddon.

Despite these distinctions, it was maintained often that there is an equality of classes in the sense of the equal priesthood of all believers. In our interviews with individual members it was always held by them that these distinctions are unimportant, that "no one cares what you are except yourself." However, other observers maintain that there is a great deal of speculation and concern among Witnesses as to who falls into what category.

From the standpoint of sociological theory, one would expect a good deal of attention paid to status definitions in times of organizational crises, and it might be well to discuss briefly the logic of this assertion. As was stated, the distinctive sign of the Remnant is self-knowledge. This is a very selective criterion. As was said to the writer by one member, "if any doubt exists in your mind at all, then you are not one." Considering the awe in which this class is held by the rank and file Witness, probably few indeed would presume to claim the title for themselves. Those who do claim it would tend to be one of two kinds of people: the very devout and unworldly type who aspire to no particular earthly benefits from their status, and those who are possessed by a strong egocentric sense of personal mission and importance. A theocratic organization must protect itself against the ambitions of the second type while reaping the devotional loyalties and other benefits from the first. The second type could present a distinct potential threat to any established authority. Hence a central elite can most effectively protect itself only if it manages to counter-balance the potential threat of one segment of the social structure with one or more other segments. Signs of this technique can be found in the Witness literature.

In two issues of the *Watchtower* of 1932 there appeared clear operational statements of the rights and duties of each category.[29] The Remnant were defined as accountable directly to the Society itself whose instructions they were commissioned to carry out. To all intents and purposes this meant legitimacy of authority over the religious lives of all other categories of Jehovah's Witnesses. Theologically, the authority of the Remnant is rooted for the Witnesses in the position of Noah, and the Jonadebs were foreshadowed by those with Noah in the ark. This relationship is worked out in the *Watchtower* commentary cited above in specific detail with reference to the Jonadeb category. The salvation of the Jonadebs, it was now made clear, was conditional upon their obedience to the rules as laid down by the organization as the church of Jehovah. As it is the function of the Remnant to interpret to the Jonadebs what these rules are, and as it seems the Jonadebs have little to say regarding what these rules and interpretations shall be, this commentary signified the subordination of a majority of the members to a definite source of legitimized authority located within the local congregational level itself. A doctrine of conditional salvation of this type is, of course, an effective mechanism of social control.

The same commentary, however, goes on to provide for protection against usurpation of authority by the derivative elite, for the instructions to the Jonadebs include a virtual invitation to keep watch at all times over the orthodoxy of the Remnant as well. This invitation is in the form of the right of the local congregation to request the resignation of any who seem to possess the "elective elder spirit."

The policy of social control through status crystallization seems to have come to a head in 1945 in the form of a letter from Hayden Covington, the eminent legal counsel, removing himself from consideration for nomination to the post of vice-president of the board of directors of the Society on the ground that he did not consider himself a member of the Remnant class. On the basis of gradual "enlightenment" it now appeared to all, including himself, that officers as well as directors of the Society should be of the Remnant.

Thus we have traced a pattern of integration through system consolidation based on the combining of secular processes of professionalization with status distinctions rooted in a sacred world-view. It is, of course, an organizational history not very dissimilar from that of the Roman Catholic church except that, apart from the office of the papacy, the Roman church was laid out on a secular administrative model while the Witness movement achieved a functioning theocracy reflecting a sacred dualistic world of good and evil in the ideological and social context of secular modernism. This makes the Witness achievement something of an innovation in social engineering and one not compatible with the notion of "churchliness" since little evidence of "compromise" other than rhetorical exists regarding the integrity of the primary message, evidence which is plentiful in Roman Catholic history. How this achievement was possible carries us into considerations of boundary-maintenance beyond simple structural alterations.

Role structure is only one dimension of a total human community. As has always been recognized in classical social theory, the ritual dimension of behavior in which meanings are acted out are crucial to the maintenance of solidarity. The cultic problems attendant upon demographic growth and ecological diffusion within an urban environment are notoriously severe. Here again the Witness movement showed itself proficient in matching continuity and innovation in a blend capable of ensuring integration while preserving the core of the message. There seem to be five key elements in this process worth reviewing briefly in turn.

A) One key is the transformation of societal ceremonials into forms appropriate to an age of mass secondary interaction. There are two such important rituals. One is the so-called Memorial Supper which goes back to the days of Russell. It began as an annual event for which all members who could possibly do so gathered to be with their leader. The ceremony itself consists essentially of the passing, by a "pioneer" (a full time active member) of the body and blood of Christ to the congregation. Unlike Communion, which it resembles, it was an annual event, somewhat more elaborate, and was carried out in one place in the presence of Russell. The event was of powerful integrative emotional significance for Russell's followers and remains so.[30] As the movement grew in size, and especially after Russell's death, it was no longer possible to hold the ceremony in one place. Rather than abandon this important cultic asset, it was decided to alter it. With the organization of the Kingdom Halls, the local "congregation servant" began to take over the primary duties connected with the ceremony, and the ritual detail was tied in with the growing centralization of authority.[31] This signified the development of two related trends by means of which the ceremony was preserved and yet utilized for solution of the new integrative problems: a liturgical orientation was being evolved ensuring standardization, and the *Watchtower* was becoming the actual vehicle of standardization similar to the Missal in the Roman church.

The second ceremonial is the famous conventions of which the first was held in 1893 in Chicago. The convention system has been elaborated into a series of local, national and world events with considerable publicity in the secular environment. They are models of expertise in infra-structural organization and their integrative functions are too evident to warrant detailed analysis.

B) A second key to communal integration is the institution of the *Watchtower* itself. The journal has never missed an announced issue since its inception. It continued publication even after the arrest of the leaders in 1918. This magazine, reaching out in forty languages, required reading for all members on direct order of the Society, is the major channel of communication. It contains long discussions of religious topics written in an intimate discursive style, letters from Witnesses on every topic from questions of doctrine to personal experiences, "official" replies to questions of doctrine, and hints, suggestions and announcements pertaining to almost every aspect of Witness life. In addition, its use in semi-liturgical ceremonials gives it a special emotional-religious importance for the individual which no publication used in a purely rational communicative way can do. In it, the individual member sees his duty and functions in Jehovah's organization as clearly interpreted for him by the Society.

C) A third integrative mechanism has been the special esoteric terminology with which ritual communication is carried on. It is a sociological truism that all political and ideological movements have their specific terms which have standardized functions of sometimes almost purely emotional rather than cognitive significance. The Witness movement is no exception and, properly understood, its terminology has definite reference to its theology. Some examples are "accurate knowledge," "rock-mass," "inhabited earth," "The Lord's Evening Meal," "sacred secret," "declared righteousness," "the elective elder spirit." In addition there are words and phrases which, though in common use, denote and connote special meanings for Witnesses. Among such are "truth," "born in the truth," and "evil." Such esoteric language has at least three integrative functions. First, it isolates the speaker from those around him who cannot understand what he is referring to. Second, it is a filter through which the speaker sees the world and is different from all other filters. Third, it binds the speaker together with other speakers as possessors of an esoteric knowledge understood only within the community of meaning. This enhances the self-image of the speaker as a member of an elite in the environment.

D) A fourth integrative factor is that complex of meaning-elements in the Witness message which together constitute a self-image which each member shares with others. There seem to be three such themes. The first is the notion of the "representative-role" derived from the Witness theology of mission. Cast in this cosmic role of the messenger of Jehovah, the individual member is invited indirectly not to worry too much about the particular status differentiations in his own organization. Sprague had this in mind in his commentary on the New World Society theology.[32] The sacralization of an organizational bureaucracy, he suggests, functions to reduce the likelihood that the members may perceive themselves as groveling before the authority of mere mortals, thus reinforcing the representative-role image by removing the paradox of divine missionaries subservient to mortal authority.

The second theological element is the revival of the notion of persecution as a historical theory of martyrdom. The Witnesses, it must be remembered, trace their movement back not to Russell but to Christ and thus identify themselves with all the known persecuted sects such as the Arians, the Waldenses, the Lollards, the Hussites, etc., each of which could claim a part of the total revelation as to Jehovah's purposes which are now to be fulfilled through the Witness movement itself. This notion of persecution as a divine sign of favor is not innovation but it operates with apparent effectiveness in lending a sense of drama in cosmic proportions to a group only ninety years old.

The third theological element is the emphasis on militaristic esprit-de-corps and the notion of the world as enemy. During periods of persecution, Witness literature abounded with descriptions of Armageddon stressed with utmost attention to detail. The military role of Christ was emphasized with barely suppressed savor. Under the rubric of Satan's organization appeared clearly all the classes, individuals and institutions which had earned the hatred and perhaps envy of the disinherited and unfortunate.[33] The theme of the common enemy played a role in welding together people whose perception of themselves as a chosen elite might perhaps otherwise have dimmed under the pressures of scorn. The common enemy was variously "far below the standards of perfect human nature"[34] and "unbearable to decent human beings."[35] In face of such an enemy, how many stood before their Society and said, "I thank God. . . . for your love for the little army in the field."?[36] It is hard to say, especially in these present days of shared terror when peace-of-mind themes replace many of the class enmities of yesterday.[37] But it is not difficult to imagine the integrative comforts of the military metaphor when the world seemed more simply divided between the chosen and the outcast, and the ancient Christian promise of the "first shall be last" still found resonance in experience.

E) Finally, there were those occasional Durkheimian rituals of ostracism which reinforce the existence and visibility of a normative order. These have diminished in significance of late, or at least it has not been considered necessary to utilize the *Watchtower* as the sounding board. But earlier, traces of this mode of integration could be found there.[38]

Credibility. When a message such as that of the Witness movement is carried into an environment whose cognitive and normative coordinates threaten at every moment to reduce the plausibility of the message to absurdity, the problem of credibility becomes serious both for the fate of the message and its missionaries. What aspects of Witness activity appear functionally relevant to this problem?

Even a cursory exposure to the movement's style of communication in the environment is sufficient to impress one with the camouflage of Weberian rationality which conceals the anti-modernist core of its message. We have already noted the legal-rational expertise with which survival was ensured in whatever environments lent themselves to this technique. This proficiency with secularist symbolism is evident in many other ways as well. Few organizations are as adept at allocating resources for the manipulation of modern communications technology.

Notable here is the function of *Awake* magazine. Unlike the theological orientation of *Watchtower, Awake* is concerned with many fields of knowledge from government, history, geography, through "natural wonders." [39] To the uninitiated, it appears more than anything else like a current affairs journal. *Awake,* with its "objective" reporting, its familiar secular interests (it has carried articles on such diverse topics as control of cockroaches in the kitchen and cloth dyes) seems to serve as a kind of credibility-buffer or shock-absorber that blunts the effects of the radically non-secular and unfamiliar doctrines of Witness theology. Surely, it seems to say, a people so sophisticated in the "ways of the world" must also have reason to believe as they do in the realm of religion, however strange at first sight their beliefs may appear. The movement is equally adept with the organization of radio communications. Sophisticated techniques of role-playing and virtually Jesuitic standards of rhetoric are standard features of missionary training.

Most striking, in a way, is the Witness emphasis on rational bookkeeping and appeal to secular pseudo-scholarship. For an organization which releases no membership rolls, no dues lists, nor any other information of real use to the sociologist, the movement turns out seemingly endless sets of statistics. Theological writings are replete with meticulous detail in the computation of various dates and doctrines. From the standpoint of the secular scholar, this concern with quantification in the larger context of speculation and imagination can only be called pseudo-scholarship. This characteristic extends to the keeping of records. There are hardly any round figures quoted in Witness reports. Total number of hours spent in the ministry in the United States in 1953, for example, was quoted as being 21,978,943 hours. In Western Samoa, 3,873 hours in the ministry were claimed.[40] All formal organizations keep records, and accuracy is one of the major mystiques of a rational "bookkeeping" society. The Witness organization is highly adept at this "mystification through quantification" which conceals even as it seems to reveal.

Another example of this appeal to credibility is the constant reference to secular scholarship which seems to appear more in recruitment literature than the theological core writings. Recruitment literature is the "cutting edge" of communication with the environment. Thus, it seems recognized that to the uninitiated, and perhaps to many of the initiated, it is important if a noted secular biblical authority claims that the concept "soul" has been mistranslated whereas the truly initiated presumably recognize the Satanic origin of all non-Witness claims to scholarship. The uninitiated would be impressed when men as noted as

President Sukarno and General Eisenhower comment upon the world's woes;[41] the truly initiated are supposed to know that even if no man living recognized the impending Armageddon, it would nevertheless come about since Jehovah has willed it. And certainly no true Witness is supposed to care much if the Satanic non-Witness scholars "give the Bible the highest rating as the world's finest literature" or say that it "surpasses the writings" of Homer, Cicero, Pindar and Plato.[42]

Goal Achievement. The goal of this movement is the perpetuation of Jehovah's message and its dissemination to the four corners of the earth until all men have had the chance to freely choose their destiny. For this, a community must be preserved capable of sufficient segregation to ward off doubt and ensure absolute conviction, but capable too of sufficient diffusion in the world to bring the message to those who await it. Peter Berger has expressed this problem recently in succinct terms worth quoting here:[43]

> The socially produced world attains and retains the status of objective reality in the consciousness of its inhabitants in the course of common, continuing social activity. Conversely, the status of objective reality will be lost if the common social activity that served as its infrastructure disintegrates.

In short, goal achievement is possible only through the maintenance of community. The key to community among the Witnesses is the institution of the local Kingdom Hall.

In her participant-observer study of a Kingdom Hall in New York City in 1954, Schwartz[44] has provided a detailed picture of the inner life of one such congregation, sufficiently rich to outline the process of socialization into the movement. The individual who has already become sufficiently interested to seek to learn more about the Witnesses is first introduced to a Bible-study class. These groups usually contain a few expert missionaries to answer questions, and it is in these groups that the deeper processes of recruitment begin since in them the prospective Witness learns the Bible thoroughly and his initial confidence is reinforced through the gradual implantation of his missionary role. Apparenly, then, these study units are of strategic significance in the socialization process.

A good part of the formal aspect of the congregational meeting is taken up with a combination of liturgical recitation and mutual criticism of rhetorical presentation. Schwartz reports a strong emphasis on common participation circumscribed by a constricted range of legitimate commentary (the *Watchtower* is the constant standard).

Various opportunities exist for the individual to broadcast cues to the leadership that he is ambitious for upward mobility in the movement. The first step is vigorous involvement in and facility with the general question-and-answer periods, since this requires considerable preparation at home. Further, there are innumerable little functional groups such as the cleanup committee, the subscription crew, the book study conductors, field service teams, etc., which offer opportunities for visibility to the interested individual. (Stroup claims that Witnesses are keenly aware of status differentials and watch the progress of particular individuals with considerable interest, for it is commonly recognized that no significant appointment such as Congregation Servant Assistant is made without specific approval from superior authorities such as the Zone or even Regional Servant.) Gifted individuals are sent on to the Gilead School for full time mission personnel and are prepared for a career in the movement. As is commonly known, however, contrary to most voluntary associations, there are very few apathetic Witnesses. The movement has experimented self-consciously and vigorously in ways of combining the principles of professionalization with optimum retention of the priesthood-of-all-believers psychology of common involvement and action.

Schwartz was not able to gather systematic data about the social history of the members of her congregation, but her comments suggest considerable difficulty with arriving at any significant generalizations. Our own personal experiences with Witnesses and observations at Yankee Stadium conventions inspire equal caution, especially with the older sociological hypotheses about links between sect membership and socio-economic deprivation, at least as far as present patterns of membership is concerned. Schwartz observed many lapsed Catholics, Protestants and some Jews among the membership of her congregation and heard a number of reports about defection from the movement, especially among second generation members. The only generalization she felt safe in advancing was that theological conviction was not at equal pitch among all the members and that the anti-anomic participation dimension of life in the movement had to be considered as a powerful explanatory variable in the social-psychology of affiliation. To move beyond this would require data not yet possible to gather.

Summary and Conclusions

This case study was presented in support of an argument that the sociological neglect of the infra-culture of social existence in the great metropolitan centers of modern society is theoretically fallacious. There are reasons for suggesting, at risk of exaggeration, that the Witness movement is one of the most significant religio-political phenomena since the rise of the Roman Catholic church. For while the latter arose in an environment not uncongenial to its ontology, the Jehovah's Witnesses repeated part of this success, with innovations, in a science-oriented environment allegedly almost completely hostile to its basic assumptions about reality. History suggests that if the scientific neglect of such movements in the heartland of urban modernism continues, we may perhaps learn of such matters more by surprise than by design.

Our analysis implies that the Witness movement in North America may be regarded as something of a triumph in social engineering. The basis for this achievement seems to lie in four related features:

a. Refined legal skills possessed by a lawyer-elite.

b. Virtuosity in the use of modern techniques of communication.

c. A technique of social organization which achieves complete centralization in combination with a de-centralized opportunity structure for upward mobility in place of the de-centralized decision procedures associated with congregational democracy.

d. A primary message which is apparently not so implausible even in a very diluted Christian environment as to be totally incompatible with secular events. The apocalyptic tradition has always been a latent theme in Christendom and has its secular representatives in social theory. The Witnesses have chosen to specialize in this option and seem to have found that for many people, events can be explained in this manner at least as well as in the liberal-secular outlook which increasingly seems at odds with current trends even for those not prone to apocalyptic theologies.

The future of such movements, then, should be seen as providing important clues to the possible transmutations of the modern mentality, much as the Gnostic sects of old foreshadowed the crises of modernism among the ancients.

Notes

1. In England this literature is associated with the names of Bott, Young and Wilmott, J. C. Mitchell, and Frankenberg. In the United States, Gans and Lenski among others may be noted in this connection.

2. In the history of Western civilization, the rise of the Gnostic sects is instructive. *Cf.* Hans Jonas, *The Gnostic Religion,* Boston: Beacon Press, 1958.

3. *Cf.* Bryan R. Wilson, *Sects and Society,* New York: Oxford University Press, 1961, and Thomas F. O'Dea, The *Mormons,* Chicago: University of Chicago Press, 1957.

4. *Cf.* N. J. Demerath III and Richard A. Peterson, eds., *System, Change and Conflict: A Reader on Contemporary Sociological Theory and the Debate Over Functionalism,* New York: The Free Press, 1967.

5. The author is in general agreement with the position set forth in Thomas Luckmann, *The Invisible Religion: The Transformation of Symbols in Industrial Society,* New York: Macmillan, 1967.

6. Exegesis of Parsons' social theory is always difficult, due both to its richness and the frequent opaqueness of his writing style. However two tendencies of Parsonian sociology are being questioned here. One is the degree of analytic separation of the "cultural" realm of life from the "social" and "personality" realms. This separation, especially in view of Parsons' stakeout of the "social system" as the focus for sociology proper, has made it difficult to build bridges between structural-functional sociology and the newer tendencies toward phenomenological analysis of social behavior which seeks to approach society itself as levels and fields of meanings, *among which* are the models of the scientific observer. (This does not mean, it should be added, that we feel there to be *no* distinction between culture and society. Rather the issue of how they interpenetrate in concrete behavior is not as simply disposed of, in our view, as the Parsonian division of labor would have it.) The other questionable feature of Parsonian sociology is the emphasis upon societal integration and equilibrium with its correlate vocabulary of deviance. This realm of theory is currently undergoing rapid alteration. And here too, it is not helpful to apply to the Witnesses the terminology of deviance. It is sufficient to point to the problems raised for them by *their* particular way of looking at the world in light of the

relative credibility of world-views in the present context of Western intellectual history. And we deirve our social system problems from this examination. It follows that were one to study the same Witness movement in a completely different environment, such as Asia or rural Africa, one might find oneself dealing with quite different social system problems. At least this should be left to empirical determination and not to some pure inner logic of functionalism. Having said this, however, we should note as well how deeply this present analysis is inspired by much of the theory and insight in Parsons' work.

7. For the present purpose, such an environment may be defined by way of four factors: large ecological scale, wide demographic dispersion, heterogeneity of stimulus fields, and—following upon such centrifugal variables—a certain political self-consciousness born of vulnerability to threats of disunity. This environment is dominated by scientific technology and its mystique, plus bureaucratic social organization which together have made possible the emergence of the four variables to which social movements like the Witnesses must adapt themselves.

8. The most useful of these turned out to be a full-length volume by a virtually life-long member who wrote it in his eightieth year, A. H. Macmillan, *Faith on the March,* N. J.: Prentice-Hall, 1957.

9. This material is available in the main (42nd Street) branch of the New York City Public Library. It is next to impossible for an outside observer to obtain access to Witness archives. However, because of the peculiar functions of the *Watchtower* detailed in the text of this essay, it is an unusually rich source of data (albeit of a "top of the iceberg" variety) for an analyst with a command of social theory in organizations and social movements.

10. Miriam Schwartz, *Jehovah's Witnesses: Study of a Religious Sect,* unpublished Bachelor of Arts Honors Thesis, Department of Sociology and Anthropology, College of the City of New York, 1954.

11. *Cf.* Milton S. Czatt, *The International Bible Students: Jehovah's Witnesses,* Yale Studies in Religion #4, Scottsdale, Penna.: Mennonite Press, 1933. Herbert H. Stroup, *Jehovah's Witnesses,* N. Y.: Columbia University Press, 1945. Werner Cohn, *The Jehovah's Witnesses as a Proletarian Sect,* unpublished Master of Arts Thesis, Department of Sociology, New School for Social Research, 1954. Marley Cole, *Jehovah's Witnesses,* N. Y.: Vantage Press, 1955. Theodore Sprague, "Some Notable Features in the Authority Structure of a Sect," *Social Forces,* March 1943. Theodore Sprague, "The World Concept Among Jehovah's Witnesses," *Harvard Theological Review,* April 1946.

12. The details are summarized in Cole, *op. cit.* Chapter VII. Cole is a good source for certain kinds of details despite his apparent bias in favor of the movement which leads him to accept Witness statistics uncritically.

13. One way of ascertaining an elite's awareness of social system problems is to look for evidence of deliberate "re-writing of history," measurable by close textual analysis of different editions of the same published works. We have not recorded this type of data, but it is a technique recommended for anyone wanting to penetrate the internal dynamics of a movement by means of its published documents.

14. For one example of the kind of data on which observers must rely in the study of conflict within quasi-secret societies, very similar to the clues which constitute "Kremlinology," see the record of the "Salter" affair in the *Watchtower,* May 1, 1937, and the letters in some subsequent issues of that year.

15. David Sills, *The Volunteers: Means and Ends in a National Organization,* Glencoe, Ill., The Free Press, 1957.

16. *Cf.* Allan W. Eister, "Toward A Radical Critique of Church-Sect Typologizing," *Journal for the Scientific Study of Religion,* Volume VI, #1, Spring 1967, pp. 85–90.

17. For details, *cf.* Cole *op. cit.,* pp. 179–89, 194–206.

18. *E.g.,* J. R. Hooker, "Witnesses and Watchtower in the Rhodesias and Nyasaland," *Journal of African History,* Volume VI, #1, 1965, pp. 91–106.

19. The corporate framework is outlined in Cole, *op. cit.,* pp. 173–79.

20. *Cf.* Hooker, *op. cit.,* and note 14 above.

21. See for instance any of the issues of the *Watchtower* prior to Russell's death and note the style of letters to the editor. Also, a good example of the impact of the death of a charismatic figure is provided in Macmillan, *op. cit.,* p. 61.

22. *Cf. Watchtower,* March 1, 1923.

23. *E.g.,* letter in *Watchtower,* June 15, 1925.

24. *Cf.* letter in *Watchtower,* August 15, 1938.

25. *Cf.* letter from editor in *Watchtower,* November 1, 1938.

26. *Cf. Watchtower,* December 1, 1938.

27. Charles Taze Russell, *Studies in the Scriptures, Volume I,* pp. 235–38.

28. For an application of this doctrine to the training of the ministry, see the Witness volume, *Qualified to Be Ministers,* 1954.

29. *Cf. Watchtower,* August 15th and September 1st, 1932.

30. *E.g.,* Stroup, *op. cit.,* p. 146.

31. In 1939, one year after the establishment of theocracy, there appeared an essay on the Memorial Supper (*cf. Watchtower,* March 15) in which it was stated that if there was no one present qualified to deliver a brief discourse before partaking of the emblems, then someone should read aloud either that article or another one directly from the Watchtower.

32. Sprague, "Some Notable Features. . . ." *op. cit.,* p. 345.

33. For a striking example of the class conflict variation of the Armageddon doctrine, see Czatt, *op. cit.,* p. 30. That Russell himself shared some of this class consciousness is suggested by a passage in his volume, *Thy Kingdom Come,* p. 23.

34. *Cf. Watchtower,* April 1897.

35. *Cf. Watchtower,* April 1933.

36. *Cf.* letter in *Watchtower,* October 1929.

37. The interplay between peace-of-mind themes and aggression in Witness writings and recruitment literature in particular is interesting to note. Typical

recruitment pamphlet titles during the 1950's included, "Can You Live Forever in Happiness on Earth," "This Good News of the Kingdom," "Healing of the Nations Has Drawn Near," "The One Hope for Peace," and "Hope for the Dead." These are all largely peace-of-mind themes with little expression of aggression to be found in the pamphlets. An apt summary of this type of appeal occurs in a Witness volume entitled *Let God Be True,* 1952, Chapter on "The New Earth." Further, the writer's experience with Witness proseletyzers suggests adeptness at utilizing secular threats like atomic war, overpopulation, race problems and so forth as part of the theological framework of analysis of history. That the theme of aggression is not dead, however, is indicated by occasional striking passages in various places, as for instance *Let God Be True,* p. 258, and *New Heaven and a New Earth,* 1953, p. 359. Without research directed specifically toward the issue, it is naturally difficult to evaluate the success of such carefully planned missionary communication. But it is perhaps not without significance that a close friend of the writer, whose judgment he considers trustworthy, relates an encounter some years ago with a couple on board ship bound for Europe who claimed that they were going to Europe with the sole intention of converting their parents to the Witness faith. The husband was a relatively high corporate official in an oil company and had an excellent income. The writer has himself encountered a dedicated Latin American Witness who was a graduate student in an American university's graduate school of business administration. Such isolated incidents prove nothing but, like the Cadillacs at Yankee Stadium Witness conventions, invite empirical attention to the dynamics of mass public mentality as argued for recently by Philip E. Converse, "The Nature of Belief Systems in Mass Publics," David E. Apter, ed., *Ideology and Discontent,* New York: The Free Press, 1964, pp. 206–61.

38. *Cf.* for one example, the affair of Mr. Salter who was accused by the leadership of forgery, fraud and disobedience, recorded in issues of the *Watchtower* beginning May 1, 1937 and extending through some of the subsequent issues in 1937.

39. *Cf.* the statement "The Purpose of Awake" in every issue of *Awake.*

40. *Cf.* Cole, *op. cit.,* pp. 220–21.

41. *Cf.* the recruitment pamphlet, "Healing of the Nations Has Drawn Near," 1957.

42. *Cf.* the Witness tract, "How Valuable is the Bible," 1957.

43. Peter L. Berger, "A Sociological View of the Secularization of Theology," *Journal for the Scientific Study of Religion,* Volume VI, 1, (Spring, 1967) p. 10.

44. Schwartz, *op. cit.*

URBAN STRUCTURE IN FRANCE

Theodore Caplow

This report is principally concerned with the recent work of European investigators, and represents an attempt to bring their findings into the perspective of urban ecology as we know it in this country.

The first studies by American sociologists of metropolitan communities outside the United States began to appear only a few years ago.[1] They demonstrated clearly that the modern patterns of the Latin American city were derived from a colonial formula marked by rigorous city-building specifications, both legal and customary. Generalizations based upon our own cities, which have been characterized by violent and irregular growth, by very little planning or construction control, and by speculation in land values, are not applicable elsewhere in the hemisphere. Thus, for example, North American cities almost invariably exhibit a rough correlation between the status of residents and their distance from the commercial center, as well as decreasing residential density toward the periphery. These gradients are usually reversed in Latin America. The more subjective aspects of urbanism also appear in a different light south of the border. A considerable degree of community integration and cultural stability may often be found within the semi-autonomous structure of the *barrio*.

We have often proceeded on the assumption the American city illustrated the normal urban configuration and that Chicago epitomized the American city.[2] Although the literature of urban sociology includes an impressive amount of fragmentary material on foreign cities,[3] it was difficult until recently to cite a single ecological study of a European city, that is, a study in which the object of analysis is the functional entity composed of a social structure in a particular physical setting.

It seems to the writer that such research is crucial to this specialty at the present time. A good many principles can be formulated on the basis of the great mass of more or less ecological research published in this country, but we do not know what degree of generality to attach to them. It is still impossible to determine which of the recorded phenomena are local accidents and which are essential to the urban way of life.

Until quite recently, urban sociology had only a shadowy existence on the Continent. In part this indifference seems to have stemmed from the identification of sociology as a branch of speculative philosophy, which still inhibits empirical research everywhere in Europe. Then too, the scarcity of funds and facilities for empirical work has scarcely been favorable for large-scale team projects.

Despite this persisting handicap there has been an impressive development of urban research in France (and elsewhere in Europe) in the few years since the war.[4] Among recent publications are the survey of Auxerre by Bettelheim, Frère, and their associates,[5] the work of George, Agulhon, Lavandeyra, Elhai and Schaeffer,[6] on the suburbs of Paris, the migration analyses of Chevalier,[7] and the

Reprinted by permission of the author and publisher from *American Sociological Review*, **17** (October, 1952) pp. 544–550.

charting of ecological distributions by Bardet.[8] Among the significant studies in progress should be cited the interesting work of Jean LaPierre in the Marseille region, and the monumental study of the "social ethnography" of Paris by a team headed by P. H. Chaumbart de lauwe.[9] Meanwhile, and beginning somewhat earlier, the human geographers have developed an impressive literature on dwelling types, the distribution of economic functions, and the evolution of street plans—including the methodologically valuable work of Tricart and his students in Strasbourg.[10]

These data are still limited and somewhat disconnected, but taken together, they permit certain tentative statements about urban structure in France:

(1) The familiar ecological principles which explain urban structure in the United States do not adequately account for urban structure in France.

The degree of centralization in France appears to depend upon a variety of local circumstances, but is always less marked than would be expected in an American community of comparable size. It is not a function of increasing community size in any regular relationship and, in the major metropolitan areas, there is some evidence that centralization has declined since the Middle Ages. Schaeffer and Chaumbart de Lauwe are able to demonstrate the absence of any single point of concentration in Paris,[11] and the absence as well of the radical daily movement of population which characterizes Chicago.[12] Instead there is a sort of general spiral movement, inwardly directed, but without convergence to a central point, and the volume of this spiral movement appears to be diminishing.

The maximum height of buildings in French cities has been limited at least since the fourteenth century, and the only skyscrapers in the country are in semi-suburban housing projects. When to this factor are added the extreme durability of construction and the historical autonomy of specialized urban districts, it is easy to understand why invasion and succession are not conspicuous aspects of the French pattern.

Indeed, without the influence of uncontrolled land values, spatial distributions in France are often singularly inexpressive of social structure. The writer has studied a community of moderate size in Southern France which, almost at first glance, shows an unusually distinct social cleavage and an equally marked physical division. Yet, upon careful examination, the association of the social structure with the spatial pattern is found to be quite irregular. Neither the distribution of the population by social class, nor the distribution of institutions by class affiliation, conforms to the fundamental spatial division of the community or to any other precise demarcation.[13]

Dispersion of population is similarly inconspicuous in the French city. There is no uniform tendency for density to decrease toward the periphery, even in Paris with its long history of expansion. Finally, there is no reason to believe that as the urban population increases, the average density of settlement within the urban community decreases, as happens in Minneapolis or Dubuque. The point has not been made more often only because dispersion of population is readily confused with suburbanization. Many French suburbs are of ancient origin: Nîmes, for example, must have been extensively suburbanized in Roman times. These suburbs, however, do not seem to be associated with a continuously declining density in the central city.

A tentative explanation can, perhaps, be approached by a return to the topic from which urban sociology originally sprung—a consideration of land values. Differential land values are sharply limited in France by the limitation of building heights, which has been continuously enforced for centuries. In many cities variations of land values are further restricted by the presence of historical monuments, palaces, churches and parks, which are almost completely immovable, in what might otherwise be a central commercial district.

Without the sorting out of land-uses and population types under the influence of differential land values, questions of ecological location take on an entirely different significance. The siting of slums, factories, ethnic colonies, or apartment houses cannot be explained in simple monetary terms. The real estate market can no longer be regarded as the principal agency regulating urban growth and no equally simple mechanism takes its place.[14]

The variety of structure found in European cities is not fundamentally explicable in the elementary terms of zonal analysis and density gradients. Any serious attempt at comparative ecology would require the substitution of a whole range of determining factors for the monistic land-value device which works so well on the American scene.

It should be noted in passing that the dominance of land values over site-determination is no longer what it used to be even in the United States. The constriction of central business districts, the deconcentration of industry, the suburbanization of the lower income groups, and the vast expansion of urbanized areas in the last twenty years, all tend together to increase the number of alternate locations for any particular group or function, and therefore compel us to pay increasing attention to more subtle factors than the straightforward compulsions of land-value.

(2) Rural-urban migration in France has not depended upon the growth of the total population, and mobility of the urban population has not been a function of expansion of the urban population.

The inadequacy of the blanket concept which equates varieties of behavior ranging from status achievement to migratory farm work under the general heading of social mobility is nowhere better illustrated than in the social history of France since the Revolution.

As everyone knows, the population surge which has since overtaken the rest of the world came to France and ran its course early, so that even without the catastrophic losses of World War I, it would have been the first Western country to show an absolute decline of population. The demographic history has actually been somewhat more complicated than this suggests, but it remains true that no civilized area had so limited a growth of population after 1800. (The relative stability of population and a certain stability of resources account perhaps for the great rigidity of social classes, and for the preservation of rural and village subcultures throughout the country.) What emerges surprisingly in the studies of Bettelheim and Chevalier is that none of this interfered with a very high rate of internal migration. For centuries the Himalayan isolation of the provincial town has been a literary and popular theme in France. However, the survey of Auxerre, a provincial city of 30,000 selected on a series of neutral criteria similar to those used in the selection of Middletown, "revealed the falsity of the stereotype of the procincial city, isolated, closed in, and maintaining a minimum contact with the exterior."[15] They found instead that three-fourths of the population were not native to the town, that 92 percent of all married couples included at least one non-native. It should be remembered that this refers to a community whose population has not increased sharply since 1801.

Similarly, Chevalier is able to show, using documentary sources which any American investigator would envy, that throughout the nineteenth century the proportion of Parisians born in Paris remained at about one-third, that in-migration (in concordance with Stouffer's intervening opportunity hypothesis) was based on real differences in wages and working conditions, was specialized by occupation by region, and was directed from each province toward particular sections of the metropolis.

(3) A third finding which may be drawn from the French data is that France —and perhaps Europe generally—presents more alternative types of urban settlement than can be found in the United States; more varieties of internal adaptation, of spatial patterning, of architectural structure, and of change. This may be only an elaborate statement of the obvious, but some of its implications are interesting.

It is difficult to estimate the extent to which the physical uniformity of our own cities has colored our general view of the urban environment. It is probable, for example, that many of the features of the conventional ecological diagram depend in large measure upon an undifferentiated gridiron plan, with almost uniform street design and essentially temporary buildings.

French cities show a much greater variety of forms. Of the types of street plans and block arrangements described by Lavedan[16] only a very few are commonly utilized in this country. Thus, only one of our large cities has a radial plan; none, to the writer's knowledge, shows the separated sector plan, the fish-bone plan, a system of related terraces, a regular elliptical plan, or even a ribbon pattern. (The case of Duluth, Minnesota, where a gridiron plan has been imposed on a steep precipice, is fairly representative.) In addition to the variety of formalized plans, European cities are conspicuous for the variations occasioned by widely-separated periods of growth.

Even apart from the walls and fortifications, the historical squares and formal gardens, the canals, and other specific antiquities, the sheer diversity of spatial patterns in French cities points up, by contrast, the startling uniformity to which we are accustomed from Maine to Texas. Thus, the *modern* streets in Paris include some which are much wider and others which are much narrower than any streets in New York. We are unfamiliar, in the United States, with the double street, the covered street, the pedestrian street, or the stairway street. Such a simple device as the arcading of a shopping area is uncommon in this country, although arcades would be far more functional in Minneapolis than in Toulouse. Much the same thing may be said of the numerous forms of the public place, the park, the promenade, the patio, the riverfront quai, the bridge, the hillside terrace, and most important, the family dwelling unit.

(4) The fourth finding from these studies has to do with the continued social viability of the *quartier*, in both large and small cities, although not in all of them.[17]

All of the investigators of the Latin-American city have been struck by the former significance of the *barrio* as a community of identification and as a functional unit, and have documented the disappearance of its autonomy within the last generation or so. As the writer has noted in a report on Guatemala City,[18] if we arrange the Middle American cities on which ecological information is available by size, the rank order of size will correspond to the rank order of disappearance of *barrio* autonomy and differentiation.

The French situation is far more complex. Anciently, all cities of any consequence were divided into quarters, and these survive in the largest cities (Paris, Marseilles, Lyons), in many of the middle-sized cities (Nice, Poitiers), and in some of the smaller ones. Throughout France and the Low Countries, differentiation by *quartier* seems to be even more conspicuous than in modern Latin America.

The *quartier* is in a real sense a community. Fully developed, it has its distinct appearance, its local industry and commerce, its housing forms, family types, collective attitudes, formal associations, and often its own dialect and folklore. The *quartier* tends to be clearly demarcated even where it does not correspond to an administrative division. In Paris, where the *arrondissement* is both an administrative and an electoral unit, some *arrondissements* like the XVIth and the Xth correspond to *quartiers*, others do not.

It appears that *quartiers*, once fully developed, tend to be exceedingly stable, perhaps more so than rural settlements. Thus the Faubourg St. Antoine, the Latin Quarter, or the Temple, retain local traditions which have been continuous since very early times. Whether such a tradition can survive in a peripheral district is less certain. One of the two suburban studies previously cited traces the development of a recognizable social type in a low-rent public housing project,[19] another documents the disappearance of community indentification in a dormitory suburb.[20] Even in the latter case, however, what remains is a greater intensity of interaction than we should expect to find anywhere in an American city. This is likely to remain so as long as the separation of home from workplace is far less complete in France than in the United States.

(5) It appears very clearly from the analysis of foreign studies that there is no framework of general categories into which knowledge of particular cities can be fitted. With an increasing volume of studies from many parts of the world [21] such conceptual vagueness becomes increasingly wasteful. Studies of foreign cities will soon have served their initial purpose of widening the perspective of American scholars, but this can hardly be justified as their sole or principal objective. Merely as "political arithmetic," information about the urban settlements of the world has immediate value. Because each city is a social configuration of some importance, the classification of data on individual cities has a double function—preservation of particular local data in convenient form, and the formulation of generalizations which will hold for given conditions, regardless of locality. But unless different studies accumulate data in more or less standard form, neither the descriptive nor the experimental possibilities of comparative data can be developed.

It is obvious that any scheme for the construction of an urban profile, applicable to any urban agglomeration, must take into account a number of factors which lie in the usual province of geography. Thus a possible division of the material might run as follows:

(1) Gross Characteristics—Population, Area, and Density
(2) Locational Elements
(3) Site Elements
(4) Migration and Spatial Mobility
(5) Ecological Structure
(6) Social Structure

This is by no means a logically inevitable schema but it may serve to indicate the general area which must be included in such a profile. It will be noted that each of the six categories contains items conventionally drawn from the academic provinces of both sociology and geography.

Thus, the measurement of density should include both land density and room-crowding. Locational elements include natural water routes as well as the delineation of service areas. Site elements, although largely geographic, will include a specification of housing forms, which are culturally imposed. The comparative study of migration can scarcely ignore the effect of the distribution of resources upon the selection of migrants. The analysis of structure, which involves close study of distributions of all kinds, requires techniques which combine cartography and statistical reporting. Even the description of social structures include such geographic elements as are necessary to establish the relationship between behavior and the physical setting in which it takes place.

It might well be maintained that the need for a close liaison between sociology and geography in the study of city life existed from the beginning, and that the curious insulation of the two literatures from each other is an unfortunate accident. Actually, however, there seem to have been a number of cogent reasons for the separation of the field of urban studies into two compartments. In the first place, the general uniformity of urban plans in the United States had somewhat the effect of holding the physical setting constant. In the second place, the immediate objectives of the earlier studies somewhat transcended the description of particular communities.

At the time of its introduction, urban sociology was devoted to the demonstration of such matters as the fundamental orderliness with which social characteristics were distributed in space, and with the importance of sub-cultural differences within the apparently unstructured urban milieu.

These points well established, little remains of the original objectives to which the early studies were directed. Nevertheless, a change of focus is never easily achieved. Recent research has continued to follow the traditional paths with progressively more esoteric terminology, and progressively less interesting results.

It would appear from both foreign and domestic data that the most promising future for urban research lies in the comparative description and analysis of urban places. If this is so, sociologists and geographers interested in the city might do well to abandon their mutual distrust in favor of active cooperation.

Notes

1. See, among others, Norman S. Hayner, "Mexico City: Its Growth and Configuration," *American Journal of Sociology,* L (January, 1945). "Criminogenic Zones in Mexico City," *American Sociological Review,* XI (August, 1946). Asael T. Hansen, "The Ecology of a Latin American City," in E. B. Reuter (ed.), *Race and Culture Contacts,* New York: McGraw-Hill, 1934. Harry B. and Audrey E. Hawthorn, "The Shape of a City: Some Observations on Sucre, Bolivia," *Sociology and Social Research,* 33 (November–December, 1948). Theodore Caplow, "The Social Ecology of Guatemala City," *Social Forces,* 28 (December, 1949).

2. With the launching of urban sociology as a specialty, Burgess wrote, "In the United States, the transition from a rural to an urban civilization, though beginning later than in Europe, has taken place, if not more rapidly and completely, at any rate more logically in its most characteristic forms." Ernest W. Burgess in "The Growth of the City: An Introduction to a Research Project," *The City,* Chicago: University of Chicago Press, 1925.

3. Two of the older textbooks and a recent treatise have been the sources usually drawn upon for European material: See Niles Carpenter, *The Sociology of City Life,* New York: Longmans, Green, 1931. Pitirim Sorokin and C. C. Zimmerman, *Principles of Rural-Urban Sociology,* New York: Henry Holt, 1929. Robert E. Dickinson, *City Region and Regionalism,* New York: Oxford University Press, 1947.

4. A useful summary of the present state of knowledge and research in this area will soon be available in the published proceedings of the Deuxième Semaine Sociologique held in Paris in March 1951. Georges Friedmann (ed.), *Villes et Campagnes: Civilisation urbaine et civilisation rurale en France,* Bibliothèque Générale de l'Ecole Pratique des Hautes Etudes, 1952.

5. Charles Bettelheim and Suzanne Frère, *Une ville Française moyenne: Auxerre en 1950: Etude de structure sociale et urbaine.* Paris: Armand Colin, 1950.

6. Pierre George, "La banlieue: une forme moderne de développement urbain"; Maurice Agulhon, "L'opinion politique dans une commune de banlieu sous la Troisième République. Bobigny de 1850 a 1914"; L. A. Lavandeyra, "Saint-Maur-des-Fossés"; H. D. Elhai, "Les H.B.M. de la Porte d'Aubervilliers"; R. Schaeffer, "La répartition géographique du personnel d'une grande usine de la banlieue parisienne." Published together as *Etudes sur la Banlieue de Paris,* Paris: Armand Colin, 1950.

7. Louis Chevalier, *La formation de la population Parisienne au XIX siècle,* Presses Universitaires de France, 1950.

8. Summarized in Gaston Bardet, *Le Nouvel Urbanisme,* Paris: Vincent Fréal, 1948.

9. Organized under the general heading of "Ecologie de l'Agglomeration Parisienne," the project is the work of a social ethnography team housed at the Musée de l'Homme (Centre d'Etudes sur la Région Parisienne) under the

general sponsorship of the Centre d'Etudes Sociologiques. The methods used in the construction of base maps, and the recording of long-term and diurnal population movements represent, in the opinion of the writer, a distinct refinement of current American practice.

10. J. Tricart, *L'Habitat Urbain,* Volume 2 of his *Cours de Géographie Humaine,* Paris: Centre de Documentation Universitaire, 1951. This volume, strongly Marxist in its interpretation, contains an excellent general bibliography of urban geography.

11. *Op. cit.,* p. 7.

12. Gerald Breese, *The Daytime Population of the Central Business District in Chicago,* Chicago: University of Chicago Press, 1951.

13. Aix-en-Provence. The city, which has a population of 27,000, is characterized by extreme social differentiation. The number of *rentiers,* professionals and white-collar persons is high, and they are as a class, extraordinarily secure, while at the same time the working class is extremely solidary. The community possesses a small university, a court of appeals, limited health resort facilities, some local industry, a medical center, some suburban functions, and serves as a market center for a very large rural area. About 40 percent of the electorate are communist; nearly the same number belong to parties of the extreme right, including a substantial royalist faction. Public opinion studies show an almost complete dichotomization of opinion. The real separation of these two halves of the community is illustrated by the tendency to double all institutions. To match the middle-class university, there is a strong "popular" extension university; the theatres, the bus-lines, and the restaurants are as unequivocally segregated as they might be under a caste system. The religious activities of the Church are matched down to such details as lotteries for school children by the parallel activity of the Communist Party.

The community is topographically divided as well, into an Old Town and a New Town, separated by the principal street. The Old Town conserves the medieval street plan and has many 14th century houses, while the New Town, designed under Cardinal Mazarin is an early example of "modern" city planning, with broad rectangular streets, architectural unity, and a partial greenbelt.

14. The functioning of the real-estate market in France is admirably described in Jules Romains' novel *Men of Good Will,* in connection with the career of Haverkamp.

15. Bettelheim and Frere, *op. cit.,* p. 258 (above translation by the present author).

16. Pierre Lavedan, *Geographie des Villes,* Paris: Gallinard, 1936.

17. It is significant that we lack an English word with the same meaning. The *quartier* is larger and far more definitely defined than the *neighborhood,* although McKenzie used *neighborhood* in this sense in his pioneer study of Columbus and it is what most of our census tracting is designed to get at.

18. *Op. cit.*

19. Elhai.

20. Lavandeyra.

21. Note, among others, the Lund Studies in Geography, published by the Royal University of Lund in Sweden, especially Series B. No. 3; Edgar Kant and others, *Studies in Rural Urban Interaction,* 1951; the work of Rene Koenig and his students on conurbanization in Switzerland; recent papers in *Plan* (*Schweizerische Zeitschrift für Landes, Regional und Ortsplanung*); Fr. Houtart, "Urbanisme, science sociale," *Les Dossiers de l'Action Sociale Catholique,* Bruxelles: February, 1950.

AFRICAN URBAN FAMILY LIFE AND THE URBAN SYSTEM

Peter C. W. Gutkind

Although there are some significant landmarks in the history of sociological and anthropological studies of African urban life, such as Hellmann's *Rooiyard* study in 1939 [1] and Wilson's work in Broken Hill published in 1941–42,[2] it is only recently that we have entered a far more creative period of research and orientation. To understand this we must look back a little.

In the first case, while nowadays African urban studies are generally conducted by social anthropologists, an earlier generation of fieldworkers, as Gluckman has pointed out, were "reared on the rural tradition of the tribe." [3] Indeed, Audrey Richards reports:

> In 1931 I first left the under-populated bush inhabited by the Bemba of north-eastern Rhodesia to study the men and women of this tribe who had migrated to the copper mining towns to the south. My conduct was then thought rather unusual in a social anthropologist. I was even told by one of my professors not to meddle with those modern urban problems, but to stick to "really scientific work" in an unspoilt tribe! [4]

Likewise, the whole outlook of colonial policy and administration, particularly in ex-British East Africa, supported the view that an urban habitat for Africans was basically unsuitable and undesirable. Thus, in 1955, the *East Africa Royal Commission Report* pointed out:

> The theory of indirect rule as well as personal inclinations of many administrators led to a concentration on the development of rural tribal societies rather than the training of an educated elite, and also to the view that the town was not a suitable habitat for a permanent African society: there has, indeed, been a tendency to look on the westernized African with suspicion. The towns have, therefore, been regarded rather as bases for administrative and commercial activities than as centres of civilizing influence, still less of permanent African populations.[5]

Reprinted by permission of the publisher and the author from *Journal of Asian and African Studies,* 1 (January, 1966), pp. 35–42.

If we combine these two approaches, it becomes clear that anthropologists had neither the inclination, nor did they receive any support, to work in urban areas in Africa.[6] But there were additional reasons why it has taken some time for anthropologists to view urban communities in Africa as legitimate areas for research. Perhaps the simplest explanation is that, with the exception of certain West African urban areas, the towns of Eastern and Southern Africa are of very recent origin and were, until recently, inhabited predominantly by non-Africans. Thus, it might be argued, field research opportunities were limited and, combined with the non-African character of the towns, anthropologists were not particularly interested in studying Europeans or Asians. They could study the former in the metropolitan countries and the latter in Asia proper.[7]

More fundamentally, however, it seems to me, anthropologists supported a vague recognition that they lacked the conceptual orientation and the methodology as both were likely to differ from their basically rural interest and experience. In many ways this is still true although it is the view of this writer that we have made very creditable progress.[8] Finally, perhaps the greatest obstacle that had to be overcome, and still acts as a substantial brake on the development of a more extensive and broad coverage, is the view that anthropological studies are by definition confined to non-industrial societies and that African urban studies do not significantly contribute to "pure" theory building. Professor Clyde Mitchell, one of the few who has combined traditional anthropological research with a major interest in the new urban communities of the Rhodesias, has discussed the "Paucity of Urban Studies in Africa." He concludes that "probably the greatest opposition comes from those who look upon urban studies as being somehow concerned with administrative and social problems. . . ."[9]

What, then, accounts for an increased interest, and some of the significant developments in, African urban research? I think the explanation may be obtained from the very traditional interests which social anthropologists have had in rural people and rural-based institutions. Thus, while few anthropologists have shown any inclination to follow the migrant African on his temporary urban sojourn, nevertheless many research workers noticed that the habits, ideas, and social organization of city life were having some modifying influence on the institutions of the rural people. Likewise, few anthropologists could ignore that even without extensive labor migration, subsistence economies were not infrequently supplemented by income from cash-cropping, wage employment in mines, on plantations, in industry generally, and in commerce or administration. In short, what was inescapably evident was that town and country were being rapidly linked by means of complex new forms of association. This in turn seems to have led to the recognition that the development of urban life, in those areas of Africa where cities came into being with colonial expansion, was part of a far more fundamental modernization, the effect of which was to transform African societies as a whole.

Possibly the first response to this recognition was to ignore and set aside the small urban communities on the grounds that they were strongly atypical. They were certainly not recognized as possibly representing early models which were likely to influence African society ever more strongly. After all, in Eastern and Southern Africa, colonial rule was still very much in the saddle and political agitation, now strongly concentrated in the cities, had hardly begun in the interwar years.

Yet another response of these anthropologists showing an interest in migrant workers and the spread of modernization [10] was to view urban resident Africans as essentially rural-oriented tribesmen in a strange and new setting; [11] a setting which certainly did not warrant the kind of close inspection devoted to a rural people whose culture and society revealed an intricate and complex institutional arrangement. Of course, it is true, that urban communities are of a different order, that the parts which comprise the whole are arranged in a different manner. Perhaps this arrangement is less neat and tidy, perhaps it is more amorphous, perhaps there is less regularity and predictability of behavior and organization. Nor can we view the urban community, certainly not those of larger scale, as a "microcosm of culture" as we can an isolated village as basically representative of the ethnic and linguistic unit of which it tends to be an intimate part. But these are matters which are being studied now with a fresh mind and increased precision.

It is the view of this writer that the social structure of African urban areas is not a mere modification and adaptation of a rural model. Urbanism in Africa, as elsewhere, is a distinct way of life productive of distinct urban institutions which exert strong pressures on individuals and groups alike to act as urban men. Thus, as Gluckman has pointed out, we are dealing with townsmen in towns and not with tribesmen in towns.[12] This formulation has helped us immeasurably to achieve that vital breakthrough which alone is the source of greater creativity. However, at this stage, what is needed is systematic documentation which gives body to this approach. The recent work by Pauw [13] and Mayer [14] in particular has given us an excellent start as have contributions by Epstein [15] and Banton,[16] Southall [17] and Mitchell.[18]

I should like to suggest in the remainder of this paper that the institutions and behavior of urban Africans, whether of recent or short urban residence, whether they constantly circulate between town and country as the Ganda of Uganda do, or whether they are urban residents of 10 years or more, can be analyzed in terms of two formative processes. First, the polarization based on tribal and ethnic identity—social/psychological processes—in an *urban context* and, secondly, the polarization based on a distinctive urban style of life, namely economic and political processes. Perhaps this characterization is a complementary approach to Mitchell's analysis of the causes of labor migration [19] which demonstrates two characteristics: centrifugal forces and centripetal forces; the former taking people away from the rural areas and the latter drawing them back to these areas. In many respects these two characteristics are a very marked feature of African urban life for it is a common characteristic of African cities generally to pattern their institutions in such a manner that opposing tendencies exist side by side. This has certainly been demonstrated with considerable clarity by virtually all the authors mentioned earlier as well as Powdermaker,[20] Elkan [21] and, more recently, by Leslie.[22]

As far as African urban family life is concerned, I would like to suggest that polarization based on local and ethnic identity may predominate in the nexus of family and face-to-face neighborhood relations. On the other hand, polarization around distinctly urban behavior and organization increasingly dominates African urban family life whereby non-local and non-ethnic associations are functionally more appropriate.[23] I believe that the conditions which produce this polarization are mutually dependent and compatible, and contribute to social and economic stability of urban family life. Neither does polarization appear to be significantly related to either length of urban residence, education or income. Yet over time an African urban family may be more strongly influenced by ethnic and local identity than attitudes and behavior which reflect "urbanism as a way of life." But even among this latter group distinctly ethnic values still find support. Thus, Pauw,[24] studying the urban-born Africans in East London, South Africa, found that certain traditional values, such as boys' initiation and *lobolo,* still had considerable "emotional" importance contributing to the status and role of the African urban resident who knew no other social environment but urban life.

The families which I studied in the peri-urban African area of Kampala,[25] the *kibuga,* constantly moved back and forth from the world of association based on kin and ethnic similarity and familiarity, to participation in groupings which cut right across such association, particularly in economic and political activity and leisure pursuits. To understand this one must have a clear appreciation of the two important networks of contact and reciprocal relations which are at work.

Family life, kin ties, neighborhood associations, or a group of friends are all constituted and bounded by a small-scale social field which is explicitly designed to assist and meet the needs of those, who of their own free will, have come into association, or those whose social position is fixed as, for example, young children under the protection and guidance of parents, siblings, or other kin in important reciprocal positions. In such a world, the core of cultural and social activities (i.e., intimate social and psychological processes), is the cement of the social networks which act as support, protection, and guidance of the individual and the group alike.[26] Identification based on kin, culture, language or religion takes precedence, be this in the East-End of London or in Lagos, Nigeria, over the continually changing large-scale environment, participation in which is determined by quite different, if not less important, demands. Thus, while the tribal community is often an isolated and culturally self-sufficient unit, the urban community has no real independent existence being invariably part of a far wider system of a regional, national, or international nature. In this kind of world the scale of the social field is determined by modern economic and political processes and polarization of activity takes place around these. Each town, anywhere, gives expression to these processes under a distinctive yet variable urban style of life. Above all, in the local community, decisions which affect its life are taken by members who are known to one another. Not so in the larger social field of urban life, the structure of which is largely determined by agents external to it. Thus, while the social-psychological processes give the African urban family the opportunity to adjust to a new social environment, the urban institutions provide the same family with the opportunities of educational and economic mobility. But in either world, Africans resident in towns are not merely rural residents transplanted who seek a conscious modification of rural ideas and habits suitable under new conditions. Rather, where, for example, tribalism prevails, or tribal settlements come into being,[27] the reason is that this form of association is as purposeful a part of urbanism and a style of life as it is for a New Yorker not to know his neighbor.[28] Both styles of life meet certain expectations. Both styles of life are not incompatible with their opposites, i.e., the increasing importance of non-tribal and non-ethnic based associations in Africa, or the neighborhood association aiming at a development of neighborliness and face-to-face contact in a New York City housing development.

What practical alternative does an African migrant laborer have on arrival in an urban area? What is the most intimate and protective form of association for him at the moment? It is almost certain to be the tribe. Leslie, in his *A Survey of Dar es Salaam,* writes: "A more compact community from which the immigrant is never completely divorced is his tribe." [29] It is in this context that the polarization based on small-scale units as part of a larger social field, the tribe or kin, becomes an adaptive mechanism, as well as being a constant in any social order, in a way quite similar to the role of the voluntary associations described by Little, particularly in West Africa.[30]

However, the urban world represents a different yet complimentary network of relations. It is a world of goods and services, of mobility and chance, of opportunity and failure. It is a world whose people shape their universe, very assuredly, yet who have only limited control of its influence over them. To many observers-interpreters, this influence is highly undesirable: an influence away from the ordered small-scale world to the bedlam and anarchy of the urban jungle. But this alleged jungle has as many adaptive and supporting characteristics as the kin group or the small-scale urban voluntary association.

This is so because, in the first case, an urban area is itself the creation of those who seek a different social order. Man is the creator of the kind of habitat which combines opportunity with choice, determinism with free will. Secondly, the large-scale social field of the urban area offers scope for the kind of activity which is the force behind modernization.[31] Quite clearly the range of choice of job and style of life in an urban area is immensely increased.[32] The individual freed from the economic and political control of the tribe creates the kind of institutions which will help him not only to adapt and adjust but also to consolidate and expand distinctly urban ways. And, in this regard, every townsman, however short his urban sojourn, leaves a cumulative imprint. Indeed, some observers might offer the view that the forces of modernization are so strong that over much of Africa the townsman is more important than the countryman as the former may act as a "reference group" to the latter.[33]

These two social fields then, and their innumerable sub-fields, provide the basis of African urban family life. Convergence and separation of these fields is constant. Or, to put it another way, small-scale group activity needs the large-scale social field for individuals and groups to achieve new goals. Likewise, a large-scale social field largely depends on the existence of smaller and more intimate social ties to provide the kind of environment in which units such as family, kin and neighborhood can and do operate. In this sense detailed analysis of African urban family life can provide us with a wide range of data relating both to theory and basic documentation of the kinds of institutions and patterns which comprise the African urban system. Taking the view I have suggested, it becomes far clearer why the urban-born Africans of East London continue to value and operate traditional institutions, or why some African white-collar workers have allegedly completely rejected traditional rural ways of life. If we study the latter group, more careful investigation will reveal that the values and habits of a small-scale tribal society have been replaced by the values and characteristics of small-scale modern urban values which do exist. The contracted urban family unit, largely divorced from its wider kin ties, and despite the difficulties it faces, gives ample evidence of an intimate world of feelings and values based on individual choice of partners, the devotion of parents towards the needs and aspirations of children and the whole range of new activities which, for lack of a better word, might be described as home making.[34] In my experience, some of the social problems which so startingly mark African urban life[35] are themselves an indication of the extent of individual freedom and choice in search of the kind of social environment which allows for a more certain and stable order. And this is the order of the small-scale field. If this sounds naive and lacking in sophistication and the handling of concepts, I would merely suggest that this is so because, as Epstein has observed, the African urban world still seems to present us with a "kind of phantasmagoria, or succession of dim figures caught up in a myriad of diverse activities, with little to give meaning or pattern to it all."[36]

There might be many who would contest the view that African urban areas are complex social systems necessarily comprised of innumerable sub-systems which operate in such a manner as to support the whole of which they are a part. This is not a wishful interpretation of mind or fiction, or a stubborn adherence to currently contested anthropological and sociological theory,[37] but rather a conclusion born of simple observation. The one great characteristic to which we must point, which is a major difference between Africa's new urban areas and those of the Western world, is the transitional character of much of what we see in cities such as Kampala, Nairobi, Leopoldville, Salisbury or Beira. But would anyone seriously contest the view that the older urban areas of Nigeria, for example, exhibit a well-established social structure and social relationships which have regularity and corporativeness? If we concede this to be so, then all that is required is further explanation of these relationships as they are being established in the newer urban areas of Africa. For is it not so, that wherever men congregate they must and do establish a working system which is designed both to allow for cooperation and for conflict.

The family, in Africa as elsewhere, is a sensitive barometer of change. It is also the "microcosm of culture" whether the family be in an urban or a rural context.

Notes

1. Hellmann, E., *Roøiyard,* Rhodes-Livingstone Papers 13, Capetown, O.U.P., 1948.

2. Wilson, G., *An Essay on the Economics of Detribalization in Northern Rhodesia,* Rhodes-Livingstone Papers 5 and 6, Livingstone, Rhodes-Livingstone Institute, 1941 and 1942.

3. Gluckman, M., "Tribalism in Modern British Central Africa," *Cahiers d'Etudes Africaines,* No. 1, 1960, p. 56. See also: M. Gluckman, "Anthropological

Problems Arising From the African Industrial Revolution," in *Social Change in Modern Africa,* A. W. Southall (ed.), London, O.U.P. for International African Institute, 1961, pp. 67–82. M. Gluckman, "From Tribe to Town," *Nation* (Sydney) No. 53, September 24, 1960, pp. 7–12.

4. Richards, A. I., "Foreword," in *The Royal Capital of Buganda,* by P. C. W. Gutkind, The Hague, Mouton, 1963, p. ix.

5. *East Africa Royal Commission, 1953–1955, Report,* Cmd. 9475, London, H.M.S.O., 1955, p. 250. See also: Gluckman, *op. cit.* 1960, p. 56.

6. I believe the same can be said of Portuguese, French and Belgian scholars. However, it is quite possible that very considerable information was collected by colonial administrative officers which has never seen the light of day. For example: E. C. Baker (District Officer), *Memorandum on the Social Conditions of Dar es Salaam,* June 4, 1931. Typescript in my possession.

7. There is still a great need to study the non-African communities in the major cities of Africa. The work by the Sofers (*Finja Transformed*) and Gussman (*Out in the Midday Sun*) are exceptions. No published studies of which I am aware exist on the Goan in East African cities or the Syrians in West African urban areas.

8. It is obvious that we have finally turned our backs on the mammoth African urban social survey. Of these numerous exist although, even today, a good case can be made for surveys of the smaller urban areas. As is well known, African countries have one or two large urban areas, but a large number of small "townships" in the under 5000 population category. We know little of them. The best examples of the creditable progress made, the theoretical problem orientation studies, are: A. W. Southall (ed.), *Social Change in Modern Africa, op. cit.,* P. Mayer, *Tribesmen and Townsmen,* Capetown, O.U.P., 1961, H. J. de Blij, *Dar es Salaam,* Northwestern University Press, 1963, B. A. Pauw, *The Second Generation,* Capetown, O.U.P., 1963, A. L. Epstein, "The Network and Urban Social Organization," *The Rhodes-Livingstone Journal,* No. 29, June 1961, pp. 29–62.

9. Mitchell, J. C., "Theoretical Orientations in African Urban Studies," Paper presented to the Association of Social Anthropologists (U.K.) on The Anthropology of Complex Societies, Cambridge, June 29, 1963 (mimeographed).

10. In this regard an early work of great distinction was: Schapera, I., *Migrant Labour and Tribal Life,* London, O.U.P., 1947.

11. This also led to the development of the concept of "detribalization" and of studies based on such a framework. See: M. J. B. Molohan, *Detribalization,* Dar es Salaam, Government Printer, 1957. For a critique of this concept see Gluckman, 1961, *op. cit.,* p. 69.

12. Gluckman, 1961, *op. cit.,* pp. 68–70.

13. Pauw, 1963, *op. cit.*

14. Mayer, 1961, *op. cit.*

15. Epstein, A. L., 1961, *op. cit., Politics in an Urban African Community,* Manchester, Manchester U.P. for Rhodes-Livingstone Institute, 1958, "Immi-

grants to Northern Rhodesian Towns," Paper read to Section N of the British Association for the Advancement of Science, 1962, *The Administration of Justice and the Urban African,* Colonial Research Studies, No. 7, London, H.M.S.O., 1953.

16. Banton, M., *West African City,* London, O.U.P., for International African Institute, 1957.

17. Southall, A. W., "Introductory Summary" in *Social Change in Modern Africa, op. cit., The Theory of Urban Sociology,* Unpublished typescript, n.d.

18. See particularly: *The Calela Dance,* Rhodes-Livingstone Paper, No. 27, Manchester U.P., for Rhodes-Livingstone Institute, 1957.

19. Mitchell, J. C., "Labour Migration in Africa South of the Sahara: The Causes of Labour Migration," *Bulletin of the Inter-African Labour Institute,* Vol. 6, No. 2, March 1959, pp. 8–32.

20. Powdermaker, H., *Copper Town: Changing Africa,* N. Y., Harper and Row, 1962.

21. Elkan, W., *Migrants and Proletarians,* London, O.U.P., for East African Institute of Social Research, 1960.

22. Leslie, J. A. K., *A Survey of Dar es Salaam,* London, O.U.P., for East African Institute of Social Research, 1963.

23. Little, K., "The Role and Voluntary Associations in West African Urbanization," *American Anthropologist,* Vol. 59, No. 4, August, 1957, pp. 579–596.

24. Pauw. 1963, *op. cit.*

25. See: Gutkind, P. C. W., "African Urban Family Life: Comment and Analysis of Some Rural-Urban Differences," *Cahiers d'Etudes Africaines,* No. 10, 1962, pp. 149–217; "La Famille Africaine et son Adaptation à la Vie Urbaine," *Diogene,* No. 37, Spring 1962, pp. 88–104; "African Urban Marriage and Family life: A Note on Some Social and Demographic Characteristics from Kampala, Uganda," *Bulletin Institut Français d'Afrique Noire,* Series B., Vol. 25, Nos. 3–4, July-October 1963, pp. 266–287.

26. See: Young, M. and Willmott, P., *Family and Kinship in East London,* London, Routledge and Kegan Paul, 1957; Litwak, E., "Geographic Mobility and Extended Family Cohesion," *American Sociological Review,* Vol. 25, 1960, pp. 385–394; Axelrod, R. N., "Urban Structure and Social Participation," *American Sociological Review,* Vol. 21, 1956, pp. 13–18; Bell, N. W. and Boat, M. D., "Urban Neighbourhoods and Informal Social Relations," *American Journal of Sociology,* Vol. 62, 1957, pp. 391–398.

27. Gutkind, P. C. W., "Urban Conditions in Africa," *The Town Planning Review,* Vol. 32, No. 1, April 1961, pp. 20–32.

28. See particularly: Epstein, 1961, *op. cit.,* pp. 224–240.

29. Leslie, 1963, *op. cit.,* p. 37; see also: Southall, 1961, *op. cit.,* pp. 25–45.

30. Little, 1957, *op. cit.*

31. Gutkind, P. C. W., "The African Urban Milieu: A Force in Rapid Change," *Civilizations,* Vol. 12, No. 2, pp. 156–195.

32. Mair, L., *New Nations,* London, Weidenfeld and Nicolson, 1963, pp. 11–31.

33. Van Velsen, J., "Labour Migration as a Positive Factor in the Continuity of Tonga Tribal Society," *Economic Development and Cultural Change,* Vol. 8, No. 3, April 1960, pp. 265–278.

34. Bird, M., "Urbanization, Family and Marriage in Western Nigeria," *Urbanization in African Social Change,* Centre of African Studies, University of Edinburgh, 1963, pp. 59–74.

35. Southall, A. W., and Gutkind, P. C. W., *Townsmen in the Making,* East African Studies, No. 9, Kampala, East African Institute of Social Research, 1957.

36. Epstein, A. L., *Some Problems in the Study of Urban Communities in Africa,* p. 2. Unpublished, n.d.

37. Apart from the work by Gluckman (*An Analysis of the Sociological Theories of Bronislaw Malinowski,* Rhodes-Livingstone Papers No. 16, London, O.U.P. for Rhodes-Livingstone Institute, 1949). See also: Davis, K., "The Myth of Functional Analysis as a Special Method in Sociology and Anthropology," *American Sociological Review,* Vol. 24, No. 6, 1959, pp. 757–772.

YOUTH CLUBS IN A WEST AFRICAN CITY

Robert Bogdan

Introduction

The urbanization literature suggests that the rapid growth of urban areas in developing nations is accompanied by social disorganization and that individuals living in these urban centers experience great stress as a result of their being caught between two worlds—the modern and the traditional. They are said to lack clear and meaningful ties to either of these worlds as well as to the urban environment. While this is the general picture, some authors suggest that in developing nations, moving to or living in cities may not be so traumatic as one might imagine, and that a number of factors exist which help the urbanites to adopt new living patterns and establish roots in their urban environment. It has been pointed out that many traditional living patterns are followed in these cities, and that life styles may not be so discontinuous as one might think.

Inhabitants of urban centers may lean on traditional patterns, learning and adopting new patterns from this secure base. Kenneth Little has written about certain organizations which have developed in West African urban areas. These take the form of voluntary associations which are either rooted in traditional patterns or are Western in form.[1] They are said to provide meaningful substitutes or continuations of traditional identities and patterns of living and to act as

Written for this volume.

socializing agents for the adoption of new roles more in harmony with the urban environment and a modern society. Religious organizations, tribal unions, friendly societies, occupational associations, and cultural associations are some of the voluntary associations discussed by Little. These associations range from rather formal organizations with written constitutions to informal get-togethers of individuals who were born in the same village or have come from the same geographic area. In Little's discussion he fails to mention one group of organizations which has a large membership in at least one West African nation, one which appears to be of special interest in understanding the adjustment to the urban environment and the process of modernization of urban youth. These are the youth clubs organized by the government. The Nigerian Government has been instrumental in establishing and directing the activities of a large number of Youth Clubs throughout the Federation. These clubs are mainly social and recreational.

The purpose of this paper is to offer a description of these Youth Clubs, their activities, and their members in the city of Ibadan which is the capital of Nigeria's Western Region, the home of the Yoruba speaking peoples. The paper is a first attempt to record some of the observations I made as a "community development worker" in Ibadan, attached to the Ministry of Economic Planning and Community Development, the Ministry by which the Youth Clubs are administered. The great majority of my time during the two-year period there was spent working with these clubs.

The comments and descriptions in this paper apply to the time period between the fall of 1964 and the summer of 1966, of course, and do not reflect the current Youth Club picture in Ibadan. This was a time of great political and social unrest. The elections held in 1964 and 1965 were greatly disputed, and the accuracy of the reported results was strongly questioned by the electorate. In the latter year, federal troops were brought into Ibadan two weeks before the elections to quell disturbances. The city was under dusk-to-dawn curfews for three weeks during this period. The Governor of the Western Region was slain along with many high ranking politicians during the military coup which occurred a few months after the 1965 election.

Ibadan

Before discussing the Youth Clubs in Ibadan, let me say a word regarding the nature of this city. Living in densely populated centers is a traditional pattern for the Yoruba. Their cities are often referred to as tribal towns or large villages rather than as urban centers because of the relative homogeneity and stability of their populations and their social, political, and economic structure.[2] A culture appropriate to living in densely populated areas has been handed down through the years, and while it has been modified as a result of Western influence, living patterns today are presented as offering no great disrupture from those of the past. Social and psychological disorganization consequently are not so characteristic of Yoruba cities as they are of other new African cities. These generalizations, which apply to many Yoruba cities, do not apply equally well to Ibadan.

Ibadan was founded in the early part of the nineteenth century before European explorers visited the area. In growth, character, and importance it has been influenced by Western contact to a larger extent than have other Yoruba cities. In the last fifty years its population has more than tripled, largely as a result of migration.[3] Its population at present is somewhere between 600,000 and 1,000,000, making it the largest city in Nigeria. While traditional social and political organizational patterns are found in the city, they play a decreasingly significant role in the lives of the inhabitants as modern forms increase in importance.

The 1952 Nigerian census indicated that 94.7% of the inhabitants of Ibadan were of Yoruba ancestry,[4] but these figures, I believe, do not give accurate picture of the heterogeneity of the population today. There are no statistics to show the present numerical composition of various ethnic groups, but diversity is evident. While the great proponderance of Ibadan's inhabitants are Yoruba there are distinct sub-tribal groups among the Yoruba. Traditionally, these groups have never been united or completely homogeneous in regard to their cultural patterns although they speak the same language and their history indicates that they are all descendents of the same ancestry. While other Yoruba cities tend to be homogenous in regard to sub-tribal groups, Ibadan is diverse in its sub-tribal stock, the groups most strongly represented are Oyo, Egbe, Ijesha, and Ijebu. The city contains a large Hausa settlement, a large number of Ibos, and members of various tribes from the Midwest Region. Many expatriates also live in the city and its environs.

Although Ibadan cannot be considered industrialized in comparison with younger West African cities, much of its labor force is dependent upon modern forms of production. The Nigerian Tobacco Company, the Adutola Tire Company, and the Lafia Canning Company have factories in the city, to mention three of the larger ones. Industry, however, employs only a small proportion of the labor force. Ibadan's commercial importance in part derives from the fact that it is located in the main cocoa producing area of Nigeria. Most cocoa produced in the country passes through the city where it is sorted before it reaches the port city of Lagos ninety miles to the south. Ibadan is a trade center with a large number of shops and markets. It is also a railroad center, and a number of tarred roads radiate from the city to major cities throughout the country. Many people are involved in occupations related to trade and transportation. Ibadan is the home of the Western Region's Secretariat which supplies white-collar jobs for many of the city's inhabitants and serves as a magnet for young migrants looking for white collar jobs. Traditional industries such as cloth weaving, pottery making, and cloth dyeing are carried on in Ibadan, but they are steadily declining as these products are being replaced by machine-made goods. An increasingly smaller percentage of the city's inhabitants are farmers who follow the traditional pattern of maintaining a home in the city and traveling to their farms.

Western organizations and institutions are numerous in the city and its environs. Ibadan is the home of the University of Ibadan, a branch of the University of Ife, of a host of secondary schools, and of the University Teaching Hospital which is said to be the largest and best equipped hospital and medical research center in West Africa. Ibadan is also the home of WNTV, the Western Region's television station, "The First in Africa." It has a sports stadium with a seating capacity of 35,000 and a modern 400-acre housing estate. A large air-conditioned Kingsway department store is located in the city along with a number of self service food stores dealing mainly in imported canned goods.

Modern buildings appear in patches in the city and its immediate environs. Aside from these patches, Ibadan is a sea of rusted metal roofs which seem to touch when viewed from one of the city's many hills. The streets are lined with petty traders selling from their small stock of foods and dry goods, and with beggars seeking alms. Ibadan's population density in 1960 was 55,555 per square mile, which is more than twice the population density of New York City.[5] Open sewers and communal water taps epitomize the stage in development of public utilities. Not a traditional village and not a new African urban center, Ibadan is a mixed breed. Priests for Shango, the god of thunder, perform sacrifices in a temple more than a hundred years old, while young men and women "twist" to Chubby Checkers in one of the many night spots. Though many Ibadanites may be thought of as traditional in orientation, the city is modern in the eyes of Nigerians. From his perspective nothing swings like Lagos on Saturday night, but Ibadan shares much of the glamour associated with this city. It is an urban magnet which draws youth in search of bright lights, modern living, and employment. It may not be typical as far as new African cities go, but it shares much of what a new African city is. Its youth are caught between the modern and the traditional. They are directly confronted with and may aspire to modern patterns and styles, but they still have a foot in the door of the traditional. Youth clubs provide for some of these youths an organization which facilitates their adjustment to an environment split between two worlds.

Youth Clubs in General

There were approximately 75 Youth Clubs in Ibadan registered with the Ministry of Economic Planning and Community Development in 1965, with a total enrollment of over 2000 according to official Ministry figures. These figures vary considerably in any given time period. Clubs may have their registration taken away by the Ministry for a number of reasons which include members' being delinquent in attendance or engaging in fights at club activities. New clubs may register at any time. Clubs are usually required to pay a registration fee each year, which is used by the Ministry to finance activities. When registration fees are determined by the number of club members in a given club rather than a set fee for all clubs regardless of the number enrolled, the official number of club members declines.

While 75 clubs were registered with the Ministry and the names of members appeared in a Ministry file, it is difficult to estimate the number of *active* clubs and *active* club members in the city. Many young people who are not listed on the register participate in club activities. Some clubs register and are never heard from again. Others register just so they may participate in one athletic competition being organized for the clubs by the Ministry. Of the 75 clubs in 1965 there were perhaps 50 which held weekly or biweekly meetings and could be considered active in that the club and its activities played an important role in the lives of its members.

Being a "registered club" means that a given club has made application as a club and has been duly recognized by the Ministry. The Ministry is indiscriminate in registering clubs and accepts almost all applications without question. There is an unenforced law that all organizations must register with the government, but a good number of Youth Clubs similar to the ones discussed are not registered. These clubs may not be registered because they have been suspended from the club system, because they don't know about the Ministry and its registration procedure, because they cannot afford the registration fee, or because they choose not to register for other reasons. Registration forms, announcements of activities, and other communications that the Ministry officials send to clubs are without exception in English. They are formal in wording and structure and are difficult for semi-literate youth to understand, thus making it difficult for groups of illiterate or semi-literate youth to become registered clubs or to keep active in club affairs when they do register.

A registered club is eligible to engage in any activity organized by the Ministry or by the Members Council which is the clubs' representative body composed of two representatives from each club. At some activities club members are asked to pay entrance fees, and clubs are often asked to pay entrance fees for competitions. Clubs organize activities on their own in addition to those organized by the Ministry and the Members Council.

When the colonial administration introduced Youth Clubs to Nigeria in the mid-forties they patterned the Nigerian clubs (with some modifications) after the constitutions, programs of activities, and the general goals of the English youth club movement. While the clubs are, therefore, basically Western in form and character, age set groups resembling Youth Clubs exist in traditional Yoruba society [6] and have been responsible for some deviations from the English model. Age set groups composed of men in their late teens and early twenties have had traditional leaders as patrons. Similarly, many of the Youth Clubs have patrons who are traditional leaders. It would perhaps be revealing to compare in detail traditional age set groups with Youth Clubs, but this would be beyond the scope of this discussion. To some extent, becoming a member of a Youth Club means adopting certain Western ways. The boys and girls who join the clubs have a propensity to adopt Western ways, and many are on the road to developing a Western mentality.

Clubs are in no way political organizations. Politics is a subject which is not discussed at club meetings or by Ministry officials in the presence of club members.

The official purpose of the Youth Club movement is to nurture the "moral, physical and spiritual growth of youth club members through play, comradeship and self government." [7] Over and over again the phrase "the youth of today are the leaders of tomorrow" is echoed throughout the Youth Club literature and voiced by Ministry officials. This phrase is accompanied by words to the effect that the Youth Clubs movement is to build "good" citizens and leaders and therefore a stronger Nigeria. While abstract goals may be presented in the literature and by higher officials in the Ministry, on an operational level Ministry officials see the clubs as providing youth with something positive to do in their spare time to keep them out of trouble. Youth Clubs are seen by some Ministry officials as adding to the prestige of the country or area in which they are established because they are Western and indicative of sophistication.

The officials who administer the clubs are generally Western in orientation, and many have been Youth Club members or instrumental in the early development of the Youth Club movement. The fact that they are committed to the Youth Clubs in their present form and function stabilizes the clubs in their basic Western form.

Various symbols of club affiliation are displayed. Membership badges are bought from the Ministry, and club members display these badges on their chests with great pride. In front of their meeting places clubs erect large, colorful wooden signboards with the names of their clubs.

Youth Club Members

Age. Although it is official Ministry policy and a written rule that club members must be between the ages of twelve and nineteen, many members are over nineteen are some are in their mid-twenties. A large number of boys and girls under the age of twelve, not considered club members either by the Ministry or by the club members, hang around club meeting sites. While not playing an active part in club affairs they attend and observe the proceedings of meetings and other club activities. Most club presidents are over nineteen, and the chairman of the city Members Council was twenty-five years old when I was in Ibadan. With few birth certificates in the country it is difficult to ascertain the exact age of club members. The only time when age is a point of concern is when a talented older boy represents a club team in an athletic competition. Most boys in the clubs are between the ages of sixteen and twenty-three, although there are some clubs whose membership is predominantly of younger boys. The age range of sixteen to twenty-three represents a time in the Yoruba boy's life when he has completed school and/or is supposed to be out establishing a life for himself. The clubs function to provide an identity for these boys who are of an age and in an environment where their identity is not clear.

Sex. There are many more male club members than female, and male members will be the main focus of this discussion. Girls are not very active in club affairs even when they are members, because traditionally a Yoruba girl's place is at home taking care of her younger brothers and sisters or in the market selling wares. The great majority of girls who are of the age for Youth Club membership live with their families. Some parents of Yoruba girls hold tight reins on their daughters and often do not approve of their attending meetings and club activities. For the more traditionally oriented parents, the club's Western flare is associated with immorality. Adopting Western social patterns is judged by them to be good for boys, however, in that the social skills of the Western world are assets to their sons in the labor market. Girls are thought not to need these skills, so that the danger of becoming immoral outweighs any positive skills that the girls might derive from club membership. It is not a common practice in the traditional Yoruba way of life for men and women to mix socially and to have friendship relations. Men travel socially with men, and women with women. The co-ed club is Western, and for male club members, having girls as club members is desirable and prestigeful in that being sophisticated in Western ways is desirable. To some extent the clubs function to alter the traditional man-woman relationship.

Tribe. Although there are a large number of individuals living in Ibadan whose tribal origin is not Yoruba, club members are Yoruba almost without exception. The few boys who come from other tribal groups speak fluent Yoruba, however, and have lived among the Yoruba for the greater part of their lives. In the city there is little social mixing between members of different tribal groups, and the Youth Clubs follow this pattern. While members of other tribes are free to be members of existing clubs or to form their own clubs, they do not do so. The clubs do not act as instruments of integration of different tribal groups and may serve to increase Yoruba tribal identity instead. The Youth Clubs, although existing throughout the federation, are organized on a regional basis. It seems that the clubs tend to build an identification with the region (which is basically a tribal unit) rather than with the nation. Building this feeling of regionalism might be a step in the direction of nationalism, however. While a few clubs in the city are made up of individuals whose ancestry is primarily from one sub-tribal group, Youth Clubs in general are not formed on the basis of sub-tribal identities. Clubs are formed for the most part on the basis of geographic proximity—youths living in the same area get together and form a club. This pattern tends to integrate sub-tribal groups.

Education. Facilities and opportunities to obtain free primary education are fairly well distributed throughout the Western Region of Nigeria, and most club members have had at least a primary school education. Most migrants who are club members have had some secondary school training. Some club members are still attending secondary school but these are a small minority. The great majority are school leavers or have completed their education. ("School leaver" is used here to refer to young people who have left school before obtaining one of the post-primary school certificates.) Approximately sixty-five percent of the club members are school leavers. Some of these completed primary school but found that their families did not have the financial resources to send them further in school. Others started secondary school and after completing a year or two had no money with which to continue. The reason for not remaining in school is with very few exceptions a function of not having passed the exam needed to enter a higher level or a function of finances. Virtually every young person desires as much education as he can get, for he believes that education increases his chances for employment. The clubs provide for their members who have learned English in school and whose vistas have been expanded by their educational experience a chance to practice some of the skills they have learned and an opportunity to meet with boys of a similar educational background.

Employment. The type of employment for which a school leaver is eligible or likely to find in Ibadan is extremely limited. Many of the club members are thus unemployed or marginally employed. Most of these youths who have had some secondary school education would rather be unemployed than perform *low-paying* manual labor. The desirable position a school leaver is *likely* to get is an apprenticeship, but virtually all wish to obtain white-collar jobs. Common apprenticeship positions held by club members are in carpentry, tailoring, auto mechanics, and surveying. Many desirable apprenticeship positions require that the apprentice pay the master for his period of apprenticeship. Many of the boys have no money to live on, let alone pay a master; so these positions are out of their reach. In some apprenticeship programs such as for auto mechanics, the apprentice is paid a small amount. This situation occurs in fields in which the master can use a good deal of help. The apprentice usually has little chance to learn more than simple operations, however, and the labor market becomes flooded with an excess of workers who are only marginally trained. School leavers are employed in other areas, such as in assisting the owner of a small shop as clerk-messenger. A few club members are hawkers, but this is a lowly occupation in the view of the school leavers.

Many club members who have West African School Certificates or commercial diplomas work in various offices in the city. Some work in the regional Secretariat. Others who have attended teacher's training college teach in Ibadan primary schools. Many higher club officers and officers of the Members Council have secondary school certificates and hold minor clerical positions with the government or in private firms.

It is becoming more and more difficult to find employment in Ibadan even for those who hold secondary school certificates. Education is advancing faster than industrialization in Nigeria, and with the migration of many educated young people from rural areas to Ibadan employment is by-passing young men whose educational qualifications would have ensured their employment only a short time ago. Many club members who hold lower secondary school certificates cannot find employment and they, along with other unemployed youths, spend their days listlessly seeking out employment leads or just hanging around.

The high rate of unemployment among the Youth Club members is a major source of frustration. The literate or semi-literate club member has a good deal of self-esteem. He attended school with the belief that his education would ensure his value in the employment market. He sees his education as making him privileged and deserving of recognition and rewards. The Youth Clubs give the unemployed something to do with their time and energies, but more important they give them a feeling of belonging which is very much needed, providing a meeting ground for boys with similar frustrations. They develop a group perspective as to the nature and causes of their plight.

Club members focus on three factors when discussing the cause of their unemployed state. The first of these is covered by the phrase *long leg*. This is the expression club members use in referring to the use of personal influence in securing jobs. They believe that nepotism and favoritism play an important role in securing employment in the city and that their state of unemployment is a result of not having the proper connections. While they indicate that they themselves would quickly make use of connections if they had any, in their unemployed state they resent the fact that others with the same or lesser qualifications find positions through the use of personal influence.

Giving a *dash* is another common means of securing employment and is viewed in a similar way as is the practice of the "long leg." "Dash" in this sense refers to money given to someone with the understanding that the receiver will do the giver a favor. For young people with some education and no money for a "dash" this method of securing employment adds to their frustration and is given as a reason for their unemployment.

The third factor that the unemployed club members focus on in explaining their state is the corruption, embezzlement, and poor use of public funds on the part of the government. High officials enjoying a high standard of living provide evidence, valid or not, that public funds are going into the pockets of the politicians rather than toward the creation of jobs through industrial planning and development. In the city the evidence confronts the jury daily. They see some of the government's development projects as being ill-considered. The fifteen-storey government-financed Cocoa House is thought of as such. The young people in the clubs are attuned to corruption and government waste, and see their unemployed state as a result of it. They appear suspicious of the activities of government officials at all levels and survey them carefully.

Religion. There are an approximately equal number of Christian and Muslim Youth Club members. This corresponds to the proportion of Christians and Muslims in the city as a whole. Some youths are members of church youth groups in addition to belonging to government registered clubs. A small minority of club members still practice traditional religions and take part in traditional ceremonies, but for the most part this is done in addition to practicing the Christian or Muslim faith. Idol worship and the less sophisticated forms of Christian worship (prophet churches) are generally looked down upon by club members, and those who participate in these forms of religion do not talk about it freely with other club members.

Although the club members disparage traditional forms of worship, they believe in (the traditional) remedies for curing illness and aiding with personal problems. Consulting herbalists and using their medicine is most often done in conjunction with the use of Western medicine and doctors. Juju, charms or magic to keep away evil or to inflict harm on others, is believed in by virtually all club members. Lower-level Ministry officials believe in juju and discuss the supernatural in relation to club affairs as part of their logical reasoning.

Youth Club Members in General. In appearance Youth Club members are a diverse group. Those who are employed usually buy clothes with whatever funds remain after giving part of their salary to relatives, paying rent for their single room, and buying food. Some are able to save a small part of their salary and buy a radio and/or a bicycle. Dress is an important status symbol among the Yoruba and among youth club members. While some club members who can afford to purchase clothes buy traditional Yoruba clothing, the majority buy either imported Western outfits or buy cloth which local tailors make into Western style outfits. Tapered trousers, long-sleeved dress shirts, and loafers or saddles are the common attire. Club members who do not have money to spend on clothes often go barefoot and wear one outfit of clothing day after day. This group often wears tattered traditional dress, but some wear shorts as do many of the younger club members. No matter what their dress, their Youth Club badge is worn proudly.

If a club member's family is resident in Ibadan, he most often lives in the family compound. If the boy is a migrant and employed, he most often lives in a rented room. An unemployed migrant usually lives with relatives or in any house that will provide him a place to sleep. Approximately fifty percent of the Youth Club members are migrants from other Yoruba towns and villages. They are in the city either seeking employment or trying to further their education.

Activities

To understand the nature of clubs and their function, and more importantly, to get a feeling for what these clubs are to their members, a discussion of the activities Youth Clubs participate in is in order.

Meetings. Although the official function of meetings is to plan activities and to discuss club affairs, they also serve as an activity in themselves and are of great importance to Youth Club members. Some clubs engage in no activity other than meetings. The meeting that the Youth Club members are attending may be the topic of discussion for the same meeting. Club members often engage in lively and lengthy debate over such matters as fines for members who came late or engaged in disorderly conduct at the meeting. Sometimes this type of discussion goes on week after week with little other business discussed. While some clubs do not see as the purpose of the meeting getting something done (in a Western sense), others do see this as their purpose and might be thought of as effective by these standards. There is great formality at these meetings. Their proceedings closely follow parliamentary procedure as understood by club members. The Ministry distributes literature to clubs concerning the proper form meetings should take and how to write constitutions, and giving an outline of how to run clubs effectively. This literature is consulted and followed closely. Clubs very often get bogged down in procedure, however.

Meetings serve as a learning situation for participation in Western institutions and in the democratic process. Club members get an opportunity to form opinions and to express them in front of a group. Being able to express an opinion and have that opinion discussed and voted upon gives the club members a feeling of worth as well as practice in performing Western roles.

At weekly meetings Yoruba is spoken as a rule. Probably fifteen percent of the clubs conduct their meetings in English. Since all members speak Yoruba and can converse in that tongue much more fluently than in English, the only apparent reason for holding a meeting in English is that it gives the club a special Western atmosphere and adds to the club's self-image of sophistication. Minutes are recorded at all meetings, and these are usually in English although there is an occasional minute book with entries in Yoruba.

Elections of club officers are usually held twice a year and are important occasions, as offices are sought by most members. Results are reported to local newspapers and to the *Young Nigerian* for publication. There are many offices in every club, and this fact assures most members that they will hold a position of importance and have a title to add to their name. These titles are used frequently. A club member may be referred to as the "honorable corresponding secretary" or as the "distinguished recording secretary," etc.

Each club elects two representatives to attend meetings of the Members Council which meets approximately every three weeks. Parliamentary procedure is followed, and meetings are usually lively and two hours in length. The Members Council elects its own officers. Ministry officers attend all the meetings and often give impromptu lectures on points being discussed or on the general proceedings of the meeting. The members discuss club affairs and plan activities. Attendance at these meetings varies considerably. If an important activity is under discussion, up to forty clubs may be represented. At other times as few as twenty clubs may be represented. The delegates report to their own club on the proceedings of the Members Council.

Dances. Dances are one of the most popular activities. Major dances on such holidays as Christmas, Independence Day, Big Isala, and Little Isala are sponsored by the Members Council and are gala affairs. Individual clubs also organize their own dances. The dances exemplify the Western tone of the clubs. The music is provided by one of the ten or more tape recording services in the city. (A tape recording service is composed of an individual who owns a tape recorder, amplifying equipment, and pop music tapes and his assistant. He rents his services at an hourly rate to individuals or organizations having dances and parties. Tape recorder services have such colorful names as "Aro Dandy," "Hi Fi," and "Jolly Time." The tape recorder operator is somewhat of a celebrity at the dances, filling a position similar to that of a famous American disc jockey. Tape recording services which have the latest music are the most popular and demand the highest prices.) The music is "high life," is a modern indigenous music, and American pop music. "My Boy Lollipop" was the number one tune during both years I spent in Nigeria. The club members twist and do the "high life" and an occasional foxtrot. Since there are always about twice as many boys as girls at these affairs, the girls are in great demand as dance partners. Boys dance with boys—partly because of the lack of girls and partly because of the friendship patterns among males in traditional Yoruba society. Occasionally a boy will bring a girl to a dance and pay her way, but the girl is often a relative. Dating of a type resembling the American form is an oddity. The great majority of boys and girls come to dances in groups made up of members of their own sex. To encourage girls to attend dances they are often admitted without an entrance fee.

At most dances an admission charge is collected at the gate. This admission fee to some extent limits the participation of unemployed youth in this activity, but when their own club sponsors the dance all its members are allowed to enter free. At other clubs if a friend of a boy who has no money is collecting tickets, he will often allow the boy without money to slip by without paying the fee. The admission fee of boys who do not have money is often paid by friends and club members who have money. Many boys who are unable to gain admission stand around at the gate listening to the music and socializing.

Club members wear their finest clothes to these dances. Approximately half of the boys who attend these dances wear traditional formal Yoruba dress. The other half wear Western clothes. White shirts and ties with tight tapered slacks are common dress clothes for the boys. Some wear woolen English suits in spite of the fact that temperatures reach well over 100 degrees at these dances. Other boys wear Western style sport shirts. One member attended all dances in a sweatshirt with a picture of the Beatles on the front. Most girls wear traditional Yoruba dress to the dances; perhaps a quarter wear Western style dresses. Sunglasses are common accessories for the boys. Many boys smoke at the dances although they would not ordinarily do so. One has to attend one of these dances to appreciate the degree to which they are an expression of young people's desire to be Western and the extent to which these dances allow them to act out Western roles.

Many dances are rather formal. While tickets may be sold to the dances, special engraved invitations are sent to "important personalities" affiliated with Youth Clubs or prominent people in the neighborhood. A program is usually provided for the dance with the name of the honorary chairman printed on it and the sequence of activities planned for the dance. Sometimes a photographer is hired to take "group photographs" at dances and other special activities. The professional photographer sells these pictures and they are kept as proud possessions by Youth Club members.

Sports. Soccer is the most popular sport and the most important activity engaged in by Youth Club members. All clubs have soccer teams which play in competitions and against other clubs in friendly matches. Youth Clubs members also participate in ping pong, boxing, and track and field. Many clubs own their own soccer ball, boxing gloves, and ping pong equipment. These are very important possessions. Some clubs have jerseys for their team members. While the importance of fair play and sportsmanship is preached by Ministry officials and verbalized by club members, there is intense competition between clubs, and fair play is often overlooked in the furore of the competition. Tempers run high, especially at soccer matches. Referees are subjected to a good deal of verbal and occasionally physical abuse. Many, if not the majority of soccer matches, are accompanied by at least one fist fight, and a good number end in brawls. Some clubs have developed a bad reputation in the city for their behavior at soccer matches. Attempts have been made by the Ministry and the Members Council to lessen the physical violence at these matches by imposing disciplinary measures on individuals and clubs engaging in acts of violence. These have not been successful. Aside from their delinquent acts at sports competitions, the clubs do not form units for anti-social activity in the community.

Soccer and boxing matches afford the Youth Club members an opportunity to release some of their pent-up energy and aggression. Sports is an area in which individuals in the clubs can achieve status in their community and among their peers. Accomplished athletes in the clubs derive a great deal of prestige from their prowess.

Film Shows, Debates and Speakers. Film shows are a common activity among Youth Clubs. Upon request, films are shown to the clubs by the British Information Service or the United States Information Service, both of which have offices and libraries in Ibadan. The clubs can choose the type of film they wish to have shown. The most popular selections are films dealing with sports or music. The film of the Dick Tiger-Gene Fulmer fight was by far the most popular. "Louis Armstrong in Concert" was another that was constantly in demand. Films dealing with J. F. Kennedy were also frequently shown. The films might be thought of as more entertaining than educational, but they expand the world in which the club members live and provide Western models to emulate.

The Youth Club organizes the film show, but this activity is a neighborhood event. The films are usually shown outdoors in a large open area in the neighborhood and attract many residents of all ages. With a microphone provided by one of the information services the club president explains to the audience that the Youth Club is the organization responsible for the show. Prominent men in the area are often provided with seats and issued special invitations to the film shows. Through film shows and semi-public activities the clubs become known as neighborhood residents and to some extent receive recognition in the community.

On occasion debates and lectures are held by clubs, but these are not very common. The lectures always relate to the role of youth in the "new" Nigeria, and are given by prominent men in the community.

Anniversary Celebrations. The importance that the Youth Club members attach to their club affiliation is exhibited in the practice of holding elaborate yearly anniversary celebrations at a time near the day their club was originally organized. The celebration usually consists of a series of activities held on consecutive days. The finale of the celebration is most often a dance.

Community Development Activities. As has been suggested by the discussion thus far, the Youth Clubs are mainly social and recreational in character. Although on suggestion from higher officers in the Ministry attempts made to get the youth involved in community development projects or to initiate ones in their own neighborhoods, have met with little success. On occasion clubs will participate in road-building projects, clean-up campaigns, or other Ministry organized "self-help" projects, but this participation is of a superficial nature and usually involves only a few club members who work on a project for a few hours and then leave. Most of the Youth Club members think in terms of what they will get in return for their labors, and the spiritual rewards or the benefits they see as deriving from the work are not sufficient to warrant the labor. The boys feel that the government should finance various development projects and pay for the labor. They do not want to "*give*" the government what it should provide itself.

Many clubs are not action-oriented as suggested by the discussion of meetings. They would lack the organizational ability to initiate and carry out projects even if they had the motivation. One club in the city which was an exception to this rule—it was extremely well organized and was very much action-oriented—was successful in organizing and carrying out a neighborhood self-improvement project. They organized adult literacy classes for elderly people in their neighborhood, and these proved to be quite successful. A good many of the boys in this particular club were employed as teachers, and the club's officers had the ability to organize. They anticipated that this project would bring prestige to their club by providing a needed service for the community, and that the residents would be grateful. Other clubs have not developed this orientation for any of several reasons. They may be too troubled by internal disorders or by the fact that their members have too many personal problems (unemployment, etc.), they may lack organizational ability, or they may feel too much hostility toward the government to initiate or participate in community development work.

The Festival of the Arts. The Festival of the Arts is an annual competition organized by the Ministry in which the clubs throughout the region compete for awards for the best performance in such events as traditional Yoruba drama, Yoruba story telling, traditional music, English drama, and English recitation. A competition is held in Ibadan for Ibadan clubs to determine who will represent the city in the regional competition. The festival functions to promote interest and respect for indigenous art forms, but it also encourages participation in Western art forms. The members of the Ibadan team do poorly in the traditional part of the competition in that their productions are usually bastardized versions of traditional art forms, whereas a good amount of the judging is based on authenticity. Their poor showing can be attributed to the diversity of sub-tribal backgrounds of their members to the fact that less prestige is associated with the traditional part of the competition than with the English portion. The Ibadan clubs do well in the English sections of the competition, and this is their claim to fame. This can be explained by the large number of literate boys and girls in the clubs in the city, and the importance of English skills to club members. This competition is clearly a conglomeration of the old and the new; the Ibadan clubs use it to express their Western orientation.

The "Young Nigerian." The "Young Nigerian" is the newspaper published monthly by the Ministry and distributed to club members free of charge. It contains mainly information concerning club activities, but it also reports non-club activities that the Ministry is inolved in. On occasion Youth Club members write articles and short stories for the paper, but this is rare; most of the writing is done by Ministry officials although it is based on information submitted by club members and field officers. The results of various sports competitions are reported, with the names of prominent athletes and details of the competitions. Articles concerning other activities of the clubs are found in the "Young Nigerian," as are the results of various club elections. The club members eagerly await the days that the paper is distributed and check carefully to see whether their name, their club's name, or the name of a friend or familar club is in print.

Leadership Training Courses. The federal government maintains two leadership training camps, one on the Jos Plateau in the Northern Region and one on an island twenty miles west of Lagos. Both camps are known as Man o' War Bay. At these camps training courses are held consecutively throughout the year except during the rainy season. Each course caters to a special category of students. These categories are based on age and occupational affiliation. A number of the courses are open each year to boys and girls who are Youth Club members; the regional government sponsors Western Region Youth Club members as participants in the course. Approximately ten youth club members attend these courses each year from Ibadan. Both the training camp and the course are styled after the Outward Bound camps in Britain, and emphasize building self-confidence through participation in challenging outdoor activities such as long distance hikes, mountain climbing, canoeing, and swimming. Not designed to increase specific leadership skills, these courses do not make a direct impact on the clubs in Ibadan but do afford the few participants a world-expanding experience which has an effect on them as individuals and indirectly on the clubs. The fact that a club member has been to one of these training courses raises his prestige considerably and increases his self-esteem. Boys who have been to Man o' War Bay wear to club affairs their tee shirts with the camp name.

The provincial office of the Ministry of Economic Planning and Community Development organizes a number of training courses for Youth Club members. Although these courses place more emphasis on learning skills relevant to Youth Club organization, they tend to copy the Man o' War Bay type training which detracts from their specific educational purpose. Lessons designed to train youth to develop stronger Youth Clubs are taken almost verbatim from the government pamphlets distributed to clubs, which emphasize the structure of clubs rather than action programs. A good number of the youths in Ibadan clubs get an opportunity to attend these courses which usually last a week and are held at the government-owned Sha Sha River Training Camp located about ninety miles east of Ibadan. After having participated in a Sha Sha River training course the club members develop a greater feeling of belonging to their club and the club system in general. Their training course graduate status gives them prestige among fellow club members.

Finance

Aside from literature and membership cards the government gives no material aid to the Youth Clubs. The government emphasizes that clubs must be self-sufficient as to finances. This causes some resentment on the part of the clubs. Many members think that the Ministry should supply equipment as a way of encouraging club activities. With registration fees to be paid, money needed to organize activities, and money needed to buy sports equipment, finance is an important problem for the clubs. Solving or dealing with financial problems does provide learning experience, however. The effect is to alter some traditional patterns which are detrimental to the economic progress of the clubs and to foster discipline in regard to financial matters. Questions regarding embezzlement and misuse of club funds are constantly raised and discussed. Precautions are introduced by the members to prevent such practices and negative sanctions have been instituted to punish offenders.

Money for support of the club and its activities is raised in a number of ways. Weekly dues are collected by most clubs. The dues amount to only a few pennies, but even that many club members are unable to pay. Since a large number of the club members are unemployed and the majority of the members are poor, treasuries do not build up very quickly. A second way of collecting funds is by organizing activities such as dances, opening them to the public, and charging admission. Some clubs are quite successful at this method, but others less skilled in planning fail miserably. Another cause of failure of many activities designed to show a profit is the traditional obligation among the Yoruba to do favors for friends and relatives. One favor which club members can do for friends and relatives is to allow them in without charge to the premises where activities are being held. Friends and "brothers" of the ticket collectors sometimes outnumber the paid entrants. Many clubs have become aware of this problem which results in debts from activities which were designed to raise money. Some clubs have developed remedies for this situation, such as having a boy who is new to the city as the ticket collector or having a general agreement among members that friends will not be allowed to enter without paying.

A third method of collecting money is by soliciting it from relatively wealthy people in the community who are club "patrons." Patrons of the clubs are often progressive and influencial men in the neighborhood who support the idea of Youth Clubs. Some of the patrons are consulted when the club is experiencing difficulties other than financial, and they act as advisors to the clubs. Some of the patrons are traditional rulers to whom people in the neighborhood come for advice as is the traditional pattern. Having patrons and encouraging the elders of the area to be club supporters, integrates the club into the neighborhood and provides for some continuity with traditional organizational patterns.

The Ministry and Club Members

Through their participation in clubs the members have a good deal of contact with civil servants working for the Ministry of Economic Planning and Community Development. Club members visit the Ministry office which is located in central Ibadan and meet with officials to discuss club matters. Ministry officials meet with club members when they attend, supervise, and organize various activities, and when they visit club meetings. As has been mentioned earlier the civil servants who work with clubs are most often Western in their orientation and to some extent serve as models to emulate.

This is not the whole picture, however, for these officials also serve as objects of hostility. The youth are generally dissatisfied with the government in power, and the frustrations they feel as a result of unemployment and related factors are intense. While the club members do not think of the civil servants as politicians or as being part of the regime in power, they do have a general suspicion regarding all government officials. The Ministry officials are under constant scrutiny by club members as they go about their club work. The youth often covertly charge these officials with irresponsibility, favoritism, and corruption. On occasion these charges are overt and manifested in open defiance of officials and their rules. Talking back is a mild form of this defiance; stoning is an extreme form. (I observed the stoning of a Ministry official once. It occured after a track and field meet at which the officer was accused of showing favoritism while acting as a judge.) The Ministry officials were charged, for example, with tampering with club funds, with choosing members to go to training courses on the basis of personal ties, and with not spending enough time at their work.

In addition to criticizing specific officials, club members often questioned and debated the practices and policies of the Ministry. The fact that the Ministry did not provide the clubs with sports equipment and with transportation to competitions was a favorite source of complaint. Whether these criticisms and charges were justified is not important—what is important is that this scrutiny and critism of officials and the Ministry was a challenge to the traditional Yoruba pattern in which adults and individuals in important positions were accorded blind deference. This new attitude gave the club members a feeling of power which sometimes moved them to responsible action. During one period of intense dissatisfaction with two officials the clubs held secret meetings to discuss the matter. These meetings resulted in a decision to boycott a Ministry-sponsored activity and to write a letter to high-ranking officials in the Ministry regarding the matter.

Conclusion

The government-organized Youth Clubs in the city of Ibadan perform a number of functions in facilitating the adaptation of young people to the urban environment and to the modern world.[8]

1) The clubs provide an identity for club members which serves as a real tie to the urban environment and to the modern world. Many of the members are unemployed, many lack other secondary group affiliations as well as primary group affiliations and have no roots in the urban environment.

2) The clubs provide for their members an opportunity to learn modern behavior patterns and skills. They also provide young people with an opportunity to exhibit and practice any modern skills and behavior patterns which they might have learned previously.

3) Clubs provide members with an opportunity to mix with individuals outside their family, sub-tribal, or neighborhood groups, and function to integrate members into the larger urban environment.

4) The clubs help members attain a feeling of importance. Participation in representive government and democratic meetings develops a feeling that one's voice can be heard and that it has some meaning in determining policies and procedures.

5) The clubs work, to some extent, to erode traditional patterns of behavior and authority among club members and in the larger urban community.

6) The clubs provide the members with outlets for pent-up energy and aggression and give them something to do with their time. They provide boys and girls with the companionship of young people who are in similar situations and under similar strains. Since many boys are unemployed and have an excess of time on

their hands they could very well turn their energies to anti-social activities and add to the political instability. Clubs direct energy to constructive forms of activity and generally keep members out of trouble.

7) The clubs provide avenues by which members can gain recognition through achievement. For urban youth few avenues are open through which they can achieve status. In the club, members may become officers or win acclaim through participation in the various competitions.

The large number of unemployed, educated or semi-educated youth in the urban areas of Africa poses many problems for these countries. These young people are dissatisfied with their state and lack significant ties to either traditional institutions or to modern institutions. In their unattached state they are prone to be attracted to the first group that calls for their alliance and offers them the opportunity for recognition. Often this group is a political one. Their presence detracts from the political stability of new African nations. Without money and ties they also tend to become involved in anti-social behavior.

It does not appear that in the near future these countries will be able to improve the employment opportunities for these young people significantly. Both the number of unemployed young people in urban centers and their dissatisfaction will most likely increase. There is a need to avert the disaster which appears to be on the horizon and which is being experienced to some extent today. Formation of Youth Clubs, though it may seem to be only a superficial answer to the problem of supplying these youth with a tie to the environment, and might be thought of as treating the effects and not the cause of the problem, may be an effective approach. In fact, the program could be expanded without a great increase in cost. Only three salaried government officers are working with the clubs, and their work with the clubs represents only part of duties. The club program, aside from officers' salaries, is almost entirely self-supporting. While club members resent paying fees, they have come to accept them. The fact that they are willing to participate in such a program in spite of the fees perhaps attests to its need.

It is the author's observation that these clubs do facilitate the adjustment of youth to the urban environment and act as socializing agents for the adoption of modern roles. The extent to which this is true and the depth and nature of the effects is a matter for further empirical investigation. Studies in this area might suggest effective programs that government agencies in developing countries could institute to reduce the strains suffered by urban areas and facilitate the modernization of their inhabitants.

The clubs may, of course, ease the immediate adjustment of members to the city for the period during which they are members, but may function to build attitudes which are not conducive to later adjustment and making a positive contribution to national development. The club system may lead to stability and alleviate social disorganization to some degree for the time being, but may, by bringing together dissatisfied youth, solidify and intensify hostilities and thus be a potential source of instability. Clubs, by promoting Western attitudes and allowing members to act out Western roles, may raise the aspirations and expectations of their members to an unrealistic level, leading to frustration and dissatisfaction.

A more detailed inquiry is needed as to the effects of club participation on the members if we are to understand the long-term effects clubs have in molding a citizenry and providing a climate which supports and contributes to sound national development.

Notes

I would like to thank Dr. Sandor Halebsky and members of his seminar in *Development* for their comments on an earlier draft of this paper.

1. Kenneth Little, "The Role of Voluntary Associations in West African Urbanization," *American Anthropologist,* **59,** No. 4, (1957), pp. 579–595.
   —, *West African Urbanization,* Cambridge University Press, 1965.

2. P. C. Lloyd, "The Yoruba Town Today," *Sociological Review,* **7,** (July, 1959) pp. 45–63.

3. Kenneth Little, *West African . . . , op. cit.,* p. 18.

4. William Bascom, "Some Aspects of Yoruba Urbanism," *American Antropologist,* **64,** (1962) p. 703.

5. *Ibid.* p. 699.

6. Lloyd, *op. cit.,* p. 51.

7. Oba C. D. Akran, *Concept of Community Development in Western Nigeria and Its Historical Perspective,* pamphlet, (Ibadan: Western Nigerian Ministry of Information Printing Office, 1961).

8. These closely parallel the functions of voluntary associations suggested by Kenneth Little, *op. cit.*

CHAPTER FOUR

THE SOCIAL CONSEQUENCES OF URBAN LIFE: LIFE STYLES

INTRODUCTION

Participation in the social life of urban settlements has manifold consequences for urban dwellers. However, there is still much uncertainty regarding the qualities of the effects that living in cities has on the inhabitants, particularly the extent to which these consequences influence their total life situation. This chapter explores some of the sociological consequences of urban life in terms of the organizations which emerge, and the social-psychological phenomena associated with these consequences.

It has long been held that urban life, in contrast to folk and rural life, has had an unfavorable effect on people. That this image is doubtful has been suggested by a number of recent observers of the urban scene. Generally, as Sjoberg has suggested in his studies of preindustrial cities, "the lot of the peasants has usually been worse than that of city dwellers, even those in the lower class" (in Faris, *op. cit.*, p. 139). Indeed, it is clear that our images of urban life have been based upon a host of myths which are now dissolving under the scrutiny of the scientific investigator.

In Mizruchi's paper, published here for the first time, the romantic notions which influenced the urbanization-disorganization school are exposed to an empirical assessment. The data gathered to test an hypothesis do not support the sociological romanticists, nor do other data assembled in other studies. However, it is suggested that researchers who take different conditions into account might provide more meaningful theoretical generalizations.

Treating education as a variable, Guillermo Briones and Frederick Waisanen focus on the effects of modernization on urban integration and educational aspirations. Charles Willie describes how educational processes affect deprived urban Negroes and how alienation ensues. Louis Kriesberg's study of public-housing tenants and Lee Rainwater's analysis of the role of fear in urban life convey the profound impact of their experiences on those in the relatively lower class categories, experiences which are foreign to the largest segment of the urban population.

Finally, Robert Perrucci describes how the constraints imposed on dwellers in slum areas of cities lead to the selection of illegitimate channels of social mobility in their efforts to attain the rewards which are so integral a part of the American dream. This paper is also published here for the first time.

ROMANTICISM, URBANISM, AND SMALL TOWN IN MASS SOCIETY: AN EXPLORATORY ANALYSIS

Ephraim H. Mizruchi

Sociologists have, in recent years, turned to an examination of some romantic conceptions regarding the mental life of urban dwellers which were at one time widely shared. At the core of these ideas was the image of urban life reflected in the works of Georg Simmel, Louis Wirth, and some of their intellectual offspring. Our objective, in this paper is to lend clarity to the issues surrounding this image by focusing on recent research on anomie, including our own empirical explorations, and to describe the nature of some of the problems involved in our conceptions of both urban and rural life.

Conceptions of the City

The most widely held image of the nature of social interaction and personal reaction in the urban milieu was the one described by Louis Wirth in his essay "Urbanism as a Way of Life." [1] Directly influenced by Georg Simmel's, "The Metropolis and the Mental Life," [2] Wirth describes urban life in the following way.

> The superficiality, the anonymity, and the transitory character of urban social relations make intelligible, also, the sophistication and the rationality generally ascribed to city-dwellers. Our acquaintances tend to stand in a relationship of utility to us in the sense that the role which each one plays in our life is overwhelmingly regarded as a means for the achievement of our own ends. Whereas the individual gains, on the one hand, a certain degree of emancipation or freedom from the personal and emotional controls of intimate groups, he loses, on the other hand, the spontaneous self-expression, the morale, and the sense of participation that comes with living in an integrated society. This constitutes essentially the state of *anomie*, or the social void, to which Durkheim alludes in attempting to account for the various forms of social disorganization in technological society.[3]

These conceptions of urban life, it should be noted, reflected a more fundamental set of images encompassed by what Shils called "German sociological romanticism." [4]

Although Wirth's view of this aspect of urban life has recently come under attack by non-students and students of Wirth alike [5] it is still an influential position.[6] However, within the past several years empirical assessessment of some

Synthesis, revision, and extension of papers read at the annual meeting of the Eastern Sociological Association, Philadelphia, April, 1966 and the American Sociological Association, Miami Beach, August, 1966.

aspects of this image has emerged in the sociological literature, particularly the assumption that anomie is a characteristic of urban life.

Urbanism and Anomie

Several studies have been done in which Srole's anomia scale [7] has been used as an indicator of personal reactions to the structural condition of anomie as described by Durkheim. These studies provide empirical data for an assessment of the classical images of the city.

In reviewing the literature it appears that the relationship between anomie and urbanism is not at all clear. An earlier study by this writer presented data indicating that anomia rates were relatively high (in a small city of 16,000 which is in the heart of a rural upstate New York area) when compared with rates found in earlier studies.[8] Greer and Kube's studies provide data which suggest to this writer that anomia rates in urban areas tend to be relatively low.[9] Still other studies suggest that what is required in this context is a direct comparison of distributions of anomia by type of community. This could lead to a meaningful theoretical framework for the interpretation of data and formulation of significant hypotheses.[10]

Accordingly, the writer designed a limited study of three samples in areas selected by inspection in three central upstate New York communities, excluding the small city studied earlier. The communities were assumed to represent points on a hypothetical *continuum* from rural to urban, without including either a "pure" urban or rural sample set. A section of a suburb adjoining Syracuse was our most urban while a section of a village near Cortland was our most rural. A section of a small town in the "Southern tier" which has both rural and suburban characteristics was included to provide a midpoint on the continuum. In addition, the shortest distance between any two communities was 30 miles, while the longest was 75 miles. In the communities selected for interviewing an attempt was made to find a section with natural boundaries (similar to "natural areas" in cities) and to select systematically for respondents adults in 2 of 3 and 3 of 4 dwelling units. Thus, within each section a very high proportion of households were sampled. Although our choices of communities leave much to be desired, particularly with respect to our urban sample, we hold that they are adequate for the attainment of our limited objectives.

Demographic data were also included in the interview schedules, as were data on values, social involvement (formal and informal), anomia, prejudice, and authoritarianism.

As our data indicate (Table 1) there is an association between type of community and anomia, with discrepancy between observed and expected *highest* in the *rural*-village and lowest in the suburb ($\chi^2 = 21.01$, P .001). This result is just the reverse of what was expected on the basis of the Simmel-Wirth assumption. Because we observed a strong association between socio-economic position and anomia in earlier studies we analysed our data conditionally by class.

Since our sample was relatively small, it was necessary to collapse the data and dichotomize those who scored 0 on the Srole scale and those who scored from 1–5. Furthermore, the small number of cases yields small theoretically expected

TABLE 1. TYPE OF COMMUNITY STRUCTURE AND ANOMIE

Anomia	High-Urban	Urban-Rural	Rural-Village	Total
0	29 (21.9)	25 (20.9)	11 (22.2)	65
1–2	28 (31.0)	28 (29.6)	36 (31.4)	92
3–5	13 (17.1)	14 (16.5)	24 (17.4)	51
Total	70	67	71	208

Chi-square = 21.01, 4 d.f., p < .001

TABLE 2. TYPE OF COMMUNITY AND ANOMIE, BY SOCIAL CLASS

Anomia	High-Urban	Urban-Rural	Rural-Village	Total
		I, II, III		
0	24 (48%)	18 (47%)	8 (38%)	50
1–5	26 (52%)	20 (53%)	13 (62%)	59
TOTAL	50	38	21	109
		IV, V		
0	3 (21%)	7 (28%)	2 (5%)	12
1–5	11 (79%)	22 (72%)	39 (95%)	72
TOTAL	14	29	41	84

frequencies in these tables and thus advise against a chi-square analysis (see Table 2).

In addition to the problems associated with size of distribution by cells is the problem posed by the influence of the association between class and anomia. Because the association between class and anomia tends to be significant in the total sample (chi-square = 59.6, 8 d.f., P .001) and has indeed been marked in our other studies, the class effect tends to obscure the association between other variables. Nevertheless, keeping this potential pitfall in mind, the data are still compatible with our overall observation that the frequency of relatively high anomia scores is greater in the *less* urbanized areas.

The percentage of anomics in the rural village is much greater than the percentage in the urban and the urban-rural samples (village, 95%; urban-rural, 72%; urban, 79%). Similarly, for the middle class samples the percentage of anomics is greater for those in the rural village (62% compared with 53% and 52% in each of the other samples). Thus it would appear that although the data are not so clear and marked with respect to the independent effect of type of community setting and anomia there is a tendency for the data to reinforce our observations to Table 1.

Although our data and those of others (Greer and Kube, *op. cit.*) cast doubt on the asumption that anomie is a characteristic of urban life, we still lacked a meaningful explanation for our observation. A review of Durkheim's analysis of the relationship between Catholics in Protestant countries and Protestants in Catholic countries [11] provides an hypothesis at a macroscopic level. Perhaps the malaise of the urban dweller during the latter part of the 19th and early 20th centuries was not simply a figment of the imagination. The conditions described may have indeed been characteristic of those periods and may be attributable to the nature of the relationship between the larger societal structure and the smaller sub-structures, the cities, within the same societies. Thus urban life within a predominantly *rural* society would be subjected to strains and relatively high anomie while rural life within an *urban* society would be exposed to somewhat similar strains. The dynamics of rural small town life as described by Vidich and Bensman provide ample data for such an interpretation.[12]

Our specific thoughts revolved about the question of the relationship between opportunity and attainment, an outgrowth of our more general interest in Merton's social structure and anomie hypothesis which is derived from one aspect of Durkheim's more general theory.[13] We reasoned that the strains between larger and smaller structures within the same society would be reflected in greater limitations felt by those who did not reside in structures which shared in the dominant patterns of societal emergence. Thus the higher anomia rate as one went from metropolitan to rural community would be a result of greater discrepancy between aspiration and attainment for those in the rural communities.

Although our samples were relatively small, thus making the process of conditional analysis difficult, we explored the relationship between level of *education,* as an index to aspiration, and *income,* as an index to attainment, within each community. As Table 3 indicates, the association between the two factors is clearer and more marked in the rural-small town sample than in the others ($\chi^2 =$ i,31, P .01).[14] However, there appears to be a "better fit" between aspiration and attainment in the rural community as measured by our indices. This clearly runs counter to our hypothesis since *fewer* than the number expected by chance were observed in the rural sample of college respondents earning under $5000. Further analysis of our data in which age and formal social participation were conditionally analysed indicated that (1) anomia was significantly associated with type of community for high participators only ($\chi^2 = 9.35$, 2 d.f., P .05) with the greatest difference between theoretically expected and observed occurring in the rural village; and (2) anomia was significantly associated with type of community for the 50 and under age group only ($\chi^2 = 7.56$, 2 d.f., P .05) with the greatest difference between theoretically expected and observed in the rural village. Thus the association between anomia and type of community is marked for those who tend to be most involved in the organized activities *of the rural community,* and who are 50 years of age and younger even though there is less discrepancy between preparation for personal advancement and attainment in the rural community.

How, then, do we interpret these data? Our observation that there is a marked association between anomia and type of community structure suggests the hypothesis that *malaise is more likely to characterize selected segments in the rural*

TABLE 3. EDUCATION AND INCOME BY TYPE OF COMMUNITY

	Grade school	High school	College	Number
		High-Urban		
5000+	2	19	33	54
Under 5000	0	3	2	5
TOTAL	2	22	35	59
		Urban-Rural *		
5000+	5	24	18	47
Under 5000	3	10	1	14
TOTAL	8	34	19	61
		Rural-Village *		
5000+	4 (7.2)	10 (11.4)	14 (9.3)	28
Under 5000	10 (6.7)	12 (10.6)	4 (8.7)	26
TOTAL	14	22	18	54
		Chi-square = 8.31, 2 d.f., $p < .01$		

* Distribution of Expected Frequencies too small for chi-square analysis.

community. Certain segments of the population in these communities appear particularly more likely to be anomic than others. Given the observation that discrepancy between aspiration and attainment, as measured by our indices, is not an influential factor in this community, it may be that the malaise is associated with the larger social structure rather than with the social situation of the person. Thus, those who are more involved and those who are most likely to be concerned with the future (the younger respondents) are more sensitive to the general societal "currents" which reflect the rapid transformation from a rural to an urban society.

Photiadis in one of a number of studies in rural Appalachia has made a similar observation about an actively involved group, ". . . alienation, at least among businessmen, is associated with smaller community size, and further, that although part of this alienation is due to dysfunctions of the economic system, the remainder is due to dysfunctions of other aspects of the community and most probably the social system."[15]

Vidich and Bensman suggest the following with respect to their study of the rural village.

> But the people of Springdale are unwilling to recognize the defeat of their values. . . . Because they do not recognize their defeat, they are not defeated. The compromises, the self-deception and the self-avoidance are mechanisms which work; for in operating on the basis of contradictory, illogical and conflicting assumptions, they are able to cope in their day-to-day lives with

their immediate problems in a way that permits some degree of satisfaction, recognition and achievement. There are many ways in which one could note that Springdalers do not achieve the optimum material and psychological rewards for their strivings, but such achievement does not appear to lie within the framework of their social structure. Life, then, consists in making an adjustment that is as satisfactory as possible within a world which is not often tractable to basic wishes and desires.[16]

Although the people of Springdale may not be willing to consciously recognize their critical condition they *do* realize that "all is not well in rural America." Neither their compromises nor their devices for personal adaptation are sufficient to obscure the great societal transformation which thrusts them into the dark pit of malaise. Indeed the very questions in the Srole anomia scale strike at the heart of their social condition: "Most public officials are not really interested in the problems of the average man," "These days a person doesn't really know whom he can count on," "Nowadays a person has to live pretty much for today and let tomorrow take care of itself," "In spite of what some people say, the lot of the average man is getting worse, not better," and finally, "Most people don't really care what happens to the next fellow." [18]

The devices noted by Vidich and Bensman are breaking down under the impact of urbanization and like the urban dweller of the past, responding to rapid changes and dislocations, the rural dweller of the present reacts to the impact of social structures upon him.

Urbanism, Romanticism and Sociological Analysis

Still another problem remains in our analysis of urban and rural differentials. What about urban social relations and anomie? What are some of the problems associated with objective analysis of the mental states of urban dwellers? Two selected issues appear to be worthy of serious reflection.

First, there continues to be an assumption of homogeneity regarding the nature of urban life in spite of the great diversity of groups and life patterns within cities. Our most urban sample is admittedly from a dwelling area which is suburban. Nevertheless we feel confident that there are sections in most large American cities in which the ecological, class, and normative patterns are much the same. Our orientation to the study of urban life has often been much akin to the proverbial blind men holding various parts of the elephant. The study by Dotson, for example, provides data to suggest that the stereotype of a sprawling impersonal, anomic city suggests a kind of homogeneity which is incompatible with our awareness of the heterogeneity of urban life.[18]

Still other studies tend to throw some doubts on other qualities of urban life traditionally described by earlier sociologists. Bruner, in a study in North Sumatra, observes that "Contrary to the traditional theory, we find in many Asian cities that society does not become secularized, the individual does not become isolated, kinship organizations do not break down, nor do social relationships in the urban environment become impersonal, superficial and utilitarian." [19]

Secondly, there is all too often an assumption made of a one-to-one correlation between social structure and mental state. Simmel's ideas regarding the mental state of the urbanite was a logical extension of his quantitative approach to interpersonal relationships. If, he reasoned, as size of group increased there is more impersonality than in structures characterized by the greatest concentration of members, there will be greater impersonality. In Wirth's approach impersonality leads to anomic and other maladaptive conditions.

Much research has shown that there is a great deal of informal, personal interaction in urban areas regardless of size. It is true that we have had cases where people have avoided "getting involved" in the affairs of their neighbors, but as sociologists, we know that the most dramatic occurrence in a community's activities is not likely to be typical of its life in general. Indeed, the drama of neighbors standing by while one of their number is murdered achieves significance *because* it is typical. What is necessary here is to specify the conditions under which certain social structures mitigate the effects of increasing size on interaction.

In sum, many sociologists, although having attained a good deal of objectivity and introspective self-control over our perceptions, are nevertheless still somewhat encumbered by romantic conceptions of social life. We have attempted to fashion of ourselves, and particularly our perceptual apparatus, sensitive instruments of sociological observation. Although it is hazardous to generalize about such a matter, we have not all been able to attain as much detachment from our involvement in the myths and values of the societies in which we live as we might desire.[20] There is much unevenness in our capacity to be objective, and thus we are more detached in some areas than in others.

What we have been suggesting here is that there are a number of spheres of sociological thought which require careful assessment on theoretical, empirical, and sociological self-analytical grounds. The classical propositions of sociology, particularly those of Durkheim and Simmel, are worthy of reassessment in terms of their theoretical implications and the social context out of which they emerged. To suggest that this is "a problem for the sociology of knowledge" or some other area of social thought is often an inadvertent means by which we cast some of our most significant questions into a sociological limbo. Ideas assumed to be important should direct us to devising observational techniques for their systematic assessment.

Finally, the issue of urban impersonality and anomie is not simply a theoretical one. The future development of society requires that we anticipate the diverse needs of manifold segments of society. The assumptions we make today will influence the decisions made by the many who will alter our society tomorrow.

Notes

I thank George Christie, Marguerite Hurley, Roslyn Gerard, John Hudson, Sandor Halebsky, Robert Perrucci, Lawrence Cagle, and Mark Abrahamson who made a variety of contributions to earlier drafts. I thank Mary Belle-Isle, Joy Meadows, and Janet McNair who typed various drafts of this and earlier papers and James O'Hair for assistance in a variety of tasks related to the completion of this paper.

1. *American Journal of Sociology*, **44** (July 1938).

2. In Kurt Wolff, editor and translator, *The Sociology of Georg Simmel,* New York: The Free Press, 1950.

3. *Ibid.,* p. 12.

4. Edward Shils, "Daydreams and Nightmares: Reflections on the Criticism of Mass Culture," *Sewanee Review,* **65** (Fall, 1957), 599. *Cf. also,* Ephraim H. Mizruchi, *Success and Opportunity: A Study of Anomie,* New York: The Free Press, 1964, pp. 11–16. On romanticism in general, see Morton White, "The Two Stages in the Critique of the American City," in O. Handlin and J. Burchard, eds., *The Historian and the City,* Cambridge, Mass.: The M.I.T. and Harvard University Press, 1963, pp. 84–94.

5. *Cf.* Anselm Strauss, *Images of the American City,* New York: The Free Press, 1961, Appendix, p. 257, in which Albert Reiss, one of Wirth's most prominent students of urban sociaology, is quoted as rejecting these ideas.

6. *Cf.* C. Wright Mills, *White Collar,* New York: Oxford University Press, 1951, and, more recently, Edwin H. Powell, "The Evolution of the American City and the Emergence of Anomie," *British Journal of Sociology,* **13** (June, 1962), 156–167.

7. Leo Srole, "Social Integration and Certain Corollaries: An Exploratory Study," *American Sociological Review,* **21** (December, 1956), 709–716. *Cf. also,* Mizruchi, 1964, Chapter 3.

8. Ephraim H. Mizruchi, "Social Structure and Anomia in a Small City," *American Sociological Review,* **25** (October, 1960), 645–654.

9. Scott Greer and Ella Kube, "Urbanism and Social Structure: A Los Angeles Study," in M. Sussman, *Community Structure and Analysis,* New York: Thomas Y. Crowell, 1959, pp. 93–112, especially pp. 106–112.

10. Lewis Killian and Charles Grigg, "Urbanism, Race, and Anomia," *American Journal of Sociology,* **67** (May, 1962), 661–665; and Lewis Rhodes, "Anomia, Aspiration and Status," *Social Forces,* (May, 1964), 434–440.

11. Emile Durkheim, *Suicide,* New York: The Free Press, 1951, Ch. 2. I thank Lawrence Cagle for seeing this relationship during a discussion in one of my graduate seminars.

12. Arthur Vidich and Joseph Bensman, *Small Town in Mass Society,* Princeton: Princeton University Press, 1958. "Springdale," it is interesting to note, is a village within the same area of upstate New York in which our samples were taken.

13. Robert K. Merton, "Social Structure and Anomie," in *Social Theory and Social Structure,* New York: The Free Press, 1949 and 1957, Revised. *Cf.* Mizruchi, 1960 and 1964, cited above.

14. Small expected frequencies in the cells of the suburban and rural-suburban tables make chi-square analysis questionable. This observation, it should be noted, is congruent with those of G. Hochbaum, J. Darley, E. Monachesi and C. Bird in their paper, "Socioeconomic Variables in a Large City," *American Journal of Sociology,* **51** (July, 1955), 34–35.

15. John D. Photiadis, "Social Integration of Businessmen in Varied Size Communities," Office of Research and Development, West Virginia University, no

date. The sensitivity of the participant to general "societal currents" is noted by Daniel Lerner, *The Passing of Traditional Society,* New York: The Free Press, 1958.

16. *Op. cit.,* p. 314.

17. Mizruchi, 1960, p. 647. It is well at this point to consider the observations made in two other studies in which anomia and urban-rural factors were assessed. Killian and Grigg in their study of samples from two southeastern communities suggest that level of education, rather than urban residence, accounts for apparent urban-rural differences in anomia among whites, and that for Negroes no significant differences were found between urban and rural respondents. That education and anomia are directly associated is suggested by our data (1960 and 1964) showing significantly higher amonia responses in successively higher educational categories with low income, the association appearing stronger as education increased. Our integration of these data in 1964 was that the higher the expectation the greater the effect of low income on the person's morale. In this study our assumption is that expectations are realistically lower in the rural and rural-small town populations regardless of education. This is consistent with our data in Table III where income and education enjoy their best fit in the rural community as reflected in the χ^2 test. It should also be noted that our analysis of theory and data in our 1964 work suggests a marked difference between anomia in the relatively lower classes and the relatively higher. Finally, Killian and Grigg fall into the romantic trap to which we are directing our attention in this paper when they, perhaps unknowingly, paraphrase Wirth in their conclusion when they refer to "the greater impersonality of the city, the more extensive political participation, and the greater freedom to participate in protest organizations may soften somewhat the impact of minority status" (p. 665). I doubt that any of these assumptions, including the latter are supported by data. My own studies suggest, in general, that the *greater* the aspiration regardless of the *corresponding opportunity*—which I think characterizes the situation of the urban Negro—the greater the frustration. Lewis M. Killian and Charles M. Grigg, "Urbanism, Race and Anomia," *American Journal of Sociology,* **67** (May, 1962), 661–665.

Rhodes, in one of several studies on anomia among high school seniors, focuses on discrepancies between aspiration and status. His comparative data indicate that "anomia is maximized in just those rural and rural-nonfarm contexts where distance between aspiration and life chances for success is maximized," (p. 439). Although they do not support our findings with respect to the more general problem of discrepancy between aspiration and attainment *within* the context of our small city studied earlier (*cf.,* Mizruchi, 1964, Chapter V), the framework within which they are interpreted, the rural-urban comparison, suggests a possible contradiction. Lewis Rhodes, "Anomia, Aspiration and Status," *Social Forces,* **42** (May, 1964), 434–440.

18. Floyd Dotson, "Voluntary Associations Among Urban Working-Class Families," *American Sociological Review,* **16** (October, 1951), 687–695.

19. Edward M. Bruner, "Urbanization and Ethnic Identity in North Sumatra," *American Anthropologist,* **63** (June, 1961), 508 (this paper is reprinted in this volume). *Cf. also,* Mizruchi, 1964, pp. 11–16.

20. *Cf.* Strauss, *op. cit.,* p. 258, for a similar view.

EDUCATIONAL ASPIRATIONS, MODERNIZATION AND URBAN INTEGRATION

Guillermo Briones and F. B. Waisanen

It is well known that the urbanization process in Latin America generally includes the forming of populations fringing the large urban centers and marginal to the larger urban culture. This report deals with the impact of an urban marginal situation on the value orientations of the inhabitants, and through value orientations, on the process of modernization.

In organized preoccupation with development, one research perspective refers to the role of education in the modification of social stratification, particularly through the process of social mobility. The work of Hyman on the different value systems of North American social classes serves as an example within this orientation.[1] Hyman's central hypothesis asserts that differential measures of mobility within different social strata are associated with certain strategic values which serve as instrumental means for self progress. He writes:

> It is our assumption that an intervening variable mediating the relationship between low position and lack of upward mobility is a system of beliefs and values within the lower classes, which in turn reduces the very *voluntary* actions which would ameliorate their low position . . . Of course, an individual's value system is only one among many factors on which his position in the social hierarchy depends. Some of these factors may be external and arbitrary, quite beyond the control of even a highly motivated individual. However, within the bounds of the freedom available to individuals, this value system would create a *self-imposed* barrier to an improved position.[2]

One of our objectives is to determine whether the relationships reported by Hyman are maintained outside the North American cultural frame. The problem has special significance for countries in transition, as it can lead to further theoretical exposure of the factors which act upon social change and the process of modernization. In regard to these broad issues, we wish to investigate how the process of urbanization, particularly as it concerns the integration of migrants to cities, reflects on modernization by means of orientation toward education. Our general hypothesis asserts that conditions of ecological marginality are manifested in cultural marginality, the latter defined according to special forms of value orientations (which may not be in fit with the values of the larger urban

Paper read at the Annual Meetings of the American Sociological Association, Miami, 1966. This research was supported by Programa Interamericano de Informacion Popular (PIIP), San Jose, Costa Rica and the University of Chile, Santiago de Chile. PIIP is a Cooperative Program between the Institute of Agricultural Sciences of the OAS and the American International Association, the latter a philanthropic and technical assistance entity founded by Mr. Nelson Rockefeller and his brothers. The authors gratefully acknowledge project support from PIIP, the Institute of Economic Planning, University of Chile, and from Michigan State University, particularly from International Programs, the International Communication Institute and the Department of Communication.

culture). Further, we expect that this condition of cultural marginality will relate to educational aspiration levels, to optimism regarding attainment of aspirations, and to perception of the functions of education.

Methodology

The data for the present paper come from a larger project on communication and migration in Chile and are derived from two samples: (1) 160 migrants residing in the city of Santiago and (2) 108 migrants now residing in marginal residential areas (or "callampas") of Santiago.

The Gran Santiago subjects were selected randomly from a larger sample of 1540 persons born outside of Santiago. The larger sample was designed for another study by the Institute of Economics at the University of Chile.

The sample of slum migrants was randomly selected from a registration of households in 30 different callampas areas, all of which are located on the periphery of Gran Santiago. In this subsample, as in the Gran Santiago case, heads of households were interviewed.

The interviewers were students at the University of Chile and were trained at the Institute for Economic Planning at the University. Interview time averaged 75 minutes. Interviewing was done in December, 1964.

Educational Aspiration Levels

Investigating the relation between value systems and social mobility is, of course only one way of approaching the more general relationship between education and economic development. When the relationship between education and development is approached directly, the problem can focus upon the training and allocation of sufficient talent to satisfy the requirements for expansion of the economic system (industrialization, development of agricultural technology, reorganization and integration of services, and the like). In facing this problem, the policy of some Latin American countries has consisted of searching for means to increase the availability of classrooms, teachers, etc. Although we do not question the significance of such measures, one could argue that the mere increase of these is not sufficient guarantee that they will be fully utilized. On this point Tumin and Feldman contend, "It is critical . . . to investigate the extent to which becoming educated, skilled, and mobile *matters to different segments of the population.*"[3] In accordance with these notions, we assume that educational goals and their economic and social consequences are connected with diverse motivations toward education, and, more specifically, with different levels of educational aspiration.

Higher or lower motivation toward a certain goal must, of course, be considered in connection with the class to which the individual belongs.[4] In this sense, when a person belonging to the labor class aspires to a college education his "ambition" is higher than that of an individual of the middle class with an equal goal. In strict sense, therefore, our data do not permit us to deal with motivations, per se, but rather with orientations toward educational levels, which, in turn, can say something about aspiration levels.

Table 1 shows the expected relationship between level of education and level of educational aspiration for his children. For migrants living in Gran Santiago, 51% of those who have had elementary education want their children to have a college education, the corresponding percentage for secondary school graduates is 76%, and 100% for those with university education.

TABLE 1. EDUCATIONAL ASPIRATIONS FOR CHILDREN IN RELATION TO EDUCATION LEVEL: SANTIAGO AND CALLAMPAS

Aspiration Level	Santiago			Callampas
	Primary	Secondary	University	Primary *
Primary	9 (7)			10 (9)
Secondary	41 (32)	24 (10)		56 (48)
University	51 (40)	76 (31)	100 (20)	34 (29)
Total	100.0 (79)	100.0 (41)	100.0 (20)	100.0 (86)

* The only educational level existing in the callampas is the elementary level.

More importantly, and considering the impact of the socio-ecological medium upon aspirations, the data show that the educational aspiration levels of the callampas population are generally lower than the aspiration levels of those living in the city, and who are, we assume, more integrated to the urban culture. Only 34% of the callampas population want a college education for their children in comparison to 51% for integrated migrants of the same (primary) educational level. (The difference is significant at the .05 level; $x^2 = 5.16$.)

The data in Table 1, showing a strong orientation of college graduates toward university education for their children, implicitly confirm the importance of the professions in the structuring of new societies. There is little cause to doubt that the achievement of a high educational level by an individual will lead to a perception of higher educational achievement as a characteristic ascribable to his position and, because of this, he will consider it both obligation and privilege that his children obtain a university education. The same conclusion is warranted from responses to a question on the types of occupations desired for children: All subjects with a college education chose professions (medicine, law, engineering, etc.); at other educational levels, especially in the elementary, the predominant preferences were nonprofessional, e.g., carpenters, mechanics, electricians, and laborers.

Table 2 shows that income relates to educational aspirations for children in the same manner as education. In short, and as one would expect, the higher the income, the higher the educational aspirations. For children of those Gran Santiago subjects earning more than 600 Escudos per month, 89% aspire to university education for their children. These percentages reduce to 76% for middle income persons and by 46% for lower income persons within the same sample. The percentages for the callampas subjects reporting university aspirations for children are 38, 39 and 26 at the respective income levels (see Table 2).

TABLE 2. EDUCATIONAL ASPIRATIONS FOR CHILDREN ACCORDING TO INCOME LEVEL: SANTIAGO AND CALLAMPAS *

Aspiration Level	Income Level					
	Santiago			Callampas		
	High	Medium	Low	High	Medium	Low
Primary		2 (1)	12 (7)	8 (2)	6 (1)	18 (14)
Secondary	11 (2)	22 (13)	42 (25)	54 (14)	55 (10)	56 (43)
University	89 (17)	76 (44)	46 (27)	38 (10)	39 (7)	26 (20)
Total	100.0 (19)	100.0 (58)	100.0 (59)	100.0 (26)	100.0 (18)	100.0 (77)

* Income categories are defined as follows:
High: More than 600 Escudos (E°) monthly.
Medium: From 151 Escudos to 600 monthly.
Low: 150 Escudos or less.
The values refer to December, *1964, when U.S. $1.00 = 3.6* Escudos.

Considering the influence of the two variables jointly, we see (Table 3) that education is related to educational aspirations for children even though economic position may be similar. Individuals having higher education generally have higher educational aspirations for their children. In the middle income category, for example all persons with a college education want a college education for their children, as against 79% of those with a high school education and 69% of those having an elementary education. The same tendency appears in the two remaining income categories.

In commenting on Table 1, we pointed out that reference to different educational levels of individuals interviewed does not necessarily imply a difference in motivation toward those levels. It could well be that orientation toward a college education of individuals with less education and less income is an index of greater motivation, if we consider—as do Keller and Zavalloni—the distance and the number of obstacles between the goal and the present position. In any case, the data suggest that educational level does have an effect upon social mobility; i.e., in the lower classes there is, by the fact of orientation toward lower educational levels, a "built-in" obstacle, or self-limitation, to social ascent.

TABLE 3. EDUCATIONAL ASPIRATIONS FOR CHILDREN BY EDUCATION ATTAINED AND INCOME: SANTIAGO

Level of Education Attained	Aspiration Level by Income								
	High			Medium			Low		
	Primary	Secondary	University	Primary	Secondary	University	Primary	Secondary	University
Primary	—	*	— (1)	3	34	69 (29)	14	48	39 (44)
Secondary	—	20	80 (5)	—	21	79 (24)	—	44	56 (9)
University	—	—	100 (13)	—	—	100.0 (3)	—	—	— (0)

* Number of cases too small for percentage summarization.

It is probable that such a limitation is based in a recognition of obstacles as well as in different levels of "educational visibility" (that is, in the perception of the structure, duration and requisites of the national educational system). According to this, education ends, for many persons, with the elementary system; they may not perceive all of the diverse forms and possibilities for continuing studies and how these possibilities are connected with the educational structure. Whatever the basis of lower aspiration levels, it appears that Hyman's hypothesis is supported by our data, and specifically, that persons less integrated to urban culture have a greater self-limitation for change in social status than do the integrated individuals.

The "Multiplying" Function of Education

The data discussed above show covariations between educational and economic characteristics on one side, and aspirations on the other. Faced with this situation, we must ask about the minimum level of education that a person attains before he begins to consider education for his children as a dynamic factor in social ascent, be it in relation to social prestige or as a factor instrumental in increasing income. For Tumin and Feldman, the problem consists in

> . . . Locating a point, if it exists, in the educational exposure of the parent, at which his horizons have been sufficiently broadened and his perspectives on the changing social system sufficiently altered for him to have a reasonably well integrated commitment to that new system.[5]

In other words, the problem is to determine the minimum level of education required by an individual before education itself becomes a significant social object, and, as such, produces a dynamic attitudinal configuration in the parents that will lead the children to higher educational levels than that of the parents.

Previous research, particularly that of Tumin and Feldman,[6] suggests that educational achievement of parents and educational aspirations for children are not in unilinear relationship. With data based upon (1) perceived importance of education to status maintenance or ascent and (2) perceived ability to support children in the formal educational process, Tumin and Feldman assert that a point of significant change in orientation toward education may occur after the fourth year of elementary education. Our data support this assertion.

The relationship between parental educational achievement and educational aspirations for children could be expressed as an "s" curve, with a significant point of aspirational "take-off" occurring somewhere between the fifth year of elementary and the second year of secondary school. At this point, a kind of rupture with traditional belief systems may occur and a more "modern" or urban outlook, committed to processes of ascent and accompanied by perception of opportunities, may start to take form.

The data on mean aspiration levels by educational achievement provide additional support for the possibility that this point of significant attitudinal change may occur between the fifth year of elementary and the second year of high school. Table 4 summarizes the relevant data, and shows the greatest relative aspirational shift within the 4–6 primary and the 1–3 secondary categories.

TABLE 4. MEAN ASPIRATION LEVELS BY LEVEL OF EDUCATION ACHIEVED

Education	X Aspiration (years)	Difference
0 *	10.90	
1–3 primary	11.21	0.31
4–6 primary	12.35	1.14
1–3 secondary	14.49	2.14
4–6 secondary	16.04	1.55
1–3 university	17.0	0.96
4 or more university	17.0	0.0

* Includes "refusals" and "indeterminants"

Plotting level of education of household head against mean aspirational level (years of school desired for children) produces an approximation of the expected "s" curve as shown in Figure 1. These data, as do those of Tumin and Feldman, suggest that similar curves might obtain in plotting educational level against other aspects of a general orientation toward education, e.g., importance attached to education, its visibility as a means to social ascent, the emergence of strategies regarding resource management (as in saving money for the education of children), and in a more general sense, a futuristic time orientation, and an awareness of arenas of self autonomy. In short, the five- to seven-year educational achievement level may represent the point of significant emergence of an attitudinal configuration of modernity.

FIG. 1. MEAN ASPIRATION LEVELS BY EDUCATION ACHIEVED.

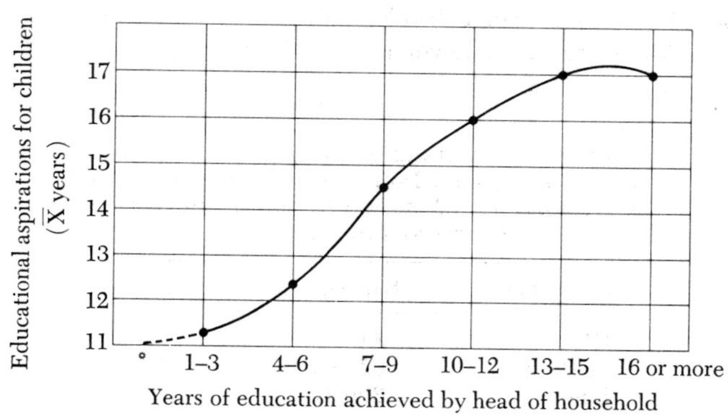

° No subjects reported no education; the mean aspiration level for 27 subjects in "no answer" and "indeterminate" categories is 10.9 years.

It is clear, however, that the existence of a "point of psychological mobilization," determined by a certain quantum of schooling, as well as the magnitude of this quantum, remains a proposition to be submitted to test through additional research.

It should be noted that the point of "take-off" in educational aspirations may be at the same time the point which marks a higher grade of rigidity in the social structure. Following Tumin and Feldman, we could consider that once this point is overcome, processes of integration could be produced that would result in a higher social homogeneity.[7] In any case, we could say that the problem of low educational levels does not appear to consist only in the lack of schools, but also in the capacity of the system to retain the children.

Educational Achievement Expectations

Differences in levels of educational aspiration for children represent only one aspect of the stratification of life chances. Another aspect refers to confidence in the possibility that children can attain the desired level. We assume that that degree of optimism, particularly in the case of the lower classes, would represent one strain of influence in the ordering of behavior toward future states.

In the low income group, 57% in Santiago and 55% in the callampas population believe their children will obtain the level of education to which they aspire (figures corresponding to high and middle income groups of Gran Santiago are 89% and 78%, respectively; for the callampas the percentages are 75% and 72%, respectively).

Clearly, confidence in the possibility of attaining an educational aspiration level depends on economic as well as educational level, but the situation of urban marginality in which many of the migrants find themselves also places a limitation on optimism. This limitation effect is supported by the data in Table 5 which summarizes the percentages of persons of different economic status who believe their children will attain a college education. The data show an expected limitation of aspirations by the individual's economic situation, but they also show that the social context in which he finds himself, in this case a situation of urban marginality (defined by residence in callampas populations), adds to the economic barrier. For equal income levels, expectations regarding a college education for the children are much lower among the groups living in these marginal

TABLE 5. PERCENTAGE OF PERSONS OF DIFFERENT INCOME LEVEL WHO INDICATE THEY BELIEVE THEIR CHILDREN WILL ATTAIN A COLLEGE EDUCATION: SANTIAGO AND CALLAMPAS

Income level	Santiago	Callampas
High	83(16)	38(8)
Medium	62(60)	17(17)
Low	30(64)	13(72)

$\chi^2 = 19.6$ $p < .001$

populations. While 83% of the Santiago migrants in the higher economic category believe that the indicated aspirational level is attainable, the corresponding figure is only 37% for nonintegrated migrants. In the lower income level, the figures are 30% and 13% respectively.

Lower optimism regarding possibility of achievement of educational aspirations, in the context of ecological and cultural marginality, could be rooted in a weaker system of informal sanctions toward education than exists in the central society; there may be insufficient socio-cultural "pressure" *on* parents (and consequently insufficient pressure *from* parents) to send their children to school. This could explain in part why educational aspiration levels expressed verbally are not realized in expected proportion.

TABLE 6. PERCENTAGE OF INDIVIDUALS IN DIFFERENT EDUCATIONAL LEVELS WHO INDICATE A BELIEF THAT THEIR CHILDREN WILL ATTAIN A COLLEGE EDUCATION: SANTIAGO AND CALLAMPAS

Educational level	Santiago	Callampas
Primary *	33(79)	18(86)
Secondary	65(41)	—
University	100.0(20)	—

*χ^2 (primary level only) = 5.23 $p < .05$

The confidence in the possibility of children's attaining a determined level of education is related to the subject's educational level in the same manner as income. Holding education constant, the callampas population has less confidence that their children will attain the aspired educational level. In Table 6 comparison can be made only for persons with an elementary education.

Images of Education

To this point, we have discussed some possible relationships between economic and social variables and educational aspirations. Now we wish to examine another element of orientation toward education, that which is constituted by the image of education and more specifically, by the perception of the goals which can be attained through education.

The data confirm the results of other investigations that groups having a lower economic status have, in greater proportion, a materialistic orientation toward education, perceiving it predominantly as a medium to attain better salaries, and thus a higher level of living. In the higher income groups, by contrast, education may be considered (in addition to its materialistic functions) as an instrument to obtain prestige and to acquire more knowledge about community affairs, that is, as a process which performs a general self-enhancement function.

Table 7, dealing with integrated migrants of Santiago, shows that 66% of the individuals of the lower stratum assign education a materialistic function as

TABLE 7. PERCEPTION OF THE FUNCTIONS OF EDUCATION ACCORDING TO INCOME LEVEL: SANTIAGO

Perceived Function	High	Santiago Medium	Low
Materialistic *	19	45	66
Nonmaterialistic	81	55	34
Total	100.0(16)	100.0(60)	100.0(64)

$\chi^2 = 12.96$ $p < .01$

compared to only 19% of individuals in the higher stratum, and 45% in the middle stratum. The effect of marginality (callampas) on these perceptions or images of education will be discussed later.

These data appear to present a contradiction between materialistic orientation and low levels of educational aspiration in the lowest income group. Mizruchi has observed:

> In the rational or cognitive sphere, education is viewed realistically by the lower classes as a means for the attainment of success. In the non-rational, evaluative sphere, education is not highly valued. There is thus a disparity between the cognitive and evaluative dimensions that fosters a greater tendency to limited achievement in the lower classes.[8]

This may well be the nature of the case; however, differences in aspiration levels do not necessarily indicate differences in motivation toward those levels. Therefore, Mizruchi's explanation might be complemented by noting that while the lower classes could perceive realistically that education permits earning more money or obtaining better jobs, they might not perceive the means to attain the education that would permit them to obtain these jobs or occupations or higher incomes. It may also be that they do not perceive the *level* at which education manifests itself in these advantages, in accordance with the concept of educational visibility mentioned above.

These differing perceptions are elements of differing symbolic worlds. Individuals cannot adequately value what they do not possess or do not know. The amount of education received by individuals in the lower ranges of the economic scale is insufficient to enable personal confirmation that education has diverse functions, among others that of providing self-satisfaction by putting the individual in contact with other sectors of the larger culture. On the other hand, when a laborer, for example, compares his situation with that of a professional, differences in education are apparent to him, and he takes these differences into consideration in explaining the better job and better economic situation.

The reverse of the case is apparent in individuals who have a higher income and higher education. They recognize the diverse functions of education and place these functions on a multiple criteria scale, ranging from the economic to general self-enhancement functions. While the person of higher socio-economic status may perceive that a significant attribute of education is the economic betterment of the individual, he also recognizes other functions.

TABLE 8. FUNCTIONS ATTRIBUTED TO EDUCATION, ACCORDING TO YEARS IN SCHOOL: SANTIAGO AND CALLAMPAS

Perceived Function	Primary	Santiago Secondary	University	Callampas Primary
Materialistic	58	42	32	66
Non-materialistic	42	58	68	34
Total	100.0(85)	100.0(41)	100.0(19)	100.0(97)

Similar conclusions can be drawn from a consideration of the effect of the number of years in school on the images of education, as in Table 8. The lower the educational level, the greater the emphasis placed on the materialistic function of education: the Santiago figures fluctuate from 32% at the college level to 58% at the elementary level. In any case, it can be noted that nonintegrated migrants with the same level of instruction as those residing in the city have a greater materialistic orientation. There exists, then, a "level of integration" influence regarding the materialistic perception of education.

Education and Satisfaction with Job

The relationships of educational achievement and occupation can be examined in the context of levels of satisfaction with one's job. In general there appears to be a tendency for these levels to be rather high, because the main referent may be the nature of the job itself and not the factors surrounding it.[9] As one would expect, variations exist according to income and education of the individual. When the latter variable is considered it is interesting to note that the relation obtained is not linear but curvilinear, which seems to indicate that not only the quantity but the quality and type of education is involved.

Table 9 shows that individuals with a high school education tend to express less satisfaction with their life situation (in relation to years of school completed) than individuals with only elementary education. For those who answered that they were fully or somewhat satisfied, the corresponding figures are 62% and

TABLE 9. LEVELS OF SATISFACTION IN RELATION TO PRESENT ECONOMIC SITUATION AND EDUCATION RECEIVED: SANTIAGO AND CALLAMPAS

Level of satisfaction *	Primary	Santiago Secondary	University	Callampas Primary
Highly satisfied and satisfied	71(63)	62(26)	80.0(16)	40(32)
Dissatisfied and highly dissatisfied	29(26)	38(16)	20.0(4)	60(49)
Total	100.0(89)	100.0(42)	100.0(20)	100.0(81)

* The subject was asked: "Considering the number of school years you have completed, are you satisfied or dissatisfied with your present economic situation?" An intensity probe followed.

71%, respectively. The percentage for individuals with a college education is 80%.

Following the tendency established in previous tables, the nonintegrated callampas populations have lower levels of satisfaction than those corresponding to migrants integrated to urban culture. (The χ^2 for primary educational level is 17.9, with $p < .001$.) Only 40% expressed some degree of satisfaction, a lower percentage than any given by the integrated migrants. This predominant dissatisfaction may relate to prevalent occupations within the slum areas, where "residual" jobs, (e.g., buyers of waste paper and empty bottles) are common.

The greater dissatisfaction of persons with high school education poses questions regarding the function of high school education in relation to individual economic aspirations and the requirements of productivity in general. It appears to be clear that "economic frustrations" are common at the secondary educational level, and that there are relatively higher income aspirations (based on education) than have been presently achieved.

Table 10, relating satisfaction with salary to education, shows that the greater proportion of unsatisfied subjects is again in the high school category. We find that with equal number of school years, the marginal populations have higher levels of dissatisfaction than the migrants residing in the city.

TABLE 10. SATISFACTION WITH SALARY ACCORDING TO EDUCATIONAL LEVEL

Level of Satisfaction *	Primary	Santiago Secondary	University	Callampas Primary
Highly satisfied and satisfied	55(37)	50(15)	80(12)	34(22)
Dissatisfied and highly dissatisfied	45(30)	50(15)	20(3)	66(43)
Total **	100(67)	100(30)	100(15)	100(65)

* The subject was asked, "Regarding the effort required in your job, are you satisfied or dissatisfied with your present income?" An intensity probe followed.

** The reduction in N results predominantly from unemployed (not applicable) and "no answer" cases. The number of undefined cases will, of course, differ with the variable at issue in any table.

A final demonstration of the curvilinear form of the correlation obtains when we consider the variables of educational level and "global" satisfaction in the job, as is done in Table 11. Again, the persons with a high school education are the ones who manifest the greater degree of dissatisfaction. At another level, and showing again the intrusion of the place of residence variable, fewer callampas residents (compared with persons of equal education living in Santiago) manifest satisfaction with their work.

The lower levels of adaptation to work manifested by individuals having a high school education, when compared with individuals with elementary and college educations, pose an interesting and possibly significant theoretical problem. The problem is directly connected with educational process and ideology, and points to the need for investigating (as does Merton with respect to divergent

TABLE 11. GLOBAL SATISFACTION WITH JOB, ACCORDING TO EDUCATION LEVEL: SANTIAGO AND CALLAMPAS

Level of Global Satisfaction *	Primary	Santiago Secondary	University	Callampas Primary
Highly satisfied and satisfied	79(52)	68(21)	93(14)	67(44)
Dissatisfied and highly dissatisfied	21(14)	32(10)	7(1)	33(22)
Total	100.0(66)	100.0(31)	100.0(15)	100.0(66)

* The subject was asked, "Taking all things into account, are you satisfied or dissatisfied with your present job?" An intensity probe followed.

conduct[10]) the manner by which social structure itself generates dissonance in individuals. Whatever the theoretical complications at psychological and social-psychological levels, the data clearly indicate that persons who are not at the educational achievement base of the social structure are nevertheless the ones who manifest less satisfaction with their work.

Conclusions

Our objective was to test the hypothesis that residence in an area of ecological marginality (in the present case, the peripheral slums of Santiago) is related to cultural marginality and attendant lower educational aspirations for children, greater pessimism regarding the possibility of achieving these aspirations, and more materialistic orientation toward the function of education. In general, the data support these propositions.

The findings support the assertion of Hyman and others that different social strata generate different orientations toward education. Moreover, the situation of ecological marginality appears to compound the class-related limiting effects upon aspirations, optimism, and visibility of education as a means to social ascent.

A basic factor within the general relationship between education and social development may be a minimum educational level for the development of an orientation which includes the perception of relationship between education as a means and self progress (or perhaps better, the social ascent of children) as a goal. The data in this Santiago case suggest, although by no means conclusively, that this point of attitudinal "take-off" may occur between the fifth year of elementary and the first year of secondary school. If further research shows this to be so, we could be led to crucial questions regarding the relationship between literacy and modernization. It may not be literacy per se that transforms the perceived boundaries of one's present and future worlds, but rather an accumulation of experiences (within which the function of literacy may be crucial, to be sure) which leads to a self concept rooted in broader boundaries and which is future oriented and mobility inclined.

Finally, the data show that degree of urban integration is related to degree of work satisfaction, with education held constant. Equally interesting, and perhaps theoretically more important, is the condition of low levels of job satisfaction expressed by subjects with secondary, as compared with primary and university levels of education. The data pose relevant questions regarding the functions and dysfunctions of secondary education in developing societies. Continuing examination is warranted into the possibility that such job satisfaction may be related to political ideological commitment, to participation in reform movements, and to different perceptions regarding channels for mobility and maintenance and enhancement of the self.

Notes

1. Herbert H. Hyman, "The Value Systems of Different Classes," in Reinhard Bendix and Seymour M. Lipset, *Class, Status and Power,* (Glencoe, Free Press, 1953).

2. *Ibid.*, pp. 426–427.

3. Melvin M. Tumin & Arnold S. Feldman, "Status, Perspective and Achievement: Education and Class Structure in Puerto Rico," *American Sociological Review* **21**, August, 1956, 465. Italics are ours.

4. Suzanne Keller & Marisa Zavalloni, "Class Sociale, Ambition et Reussite," Sociologie du Travail. **1**, 62, pp. 1–14.

5. Tumin and Feldman, *loc. cit.*, p. 468.

6. Tumin and Feldman, *loc. cit.*, p. 467. While the Tumin and Feldman data are based upon different variables and different modes of analysis, they report: ". . . It would appear that while education up to four years of school may matter, and though its effects may be cumulative, once the fourth year is passed, a new vista of life possibilities seems to be opened." The problem stated has clear implications to social and economic development. Given a point of "psychological mobilization," basic questions can be asked about educational planning; what is the minimum schooling a population should have to become actively incorporated into the development process?

7. Tumin and Feldman, *loc. cit.*, p. 472.

8. Ephraim H. Mizruchi, *Success and Opportunity: A Study of Anomie,* (Glencoe, Free Press, 1964), p. 81.

9. See Guillermo Briones y Jose Mejia, *El Obero Industrial,* (Lima, Universidad de San Marcos, 1964), pp. 41–42.

10. Robert K. Merton, "Social Structure and Anomia," in *Social Theory and Structure,* (Glencoe, Free Press, 1957), pp. 131–160.

EDUCATION, DEPRIVATION AND ALIENATION

Charles V. Willie

Today our nation is host to three separate but interrelated revolutions. There are radical and fundamental changes in the United States in the production of goods and services, in the geographic distribution of the population, and in the patterns of social interaction in local communities. In short, we are in the midst of the automation, urbanization and human relations revolutions.

A revolution is a social movement. It grows through collective effort, may be controlled and directed by human intelligence, but neither started nor stopped by choice of a single person. It was not the privilege of any single person to start these revolutions. It is not his prerogative to stop them. But it is each person's responsibility to participate in guiding them toward the fulfillment of goals that benefit all people. Whether we like it or not, three revolutions are upon us to which our society and its schools must respond.

Automation Revolution

With the introduction of power-driven machinery in England after 1750, we have increasingly found ways of replacing hand labor. Today there are a multiplicity of devices in agricultural and manufacturing industry designed to perform actions formerly performed by human beings.

The wealth of this nation can be attributed, in part, to increasing automation. The gross national product (which is the total national output of goods and services) rose from about 100 billion dollars in 1929,[1] before the Great Depression, to over 600 billion today. Personal income has steadily increased and so has the number of employed. Computed in 1962 dollars, the average annual income of families and individuals rose from $4,200 in 1929 to $6,400 in 1962. Moreover, 19 percent of the nation's families have incomes over $10,000 a year.[2] The number of jobs increased from 55 million in 1940 to more than 70 million today.[3]

Change in agriculture is a good example of the contribution of automation to the production of goods and services. In a report prepared for the Twentieth Century Fund, Edward Higbee points out that "an hour of farm labor now produces four times as much as it did in 1919–1921." [4] This increase in production capacity is associated with a decrease in the number of agricultural workers. Horses and mules are obsolete and so are the unskilled hands that drove them. The airplane has become a farming implement, spraying fertilizer, pesticides and buzzing blackbirds away from the fields.[5] Thus automation not only has replaced the limited skills of farm hands, it also has displaced the scarecrow. The limited skills of laboring men have been rendered obsolete on the farms and in the cities, too. For example, less than six percent of the employed labor force in Washington, D. C. are laborers.

Although the automation revolution has generated new wealth and more work, it also has generated a residue of poor and unemployed. One-fifth of the nation's

---

Reprinted by permission of the author and publisher from the *Journal of Negro Education,* Summer 1965, pp. 209–219.

households are impoverished, having incomes under $3,000 a year and four to six percent of the labor force who may want to work cannot find work because they are unskilled, uneducated, nonwhite, adolescent or elderly. The unemployment rate among nonwhites and the unskilled is twice the national rate; the unemployment rate among persons in the labor force in their late teens is three times the national rate. Elimination of the circumstances which generate this residue is a challenge to automation and should be a major concern of the total nation. Michael Harrington describes this residue as a "monstrous example of needless suffering. . . ."[6] John Galbraith calls it a "disgrace."[7]

The mythology of poverty has been one among several deterrents to a solution to the problem. While only four to six percent of the labor force have remained unemployed in recent years, 20 percent of the households exist on less than $3,000 a year. Nevertheless, the myth persists that poor people are those who will not work. A 1963 survey of 1,000 households in the four-square mile area surrounding Cardozo High School in the District of Columbia revealed that 190 of the households have *employed* heads who earn less then $3,000 per year. In most instances, the head is an unskilled worker who continues to work even though his earnings are insufficient to support his family. His is the lot of the employed poor. There are children of all age levels in these families which means they are a legitimate concern of the schools. The problem can not be simplified to one of motivation. The heads of these families want to work and do work but their earning capacity is limited and, as a result, their children are deprived of many opportunities that would prepare them to move out of a condition of poverty when they become adults.

Urbanization Revolution

The industrial-automation revolution could not have occurred without the urbanization revolution. The late Louis Wirth, professor of sociology at the University of Chicago, has stated that "the beginning of what is distinctively modern in our civilization is best signalized by the growth of great cities."[8] He has defined the city as a relatively large, dense, and permanent settlement of socially heterogeneous individuals.[9]

The congregating of large numbers of persons with diversified talents is necessary for mass production. Hence, the congregating of people in cities has increased as the economy has shifted from farming to manufacturing.

The enrichments of urban living are many. Specialization and division of labor have brought together people of diversified talents who have easy access to each other. One person is available and employed to do for another what the other cannot do for himself.

The heterogeneous population, so essential in sustaining urban life, often has been the basis for contemporary community strife. As pointed out several years ago by sociologist Louis Wirth, increase the number of inhabitants in a settlement and you affect the relationships between them.[10] Typically, in the urban community, "our physical contacts are close but our social contacts are distant."[11] Symbolically, Negro author James Baldwin entitles a book, *Nobody Knows My Name*.[12] The lot of the urban dweller is like that of the Ancient Mariner who cried out on the high salty sea: water, water, everywhere; and not a drop to drink. There are people, people everywhere; but city dwellers are lonely. They are distrustful of people who are different from themselves. And yet, these are people whom they need; diversity is a necessity in city life. Suburbanities cannot say, in truth, to slum dwellers: "You are not part of us." The affluent cannot say, with honor, to the poor: "We are not responsible for your condition." Whites cannot say, with sincerity, to nonwhites: "We have no need of you." We are all inextricably connected and must bind ourselves together in ways that help each other.

If city people must do for each other what one cannot do for himself, they must learn to trust each other. But persons tend to trust each other whom they know and can call by name. There is always an element of doubt about the strange face in the "lonely crowd." Persons may get to know each other and feel free and easy only when they have met each other. Meeting persons of different backgrounds is becoming increasingly difficult. The slums and suburbs are in separate locations. Whites and nonwhites have different associations. The poor and affluent are isolated. Neighborhood-based associations are becoming increasingly homogeneous in the characteristics of persons who participate in them and at a time when the total urban community is becoming more heterogeneous with its members dependent on strangers whom they do not know. These two trends are incompatible and are on a collision course. Segregation creates a dilemma for urban community organization; the proportion of community persons whom we know decreases as our need to know them increases. What is the responsibility of the schools to homogenize the people of the city which of necessity is heterogeneous?

Human Relations Revolution

The revolution in human relations has been stimulated by the concentration of diversified populations in the big cities of our nation. Abraham Lincoln reminded the nation several decades ago that a house divided against itself cannot stand. This principle also applies to local urban communities. The city accepts the people of all ages, races, religions, nationalities and social classes because their talents are needed. This acceptance has been its strength. Some cities cannot tolerate the kinds of people who have come to serve the community and relegate them to segregated sections cut off from the mainstream of society. This rejection has been its weakness. We cannot divide the people, set them against each other, and remain strong.

Oppressed people who live in the company of free people will not endure their oppression forever. Poor people who exist in a society of plenty, lose patience and eventually rebel. Current demonstrations by the oppressed and uprisings of the poor have human relations implications. The causes for these disturbances cannot be resolved without effecting major changes in the social relations of people in our society. We do a disservice to the students whom we teach if their exposure is only to situations of racial segregation and social class separation. Students with these limited experiences may be unaware of the changes needed. Moreover, this is the city of the present and the past which most assuredly is passing away. The new city will be a mixture of many interdependent people who need and, therefore, must trust each other. We must teach our students this truth today, that we are all entangled together in the "sweet fly-paper of life." Yet we continue to educate our children in schools where the races of mankind are segregated and different social classes are separated from each other. Our continuing segregated schools are nothing less than a cultural lag.

Response of the Schools

It seems to me that the schools must respond to these three revolutions by eliminating all conditions, within their authority, which contribute to deprivation of and alienation between persons and the separation of different races and social classes. For too long the schools have compromised and denied that they have a responsibility.

We consider a person or a category of persons to be deprived when their financial resources are insufficient to obtain the goods and services considered necessary for a normal standard of living in the local community. We consider a person or a category of persons to be alienated when they are cut off from the mainstream of a society and the helpful supports of a community. Racial segregation as practiced in the United States for more than a century has been a powerful form of alienation, cutting off Negro youth from the helpful assistance of the society-at-large. There are other forms of deprivation and alienation, but economic and racial forms are what we shall discuss now.

The theme of this part of the discussion is that deprivation and alienation are compounded circumstances; you can't solve one and keep the other. Failure to recognize this fact has brought us to our current crisis.

Even the clear thinking Dr. James B. Conant has contributed to the confusion concerning the school's responsibility for racial integration. In 1961, Dr. Conant publicly endorsed the statement of a city superintendent of schools who insisted that "he was in the education business and should not become involved in attempts to correct the consequences of voluntary segregated housing."[13] Viewed historically, one hardly could call racially segregated housing in the United States voluntary. But that is another issue. The main point of this school superintendent is that he is in the business of overcoming deprivation, not alienation, as if deprivation because of race could be solved within the framework of alienating racial segregation. Many educators have suggested that Negro youth can be upgraded educationally and economically without dealing with the social problem of segregation. This assertion is a "bad pitch."

Even Dr. James B. Conant swung at this bad pitch and almost struck out in his book, *Slums and Suburbs*. He counseled those who are agitating for the deliberate mixing of children to accept *de facto* segregated schools as a consequence of a present housing situation and to work for the improvement of slum schools whether Negro or white.[14] The fact is that most slum schools serve a predominantly Negro population and, in general, communities unwilling to desegregate their Negro population have been unwilling to upgrade it economically and educationally. We have several decades of proof that separate facilities are seldom equal. The only reason for separating persons in the first place is to accord them differential treatment.

As Dr. Conant has said, "more money is needed in slum schools." [15] But more money will never be spent in slum schools so long as they are schools reserved for minorities who are unwelcome in the mainstream of community life. Consider the programs designed to upgrade slum schools throughout the nation; they are largely supported by foundation or Federal Government funds that originate outside the community. While some localities have provided matching funds from local tax revenue, by and large there is an absence of large-scale commitment to expending a disproportionate amount of the school budget in slum schools. I do not expect this situation to change for the better so long as slum schools are part of the overall community pattern of racial segregation, *de facto* or deliberate.

Washington, D. C. is a prototype of what may be experienced in many big cities of the nation. The best high school in the community is in a predominantly white neighborhood; the poorest high school in the community is in a predominantly Negro neighborhood.

Washington, D. C. schools operate on a track system in which children within a specific grade are grouped according to their ability. The tracks range from basic, general, and college preparatory, to honors. Yet, in 1964, not all senior high schools in the predominantly Negro inner-city section of Washington had honors tracks. What are the provisions for bright students in some inner-city high schools who deserve advanced study?

According to a study of the Washington, D. C. schools, using 1962 data, one-third of the grade-school students in a predominantly Negro inner-city district attended elementary schools erected before 1900, as compared with only one-sixth of the citywide enrollment at this level. Also, 16 percent of the elementary children attend school on a part-time schedule because of overcrowding, as compared with only three percent of the citywide elementary school population. In this same predominantly Negro inner-city district, 26 percent of the elementary school children are in classes of 36 or more children, as compared with 18 percent of the elementary school children in the citywide population.

Public Affairs Pamphlet #316, entitled "School Segregation, Northern Style," clearly states that "segregated schools in the North are poorer"; they tend to be older, less well equipped and more crowded than schools in the white neighborhoods.[16] In Chicago as late as 1960, Negro schools were assigned a disproportionate number of inexperienced teachers, and "81 percent of the children in the all-Negro schools" as in contrast to only "2 percent of the 'white' schools" were on "double session." [17]

It is true that in some localities the conscience of the community has been pricked by the current civil rights revolution. A few new schools have been built in Negro neighborhoods. These one or two schools have not upset the pattern. I would advise you to keep your eye on the pattern. It is also true that selected schools in predominantly Negro neighborhoods have been singled out for "higher horizons" programs. This is a laudable beginning, if it is clearly understood as a beginning. Until higher horizons schools are the rule rather than the exception in slum sections of the city, they still will not have transformed the pattern of a poor quality of education in slum schools.

In his book, the *Affluent Society*, Dr. John Galbraith states that "we ought to invest more than proportionately in the children of the poor community. It is there that high-quality schools . . . are most needed to compensate for the very low investment which families are able to make in their offspring. . . ." [18]

We ought to do this. But are we likely to do so when it is recognized that many of the poor are Negro and that for several years our institutions have deliberately separated Negroes and other minorities from the mainstream of community life so that they could be treated differently?

In 1961, Dr. Conant's published position was that *de facto* segregation should be accepted as a consequence of the present housing situation and that groups agitating for a deliberate mixing of schools could spend their energies best working for the improvement of slum schools, whether Negro or white. Fortunately, in February 1964, in a Chicago news conference, Dr. Conant altered his views and allegedly said, according to the Associated Press, "I was clearly wrong when I suggested several years ago that bussing high school youngsters around a big city was impractical." He allegedly further said the big cities should strive to have as many racially and economically mixed high schools as possible and that the comprehensive high school should become truly comprehensive.[19]

Although the statement in *Slums and Suburbs* has probably been used by some communities as the basis for attempting to do something about deprivation without changing community patterns of segregation, even then, back in 1961, Dr. Conant approached the subject with ambivalence. In that same book, he observed that "nearly a hundred years ago our ancestors—North and South, East and West—accepted, almost without protest, the transformation of the status of the Negro from that of a slave into that of a member of a lower, quite separate caste." And then he admits that "we now recognize so plainly but so belatedly, a caste system finds its clearest manifestation in an educational system." [20] Persons unprepared to do something about racial segregation ignore this section of Dr. Conant's book. But we ignore it today at our own peril. This is what the civil rights revolution is all about. It is concerned with the mainstream of American society, and the abrogation of a semicaste system. This is why we call deprivation and alienation a compounded situation. To eliminate deprivation, we must eliminate alienation due to segregation and discrimination.

How do we go about eliminating the compound problems of deprivation and alienation? First, we must begin to identify the problem as it is and do away with a lot of camouflaging verbiage.

The reason that Negro children were one to two years behind white children in some subjects when some school systems desegregated after 1954 is because Negro children for many years had received the short end of the deal. For years, Negro youngsters in communities throughout the nation have been segregated, discriminated against, and herded into a separate caste-like status. As Dr. Conant points out, "a caste system finds its clearest manifestation in an educational system." [21]

I am reminded of a young social scientist in Washington who came to us at Washington Action for Youth for financial assistance for his project designed to teach Negro youth good work attitudes so that they could find jobs. Here was a purveyor of a project who knew but tried to ignore the fact that the unemployment rate is twice as high among Negro males as it is among white males to learn marketable skills, and on the other hand, white employers are inclined to hire white workers first. It seemed to us that the primary problem was not to expend our energy developing good work attitudes but to redouble our efforts to provide a meaningful education for these youth, providing them with marketable skills, and to eliminate discrimination against them. The opportunity to earn money is usually a good antedote for poor work attitudes.

As a matter of fact, we proved this during the summer of 1963. Washington Action for Youth, in cooperation with the D. C. Public Schools, the D. C. Recreation Department, the U. S. Employment Service and the Washington Urban League, sponsored a summer job program for deprived youth. Jobs were obtained in government and in private business for approximately 1,100 youth 16–18 years of age. Most youth earned $1.25 per hour for a period of eight weeks with wages being paid by the employing organizations. Seventy-two percent of the youth lived in poor neighborhoods. Two-thirds came from families in which the head was a manual worker. Eighty percent had not worked previously. About six percent had parents currently receiving public welfare. Ten to fifteen percent had court records. These were deprived youth who had experienced limited opportunity in the past. In general, they turned in high-level performances when the opportunity to work was provided.

At the close of the summer, employers were requested to evaluate the performance of each youth and to indicate whether he would hire the youth again. Eighty-seven percent of the youth achieved job performance ratings of average to excellence and employers were sufficiently satisfied to state that they would rehire three out of every four youth. Nearly all of the youth were Negro.

In the Summer of 1964, Georgetown University proved that youth from inner-city areas of Washington respond well when opportunities to participate in the educational mainstream of community life are offered. Fifty-one high school seniors were invited to the Georgetown University campus during the Summer Session to participate in an eight-week College Orientation Program consisting of English, chemistry and mathematics courses and field trips. Ninety-eight percent of the youngsters remained in the program the entire period. They had a full day of classes but did not receive high school or college credit. One-fourth of the children with averages below B for the spring semester in high school performed at B or A levels during the summer at Georgetown. Chemistry and English were the courses in which the most dramatic improvement occurred. More than half of the youth with below B averages for the spring semester in high school worked at B or A levels in chemistry during the summer. Moreover, the University faculty who taught these high school seniors felt that they could recommend three out of every four for college on the basis of their summer's performance.

So the phrases, "poor motivation" and "poor attitude," are but camouflaging verbiage that cover up the poor effort of the adult affluent society to reach out to deprived youth and to provide opportunities for them in the mainstream of society. When this is done in good faith, our experience is that these youngsters respond well.

Low aspiration is another camouflaging phrase that covers up the fact that in our society all are encouraged to succeed but some are denied the opportunity. We know that low-income Negro families are acquainted with the good life and want it for their children. In the summer of 1963, we surveyed a randomly selected sample of 1,000 households in a deprived and predominantly Negro neighborhood in Washington. Respondents were asked to tell what they hope each of their children would do when he grows up. About half replied that job preference is for the child to decide. Of the remaining number who had specific occupational preferences, 90 percent wanted their child to be a professional worker such as a doctor, lawyer, engineer, minister, teacher, nurse, or social worker. Moreover, these low-income, unskilled or unemployed workers in our sample were aware of the educational requirements for professional work. These families have dreamed no small dreams. Their aspirations are high. But their means for fulfilling these aspirations are few. Their financial resources are small. Their experience of discrimination is great. In summary, the opportunity system is blocked.

We tend to attribute to others the problems that are our own. Thus, youth who are pushed out of school because schools are not flexible enough and sufficiently creative to accommodate their special needs are labeled "dropouts." This label places the onus on the youth and not on the school. Poor, fearful, lower-class, Negro families that are rejected by community social service agencies are classified as "uncooperative clients." This label places the responsibility on the family and not on the agency. These and other techniques we have used to rationalize the inadequacies of an affluent society that cares but does not care enough for the poor, oppressed, and the afflicted.

Conclusions and Recommended Changes

After facing up to the problem as it actually is, the next task is to devise an appropriate methodology for solving it. In general, two alternatives lie before us —one, change the individual, and the other, change the system. Attempts to change the individual are easier because a person is vulnerable and defenseless. Attempts to change the system are more difficult because institutions are rigid and time-honored. But change the institutional system we must, if school people are to be more than a band-aid brigade.

Helping deprived youth is necessary and essential. However, these efforts must be viewed in proper perspective as acts of rehabilitation. Changing the system that generates segregation, alienation, and deprivation is an act of prevention. While tackling the backlog of past misdeeds requires much of our time and may appear to be overwhelming, we must at the same time assign part of our energy to preventive activities if the same problems we are working so hard to overcome today are not to be visited upon future generations.

The deprivation of the present was contributed to by the social system of the past. Dr. Conant recognized this when he said that "public schools for Negroes and whites together might have softened the caste lines" had these been established long ago when slavery had just vanished.[22]

Of crime control, Dr. Leslie Wilkins of Great Britain has reminded us of the limitation of our approach. Like other community efforts, those designed to suppress crime have focused largely on individuals. As Dr. Wilkins points out in the book, *Society Problems and Methods of Study,* it is easy to say of the criminal "He did it—deal with him." He also points out that "crime has *not* been considered as a failure of social controls but has been simplified to the wrong doing of single persons or gangs." "It should be clear," he concludes, "that dealing with him has not solved the problem of crime and seems unlikely to do so. . . ." He points out that there are social as well as personal control mechanisms, and . . . to operate on only half of the problem (that is, the personal mechanism) may not solve even half of it, let alone the whole." [23]

The same may be said of problems of deprivation in the school. To focus only on the deprived child without considering also the social system which alienates him and contributes to his deprivation may not solve even half of the problem and certainly not the whole.

It seems to me that one of the major system changes the school must make if it desires to overcome deprivation due to alienating racial segregation due to alienating racial segregation is to renounce commitment to the concept of the neighborhood school. With reference to elementary schools, I am uncertain as to the importance of the neighborhood school. But at the secondary level, the concept of a neighborhood school contributes to segregation; and on this basis, it cannot be justified.

No one argued about the virtues of the neighborhood high school in Dallas, Texas nearly 25 years ago when I attended Lincoln High School for Negroes in that city. Although my family lived in the western sector of Dallas, in a neighborhood called Oak Cliff, my brothers and sister and all of our playmates travelled by bus several miles to the southern sector of Dallas to attend high school; and we paid our own bus fare. The only other high school for Negroes was in the northern sector. This was during the days of segregation. Then, the neighborhood school was not exhaulted.

There were, of course, high schools in the western sector of the city where I lived. One might call these neighborhood schools. But enrollment in these schools was limited to white children. The concept of the neighborhood school, therefore, was not relevant in the city of my youth. Had the little Willie boys and girl attended the neighborhood high school in Dallas in the 1930's, 1940's, 1950's there would have been unmistakable racial integration. As the Negro population in urban areas has increased during the past quarter of the century and as this increase in population has been limited to ghetto-like neighborhoods in the center of the city, the concept of the neighborhood school has assumed greater relevance in education. One suspects that the concept of the neighborhood school has been assuming increasing importance since the Supreme Court's decision in 1954 which ruled illegal officially segregated public schools.

I have still another reason for suspecting the concept of the neighborhood school is not as great as it's said to be. It seems the concept of the neighborhood school is most rigidly adhered to in lower-class and in lower-middle-class neighborhoods, but is more flexible and relaxed for residents of the affluent neighborhoods. In the District of Columbia, for example, one of the better elementary schools is the Amidon school in southwest Washington. The superintendent of the city school system has a special interest in that school and its curriculum. In fact, he has written a book about the beneficial effects of its curriculum and the method of teaching that goes on there. Some of the finest teachers in Washington are employed at the Amidon School. In 1962 and 1963 when I lived in southwest Washington, Amidon was an open school. Children attended it from all over the city. By taxi, late-model car, and other means of transportation, well dressed children from all over the city descended each day on Amidon. For these more affluent children it would appear that the quality of education they received was considered more important by their parents than the geographic location of the school.

Even another example is the boarding school. Some of the presidents of this country graduated from these schools. Boarding schools certainly are not neighborhood schools. Yet, they turn out persons of good character and sound mind. But boarding schools are for the affluent. Could it be that neighborhood schools are recommended for the alienated and poor? The concept of the neighborhood school should remain an open issue in public education. It is in need of more study and analysis, particularly from the point of view of its association, if any, with segregation, alienation, and deprivation.

Another kind of change in the current system of schools and education could be in the deployment of personnel. The racial composition of the teaching staff in many big city schools tends to reflect the racial composition of the neighborhoods in which these schools are located. In Washington, D. C., for example, there are high school principals who are Negro; but none were principals of schools in predominantly white neighborhoods during the 1963–64 school year. Moreover, the high schools in predominantly Negro neighborhoods had predominantly Negro faculties and the high schools in predominantly white neighborhoods had predominantly white faculties. This same pattern exists in other big cities. The argument is frequently given that teachers prefer to teach in schools that are near their homes. This reasoning suggests that one of the primary variables in education is the residential location of the instructor. I beg to differ with this reasoning. No reliable study has found any correlation between the teaching talents of an instructor and his residential address. Furthermore, a diversified teaching staff is a distinct educational experience for the student.

Every school within the city could have an integrated teaching staff of white and Negro teachers. This is within the power of most school administrations; and they should exercise this power with all deliberate speed. What better way to teach children that Negro and white persons should live together as brothers and sisters than to show them daily that Negro and white persons work together as teaching colleagues.

These and other changes in the school as a system we must make to overcome the festering problem of deprivation compounded by alienating segregation. Changes in the behavior of an individual may or may not affect the institutional systems of a community. But changes in the institutional system usually produce changes in individual behavior. This kind of change tends to be more enduring because it is sanctioned and supported. The time has come not only to redeem the individual who has fallen but to modify the system that contributed to his downfall.

Teachers and administrators are not expected to remake the world. But they can certainly influence the direction in which it is moving by demonstrating what is attainable within the institution in which they work.[24] If a caste system finds its clearest manifestation in an educational system, then the schools are a good place to start in eliminating racial segregation, alienation, and deprivation.

Notes

1. U. S. Bureau of the Census, *Statistical Abstract of the United States,* 1963 (Washington: U. S. Government Printing Office, 1963), p. 321.
2. Herman P. Miller, *Rich Man, Poor Man* (New York: Thomas Y. Crowell, 1964), pp. 26, 29.
3. U. S. Bureau of the Census, *op. cit.,* p. 219.
4. Edward Higbee, *Farms and Farmers in an Urban Age,* (New York: The Twentieth Century Fund, 1963), p. 21.
5. *Ibid.,* p. 10.
6. Michael Harrington, *The Other American* (New York: The MacMillan Co., 1962), p. 191.
7. John Kenneth Galbraith, *The Affluent Society* (New York: Mentor Books, 1958), p. 258.
8. Louis Wirth, "Urbanism as a Way of Life," in Paul K. Hatt and Albert J. Reiss, Jr. (eds.) *Cities and Society* (New York: The Free Press of Glencoe, 1957), p. 46.
9. *Ibid.,* p. 50.
10. *Ibid.,* p. 52.
11. *Ibid.* p. 55.
12. James Baldwin, *Nobody Knows My Name* (New York: Dell Publishing Co., 1961).
13. James Bryant Conant, *Slums and Suburbs* (New York: McGraw-Hill Book Co. 1961), p. 30.
14. *Ibid.,* p. 31.
15. *Ibid.,* pp. 145–146.
16. Will Maslow and Richard Cohen, *School Segregation, Northern Style* (New York: Public Affairs Pamphlet, 1961), p. 5.
17. *Ibid.,* p. 6.
18. John Kenneth Galbraith, *The Affluent Society* (New York: Mentor Books, 1958), pp. 256–258.
19. *Associated Press,* news story, February 11, 1964.
20. James B. Conant, *op. cit.,* pp. 11–12.

21. *Ibid.*

22. *Ibid.*

23. Leslie T. Wilkins, "Criminology: An Operational Research Approach," in A. T. Welford *et al.* (eds.), *Society Problems and Methods of Study* (London: Routledge and Kegan Paul, Ltd., (no date), p. 329.

24. Charles V. Willie, "Anti-Social Behavior Among Disadvantaged Youth: Some Observations on Presentation for Teachers," *The Journal of Negro Education,* XXXIII (Summer, 1964), 180–181.

NEIGHBORHOOD SETTING AND THE ISOLATION OF PUBLIC HOUSING TENANTS[1]

Louis Kriesberg

Underlying many controversies about the desirable location of low-income public housing projects are varying beliefs about the consequences of placing low-income families in middle-income neighborhoods. Locating public housing projects in a middle-income neighborhood might offer project tenants an opportunity to learn, develop, and express the life style of middle-income families. This could occur through several processes. Members of low-income families may participate in churches, schools, and other institutions serving middle-income persons. Such participation could provide new models, new opportunities for action, and better services than those available in low-income neighborhoods. Residence in a middle-income neighborhood could make possible the observation of models of behavior rarely seen in low-income neighborhoods and less exposure to models of conduct low-income families think disreputable. The very circumstances of a different neighborhood style of life could facilitate new forms of conduct. For example, in low-income urban neighborhoods, mothers may believe that their children are subject to undesired influences from other children and their children are highly involved in peer relations; in the face of these circumstances the mother may fight a losing battle to exercise parental authority. In a middle-income neighborhood, the peer life may be less intense and the children's conduct more supervised by parents; a low-income mother may not be thrust into such direct conflict with her children and exercise indirect supervision more successfully.[2] Finally, new desires, knowledge, and skills may be acquired through personal acquaintanceship and friendship. Such personal relationships would make more effective each of the other processes.

Placing low-income public housing in middle-income neighborhoods, however, may have other consequences. The social differences between tenants and the neighborhood residents may be so great that the project tenants are socially

Reprinted by permission of the author. A version of this paper is to be published in *The Journal of the American Institute of Planners,* 1968.

isolated. They may be barred from participating in the neighborhood life and thrust upon themselves to such an extent that the processes listed above would not be operative. They may even become more resigned, discouraged, and frustrated. Furthermore, middle-income neighborhood residents may be fearful or antagonistic to the project tenants and feel that their interests are threatened by the location of a housing project in the area. The isolation of the project tenants may follow from this.

Obviously, many profound value issues are at stake. But there are also factual questions whose answers at least would clarify the policy alternatives. In this paper, I will analyze the extent to which social isolation between project tenants and residents in the surrounding area exists and is affected by the socio-economic differences between them. In order to make such an assessment, it is necessary to examine housing projects which vary in neighborhood settings. It is also necessary to consider conditions other than socio-economic status differences which may account for the extent of isolation of project tenants.

The analysis is based upon a survey of families in four low-income public housing projects and the neighborhoods surrounding each, in Syracuse, New York.[3] All the projects in Syracuse are small and have low density, compared to most low-income public housing projects of America's largest cities. Even within Syracuse, however, the projects differ in significant ways. It is the variation among the four public housing projects and particularly the variation in their surrounding neighborhoods which makes possible the investigation of the issues raised. I shall refer to the four projects as Park, Grant, Evans, and Stern. The projects and surrounding neighborhoods are depicted in the maps below.

The Four Projects and Surrounding Neighborhoods

The social composition of a housing project is affected by the rules defining eligibility, by the processes which affect who applies from among the eligible families, by housing authority rules and practices which select among the applicants those who will be offered an apartment, and by the length of time different kinds of families remain in public housing.

Of the four public housing projects in Syracuse, two are federally subsidized projects and two are state subsidized. The federal projects, Evans and Stern, have slightly higher maximum income limits for eligibility and continued residence than do Park and Grant, the two state projects. Among the eligible families, those who are particularly disadvantaged in the private housing market because of inadequate income, social discrimination, or the lack of housing suitable to their family needs are most likely to apply.[4] Some of these families, however, may also have extra difficulty in being accepted for public housing, as do, for example, families with a history of rent delinquency, with persons who have a criminal record, or with unwed mothers.[5] In the past, the local housing authority permitted accepted applicants some choice among apartments, within the limits set by the efforts of maintaining low vacancy rates. An applicant could refuse a vacancy for the next available one if he wished. This probably has resulted in more homogeneity within a project and between a project and its surrounding neighborhood than would otherwise be the case.

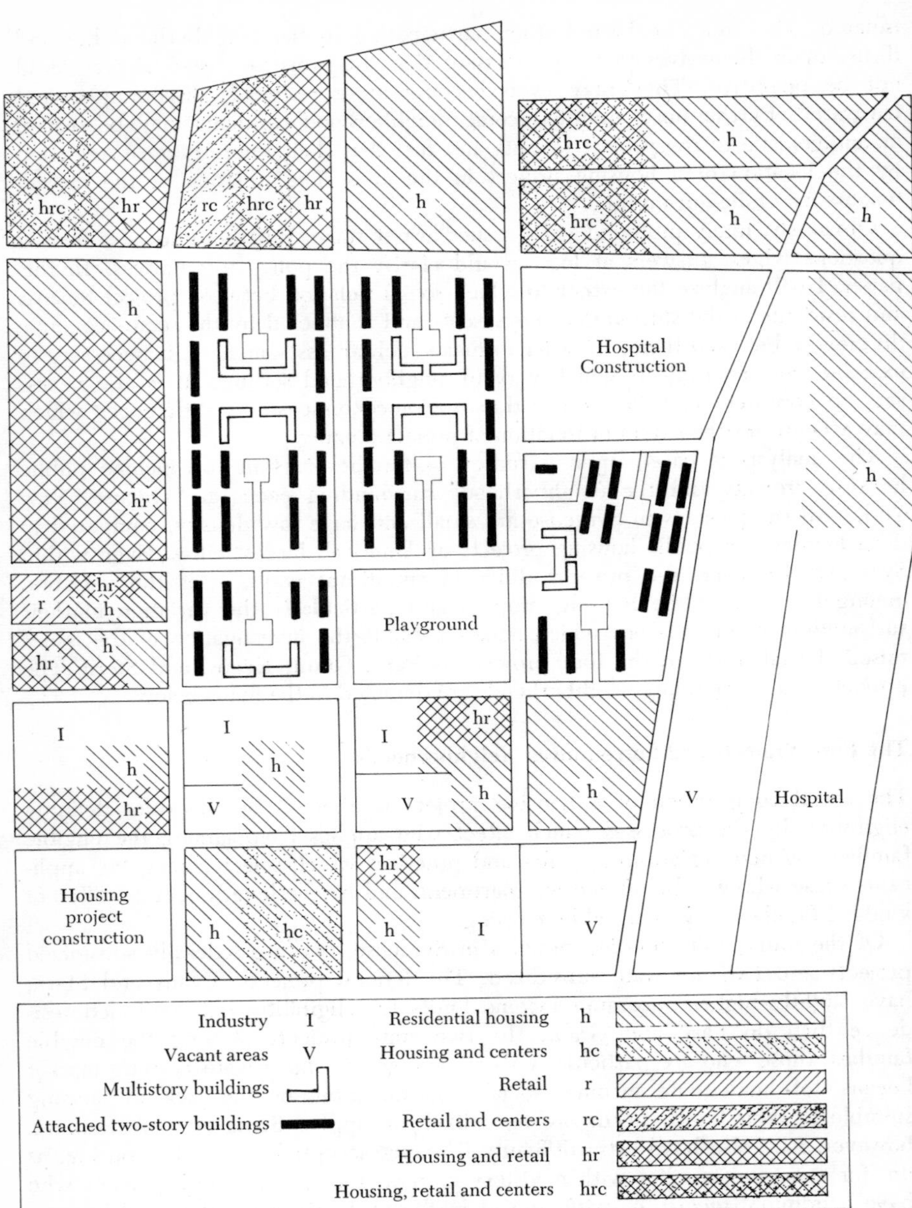

Map 1. Project Park

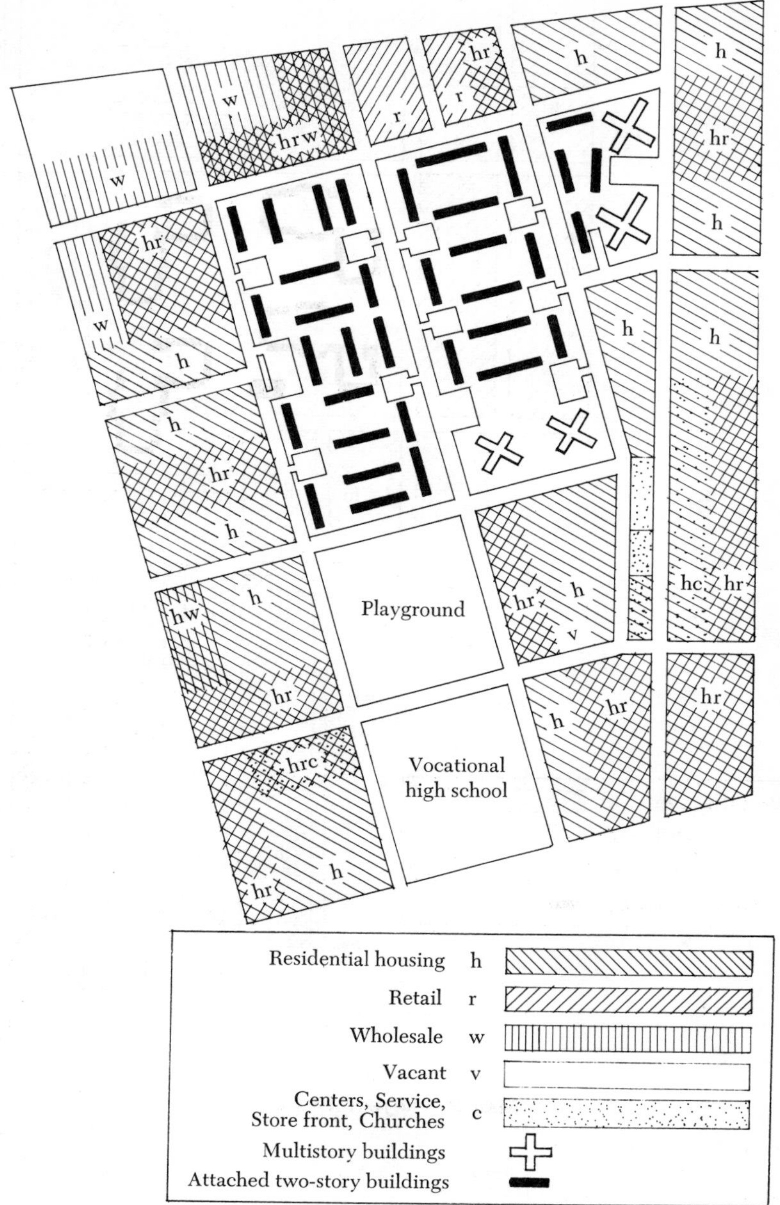
w
w
hr w
r
hr
r
h
h
hr
h
hr
w
h
h
h
h
hr
h
h
hw
Playground
hr
h
v
hc
hr
hr
hr
h
hr
hrc
Vocational
high school
hr
h
Residential housing h
Retail r
Wholesale w
Vacant v
Centers, Service,
Store front, Churches c
Multistory buildings
Attached two-story buildings

MAP 2. PROJECT GRANT

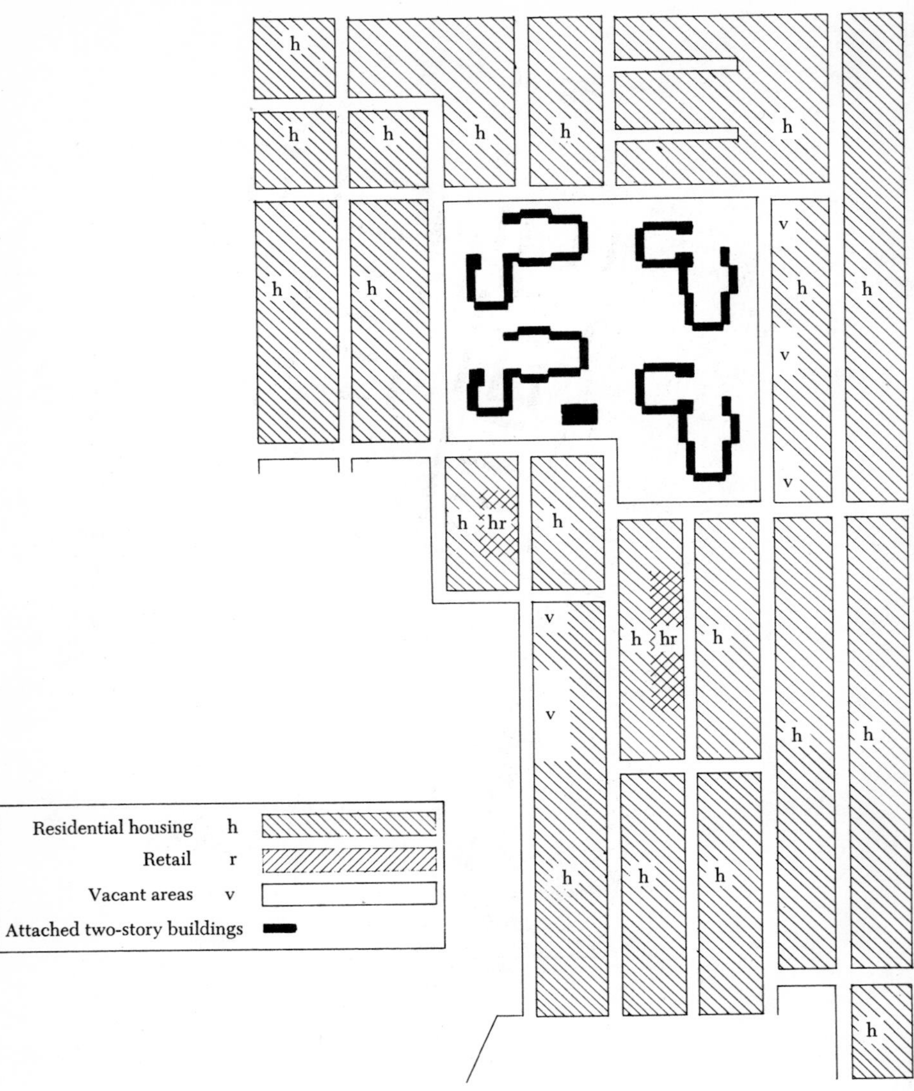

Map 3. Project Evans

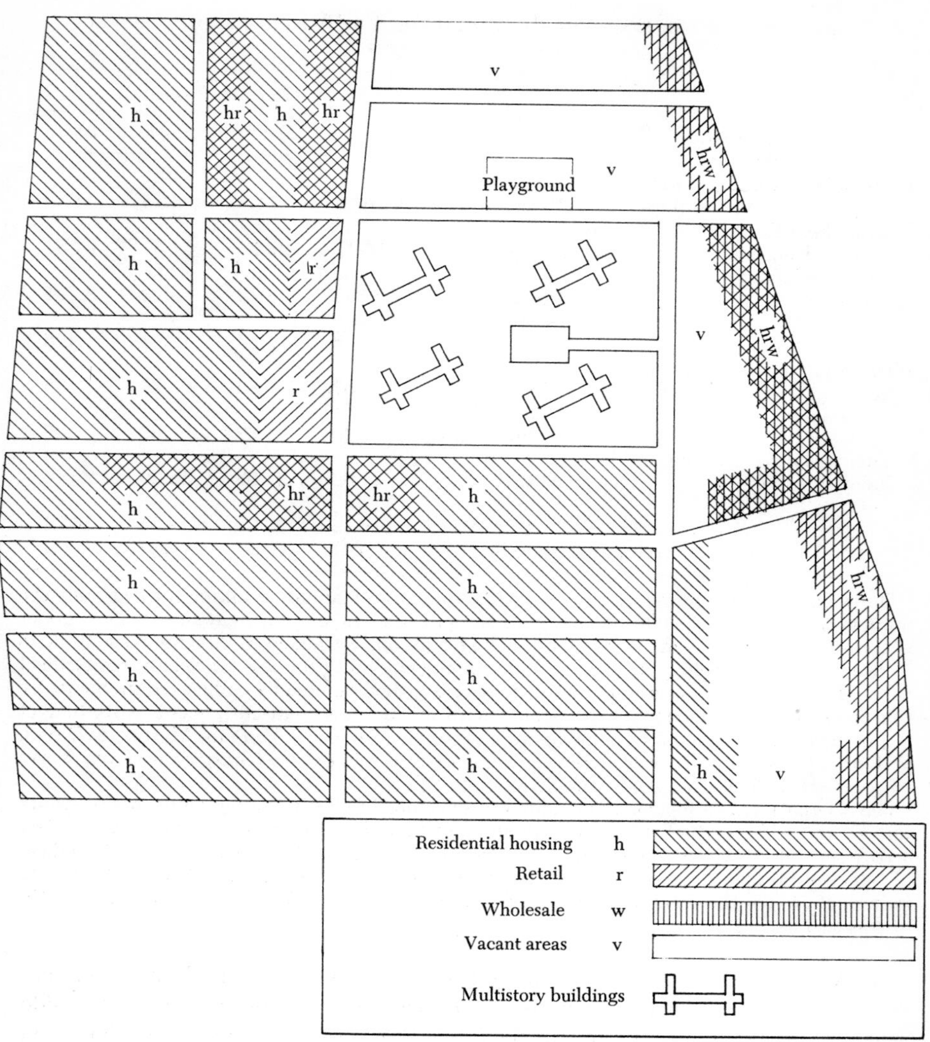

Map 4. Project Stern

TABLE 1. SOCIAL AND ECONOMIC CHARACTERISTICS OF FAMILIES AND HOUSEHOLD BY HOUSING PROJECT

Characteristic		Housing Projects			
		Evans	Grant	Park	Stern
Households including a married couple with minor children	Percent	67.3	34.5	41.5	57.6
Households with some or all income from public welfare	Percent	16.4	26.7	51.3	24.8
Annual household income in dollars	Means	4,195	3,072	3,023	3,791
	Standard deviations	1,408	1,757	1,584	1,498
Welfare ratio—(.90 = poverty line)[1]	Means	1.02	.86	.75	.95
	Standard deviations	.29	.32	.26	.35
Occupational socio-economic index of family [2]	Means	29.82	31.89	18.20	25.16
	Standard deviations	16.12	22.32	12.25	16.74
Total number of households in sample		(104)	(206)	(123)	(113)

[1] The welfare ratio is based upon a budget of minimum standards, taking into account the number of persons in the household, and their ages, sex, and employment status. The budget is adapted from a schedule developed by the Community Council of Greater New York to be used by private welfare agencies in determining eligibility for assistance and free medical care. The welfare ratio was constructed by dividing the household's budget requirements by the gross household income. A household with income less than 90 percent of its budget requirements is considered to be living in poverty. See James N. Morgan, Martin H. David, Wilbur J. Cohen, and Harvey E. Brazer, *Income and Welfare in the United States* (New York: McGraw-Hill Book Company, 1962), 189.

[2] The occupational socio-economic index was developed by Otis Dudley Duncan. See Chapters VI and VII by Otis Dudley Duncan and Appendix B in Albert J. Reiss, Jr., *Occupations and Social Status*, (New York: The Free Press of Glencoe, 1961). Occupations with indices of between 66 and 96 constitute the highest decile of the national population; those with indices of 50–65, the second highest decile; and those with indices of 0–13 and 14–18, the lowest two deciles.

Park, with 677 units, is the largest project; about one-third of which are reserved for the elderly. The units for the elderly are high-rise buildings; aside from these, the units are in attached two-story, single-family houses grouped around courtyards. Fewer than half of the households contain a couple with at least one minor child (See Table 1). This is accountable for not only because of the elderly; 42 percent of the mothers living with minor children are husbandless. Park has a relatively high percent of the families receiving public assistance; the families are relatively poor and of low socio-economic origins. Seventy-five percent of the adults are Negro; most of the whites are elderly. The area surrounding the project has a higher proportion of Negroes. The surrounding area is of generally low income. (See Table 2).

Grant is almost as large as Park and has half of its units reserved for the elderly, with the same physical structure. The families are not, on the average, so poor as those in Park, and the variability in income is greater. Only ten percent of

TABLE 2. SOCIAL AND ECONOMIC CHARACTERISTICS OF FAMILIES AND HOUSEHOLDS BY NEIGHBORHOOD

Characteristic		Neighborhoods			
		Evans	Grant	Park	Stern
Households including a married couple with minor child(ren)	Percent	59.0	32.7	37.6	44.2
Households with some or all income from public welfare	Percent	1.1	18.7	23.0	3.0
Annual household income in dollars	Means	7,562	4,887	5,369	9,492
	Standard deviations	3,150	2,819	3,796	5,486
Welfare ratio—(.90 = poverty line)	Means	1.84	1.41	1.37	2.56
	Standard deviations	.75	.82	.99	1.86
Occupational socio-economic index of family	Means	40.21	24.78	20.21	54.35
	Standard deviations	19.64	18.60	16.80	25.01
Total number of households in sample		(95)	(98)	(109)	(104)

the adults are Negroes. The surrounding neighborhood is a low-income, white area.

Physically, Evans is the smallest and most attractive project. It consists of 200 dwelling units grouped into four courts. Small porches frame the main entranceways which face outward into the street. Evans is predominantly a project of small complete families. As can be seen in Table 1, Evans families are least likely to receive public assistance and have the highest average income. Nearly all the families are white. The project is located in a relatively homogeneous, white, middle-income residential area.

Stern is quite different from the other projects. Its 213 units are in four buildings which are three and four stories high, without elevators. Children's courtyard play cannot be controlled from within the apartment, and the dark, windowless hallways are often used as play areas. In a survey of complete families that had applied for public housing, Stern was least preferred of all four projects.[6] A majority of the households consist only of a couple with minor children, but it is more varied than Evans, having a higher percentage of incomplete families. On the average, the families are a little poorer than those in Evans. About one-third of the adults are Negro. The neighborhood around Stern is heterogeneous, but is generally of middle and upper-middle income white families.

Conditions Affecting Project Isolation

Four major conditions affect the likelihood that tenants of a low-income public housing project will be isolated from the surrounding neighborhood. First, the socio-economic status differences between project tenants and neighborhood residents may vary; presumably, the greater the differences, the less likely is interaction to occur. Second, there may be varying physical barriers separating the project from the neighborhood. Third, projects and neighborhoods can have varying levels of social interaction; presumably, the higher the level of interaction within the project relative to the level outside, the greater the tenants' isolation. Finally, tenants may have moved from the surrounding neighborhood into the project; in that case they can easily maintain old ties to the neighborhood.

In terms of socio-economic status, Stern tenants are most dissimilar from the neighborhood residents. For example, the average gross income of Stern households is only 25 percent of the average income of Stern neighborhood households. At the other extreme, the average income of Grant project household is over 60 percent that of Grant neighborhood households. For Evans and Park projects, the household incomes are a little over 50 percent of the average income of the households in the adjacent neighborhoods. Similarly, for every social status characteristic—education, father's occupation, race, and religion—Stern project tenants are more often unlike residents in the surrounding neighborhood than are the tenants of any other project. Even the difference in the distribution of types of families is greater between Stern project and neighborhood than between the other projects and their adjacent neighborhoods. The relative dissimilarity of the other projects and their respective neighborhoods is difficult to rank. On the whole, the tenants are similar to the residents in the surrounding neighborhoods. In terms of the distribution of family types and household composition, Grant project and its neighborhood are most similar. In terms of the various social status measures, one or another project-neighborhood pair is most similar.

These objective similarities and differences between the projects and their adjacent neighborhoods are reflected in the perception of the neighborhood residents. The respondents in each neighborhood were asked about the nearby housing project, "Do you think you have a lot in common, quite a bit in common, little in common, or nothing in common with the people living in ———?" It is clear that simply living in public housing constitutes a barrier. A substantial minority in each neighborhood replied that they did not know how much they had in common with the people in the nearby project: 30 percent in Park, 25 percent in Stern, 24 percent in Evans, and 21 percent in Grant neighborhoods. When asked about persons in their own neighborhoods outside of public housing, the percentage who said they did not know how much they had in common with their neighbors was much lower, varying from 12 to 7 percent. Furthermore, considering only those persons who could say how much they had in common with persons in the adjacent projects, only a small minority said they had a lot or quite a bit in common with the project tenants: 28 percent of the Park neighborhood residents, 19 percent of those in Grant neighborhood, 18 percent in Evans neighborhood, and only 9 percent in the Stern neighborhood. More felt they have quite a bit or a lot in common with people living in their neighborhood outside of public housing. In terms of the relative isolation of the four projects, clearly Stern is seen as most different by the neighbors outside, as we would expect from the data already considered.

Physically, residents of Stern housing project have the greatest barriers to interaction. Neighborhood houses front only one side of Stern. The project itself faces inward, and most of the tenants do not live on the street level. The other three projects are more difficult to rank. The units of Evans face out towards neighborhood housing of similar style. This is less true for Park and Grant, but the streets and the stores of Park and Grant neighborhoods are more active centers of neighborhood life than is true in Evans neighborhood.

In the neighborhood surrounding Park and Grant housing projects, the small owner-operated stores serve only the local market, unlike the supermarkets and specialty stores in the areas near Stern and Evans. Bars and pool halls provide hangouts for adult men. Moreover, streets run through Park so that neighborhood residents are more likely to walk or drive through this project to use neighborhood facilities. Grant project, on the other hand, has several nonresidential areas on its perimeter: a Catholic school, a city high school, and a playground.

The third condition to be considered is the degree to which the projects and neighborhoods provide opportunities for desirable associations. Presumably, in large, homogeneous projects where physical arrangements of the housing units are conducive to neighboring, the opportunities for interaction within the project would be great.[7] Evans project is small, but it is most homogeneous. Grant and Park projects are heterogeneous, but the major categories within each are large. Stern is small and heterogeneous. As a subjective measure of the opportunities for interaction, we can look at the responses to the question about how much the tenants in each project feel they have in common with others in the same project. A large proportion in Evans and Grant feel they have a lot or quite a bit in common with others in the same project (40 percent and 50 percent, respectively). The proportion in Stern is expectedly lower than in Evans and Grant (27 percent of the tenants feel they have a lot or quite a bit in common with others). Park is surprising; the same proportion as in Stern feel they have a lot or quite a bit in common with others in Park housing project. This is lower than one would expect, given the objective characteristics of the population in Park housing project. One reason for this peculiarity is that Park tenants and neighborhood residents are highly involved in kinship relations and in friendship networks of limited scope. In this privatized network there is less room for extensive identification. Another explanation arises from the lack of distinction between Park and the surrounding neighborhood. As noted previously, Park neighborhood residents are most likely to feel they have something in common with Park housing tenants. Park housing project does not appear to have as great a separate identity as do the other projects. Consideration of the last factor affecting project isolation will help explain these findings.

If project tenants are drawn from the neighborhood immediately surrounding the project, they would be able to maintain associations with their old friends in the neighborhood. The project tenants would be less likely to form close relations with their new neighbors and develop a sense of commonness with others in the project. Most of the Park tenants previously lived in the neighborhood around Park. Only a small minority of the Evans and Stern tenants previously lived in the immediate vicinity of their respective projects. A majority of the Grant tenants previously lived in the immediate surrounding area. We should also note that it takes time to get to know people, and Park project is the oldest in Syracuse, having been opened in 1939. Stern was opened in 1949, Evans in 1952, and Grant in 1954. A higher proportion of Park tenants than those in the other projects have lived at their present address for several years.

The Degree of Project Isolation

Isolation means several things: that housing project tenants know few people in the adjoining neighborhoods and interact infrequently with those they know; that few persons in the surrounding area know any tenants and interact little with those they know; and that a high proportion of the tenants' neighboring and friendship interactions are with persons living in the project rather than with persons in the adjoining neighborhood. Of course, isolation also may mean lack of visibility and opportunity to observe the life of the people in the surrounding neighborhood. At this time, however, we will restrict the discussion to the social-interactional isolation of the projects from the surrounding neighborhoods.

The ranking of the projects in terms of isolation may differ, depending upon the measure of social-interactional isolation. We will examine several measures of project isolation separately. All the tenants in each project were asked, "Do you know anyone in the neighborhood around ——— (NAME OF PROJECT) well enough to talk to?" As can be seen in Table 3, more than half of the respondents in every project knew at least one person in the immediate neighborhood well enough to talk to. In Park project, three-fourths so reported. Furthermore, half of the Park tenants reported knowing seven or more persons in the neighborhood; about one-fifth to one-fourth of the tenants in the other projects reported knowing as many. The other three projects are very similar, there is only a slight tendency for Grant tenants to report knowing twenty or more persons in the surrounding area.

When we consider the number of persons in the neighborhood who reported their acquaintanceship with persons in the adjacent project, also shown in Table 3, the pattern is slightly different. Only in Park neighborhood does more than a majority claim to know someone in the project. Park neighborhood residents are most likely to know someone and to know many persons in the adjacent project

TABLE 3. NUMBER OF NEIGHBORS KNOWN ACROSS PROJECT LINES BY AREAS

Number of Neighbors Known	*Areas*							
	Project Tenants Knowing Neighbors Outside				Neighborhood Residents Knowing Project Tenants			
	Evans	Grant	Park	Stern	Evans	Grant	Park	Stern
None	41.0	46.4	22.7	42.9	73.9	58.9	44.9	72.6
1–6 persons	39.8	30.6	25.3	33.3	21.6	34.9	33.3	25.5
7–19 persons	11.8	9.4	20.0	15.7	3.9	4.7	11.6	1.3
20 or more persons	7.5	13.7	32.0	8.2	0.7	1.6	10.2	0.7
Totals %	100.1	100.1	100.0	100.1	100.1	100.1	100.0	100.1
(N)	(161)	(278)	(150)	(147)	(153)	(129)	(147)	(153)

than are the residents in any other neighborhood. Grant neighborhood residents are more likely than Evans or Stern residents to know persons in the adjacent project. One difficulty in interpreting these results is that Park and Grant projects are much larger than Evans and Stern; the chance of knowing someone in one of those projects is considerably greater than in the smaller projects of Stern and Evans. Computing the percentages in terms of the relative sizes of the projects reveals no differences among the four neighborhoods in the proportion knowing someone in the adjacent project.

Project tenants who said they knew at least one person in the surrounding neighborhood and neighborhood residents who said they knew at least one person in the adjacent project were asked a series of questions about the one person with whom they had most to do. One question was, "How often do you usually get together with (him) (her)?" The area variation in response to the question is presented in Table 4. The patterns are the same. Park tenants are most likely to get together more often than once a week with the neighborhood resident with whom they have most to do; the other projects do not differ from each other. Looking at the proportion of the neighborhood residents who get together often with the most frequently seen person in the adjacent neighborhood, we find again that Park is highest, followed by Grant, and followed by Stern and Evans, which are alike. Again, taking into account the relative size of the projects, there is no real difference among the neighborhoods.

Racial characteristics are relatively visible and therefore may be of particular importance in the interaction between project tenants and the residents in the surrounding areas. Among Park tenants, it is true that white men and women are less likely to know someone, to know many persons, or to interact frequently with someone they know in the surrounding area, compared to Negroes. This may be due to the fact, however, that whites in Park are generally elderly persons. In Grant and Stern projects, where the number of Negroes makes a comparison possible, there is no clear evidence that race is a barrier. Indeed, Negro men are more likely than white men to know someone and interact often with someone in the surrounding neighborhood; they are just as likely to know many persons in

TABLE 4. FREQUENCY OF GETTING TOGETHER WITH PERSON ACROSS PROJECT LINE BY AREAS

	Areas							
	Project Tenant and Person Outside				Neighborhood Resident and Project Tenant			
Frequency of Getting Together	Evans	Grant	Park	Stern	Evans	Grant	Park	Stern
Never get together								
Never get together or do not know anyone	46.9	51.9	26.0	45.6	81.6	62.5	50.7	80.2
Less often than once a week	18.1	15.2	10.0	21.5	10.9	18.0	17.1	12.5
Once a week	14.4	7.8	20.7	4.1	4.1	7.8	15.8	2.0
More often than once a week	20.6	25.1	43.3	18.8	3.4	11.7	16.4	5.3
Totals %	100.0	100.0	100.0	100.0	100.0	100.0	100.0	100.0
(N)	(160)	(283)	(150)	(149)	(147)	(128)	(146)	(152)

the surrounding area. Among the women, there are no consistent differences between Negroes and whites. A somewhat higher proportion of white women in Stern frequently see someone in the surrounding area, compared to Negro women; but Negro women in Grant are more likely than white women to know many persons in the surrounding area. Otherwise, there are no differences between Negro and white women in Stern and Grant in terms of these measures.

The respondents were asked about friends as well as neighbors. They reported how many friends they had. Then they were asked a series of questions about the two friends with whom they felt closest; in this series, they were asked if each friend lived in the housing project, the adjacent neighborhood, or elsewhere. Among the Park tenants, 39 percent have at least one of their closest friends in the neighborhood around Park project; the corresponding percentages for Evans, Grant, and Stern are 15, 16, and 13, respectively.[8] Conversely, 13 percent of the Park neighborhood residents have at least one friend in the Park project; among the Grant and Evans neighborhood residents, only 2 percent have at least one of their two closest friends living in the adjacent project; none of the Stern neighborhood residents in the sample had either of their two closest friends in Stern project. By every measure, there is more interaction between the Park tenants and their neighbors in the adjacent area than is the case for the other three projects and their adjacent areas.

Does this necessarily mean that Park tenants are least likely to have their closest friends in the housing project? Actually, almost two-thirds of the Park tenants have at least one of their two closest friends living in Park project (one-third have both of their closest friends in the project). In Evans, Grant, and Stern, only one-third of the tenants have even one of their closest friends in the project. Interestingly, the pattern in the adjacent neighborhoods is similar, if less marked; the proportion in each neighborhood who have at least one close friend in the neighborhood is 57 percent in Park neighborhood, 41 percent in Evans and Grant neighborhoods, and 36 percent in Stern neighborhoods.

What accounts for this apparent discrepancy is the proportion of persons in each area who have close friends *elsewhere than in the project or the neighborhood.* Among the Park tenants, only 37 percent have one of their two closest friends living elsewhere; the percentages are 71, 70, and 74 for Evans, Grant, and Stern, respectively. Again, the pattern is the same for the adjacent neighborhoods; the proportion of neighborhood residents with friends elsewhere is 53 percent for Park neighborhood, but 82 percent for Evans and Grant, and 87 percent for Stern residents.

In short, it appears that most of the Park tenants and neighborhood residents live in a social world with relatively narrow physical boundaries, but the project itself is not an important barrier to social interaction. Neighbors and friends are likely to be the same people. Racial segregation in housing tends to restrict friends and relatives to the same section of the city.[9] In the other three projects and adjacent neighborhoods, most persons have their closest friends outside their immediate areas of residence. As a matter of fact, over 50 percent in each of the three projects and each of the three adjacent neighborhoods have *both* their closest two friends living elsewhere. Apparently, persons whose friends live elsewhere are likely to engage in casual neighborly interaction but the project boundary is a barrier to such interaction for most of them—the neighborly interaction is confined to immediate neighbors.

Conclusions

The kinds of people living in a low-income public housing project vary a great deal—even in four projects in one medium-sized city. The physical characteristics of the projects and the surrounding areas, and the processes of self-selection by tenants and of admission by the housing authorities all affect the social composition of each project.

Given such variability, it is possible to study how certain conditions affect the social isolation of project tenants from residents in the surrounding area. Of course, studying only four cases does not permit assessing the relative importance of each condition. The results of the analysis, nevertheless, yield some clear findings. First of all, residence in public housing does constitute a barrier to social interaction. This seems to be the case unless the project tenants are largely drawn from the surrounding neighborhood and no marked physical impediments to interaction exist, no major social differences exist (which is likely to be true if the tenants are drawn from the surrounding area), and the project tenants do not develop a strong community.

Considerable differences in socio-economic status between project tenants and residents in the surrounding area is not, however, an important impediment to social interaction. Thus, in the case of Stern, socio-economic differences were most marked. Nevertheless, the social isolation of project tenants was not higher than in the case of Evans or even Grant. This was true despite the fact that the physical conditions conducive to interaction were least between Stern tenants and the residents in the surrounding areas. Apparently the reservoir of possible associations in the neighborhood outside Stern was sufficiently large that interaction could occur at the same low level as for the Evans and Grant tenants. Perhaps if the socio-economic differences were much greater they would have a noticeable effect despite the importance of so many other factors affecting the level of interaction. On the basis of the evidence from this analysis, however, it seems that the heterogeneity within a project and within the area surrounding a project is often large enough to provide the basis for establishing neighborly relations and even friendships. After all, people are not alike only because they have similar incomes or levels of education. They are also alike and share interests because they have other qualities as men, women, mothers, fathers, shoppers, wives, husbands, renters, residents in a general area of a city, and consumers of popular culture.

In the beginning of this paper, I listed a variety of ways in which low-income families living in middle-income neighborhoods might learn, develop, and express the life-styles of middle-income families. The social isolation of project tenants would impede some of the processes by which such changes occur. The evidence of this analysis indicates that socio-economic status differences are not a particularly important barrier to social interaction between project tenants and neighborhood residents. I believe that the resolution of such factual controversies will contribute to the reasoned discussion of policy alternatives.

Notes

1. This paper is based upon a study of public housing and social mobility, supported by funds from the Ford Foundation and the Welfare Administration of the U. S. Department of Health, Education, and Welfare, Grant number 042. Analysis conducted at the Syracuse University Computing Center was aided by the National Science Foundation under Grant GP-1137.

   This paper has benefited from the comments of and discussions with: Seymour S. Bellin, Irwin Deutscher, Helen Icken Safa, Laurence Cale, and Alphonse Sallett.

   An abridged version of this paper was presented at the Eastern Sociological Society annual meetings, April, 1967.

2. Louis Kriesberg, "Rearing Children for Educational Achievement in Fatherless Families," *Journal of Marriage and the Family*, forthcoming.

3. Separate samples were drawn of families in each project and the area within four or five blocks surrounding each project. Varying sampling ratios were used to yield approximately equal number of cases in each project and neighborhood. A new 500 unit housing project restricted to large families was constructed since the survey was completed.

   In all, 1,274 respondents were interviewed; husbands and wives in the same families were interviewed. The personal interviews averaged about an hour and a half for the women and a little over an hour for the men. The survey was conducted in the Spring of 1963. For additional information about the sample and the data collection procedures, see Louis Kriesberg and Seymour S. Bellin, "Fatherless Families and Housing: A Study of Dependency," Syracuse University Youth Development Center, November, 1965, offset.

4. As part of the study of public housing and social mobility, a survey was made of families eligible for low-income public housing who were living in an area about to undergo urban renewal and who therefore faced relocation. Some of the findings from the survey are reported in Seymour S. Bellin and Louis Kriesberg, "Relations among Attitudes, Circumstances and Behavior: The Case of Applying for Public Housing," *Sociology and Social Research*, forthcoming, and in Irwin Deutscher and Laurence T. Cagle, "Housing Aspirations of Fatherless Families," Syracuse University Youth Development Center, 1964, mimeographed.

5. Irwin Deutscher, "The Bureaucratic Gatekeeper in Public Housing," Irwin Deutscher and Elizabeth Thompson, eds., *Among the People: Studies of the Urban Poor* (New York: Basic Books, forthcoming).

6. Stern is unpopular among both Negroes and whites, unlike the other projects which differ in appeal or acceptance for Negroes and whites. Among white applicants, Park has the lowest rank preference; among Negroes, Evans ranks lowest. See Ronald Ley, "An Analysis of Project Preferences of Applicants for Public Housing," Syracuse University Youth Development Center, 1961.

7. For the classic demonstration of the effects of physical design of a housing complex upon neighborhood interaction, see Leon S. Festinger and Kurt Back, *Social Pressures in Informal Groups* (New York: Harper & Bros., 1950).

8. Respondents who said they had no friends are excluded from the analysis. Persons who said they had only one friend were classified by the location of that one friend. That is, when we say both friends are located in a particular place, we mean both of the two friends mentioned or, in the few cases in which only one friend was mentioned, where his or her one friend lives.

9. Alan K. Campbell *et. al.*, *The Negro In Syracuse* (Syracuse, N. Y.: University College of Syracuse University, 1964), pp. 25–30.

FEAR AND THE HOUSE-AS-HAVEN IN THE LOWER CLASS

Lee Rainwater

Men live in a world which presents them with many threats to their security as well as with opportunities for gratification of their needs. The cultures that men create represent ways of adapting to these threats to security as well as maximizing the opportunities for certain kinds of gratifications. Housing as an element of material culture has as its prime purpose the provision of shelter, which is protection from potentially damaging or unpleasant trauma or other stimuli. The most primitive level of evaluation of housing, therefore, has to do with the question of how adequately it shelters the individuals who abide in it from threats in their environment. Because the house is a refuge from noxious elements in the outside world, it serves people as a locale where they can regroup their energies for interaction with that outside world. There is in our culture a long history of the development of the house as a place of safety from both nonhuman and human threats, a history which culminates in guaranteeing the house, a man's castle, against unreasonable search and seizure. The house becomes the place of maximum exercise of individual autonomy, minimum conformity to the formal and complex rules of public demeanor. The house acquires a sacred character from its complex intertwining with the self and from the symbolic character it has as a representation of the family.[1]

These conceptions of the house are readily generalized to the area around it, to the neighborhood. This fact is most readily perceived in the romanticized views people have about suburban living.[2] The suburb, just as the village or the farm homestead, can be conceptualized as one large protecting and gratifying home. But the same can also be said of the city neighborhood, at least as a potentiality and as a wish, tenuously held in some situations, firmly established in others.[3] Indeed, the physical barriers between inside and outside are not maintained when people talk of their attitudes and desires with respect to housing. Rather, they talk of the outside as an inevitable extension of the inside and of the inside as deeply affected by what goes on immediately outside.

Reprinted by permission of the author and publisher from the *Journal of the American Institute of Planners,* **32** (January, 1966), pp. 23–30.

When, as in the middle class, the battle to make the home a safe place has long been won, the home then has more central to its definition other functions which have to do with self-expression and self-realization. There is an elaboration of both the material culture within the home and of interpersonal relationships in the form of more complex rituals of behavior and more variegated kinds of interaction. Studies of the relationship between social class status and both numbers of friends and acquaintances as well as kinds of entertaining in the home indicate that as social status increases the home becomes a locale for a wider range of interactions. Whether the ritualized behavior be the informality of the lower middle class family room, or the formality of the upper middle class cocktail party and buffet, the requisite housing standards of the middle class reflect a more complex and varied set of demands on the physical structure and its equipment.

The poverty and cultural milieu of the lower class make the prime concern that of the home as a place of security, and the accomplishment of this goal is generally a very tenuous and incomplete one. (I use the term "lower class" here to refer to the bottom 15 to 20 percent of the population in terms of social status. This is the group characterized by unskilled occupations, a high frequency of unstable work histories, slum dwellings, and the like. I refer to the group of more stable blue-collar workers which in status stands just above this lower class as the "working class" to avoid the awkwardness of terms like "lower-lower" and

FIG. 1. VARIATIONS IN HOUSING STANDARDS WITHIN THE LOWER AND WORKING CLASSES

Focus of Housing Standard	Core Consumer Group	Most Pressing Needs in Housing: Inside the House	Most Pressing Needs in Housing: Outside Environs
Shelter	Slum dwellers	Enough room Absence of noxious or dangerous elements	Absence of external threats Availability of minimum community services
Expressive elaborations	Traditional working class	Creating a pleasant, cozy home with major conveniences	Availability of a satisfying peer group society and a "respectable enough" neighborhood
All-American affluence	Modern working class	Elaboration of the above along the line of a more complex material culture	Construction of the all-American leisure style in terms of "outdoor living" "Good" community services

"upper-lower" class.) In the established working class there is generally a somewhat greater degree of confidence in the house as providing shelter and security, although the hangovers of concern with a threatening lower class environment often are still operating in the ways working class people think about housing.[4]

In Figure 1, I have summarized the main differences in three orientations toward housing standards that are characteristic of three different consumer groups within the lower and working classes. I will elaborate below on the attitudes of the first group, the slum dwellers, whose primary focus in housing standards seems to be on the house as a shelter from both external and internal threat.

Attitudes toward Housing

As context for this, however, let us look briefly at some of the characteristics of two working class groups. These observations come from a series of studies of the working class carried out by Social Research, Inc. over the past ten years. The studies have involved some 2,000 open-ended conversational interviews with working class men and women dealing with various life style areas from child rearing to religion, food habits to furniture preferences. In all of this work, the importance of the home and its location has appeared as a contant theme. These studies, while not based on nationally representative samples, have been carried out in such a way as to represent the geographical range of the country, including such cities as Seattle, Camden, Louisville, Chicago, Atlanta, as well as a balanced distribution of central city and suburban dwellers, apartment renters, and home owners. In these studies, one central focus concerned the feelings working class people have about their present homes, their plans for changes in housing, their attitudes toward their neighborhoods, and the relation of these to personal and familial goals. In addition, because the interviews were open-ended and conversational, much information of relevance to housing appeared in the context of other discussions because of the importance of housing to so many other areas of living.[5] In our studies and in those of Herbert Gans and others of Boston's West End, we find one type of working class life style where families are content with much about their housing—even though it is "below standard" in the eyes of housing professionals—if the housing does provide security against the most blatant of threats.[6] This traditional working class is likely to want to economize on housing in order to have money available to pursue other interests and needs. There will be efforts at the maintenance of the house or apartment, but not much interest in improvement of housing level. Instead there is an effort to create a pleasant and cozy home, where housework can be carried out conveniently. Thus, families in this group tend to acquire a good many of the major appliances, to center their social life in the kitchen, to be relatively unconcerned with adding taste in furnishings to comfort. With respect to the immediate outside world the main emphasis is on a concern with the availability of a satisfying peer group life, with having neighbors who are similar, and with maintaining an easy access back and forth among people who are very well known. There is also a concern that the neighborhood be respectable enough—with respectability defined mainly in the negative, by the absence of "crumbs and bums." An emphasis on comfort and contentment ties together meanings having to do with both the inside and the outside.

Out of the increasing prosperity of the working class has grown a different orientation toward housing on the part of the second group which we can characterize as modern instead of traditional. Here there is a great emphasis on owning one's home rather than enriching a landlord. Along with the acquisition of a home and yard goes an elaboration of the inside of the house in such a way as not only to further develop the idea of a pleasant and cozy home, but also to add new elements with emphasis on having a nicely decorated living room or family room, a home which more closely approximates a standard of all-American affluence. Similarly there is a greater emphasis on maintenance of the yard outside and on the use of the yard as a place where both adults and children can relax and enjoy themselves. With this can come also the development of a more intense pattern of neighborhood socializing. In these suburbs the demand grows for good community services as opposed to simply adequate ones, so that there tends to be greater involvement in the schools than is the case with traditional working class men and women. One of the dominant themes of the modern working class life style is that of having arrived in the mainstream of American life, of no longer being simply "poor-but-honest" workers. It is in the service of this goal that we find these elaborations in the meaning of the house and its environs.

In both working class groups, as the interior of the home more closely approximates notions of a decent standard, we find a decline in concerns expressed by inhabitants with sources of threat from within and a shift toward concerns about a threatening outside world—a desire to make the neighborhood secure against the incursions of lower class people who might rob or perpetrate violence of one kind or another.

As we shift our focus from the stable working class to the lower class, the currently popular poor, we find a very different picture. In addition to the large and growing literature, I will draw on data from three studies of this group with which I have been involved. Two studies deal with family attitudes and family planning behavior on the part of lower class, in contrast to working class couples. In these studies, based on some 450 intensive conversational interviews with men and women living in Chicago, Cincinnati, and Oklahoma City housing was not a subject of direct inquiry. Nevertheless we gained considerable insight into the ways lower class people think about their physical and social environment, and their anxieties, goals, and coping mechanisms that operate in connection with their housing arrangements.[7]

The third study, currently on-going, involves a five year investigation of social and community problems in the Pruitt-Igoe Project of St. Louis. This public housing project consists of 33 11-story buildings near downtown St. Louis. The project was opened in 1954, has 2,762 apartments, of which only some 2,000 are currently occupied, and has as tenants a very high proportion (over 50 percent) of female-headed households on one kind or another of public assistance. Though originally integrated, the project is now all Negro. The project community is plagued by petty crimes, vandalism, much destruction of the physical plant, and a very bad reputation in both the Negro and white communities.[8] For the past two years a staff of ten research assistants has been carrying out participant observation and conversational interviewing among project residents. In order to obtain a comparative focus on problems of living in public housing, we have also interviewed in projects in Chicago (Stateway Gardens), New York (St. Nicholas), and San Francisco (Yerba Buena Plaza and Westside Courts). Many of the concrete examples which follow come from these interviews, since in the course of observation and interviewing with project tenants we have had the opportunity to learn a great deal about both their experiences in the projects and about the private slum housing in which they previously lived. While our interviews in St. Louis provide us with insight into what it is like to live in one of the most disorganized public housing communities in the United States, the interviews in the other cities provide the contrast of much more average public housing experiences.[9] Similarly, the retrospective accounts that respondents in different cities give of their previous private housing experience provides a wide sampling in the slum communities of four different cities.

In the lower class we find a great many very real threats to security, although these threats often do seem to be somewhat exaggerated by lower class women. The threatening world of the lower class comes to be absorbed into a world view which generalizes the belief that the environment is threatening more than it is rewarding—that rewards reflect the infrequent working of good luck and that danger is endemic.[10] Any close acquaintance with the ongoing life of lower class people impresses one with their anxious alienation from the larger world, from the middle class to be sure, but from the majority of their peers as well. Lower class people often seem isolated and to have but tenuous participation in a community of known and valued peers. They are ever aware of the presence of strangers who tend to be seen as potentially dangerous. While they do seek to create a gratifying peer group society, these groups tend to be unstable and readily fragmented. Even the heavy reliance on relatives as the core of a personal community does not do away with the dangers which others may bring. As Walter Miller has perceptively noted, "trouble" is one of the major focal concerns in the lower class world view.[11] A home to which one could retreat from such an insecure world would be of great value, but our data indicate that for lower class people such a home is not easy to come by. In part, this is due to the fact that one's own family members themselves often make trouble or bring it into the home, but even more important it is because it seems very difficult to create a home and an immediate environment that acutally does shut out danger.[12]

Dangers in the Environment

From our data it is possible to abstract a great many dangers that have some relation to housing and its location. The location or the immediate environment is as important as the house itself, since lower class people are aware that life inside is much affected by the life just outside.

In Figure 2, I have summarized the main kinds of danger which seem to be related to housing one way or another. It is apparent that these dangers have two

FIG. 2. A TAXONOMY OF DANGERS IN THE LOWER CLASS HOME AND ENVIRONS: EACH OF THESE CAN INVOLVE PHYSICAL, INTERPERSONAL, AND MORAL CONSEQUENCES

Source of Danger	
Non-Human	*Human*
Rats and other vermin	Violence to self and possessions
Poisons	Assault
Fire and burning	Fighting and beating
Freezing and cold	Rape
Poor plumbing	Objects thrown or dropped
Dangerous electrical wiring	Stealing
Trash (broken glass, cans, etc.)	Verbal hostility, shaming, exploitation
Insufficiently protected heights	Own family
Other aspects of poorly designed or deteriorated structures (e.g., thin walls)	Neighbors
Cost of dwelling	Caretakers
	Outsiders
	Attractive alternatives that wean oneself or valued others away from a stable life

immediate sources, human and non-human, and that the consequences that are feared from these sources usually represent a complex amalgam of physical, interpersonal, and mortal damage to the individual and his family. Let us look first at the various sources of danger and then at the overlapping consequences feared from these dangers.

There is nothing unfamiliar about the non-human sources of danger. They represent a sad catalogue of threats apparent in any journalist's account of slum living.[13] That we become used to the catalogue, however, should not obscure the fact that these dangers are very real to many lower class families. Rats and other vermin are ever present companions in most big city slums. From the sense of relief which residents in public housing often experience on this score, it is apparent that slum dwellers are not indifferent to the presence of rats in their homes. Poisons may be a danger, sometimes from lead-base paints used on surfaces which slum toddlers may chew. Fires in slum areas are not uncommon, and even in a supposedly well designed public housing project children may repeatedly burn themselves on uncovered steampipe risers. In slums where the tenant supplies his own heating there is always the possibility of a very cold apartment because of no money, or, indeed, of freezing to death (as we were told by one respondent whose friend fell into an alcoholic sleep without turning on the heater). Insufficiently protected heights, as in one public housing project, may lead to deaths when children fall out windows or adults fall down elevator shafts. Thin walls in the apartment may expose a family to more of its neighbor's goings-on than comfortable to hear. Finally, the very cost of the dwelling itself can represent a danger in that it leaves too little money for other things needed to keep body and soul together.

That lower class people grow up in a world like this and live in it does not mean that they are indifferent to it—nor that its toll is only that of possible physical damage in injury, illness, incapacity, or death. Because these potentialities and events are interpreted and take on symbolic significance, and because lower class people make some efforts to cope with them, inevitably there are also effects on their interpersonal relationships and on their moral conceptions of themselves and their worlds.

The most obvious human source of danger has to do with violence directed by others against oneself and one's possessions. Lower class people are concerned with being assaulted, being damaged, being drawn into fights, being beaten, being raped. In public housing projects in particular, it is always possible for juveniles to throw or drop things from windows which can hurt or kill, and if this pattern takes hold it is a constant source of potential danger. Similarly, people may rob anywhere—apartment, laundry room, corridor.

Aside from this kind of direct violence, there is the more pervasive ever-present potentiality for symbolic violence to the self and that which is identified with the self—by verbal hostility, the shaming and exploitation expressed by the others who make up one's world. A source of such violence, shaming, or exploitation may be within one's own family—from children, spouse, siblings, parents—and often is. It seems very likely that crowding tends to encourage such symbolic violence to the self but certainly crowding is not the only factor since we also find this kind of threat in uncrowded public housing quarters.[14] Most real and immediate to lower class people, however, seems to be the potentiality for symbolic destructiveness by their neighbors. Lower class people seem ever on guard toward their neighbors, even ones with whom they become well-acquainted and would count as their friends. This suspiciousness is directed often at juveniles and young adults whom older people tend to regard as almost uncontrollable. It is important to note that while one may and does engage in this kind of behavior oneself, this is no guarantee that the individual does not fear and condemn the behavior when engaged in by others. For example, one woman whose family was evicted from a public housing project because her children were troublemakers thought, before she knew that her family was included among the twenty families thus evicted, that the evictions were a good thing because there were too many people around who cause trouble.

Symbolic violence on the part of caretakers (all those whose occupations bring them into contact with lower class people as purveyors of some private or public service) seems also endemic in slum and public housing areas. Students of the interactions between caretakers and their lower class clients have suggested that there is a great deal of punitiveness and shaming commonly expressed by the caretakers in an effort to control and direct the activities of their clients.[15]

The defense of the client is generally one of avoidance, or sullenness and feigned stupidity, when contact cannot be avoided. As David Capolvitz has shown so well, lower class people are subjected to considerable exploitation by the commercial services with which they deal, and exploitation for money, sexual favors, and sadistic impulses is not unknown on the part of public servants either.[16]

Finally, outsiders present in two ways the dangers of symbolic violence as well as a physical violence. Using the anonymity of geographical mobility, outsiders may come into slum areas to con and exploit for their own ends and, by virtue of the attitudes they maintain toward slum dwellers or public housing residents, they may demean and derogate them. Here we would have to include also the mass media which can and do behave in irresponsibly punitive ways toward people who live in lower class areas, a fact most dramatically illustrated in the customary treatment of the Pruitt-Igoe Project in St. Louis. From the point of view of the residents, the unusual interest shown in their world by a research team can also fit into this pattern.

Finally, the lower class person's world contains many attractive alternatives to the pursuit of a stable life. He can fear for himself that he will be caught up in these attractive alternatives and thus damage his life chances, and he may fear even more that those whom he values, particularly in his family, will be seduced away from him. Thus, wives fear their husbands will be attracted to the life outside the family, husbands fear the same of their wives, and parents always fear that their children will somehow turn out badly. Again, the fact that you may yourself be involved in such seductive pursuits does not lessen the fear that these valued others will be won away while your back is turned. In short, both the push and the pull of the human world in which lower class people live can be seen as a source of danger.

Having looked at the sources of danger, let us look at the consequences which lower class people fear from these dangers. The physical consequences are fairly obvious in connection with the non-human threats and the threats of violence from others. They are real and they are ever present: One can become the victim of injury, incapacitation, illness, and death from both nonhuman and human sources. Even the physical consequences of the symbolic violence of hostility, shaming, and exploitation, to say nothing of seduction, can be great if they lead one to retaliate in a physical way and in turn be damaged. Similarly there are physical consequences to being caught up in alternatives such as participation in alcohol and drug subcultures.

There are three interrelated interpersonal consequences of living in a world characterized by these human and nonhuman sources of danger. The first relates to the need to form satisfying interpersonal relationships, the second to the need to exercise responsibility as a family member, and the third to the need to formulate an explanation for the unpleasant state of affairs in your world.

The consequences which endanger the need to maintain satisfying interpersonal relations flow primarily from the human sources of danger. That is, to the extent that the world seems made up of dangerous others, at a very basic level the choice of friends carries risks. There is always the possibility that a friend may turn out to be an enemy or that his friends will. The result is a generalized watchfulness and touchiness in interpersonal relationships. Because other individuals represent not only themselves but also their families, the matter is further complicated since interactions with, let us say, neighbors' children, can have repercussions on the relationship with the neighbor. Because there are human agents behind most of the non-human dangers, one's relationships with others—family members, neighbors, caretakers—are subject to potential disruptions because of those others' involvement in creating trash, throwing objects, causing fires, or carrying on within thin walls.

With respect to the exercise of responsibility, we find that parents feel they must bring their children safely through childhood in a world which both poses great physical and moral dangers, and which seeks constantly to seduce them into a way of life which the parent wishes them to avoid. Thus, childrearing becomes an anxious and uncertain process. Two of the most common results are a pervasive repressiveness in child discipline and training, and, when that seems to fail or is no longer possible, a fatalistic abdication of efforts to protect the children. From the child's point of view, because his parents are not able to protect him from many unpleasantnesses and even from himself, he loses faith in them and comes to regard them as persons of relatively little consequence.

The third area of effect on interpersonal relations has to do with the search for causes of the prevalence of threat and violence in their world. We have suggested that to lower class people the major causes stem from the nature of their own peers. Thus, a great deal of blaming others goes on and reinforces the process of isolation, suspiciousness, and touchiness about blame and shaming. Similarly, landlords and tenants tend to develop patterns of mutual recrimination and blaming, making it very difficult for them to cooperate with each other in doing something about either the human or nonhuman sources of difficulty.

Finally, the consequences for conceptions of the moral order of one's world, of one's self, and of others, are very great. Although lower class people may not adhere in action to many middle class values about neatness, cleanliness, order, and proper decorum, it is apparent that they are often aware of their deviance, wishing that their world could be a nicer place, physically and socially. The presence of nonhuman threats conveys in devastating terms a sense that they live in an immoral and uncontrolled world. The physical evidence of trash, poor plumbing and the stink that goes with it, rats and other vermin, deepens their feeling of being moral outcasts. Their physical world is telling them they are inferior and bad just as effectively perhaps as do their human interactions. Their inability to control the depredation of rats, hot steam pipes, balky stoves, and poorly fused electrical circuits tells them that they are failures as autonomous individuals. The physical and social disorder of their world presents a constant temptation to give up or retaliate in kind. And when lower class people try to do something about some of these dangers, they are generally exposed in their interactions with caretakers and outsiders to further moral punitiveness by being told that their troubles are their own fault.

Implications for Housing Design

It would be asking too much to insist that design per se can solve or even seriously mitigate these threats. On the other hand, it is obvious that almost all the nonhuman threats can be pretty well done away with where the resources are available to design decent housing for lower class people. No matter what criticisms are made of public housing projects, there is no doubt that the structures themselves are infinitely preferable to slum housing. In our interviews in public housing projects we have found very few people who complain about design aspects of the insides of their apartments. Though they may not see their apartments as perfect, there is a dramatic drop in anxiety about nonhuman threats within. Similarly, reasonable foresight in the design of other elements can eliminate the threat of falling from windows or into elevator shafts, and can provide adequate outside toilet facilities for children at play. Money and a reasonable exercise of architectural skill go a long way toward providing lower class families with the really safe place of retreat from the outside world that they desire.

There is no such straightforward design solution to the potentiality of human threat. However, to the extent that lower class people do have a place they can go that is not so dangerous as the typical slum dwelling, there is at least the gain of a haven. Thus, at the cost perhaps of increased isolation, lower class people in public housing sometimes place a great deal of value on privacy and on living a quiet life behind the locked doors of their apartments. When the apartment itself seems safe it allows the family to begin to elaborate a home to maximize coziness, comfortable enclosure, and lack of exposure. Where, as in St. Louis, the laundry rooms seem unsafe places, tenants tend to prefer to do their laundry in their homes, sacrificing the possibility of neighborly interactions to gain a greater sense of security of person and property.

Once the home can be seen as a relatively safe place, lower class men and women express a desire to push out the boundaries of safety further into the larger world. There is the constantly expressed desire for a little bit of outside space that is one's own or at least semiprivate. Buildings that have galleries are much preferred by their tenants to those that have no such immediate access to the outside. Where, as in the New York public housing project we studied, it was possible to lock the outside doors of the buildings at night, tenants felt more secure.

A measured degree of publicness within buildings can also contribute to a greater sense of security. In buildings where there are several families whose doors open onto a common hallway there is a greater sense of the availability of help should trouble come than there is in buildings where only two or three apartments open onto a small hallway in a stairwell. While tenants do not necessarily develop close neighborly relations when more neighbors are available, they can develop a sense of making common cause in dealing with common problems. And they feel less at the mercy of gangs or individuals intent on doing them harm.

As with the most immediate outside, lower class people express the desire to have their immediate neighborhood or the housing project grounds a more controlled and safe place. In public housing projects, for example, tenants want project police who function efficiently and quickly; they would like some play areas supervised so that children are not allowed to prey on each other; they want to be able to move about freely themselves and at the same time discourage outsiders who might come to exploit.

A real complication is that the very control which these desires imply can seem a threat to the lower class resident. To the extent that caretakers seem to demand and damn more than they help, this cure to the problem of human threat seems worse than the disease. The crux of the caretaking task in connection with lower class people is to provide and encourage security and order within the lower class world without at the same time extracting from it a heavy price in self-esteem, dignity, and autonomy.

Notes

1. Lord Raglan, *The Temple and the House* (London: Routledge & Kegan Paul Limited, 1964).

2. Bennett M. Berger, *Working-Class Suburb* (Berkeley: University of California Press, 1960) and Herbert Gans, "Effect of the Move From the City to Suburb" in Leonard J. Duhl (ed.), *The Urban Condition* (New York: Free Press, 1963).

3. Anselm L. Strauss, *Images of the American City* (New York: Free Press, 1961).

4. In this paper I am pulling together observations from a number of different studies. What I have to say about working class attitudes toward housing comes primarily from studies of working class life style carried out in collaboration with Richard Coleman, Gerald Handel, W. Lloyd Warner, and Burleigh Gardner. What I have to say about lower class life comes from two more recent studies dealing with family life and family planning in the lower class and a study currently in progress of social life in a large public housing project in St. Louis (being conducted in collaboration with Alvin W. Gouldner and David J. Pittman).

5. These studies are reported in the following unpublished Social Research, Inc. reports: *Prosperity and Changing Working Class Life Style* (1960) and *Urban Working Class Identity and World View* (1965). The following publications are based on this series of studies: Lee Rainwater, Richard P. Coleman, and Gerald Handel, *Workingman's Wife: Her Personality, World and Life Style* (New York: Oceana Publications, 1959); Gerald Handel and Lee Rainwater, "Persistence and Change in Working Class Life Style," and Lee Rainwater and Gerald Handel, "Changing Family Roles in the Working Class," both in Arthur B. Shostak and William Gomberg, *Blue-Collar World* (New York: Prentice-Hall, 1964).

6. Marc Fried, "Grieving for a Lost Home," and Edward J. Ryan, "Personal Identity in an Urban Slum," in Leonard J. Duhl (ed.), *The Urban Condition* (New York: Free Press, 1963); and Herbert Gans, *Urban Villagers* (New York: Free Press of Glencoe, Inc., 1962).

7. Lee Rainwater, *And the Poor Get Children* (Chicago: Quadrangle Books, 1960), and Lee Rainwater, *Family Design: Marital Sexuality, Family Size and Family Planning* (Chicago: Aldine Publishing Company, 1964).

8. Nicholas J. Demerath, "St. Louis Public Housing Study Sets Off Community Development to Meet Social Needs," *Journal of Housing,* XIX (October, 1962).

9. See, D. M. Wilner, *et al., The Housing Environment and Family Life* (Baltimore: Johns Hopkins University Press, 1962).

10. Allison Davis, *Social Class Influences on Learning* (Cambridge: Harvard University Press, 1948).

11. Walter Miller, "Lower Class Culture as a Generating Milieu of Gang Delinquency," in Marvin E. Wolfgang, Leonard Savitz, and Norman Johnson

(eds.), *The Sociology of Crime and Delinquency* (New York: John Wiley Company, 1962).

12. Alvin W. Schorr, *Slums and Social Insecurity* (Washington, D.C.: Department of Health, Education and Welfare, 1963).

13. Michael Harrington, *The Other America* (New York: MacMillan Co., 1962).

14. Edward S. Deevey, "The Hare and the Haruspex: A Cautionary Tale," in Eric and Mary Josephson, *Man Alone* (New York: Dell Publishing Company, 1962).

15. A. B. Hollinghead and L. H. Rogler, "Attitudes Toward Slums and Private Housing in Puerto Rico," in Leonard J. Duhl, *The Urban Condition* (New York: Free Press, 1963).

16. David Caplovitz, *The Poor Pay More* (New York: Free Press of Glencoe, 1963).

THE NEIGHBORHOOD "BOOKMAKER": ENTREPRENEUR AND MOBILITY MODEL

Robert Perrucci

Much of the work on social stratification and social mobility has provided ample documentation of the manner in which persons of lower socio-economic origins are hampered with respect to educational and occupational achievement. In addition to the constraining factors of community organization [1] and poor quality schools in low income areas,[2] there has also been ample documentation of the role of family structure,[3] and of individual values and achievement orientation [4] in inhibiting mobility. The most influential work in this area has been that by Hyman, Rosen, and Stodtbeck. Hyman has argued that lower class youth do not value those educational and occupational elements that are essential for upward mobility. As he has put it:

> The components of this value system, in our judgment, involve less emphasis upon the traditional high success goals, increased awareness of the lack of opportunity to achieve success, and less emphasis upon the achievement of goals which in turn would be instrumental for success. To put it simply the lower class individual doesn't want as much success, knows he couldn't get it even if he wanted to, and doesn't want what might help him get success. Of course, an individual's value system is only one among many factors on which his position in the social hierarchy depends. Some of these factors may be external and arbitrary, quite beyond the control of even a highly motivated individual. However, within the bounds of the freedom available to individuals, this value system would create a *self-imposed* barrier to an improved position.[5]

Working paper Number 10, *Institute for the Study of Social Change,* Purdue University, Lafayette, Indiana. Published by permission of the author.

Rosen, on the other hand, noted that a personality dimension referred to as achievement motivation is directly related to social class. The lower the socio-economic status of male high school students the less likely they were to describe the content of Thematic Apperception Tests in terms of "achievement based upon a standard of excellence." [6] The particular stress in Strodtbeck's work was upon the distribution of power within the family and the manner in which socialization within different family structures can aid or inhibit the development of a view of the world as orderly and amenable to influence and mastery by individuals.[7]

In much of this work the particular individual attributes and social values that are examined are those that reflect the generally accepted institutionalized means for mobility. Rosen's procedures did allow for the possibility that the boy who might want to become the "best crapshooter on the block" rather than a doctor or a lawyer would also be described as having a strong achievement motivation. However, the overwhelming feeling one gets from much of the work on social class, values, and aspirations is that many of the lower class youth have simply been unable to separate out what they want to say or what they believe, from what is socially acceptable.

This emphasis upon middle class values and aspirations does tell us that the lower class boy does not embrace them, but it does not tell us much about what values and aspirations he does embrace.[8] This latter concern would turn our attention away from the "deficiencies" of the lower class youth to an examination of how the things he is "rich" with may be related to the dynamics of mobility.

The purpose of the present paper is to examine the occupational role of the neighborhood bookmaker in terms of work setting, recruitment patterns, relations with employees, relations with customers, and his connections with competitors and the law as persons most relevant to his own business success. Special attention will be given to the bookmaker as a mobility model for youth in low income areas and to how the role requirements of the occupation tends to select persons with skills and personal qualities similar to those required for more socially desirable occupational pursuits. Finally, it will be suggested that the bookmaker as a mobility model has a self-defeating aspect which may have more general applicability to other mobility models in low income neighborhoods.

The Horseroom and the Betting Context[9]

The bookmaker that is the subject of this paper is primarily concerned with taking bets on horse races. Although he may also take bets on boxing matches and ball games of all sorts, run "crap games," "bankroll" bowling matches, these activities occupy a much smaller proportion of his time and energy and are most often nighttime activities which border on leisure. He works the year around as the tracks in the New York–New England area, Louisiana, Florida, Maryland, Illinois, and California provide ample opportunity for bettors. His customers are to be found in that psychological-physical area known as the neighborhood, where one feels known and safe.

The bookmaker operates under two general conditions which are controlled by the larger society—when things are "open" and when they are "tight." When open, the bookmaker carries out his activities in a "horseroom" which is generally a lower-level store front or one-flight-up vacant apartment. The horseroom has little furniture, the most prominent piece being the writers' table with from two to four writers taking bets. The other prominent part of the room is a large section of wall space where "scratch sheets" giving listings of horses entered in various races at major tracks about the country with the "morning line" odds for each horse; horses who have been removed from races, i.e., "scratched," are also listed.

Customers place their bets with the writers who record their bets, the date, the time, and the bettor's initials or code name in original and duplicate. The original is retained for the bookmaker's record, and the "dupe" constitutes the bettor's receipt. The bookmaker's function at such times is largely executive and public relations. He spends much of his time moving among the customers talking, kidding, and "cutting up jackpots" with friends (recalling humorous situations involving themselves and others, or serious yet humorous situations which they had been through). He is automatically consulted by the writers in the event of large bets, either individually or cumulatively on a horse, that might "hurt" him. He is also available when a customer requests a "marker" (bet on credit).

Other bets are brought to the horseroom by "runners" from various "drop off" spots in the neighborhood like barbershops and grocery stores, or bets he picks up from small businesses like a dress factory or meat packaging plant each day at lunch. (There is usually an employee at the plant also in the bookmaker's employ who gathers the bets and gives them to the runner.)

The bookmaker keeps track of the volume and pattern of the betting in order to decide whether to "hold" all bets or to "lay off" bets with another bookmaker or at the race track if there is a local track in operation. He makes these decisions in a way which minimizes the possibility of large losses while also maximizing his chances for gain. In so doing, he often must draw upon his own knowledge of horses in deciding which horses he believes do or do not have a reasonable chance of winning. The bookmaker's ability to "dope" the races himself with systematic and serious analysis of the racing form (referred to as the "bible"), which contains elaborate past performance information on all horses running that day, often becomes a source of personal prestige, and of the respect that his customers have for him.

When the bookmaker's relations with the larger society become "tight" the horseroom is closed down. The police who cooperate with the bookie in his activities inform him that they can no longer assure the safety of his operation with respect to arrests if he chooses to remain open. Although the horseroom is closed, the bookmaker may still conduct his business from an automobile or from a neighborhood bar. When things become extremely tight the bookie himself is closed down, and the understanding is that he is a target for arrest. Under such conditions the bookie's business is severely curtailed. When unable to maintain a stable location, customers cannot place bets with him unless he contacts them. The number of customers and runners that he can contact is sharply reduced as is the volume of his business. Bettors must make all their bets for the day at one time as they may not be able to bet again later in the day. This eliminates the possibility that the bookmaker can recoup if he suffers losses in early races, and he cannot play possibilities by "moving" bets around to maximize his own potential gains.

The bookmaker's chances to stay open or closed are determined by the distribution of pressure at various levels of the police hierarchy. The bookmaker's relations with the authorities are limited to authorities at the precinct level. Weekly "payoffs" to precinct officials protect the bookie against harassment at the precinct level, and carry the promise of being informed if division men are moving into an area to "bust the bookies." From time to time division officials put pressure on the precinct officials to show evidence that action is being taken against bookmakers. In such cases the bookmaker learns that he is to be raided and that someone will have to "take a pinch" (be arrested). The bookie will then hire someone to take the pinch during the raid. Little difficulty is encountered in finding someone among those who "hang out" at the horseroom who is willing to take a pinch. Men without records or with minor records are virtually guaranteed a suspended sentence with a fine. The bookmaker will handle the fine and pay his stand-in anywhere from two hundred to five hundred dollars for his service. While this practice of using substitutes to take a pinch is well known to precinct authorities, it is overlooked since their main concern is to demonstrate to division authorities that horserooms have been closed down and bookies arrested.

The Bookie as the "Mark"

On the face of it, the betting context seems to present a fairly simple and straightforward relationship between the bookie and his customer. Beneath the surface of this betting relationship between the bettor and the bookmaker is a highly competitive set of expectations and behaviors. Both participants in this competitive relationship maintain a conception of what they consider a worthy opponent. Bookies show little respect for the foolish bettor, whose wagers are small and are based upon multiple winning choices for a payoff. Such bets give maximum advantage to the bookie since the probabilities of multiple winning choices are low, and even if successful, the small initial bet keeps bookmaker losses to a minimum.

At the same time that the bookie shows his lack of respect for the small and foolish bettor, he is well aware that such bettors can be a stable source of income for him. This disrespect for such bettors is reflected in the oft-repeated humorous remarks that the bookie directs toward them in the betting situation: "Well, here's two bucks I can spend right now," or "If I had another hundred just like you, I could retire."

The bookie who actually does have an abundance of two-dollar bettors may often find that he does not have much prestige in the eyes of his fellow bookies, or in the eyes of the seasoned and skilled bettor. The competitive nature of the betting relationship is nonexistent, as the bookie has all the "percentages" in his favor, and he need not exhibit his own skills "doping" races and deciding which bets to hold and which to "lay off." The bookie who does not earn the respect of his bettors due to his own knowledge of betting is often left with very few skilled, "heavy" bettors.

The competitive nature of the bookmaker-bettor relationship leads to an elaboration of the competition which may function to give the bettor an advantage in his individual bet similar to that which the bookmaker enjoys in terms of aggregate probabilities. This new form of competition is found in the art of "past-posting," where the customer attempts to transform the bookie into the "mark." Past-posting is the practice of placing a bet on a horse after the start of a race. In its most complex form it requires someone at the race track, or in close proximity to it, to relay information on a race as it is in progress, over the telephone or by a special wire service to someone at a phone booth or receiving set very close to the horseroom. The person receiving the information on the horse who has won the race, or the horse who has a sufficient lead close to the completion of the race, immediately places a bet on this horse with the bookie.

The success of this operation depends upon the bookie's willingness to accept a bet so close to the scheduled post-time of a race. The situation here is much like the confidence game which depends so heavily upon the existence of "larceny in the heart of the mark." Getting the bookie to accept "past-posted" bets is accomplished in several ways. It may be tried only with bookmakers who are known not to record the time of the bet on a betting slip, but who simply check the "post-times" for each race from the scratch sheet and accept only those bets that are close to the listed post-time. The actual post-time of a race is often several minutes later than the listed post-time and may be as much as ten minutes later due to the accumulated delays of getting races started at the race track. This fact encourages many bookies to be a little cavalier in accepting bets on races so close to the listed post-time. On the other hand, if past-posting is tried with a bookie who is known to record the time on all bets, the strategy is to get him to suspend this rule in order not to lose the bet. This is accomplished by the "conman" rushing into the horseroom with a long list of bets, most of which are on different horses on the past-posted race with the heaviest concentration of bets on the horse who is known to have already won. He will display the list while asking if he "still has time for the 3rd at Belmont." In order not to lose the "action," the bookie often takes the bet without recording the time. For if he records the time, and the race actually started before that time, then the entire bet is cancelled. Rather than risk this loss, the bet is accepted. The fact that all this takes place within a few minutes of the listed time of the race makes the bookie less suspicious of such activities. It is also important that past-posting is not attempted by complete strangers, but by persons who are regular bettors with a bookie, and who use betting patterns close to the one that will be used in the past-posted race; they have also often placed bets on other races close to post-time, all of which makes his "rigged" bet appear like any other bet.

In addition to the bookie's vulnerability to attempts by his bettors to treat him as the "mark," are the attempts by his writers and runners to exploit their positions to their own rather than his advantage. Writers, as a matter of standard practice, write betting slips for friends on horses that have already won their races. This is done by having a friend in the horseroom at the time when the bookie is not present, at which time the writer will write a slip for a horse in a race that has already been run and for which the winner is known. The friend and the writer split such winnings between them.

This practice is known to the bookmaker, and it is a hazard he accepts but nonetheless tries to eliminate. He keeps close tabs on the weekly losing bets taken by each writer, hoping to uncover unusually large losses for one of the writers that occur with some regularity. The bookie also keeps himself informed as to the people that the writers are "tight" with (i.e., close friends) in order to uncover unusually "lucky" friends.

The main protection available to the bookie against his writers' past-posting activities is to stay on the betting premises and to pick up all duplicates of the betting slips from the writers at numerous times during the day. This will seriously limit the chances that a writer can write a winning bet for a friend after the race has been completed. Such survillance activities, however, restrict the bookie's activities to the horseroom, limiting his public relations work and his own betting at the race track itself. Moreover, keeping close tabs on writers is analogous to "close supervision," and may engender work dissatisfaction among writers.

The main problem found by the runners is their tendency to "hold" certain bets rather than turn them in to the bookie. Holding bets by runners is, in effect, acting as the bookie. This tendency can be traced to the fact that runners are themselves very knowledgeable bettors who cannot restrain themselves from holding bets that they believe are "sure" losers. This is a dangerous practice, of course, since the runner does not hold many bets and a bad guess may cost him a good deal of his own money. This behavior is, in a very real sense, analogous to a "pre-professional internship," whereby the runner hopes to get together enough of a bankroll and enough potential bettors to start his own small book.

Tension with Clients: Minimizing the Visibility of Success

The neighborhood bookmaker is a long-standing resident of the area in which he practices, and he generally shares the ethnicity of the dominant group in the area. Both of these attributes help contribute to the success of the bookmaker by making him more acceptable to potential bettors, and giving him access to neighborhood storekeepers who allow their establishments to serve as pick-up spots for bets. Strong neighborhood and ethnic ties also help to minimize the possibility that complaints about bookmaking activities will be made to local police authorities.

The fact that the betting relationship is based upon elements of primary-type relationships places the bookmaker in paradoxical situations. Since he is a person of some prestige in the neighborhood he must behave in a manner that is consistent with his high position. Moreover, if he wishes to represent success in an occupation that demands considerable ability—either for reasons of personal pride or to demonstrate to bettors that he is an economically stable person with which to bet—he is expected to validate this success with the usual symbols.

At the same time that he is expected to validate his success, he must be careful not to overdo it. Thus, he is expected to be a "good spender," while not appearing overprosperous to customers who have themselves suffered considerable losses; he must be understanding to his losing customers by extending betting credit, while not becoming a target for all would-be borrowers; and he must exhibit his proficiency in his field, while not boasting and offending customers. The balance is often maintained by the bookmaker's practice of "moaning" and "packing two BR's." Moaning is the art of deploring a current run of bad luck in a most convincing manner, and it is practiced primarily on those customers who might become envious of obvious prosperity or who might wish to borrow money from the bookie. Moaning is often validated by the bookmaker's practice of carrying two bankrolls, one for public display and the other for private use. In response to ribbing from customers that "he must be getting fat" (i.e., prosperous), or the inquiry of a would-be borrower of "how are you holding," the bookie is quick to display his public bankroll of a few one and five dollar bills.

A very close parallel to this situation for the bookmaker is revealed in a description of the relationship between crew-leaders and pickers in migrant labor camps. Truman Moore describes the crew-leader as follows:

> His dealings with the migrant crew were complex. For one thing, he lived closely with them. His impression on them was important. If a crew-leader looked too prosperous, the crew might think he was crooked. If he looked too poor, they might doubt he was a good crew-leader. Hamp managed to look just right. He had a pair of brown pants and a red shirt that were ragged to the point of fascination. He was the raggedest man they'd ever seen. Close examination of this costume would have revealed patches sewn over whole cloth, but the effect was one of arresting poverty. To contrast with this, Hamp drove a Cadillac. His garments attested to his humility and his car to his success.[10]

Both the bookmaker and the crew-leader find themselves in a situation where success can be like the kiss of death. Their success is in large part connected to the fact that they share common emotional bonds with the group members they "serve." This very same fact, however, restricts them in the overt display of success; for to profit excessively from economic relationships with in-group members may smack of exploitation.

Particularism, Envy and Controlled Mobility

It has been suggested in this paper that the occupational role of the bookmaker has many elements in common with more acceptable occupational pursuits. Recruitment into the occupation tends to be orderly, and reflects elements of pre-professional apprenticeship roles. Moreover, the technical and human relations skills associated with the role are as demanding and complex as many other high level entrepreneurial roles. The particular combination of elements in the occupational role of bookmaker operate as a visible mobility model for lower class youth; much as the teacher, doctor, or lawyer serves as a mobility model for the middle class youth.

The peculiarity of the bookmaker role as a mobility model, in contrast to middle class models, is that aspirations to become a bookmaker require a person to become more closely tied to his communal group rather than to break such ties. (Middle class mobility models require educational achievements which often serve to maximize differences between the mobile person and his origins.) His prospects for success as a bookmaker are heavily dependent upon *particular-*

istic criteria of friendship, ethnicity, and communal ties. Another of the pattern variables also distinguishes this lower class mobility model from middle class models: the role is characterized by *diffuse* interactions rather than specific ones. That is, the bookmaker-customer relationship is not confined to a betting transaction, but tends to spill over into other interests and obligations outside the betting context.

It is tempting to use the elements of this case material on the bookmaker to reflect a more general feature of social relationships in lower class settings. There is some fragmentary evidence that relationships in the lower classes are governed by ties and obligations to particular persons and groups, rather than by abstract normative systems. A paper by Muir and Weinstein [11] on class differences in norms of social obligation indicates that middle class respondents are more likely to subscribe to reciprocity norms ("Do you eventually quit doing favors for people like this—who never repay although able?"); they feel less close to persons whom they owe and those who owe them ("In general do you feel closer or less close to someone who never repays his social obligations, although he can?"; and "In general, do you feel closer or less close to someone you owe a large favor to?"); and they feel more obligated to return favors for someone outside the family rather than someone in the family ("Do you feel as obligated to do a favor for someone in the family—like an aunt, uncle, father, daughter, etc.—as you would someone outside the family?").

The significance of differences in orientations to individuals or to normative obligations is found in the fact that mobility is apparently facilitated by the ability to break old ties and easily establish new ties,[12] a pattern that can be more readily followed where there are fewer obligations to specific persons. Very similar observations have been made on the significance of universalistic norms governing relations with strangers for the establishment of economic relationships in developing societies.[13]

What we are suggesting, then, is that particularism and diffuseness in social relationships are very much associated with success in certain occupations in lower class communities; the case of the bookmaker clearly underscores this hypothesis. However, the very conditions which promote the success also severely limit the extent of the success. The specific mechanism that seems to produce this controlled mobility is the group response of *envy* to a successful person. Envy operates as a negative sanction which has the function of criticizing a group member who has attempted to distinguish himself from other group members. In many ethnic communities people take great pains to avoid producing envy in others as it is often associated with the "evil eye." The envious person, in effect, puts a curse of bad luck upon the object of his envy. It is important to note that the envious person is not the guilty party (as he would be in the middle class community) but the person who has behaved in a way to encourage envy.

This concern with envy has been noted by others who have studied tight-knit ethnic communities. Madsen,[14] in a study of Mexican Americans in South Texas describes the care that people take to avoid being too different from other group members in behavior, dress, or Anglo-type mannerisms. "As personal shortcomings or failures are easily admitted, so personal gains or advancements may be concealed. Such concealment prevents *envidia* or envy in others." [15]

Thus, while mobility behavior can be encouraged within lower class communities, it is suggested that such mobility is highly controlled by the same conditions that induced the mobility in the first place. The constraints placed upon the person in a community mobility role can produce results very much like those associated with the Protestant ethic. The compulsion to work combined with asceticism produced wealth; similarly, the neighborhood bookmaker by hiding his success can also produce wealth. With the consumption of this wealth, however, he would be faced with envious and unhappy bettors, and increased efforts by runners and writers to get a larger share of the pie. In contrast to success in the middle class community, success based upon economic transactions with members of the lower-class community is not supported by justifying economic norms that approve his rights to the success.

Notes

1. William H. Sewell, "Community of Residence and College Plans," *American Sociological Review,* **29** (February, 1964), 24–38; Natalie Rogoff, "Local Social Structure and Educational Selection," in A. H. Halsey, J. Floud, and C. Arnold Anderson, *Education, Economy, and Society,* New York: Free Press, 1961, pp. 241–251.

2. Patricia C. Sexton, *Education and Income,* New York: Viking Press, 1961.

3. Fred L. Strodtbeck, "Family Interaction, Values and Achievement," in David C. McClelland, *et al., Talent and Society,* Princeton, New Jersey: D. Van Nostrand Co., 1958; Robert A. Ellis and W. Clayton Lane, "Structural Supports for Upward Mobility," *American Sociological Review,* **38** (October, 1963), 743–756; Irving Krauss, "Sources of Educational Aspirations Among Working-Class Youth," *American Sociological Review,* **29** (December, 1964), 867–879.

4. Herbert H. Hyman, "The Value Systems of Different Classes: A Social Psychological Contribution to the Analysis of Stratification," in R. Bendix and S. M. Lipset, eds., *Class, Status and Power,* New York, Free Press, 1953; Bernard C. Rosen, "The Achievement Syndrome: A Psychocultural Dimension of Stratification," *American Sociological Review,* **21** (April, 1956), 203–211; Harry J. Crockett, "The Achievement Motive and Differential Occupational Mobility in the United States," *American Sociological Review,* **27** (April, 1962), 191–204; Murray A. Straus, "Deferred Gratification, Social Class, and the Achievement Syndrome," *American Sociological Review,* **27** (June, 1962), 326–335.

5. Hyman, *op. cit.*, p. 426.

6. Rosen, *op. cit.*

7. Strodtbeck, *op. cit.*

8. Some notable exceptions in this connection are Frank Reissman, *The Culturally Deprived Child,* New York: Harper and Row, 1962; Richard A. Cloward and Lloyd E. Ohlin, *Delinquency and Opportunity: A Theory of Delinquent Gangs,* New York: Free Press, 1960; and Irving K. Zola, "Observations on Gambling in a Lower-Class Setting," *Social Problems,* **10** (Spring, 1963), 353–361.

9. The material contained in this paper is a part of the author's experiences as a "runner" and "writer" for bookmakers in New York City during the late 1940's and early 1950's. It also reflects his involvement with an active "gambling culture" during his late teens and early twenties.

10. Truman Moore, "Slaves for Rent," *Atlantic Monthly* (May, 1965), 109–122.

11. Donal E. Muir and Eugene A. Weinstein, "The Social Debt: An Investigation of Lower-Class and Middle-Class Norms of Social Obligation," *American Sociological Review,* **27** (August, 1962), 532–539.

12. See, e.g., Peter M. Blau, "Social Mobility and Interpersonal Relationships," *American Sociological Review,* **21** (June, 1956), 290–295.

13. Arthur Stinchcombe, "Organizations and Social Structure," in James March, ed., *Handbook of Organizations,* Chicago: Rand McNally, 1966.

14. William Madsen, "Value Conflicts and Folk Psychotherapy in South Texas," in Ari Kiev, ed., *Magic, Faith, and Healing,* New York: Free Press, 1964, pp. 420–440.

15. *Ibid.,* p. 426.

CHAPTER FIVE

STRAIN AND CONFLICT IN URBAN LIFE

INTRODUCTION

The most dramatic aspects of urban social research revolve about the manifold problems which are perceived by laymen and sociologists alike as "the crises of cities." Many of the problems singled out by the sociologists for intensive research and efforts at solution are also attacked by laymen with whatever procedures are at hand. The sociologist, however, remains somewhat detached in order to understand how a given problem fits into the broader spectrum of social life and what its unique and common aspects are. By analyzing strain and conflict in this manner, we attain a more profound grasp and a clearer perspective. For example, although the public may suddenly become aware of what is perceived to be an inordinate number of suicides in the cities, there may actually be no increase in the suicide rate. Crime rates, to select another example, increase with increased enforcement of law. What is most dramatic, then, does not always reflect fundamental sources of strain and conflict.

That there *is* strain and conflict in urban life cannot, however, be disputed. Our selections in this chapter attempt to provide some idea of the breadth and depth of the strains and conflicts perceived to be of greatest concern today. Solutions to these perceived problems should be derivable from the generalizations supported by the research which these papers reflect.

William Mangin's paper on problems of mental health in the process of urban migration in South America gives us some feeling for the nature of social aspects of mental health problems generally (see also Leo Srole *et al., Mental Health in the Metropolis,* New York: McGraw-Hill, 1962, for a study of mental illness in New York City.

Nathan Goldman deals with the sociological factors which influence decisions to arrest juvenile offenders in American cities, and Walter Miller describes the processes by which violent crimes occur in urban gang conflicts. Weinberg discusses delinquency in another setting, West Africa, and shows how it is related to urbanization. Buikhuisen describes teenage riots in the Netherlands and attempts to explain how they occur. Finally, Charles Tilly takes a broad view of urban life and describes its most dramatic and chaotic aspects.

Our effort in this chapter has been to present studies dealing with the most dynamic aspects of conflict and strain. In this way, we anticipate the focus of our next chapter which deals with urban change.

MENTAL HEALTH AND MIGRATION TO CITIES: A PERUVIAN CASE

William Mangin

Large-scale internal migration in Peru is not a new phenomenon. Kubler[1] and others have commented on migration in Inca and Colonial times. Migration from the provinces to Lima is of long standing and has largely accounted for the growth of the city. García Frías[2] pointed out the extent of migration in and out of Lima in 1940, and the most causal observer in Lima today can note the large numbers of migrants arriving daily from the provinces. The migrants include people from all social classes, all types of settlements, and all regions, and are found in all sections of Lima. The few white upper-class migrants from the large haciendas and towns of the provinces are generally quite familiar with Lima and Lima culture before they migrate and therefore have little difficulty in adjusting. In many cases they are quite involved in extended families which maintain Lima residences as well as provincial ones. The small kinship-oriented upper class of Peru controls the vast majority of the wealth of the country but is relatively unimportant in terms of migration. Another group that, until the last few years, figured somewhat less in migration than others is the conservative Indian group,[3,4] that is, the people characterized by Quechua speaking, coca chewing, trial marriage, remnants of patrilineal ancestry, and homespun Indian clothing, and who generally migrate to a provincial city, a mine, or a hacienda for a number of years, even a generation, before coming to Lima.

The bulk of the migrants are mestizos, Cholos (progressive Indians who have left Indian communities and are participating in national Peruvian culture, generally a one-generation transitional group), and those who, for lack of a better term, I shall call modern provincial Peruvians. The Cholos are mostly bilingual mountaineers, but so are many of the mestizos and the modern Peruvians. As Simmons noted[5] there are two ideal types in Peru, the coastal-urban-creole (or modern Peruvian) and the mountain-rural-Indian, but there is considerable intermixture of the categories in actual fact. The dominant high-status culture pattern in Lima is certainly the urban, modern Peruvian.

Reprinted by permission of the author and publisher from *Annals of The New York Academy of Sciences,* **84** (December 8, 1960), pp. 911–917.
The investigation reported in this paper was supported by a research grant from the National Institute of Mental Health, Public Health Service, Bethesda, Md. The research in Peru was conducted from 1957 to 1959.

Some current (and ancient) writings in social science would lead us to expect that the low-status migrants whose culture differs most from that of the dominant group will suffer severe stress and exhibit disorganized and maladaptive behavior supposedly characteristic of people in the transculturation situation.[6] The problem is enormously complex and has been studied only minimally but my own four-year study in Peru does not support this expectation. The important factors in the adjustment of migrants to Lima seem to have relatively little to do with migration as such. Many are faced with the necessity of learning new patterns in a short time, but my data indicate that they do so in a manner characteristic of their response to problems in the mountains. Drastic changes in personality were not found among the respondents, and changes in the degree and nature of social participation seemed to be largely within the control of the individual; that is, a man who desires either more or less contact with kinsmen and/or *paisanos* can usually arrange it either way. A man who wants the primary-group relationships of a small community in Lima can usually satisfy this want even as a man who desires to escape from precisely these relationships can usually escape. It is also possible for a man to cut himself off completely from contacts with his home locality, or to participate intensely with people from that locality in Lima and stay in almost daily contact with the actual home town through seeing visitors and making visits.[7] The most important "migration" in Peru, in terms of culture change, is not the move from the provinces to Lima but the sociopsychological change from a conservative Indian cultural group to modern Peruvian national culture. This may or may not be accompanied by geographical relocation.

For many people migration is a response to a change in level of aspiration; for others it is a continuation of some early aspiration; for still others it is forced by economic or political conditions. For some it reflects hope, for others despair. There are migrants who try to carry their mountain cultural patterns over into Lima, and among them are those who succeed and those who fail. There are also those who try to change markedly, usually in the direction of modern Peruvian culture and social class mobility, and among them there are those who succeed and those who fail. Actually most people fall somewhere in between. The largest numerical group, those who preserve a semblance of mountain culture in Lima, appears to be only a one- or two-generation category, since most of the individuals involved do not want their children to remain in the same condition. They are in fact markedly and unrealistically upwardly mobile for their children while maintaining low levels of aspiration for themselves.[8] One place to study most types of migrants from the mountains to Lima that satisfies the anthropological bias for community studies and has the practical advantage of localizing informants is the "clandestine urbanization," or squatter settlement, called a *barriada*. After residing in Lima for some time many of the migrants discover the *barriadas* that ring Lima on the hillsides and river banks. The backgrounds of the residents vary tremendously, but one *barriada* does not seem very different from another.

Barriadas are located on state, municipal, or church lands in or near the city. They were originally formed by some sort of an organized invasion and each has a formal association and is considered a community by the residents.

At its worst a *barriada* is a crowded, helter-skelter hodge-podge of inadequate straw houses with no water supply and no provision for sewage disposal; parts of many are like this. Most do have a rough plan, and most inhabitants convert their original houses to more substantial structures as soon as they can. Construction activity, usually involving family, neighbors, and friends, is a constant feature of *barriada* life and, although water and sewage usually remain critical problems, a livable situation is reached with respect to them.

In a 1956 census Matos Mar of the University of San Marcos showed a population of approximately 120,000 in 56 *barriadas* of Lima-Callao.[10] In 1958, a somewhat less-carefully taken census of roughly the same area showed a population of 276,600 in 129 *barriadas*. The latest official census [9] figure for Lima-Callao is 592,347, taken from the 1940 census. The calculated population for 1957 for Lima-Callao is 1,260,729.[11] Granting considerable leeway for error in all the figures, it would seem that from 10 to 20 percent of the population of Lima lives in *barriadas*.

Lima is changing rapidly, as are the *barriadas*, and it is difficult to compile a list of characteristics that will apply to all *barriadas* or to any one *barriada* over a period of time. It is possible, however, to describe an ideal type of *barriada* and indicate the direction of change. There is variation between *barriadas*, of course, but their histories are remarkably similar.

A typical *barriada*, allowing for a few months' settling period, exhibits the following characteristics:

(1) The overwhelming majority of the adults are provincial-born, and the majority of these are from the mountains. They are usually young people with children; there are few adolescents or aged.

(2) Few residents have come to the *barriada* directly from the province, but have resided for some time in Lima.

(3) The residents are all "owners" of the lots and the straw-mat houses they themselves have constructed. In some cases there has been land speculation from the beginning, but generally speculators have been rare among the original settlers. There are no units that are not dwellings, and the usual household group is the nuclear family. In many cases the association will allow only nuclear families and married couples to build.

(4) There is a feeling of separateness from the city, a feeling of being under attack, which is reinforced by the lack of municipal services and protection and by unfavorable public attitudes toward *barriadas*.

(5) There is a relatively high degree of integration and "belongingness," and considerable pride in achievement and satisfaction with home ownership.

(6) The *barriada* associations (such as Fathers of Families of Mariscal Castilla, Defenders of Mirones, and Home Owners of Santa Clara de Bella Luz) consist of self-appointed groups, usually the leaders and organizers of the original settlements, and leadership is based chiefly on the personality of the members plus kinship and regional loyalty.

The direction of change for each of the above items seems to be as follows:

(1) The percentage of provincial-born goes down as more children are born in a *barriada*. The heads of new families, both those who construct new homes and those who replace moving families, continue to be provincial-born, and many people come from the provinces to reside in the new house of a relative.

(2) More people come directly to the *barriadas* from the provinces, often upon the advice and with the assistance of relatives and kinsmen.

(3) Renting becomes more frequent, and many individuals sell, lease, or lend their houses, almost always without having clear title. The number of boarders goes up as does the number of extra people in the household. The open conflicts over lot ownership characteristic of the early period give way to litigation before the *barriada* association or in the police stations and courts. Many open stores or bars in houses and some public buildings (school, assembly hall, office for association, movie) are constructed. A half-finished chapel is a common sight. Most houses are gradually converted to cement and brick. The nuclear family is augmented by relatives of various degrees of closeness; desertion by husbands is common enough to make the woman-children household a frequently encountered phenomenon.

(4) Generally the feeling of separateness lessens and services increase, but there is considerable variation on this point. In many cases, where there has been no continued pressure for the land from outsiders or where the inhabitants have successfully resisted such pressure, the area gradually becomes "urbanized" and blends into the city, as in the case of Zarumilla and parts of Fray Martin de Porres and Mirones. The electric company serves the area, branch banks and stores appear, movies are opened, bus lines operate, priests come, and finally the government recognizes the existence of the *barriada* for more than tax collection by appointing school teachers and, in one case, even appointing two mounted police to patrol an area of five square miles and 20,000 people.

(5) Belongingness and integration tend to be replaced by coresidence. The original settlers are swallowed up by the growing population, and some of them move out. The need for unity in defense against outside threats to the *barriada* lessens, and internal tensions increase. Many more people rent, and many of the older inhabitants, who were pleased with their situation at first, begin to complain of the surroundings, quarrel with their neighbors, and comment unfavorably on new arrivals ("Too many brute-Indians," "Too many brute-Negroes," and "Too many bad people"). Many individuals also develop new, or reinforce old, relationships with outsiders on the basis of such ties as kinship, region, occupation, and politics.

(6) The association takes on a more political character and, even though personality and regionalism continue to be important in the local elections, national politics and national issues play a larger part. The original leaders often move out (in which case they may or may not continue to exert influence) or, following a time-honored Peruvian tradition, a reform faction accuses them of stealing money and they, in turn, can choose to fight, flee, or sulk. As the *barriada* becomes more a part of Lima the association usually loses power.

For most of the migrants the *barriada* represents a definite improvement in terms of housing and general income, and Lima represents an improvement over the semifeudal life of the mountain Indian, Cholo, or lower-class mestizo.

There is very little violence, prostitution, homosexuality, or gang behavior in *barriadas*. Petty thievery is endemic throughout Lima, but *barriadas* seem somewhat safer than most neighborhoods in this respect, perhaps because there is less to steal.

In collaboration with Humberto Rotondo, psychiatrist from the Ministry of Health, and José Matos Mar, an anthropologist from the University of San Marcos, a study of one *barriada* was carried out during 1958 and 1959. In addition to traditional anthropological methods such as observation, conversation, and participation, we administered five questionnaries, including the Cornell Medical Index, to a selected sample of 65 of the 600 families. In 1959 I also assisted Walter Slote, a psychoanalyst, in the collection of Rorschach and partial TAT records from an arbitrarily-chosen group of residents.

The material has yet to be systematically analyzed but, in regard to pathological behavior, it does not seem to be directly related to migration. The high percentage of "yes" answers on the Cornell Medical Index indicating the presence of neurotic and psychotic symptoms does not seem very different from the percentage on records of mountain residents from Huancavelica and Puno. In fact my own work and that of Wellin[12] indicate that a general preoccupation with illness (real and imagined), panic reaction to illness, and a belief in the relatedness of personal responsibility to illness through witchcraft and taboo violation seem characteristic of both Indian and Mestizo culture throughout Peru.

Rotondo's interviewers administered a modified inventory of symptoms of childhood behavior problems to mothers in the sample, and they found a very high frequency of fear of the dark and bed-wetting in children up to the age of 12.[13] At my suggestion some local disease categories were added to the list (such as evil eye, fright, and bewitchment), and most of the symptoms of illness such as vomiting, diarrhea, and fever were classified by the mothers into these categories, which are also the common diseases of children outside of Lima.

Rotondo has noted, in another study,[14] the incidence of respondents who, although in precarious situations economically and socially, felt themselves to be objects of envy. This is also true in the *barriada* we studied. Assuming a certain amount of projection, it would seem that there is considerable envy of those whose dependency needs are satisfied. I encountered this phenomenon frequently in my work in the mountains of Ancash.

Another characteristic we noted in the *barriada* that is also commonly noted throughout Peru is relatively severe depression. Descriptive words such as "depressed," "sad," and "pitiful" occur with great frequency in our interviews and field notes. The humble, passive, tranquil, modest individual described by many informants as the ideal personality type is not strong and forbearing but rather frightened and ineffective.

Another set of phenomena that have their mountain counterparts but are more extreme in Lima and are more Creole or Mestizo than Indian are the following ambivalent attitudes about marriage and the family:

(1) A large number of men and women, both in and out of the sample, say that marriage is desirable and to be sought, but at the same time say that the bachelor has more possibilities than the married man and "My failure was caused by marrying too young." This is also illustrated by frequent contradictory statements about spouses in the same interview, for example, "My husband is a good man with me and with the children"; "If my husband hadn't abandoned us when I had epilepsy I would have recovered faster"; and "He has been a disillusion for me."

(2) Many respondents express open ambivalence about children, which is quite rare in the mountains. "My happiness is with my children"; "My children are a burden to me"; "My children will take care of me when I am old—I can call on them for anything"; "I am disenchanted with my children—they care only for themselves"; "I am happy only in my home with my wife and children"; and "I am unable to progress because of too many children."

(3) A common contradiction that may not be as contradictory as it first appears is that in which one encounters verbalizations about happiness and enjoyment only with wife and children from the very same men who habitually beat their wives and children. Violence toward wife and children is the most frequently encountered form of violence in Peru and, in many cases, there was no hint of it in the questionnaires. This was one of the many occasions where the questionnaires became valuable only in conjunction with the observational data of the anthropologist.

(4) Although fathers are quite indulgent and loving toward sons during the first six or seven years, avoidance and tension are common in the relationship from that time on. Fathers often assert their authority verbally and physically, but the children generally side with the mother; the father's intimate relationships tend to be with male peers and with his own sisters and, to a lesser extent, his brothers.

The perception of the mother seems to be represented by two extremes: the good mother and the bad mother. One image is the nurturing, comforting mother one can depend upon for support and counsel; the other is the mother who says, "Go out and succeed" but who also communicates in other ways that the child had better not leave or he will be a social and moral failure. Abandonment by the parents, especially by the mother, is one of the most commonly encountered themes in the *barriada* data and in Peruvian folklore. The search for someone to depend upon is carried on in many situations, constantly ending in disillusionment.

One informant, a 30-year-old mestizo married man with two children, who migrated from the mountains of Ancash to Lima and was unemployed at the time of the interview, expressed a view of his plight that in addition to being poetic, is a prototype of the sociopsychological situation of many lower-class Peruvians. The following story, a combination of Hansel and Gretel, a Peruvian folktale,[15] and the informant's own projections, was given as a response to the blank TAT card. Among other things it brings out the theme of abandonment by the parents and disillusion in other substitute authority figures.

"These are monsters, very ancient things. The monster had power because he was from God—against human beings. There was a married couple in a place where there was nothing to eat—a poor family. They had two children, a little girl and a little boy. The parents went far away to look for food. They found only one piece of bread for themselves at night. The children were waiting for their parents. When the parents arrived the children woke up asking them for bread. Not finding any food for themselves, the parents decided to throw the children off a precipice far away. The mother said it was better to kill them; the father said it was not better. They decided not to kill the children there but to put them in a bag and to take them to the precipice. They left them hanging in the air by a rope over the precipice. During the day the children cried for help. Hearing this, a condor came and took them, carrying them down to the ground. The children got out of the bag and started to walk. The condor flew away, scared. The children walked alone to an unknown place. The little girl was 10 and the boy only 5. The girl spoke perfectly and could walk. During that whole day they found only one kernel of corn, which somebody had thrown out; they divided it in two and ate. In that lonely place they cried in the night for their mother and father. A high voice answered their call. A little while later the monster presented himself to the children and took them to his cave. Then the monster spoke. He said, 'Who are you and from where did you come?' The children said they had lost their parents, and the monster said, 'I'll take care of you.' The monster put rocks in a pot and boiled them as though they were potatoes, but the children couldn't eat them because they were rocks. The monster began to eat the rocks as though they were stewed potatoes, trying to show them how to eat, but they couldn't eat them. He said, 'If you can't eat these potatoes, I'm going to eat you.' While the monster was asleep in his cave, the children escaped. The children, fleeing, found a wooden cross, and they said, 'Sir, save us from this danger, we've lost our parents.' They heard the monster coming. They went to hide under the cross, and when they hid under the cross there was no monster. They heard a voice from the sky that said, 'My children come up.' Looking up they saw nothing but a rope ladder. They went up the ladder to the sky—into space. Then the monster came and asked the cross to put the ladder down so he could follow the children. The cross did, and he started up the ladder after the children. The monster said, 'Just as you have God, I also have God, and when I catch you I'll eat you.' But on the ladder the monster was climbing there were two rats and they were tearing the rope ladder. The monster said to them 'Brothers, don't destroy my ladder, I have to destroy my prisoners.' The rats answered, 'For a bad person there is no ladder to God.' Then they tore through the ladder, and the monster fell to the ground, landing on the edge of a hill. His blood splashed all over one tremendous hill and on to others; the hill he landed on exploded like a bomb. The story ends now. Whenever anybody calls, the hills answer or, better said, they echo. When somebody calls, he thinks it is a person answering, but it is not a person."

Notes

1. Kubler, G. 1952. The Indian Caste of Peru, 1795–1940. Publ. 14, Institute of Soc. Anthropol. Smithsonian.

2. García Frías, R. 1947. Intensidad absoluta y relativa de la emigración provinciana al Departamento de Lima. Estadística Peruana. **5**:54–66.

3. Beals, R. 1953. Social stratification in Latin America. Am. J. Sociol. **58**:327–339.

4. Mangin, W. 1955. Estratificacion social en el Callejón de Huaylas. Revista museo Nacional. **24**. Lima, Peru.

5. Simmons, O. 1952. El uso de los conceptos de aculturación y asimilación en el estudio del cambio cultural en el Perú. Perú Indígena. **2**(4):40–47.

6. Fried, J. 1959. Acculturation and mental health among migrants in Peru. *In* Culture and Mental Health, M. K. Opler, Ed. Macmillan. New York, N. Y.

7. Mangin, W. 1959. The role of regional associations in the adaptation of rural population in Peru. Sociologus. **9**:21–36. Berlin, Germany.

8. Mangin, W. Conflictos Culturales y Salud Mental. Paper presented at 2° Latin American Congres for Mental Health, Lima, 1959. In press.

9. Censo Nacional de Población del Perú. 1940. Ministerio de Hacienda. Lima, Peru.

10. Matos Mar, José, Censo de las Barriadas de Lima, 1956 (unpublished manuscript).

11. Estadística Peruana. 1958. Ministerio de Hacienda. Lima, Peru.

12. Wellin, E. 1955. Water boiling in a Peruvian town. *In* Health, Culture and Community, B. Paul, ed. Russell Sage. New York, N. Y.

13. Gildea, M., H. R. Domke, I. N. Mensh, A. D. Buchmueller, J. C. Glidewell & M. B. Kantor. 1958. Community mental health research: findings after 3 years. Am. J. Psychiat. **114**:970–976.

14. Rotondo, H. *et al.* 1959. Estudios de psiquiatría social en áreas urbanas y rurales. Mendocita. (Mimeographed.)

15. Arguedas, J. M. & F. Izquierdo Ríos. 1947. Mitos, Leyendas y Cuentos Peruanos Lima, Min. Educ. See story "El Achiguée," pp. 130–134 for similar themes.

DIFFERENTIAL ARRESTS OF JUVENILE OFFENDERS IN URBAN AREAS

Nathan Goldman

The fact of differences in official delinquency rates in urban and rural areas has long been recognized. Studies have consistently shown a lower rate of court appearance of juveniles in rural areas than in urban areas. Reports from the U.S. Children's Bureau indicated that the urban case rate in 1956 was about 3.5 times that of court appearances in rural areas. In urban areas 43.8 children per 1,000 of the child population between the ages of 10 and 17 were charged in court with delinquency while in semiurban areas the rate was 25.7, and among rural children the rate was 12.5.[1]

This paper is derived from the author's Ph.D. dissertation, "The Differential Selection of Juvenile Offenders by Police for Court Appearance," Sociology, 1950.

Delinquency cases disposed of by children's courts in New York State in 1953 show some interesting variations in the distribution of kinds of offenses in upstate New York as compared with offenses reported in New York City. In Table 1 are presented the relative proportions, for upstate New York, for New York City, and for the total state, of various offenses for which children were brought before the courts in 1953. It may be seen that in New York City there are proportionately more cases reported of robbery, sex offenses, and injury to the person than in upstate New York. On the other hand, cases of stealing, running away, and carelessness or mischief appear relatively more frequently in upstate courts.

TABLE 1. DELINQUENCY CASES DISPOSED OF BY CHILDREN'S COURTS BY REASON REFERRED, NEW YORK STATE

Offense	Upstate		New York City	
	Number	Percent of Total	Number	Percent of Total
Automobile theft	300	8.26	539	10.02
Robbery	51	1.40	303	5.63
Other stealing	804	22.15	582	10.82
Burglary or unlawful entry	956	26.34	1,679	31.21
Truancy	228	6.28	389	7.23
Running away	75	2.07	68	1.26
Ungovernable	216	5.95	432	8.03
Sex offense	105	2.89	286	5.32
Injury to person	117	3.22	407	7.57
Act of carelessness or mischief	665	18.32	637	11.84
Other	113	3.11	58	1.08
Total	3,630	100	5,380	100

SOURCE: State of New York, *Report of the Department of Correction 1953 and 1954, p. 155.*

It appears that not only the amount of recorded delinquency but the kind of offenses charged against children may vary in large and in small communities. Offenses for which metropolitan New York children were charged in court are generally more "serious" than those for which children in smaller upstate New York communities were seen in court. Such observed differences might be the result of a large variety of variables: differences between community value orientations; more severe policing in large urban areas; the more frequent use in large urban areas of public agencies to solve community problems; differences in police organization, etc.

It is our intention to analyze, in this paper, the differential selection in large and small urban areas of arrested juveniles for court referral. It is hypothesized that police selectively refer arrested juvenile offenders to court, and that this selection is different in urban areas of different population size. This broad hypothesis, based on experience with institutionalized delinquents and on the research literature, might be tested by a consideration of certain differences between a population of juvenile offenders known only to the police and those reported by the same police to a juvenile court. In the study summarized below, statistical evidence will be adduced to show that only a portion of the juvenile offenders known to the police are referred to the juvenile court and that this sample of offenders officially reported to the juvenile court by the police varies from community to community.

Data were obtained directly from the police files in each of four municipalities in Allegheny County, Pennsylvania. From these files were recorded the name of the offender, the age, race, sex, home address, nature of the offense, and disposition of the case. A conference was held with the man principally responsible for the records in which all cases were discussed and questionable cases clarified. The records were, in the main, those of male offenders, with only a scattering of girls. Data from one of the communities contained no records of female offenders. In another, no Negro juveniles were arrested.

In the following discussion, the data will be analyzed according to the disposition of the case by the police. We shall compare cases released by the police without referral to the court with those which become known to the juvenile court through the police. Cases reported informally for the information of the court will be included in the latter category, together with cases referred by a petition or other form of official paper. The data for each municipality will be examined for the proportion of all arrests which become known to the juvenile court, and the selective handling of different offense categories. Finally, an analysis of the similarities and differences found in the treatment of juvenile offenders in these different kinds of cummunities will be made. The statistical significance of the difference found between the proportions of a given offense category disposed of by the police by court referral and such disposal of all other arrests will be estimated by the use of the critical ratio. A P value of .01, corresponding to a critical ratio of 2.6, is used as the criterion for the rejection of the null hypothesis. The critical ratio was not computed in cases where any cell value was below 5.

Steel City

Steel City is a large industrial community, with a population of about 55,000 in 1940. Of this population 15.8 percent were foreign born, and 4 percent were Negro. The majority of foreign-born persons came from Hungary and Czechoslovakia. The major occupational groups are laborers and operatives. It contains a large business center which serves residents from the smaller neighboring towns. It has a densely populated slum area, and several old "respectable" upper-class areas near the outskirts of the city.

The records of the 484 male juveniles arrested in Steel City during the period from January, 1946, to November, 1949, were studied. Female juvenile arrest data were not available. During this period 581 juvenile arrests were recorded by the juvenile officer in Steel City. The average arrest rate per year was 18.6 per 1,000 children aged 10 to 17. The distribution of these arrests by type of offense is indicated in Table 2.

Among juvenile offenders in Steel City, the offense of larceny occurs most frequently, including 30.9 percent of the juvenile offenses recorded by the

TABLE 2. DISPOSITION OF CASES BY STEEL CITY POLICE

Offense	Total Arrests	Released	To Court	Percent to Court		Critical Ratio	Percent of Arrests	Percent to Court
Larceny	180	117	63	35.0	34.6	3.73	30.9	23.5
Receiving stolen goods	2	2	0	0			0.3	0
Burglary	92	23	69	75.0	75.3	6.18	15.8	25.7
Robbery	1	0	1	100.			0.2	0.4
Larceny, motor vehicle	16	0	16	100.	100.	....	2.8	5.9
Riding in stolen car	7	0	7	100.			1.2	2.6
Assault	2	0	2	100.	80.0	4.48	0.3	0.7
Sex	35	7	28	80.			6.0	10.4
Concealed weapon	3	1	2	66.7			0.5	0.7
Incorrigible, delinquent	32	7	25	78.1	62.5	2.59	5.5	9.3
Runaway	24	14	10	41.7			4.1	3.7
Disorderly	17	7	10	58.8	25.0	3.73	2.9	3.7
Drunk	2	2	0	0			0.3	....
Gambling	24	23	1	4.2			4.1	0.4
Violating borough ordinance	22	18	4	18.2			3.8	1.5
Violating motor vehicle law	3	1	2	66.7			0.5	0.7
Mischief	23	20	3	13.0	23.5	5.57	4.0	1.1
Malicious mischief	24	14	10	41.7			4.1	3.7
Property damage	70	56	14	20.0			12.0	5.2
Arson	2	1	1	50.0			0.3	0.4
Total	581	313	268	46.1			99.6	99.6

police. Burglary and property damage are the next most frequent offenses, comprising 15.8 percent and 12 percent respectively of the total number of offenses. Sex offenses make up only 6 percent of the total offenses officially recorded by the police.

Of the 581 juvenile arrests officially recorded by the police in Steel City, 268 or 46.1 percent were disposed of by court referral. However, the proportions of different offenses thus referred ranged from total referral of some offenses to no referral in two offense categories. All cases of theft of a motor vehicle, riding in a stolen car, robbery, and assault were reported to the juvenile court. Eighty percent of the sex offenses, 75 percent of the burglaries, and 78 percent of the "delinquent and incorrigible" category were disposed of by court referral. None of the cases of drunkenness or of receiving stolen goods were reported to the court. Thirty-five percent of the cases of larceny known to the police were

TABLE 3. DISPOSITION OF SERIOUS AND MINOR JUVENILE CHARGES BY STEEL CITY POLICE

Degree of Crime	Number	Percent of Total Arrests	Percent to Juvenile Court	Critical Ratio
Serious	125	26.9	80.1	9.89
Minor	456	73.1	33.6	....
Total	581	100.0	46.1	....

referred to court authorities. The remainder of the arrests were disposed of by the police themselves on an unofficial basis, without court referral.

It appears, from Table 2, that the various offense groups are differentially or selectively disposed of by the police. In only one case, that of the combined offenses of being incorrigible and delinquent, and of running away from home, was the critical ratio below the criterion value of 2.6 set in this study.

The differential handling of the various offenses can be further observed by comparing the portion which a given offense constitutes of the total number of arrests and also of the total number of court cases. It may be seen in Table 2 that although larceny makes up 30.9 percent of the number of arrests, it comprises only 23.5 percent of the cases referred to the court. On the other hand, theft of a motor vehicle, which makes up 2.8 percent of the total offenses, contains twice this proportion of the total court referals. A similar relationship may be observed for the offense of riding in a stolen car. Burglary also forms a much larger proportion of the court group than of the arrest group. The converse is true of such offenses as gambling, violating a borough ordinance, running away from home, engaging in mischief and property damage. Some offenses known to the police are thus proportionately overrepresented in the court sample, and some are underrepresented.

Offenses generally considered serious, such as burglary, robbery, theft of a motor vehicle and riding in a stolen car, assault, sex offenses, and carrying concealed weapons, were reported to the court by the Steel City police much more frequently than other offenses (Table 3). Of the 156 such serious cases in Steel City, 125 or 80.1 percent were disposed of by the police through court referral. Although the minor offenses in Steel City accounted for 73.1 percent of the total arrests, only 33.6 percent were referred to the juvenile court. Thus, although there are almost three times as many arrests for minor offenses as for serious, many fewer are reported to court.

Trade City

Trade City with a population of about 30,000 in 1940 is a residential area with some light industry and a flourishing shopping district. It is generally a middle-class community with no defined slum area. Seven per cent of the population are foreign; less than 2 percent are Negro. The major foreign-born groups are

TABLE 4. DISPOSITION OF CASES BY TRADE CITY POLICE

Offense	Total Arrests	Re-leased	To Court [1]	Percent to Court		Critical Ratio	Per-cent of Arrests	Per-cent to Court
Larceny	52	18	34	65.4	68.9		30.6	28.1
Receiving stolen goods	6	0	6	100.		0.46	3.5	4.9
Burglary	42	14	28	66.7	68.9	0.39	24.7	23.1
Robbery	3	0	3	100.			1.8	2.5
Larceny, motor vehicle	14	3	11	78.6	78.6	....	8.2	9.1
Riding in stolen car	1	1	0	.....			0.6	....
Sex	3	0	3	100.		....	1.8	2.5
Incorrigible, delinquent	8	0	8	100.	86.3	....	4.7	6.6
Runaway	14	3	11	78.6			8.2	9.1
Disorderly	12	4	8	66.7	65.0		7.1	6.6
Vagrancy	1	0	1	100.			0.6	0.8
Drunk	1	0	1	100.			0.6	0.8
Prowling	1	0	1	100.		0.65	0.6	0.8
Violating borough ordinance	3	3	0	....			1.8	....
Violating motor vehicle law	1	0	1	100.			0.6	0.8
Army uniform violation	1	0	1	100.			0.6	0.8
Malicious mischief	7	3	4	57.1		....	4.1	3.3
Total	170	49	121	71.2		....	107.1	92.8

[1] Including cases referred to the squire for official action.

English and German. The labor force is made up primarily of clerical, sales and kindred workers, together with craftsmen and foremen.

Information on juvenile arrests in Trade City was obtained for a four-year period during which time there were 170 arrests of 162 boys and girls. The average annual arrest rate was 12.4 per 1,000 children between the ages of 10 and 17. The distribution of arrests by type of offense, and the disposition of these cases may be found in Table 4.

Most of the arrests in Trade City were for larceny and robbery, these two offenses accounting for 55.3 percent of the total. Theft of a motor vehicle, running away from home, and disorderly conduct were charged in an additional 23.5 percent of cases. Thus, these five offenses make up about 78 percent of all arrests in Trade City. Of the 170 arrests recorded, 121 or 71.2 percent became known to the juvenile court either through direct referral by the police or through a report filed by the local squire to whom the police had referred the case for judicial action.

TABLE 5. DISPOSITION OF SERIOUS AND MINOR JUVENILE CHARGES BY TRADE CITY POLICE

Degree of Crime	Number	Percent of Total Arrests	Percent to Juvenile Court	Critical Ratio
Serious............	45	37.1	71.4	0.56
Minor............	125	62.9	71.0	....
Total...........	170	100.0	71.2	....

It appears from Table 4 that no one offense or offense group is differentially reported by the police to court. In Table 4 it may be seen that there are only slight differences between the proportion which any offense category comprises of the total of all offenses, and the proportion which this category is of the total court referrals. When serious and minor offenses are examined separately, in Table 5, it appears that referral of serious offenses is only very slightly more frequent than referral of minor offenses. It may be concluded, therefore, that in Trade City there is little differential disposition of arrests according to offense type.

Milltown

Milltown, the third of our sources of information, had a population of about 12,700 in 1940. Of these, 13.77 percent are foreign-born, and 3.28 percent Negro. The major foreign-born groups come from Italy and Poland. Milltown is a small, highly industrialized community containing several very large industrial plants, the major occupational groups being laborers, and clerical and sales workers.

Information was obtained on juvenile arrests from March, 1948, through September, 1949, from police records. The name, sex, age, race, residence, nature of the offense, and disposition were obtained for each case. During this 19-month period there were 107 boys and girls arrested for a total of 114 offenses. The average annual arrest rate for Milltown was 34.8 per 1,000 children aged between 10 and 17.

Larceny, the violation of a borough ordinance, and malicious mischief comprise 81.5 percent of the offenses for which children were arrested in Milltown. No cases of theft of an automobile, sex offense, or incorrigibility were recorded.

Of the total 114 offenses committed by juveniles and recorded in the Milltown police records, only 17 or 14.9 percent were reported to the juvenile court. The major portion of the arrests was disposed of informally by the police. The kinds of offenses for which children in Milltown were arrested, and the police handling of the various types of offenses are presented in Table 6. Every case of burglary, robbery, and attempted robbery known to the police was referred to the court. Less than one-fourth of the cases of larceny were disposed of by court referral, and only 3.4 percent of the violations of a borough ordinance were so handled.

TABLE 6. DISPOSITION OF CASES BY MILLTOWN POLICE

Offense	Total Arrests	Re-leased	To Court	Percent to Court		Critical Ratio	Per-cent of Arrests	Per-cent to Court
Larceny	39	30	9	23.1	21.9	1.59	34.2	52.9
Receiving stolen goods	2	2	0	0			1.8	....
Burglary	1	0	1	100.	100	....	0.9	5.9
Robbery	1	0	1	100.			0.9	5.9
Attempted robbery	5	0	5	100.			4.4	29.4
Disorderly conduct	7	7	0	0	2.4	....	6.1	....
Gambling	1	1	0	0			0.9	....
Drunk	1	1	0	0			0.9	....
Vagrancy	3	3	0	0			2.6	....
Violating borough ordinance	29	28	1	3.4			25.4	5.9
Malicious mischief	25	25	0	0		....	21.9	....
Total	114	97	17	14.9		....	100.0	100.0

All of the other offenses were disposed of by the police without official action. Except for the combined offenses of larceny and receiving stolen goods, the differential reporting of offense groups to juvenile court appears to be the rule in Milltown. The critical ratio values for the serious and disorderly conduct groups are above the 2.6 value. The malicious mischief category is only very slightly below this significance criterion.

Of those cases reported to the juvenile court the offense of larceny appeared in the largest portion, 52.9 percent, although it constituted only 34.2 percent of the arrests. Burglary, robbery, and attempted robbery, when combined, make up only 6.2 percent of the arrests but contribute 41.2 percent of the court cases. On the other hand, violation of a borough ordinance appears more than four times as often, proportionately, in the arrest column as in the court column of Table 6.

In Table 7 it may be seen that every arrest for a serious offense resulted in a court referral. Each of the arrests for burglary, robbery, and attempted robbery

TABLE 7. DISPOSITION OF SERIOUS AND MINOR JUVENILE CHARGES BY MILLTOWN POLICE

Degree of Crime	Number	Percent of Total Arrests	Percent to Juvenile Court	Critical Ratio
Serious	7	6.1	100.	....
Minor	107	93.9	9.3	....
Total	114	100.0	14.9	....

were reported to the juvenile court. Although about 94 percent of the arrests were for minor offenses, only 9.3 percent of these were referred to court. There seems to be very definitely a differential reporting to court from Milltown, according to offense type, except for larceny.

Manor Heights

Manor Heights, the fourth of our sources of data, is a relatively new residential area with a median rental more than three times that of the county average. The major foreign-born come from the British Isles and from Germany, and compose 4.84 percent of the total population. Negroes make up only 0.45 percent of the total. The population of Manor Heights was about 20,000 in 1940. The major occupations are clerical and sales workers, proprietors, managers, officials, and professional workers. Manor Heights has only a small commercial center, and no slum area.

Police records of juvenile arrests were obtained from Manor Heights for the period beginning January, 1947, and ending October, 1949. There was a total of 371 juvenile arrests of 330 boys and girls during this 34-month period in Manor Heights. No Negro juveniles were arrested in the community during this period. The average annual rate of arrest was 49.8 per 1,000 children aged 10 to 17. This is the highest rate obtained in any of the four communities studied.

The charge found most frequently in Table 8 is that of violating a borough ordinance. This constitutes 26.7 percent of the total offenses known to the police in Manor Heights. Arrests for property damage, malicious mischief, and trespassing follow next in descending order, including 15.6 percent, 12.9 percent, 11.1 percent, and 10.5 percent of the total, respectively. There were no arrests of juveniles for robbery in Manor Heights.

Only 32, or 8.6 percent, of the offenses known to the police in Manor Heights were disposed of by juvenile court referral. More than half of these cases, 53.2 percent, were referred for the two offenses of theft of a motor vehicle and riding in a stolen car. All cases of burglary, sex offense, and running away from home were reported to the juvenile court. Ninety-four percent of the cases of theft of a motor vehicle were referred to the court. None of the 13 cases of larceny, nor any of the cases of drunkenness, gambling, trespassing, mischief, malicious mischief, or property damage were ever made known to the court either by commitment or by report, although these offenses constituted 56.3 percent of the total arrests. The statistical reliability of the differences in reporting rates for all offenses except larceny is borne out by the high critical ratio values.

In Table 8 may be seen further the disproportionate representation of certain offense categories in the cases referred to the juvenile court. Although theft of a motor vehicle was the charge in only 4.3 percent of the juvenile offenses in Manor Heights, it appeared in 46.9 percent of the court referrals. Sex offenses made up only 1.1 percent of the total arrests. However, they constituted eleven times this proportion of the court cases, 12.5 percent. The offense of burglary, comprising less than 1 percent of the arrests, occurred in 9.4 percent of the cases referred to the court. On the other hand, several offense categories were lightly dealt with. Violation of a borough ordinance, accounting for more than one-fourth of the arrests, is found in only 9.5 percent of the court referrals. Although the

TABLE 8. DISPOSITION OF CASES BY MANOR HEIGHTS POLICE

Offense	Total Arrests	Released	To Court	Percent to Court		Critical Ratio	Percent of Arrests	Percent to Court
Larceny	13	13	0	0		....	3.5	....
Burglary	3	0	3	100.		....	0.8	9.4
Larceny, motor vehicle	16	1	15	93.8	94.4	13.3	4.3	46.9
Riding stolen car	2	0	2	100.			0.5	6.3
Sex	4	0	4	100.		....	1.1	12.5
Incorrigible, delinquent	2	1	1	50.	75.0	....	0.5	3.1
Runaway	2	0	2	100.			0.5	6.3
Disorderly conduct	18	17	1	5.6			4.9	3.1
Drunk	4	4	0	0			1.1	....
Gambling	6	6	0	0			1.6	....
Trespassing	39	39	0	0	2.7	4.0	10.5	....
Violating borough ordinance	99	96	3	3.0			26.7	9.4
Violating motor vehicle law	16	15	1	6.3			4.3	3.1
Mischief	41	41	0	0			11.1	....
Malicious mischief	48	48	0	0		....	12.9	....
Property damage	58	58	0	0			15.6	....
Total	371	339	32	8.6		....		....

combined offenses of larceny, trespassing, mischief, malicious mischief, and property damage were responsible for more than half (53.6 percent) of the arrests, none of these offenses are to be found in the court referrals. When the violation of a borough ordinance, drunkenness, and gambling are added to these five offenses, it appears that the offenses responsible for 83 percent of the arrests contributed only 9.4 percent of the cases referred to the juvenile court. The greater bulk of the court referrals, 90.6 percent, were drawn from only 17 percent of the total arrests.

In Table 9 "serious" offenses are considered. Ninety-six percent of the serious offenses were disposed of by Manor Heights police by court referral. Of the

TABLE 9. DISPOSITION OF SERIOUS AND MINOR JUVENILE CHARGES BY MANOR HEIGHTS POLICE

Degree of Crime	Number	Percent of Total Arrests	Percent to Juvenile Courts	Critical Ratio
Serious	24	6.7	96.0	16.2
Minor	347	93.3	2.3	....
Total	371	100.0	8.6	....

remaining minor offenses comprising 93.3 percent of the total arrests, only 2.4 percent were disposed of in this manner.

Comparison of Communities

In the previous section, the data for each community were considered separately. An analysis of the differences in police disposition of cases of juvenile offenders in these four communities might reveal some significant variations in the selection of juvenile offenders for court referral, according to the size and type of town. Data for making comparisons are grouped together in Table 10.

TABLE 10. THE FOUR COMMUNITIES COMPARED, ARREST AND COURT REFERRAL DATA

Arrests and Court Referrals	Steel City	Trade City	Manor Heights	Milltown	Total
Population	50,000	30,000	20,000	12,500	112,500
Arrests:					
Total number recorded	581	170	371	114	1,236
Average annual rate per 1,000	15.9	10.9	44.9	33.8	21.8
Percent serious	26.9	37 1	6.7	6.1	20.3
Percent minor	73.1	62.9	93.3	93.9	79.7
Court referrals:					
Percent of total	46.1	71.2	8.6	14.9	35.4
Percent of serious	80.1	71.4	96.0	100.0	80.2
Percent of minor	33.6	71.0	2.3	9.3	24.1

There is a marked difference in the rate of juvenile arrests in the four communities. The highest rate of arrests per 1,000 population aged 10 to 17 was found in the economically and socially superior municipality of Manor Heights. The next highest rate of arrests appears in the small predominantly industrial town which has a high rate of foreign-born and Negroes, a high proportion of laborers, and the lowest median rental of the four communities studied. The arrest rates of the two remaining communities, Steel City and Trade City, are much lower. Thus, the two smallest communities have the highest rates of juvenile arrests.

There appears, from Table 10, to be considerable variation in the proportions of arrests disposed of by court referral by the police of the four municipalities. In the analysis of the combined data it was found that 35.4 percent of the juvenile arrests were referred to the court. Considering the communities separately, we find a wide range in the proportions of court referrals—from 8.6 percent to 71.2 percent. The highest proportion of such official dispositions is found in Trade City, the second largest of the communities studied. The large Steel City is second in the proportion of arrests referred to court—46.1 percent. Both Milltown and Manor Heights fall far below this, with referral proportions of 14.9 percent and 8.6 percent, respectively.

It seems that in our four communities the rate of court referral increases with a decrease in the rate of arrest. The two towns with the highest proportions of juveniles arrested have the lowest rates of court referral, and the two large communities, Steel City and Trade City, with the lowest rates of juvenile arrest have the highest percentage of court referral by police.

In Trade City, with the highest arrest-commitment rate, 71.2 percent, there seems to be a tendency to report all types of offenses equally, but not every case of even such serious offenses as burglary, theft of a motor vehicle, and larceny is reported to the court. The police of the other three towns, however, are more selective in the reporting of offenses to the juvenile court. All cases of theft of a motor vehicle, and of assault are reported by Steel City police to the court. Eighty percent of the known sex offenses, and 75 percent of the burglary cases are also reported. However, only about one-third of the larceny cases are disposed of by referral to the court by Steel City police. Milltown and Manor Heights police reported almost all serious offenses to the court. Milltown police referred slightly less than one-fourth of the larceny arrests to court authorities, while Manor Heights reported none of the arrests for larceny or disorderly conduct. Steel City and Trade City police referred a large proportion of cases in the delinquent-incorrigible category to court.

It appears that the police of all four municipalities consider theft of an automobile, burglary, robbery, sex offenses, and asasult serious enough for immediate court referral in almost all cases. The referral of such serious cases to court varies from 71.4 percent in Trade City to a high of 100 percent in Milltown, with an average of 80.2 percent. In Steel City, Manor Heights, and Milltown the referral rate for serious offenses exceeds that for the total of all offenses. Only in Trade City do we find no difference in the reporting of serious and other offenses.

Differences in the reporting rates of the three communities—not including the non-discriminating Trade City police—are largely the result of the differential handling of minor offenses. Violation of a borough ordinance was rarely reported to court by any of the police. Cases of malicious mischief were not reported to the court by the two smaller communities but were referred in about 42 percent and 57 percent of such arrests in Steel City and Trade City respectively. Arrests for disorderly conduct were more frequently referred to court in the larger towns than in the smaller. In Manor Heights 93 percent of the arrests were of a minor nature; only about 2.3 percent of these became known to the Juvenile Court. Thirty-four percent of the minor arrests in Steel City, which comprised 73 percent of the total arrests, were referred to court. In Trade City, 63 percent of the arrests were for minor offenses; 71 percent of these were sent to the juvenile court. Although minor offenses accounted for 93.8 percent of the total arrests in Milltown, only 9.3 percent of these were sent on to juvenile court. It seems apparent from Table 10 that offenses of a minor nature are overlooked by the police in our two small communities and treated by court referral in the two larger ones.

It appears from our data that, in the sample of four communities we studied, the two small municipalities have higher arrest rates than the two large towns, and lower court referral rates; a lower rate of arrest for serious offenses and a higher rate of court referral for serious offenses; a higher rate of arrest for minor offenses and a lower rate of court referral for minor offenses.

Arrests and Referrals

The reasons for the selective referral of different offenses might be sought in the social organization of the community, or in the organization and attitudes of the police. To obtain such information, 108 policemen in the city of Pittsburgh and in the surrounding towns, including the four on which the previous sections were based, were interviewed. Only men who had some contact with juvenile cases were contacted. They were asked a set of open-ended questions involving the general problem of the disposition of a child apprehended in, or referred to the policeman for, an act in violation of the law. The questions involved facts about the child's family, the policeman's evaluation of the behavior and attitude of the offending child, the nature of the offense, the policeman's attitude toward the juvenile court, various problems arising in the police handling of juvenile arrests, and the policeman's interpretation of the desires and attitudes of the community. Hypothetical situations were described, and the police respondents were asked how they would act in the situation and to give reasons for such action. They were encouraged to relate actual incidents from their experiences with juvenile offenders. The following is a brief summary of an analysis of these interview situations.

In general, it may be said that the policeman, in making his decision regarding the disposition in a case of a juvenile arrest is affected by a series of pressures brought to bear on him by the community. He attempts to reflect, in his handling of juvenile offenses, what he believes to be the attitude of the citizens of the town toward the offense, toward the boy, and toward his family. One police chief aptly described the situation when he said that his primary job was "to keep the public off my neck." The decision of the citizen complainant to press charges or to forgo official action defines the policeman's policy in a large proportion of arrests. Thus, serious offenses may go unreported and minor offenses may be officially referred to court.

In addition to this general sensitivity to the desires of the community it seems, from the interview data, that the police are governed by a series of other considerations, some of which seem to have no relation to the offender or the offense. Many of these are related somehow to the more general factor of the community attitude discussed above. Some appear as problems related to the job of policing. The following discussions describe some of the factors which affect the individual policeman's decision with respect to court referral of a juvenile.

Police Officer's Impression of the Family. The policeman's interpretation of the degree of family interest in and control of the offender and the reaction of the parents to the problem of the child's offense is one of the most, if not the most, important criterion determining police handling of a case. A child coming from a home where supervision is judged to be lacking, or where the parents—especially the mother—are alcoholic, or where an aggressive or "unco-operative" attitude is shown toward the police officer is considered in need of supervision by the juvenile court. Stereotypes regarding the Jewish family, the Negro, the Irish family, etc., guide the policeman's decision. Offenses committed late at night are taken to indicate a lack of home supervision. The fact that an offender comes from a broken home is considered evidence for the need of court intervention.

The Attitude and Personality of the Child. An offender who is well mannered, neat in appearance, and "listens" to the policeman will be considered a good risk for unofficial adjustment in the community. Defiance of the police will usually result in immediate court referral. Athletes and altar boys will rarely be referred to court for their offenses. The minor offenses of feebleminded or atypical children will usually be overlooked by the police. Maliciousness in a child is considered by the police to indicate need for official court supervision.

The Degree of Criminal Sophistication. The use of burglar tools, criminal jargon, a gun, strong-arm methods, signs of planning or premeditation, demands by the child for his "rights," a lawyer, etc., are generally taken by the police to indicate the need for immediate court referral of the child offender.

Groups. The group must be released or reported as a whole. Some police may attempt to single out the leader of the gang for court referral. Such action, however, exposes the policeman to the censure of the court for failing to report the others involved in the offense.

Policeman's Attitude toward Specific Offenses. The reporting or non-reporting of a juvenile offender may depend on the policeman's own childhood experiences or on attitudes toward specific offenses developed during his police career, or his interpretation of the standards of the community.

Publicity. An increase in the "visibility" of delinquency, or a decrease in community tolerance level may cause the police to feel that juvenile delinquency is too "hot" a problem to handle unofficially and must be referred to the court. In the police interviews it was often indicated that this factor might operate to bring into court an offense of even a very insignificant nature.

Various Practical Problems of Policing. The fact that no witness fees are paid policemen in juvenile court was mentioned by a small number as affecting the policy of some police officers with respect to court referral of juveniles. The distance to the court and to the detention home and the availability of police personnel for the trip were likewise indicated as occasionally affecting the treatment of the juvenile offender.

Necessity for Maintaining Respect. A juvenile who publicly causes damage to the dignity of the police, or who is defiant, refusing the "help" offered by the police will be considered as needing court supervision, no matter how trivial the offense.

Pressure by Groups. Such pressure was indicated as determining the line of action a policeman will follow in a given case, especially in communities with strong ethnic political clubs. He considers it necessary to accede to such pressures in order to retain his job.

The Impact of Past Experiences. A policeman's experiences in the juvenile court, or with different racial, ethnic, or economic groups, or with parents of offenders, or with specific offenses may condition his future reporting of certain classes of offenders or certain types of offenses.

The Policeman's Attitude toward the Juvenile Court. This may be based on actual experience with the court, or on ignorance of court policies. The policeman who feels the court is unfair to the police or too lenient with offenders may fail to report cases to the court since, in his opinion, nothing will be gained by such official referral.

Apprehension about Criticism. Cases which the policeman might prefer, for various reasons, not to report for official action may be reported because of fear that the offense might subsequently come to the attention of the court and result in embarrassment to the police officer.

The differential referral rates of the various communities may be seen as a reflection of the nature of the relation between the police and the community. In the two small communities, Manor Heights and Milltown, the chief of police handled cases of juvenile violators of the law. In Milltown the police chief was a native of the community. He was a member of church, fraternal, and service groups in the community. A Milltown child apprehended in a law violation will very probably be the child of a friend or schoolmate of the chief. Unless the offense is serious an informal rather than an official court disposition of the case is likely.

In Manor Heights the police chief handled cases of juvenile arrests in consultation with the parents. One morning each week was set aside for meetings with the parents of children who had been arrested. An arrangement was then made co-operatively with the parents for the offender to work out some penalty. He might be deprived of his allowance, or automobile driver's permit, or his evenings out, for a stated period. The citizens, mostly professionals and businessmen, supported such handling of minor offenses by children. Serious offenses, however, were almost always referred to court.

The relation between the police and the public, in Trade City, was of a secondary, rather than a face-to-face, nature. The chief was not a native of the city, and knew relatively few of the citizens. Moreover, an open political conflict between the burgess and the police chief was in progress at the time of this study. Some of the police complained that because of this breach in relations in city hall, they were ridiculed by youth in Trade City.

There was also, in Trade City, as opposed to Manor Heights and Milltown, a good deal of transience. Many people traveled through the city daily on their way to and from their jobs, shopping, or amusement tours to Pittsburgh. Police dealt with offenders in an impersonal, official manner. As the data above showed, serious and minor violations of the law by juveniles were treated, to a large extent, alike.

Steel City, although larger in population than Trade City, had a higher arrest rate, lower rate of arrests for serious offenses, a lower rate of court referral for all offenses, a higher rate of referral of serious offenses, and a lower rate of referral of minor offenses. In these it varies from Trade City in the direction of our two smaller communities. In addition, it had a lower median rental than Trade City, a higher percentage of Negro and foreign-born, a lower median school grade, and a lower percentage of college graduates. It might be expected to have a higher rate of delinquency than Trade City. It is probable that the difference in arrest and referral rates may be due to the fact that all juvenile cases were handled by one man assigned this duty by the chief of police. In Trade City many police made juvenile arrests. These were submitted to the desk sergeant and the chief, who handled the cases in a routine impersonal manner. The juvenile officer in Steel City prided himself on his efforts to help youth in trouble. He carried a number of cases on "unofficial probation" without reference to the court.

The lower rate of serious offenses in Steel City might be a function of a special attitude of police in this area toward the 18-year age ceiling for juveniles in Pennsylvania. A number of policemen stated in interviews that many of the seventeen-year-olds they arrested for serious offenses had left school and were working in the steel mills. Rather than treat him as a juvenile, as the law dictated, they preferred to release the offender, hoping to catch him again soon after his eighteenth birthday. He would then be treated, in the eyes of the police, more adequately in the criminal court.

The referral of offending juveniles to court thus appears to be a function of the kind of relation established between the police and the community. In areas where there is a close personal face-to-face type of relation between the police and the public, juvenile arrests are handled informally at the police level. As this relation becomes more formal and impersonal and as personal communication between police and public becomes minimized, more frequent use will be made of formal court procedures to solve the community problem of juvenile delinquency.

The juvenile court population is constituted largely of police referrals. Since court and public institutions for the care of adjudicated delinquents provide most of the subjects for research on the problem of juvenile delinquency, the nature of the police selection of juvenile offenders for court referral becomes a matter of crucial concern for investigators in this field. That this selection is often based on a number of factors not relevant to the behavior in question, and at times not relevant to the actor involved, the delinquent child, has been shown in this research.

Note

1. U. S. Department of Health, Education, and Welfare, *Juvenile Court Statistics, 1956* (Washington, D.C.: Superintendent of Documents, 1958), p. 4.

VIOLENT CRIMES IN CITY GANGS

By Walter B. Miller

The 1960's have witnessed a remarkable upsurge of public concern over violence in the United States. The mass media flash before the public a vivid and multivaried kaleidescope of images of violence. Little attention is paid to those who question the assumption that the United States is experiencing an unparalleled epidemic of violence, who point out that other periods in the past may have been equally violent or more so; that troops were required to subdue rioting farmers in 1790, rioting tax-protesters in 1794, rioting laborers in the 1870's and 1880's, and rioting railroad workers in 1877; that race riots killed fifty people in St. Louis in 1917 and erupted in twenty-six other cities soon after; that fifty-seven whites were killed in a slave uprising in 1831; that the Plug Uglies, Dead Rabbits, and other street gangs virtually ruled parts of New York for close to forty years; that rival bootleg mobs engaged in armed warfare in Chicago and elsewhere during the Capone era; and that the number killed in the 1863 draft riots in New York was estimated at up to 1,000 men. Nevertheless, however much one may question the conviction that the United States today is engulfed in unprecedented violence, one can scarcely question the ascendancy of the *belief* that it is. It is this belief that moves men to action—action whose consequences are just as real as if the validity of the belief were incontrovertible.

Close to the core of the public imagery of violence is the urban street gang. The imagery evokes tableaux of sinister adolescent wolf packs prowling the darkened streets of the city intent on evil-doing, of grinning gangs of teenagers tormenting old ladies in wheelchairs and ganging up on hated and envied honor students, and of brutal bands of black-jacketed motorcyclists sweeping through quiet towns in orgies of terror and destruction. The substance of this image and its basic components of human cruelty, brutal sadism, and a delight in violence for its own sake have become conventionalized within the subculture of professional writers. The tradition received strong impetus in the public entertainment of the early 1950's with Marlon Brando and his black-jacketed motorcycle thugs, gathered momentum with the insolent and sadistic high-schoolers of *The Blackboard Jungle,* and achieved the status of an established ingredient of American folklore with the Sharks and Jets of the *West Side Story.*

What is the reality behind these images? Is the street gang fierce and romantic like the Sharks and Jets? Is it a tough but good-hearted bunch of rough and ready guys like the "Gang that Sang Heart of my Heart"? Or is it brutal and ruthless like the motorcyclists in *The Wild Ones?* In many instances where an area of interest engages both scholars and the public, most of the public embrace one set of conceptions and most scholars, another. This is not so in the case of the street gang; there is almost as much divergence within the ranks of scholars as there is between the scholars and the public.

Reprinted by permission of the author and publisher from *The Annals of the American Academy of Political and Social Science,* **364** (March, 1966), pp. 96–112.

One recent book on gangs contains these statements:

> Violence [is] the core spirit of the modern gang. . . . The gang boy . . . makes unprovoked violence . . . [senseless rather than premeditated] . . . the major activity or dream of his life. . . . The gang trades in violence. Brutality is basic to its system.[1]

Another recent work presents a different picture:

> The very few [gang] boys who persist in extreme aggression or other dangerous exploits are regarded generally as "crazy" by the other boys. . . . Our conservative estimate is that not more than one in five instances of potential violence actually result in serious consequences. . . . For average Negro gang boys the probability of an arrest for involvement in instances of potential violence is probably no greater than .04.[2]

A third important work states:

> In [a] second type [of delinquent gang or subculture] violence is the keynote. . . . The immediate aim in the world of fighting gangs is to acquire a reputation for toughness and destructive violence. . . . In the world of violence such attributes as race, socioeconomic position, age, and the like, are irrelevant.[3]

What is the reality behind these differences? The question is readily raised, but is not, unfortunately, readily answered. There exists in this area of high general interest a surprising dearth of reliable information. It is quite possible that discrepancies between the statements of scholars arise from the fact that each is referring to different kinds of gangs in different kinds of neighborhoods in different kinds of cities. We simply do not know. Lacking the information necessary to make general statements as to the nature of violence in the American city gang, it becomes obvious that one major need is a series of careful empirical studies of particular gangs in a range of cities and a variety of neighborhoods. The present paper is an attempt to present such information for one inner-city neighborhood, "Midcity," in a major eastern city, "Port City."

What Are "Violent" Crimes?

The term "violence" is highly charged. Like many terms which carry strong opprobrium, it is applied with little discrimination to a wide range of things which meet with general disapproval. Included in this broad net are phenomena such as toy advertising on television, boxing, rock-and-roll music and the mannerisms of its performers, fictional private detectives, and modern art. Used in this fashion the scope of the term becomes so broad as to vitiate its utility severely. Adding the term "crimes" to the designation substantially narrows its focus. It is at once apparent that not all "violence" is criminal (warfare, football, surgery, wrecking cars for scrap), but it is less apparent to some that not all crime is violent. In fact, the great bulk of adolescent crime consists of nonviolent forms of theft and statute violations such as truancy and running away. In the present report "violent crimes" are defined as *legally proscribed acts whose primary object is the deliberate use of force to inflict injury on persons or objects, and, under some circumstances, the stated intention to engage in such acts.* While the scope of this paper prevents discussion of numerous complex issues involved in this definition, for example, the role of "threat of force" as criminally culpable, an idea of the kinds of acts included under the definition may be obtained directly by referring to Tables 3 and 4 , pages 106 and 107. Table 3 delineates sixteen forms of "violent" offenses directed at persons and objects, and Table 4 delineates fourteen legal categories. It is to these forms that the term "violent crimes" will apply.

Circumstances and Methods of Study

Conclusions presented in subsequent sections are based on the research findings of an extensive study of youth gangs in "Midcity," a central-city slum district of 100,000 persons. Information was obtained on some 150 corner gangs, numbering about 4,500 males and famales, aged twelve to twenty, in the middle and late 1950's. Selected for more detailed study were twenty-one of these gangs numbering about 700 members; selection was based primarily on their reputation as the "toughest" in the city. Study data of many kinds were obtained from numerous sources, but the great bulk of data was derived from the detailed field records of workers who were in direct daily contact with gang members for periods averaging two years per gang. Seven of these gangs, numbering 205 members (four white male gangs, one Negro male, one white female, one Negro female) were subject to the most intensive field observation, and are designated "intensive observation" gangs. Findings presented here are based primarily on the experience of these seven, along with that of fourteen male gangs numbering 293 members (including the five intensive-observation male gangs) whose criminal records were obtained from the state central criminal records division.

Detailed qualitative information on the daily behavior of gang members in sixty "behavioral areas" (for example, sexual behavior, family behavior, and theft) was collected and analyzed; however, the bulk of the findings presented here will be quantitative in nature, due to requirements of brevity.[4] Present findings are based primarily on three kinds of data: (1) *Field-recorded behavior*—all actions and sentiments recorded for the seven intensive observation gangs which relate to assault (N = 1,600); (2) *Field-recorded crimes*—all recorded instances of illegal acts of assault and property damage engaged in by members of the same gangs (N = 228); and (3) *Court-recorded crimes*—all charges of assaultive or property damage offenses recorded by court officials for members of the fourteen male gangs between the ages of seven and twenty-seven (N = 138).

The analysis distinguishes four major characteristics of gangs: age, sex, race, and social status. Of the seven intensive-observation gangs, five were male (N = 155) and two, female (N = 50); none of the fourteen court-record gangs was female. Five of the intensive-observation gangs were white (N = 127) and two, Negro (N = 78); eight of the court-record gangs were white (N = 169) and six, Negro (N = 124). The ethnic-religious status of the white gangs was multinational Catholic (Irish-Italian with Irish dominant, some French, and

Slavic). Social status was determined by a relatively complex method based on a combination of educational, occupational, and other criteria (for example, parents' occupation, gang members' occupation, gang members' education, and families' welfare experience).[5] On the basis of these criteria all gangs were designated "lower class." Three levels *within* the lower class were delineated and were designated, from highest to lowest, Lower Class I, II, and III. Gangs analyzed in the present paper belonged to levels II and III; the former level is designated "higher" status, and the latter, "lower." It should be kept in mind that the terms "higher" and "lower" in this context refer to the lowest and next-lowest of three intra-lower-class social-status levels.[6]

The Patterning of Violent Crimes in City Gangs

Study data make it possible to address a set of questions central to any consideration of the reality of violent crime in city gangs. How prevalent are violent crimes, both in absolute terms and relative to other forms of crime? What proportion of gang members engage in violent crimes? Is individual or collective participation more common? Are those most active in such crimes more likely to be younger or older? white or Negro? male or female? higher or lower in social status? What forms do violent crimes take, and which forms are most prevalent? Who and what are the targets of violent crimes? How serious are they? How does violence figure in the daily lives of gang members?

The following sections present data bearing on each of these questions, based on the experience of Midcity gangs in the 1950's. The first section bears on the last of the questions just cited: What was the role of assaultive behavior in the daily lives of gang members?

Approximately 1,600 actions and sentiments relating to assaultive behavior were recorded by field workers during the course of their work with the seven "intensive observation" gangs—a period averaging two years per gang.[7]

This number comprised about 3 percent of a total of about 54,000 actions and sentiments oriented to some sixty behavioral areas (for example, sexual behavior, drinking behavior, theft, and police-oriented behavior). Assault-oriented behavior was relatively common, ranking ninth among sixty behavioral areas. A substantial portion of this behavior, however, took the form of words rather than deeds; for example, while the total number of assault-oriented actions and sentiments was over two and a half times as great as those relating to theft, the actual number of "arrestable" incidents of assault was less than half the number of theft incidents. This finding is concordant with others which depict the area of assaultive behavior as one characterized by considerably more smoke than fire.

About one half (821) of the 1,600 actions and sentiments were categorized as "approved" or "disapproved" with reference to a specified set of evaluative standards of middle-class adults;[8] the remainder were categorized as "evaluatively neutral." There were approximately thirty "disapproved" assault-oriented actions for every instance of "arrestable" assault, and five instances of arrestable assault for every court appearance on assault changes. Males engaged in assault-oriented behavior far more frequently than females (males 6.3 events per month, females 1.4), and younger males more frequently than older.

Information concerning both actions and sentiments relating to assault—data not generally available—revealed both similarities and differences in the patterning of these two levels of behavior. Expressed sentiments concerning assaultive behavior were about one and a half times as common as actual actions; in this respect, assault was unique among analyzed forms of behavior, since, in every other case, recorded actions were more common than sentiments, for example, theft behavior (actions 1.5 times sentiments) and family-oriented behavior (actions 2.2 times sentiments). The majority of actions and sentiments (70 percent) were "disapproved" with reference to adult middle-class standards; actions and sentiments were "concordant" in this respect, in that both ran counter to middle-class standards by similar proportions (actions, 74 percent disapproved and sentiments, 68 percent). This concordance contrasted with other forms of behavior: in sexual behavior, the level of disapproved action was substantially higher than that of disapproved sentiment; family-oriented behavior, the level of disapproved sentiment, substantially higher than that of action.

Separate analysis were made of behavior oriented to "individual" assault (mostly fights between two persons) and "collective" assault (mostly gang fighting). With regard to individual assault, the number of actions and the number of sentiments were approximately equal (181 actions, 187 sentiments); in the case of collective assault, in contrast, there was almost twice as much talk as action (239 sentiments, 124 actions). Sentiments with respect both to individual and collective assault were supportive of disapproved behavior, but collective assault received less support than individual. Behavior *opposing* disapproved assault showed an interesting pattern; specific actions aimed to inhibit or forestall collective assault were over twice as common as actions opposing individual assault. Gang members thus appeared to be considerably more reluctant to engage in collective than in individual fighting; the former was dangerous and frightening, with uncontrolled escalation a predictable risk, while much of the latter involved relatively mild set-to's between peers within the "controlled" context of gang interaction.

Assault-oriented behavior, in summary, was relatively common, but a substantial part of this behavior entailed words rather than deeds. Both actions and sentiments ran counter to conventional middle-class adult standards, with these two levels of behavior concordant in this respect. Insofar as there did exist an element of assault-inhibiting behavior, it was manifested in connection with collective rather than individual assault. This provides evidence for the existence within the gang of a set of "natural" forces operating to control collective assault, a phenomenon to be discussed further.

Frequency of violent crime. The wide currency of an image of violence as a dominant occupation and preoccupation of street gangs grants special importance to the question of the actual prevalence of violent crimes. How frequently did gang members engage in illegal acts of assault and property damage? Table 1 shows that members of the five intensive-observation male gangs, on the basis of field records of known offenses, were involved in violent crimes at a rate of somewhat under one offense for each two boys per ten-month period, and that the fourteen male gangs, on the basis of court-recorded offenses, were charged with "violent" crimes at a rate of somewhat under one charge for each two boys

TABLE 1. FREQUENCY OF VIOLENT CRIMES BY MALE GANG MEMBERS (BY RACE AND SOCIAL STATUS)

Race and Social Status	Five Intensive-Observation Gangs			Fourteen Court-Record Gangs		
	Number of Individuals	Number of Involvements [a]	Rate [b]	Number of Individuals	Number of Charges [c]	Rate [d]
White L.C. III	66	154	8.4	97	81	8.3
Negro L.C. III	— [e]	—	—	58	39	6.7
White L.C. II	50	40	1.5	72	10	1.4
Negro L.C. II	39	34	2.5	66	8	1.2
	155	228	4.7	293	138	4.7

L.C. III (8.4) = L.C. II (2.0) × *4.2* L.C. III (7.7) = L.C. II (1.3) × *5.9*
White (5.4) = Negro (2.5) × *2.1* White (5.4) = Negro (3.8) × *1.4*

[a] No incidents assault and property damage × number of participants.
[b] Involvements per 10 individuals per ten-month period.
[c] Charges on fourteen categories of assault and property-damage offenses (see Table 4).
[d] Charges per ten individuals ages seven through eighteen.
[e] Not included in study population.

during the twelve-year period from ages seven through eighteen.[9] The 228 "violent offense" involvements comprised 24 percent of all categories of illegal involvements (assault 17 percent, property damage 7 percent), with assault about one-half as common as theft, the most common offense, and property damage about one-quarter as common. The 138 court charges comprised 17 percent of all categories of charge (assault charges 11 percent, property damage 6 percent) with assault charges about one-third as common as theft, the most common charge, and property damage about one-fifth as common. The total number of "violence-oriented" actions and sentiments examined in the previous section comprised something under 4 percent of actions and sentiments oriented to sixty behavioral areas (assault-oriented behavior, 3.2 percent; property-damage-oriented, 0.5 percent).

These figures would indicate that violence and violent crimes did not play a dominant role in the lives of Midcity gangs. The cumulative figures taken alone—228 known offenses by 155 boys during a period of approximately two years, and 138 court charges for 293 boys during a twelve-year age span—would appear to indicate a fairly high "absolute" volume of violent crime. If, however, the volume of such crime is compared with that of other forms—with "violent" behavior, both actional and verbal, comprising less than 4 percent of all recorded behavior, field-recorded "violent" offenses comprising less than one-quarter of all known offenses, and court charges of violent crimes less than one-fifth of all charges—violence appears neither as a dominant preoccupation of city gangs nor as a dominant form of criminal activity. Moreover, one should bear in mind that these rates apply to young people of the most "violent" sex, during the most "violent" years of their lives, during a time when they were members of the toughest gangs in the toughest section of the city.

Race and social status. The relative importance of race and social status is indicated in Table 1, with field-recorded and court-recorded data showing close correspondence. Of the two characteristics, social status is clearly more important. Lower-status gang members (Lower Class III) engaged in field-recorded acts of illegal violence four times as often as those of higher status (Lower Class II) and were charged in court six times as often. White and Negro rates, in contrast, differ by a factor of two or less. The finding that boys of lower educational and occupational status both engaged in and were arrested for violent crimes to a substantially greater degree than those of higher status is not particularly surprising, and conforms to much research which shows that those of lower social status are likely to be more active in criminal behavior. What is noteworthy is the fact that differences of this magnitude appear in a situation where status differences are as small, relatively, as those between Lower Class II and III. One might expect, for example, substantial differences between college boys and high school drop-outs, but the existence of differences on the order of four to six times between groups *within* the lower class suggests that even relatively small social-status differences among laboring-class populations can be associated with relatively large differences in criminal behavior.

Table 1 findings relating to race run counter to those of many studies which show Negroes to be more "violent" than whites and to engage more actively in violent crimes. Comparing similar-status white and Negro gangs in Midcity shows that racial differences were relatively unimportant, and that, insofar as there were differences, it was the whites rather than the Negroes who were more likely both to engage in and to be arrested for violent crimes. White gang members engaged in field-recorded acts of illegal violence twice as often as Negro gang members and were charged in court one and a half times as often. These data, moreover, do not support a contention that Negroes who engage in crime to a degree similar to that of whites tend to be arrested to a greater degree. The one instance where Negro rates exceed those of whites is in the case of field-recorded crimes for higher status gangs (white rate 1.5, Negro 2.5).[10] Court data, however, show that the Negro boys, with a *higher* rate of field-recorded crime, have a slightly *lower* rate of court-recorded crime. An explanation of these findings cannot be undertaken here; for present purposes it is sufficient to note that carefully collected data from one major American city do not support the notion that Negroes are more violent than whites at *similar social status levels,* nor the notion that high Negro arrest rates are invariably a consequence of the discriminatory application of justice by prejudiced white policemen and judges.

Age and violent crime. Was there any relationship between the age of gang members and their propensity to engage in violent crimes? Table 2 shows a clear and regular relationship between age and offense-frequency. The yearly rate of changes rises quite steadily between the ages of 12 and 18, reaches a peak of about 9 charges per 100 boys at age 18, then drops off quite rapidly to age 22, leveling off thereafter to a relatively low rate of about 3 charges per 100 boys per year. The bulk of court action (82 percent of 229 charges) involved assaultive rather than property-damage offenses. The latter were proportionately more

TABLE 2. FREQUENCY OF VIOLENT CRIMES BY AGE: 14 MALE GANGS (N = 293): COURT CHARGES (N = 229)

Age	Number of Individuals	Number of Charges [a]	Rate [b]	Assault Charges [c]	Rate	Property Damage Charges [d]	Rate
8	293	—	—	—	—	—	—
9	293	—	—	—	—	—	—
10	293	1	0.3	1	0.3	—	—
11	293	7	2.4	2	0.7	5	1.7
12	293	—	—	—	—	—	—
13	293	6	2.0	1	0.3	5	1.7
14	293	16	5.5	12	4.1	4	1.4
15	293	19	6.5	14	4.8	5	1.7
16	293	26	8.9	21	7.2	5	1.7
17	293	25	8.5	21	7.2	5	1.7
18	293	27	9.2	23	7.8	3	1.0
19	293	21	7.2	18	6.1	3	1.0
20	293	22	7.5	21	7.2	1	0.3
21	293	20	6.8	19	6.5	1	0.3
22	292	9	3.1	8	2.7	1	0.3
23	281	10	3.5	8	2.8	2	0.7
24	247	5	2.0	4	1.6	1	0.4
25	191	7	3.7	6	3.1	1	0.5
26	155	5	3.2	5	3.2	—	—
27	95	3	3.1	3	3.2	—	—

[a] Charges on fourteen categories of offense (see Table 4).
[b] Charges per 100 individuals per year of age.
[c] Categories 1, 3, 4, 5, 5, 7, 8, 9, 13, and 14, Table 4.
[d] Categories 2, 10, 13, 12, Table 4.

prevalent during the 11–13 age period, after which the former constitute a clear majority.

The age-patterning of theft-connected versus nontheft-connected violence and of intended versus actual violence was also determined. Violence in connection with theft—almost invariably the threat rather than the use thereof—constituted a relatively small proportion of all charges (14 percent), occurring primarily during the 15–21 age period. Court action based on the threat or intention to use violence rather than on its actual use comprised about one-quarter of all charges, becoming steadily more common between the ages of thirteen and twenty, and less common thereafter. At age twenty the number of charges based on the threat of violence was exactly equal to the number based on actual violence.

These data indicate quite clearly that involvement in violent crimes was a relatively transient phenomenon of adolescence, and did not presage a continuing pattern of similar involvement in adulthood. It should also be noted that these findings do not support an image of violent crimes as erratically impulsive, uncontrolled, and unpredictable. The fact that the practice of violent crime by gang members showed so regular and so predictable a relationship to age would indicate that violence was a "controlled" form of behavior—subject to a set of shared conceptions as to which forms were appropriate, and how often they were appropriate, at different age levels.

Participation in assaultive crime. What proportion of gang members engaged in assaultive crimes? [11] During the two-year period of field observation, 53 of the 205 intensive-contact gang members (26 percent) were known to have engaged in illegal acts of assault—50 out of 155 males (32 percent), and 3 out of 50 females (6 percent). Male-participation figures ranged from 22 percent for the higher status gangs to 42 percent for the lower. "Heavy" participants (four or more crimes) comprised only 4 percent (six males, no females) of all gang members. During the same period nineteen gang members (all males) appeared in court on assault charges—about 12 percent of the male gang members. While there is little doubt that some gang members also engaged in assaultive crimes that were known neither to field workers nor officials, the fact that three-quarters of the gang members and two-thirds of the males were *not* known to have engaged in assaultive crimes during the observation period and that 88 percent of the males and 100 percent of the females did not appear in court on charges of assaultive crimes strengthens the previous conclusion that assault was not a dominant form of gang activity.

A related question concerns the relative prevalence of individual and collective assault. One image of gang violence depicts gang members as cowardly when alone, daring to attack others only when bolstered by a clear numerical superiority. Study data give little support to this image. Fifty-one percent of recorded assault incidents involved either one-to-one engagements or engagements in which a single gang member confronted more than one antagonist. As will be shown in the discussion of "targets," a good proportion of the targets of collective assault were also groups rather than individuals. Some instances of the ganging-up" phenomenon did occur, but they were relatively infrequent.

The character of violent crime. What was the character of violent crime in Midcity gangs? Violent crimes, like other forms of gang behavior, consist of a multiplicity of particular events, varying considerably in form and circumstance. Any classification based on a single system does not account for the diversity of violence. The following sections use five ways of categorizing violent crimes: (1) *forms of crime directed at persons* (distinctions based on age, gang membership, and collectivity of actors and targets); (2) *forms of crime directed at objects* (distinctions based on mode of inflicting damage); (3) *forms of crime directed at persons and objects* (based on official classifications); (4) *targets of crime directed at persons* (distinctions based on age, sex, race, gang membership, collectivity); and (5) *targets of crime directed at objects* (distinctions based on identity of object).

Table 3 (column 1) shows the distribution of eleven specific forms of field-recorded assault directed at persons. In three-quarters of all incidents participants on both sides were peers of the same sex. In 60 percent of the incidents, gang members acted in groups; in 40 percent as individuals. Fifty-one percent of the incidents involved collective engagements between same-sex peers. The most common form was the collective engagement between members of different gangs; it constituted one-third of all forms and was three times as common as the next most common form. Few of these engagements were full-scale massed-encounter gang fights; most were brief strike-and-fall-back forays by small guerrilla

TABLE 3. FORMS OF VIOLENT CRIME: FIELD-RECORDED OFFENSES: SEVEN INTENSIVE-OBSERVATION GANGS (N = 205): INCIDENTS (N = 125)

Person-Directed			Object-Directed		
	Number of Incidents	% Known Forms		Number of Incidents	% All Forms
1. Collective engagement: different gangs	27	32.9	1. Damaging via body blow, other body action	10	27.0
2. Assault by individual on individual adult, same sex	9	11.0	2. Throwing of missile (stone, brick, etc.)	10	27.0
3. Two-person engagement: different gangs	6	7.3	3. Scratching, marking, defacing, object or edifice	8	21.6
4. Two-person engagement: gang member, nongang peer	6	7.3	4. Setting fire to object or edifice	4	10.8
5. Two-person engagement: intragang	5	6.1	5. Damaging via explosive	1	2.7
6. Collective assault on same sex peer, nongang-member	5	6.1	6. Other	4	10.8
7. Threatened collective assault on adult	5	6.1		37	100.0
8. Assault by individual on group	4	4.9			
9. Assault by individual on female peer	4	4.9			
10. Participation in general disturbance, riot	3	3.6			
11. Collective assault on same-sex peer, member of other gang	2	2.4			
12. Other	6	7.3			
13. Form Unknown	6	—			
	88	99.9			

bands. Assault on male adults, the second most common form (11 percent), involved, for the most part, the threat or use of force in connection with theft (for example, "mugging," or threatening a cab-driver with a knife) or attacks on policemen trying to make an arrest. It should be noted that those forms of gang assault which most alarm the public were rare. No case of assault on an adult woman, either by individuals or groups, was recorded. In three of the four instances of sexual assault on a female peer, the victim was either a past or present girl friend of the attacker. Only three incidents involving general rioting were recorded; two were prison riots and the third, a riot on a Sunday excursion boat.

The character of violent crimes acted on by the courts parallels that of field-recorded crimes. Table 4 shows the distribution of fourteen categories of offense for 293 gang members during the age period from late childhood to early adulthood. Charges based on assault (187) were five and a half times as common as charges on property damage (42). About one-third of all assault charges involved the threat rather than the direct use of force. The most common charge was "assault and battery," including, primarily, various kinds of unarmed engagements such as street fighting and barroom brawls. The more "serious" forms of assaultive crime were among the less prevalent: armed assault, 8 percent; armed robbery, 5 percent; sexual assault, 4 percent. Not one of the 293 gang members appeared in court on charges of either murder or manslaughter between the ages of seven and twenty-seven.

TABLE 4. FORMS OF VIOLENT CRIME: COURT-RECORDED OFFENSES: 14 MALE GANGS (N = 293): COURT CHARGES THROUGH AGE 27 (N = 229)

Offense	Number	Percentage
1. Assault and battery: no weapon	75	32.7
2. Property damage	36	15.7
3. Affray	27	11.8
4. Theft-connected threat of force: no weapon	22	9.6
5. Possession of weapon	18	7.9
6. Assault, with weapon	18	7.9
7. Theft-connected threat of force: with weapon	11	4.8
8. Assault, threat of	8	3.5
9. Sexual assault	8	3.5
10. Arson	6	2.5
11. Property damage, threat of	—	—
12. Arson, threat of	—	—
13. Manslaughter	—	—
14. Murder	—	—
	229	100.0

The use of weapons and the inflicting of injury are two indications that violent crimes are of the more serious kind. Weapons were employed in a minority of cases of assault, actual or threatened, figuring in 16 of the 88 field-recorded offenses, and about 55 of the 187 court offenses.[12] In the 16 field-recorded incidents in which weapons were used to threaten or injure, 9 involved knives, 4, an object used as a club (baseball bat, pool cue), and 3, missiles (rocks, balls). In none of the 88 incidents was a firearm of any description used. The bulk of assaultive incidents, then, involved the direct use of the unarmed body; this finding accords with others in failing to support the notion that gang members engage in assault only when fortified by superior resources.

Serious injuries consequent on assault were also relatively uncommon. There were twenty-seven known injuries to all participants in the eighty-eight incidents of assault; most of these were minor cuts, scratches, and bruises. The most serious injury was a fractured skull inflicted by a crutch wielded during a small-scale set-to between two gangs. There were also two other skull injuries, three cases of broken bones, three broken noses, and one shoulder dislocation (incurred during a fight between girls). While these injuries were serious enough for those who sustained them, it could not be said that the totality of person-directed violence by Midcity gang members incurred any serious cost in maimed bodies. The average week-end of highway driving in and around Port City produces more serious body injuries than two years of violent crimes by Midcity gangs.

Data on modes of property damage similarly reflect a pattern of involvement in the less serious forms. As shown in Table 3, in ten of the thirty-seven field-recorded incidents the body was used directly to inflict damage (punching out a window, breaking fences for slats); another ten involved common kinds of missile-throwing (brick through store window). Most of the "defacing" acts were not particularly destructive, for example, scratching the name of the gang on a store wall. Fire-setting was confined to relatively small objects, for example, trash barrels. No instance was recorded of viciously destructive forms of vandalism such as desecration of churches or cemeteries or bombing of residences. The one case where explosives were used involved the igniting of rifle cartridge powder in a variety store. Of the forty-two cases of court-charged property-destruction, only six involved arson; the actual nature of vandalistic acts was not specified in the legal designations.

Targets of violent crime. While much gang violence took the form of "engagements with" rather than "attacks on" other persons, additional insight may be gained by viewing the gang members as "actors," and asking: "What categories of person were targets of gang assault, and what kinds of physical objects targets of damage?" One image of gang violence already mentioned sees the act of "ganging up" on solitary and defenseless victims as a dominant gang practice; another sees racial antagonism as a major element in gang violence. What do these data show?

Table 5 shows the distribution of 88 field-recorded incidents of assault for 13 categories of target, and 43 incidents of damage for 6 categories.[13]

Of 77 targets of assault whose identity was known, a substantial majority (73 percent) were persons of the same age and sex category as the gang members, and a substantial majority (71 percent), of the same race. One-half of all targets were peers of the same age, sex, and race category. On initial inspection the data seem to grant substance to the "ganging up" notion; 44 of 77 targets (57 percent) were individuals. Reference to Table 3, however, shows that 34 of these incidents were assaults on individuals *by* individuals; of the remaining 10, 4 were adult males (police, mugging victims) and one, the famale member of a couple robbed at knife point. The remaining 5 were same-sex peers, some of whom were members of rival gangs. There was no recorded instance of collective assault on a child, on old men or women, or on females by males. There was no instance of an attack on a white female by a Negro male. Partly balancing the five cases of collective assault on lone peers were three instances in which a lone gang member took on a group.

TABLE 5. TARGETS OF VIOLENT CRIME: FIELD-RECORDED OFFENSES: SEVEN INTENSIVE-OBSERVATION GANGS (N = 205): INCIDENTS (N = 125)

Persons	Number of Incidents	% Known Targets	Objects	Number of Incidents	% All Targets
1. Groups of adolescents, other ganga, same sex, race	18	23.4	1. Stores, commercial facilities: premises, equipment	11	29.7
2. Groups of adolescents, other gangs, same sex, different race	12	15.5	2. Semipublic facilities: social agencies, gyms, etc	10	27.0
3. Individual adults, same sex, same race	12	15.5	3. Automobiles	8	21.6
4. Individual adolescents, other gangs, same sex, same race	8 8	10.4 10.4	4. Public facilities: schools, public transportation, etc.	5	13.5
5. Individual adolescents, nongang, same sex, race	6	7.8	5. Private houses: premises, furnishings	3	8.1
				37	99.9
6. Individual adolescents, nongang, different sex, same race	4	5.2			
7. Individual adolescents, nongang, same sex, different race	4	5.2			
8. Individual adults, same sex, different race	4	5.2			
9. Individual adolescents, own gang	3	3.9			
10. Groups of adolescents, own gang	3	3.9			
11. Individual adolescents, nongang, same sex, different race	2	2.6			
12. Individual adults, different sex, same race	1	1.3			
13. Target unknown	11	—			
	88	99.9			

These data thus grant virtually no support to the notion that favored targets of gang attacks are the weak, the solitary, the defenseless, and the innocent; in most cases assaulters and assaultees were evenly matched; the bulk of assaultive incidents involved contests between peers in which the preservation and defense of gang honor was a central issue. Some support is given to the notion of racial friction; 30 percent of all targets were of a different race, and racial antagonism played some part in these encounters. On the other hand, of thirty-three instances of collective assault, a majority (55 percent) involved antagonists of the same race.

Physical objects and facilities suffering damage by gang members were largely those which they used and frequented in the course of daily life. Most damage was inflicted on public and semipublic facilities, little on private residences or other property. There was no evidence of "ideological" vandalism (stoning embassies, painting swastikas on synagogues). Most damage was deliberate, but some additional amount was a semiaccidental consequence of the profligate effusion of body energy so characteristic of male adolescents (breaking a store window in course of a scuffle). Little of the deliberately inflicted property damage represented a diffuse outpouring of accumulated hostility against arbitrary objects; in most cases the gang members injured the possession of properties of particular persons who had angered them, as a concrete expression of that anger (defacing automobile of mother responsible for having gang member committed to correctional institution; breaking windows of settlement house after ejection therefrom). There was thus little evidence of "senseless" destruction; most property damage was directed and responsive.

Gang fighting. An important form of gang violence is the gang fight; fiction and drama often depict gang fighting or gang wars as a central feature of gang life (for example, *West Side Story*). The Midcity study conceptualized a fully developed gang fight as involving four stages: initial provocation, initial attack, strategy-planning and mobilization, and counterattack.[14] During the study period, members of the intensive-observation gangs participated in situations involving some combination of these stages fifteen times. Despite intensive efforts by prowar agitators and elaborate preparations for war, only one of these situations eventuated in full-scale conflict; in the other fourteen, one or both sides found a way to avoid open battle. A major objective of gang members was to put themselves in the posture of fighting without actually having to fight. The gangs utilized a variety of techniques to maintain their reputation as proud men, unable to tolerate an affront to honor, without having to confront the dangerous and frightening reality of massed antagonists. Among these were the "fair fight" (two champions represent their gangs *a la* David and Goliath); clandestine informing of police by prospective combatants; *reluctantly* accepting mediation by social workers.

Despite the very low ratio of actual to threatened fighting, a short-term observer swept up in the bustle and flurry of fight-oriented activity, and ignorant of the essentially ritualistic nature of much of this activity, might gain a strong impression of a great deal of actual violence. In this area, as in others, detailed observation of gangs over extended periods revealed that gang fighting resembled other forms of gang violence in showing much more smoke than fire.

The Problem of Gang Violence

The picture of gang violence which emerges from the study of Midcity gangs differs markedly from the conventional imagery as well as from that presented by some scholars. How is this difference to be explained? The most obvious possibility is that Midcity gangs were somehow atypical of gangs in Port City, and of the "true" American street gang. In important respects the gangs were *not* representative of those in Port City, having been selected on the basis of their reputation as the "toughest" in the city, and were thus *more* violent than the average Port

City gang. The possibility remains, in the absence of information equivalent in scope and detail to that presented here, that Port City gangs were atypical of, and less violent than, gangs in other cities. I would like in this connection to offer my personal opinion, based on ten years of contact with gang workers and researchers from all parts of the country, that Midcity gangs were in fact *quite* typical of "tough" gangs in Chicago, Brooklyn, Philadelphia, Detroit, and similar cities, and represent the "reality" of gang violence much more accurately than "the Wild Ones" or the Egyptian Kings, represented as the prototypical "violent gang" in a well-known television program.

Even if one grants that actual city gangs are far less violent than those manufactured by the mass media and that the public fear of gangs has been unduly aroused by exaggerated images, the problem of gang violence is still a real one. However one may argue that all social groups need outlets for violence and that gang violence may serve to siphon off accumulated aggression in a "functional" or necessary way, the fact remains that members of Midcity gangs repeatedly violated the law in using force to effect theft, in fighting, and in inflicting damage on property as regular and routine pursuits of adolescence. *Customary* engagement in illegal violence by a substantial sector of the population, however much milder than generally pictured, constitutes an important threat to the internal order of any large urbanized society, a threat which must be coped with. What clues are offered by the research findings of the Midcity study as to the problem of gang violence and its control?

First, a brief summary of what it *was*. Violence as a concern occupied a fairly important place in the daily lives of gang members, but was distinguished among all forms of behavior in the degree to which concern took the form of talk rather than action. Violent crime as such was fairly common during middle and late adolescence, but, relative to other forms of crime, was not dominant. Most violent crimes were directed at persons, few at property. Only a small minority of gang members was active in violent crimes. Race had little to do with the frequency of involvement in violent crimes, but social status figured prominently. The practice of violent crimes was an essentially transient phenomenon of male adolescence, reaching a peak at the age when concern with attaining adult manhood was at a peak. While the nature of minor forms showed considerable variation, the large bulk of violent crime in Midcity gangs consisted in unarmed physical encounters between male antagonists—either in the classic form of combat skirmishes between small bands of warriors or the equally classic form of direct combative engagement between two males.

Next, a brief summary of what it was *not*. Violence was not a dominant activity of the gangs, nor a central reason for their existence. Violent crime was not a racial phenomenon—either in the sense that racial antagonisms played a major role in gang conflict, or that Negroes were more violent, or that resentment of racial injustice was a major incentive for violence. It was not "ganging up" by malicious sadists on the weak, the innocent, the solitary. It did not victimize adult females. With few exceptions, violent crimes fell into the "less serious" category, with the extreme or shocking crimes rare.

One way of summarizing the character of violent crime in Midcity gangs is to make a distinction between two kinds of violence—"means" violence and "end" violence. The concept of violence as a "means" involves the notion of a resort to violence when other means of attaining a desired objective have failed. Those who undertake violence in this context represent their involvement as distasteful but necessary—an attitude epitomized in the parental slogan, "It hurts me more than it does you." The concept of violence as an "end" involves the notion of eager recourse to violence for its own sake—epitomized in the mythical Irishman who says, "What a grand party! Let's start a fight!" The distinction is illustrated by concepts of two kinds of policeman—the one who with great reluctance resorts to force in order to make an arrest and the "brutal" policeman who inflicts violence unnecessarily and repeatedly for pure pleasure. It is obvious that "pure" cases of either means- or end-violence are rare or nonexistent; the "purest" means-violence may involve some personal gratification, and the "purest" end-violence can be seen as instrumental to other ends.

In the public mind, means-violence is unfortunate but sometimes necessary; it is the spectacle of end-violence which stirs deep indignation. Much of the public outrage over gang violence arises from the fact that it has been falsely represented, with great success, as pure end-violence ("senseless," "violence for its own sake") when it is largely, in fact, means-violence.

What are the "ends" toward which gang violence is a means, and how is one to evaluate the legitimacy of these ends? Most scholars of gangs agree that these ends are predominantly ideological rather than material, and revolve on the concepts of prestige and honor. Gang members fight to secure and defend their honor as males; to secure and defend the reputation of their local area and the honor of their women; to show that an affront to their pride and dignity demands retaliation.[15] Combat between males is a major means for attaining these ends.

It happens that great nations engage in national wars for almost identical reasons. It also happens, ironically, that during this period of national concern over gang violence our nation is pursuing, in the international arena, very similar ends by very similar means. At root, the solution to the problem of gang violence lies in the discovery of a way of providing for men the means of attaining cherished objectives—personal honor, prestige, defense against perceived threats to one's homeland—without resort to violence. When men have found a solution to this problem, they will at the same time have solved the problem of violent crimes in city gangs.

Notes

1. L. Yablonsky, *The Violent Gang* (New York: The Macmillan Company, 1963), pp. 4, 6.

2. J. F. Short and F. L. Strodtbeck, *Group Process and Gang Delinquency* (Chicago: University of Chicago Press, 1965), pp. 224, 258.

3. F. A. Cloward and L. E. Ohlin, *Delinquency and Opportunity: A Theory of Delinquent Gangs* (Glencoe, Ill.: Free Press, 1960), pp. 20, 24.

4. Qualitative data on the nature of "violent" and other forms of gang behavior which convey a notion of its "flavor" and life-context will be presented in W. B. Miller, *City Gangs* (New York: John Wiley & Sons, forthcoming).

5. Details of this method are presented in *City Gangs, op. cit.*

6. IBM processing of court-recorded offenses and preliminary analyses of field-recorded assault behavior and illegal incidents was done by Dr. Robert Stanfield, University of Massachusetts; additional data analysis by Donald Zall, Midcity Delinquency Research Project. Some of the specific figures in the tables may be slightly altered in the larger report; such alterations will not, however, affect the substance of the findings. The research was supported under the National Institute of Health's Grant M-1414, and administered by the Boston University School of Social Work.

7. The definition of "violent crimes" used here would call for an analysis at this point of behavior oriented to both assault and property destruction. However, the type of data-processing necessary to an integrated analysis of these two behavioral forms has not been done for "property damage," so that the present section is based almost entirely on behavior involving persons rather than persons and property. Behavior involving property damage was relatively infrequent; 265 actions and sentiments were recorded, ranking this form of behavior forty-fifth of sixty forms; vandalistic behavior was about one-sixth as common as assaultive behavior, a ratio paralleled in officially recorded data (cf. Table 4). Most subsequent sections will utilize findings based on both assault and property damage.

8. Examples of *approved actions:* "acting to forestall threatened fighting" and "agreeing to settle disputes by means other than physical violence"; *disapproved actions:* "participating in gang-fighting" and "carrying weapons"; *approved sentiments:* "arguing against involvement in gang fighting" and "opposing the use of weapons"; *disapproved sentiments:* "defining fighting prowess as an essential virtue" and "perceiving fighting as inevitable."

9. Four types of "unit" figure in this and following tables. These are: (1) *Incidents:* An illegal incident is a behavioral event or sequence of events adjudged by a coder to provide a sound basis for arrest if known to authorities. Information as to most incidents was obtained from field records. In the case of assault incidents, this definition ruled out a fair number of moderately to fairly serious instances of actual or intended assault which involved members of the same gang or occurred under circumstances deemed unlikely to produce arrest even if known. (2) *Involvements:* Incidents multiplied by number of participants, for example: two gang members fight two others—one incident, four involvements. (3) *Court Appearances:* The appearance in court of a gang member on a "new" charge or charges (excluded are rehearings, appeals, and the like). (4) *Court Charges:* Appearances multiplied by number of separate charges, for example, an individual's being charged at one appearance with breaking and entering, possession of burglars' tools, and conspiracy to commit larceny counts as three "charges." The "violent crime" charges of Table 1 represent fourteen categories of offense involving actual or threatened injury to persons or objects. The fourteen offense designations appear in Table 4, and were condensed from forty categories of police-blotter designations.

10. This ratio obtains for males only; calculations which include the girls' gangs show higher rates for whites in this category as well as the others. Data on

field-recorded crimes on the female gangs are not included in Table 1 for purposes of comparability with court data; there were too few court-recorded offenses for females to make analysis practicable. At the time the field data were collected (1954–1957) Negroes comprised about 35 percent of the population of Midcity; court data cover the years up to 1964, at which time Negroes comprised about 55 percent of the population.

11. Findings do not include data on property damage. See footnote 7.

12. On the basis of field-recorded data it was estimated that about one-quarter of "Affray" charges involved sticks or other weapons.

13. Findings are based on field-recorded data only; official offense designations seldom specify targets.

14. A description of the gang fight as a form of gang behavior is included in W. B. Miller, "Lower-Class Culture as a Generating Milieu of Gang Delinquency," *Journal of Social Issues,* Vol. XXXI, No. 4 (December 1957), pp. 17, 18.

15. The centrality of "honor" as a motive is evidenced by the fact that the "detached worker" method of working with gangs has achieved its clearest successes in preventing gang fights by the technique of furnishing would-be combatants with various means of avoiding direct conflict without sacrificing honor.

RESEARCH ON TEENAGE RIOTS

W. Buikhuisen

Disturbances caused by Teddy-boys, *Halbstarken,* mods, rockers, etc., are no unfamiliar phenomenon in Europe. Hundreds of teenagers, generally strangers to one another assemble at certain points in the city, preference usually being given to the busy streets and squares in the centre of town where, surrounded by the general public, they form speaking choruses, shout loudly, twist and uproot traffic signs, overturn parked cars, etc.

These activities necessitate police action and the disturbances usually culminate in a clash between police and public.

Everyone who has ever witnessed this type of disturbance is deeply impressed by it. The hysterical atmosphere, the senseless destruction, etc., give rise to such questions as: who are these teenagers, what makes them act in this fashion, how do they differ from adolescents who do not participate in such activities, how do these riots start, and especially: is it possible to prevent disorders of this kind?

In order to be able to answer questions of this sort, the Institute for Social Psychology of the University of Utrecht[1] collaborated with the Netherlands Institute for Preventive Medicine at Leyden in developing a research project consisting of four interrelated programmes.

Reprinted by permission of the author and publisher from *Sociologica Neerlandica,* 4 (Winter, 1966–67), pp. 1–19.

First, a large number of disturbances in various parts of the Netherlands were studied. Systematic observation was used to trace their development. Two types of factors were sought: those that stimulate the outbreak of riots, and those that tend to impede them.

In addition, attention was given to the police-public relationship, and to the actions of the police during the disturbances.

The second progamme consisted of a comparative study of teenagers who take part in such disturbances and of a control group of teenagers who do not. A third group consisting of young juvenile delinquents convicted for property offenses was also included in the study. The object here was to determine how the hooligans differ from this type of young delinquent, a comparison that seemed necessary in view of the fact that the literature on hooligans contains explanations for their behaviour highly similar to those generally given for juvenile delinquency.

In conjunction with this comparative study, participant observation was used to determine how teenagers who take part in riots tend to spend their leisure time. To this end, two co-workers of the author visited a cafeteria that was known to be a meeting place for teenage boys who actively participate in riots. For almost four months these participant observers spent almost all their free time there, and it was not long before they succeeded in being completely accepted by the boys operating from it.

The last part of the research project was an attempt made during a field experiment to prevent the outbreak of this type of disturbance.

Specific Details of the Research Project

One of the first problems confronting those interested in teenagers who actively participate in rioting is how to find out where they live. One of the most obvious methods is to proceed from the teenagers arrested by the police during this type of disturbance. Observation during the riots, however, showed that the boys arrested were by no means representative of the boys responsible for them. Indeed, it proved to be the rule rather than the exception for the real culprits to escape arrest. So a means had to be found to enable us to discover the addresses of boys who take an active part in the initiation of such disturbances. To this end, we proceeded as follows.

A number of observers were posted in those places where irregularities were expected. All were dressed in an appropriate manner, i.e. in tapered trousers worn with a leather jacket, duffle coat, or army jacket. Each observer carried a large number of cigarette packages, on the outside of which was printed in large letters: 'A free movie ticket is enclosed.' Inside the package, in addition to the cigarettes, was a questionnaire. Two questions about smoking were asked, namely: 'Do you smoke?' and 'Which do you prefer—cigarettes, cigars, a pipe, or cigarette tobacco?'

Each person who sent in the completed questionnaire received a free movie ticket. Extra attractions, such as a portable radio or tape recorder were offered for each 25th and 100th questionnaire received. The purpose of this so-called advertisement campaign was, of course, to obtain the addresses of the trouble-makers responsible for the disturbances. So, the cigarettes were given *only* to youths who in one way or another were active participants in the riot. In all, 38 packages were handed out. 35 boys returned the completed questionnaire and thus provided us with their addresses. Of that number, two had each received two packages, and one boy later appeared to have received his package erroneously. There then remained a group of 32 boys, who formed the basis of the research project. They were compared on numerous points with a matched group of non-hooligans and a group of juvenile delinquents convicted of property offenses (hereafter referred to as delinquents).

Matching criteria were age, education, occupation, family-structure, father's occupation and socio-economic milieu.

What Was Investigated?

A great deal has been written about hooliganism in social science publications. Writers such as Bondy, Kaiser, Holmberg, Muchow, Mik, Krantz and Vercruysse, Feyt, and Racine have gone into this subject extensively. The explanations given for the behaviour of the boys, however, vary considerably. These differences are partly attributable to the fact that the groups studied could not always be compared with one another. But even in those cases where the point of departure is the same, differences may still be found.

The present study attempts to test the various hypotheses given in the literature, to which end the following subjects were included in the project: parental home, school situation, work situation, certain aspects of modern society, personality and emotional life of the subject, his interests, how his leisure time is spent, and his attitude toward the police.

As a general hypothesis, Kaiser's statement is used: '. . . man wird sich den soziologischen Ort der Jugendausschreitungen generell *zwischen* den Polen des normgemässen und angepassten Verhaltens einerseits und des hochgradig verwahrlosten oder echt kriminellen Tuns anderseits vorzustellen haben.' [2]

In terms of this study, this means that on the data we collect, the scores of the boys actively engaged in rioting may be expected to lie between those of the control group and those of the delinquents.

Kaiser's hypothesis itself, however, will not be tested as a whole. For our purposes, it will be split into three separate hypotheses:

1. On those variables where the delinquents are expected to produce low (or high) scores, the hooligans will score lower (or higher) than the boys of the control group.
2. On those variables where the delinquents are expected to produce low (or high) scores, they will score lower (or higher) than the boys of the control group.
3. On those variables where the delinquents are expected to produce low (or high) scores, the hooligans will not score as low (or high) as the delinquents.

These three working hypotheses are based on the generally-known direction in which the delinquents will score.

The Research Methods Used

To collect the data, many and various research methods were used. In addition to the usual direct and indirect questions, we also used statements, scaling, semantic differentials, forced choice techniques, projection plates (a type of T.A.T.), sentence completion, projection techniques specially designed for this project (verbal projection tests) and tests to measure certain personality characteristics. Each of these techniques was constructed in such a way as to permit objective scoring.

Different techniques were continuously applied in each test area. To measure the attitude toward the parents, for example, direct and indirect questions, sentence completion, semantic differentials, scaling, and projection tests were used.

The presence or absence of the threat-of-war factor was determined by five different techniques.

The continuous application of different techniques in each area served as an indicator of the value of the data collected. For the reliability of the data increases when it becomes evident that the same results are obtained by a number of separate, non-related methods.

Validity of the Instrument

The object of a comparative study is to find out if there are differences. Uniformity may be due to one of two things:

1. either there are no differences between the groups compared, or
2. there are differences, but the instrument of measurement is not capable of bringing them to light. It is unable to differentiate.

The ability to differentiate is indeed one of the prerequisites for an instrument of measurement. This was another reason for including the group of delinquents in this project. A great deal of research has already been done on young delinquents. Duplicated research projects have usually yielded much the same results. The instrument we have devised should, if it is at all effective, register any differences present. In this respect, the presence of the group of delinquents works as a sort of indicator of its ability to differentiate.

Methodologically, this is a great advantage. Should we find no differences in some areas between hooligans and the boys of the control group, and definite differences between the latter and the delinquents, then the absence of these differences between the hooligan and the non-hooligan can no longer be dismissed with the traditional remark that the tests used were not up to the task of distinguishing between them.

Approaching the Subjects

Much of the research on hooligans and juvenile delinquents is carried out in a situation in which the subject knows what it is all about. He is being interviewed in his role of hooligan or delinquent, many such interviews even occurring during the period in which he is held in custody. Methodologically speaking, this is an undesirable situation. The subject knows what the research worker is doing and, in certain respects, can hope to gain by his answers. If he is in the hands of the police, this is quite obvious. But even if this is not the case, he may be feeling a subsequent need to rationalize his behaviour.

In order to eliminate this undesirable mechanism in advance, it was decided to approach the subjects from a simulated direction. They were asked to assist in a research project on national leisure time habits, an approach which permitted us to broach all the desired topics (parental home, work situation, attitude towards society, etc.) in a neutral manner.

Another form of bias is that whereby the interviewer knows the type of subject (hooligan, delinquent) he is dealing with. The circumstances were so regulated, therefore, that the interviewer did not know whether he was with a boy from the control group or one of the delinquents. Nor could he determine this from the results of the interview. Indeed, seven of the nine interviewers were quite unaware of the fact that delinquents were included in the interviews.

Number of Subjects in the Research Project

In total, the project concerned 134 persons. Table I shows the number of persons in the various research groups. The participation percentage is also given.

TABLE I. PARTICIPATION FIGURES PER GROUP

	Number Approached	Number of Refusals	Number of Participants	Participation Percentage
Hooligans	31	1	30	96
Delinquents	37	2	35	94
Control I	37	2	35	94
Control II	36	2	34	94
Total	141	7	134	95

As can be seen from this Table, two control groups of non-hooligans were used in the beginning. With one exception, the two groups were identical. Unlike Control Group I, the boys of Control Group II did not come from the same neighbourhood as the hooligans. The addresses of the latter showed that many of them lived in a neighbourhood known to the police as undesirable. It was feared that if no differences were to be found between the hooligans and a control group of non-hooligans selected from the same neighbourhood, this would be 'explained' with the remark that it is not possible to form a control group of nonhooligans from that type of neighbourhood. In order to be able to test the validity of this argument in advance a second control group was selected from a socially comparable neighbourhood without such a reputation. Once analysis of the material had shown that no statistically significant difference existed between the two control groups, they were combined into one large control group for the further processing of the data.

Results of the Comparative Study[3]

Personal particulars. The study showed that the hooligans belonged predominantly in the 16 to 18 age group, that their schooling mostly consisted of primary education, that the number still at school was quite low, that most of those already working belonged to the labourer category, and that the majority derived from the lower socio-economic groups of the population. None were out of work.

Parental home. The literature[4] devotes a great deal of attention to such factors as the housing situation (Muchow, 1956; Krantz & Vercruysse, 1959; etc.), family incompleteness (Kaiser, 1959, Bondy et al., 1957), the working mother (see Rose, 1961), frequent absence of the father for occupational reasons (Mik, 1962) and position in the sequence of children (Kaiser, 1959). The study showed that as far as housing, being obliged to share a room and the mother

TABLE II. ITEMS RELATING TO THE PARENTAL HOME

	Average for: contr. N = 69	Average for: delinq. N = 35	Average for: hool. N = 30	Is this difference significant? contr.-delinq. yes/no	P	contr.-hool. yes/no	P	delinq.-hool. yes/no	P
Opinion of parents									
helpful	8.8[1]	8.0	8.7	yes	.02[2]	no	—	yes	.10
calm	8.2	7.7	8.6	yes	.10	no	—	yes	.03
understanding	7.3	6.3	7.1	yes	.05	no	—	yes	.07
self-confident	8.0	7.1	8.2	yes	.02	no	—	yes	.02
influential	7.1	5.6	7.1	yes	.005	no	—	yes	.025
strong	7.5	6.3	7.8	yes	.004	no	—	yes	.006
ideal	7.9	7.1	7.7	yes	.04	no	—	no	—
show appreciation	7.7	7.1	8.0	no	—	no	—	yes	.09
happy home	7.2	5.8	6.9	yes	.01	no	—	yes	.06
don't interfere	5.4	6.7	5.9	yes	.004	no	—	yes	.10
Appreciation of upbringing by parents	8.1	6.7	8.5	yes	.006	no	—	yes	.002
To what extent will he bring up his own children differently	3.6	4.7	3.8	yes	.05	no	—	no	.11
Relationship with parents									
talkative	6.3	5.3	7.2	yes	.05	no	—	yes	.006
helpful	7.8	6.8	7.7	yes	.02	no	—	yes	.08
honest	8.3	7.4	7.8	yes	.01	yes	.09	no	—
frank	6.4	5.2	7.4	yes	.04	no	—	yes	.002
patient	6.6	5.3	6.8	yes	.01	no	—	yes	.03
polite	7.2	6.6	7.4	yes	.09	no	—	yes	.06
obedient	6.9	5.9	7.0	yes	.01	no	—	yes	.02
discusses his problems with them	6.1	3.1	5.7	yes	.000	no	—	yes	.001

[1] The scores run from 0 to 10. The higher the score, the more significant is the point concerned.
[2] The t-test was applied. Testing was one-sided.

working outside the home are concerned, the group of hooligans were no different from the control group. The same holds for family incompleteness, while the hooligans occupy no specific position in the sequence of children.

The only difference between hooligans and the control group found here is the frequent absence of the father for occupational reasons. It appeared that on the average the fathers of the former were absent more often because of their jobs than the fathers of the members of the control group.

Questions such as family life (Seelmann, 1957), relationship with the parents (Kern, 1957), a feeling of being misunderstood (Unesco report, 1958) and the upbringing at home (Muchow, 1956) are often related to the behaviour of the hooligans. Table II shows how the different groups answered the items relating to the parental home.

This Table indicates clearly that large differences exist between the hooligans and the juvenile delinquents with respect to points such as opinion of the parents, relationship with the parents and opinion of the upbringing received.

The delinquents are more negative toward their parental home in practically all respects, while the hooligans, on the other hand, show no sign of any such attitude.

Summarizing, we may conclude that in contrast to much of the literature, this study indicates no reason to suppose that the parental home is a source of frustration for this type of hooligan.

The interviews did reveal that the hooligans place a high value on lack of parental interference while at the same time their parents have significantly stronger opinions about leaving their children free. The absence of this supervision factor may be regarded as a characteristic of the hooligan.

School Behaviour and the Attitude to Learning

Table III reveals a close similarity between the delinquents and the hooligans in their attitude to learning. The opinions of the hooligans and the delinquents are less favourable in almost every respect. So it is not to be wondered at that when

TABLE III. ATTITUDE TO LEARNING

	Average for:			Is this difference significant?					
				contr.-delinq.		contr.-hool.		delinq.-hool.	
	contr. N = 68	delinq. N = 35	hool. N = 30	yes/no	P	yes/no	P	yes/no	P
Find it enjoyable	6.3 [1]	6.4	5.5	no [2]	—	yes	.06	no	—
Consider it necessary	9.0	7.9	8.6	yes	.005	yes	.10	no	—
Continuing voluntarily	7.9	7.1	7.0	yes	.09	yes	.06	no	—
Pay attention	7.8	6.7	6.4	yes	.01	yes	.001	no	—
Consider it important	8.9	8.4	8.5	yes	.10	no	—	no	—
Find it fine	6.2	5.7	5.2	no	—	yes	.03	no	—
Find it interesting	7.6	6.4	6.7	yes	.01	yes	.05	no	—
Plan to continue as long as possible	4.9	4.1	3.9	yes	.08	yes	.04	no	—

[1] and [2] See notes following Table II.

TABLE IV. CONDUCT AT SCHOOL

	Average for:			Is this difference significant?					
	contr.	delinq.	hool.	contr.-delinq.		contr.-hool.		delinq.-hool.	
	N = 69	N = 35	N = 30	yes/no	P	yes/no	P	yes/no	P
Often played truant	1.7 [1]	4.8	3.4	yes	.0001 [2]	yes	.003	yes	.06
difficult pupil	4.1	6.4	5.5	yes	.0001	yes	.006	yes	.09

[1] and [2] See notes following Table II.

given the choice between continuing their education and going to work both categories show significantly more preference for the latter than do the boys of the control group. The fact that both the hooligans and the delinquents said they did not like school is fully consonant with this finding.

A similar attitude to learning is found amongst the parents. Significantly more parents of hooligans and delinquents consider knowledge to be of minor importance and see less need for continued education than do the parents of the boys in the control group.

Table IV shows that the hooligans and delinquents also differ from the boys in the control group in their conduct at school.

Though the hooligans were more often guilty of truancy and were more difficult at school than the boys of the control group, their record in this respect is less unfavourable than that of the delinquents.

The Work Situation

Many writers feel that hooliganism can be explained as a reaction to an unsatisfactory work situation. The work supposedly offers no opportunities for self-realization (Unesco report, 1958), has become impersonal in character (see Rose, 1961) and no longer provides status (Kaiser, 1959). The research project therefore devoted a great deal of attention to these problems. Table V shows what the members of the various groups think of their work.

TABLE V. EVALUATION OF WORK

	Average for:			Is this difference significant?					
	contr.	delinq.	hool.	contr.-delinq.		contr.-hool.		delinq.-hool.	
	N = 49 [1]	N = 28	N = 23	yes/no	P	yes/no	P	yes/no	P
Work ideal	6.1 [2]	5.1	6.6	yes	.05 [3]	no	–	yes	.04
Work satisfactory	7.0	6.1	7.9	yes	.10	no	–	yes	.02
Plans to continue in present employment	6.5	5.3	7.4	yes	.09	no	–	yes	.03

[1] This question was not put to boys still at school.
[2] and [3] See notes following Table II.

It is clear from this table that there is no difference between the hooligans and the control group in their opinions of their jobs. The delinquents, however, judge their work significantly less favourably than the other two groups.

Nor is there any difference between the hooligans and the control group as regards their attitude to work.

This tallies with the findings of Bondy et al. (1957) and Kaiser (1959). The delinquents differed significantly from the other groups in this respect as well. The p-values concerned were .02 and .001 respectively. In their relations with the people at work, there was no difference between the three groups. It is true, however, that neither the hooligans nor the delinquents cared much what the boss thought of them. No differences were found to exist between the three groups as regards the status attached to work. Consequently, Kaiser's hypothesis could not be confirmed.

Factors Connected with Persons and Types

Holmberg's study (1957) shows that there is also something to be said for taking note of personality characteristics. For this aspect of the study, tests and self-evaluation techniques were used. The following group picture of the hooligans was formed on the basis of the difference found to exist between them and the control group. They have little ambition, enjoy being conspicuous, have a large number of friends at a purely superficial level, approve wholeheartedly of adventure and fighting, are more quick-tempered, become bored more easily, dislike being alone, have a more materialistic attitude and do not feel uncertain of themselves.

As far as their emotional life is concerned, there is no reason to assume that the hooligans are any worse off than the subjects of the control group. Nor do they differ from the boys of the control group with respect to variables such as loneliness, lack of love and general frustration.

Using the same procedure for the delinquents, the following group picture emerges: they have fewer ambitions, dislike being alone, find it more difficult to make contact with others, are more hot tempered, have less self control and are more materialistic than the control group.

Their emotional life is far from ideal. They are more lonely, receive less love, feel a greater need to be cosseted, have more unfulfilled desires and feel more frustrated. In this respect they also differ greatly from the hooligans.

Comments on Society

A number of familiar, stereotyped comments on society—such as 'There's not much these days that's worth putting yourself out for'—were presented to the subjects as statements. Table VI shows how they reacted. The delinquents are significantly more in agreement with these statements than the boys of the control group. For the hooligans, this applies only to the first statement.

The extent to which the members of the three groups felt war to be imminent was also investigated. Several writers, such as Muchow (1959), Mik (1961) and

TABLE VI. OPINIONS ON CERTAIN ASPECTS OF MODERN SOCIETY

	Percentage per Group Supporting Statement			Is this difference significant?					
	contr. N = 69	delinq. N = 35	hool. N = 30:42 N = 29:63	contr.-delinq. yes/no	P	contr.-hool. yes/no	P	delinq.-hool. yes/no	P
42: There's not much these days that's worth putting yourself out for	20.3	34.3	46.7	yes	.09 [1]	yes	.007	no	—
42: If you want to get anywhere you have to leave the country	5.8	20.0	6.7	yes	.03	no	—	no	—
63: If you want to get ahead you have to be ruthless	56.5	71.4	58.6	yes	.10	no	—	no	—

[1] x^2 was applied.

TABLE VII. INTERESTS

	Average for:			Is this difference significant?					
	contr. N = 69	delinq. N = 35	hool. N = 30	contr.-delinq. yes/no	P	contr.-hool. yes/no	P	delinq.-hool. yes/no	P
Foreign affairs	3.82	3.01	1.63	no	–	yes	.008	(no	–) [1]
Politics	3.72	2.78	1.85	yes	.09	yes	.005	(no	–)
Social questions	2.79	2.15	1.22	no	–	yes	.002	(no	–)
Youth work	4.33	4.02	2.64	no	–	yes	.015	(no	–)
Technology	5.22	5.99	3.68	no	–	yes	.014	(no	–)
Space exploration	5.61	4.40	3.88	yes	.05	yes	.01	no	–
Foreign countries	6.13	6.23	4.49	no	–	yes	.009	(no	–)
Sports	8.04	6.58	6.50	yes	.006	yes	.005	no	–
Television	5.01	5.04	6.47	no	–	yes	.02	(no	–)
Classical music	3.32	2.27	0.8	yes	.063	yes	.0001	(no	–)

[1] For all values enclosed in parentheses the difference is not significant because the hooligans' score is different from that expected on the basis of the original hypothesis. This does not alter the fact that the hooligans differ widely from the delinquents on each of these variables.

Perquin (1959) set the behaviour of hooligans against the background of the possibility of a third world war. Contrary to what might have been expected, it transpired that the thought of war is a more significant factor among the control group than among the hooligans or the delinquents.

Interests

There also proved to be wide differences between the interests of various groups, as is shown in Table VII.

This Table indicates that the hooligans were less interested in each of the points listed than were the boys in the control group. That general lack of interest also extends to other areas—to associational life, for instance, which finding tallies with that of Kaiser (1959) and Seelmann (1957). They join clubs significantly less often and rarely have anything in the way of a hobby.

The delinquents occupy a middle position here.

Use of Leisure Time

This lack of interest on the part of the hooligans is reflected in the way they spend their leisure time. They differ in this respect from the boys of the control group in that they spend less time in clubs, participate less in sports, devote less time to a hobby, participate less in evening courses, donate less time to charity campaigns and visit others less often. What, then, does the hooligan actually do? He proved to spend more of his free time in the streets than at home, to be more addicted to rowdyism and fighting, and to go out, visit a cafe or cafeteria, play cards and go out dancing more often. Finally, the hooligans were found to be bored significantly more often than the boys of the other research groups.

Comparison of hooligans and delinquents reveals that the former remain home less often, spend less time on their hobbies, go to a club less often and, when they do go, find it less enjoyable. On the other hand, they hang around the streets more, stir up trouble more often and spend more time playing cards and listening to records.

Conclusion

There are a number of persistent stereotypes about hooligans. One repeatedly hears that their behaviour is related to some undesirable situation in their lives—the parental home for instance, which is depicted as an unhappy home, where they find no understanding from their parents, are neglected, do not receive enough love, etc. This in turn gives rise to the tensions and frustration later released in the streets. A similar argument is applied to the work situation of the unskilled labourer. His work is sheer drudgery, offering him no fulfilment and denying him all opportunity to be creative. He lacks the satisfaction of having produced something. He can neither be himself nor express himself in his work, with the result that he is forced to seek a sphere in which he can be himself. He finds it in the streets, which afford him the opportunity to blow off steam and to express himself.

Another cause to which hooligans' behaviour is attributed is modern society: its numerous dictums on what is permissible and what is not; its increasing depersonalization together with the loss of personal contacts, the growing isolation this involves, and so on. The hooligan is struggling to resist this process, and his conduct is aimed at drawing attention to our social ills. His misbehavior should be a warning to us. It is even claimed that these boys are the elite of our youth, refusing as they do to accept the situation and trying in their own way to bring the problem to our attention.

The final point to be mentioned here is the ever-present threat of a third world war. We are all living, so the argument goes, on the volcano of total destruction by an atomic war. It is a political situation that the young people have inherited from their elders. So why should they have any respect for those elders? Another theory advances fatalism as the cause of the problem: there's no point in anything; one bomb and it's all over. So why bother to observe restrictive norms? Do as you like. Enjoy yourself while you can.

Our research showed quite plainly that none of these 'romantic' explanations could be confirmed. The hooligans do not complain of their parents or their upbringing. They do not feel misunderstood. On the contrary, they have a rather positive attitude toward their parents. As far as their attitude toward their work is concerned, they are no different from boys who do not indulge in their sort of behaviour. The value they attach to their work is no less than that of the boys in the control group. Occasionally, there is even a reverse tendency observable. As to the status attached to their work, the hooligans place their work higher.

Moreover, there was no real difference between the hooligans and the non-troublemakers as regards their opinion of society.

The war factor can be discarded altogether: the thought of a third world war never occurs to these boys.

Our findings indicate quite clearly that hooligans' behaviour should not be regarded as an attitude of resistance, as a reaction to certain social ills. *The hooligans are characterized by a general lack of interest.* School interests them very little; they have no interest in learning; they are not concerned about what their boss may think of them; they are devoid of all ambition; they consider that there is very little nowadays that's worth bothering about. Politics, social questions, technology, sports, etc. do not interest them very much. They have little desire for club life and have virtually no hobbies. This general lack of interest might be described as their hall-mark.

The Participant Study

The interviews indicated that many of the hooligans met regularly in a certain cafeteria. Two carefully chosen participant observers were then stationed in the cafeteria. For more than three months they shared the joys and sorrows of the group, turning in daily reports on what they saw and experienced. Lack of space restricts us to a summary of the results of this part of the research project. In general it may be stated that they closely resemble those obtained from the interviews: lack of interest, much time spent just hanging about, intense boredom, uncouthness with outsiders, stirring up trouble on specific occasions and provocation, though the latter was largely confined to situations in which there was no alternative.

Another point worth mentioning here is the group structure. Unlike that of gangs of delinquents, it was not very cohesive. There was no leader in the usual sense of the word, the leadership changing as it were, according to the situation. Nor were there any seconds-in-command. The group had no fixed composition; its membership changed constantly. Group cohesion and inter-solidarity were entirely lacking, so that their association had a curious 'no-obligations' character. The interrelationships were not very close. Anyone wishing to join in was welcome and everyone was free to come and go as he pleased.

Some writers, such as Mik (1961) and Racine et al (1965) point to the presence of homosexual tendencies in groups such as these. We found no evidence of this. Heterosexual activities were frequently observed: the opposite sex, in fact, constituted one of the few subjects in which the boys were genuinely interested.

Finally, our participant observation provided a good opportunity to find out whether these hooligans also commit property offences. This turned out not to be the case.

Comparison of Hooligans and Delinquents Convicted of Property Offences

We were able to confirm what we had suspected from the results already obtained from the comparative study. For differences between the hooligans and the group of delinquents convicted of property offenses were discovered in a large number of areas (parental home, work situation, emotional life, attitude toward society, etc.).

A third method was used to determine whether these hooligans and delinquents belong to separate categories. This was the follow-up study. The police dossiers of the subjects were obtained two and a half years after the interviews for the comparative study. It turned out that half of the delinquents had again been convicted of property offenses. The relevant percentages for the hooligans and the control group were 4 and 7 respectively, while, in addition, one-quarter of the hooligans had been before the Court for acts of aggression, (molesting passers-by, obstruction, etc.).

It may thus be stated that hooligans and young delinquents convicted of property offenses from two separate categories.

Disturbance-prevention Experiment

The final part of the project was an attempt in the form of a field experiment to prevent the outbreak of collective hooliganism. Observation of a large number of such riots had shown that in this type of situation a certain recurrent pattern can be distinguished. For a riot to take place there must be a crowd; people gather at the scene of a potential disturbance in the expectation of something happening; if time passes without anything happening, they tend to disperse; this tendency is checked the moment something happens to strengthen the original expectation; an it-will-happen-now atmosphere precedes the disturbance; verbal activities (shouting, abuse) usher in acts of minor destruction (twisting and bending traffic signs). All of these events create a certain mood which is a prerequisite for the following phase: the outbreak of collective vandalism.

In short, it may be stated that two groups of factors play an important part in the development of a riot. One might be termed disturbance-stimulative (the presence of the general public, the expectation that something is about to happen, etc.) and the other disturbance-preventive (absence of preliminary activities, dispersal of the general public).

The field experiment was based on the idea of strengthening the disturbance-preventive factors and neutralizing the disturbance-stimulative factors.

Design of the Experiment

The experiment took place in a street noted for its rioting every New Year's Eve. This traditional site was chosen because it enabled us to judge the effect of our experiment by comparing the events of that year with those of the year before and the year after.

The following method was used. A group of 23 co-workers (predominantly students) was distributed in pairs along the street. They had three tasks: to undermine the expectation of the general public that something would happen;

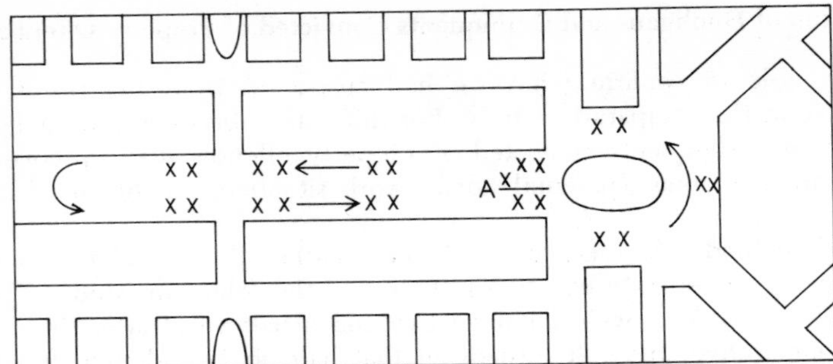

FIG. 1. DIAGRAM OF DISTURBANCE-PREVENTION EXPERIMENT. EACH CROSS REPRESENTS A CO-WORKER. THE ARROWS INDICATE THE DIRECTION IN WHICH THEY WALKED.

to stop at once any action that could lead to the definite outbreak of a riot; and to attempt to get the teenagers out of the area by drawing their attention to alternative activities.

They set about their work as follows. At a prearranged signal (given as part of a fireworks display) they mingled with the general public and began to make undermining comments to the effect that nothing was going to happen that night (It is dull here tonight; nothing is going to happen tonight; there's no chance of anything happening; nothing ever happens anymore, etc.). After a while a second theme was added: to leave (Let's go; it's late; nothing will happen now anyway; everyone is going home, I even saw the police leave; Where is Jan? Oh, he has already gone home. And Piet? He didn't bother to come. He said it would be a wash-out. Next year, you won't find me here either. Come on, there's a good programme on television, etc.).

As the pairs of co-workers walked in a pre-determined direction (see diagram) the public was constantly confronted with people announcing that nothing was going to happen. It was hoped that this theme would gradually be taken over by members of the public.

In addition, they worked their way into certain groups and then suggested going somewhere else to see if there was anything going on there. Their third instruction was to put an immediate stop to the activities that generally precede riots (speaking choruses, shouting, etc.), for which purpose they carried cigarettes. As soon as there was danger of anything happening at any point they approached and broke up these activities by offering cigarettes and wishing everyone a happy New Year, following this up with the usual conversation on the subject of how dull it all was, etc.

Results of the Experiment

Evaluation of a field experiment such as the one described is not easy. In retrospect, the following may be stated:

1. The co-workers succeeded in introducing to the general public the idea that nothing would happen.
2. This theme was taken over by part of the general public.

3. They managed to get several groups of teenagers out of the way.
4. They checked a number of preliminary activities.

Comparing the occurrences of that evening with those of the preceding and the following year, two things become obvious.

First, the atmosphere during the experiment was completely different. Generally speaking this type of disturbance is accompanied by an almost tangible tension that erupts at a given moment into collective vandalism. On this occasion there was no tension worth speaking of. Second, the number of destructive acts was confined to two of a comparatively minor nature. This was considerably less (quantitatively as well as qualitatively) than in the years immediately before and after.

On the other hand, we were unable to prevent a number of undesirable actions and the necessity for police intervention. We nevertheless feel justified in assuming that this field experiment had a positive influence on the events of the evening and we believe, therefore, that it is possible to influence mass behaviour with this type of social-psychological technique.

Hooligans' Behaviour: a Theory

As stated in the foregoing, our findings lend no support to the notion that hooligans' behaviour is a form of resistance. How, then, can that behaviour be explained? On the basis of the results of the comparative and participant studies, we incline to the view that hooligans' behaviour is simply a leisure-time activity at those moments when there is nothing else offering.

It is no longer a truism that one's spare time can be employed as one wishes. The degree of success depends on the means [4] and the amount of time available. It is clear that 'nature' has endowed the hooligan with a minimal share in most of those means. On the other hand, he has a great deal of free time.[5] That lack of means, however, creates a situation whereby his personal input as regards his use of leisure time is continuously low. Consequently, he is dependent to a large extent on others and on what happens around him. That is why hooligans are always to be found where there is a chance of something happening. This imbalance between the available means and the leisure time to be filled leads to boredom. The participant study shows quite plainly that they try to dispel that boredom with the aid of provocative action of one sort or another. The hooligan is not continuously provocative; he acts in that way only when he has nothing else to do. His provocative behaviour is instrumental in character.

Notes

1. I am indebted to Professor Mauk Mulder for his moral and technical support.

2. G. Kaiser, *Randalierende Jugend* (Riotous Youth; 1959) p. 126.
'. . . One can generally conceive of youth excesses being sociologically situated between the extremes of norm-conforming and well-adapted behaviour on the one hand, and behaviour arising from severe neglect or outright criminality on the other.'

3. In view of the large number of questions asked per topic, we must restrict ourselves to a partial description of the data.

4. By 'means' is understood everything that might be construed as a leisure time activity (hobbies, skills, interest, club membership, general knowledge, etc.).

5. We are not concerned here with the origins of the situation, though it will have considerable bearing on the prevention of hooliganism in the future.

URBANIZATION AND MALE DELINQUENCY IN GHANA

S. *Kirson Weinberg*

Along with the political emancipation and rapid technological advances in Ghana, West Africa, the concomitant processes of urbanization have brought higher standards of living, educaton, and medical care; but they have also wrought increased rates of desertion, prostitution, crime, and delinquency.[1] Our central aim in this report is to trace the effects of urbanization on male delinquency in Accra, Ghana.[2] Urbanization continuously affects the local community, the family, and the school, which in turn affect the incidence of delinquent behavior.

This approach—urbanization as a contributing factor in delinquency—is different from particularistic versions, which regard urbanization as an implicit context within which to analyze the influence of a single social unit such as the local community or family.[3] Instead, this study seeks to resolve the mode of influence of urbanization upon the loci and practices of delinquents. One view maintains that, with urbanization, delinquency predominates in urban centers and is negligible in villages and rural areas. Another view contends that delinquent behavior increases with the spread of urbanization because delinquency increases not only in urban centers but also in villages.[4]

Our theses are, first, that the disorganization resulting from urbanization affects the city, adjacent villages, and the villages from which people emigrate; second, that delinquent behavior represents a mode of adaptation to urban living by lower-class youth who have become alienated from the family and the school system and are in a marginal social position. In this situation, they often turn to deviant peers on the street for guidance.

Subjects and Procedures

We studied 107 male offenders against property in the Remand School in Accra, the capital of Ghana. We compared their histories and records with ninety-five

Reprinted by permission of the author and publisher from *Journal of Research in Crime and Delinquency,* July 1965, pp. 85–94.

male students, ten to eighteen, in primary and middle schools in and about Accra, to study their differences of adjustment to a society whose customs and institutions differ somewhat from those of Western societies.

Since we regarded male delinquent behavior as emergent from slums, we visited slum areas and villages about Accra and consulted seven adult Ghanaians on family organization, modes of social control, and juvenile behavior in the isolated as well as in the changing tribal villages.

The Urbanization Process

Ghana combines British political, legal, and educational influences with indigenous tribal customs and institutions. English is its official language, and its judicial and legal systems and correctional institutions are predominantly British in conception. But its family organization, interpersonal attitudes, and basic belief systems incline to the tribal and traditional.[5]

Accra combines both local and Western characteristics because urbanization in Africa preceded Western influence. Industrializaton, which is Western-oriented, is not widespread. Commerce, on the other hand, is widely developed; and a vast administrative bureaucracy exists. The urbanization of Accra depends less on its industrialization than on its governing bureaucracy, commerce, and retail trade. Its Western prototype would be Washington, D. C., rather than Chicago.

Consistent with the rapid, even explosive, population increase in cities in less developed nations, Accra has attracted many rural people since World War II; its resident population is about 490,000. The advent of the truck as a public conveyance and the recently built paved roads have enabled many migrants in search of work and "fortune" in the big city to flock to Accra. By 1954, 48 percent of the inhabitants of Accra were not of the Gas tribe (the aboriginal tribal group), and these migrants "were drawn from practically every tribal division in the country and beyond." The spatial proximity and mingling of culturally diverse peoples have influenced changes in social values; mobility and impersonality have led to declining community and family controls; kinship status is being replaced, increasingly, by occupational status; and cultural conflicts between immigrant parents and their children have contributed to conditions which motivate youths in the lower strata to stray into delinquency. Similar effects of urbanization in South Africa have been noted by Williamson:

> An important factor in producing criminal behavior is culture conflict. This discontinuity is seen in the movement of hundreds of thousands of Bantus from the "Veld," the native reserves, and even other parts of Africa to the cities where a new set of physical and personal associations surrounds the individual. There is a breakdown in primary controls that follows detribalization with the introduction of cash economy, accelerated mobility, personal anonymity, and new leisure time pursuits. . . . One aspect of nonconforming behavior has been gang life among the (African) juvenile offenders.[6]

Urbanization as a total process which affects the city and disrupts villages differs from the definition of urbanism which refers to urban characteristics such as size, density, heterogeneity, mobility, and impersonalism.[7] As a consequence of urbanization, youths and adults who migrated to the cities in great numbers disrupted the kinship structure and left a residual preponderance of young children, women, and aged people in the villages. Within the city, on the other hand, single men and men separated from their families are in the majority. This condition has disrupted the controls within the family and has increased the influence of the street and local community, with a consequent decline in social control.[8]

Within the city, there were so many unattached young men that the sex prestige of the women rose and the demand for prostitutes increased. This large number of unattached males also contributed to declining informal and family controls and to the increase in criminal behavior. In Accra, the Zambrama has a ratio of 65 women to 1,000 men. And though the Hausas and Fulani of Nigeria and the Liberians and Wangara who brought their wives with them had about an equal sex ratio, the Mossi and Busanga had about 300 women to 1,000 males; and the Kotokoli migrants had the relatively high female-male ratio of 511 to 1,000 because many Kotokoli women migrated to Accra to become prostitutes.[9]

Massive migration to the city created problems not only of housing, employment, and sanitation, but also of institutional controls and outlets for youths, except perhaps within the family and the school system. But the disorganized family could not fulfill this functon, and the school that did not understand and cope with wayward youth could not sustain their interest or control their behavior.

This flow of migration to the city was stimulated by the many migrants who retained their tribal village identity and who periodically returned to impress the villagers with their gifts and city exploits. For example, 71 percent of the Zambrama who had resided in Accra less than two years saved most of their earnings so they could return to the village. On the day a Zambrama returned to his village, he acted like a king; he distributed presents to the villagers until he had almost nothing left for himself. The migrant impressed the villagers by exaggerating the amount of wealth attainable in the city.[10] As a result many village youths regarded farming, village crafts, or herbalistic medicine as unappealing occupational roles. They viewed emigration to the city as a sign of adulthood. Since they no longer depended upon the father for sustenance or for the bride price, they could also be in an economic position to select the bride of their choice. Thus, youths who contemplated emigration to the city, in effect, acquired a new freedom from traditional parental controls and were more reluctant to emulate the occupations of their fathers or uncles. They became less responsive to social controls.

Roving gangs of delinquents directly affected delinquency in the village. For example, the "Pilot" boys in Sekondi-Takoradi acted as guides to sightseers and as procurers who directed European sailors to prostitutes. They were also skilled thieves who robbed drunken sailors. Periodically, they roamed the countryside and invaded nearby villages to recruit credulous youngsters to steal money from their parents and relatives. Some youths did run away to join their ranks.[11] Thus, delinquency arose in the village as well as the city as a consequence of declining social controls and of, sometimes, the influence of roving delinquent gangs.

Residence, Rendezvous, and Activities of Delinquents

The residential distribution of juvenile delinquents was more scattered than it is in American cities. As in American cities, they concentrated in and about the central business district, in established areas such as Jamestown and in areas of first settlement such as Nima. On the other hand, some delinquents resided in villages along thoroughfares. Because of nearby roads, these villages combined the characteristics of both the village and the suburb. Day or night, youths could wander to the central business district or to other places where they were not known—such as bus stations—steal, and return home. This type of village differed from the isolated village settlement (the folk society), which lacked access to roads, enabling social control of youth to remain effective.

The aforementioned residential areas of delinquents in Accra vary from those of cities in other countries. In Mexico City, delinquents are concentrated in slum areas near the center of the City. In Caracas, Venezuela, and in Timbuctoo, Mali, delinquents concentrate in slums on the outskirts of the city. In Tokyo, delinquents are distributed throughout the city.[12]

The rendezvous of delinquents, however, frequently varied from their places of abode. Consistently, older delinquents in Accra hung about places of minimal informal and formal controls, such as the cinemas, beaches, bus and train stations, and market places. Even younger delinquents who loitered near homes frequently roamed the city and beyond, straying to places where they wouldn't be known. (In American cities, the rendezvous for delinquents are street corners; in British cities, amusement arcades; in Tokyo, stores adjacent to intersecting thoroughfares.[13]) The rendezvous of delinquents were also near places where their thefts occurred. In these busy areas strangers abounded, portable goods were accessible, social controls were minimal, and escape from detection was optimal.

Thefts consisted mainly of small portable objects, such as food, small articles, or money (usually under fifteen dollars). Delinquents frequently used the money to buy food or attend the cinema. Although some youths engaged in procuring, they seldom engaged in vandalism and were seldom detected for rape or for addiction to Indian hemp or alcohol—although arrests for these offenses are on the increase. They were seldom involved in gang fights. Theft was a means of subsistence as well as an expressive pursuit of excitement. Some older delinquents and youthful vagrants, in fact, resorted to theft as a means of survival. This is the behavior of homeless marginal individuals, of adults as well as juveniles, who are uprooted from the village and kinship group. Many delinquents experienced a sense of rootlessness because of their frequent shifts to different families, their truancies away from the family and school, and their parents' or guardians' indifference to their welfare.

One boy born in Accra became an orphan at three. Placed in a government school, he was dismissed after one year because of truancy and was sent to live with his uncle in Kokampe, a small town. He subsequently left for Kumasi to work at cocoa farming. Again he was placed in school, where he reached the fifth grade. Influenced by delinquent companions he stopped attending school and resisted all efforts to renew his attendance. He spent the days with his companions roaming aimlessly about the city and was finally caught stealing food at the market place.[14]

Gang delinquents, however, sometimes develop systematic stealing practices, as illustrated in the following case:

> Akuetah, a thirteen-year old delinquent, had lived with his mother until he was eight and was then sent to his father. He fought with other boys and was expelled from school, whereupon he returned to live with his mother and grandmother. He became friendly with four older boys who had also dropped out of school; they formed a gang and engaged in predatory practices almost daily. Their routine consisted mainly of stealing money for food or for the evening cinemas. When their mothers left home in the morning for petty trading, they decided upon their activities for the day. Each boy took his turn at stealing enough for the entire group. They also practiced collective stealing. One gang member would buy some article from a woman in the market place and then return to tell her that the person who had sent him was dissatisfied with the product. The woman would follow the boy to see the person and, as soon as she left her stall, the other boys would raid it and steal money and merchandise while the lead boy would flee into the crowd.[15]

Urban Family's Influence Upon Delinquency

Within this urban setting, the traditionally extended kinship group was declining and being replaced by the more flexible conjugal family. The shrinking size of the family, decline of parental authority, and increased influences of the local community and "the street" contributed markedly to the delinquent behavior of youth. One report on African urbanization described the effect of this family change upon delinquency:

> In the past as in many rural areas today, the family or the tribal group was the center of life and the focus of all social activities, whether economic, religious, political or educational. In areas undergoing social change, such familial institutions have been greatly weakened and many reports from Africa have reported the importance of this factor with respect to the emergence of juvenile delinquency.[16]

Polygamy, which remains legal, also diminished because of the economic burden of supporting more than one wife, as well as the rising status of urban women, who demanded more from the husband.[17]

The Gas, an aboriginal tribe in the Accra area, traditionally had a matrilineal family organization in which the mates lived apart and in which family authority was vested in the maternal uncle. But the rising authority of the father in the family was creating familial conflict between the children and the uncle.

The tradition of shifting children to relatives or nonrelatives among many tribes in Ghana and other parts of West Africa became a source of parent-child stress in the urban areas.[18] In the villages, traditional family shifting meant that the child could be physically close to and reared by the extended family. In the urban community, the child's transference to a relative in a distant part of the

TABLE 1. RESIDENT ARRANGEMENTS OF MALE DELINQUENTS AND NONDELINQUENTS: BY PERCENTAGES

Resident Arrangement	Delinquents (N = 107)	Nondelinquents (N = 95)
Both Parents	11.2	38.9
Father Only	17.8	21.1
Mother Only	17.8	9.5
Sibling: Sister or Brother	6.5	7.4
Grandparent	9.3	7.4
Aunt or Uncle	15.0	12.6
Distant Relative or Nonrelative	7.4	3.1
On Their Own	15.0	.0
	100.0	100.0

city or in another city required a drastic readjustment. Thus, what constituted in a village a minor readjustment for a child in an extended family could become in an urban setting a very profound change in a conjugal family.

The comparative prevalence of these family shifts of the delinquent and nondelinquent subjects is shown in Table 1. Only 11.2 percent of the delinquents and 38.9 percent of the nondelinquents resided with their parents. At the other extreme, a significantly higher percentage of delinquents than nondelinquents—7.4 to 3.1—were residing with distant kinsmen or nonrelatives, who were more apt to exploit them than were close kin.

Delinquents were shifted—with significantly more frequency than nondelinquents—for unfavorable reasons, such as parental illness or separation, abuse or neglect by parents or guardian, disciplinary purposes, or truancy from the home. The respective percentages were 42.9 to 13.9. (See Table 2.) Nondelinquents, on the other hand, were shifted more frequently to relatives for favorable reasons, such as better access to school, to learn a trade, for company or for effective rearing, or because parents or relatives migrated and could not keep subject.

The estrangement between parents and delinquent children was more evident than between parents and nondelinquents. Thus, 43 percent of the delinquents but less than 1 percent of the nondelinquents had run away from their family—although some nondelinquents may have withheld this information. Also, with each successive family shift, the tendency toward truancy increased. Thus, the

TABLE 2. TYPE OF FAMILY SHIFTS AMONG DELINQUENTS AND NONDELINQUENTS

Type of Family Shift	Delinquents (N = 133)	Nondelinquents (N = 70)
Favorable	57.1	86.1
Unfavorable	42.9	13.9
	100.0	100.0

$X^2 = 17.471(df - 1)p < .001$

ratio for runaways was 4.1 percent, after the first family shift; 18.2 percent, after the second family shift; 33.3 percent after the third family shift; and 42.8 percent after the fourth family shift. One consequence of this was that 15.0 percent of the delinquents, but none of the nondelinquents, were homeless vagrants.

Delinquents more frequently than nondelinquents come from broken homes brought about by the death or desertion of one or both parents (50.1 and 20.5 percent, respectively). However, the broken home in Ghana (meaning the absence of one parent from the home) does not have the same effect on children as in the United States because many Ghanaian children were not living with their parents at the time of the death or desertion of one. The consequences of the absence of one parent differed for delinquents and nondelinquents. The remaining parent of the delinquents tended to shift them to other families, while the remaining parent of the nondelinquents tended to keep them at home. Furthermore, as is true in America, many families of delinquents and nondelinquents were one-parent arrangements. Fewer delinquents than nondelinquents —17.8 percent, compared with 21.1 percent—resided with the father only, but almost twice as many delinquents as nondelinquents—17.8 percent and 9.5 percent, respectively—resided with the mother only. (See Table 3.)

TABLE 3. PERCENTAGES OF MALE JUVENILE DELINQUENTS AND NONDELINQUENTS IN ACCRA (1957–61) RESIDING WITH MOTHER ONLY AND FATHER ONLY, COMPARED WITH DELINQUENTS IN PHILADELPHIA

	Mother Only	Father Only
Accra		
Nondelinquents	9.5	21.1
Delinquents	17.8	17.8
Philadelphia *		
Male White		
Delinquents	17.9	3.1
First offenders	15.5	2.6
Recidivists	22.0	4.4
Male Negro		
Delinquents	39.4	4.0
First offenders	35.2	3.8
Recidivists	42.1	4.2

* Data taken from T. P. Monahan, "Family Status and the Delinquent Child—A Reappraisal and Some New Findings," *Social Forces*, March 1957, pp. 230–58.

Another parental control of the child relevant to delinquency is the presence of the mother in the home. Since the Ghanaian mother predominantly engaged in petty trading or selling small wares outside the home, the percentages of employment among mothers of delinquents and nondelinquents were not significantly different. In fact, more mothers of nondelinquents than the mothers of delinquents (81.7 and 69.4 percent, respectively) were employed.

Role of the Urban School

The social marginality of the delinquents was reinforced by their truancy from or dropping out of school and did not differ markedly from that of certain American dropouts who remain unemployed because they have so few vocational opportunities in an automated society.[19] Ghanaian dropouts also had, in addition to few vocational outlets, few other institutionalized outlets for constructive participation. The very rapid population growth of the urban community created a condition referred to by one as "over-urbanization," because the urban community could not accommodate the many immigrants and their children with appropriate institutional outlets to help them channel their behavior along conventional lines.[20] In American society, the rapidity of automation as well as migration to the city has created a large residue of urban inhabitants who lack the skills to adjust economically to the urban community.

TABLE 4. GRADES COMPLETED BY MALE DELINQUENTS AND NONDELINQUENTS

Education	Delinquents		Nondelinquents	
	Percent (N = 107)	Percent Cum.	Percent (N = 95)	Percent Cum.
None	13.1	13.1	—	—
Prim. One	.9	14.0	—	—
Prim. Two	1.9	15.9	—	—
Prim. Three	14.9	30.8	—	—
Prim. Four	15.9	46.7	—	—
Prim. Five	17.8	64.5	—	—
Prim. Six	14.9	79.4	16.8	16.8
Mid. Form I	5.6	85.0	16.8	33.6
Mid. Form II	5.6	90.6	43.2	76.8
Mid. Form III	2.8	93.4	17.9	94.7
Mid. Form IV	3.8	97.2	5.3	100.0
Sec. School	2.8	100.0	—	100.0
Total	100.0		100.0	

Since primary education had not been compulsory in the past, 13.1 percent of the delinquents had no schooling, and 84 percent were either truants or dropouts. In addition, 79.4 percent of the delinquents had not progressed beyond the sixth grade, compared with only 16.8 percent of the nondelinquents. (See Table 4.) Social class differences between delinquents and nondelinquents may have, in part, influenced this discrepancy in school attainment. The delinquents were generally in a lower socio-economic stratum, but the disorganized family also contributed to their lack of motivation for attending school.

Peer Associates: The Deviant Outlet for Marginality

Delinquent peers provided companions for the marginal urban youth who did not attend school. These delinquents adopted the youth culture of the street and became emancipated from their parents and adult groups. Rural youths in the folk-village, despite some gang behavior, were controlled and directed by adults.[21] Urban juveniles and youths, because of their association with delinquents, absorbed techniques and rationalizations for stealing and procuring, as well as adopting other forms of deviant and subsistence behavior. Their delinquent behavior was a group practice, learned in the process of peer interaction, on the street away from adults. Of ninety-nine male delinquents about 94 percent were either directly influenced by delinquent associates or congregated at the meeting places of delinquents. Not only was the influence of peers direct, but the delinquent behavior, per se, represented a shared, socialized experience.

Because these experiences involved law violations, the boys acquired a certain solidarity and autonomy in their group behavior which varied with the ages of delinquent associates.

The most cohesive social relationships prevailed among older delinquents. Busia has reported the activities of the gangs of "Pilot Boys" in Sekondi-Tokoradi. Acquah has described the activities of the "Canoe Boys" or "Kaaya Kaaya Boys" in Accra, who slept near stores on the main street or on the beach. They were in no way connected with fishing, and spent their time gambling when not engaged in odd jobs or stealing.[22] This type of cohesive gang, while not necessarily formalized, had a certain autonomy and was motivated by a deviant set of values which alienated it from conventional society.

A looser type of association prevailed among younger delinquents who engaged in mischievous pranks and theft of small articles.

> Kwami, a fourteen-year-old of the Ewe tribes, has lived with his mother since birth, while his father, a goldsmith, has resided in another part of Ghana. At six, Kwami accompanied his mother to the town of Ito, where she sold fish in the market place. Soon after Kwami enrolled in school he became a truant because he resented the hostility of teachers and students and also began to steal pencils and other small items; he was often caught and beaten severely. Kwami also stole money from his mother and, with an associate whom he met while playing soccer near his house, habitually stole from the market place. The two planned an operation in which one would ask the lady at a stall about the cost of articles while the other tried to steal money from the box. When successful, they shared the loot, although the boy who did the actual stealing received the larger share. Kwami said they also stole tin-meats and sweets, which they either consumed or sold. With the stolen money, Kwami and his companion bought clothes and attended movies. They moved about dust bins, collecting empty bottles to be returned for money. They did not steal from farmers because they feared that some would practice juju (black magic) on them.
>
> Kwami and his companion also carried posters advertising the local movie so they would be admitted to the cinema in the evening. Sometimes they roamed to villages about three miles away during school hours or they would wander about town seeking gambling places.
>
> While helping a woman to pack some things in the market place, Kwami stole about five dollars. He was seen by two boys. He went home, buried most of the money, and took a shilling to rent a bicycle. The boys who had witnessed the theft then told him that the woman had threatened to apply juju on the

thief. Severely frightened, Kwami surrendered the money, was arrested, and was committed to the Remand Home.

A third type of social relationship among delinquents consists of aggressive, experienced delinquents inducing a novice to steal from his family or neighbors. The village and neighborhood recruits of the "pilot" boys engaged in this mode of stealing.

In the process of urban adjustment the delinquent youths' recourses to deviation as a way of life were not reactions against middle-class values but a rebellion against adult control and a channelizing of purposeful behavior in their marginal condition. In their search for subsistence and excitement, when no purposeful legitimate institutions were available, they sought guidance from the street society.

Conclusions and Discussion

Within the technologically underdeveloped society of Ghana, the processes of urbanization affect the central city, the villages from which people emigrate, and the villages which are adjacent to cities. These changes create conditions which contribute to delinquency.

The prevalence of delinquency among urban youths in Ghana contrasted with the supposed scarcity of delinquency among youth in disrupted villages does not necessarily obtain. Although delinquency within the city is more widespread than in villages, the youths in those villages adjacent to the city sometimes leave the village to steal in the city.

The rise of delinquency seems to occur when certain youths, willingly or unwillingly, are thrust away from conventional outlets and value systems and become attracted to illegitimate ones. Although this behavior involves a polarity of alternative attractions between legitimate and illegitimate opportunities, it involves, too, a tendency to combine both in a process of subsistence. In the genesis of delinquent behavior, the sequence of experiences includes tension and estrangement from the family, a defiance and an evasion of adult controls emerging from hostility between the parents and children, and an alienation from school frequently stimulated by hostility from peers and the inability of teachers to cope with the youths' misbehavior and with their general lack of motivation. Truancy puts the youths in a culturally marginal position which makes them responsive to deviant influences.

The impact of urbanization upon delinquency obtains cross-culturally in underdeveloped countries and is related to urban growth. Many immigrants who have flocked to the cities have remained unemployed or partly employed. Destitute, living in overcrowded conditions, and desperately seeking subsistence, older boys often resort to subsistence stealing, a pattern of behavior that frequently characterizes the adaptive techniques of youths as well as adults. A cultural lag exists between the needs of some youth and the lack of institutions to channelize their needs; this discrepancy places these youths in a marginal position and impels them to satisfy their needs through deviant conduct with their peers, in the process of adapting to the urban community.

Notes

1. This article was prepared with the assistance of the University of Ghana and the cooperation of the Department of Welfare of Ghana.

2. For a comparison of the differences between delinquents and nondelinquents in Ghana, in which the urban context is considered implicitly as the social framework, see S. K. Weinberg, "Juvenile Delinquency in Ghana: A Comparative Analysis of Delinquents and Non-Delinquents," *Journal of Criminal Law, Criminology and Police Science,* December 1964, pp. 471–81.

3. See, for example, Sheldon and Eleanor Glueck, *Unraveling Juvenile Delinquency* (Cambridge, Mass., Harvard University Press, 1950) pp. 120–35; B. Lander, *Towards an Understanding of Juvenile Delinquency* (New York, Columbia University Press, 1954); and C. R. Shaw and H. D. McKay, *Juvenile Delinquency and Urban Areas* (Chicago, University of Chicago Press, 1942). On the other hand, for an analysis of comparative urbanism and criminal behavior, see M. B. Clinard, "A Cross-Cultural Replication of the Relation of Urbanism to Criminal Behavior," *American Sociological Review,* April 1960, pp. 253–57.

4. "Urbanization in Asia and the Far East," *Proceedings of the Joint UN Unesco Seminar,* Bangkok, August 1956 (Unesco, 1958—S.S. 57) pp. 230–50.

5. See I. Acquah, *Accra Survey* (London, University of London, 1958), pp. 28, 29; and A. Phillips, ed., *Survey of African Marriage and Family Life* (London, Oxford University Press, 1953).

6. See R. Williamson, "Crime in South Africa: Some Aspects of Causes and Treatment," *Journal of Criminal Law, Criminology, and Police Science,* July–August 1957, pp. 187, 188; see also P. C. W. Gutkind, "Congestion and Overcrowding: An African Problem," *Human Organization,* Fall 1960, pp. 129, 130.

7. See L. Wirth, "Urbanism as a Way of Life," *American Journal of Sociology,* July 1938, pp. 1–9; M. B. Clinard, "The Organization of Urban Community Development Services in the Prevention of Crime and Juvenile Delinquency, with Particular Reference to Less Developed Countries," *International Review of Criminal Policy,* No. 19, pp. 3–12; S. K. Weinberg, *Social Problems in Our Times* (Englewood Cliffs, N. J., Prentice-Hall, 1960), pp. 20–42; and J. S. Slotkin, *From Field to Factory* (New York, Free Press, 1960).

8. Acquah, *op. cit. supra,* note 5, pp. 46–54.

9. J. Rouch, "Migrations on Ghana Enquete 1953–1955," *Journal de la Société des Africanistes,* Vol. 26, 1956, pp. 76, 77. (English translation by P. E. O. and J. B. Hangham, Accra, 1954, mimeographed, pp. 17, 18.)

10. *Ibid.,* pp. 121, 122; and M. Herskovitz, *The Human Factor in Changing Africa* (New York, Alfred A. Knopf, 1962), pp. 263–278.

11. K. Busia, *Report on a Social Survey of Sekondi-Tokoradi* (Accra, Government Printing Office, 1950), pp. 21–30.

12. See W. Middendorf, "New Forms of Juvenile Delinquency: Their Origin, Prevention and Treatment," *Second United Nations Congress on the Prevention of Crime and Treatment of Offenders* (New York, United Nations Department of Economic and Social Affairs, 1960), pp. 23–53; H. Miner, *Timbuctoo* (Princeton,

Princeton University Press, 1953); and K. Kashikuma, et al., eds., "Ecological Study of Juvenile Delinquency," *Family Court Record,* Supreme Court, 1958, cited in G. A. DeVos and K. Mizushima, *Research on Delinquency in Japan: An Introductory Review* (University of California [Berkeley], 1960), p. 34.

13. See H. Mannheim, *Juvenile Delinquency in an English Middletown* (London, Kegan Paul, 1948); and J. Abe, et al., "Sociopsychological Study of Delinquency Formation," *Tohoku Correctional Bulletin,* II, No. 1, 1957, pp. 183–211.

14. Case in the author's files.

15. Case in the author's files.

16. "Some Considerations on the Prevention of Juvenile Delinquency in African Countries Experiencing Rapid Social Change," *International Review of Criminal Policy* No. 16 (United Nations publications, No. 61 IV. 2), p. 43.

17. A. Phillips, *op. cit. supra* note 5; P. Fawahoo, "Urbanization and Religion in Eastern Ghana," *Sociological Review,* July 1959, pp. 83, 84.

18. See R. Lystad, *The Ashanti: A Proud People* (New Brunswick, N. J., Rutgers University Press, 1958), pp. 44–72.

19. See J. B. Conant, *Slums and Suburbs* (New York, New American Library of World Literature, 1964), pp. 33–38.

20. Acquah, *op. cit. supra* note 5, pp. 81–85.

21. See M. J. Field, *Social Organization of the Ga People* (London, Crown Agents for the Colonies, 1940); M. Manoukian, *Akan and Ga-Adangme People of the Gold Coast* (London, International African Institute, 1950); and M. Fortes, *The Web of Kinship among the Tallensi* (London, Oxford University Press, 1949), pp. 54–84.

22. See Busia, *op. cit. supra* note 11, pp. 32–35; and Acquah, *op. cit. supra* note 5, p. 54.

A TRAVERS LE CHAOS DES VIVANTES CITÉS[1]

Charles Tilly

Baudelaire sounded the exact note:

> *Fourmillante cité, cité plein de rêves*
> *Ou le spèctre, en plein jour, raccroche le passant.*

How admirable it is, he tells us, to be free of that spectral grasp:

> *Telles vous chéminez, stoïques et sans plaintes*
> *A travers le chaos des vivantes cités.*

"Through the chaos of the living city!" A great motto for the study of collective disorder.

"Under the aegis of the city," declares Lewis Mumford, "violence . . . became normalized, and spread far beyond the centers where the great collective

Reprinted by permission of the author and the International Sociological Association.

manhunts and sacrificial orgies were first instituted." [2] Again we encounter the image of the city as destroyer, of urban life as the solvent of social bonds, of violence as the price paid for living on the large scale. While peasant revolts leave faded souvenirs here and there, the word "revolution" recalls city streets. As deprived millions limp hopefully into the cities of Africa or Latin America, political observers hold their breaths. When will the cities explode? Urbanization, it seems to go without saying, means social disorder.

It does, in a way. Huge wars and devastating revolutions came into man's life only with the flowering of cities. But whether urbanization and collective violence have a necessary or a contingent connection—or, indeed, any genuine causal connection at all—is far from clear.

Some small observations on the nature of that connection form the substance of this essay. I want to comment on the ways urbanization might incite or transform collective violence, raise some questions about the relationship between violent and nonviolent forms of political participation, sketch some means for investigating the political consequences of urbanization, and review some relevant but quite preliminary findings from a study of the evolution of political disturbances in France since 1830.

Why and how does urbanization affect collective violence? Sociologists have some well-fixed ideas on the subject. After stressing the disruptive personal effects of migration and the "frictions" produced by the rubbing together of urban and pre-urban value systems in expanding cities, Philip Hauser tells us that:

> Another group of serious problems created or augmented by rapid rates of urbanization are those of internal disorder, political unrest, and governmental instability fed by mass misery and frustration in the urban setting. The facts that the differences between the "have" and "have not" nations, and between the "have" and "have not" peoples within nations, have become "felt differences," and that we are experiencing a "revolution in expectations," have given huge urban population agglomerations an especially incendiary and explosive character.[3]

In Hauser's view, the breaking of traditional bonds and the conflict of values feed disorder, while the swelling city's combination of misery and heightened hopes nearly guarantees it. Change produces tension, tension breaks out in collective explosions, and a form of action more frenzied than that of stable, developed countries erupts into life.

Hauser's analysis, I believe, sums up the predominant sociological position. Seen from the outside, the set of ideas looks solid and chinkless. Unpeeled, it reveals gaps and tangles. For one thing, it contains a notion of the equivalence of different types of disorder. Personal malaise, moral deviation, crime, and political upheaval are supposed to flow into each other.

Almost mystically, Louis Chevalier announces that essential unity: outside the major outbursts, he says,

> The political and social violence which has been studied so often and so minutely is replaced by other forms of violence—more continuous, more complex, harsher, involving greater numbers, taking from the rise and the bulk

of the masses their progress, their unity and their force. Here is another form of connection among crises: Private dramas, daily ones, add their weight to the public ones, developing outside them, but accumulating and culminating in them.[4]

Chevalier does not hesitate to call nineteenth-century Paris a sick city, or to consider misery, crime, suicide, street violence, and popular rebellion so many expressions of the same pervasive pathology. That is one side of the standard sociological formulation.

Turn this set of ideas over. On the other side is stamped a complementary set: that there is a sharp disjunction between healthy and pathological social states, between the normal and the abnormal, between order and disorder, which justifies treating different specimens of disapproved collective behavior as manifestations of the same general phenomenon—"deviance." The responses which other people give to the disapproved behavior win another general label—"social control."

Collective violence almost automatically receives both the complementary treatments. It is easy to treat it as the final expression of a fundamental pathology which also shows up as crime, delinquency, family instability, or mental illness. It is even easier to treat it as radically discontinuous from orderly political life. Long before Taine and Le Bon had dismissed the mass actions of the French Revolution as the work of demonic guttersnipes, Plato had shuddered over the outbreaks of man's "lawless wild-beast nature, which peers out in sleep," and James Madison had warned of "an unhappy species of the population . . . who, during the calm of regular government, are sunk below the level of men; but who, in the tempestuous scenes of civil violence, may emerge into the human character, and give a superiority of strength to any party with which they may associate themselves."

More recently, Hannah Arendt has argued that "violence is a marginal phenomenon in the political realm . . . ," that "political theory has little to say about the phenomenon of violence and must leave its discussion to the technicians," that "insofar as violence plays a predominant role in wars and revolutions, both occur outside the political realm."[5] And the political realm, to Miss Arendt's mind, contains normal social life.

Here two ideas intertwine. One is that violence appeals to the beast in man and to the beasts among men. The other is that men in becoming violent step over an abyss which then separates them from coherent rationality.

Despite their devotion to death-dealing automobiles, aggressive detectives, and murderous wars, it is true that men ring round most forms of interpersonal violence with extraordinary tabus and anxieties. Yet collective violence is one of the commonest forms of political participation. Why *begin* an inquiry into the effects of urbanization with the presumption that violent politics appear only as a disruption, a deviation, or a last resort? After all, Sorokin encountered eighty-odd significant "internal disturbances" in general histories of western European countries during the nineteenth century alone; he could, in fact, have found many more. Rather than treating collective violence as an unwholesome deviation from normality, we might do better to ask under what conditions (if any) violence disappears from ordinary political life.

That is, however, a mischievous question. The treatment of collective behavior in terms of change: tension—tension-release and the assumption of drastic discontinuity between routine politics and collective violence cling to each other. Most students of large-scale social change cling to both. Challenging either the fit between the two notions or their independent validity therefore smacks of rabble-rousing. Yet there are some alternatives we cannot simply ignore.

First, collective violence often succeeds. Revolutionaries do come to power, machine-breakers do slow the introduction of labor-saving devices, rioters do get public officials removed. The local grain riot, so widespread in western Europe from the seventeenth through the nineteenth centuries, often produced a temporary reduction of prices, forced stored grain into the market, and stimulated local officials to new efforts at assuring the grain supply. I do not mean that by some universal calculus violence is more efficient than nonviolence. I simply mean that it works often enough in the short run, by the standards of the participants, not to be automatically dismissed as a flight from rational calculation.

Second, whether or not it succeeds in the short run and by the standards of the participants, collective protest is often a very effective means of entering or remaining in political life, of gaining or retaining an identity as a force to be reckoned with. Eugene Debs boasted that "no strike has ever been lost" and American advocates of Black Power consider their appeal the only means of mobilizing Negroes as an effective political force. Although there are always Revisionists to argue that the dispossessed will gain power more cheaply by circumventing revolution, even though the Revisionists are often right, collective violence does frequently establish the claim to be heard, and feared. In that sense, too, it can be a rational extension of peaceful political action.

Third, acts of collective violence often follow a well-defined internal order. The order goes beyond the Freudian logic of dreams or that symbolic correspondence Smelser finds between the beliefs embodied in collective movements and the strains which produce them. In many cases it is sufficiently conscious, explicit, and repetitive to deserve the name "normative." Many western countries on the eve of intensive industrialization, for example, have seen a recurrent sort of redressing action against what the people of a locality consider to be violations of justice: mythical avenging figures like Rebecca or Ned Ludd, threats posted in their names, outlandish costumes (women and Indians being favorite masquerades), routine, focussed, roughly appropriate punishments inflicted on the presumed violators of popular rights. Disorder displays a normative order.

Fourth, the participants in collective violence are frequently rather ordinary people. The recent studies of popular disturbances in France and England by Rudé, Thompsom, Soboul, Rose, Cobb, Vovelle, and many others have shifted the burden of proof to those who wish to claim that mass actions recruit from the lunatic fringe. Not that these studies portray the recruitment as a kind of random sampling; real grievances, economic conditions, established paths of communication, the character of local politics all help determine who take part. But the rioters and machine-breakers commonly turn out to be fairly ordinary people acting on important but commonplace grievances. Louis Chevalier's "dangerous classes" stay out of sight.

Finally, the large-scale structural changes of societies which transform everyday politics through their effects on the organization, communication, and common consciousness of different segments of the population also transform the character and loci of collective violence. As the scale at which men organize their peaceful political actions expands, so does the scale at which they organize their violence. As workers in mechanized industries become a coherent political force, they also become a source of disorder. The correlations are obviously complex and imperfect; that is precisely why they are interesting. But they are correlations rather than antitheses.

So there are five reasons for hesitating to assume that collective violence is a sort of witless release of tension divorced from workaday politics: its frequent success as a tactic, its effectiveness in establishing or maintaining a group's political identity, its normative order, its frequent recruitment of ordinary people, and its tendency to evolve in cadence with peaceful political action. The five points are debatable and worthy of debate . . . not to mention empirical investigation. To the extent that they are valid, they lead to somewhat different expectations from the usual ones concerning the development of political disturbances in the course of urbanization.

Urbanization *could* affect collective violence in three main ways: by disrupting existing social ties and controls, by exposing more individuals and groups to urban institutions and living conditions, and by changing relations between city and country. In fact, an abundant (if largely theoretical and anecdotal) literature asserts the disturbing effects of each of these changes. The disruption of ties and controls is commonly supposed to incite disorder either by removing restraints to impulses which would under normal circumstances be muffled or by inducing anxiety in individuals detached from stable, orderly surroundings. Mass migration to cities is the standard example. Exposure to urban institutions and living conditions is usually considered to promote collective violence in two respects: (1) by imposing intolerable privations in the form of material misery and unfamiliar disciplines or (2) by communicating new goals via heightened communication within large groups sharing common fates and interests, and via the diffusion of higher standards of comfort and welfare from the existing urban population to the newcomers. Thus rapid urban growth is said to exacerbate the "revolution of rising expectations." The changing relations between city and country are often thought to engender disturbance in the country itself as cities expand their claims for goods, men, taxes, and subordination, while rural communities resist those claims. So regions of distinct tribal character presumably become ripe for rebellion.

If the disruption of existing ties and controls, the exposure of individuals and groups to urban institutions and living conditions, and the changing relations between city and country all uniformly encourage collective violence, then matters are delightfully simple: the pace and location of upheaval should be closely correlated with the pace and location of urban growth. That hypothesis easily lends itself to testing. Surprisingly, it has not yet been truly tested.

Even in the absence of good data on either side of the relationship, however, we may legally doubt whether it is so splendidly straightforward. In no western European country have the peak years of urban growth since 1800 also been the peak years of political upheaval. In trying out crude measures on various samples of contemporary nations, Eckstein, Germani, Kornhauser, Lipset, and Soares have all felt impelled to push on to more complicated explanations.

Happily, the various components of urbanization also lend themselves to separate analysis. We can to some extent isolate the political correlates of rapid migration from rural areas to large cities, of miserable urban living conditions, or of the expansion of central control into the rural backland. Rather than the amassing of case studies of violence or the statistical manipulation of general indices drawn from samples of whole countries, two strategies getting at differentials within countries seem particularly suitable. The first is to compare segments of the country—communities, regions, classes, as well as periods—in terms of the frequency and intensity of collective violence, of the forms violence takes, of the participants in it. Whereas international comparisons ordinarily make it tough to disentangle the correlates of urban poverty from those of rapid migration to cities, and case studies usually hide the significance of negative instances, systematic comparisons within countries promise the opportunity to examine the differences between turbulent and placid periods or settings in meaningful detail, with reasonable controls.

The second strategy is to separate—and, where possible, to index—the appearance of different *forms* of collective violence. This means eschewing summary indices of "turbulence" or "instability." It also means paying as much attention to variations in the form of collective outbursts as to shifts from calm to fury and back again. Here the illuminating work of George Rudé or Eric Hobsbawm, who have depicted the characteristic pre-industrial disturbances and stressed their replacement by other kinds of disturbances with the advent of industrialization, offers questions and hypotheses galore.

The power to close in on such hypotheses gives these two strategies their attraction. The ideas about urbanization and collective violence I earlier characterized as the standard sociological treatment immediately suggest predictions: those periods and regions in which the intensest urban growth goes on should be the richest in disturbances; misery, mobility, and cultural diversity will have separate and roughly additive effects; while collective violence and other forms of "deviance" will be positively correlated in gross and will recruit in the same parts of the population, at a given level of urban concentration or a given pace of urbanization they will be negatively correlated, since they are alternative expressions of the same tensions; collective violence will recede as new groups become formally organized, integrated into the nation's political life.

There is surely something to all these hypotheses. They deserve checking. But the second thoughts on the nature of collective violence we encountered earlier suggest some different predictions: a weak connection of political disturbances with crime, misery or personal disorder, a corresponding rarity of the criminal, miserable or deranged in their ranks, a strong connection with more peaceful forms of political contention, a significant continuity and internal order to collective violence where it does occur, a long lag between urban growth and collective outbursts due to the time required for socialization and formation of a common consciousness on the part of the newcomers, a tendency for disturbances to cluster where there is a conflict between the principal holders of power in a locality and more or less organized groups moving into or out of a *modus vivendi* with those holders of power, a marked variation of the form of the disturbance with the social organization of its setting. On the whole these hunches are harder to verify than those deducible from the standard sociological treatment. Still they can be tested, and should be.

Our group of sociologists and historians has during the past few years been working toward the relevant comparisons for France between 1830 and 1960. While one can hardly derive universal laws from a single case, any of the propositions nominated for general application to urbanizing societies ought at least to apply to the recent past of individual western countries.

France of the last century and a half is a good starting-point. Its territory is fairly constant, the general lines of its political history well known, its violent incidents abundant. The period 1830 to 1960 contains several important surges of industrial expansion and urban growth. And the records are remarkably rich—often richer, contrary to our sociological prejudices, for the earlier years than for the later ones.

The raw materials come from French archives, newspapers, political yearbooks, government reports and statistical publications, occasional memoirs, and specialized historical works. For information on collective violence, our basic procedures are: (1) to enumerate as many as possible of the violent disturbances above a certain scale occurring in France each year and code them all in a summary, standard way; (2) to select a systematic sample of them for intensive analysis, and, first, gather as much additional information about them as possible from the archival sources and historical works, then, code them in a very detailed fashion according to a regular scheme; (3) to organize special studies of especially informative periods or disturbances. When all is finished, there will probably be some 4000 disturbances in the general sample, 500-odd in the intensive sample, two or three full years and a dozen disturbances singled out for special study.

A good deal of general information about the social settings of disturbances, of course, enters the analysis in the form of observations on the disturbances themselves. But that way of accumulating information slights the settings with few disturbances, or none. We have tried to get around that difficulty by assembling comparable information on major social changes—for example, urban population, net migration, labor force shifts—year by year for France as a whole, for its eighty to ninety departments, and for the larger cities.

We have also begun to deal with other forms of collective conflict by putting together roughly comparable information on most of the strikes (some 50,000 of them) reported in France from 1830 to 1960. Despite this extensive standardization of the sources, however, the sorts of questions this research raises will most likely often drive us back to other sources in order to account for contrasts in violent propensities between different years, areas, and segments of the French population. In short, the data collected should provide some moderately firm tests of existing hunches concerning differentials in collective violence, plus some good leads for further investigation, but they cannot conceivably provide a total explanation of France's turbulent political history.

With the data in hand, one can do several different kinds of analysis. The first has been done most often in the past: the study of the way different characteristics of disturbances vary together, in terms of such questions as whether highly-organized disturbances tend to last longer, or peasant rebellions to kill more people. The second relates the disturbances to their immediate settings, for example by examining whether urban distrubances involve more heterogeneous populations than rural ones. The third brings out general variations in the frequency and form of disturbances from one period to another, or one place to another, perhaps by asking whether the people of mountainous areas like the Ariège are inclined to frequent, short-lived attacks on property. The fourth deals with possible connections between these variations in frequency and form and the intensity of major social changes occurring in different periods or places, as in the comparison of cities receiving many rural migrants with cities receiving many migrants from other cities. The fifth investigates correlations of the appearance of disturbances with the development of other forms of conflict or of other presumed signs of social disorder, for example by checking whether suicide and collective conflict vary in opposite directions from each other. If these analyses do identify some interesting uniformities for particular periods, then the final series will follow their changes of pattern over time—conceivably determining whether the artisans so prominent in the disturbances of the 1830's but so invisible later lose their will to protest or simply find themselves swallowed up in the mass of protesting miners and factory workers.

As my description indicates, this work is far from finished. For the moment, all we can do is cast up straws to see which way the wind blows. Let us seize the straws anyway, since there seem to be strong breezes on the way.

For any particular period and place, the rather general inquiries we have been discussing translate into four or five specific questions. Where and when did collective violence take place? Who took part? What form did it take? How did all these change? Let us survey the first thirty years of our period, from 1830 to 1860. The three decades lead us through several major upheavals and changes of regime in France: from the Restoration to the July Monarchy via the resolution of 1830, through the Monarchy with its insurrections in Paris and Lyon, from the July Monarchy to the Second Republic via the Revolution of 1848 and its turbulent aftermath, into the Second Empire through Louis Napoleon's *coup d'état*.

The thirty years also bracket an unprecedented push of economic expansion and urban growth. The expansion was slow in the 1830's, punctuated by depression in the 1840's, and extraordinarily vigorous in the 1850's; during that third decade the railroads proliferated and modern industry got underway. Correspondingly, the growth of cities accelerated from moderate in the 1830's and 1840's to feverish in the 1850's. While around 1830 the leaders were mainly the old regional capitals—Toulouse, Strasbourg, Marseille, Lyon, Paris, with St. Etienne and Roubaix-Tourcoing beginning to represent the newer industrial centers—by the 1850's the entire region of Paris and all the industrializing Northeast were full of spurting cities.

Collective violence did not dance to the rhythm of urban growth. The turbulent years of this period, even leaving the major revolutions aside, were 1830, 1848, and 1851. The principal runs of violent years went from 1830 to 1834 and 1847 to 1851. The later 1850's, those peak years for urban growth, were practically empty of violent disturbances; so were the 1860's. If anything, the correlation is inverse: rapid growth, little disturbance.

As to *where* disturbances occurred, our results to date are largely cautionary or negative. The map of collective violence depends on the definition of "collective" and "violence," and on the sources of information concerning incidents. For example, if we tally apparently violent incidents reported by the provincial correspondents of the Ministry of Justice from 1840 through 1844,[6] the departments reporting three or more of them break down as follows:

3 incidents: Ariège, Bouches-du-Rhône, Cher, Corse, Loire, Maine-et-Loire, Nord

4 incidents: Gard, Haut-Rhin, Hérault

5 incidents: Creuse, Isère, Morbhian

6 incidents: Tarn, Vendée

7 incidents: Nièvre

The list is reassuring in a small way, since all but Creuse, Loire, and Maine-et-Loire also appear in the corresponding tally for 1830 to 1834. Yet it is on the whole disconcertingly rural. The departments contributing four or more disturbances to the register of "troubles à l'occasion de la cherté des subsistances" in 1853 to 1854 compiled by the Ministry of Justice are:

4 incidents: Corrèze, Ille-et-Vilaine, Loir-et-Cher, Loiret, Manche, Seine-et-Marne

5 incidents: Finistère

6 incidents: Marne

7 incidents: Dordogne, Pas-de-Calais

8 incidents: Deux-Sèvres, Morbihan, Tarn

9 or more: Charente-Inférieure, Gironde, Haute-Vienne, Vendée, Vienne

This set is a trifle more urban than the last one. The very special case of Paris is missing by design from these tallies, but the rarity of reports from such cities as Rouen, Toulouse, Strasbourg, and even Lyon is striking.

Systematic bias in these sources may help explain the distribution. The fundamental fact they reflect, however, is the prevalence of short-lived disturbances in the smaller towns and rural areas of France in the 1830's and 1840's. Three types of events recur again and again: food riots, violent resistance to taxation, and collective invasions of forests, fields and other rural property. (The fourth frequent form of collective violence of the mid-nineteenth century—the smashing of machines by unemployed or fearful workers—did not reach its full pace until after the period of these compilations.) Here we have the recurrent and somehow coherent "pre-industrial" forms of disturbance described by Edward Thompson or Eric Hobsbawm. The bread riot, with its regular combination of grumbling against price rises, massing in markets, seizure of grains being shipped or held in storage, and forced public sale at a price locally determined to be just, sums up their character.

The very prevalence of such small disturbances, their closeness to everyday life, creates enormous problems for anyone who wishes to compare areas or periods in terms of their turbulence. To insure a degree of comparability in our study of France, we have attempted to restrict our sample of collective conflicts to events in which at least one of the participating groups included fifty people or more, and have devoted special attention to events appearing to involve at least 1000 people.

Minima of 50 and 1000 weight the sample, to some unknown extent, toward places with more people available. They probably make small towns seem quieter than they are, but they should not affect the analysis of changes over time too seriously. Certainly our samples are more urban than the compilations from Ministry of Justice files just discussed. For the year 1830, where the sample consists of all disturbances meeting our minima and mentioned in the newspapers *Moniteur, Constitutionnel, Journal des Débats,* and *Gazette des Tribunaux,* the departments having outbreaks of collective violence meeting the 100-man minimum are Cher, Gard, Gironde, Haute-Garonne, Loire-Inférieure, Seine, Tarn, and Yonne, with the Seine (and Paris) leading the list. The departments with two or more disturbances above the 50-man minimum are Ariège, Gironde, Nord, Yonne, Aisne, Seine, Manche, Gard, and Tarn, the Seine again leading the way. For the much larger lot of disturbances during 1848 and 1849, taken from the *Moniteur, Constitutionnel,* and *Le Siècle,* two or more large-scale conflicts show up from Nord, Seine, Seine-Inférieure, Tarn-et-Garonne, Rhône, and Charente Inférieure. There are three or more disturbances meeting the lower minimum in Bouches-du-Rhône, Bas-Rhin, Var, Loire, Rhône, Seine-Inférieure, Nord, Haute-Garonne, Ariège, Somme, Moselle, Gard, Basses-Pyrenées, Charente-Inférieure, Gironde, Seine, and Seine-et-Oise. This time the Seine has fourteen of the smaller disturbances and five of the larger ones.

Big cities like Lyon or Rouen stand out on these lists, as do their surrounding areas. Paris and Seine tower over all the rest. Yet very rural departments like Ariège remain in their company. Furthermore, despite the example of Paris, there is no obvious tendency for the fastest-growing cities or the most rapidly-urbanizing departments to produce more collective violence than the rest. The relationship must be more subtle.

Some interesting hints as to its character appear in the fragmentary data on strikes during the early 1830's. In Aguet's careful enumeration the most strike-prone departments are (in roughly descending order) Seine, Rhône, Seine-Inférieure, Loire, and Bouches-du-Rhône, the departments containing Paris, Lyon, Rouen, St. Etienne and Marseille.[8] These same departments stand out in the tally of disturbances. In short, strikes and collective violence went together.

Not that they were the same thing. I have already pointed out how many of this period's smaller disturbances were food riots, conflicts with tax collectors, and forcible invasions of rural property. Practically none of them began as strikes. But a significant number of the minor disturbances were simply the violent parts of series of actions pitting workers against employers: demonstrations, political agitation, threats, property damage, strikes as well. They grew from the same basic conflicts. And some of the great outbursts (the insurrections of Lyon being the best-known examples) flashed in direct response to strikes.

George Rudé considers the working-class disturbances of the 1830's to start a great new phase. "For the first time," he concludes, "we find the same workers being engaged in successive political demonstrations, wage demands being put

TABLE 1. NUMBER OF STRIKES IN FRANCE BY INDUSTRY, 1830–44

Industry	Years			Estimated Labor Force in 1840–45 (in thousands)
	1830–34	1835–39	1840–44	
Agriculture, forestry, fishing	0	0	1	7,000
Mining and extraction	3	3	8	108
Food products	3	1	3	256
Chemical products	1	0	1	20
Paper and printing	9	2	12	47
Leather products	2	3	3	235
Textiles	32	26	30	1,560
Wood products	10	6	8	502
Metal products	8	2	6	305
Construction	13	6	21	474
Services and professions	0	0	2	3,000
Totals	81	49	95	13,507

Sources: Jean-Pierre Aguet, *Contributions à l'histoire du mouvement ouvrier francais: les grèves sous la Monarchie de Juillet (1830–1847)* (Geneva: Droz, 1954); J.-D. Toutain, *La Population de la France de 1700 à 1959* (Paris: Institut de Science Economique Appliquée, 1963), Cahiers de l'institut de Science Economique Appliquée, Serie, AF, no. 3.

forward at a time of economic depression, and wage earners participating as readily in political as in economic movements." [9] He might have added that the wage-earners still came from the older crafts and established industries rather than the swelling modern factories. To return to Aguet's enumeration of French strikes, the number of strikes reported by industry for five-year intervals are shown in Table 1. The figures drastically underestimate the total number of strikes and give far too much weight to Paris, but they are the best we have so far.

By sheer bulk, the textile industry dominated both the industrial labor force and the strike scene. For their size, however, construction, mining, and especially printing seem to have produced exceptional numbers of strikes. As the century wore on, textiles and construction held their own, the mines grew in importance as sources of strikes, the printers lost their force, and the metal-working industries with their factory production came into prominence. Under the July Monarchy, the workers in modern industry were still silent. The great Parisian series of strikes in 1840 brought out the tailors, papermakers, nailmakers, carters, wainwrights, masons, stonecutters, locksmiths, turners, carpenters, shoemakers, spinners, bookbinders, and bakers—mostly men from the skilled, established crafts.

The same occupations and industries led the Parisian working-class political activity, and fed the city's violent disturbances. The city's prefects of police were aware enough of the connection to always have their spies circulating through the workmen's cafes and hiring areas around the Place de Grève and the Place du Châtelet. A prefect's report for 9 September, 1831 (the midst of a very troubled period in Paris) remarked:

> Il y a eu hier beaucoup de réunions d'ouvriers, au Châtelet, a la Grève sur les quais et aux environs des halles. Beaucoup de ceux qui en faisaient partie, paraissaient réduits au désespoir. Quelques-uns même, dans un état violent d'exaspération, parlaient de se procurer des armes. Plusieurs sergens de ville étant venus à passer auprès d'eux, ils ont crié, "A l'eau! A l'eau! A bas les mouchards!
>
> Il a fallu sur plusieurs points l'intervention de la force armée pour dissiper les Groupes.[10]

The "despair" and "exasperation" the prefect described were real enough. The point is that they are articulated and acted on by segments of the Parisian working class already politically alert, organized, integrated into the life of the city—*not,* that is, the uprooted, outcast, dangerous classes.

The studies that have been done of participants in diverse outbreaks of violence in Paris between 1830 and 1860 point in the same direction. For the Revolution of 1830, Adeline Daumard observes that "artisans on the border between the common people and the bourgeoisie were at the core of the insurgents," and David Pinkney's careful enumerations agree.[11] The violent days of April, 1834, brought into action such men as 36-year old Louis Bertembois, a shoemaker born in St. Frambourg (Oise), François Soubrebois, 29, a typographer originally from Perpignan, the wagon-painter J.-P. Etienne, 17 years old, a Parisian, the caterer Jean Pouchin, 32, from a small town in Calvados, reputed to be a member of the Société des Droits de l'Homme, and 22-year old Jean Hallot, a cabinetmaker from Paris, labeled in the police reports as an "instigator." [12] And in the revolution of February, 1848, George Rudé points out, the city's wage earners "left their workshops with their masters and, with them, jointly manned the barricades; radical journalists, students, *polytechniciens,* and National Guards had also played their part; and on the lists of those decorated for their part in the February events the names of wage earners appear alongside those of shopkeepers, master craftsmen, and members of the liberal professions." [23]

It would be tedious to keep marching from disturbance to disturbance, insisting on their continuities without really being able to detect their variations or to make the needed comparisons with disturbances outside of Paris. That finer work, those more systematic comparisons remain to be done. But there is one more Parisian case of special interest: the June Days of 1848. That bloody disturbance deserves our attention both because it had the most proletarian appearance of any up to its time, and because it left remarkably detailed evidence concerning who took part.

Table 2 summarizes the available information on the origins and occupation of more than 11,000 persons of the probable 15,000 arrested for participation in the June Days. In order to give a general sense of their relation to the labor force of the time, it also presents the number of workers in each group of industrial establishments reported by employers to the Chamber of Commerce in 1847 and 1848, and relates the arrests to the industries as a series of rates per 10,000 workers. While comparisons within the sample do display a slight tendency for construction workers to have been arrested on suspicion, then released, and a

Table 2. Persons Arrested for Taking Part in June Days, 1848, by Industry and Birthplace

Industry	BIRTHPLACE					Number of Workers Reported in 1848 Survey	Arrests per 10,000 Workers
	Seine	Other France	Foreign	Unknown	Total		
Food	53	342	21	39	455	10,428	436
Building	350	1,480	68	126	2,024	41,603	487
Furniture	210	346	67	41	664	36,184	184
Garment	154	700	85	68	1,007	90,064	112
Textile	70	246	10	16	342	36,685	93
Hides and Leather	35	110	9	10	164	4,573	361
Sadlery, Coach Building	39	135	11	9	194	13,754	141
Indus. chemicals, ceramics	44	76	10	17	147	9,737	151
Ordinary metals	316	872	44	74	1,306	24,894	526
Precious metals	93	107	8	24	232	16,819	138
Cooper	32	86	4	6	128	5,405	237
Fashion	67	125	12	9	213	35,679	60
Printing	164	211	18	41	434	16,705	260
Transportation	129	331	24	39	523	—	—
Services	67	316	29	43	455	—	—
Commerce	162	507	36	69	774	—	—
Military	110	261	15	100	486	—	—
Professions	80	189	16	36	321	—	—
Other	257	749	59	91	1,156	—	—
Not reported	21	69	9	171	270	—	—
Totals	2,453	7,258	555	1,031	11,295		

Sources: Archives Nationales F^{7}2586, *Liste générale en ordre alphabétique des inculpés de juin 1848:* Chambre de Commerce de Paris, *Statistique de l'Industrie à Paris résultant de l'enquête faite par la chambre de Commerce pour les années 1847–8* (Paris: 1851)

significantly greater tendency for arrested soldiers and persons born in Paris to finally be convicted, this tabulation represents the men and women actually implicated in the rebellion fairly faithfully.[14]

It does not show a simple cross section of the Parisian population, but it does show a wide spread across its various categories. The largest single occupational group were the 685 day laborers, who were in the company of 552 stonemasons, 463 cabinet makers and 434 shoemakers. Construction, metalworking, and the clothing trades had the largest shares in absolute numbers. Compared with their parts in the working population of the time, men from construction, food production and metalworking industries seem to have played an exceptional role. Their arrests run around five percent of all the men reported in these industries. Mechanics (especially from the railroads), leatherworkers, and printers also appear to have contributed more than their share to the rebellion. Textile workers, it seems fair to say, were under-represented.

George Duveau's sketch of the June Days has as its principal characters a mechanic of La Chapelle, a chosier of the faubourg Saint-Dénis, and a cabinet-maker from the faubourg Saint-Antoine.[15] If he had added a stonemason from the Hôtel de Ville, a daylaborer from Popincourt, and a tanner from Saint-Marcel, his cast would have been representative.

The distribution we find is remarkably like the strike activity of the time: an amalgam of the old, politically active trades with a few sections of modern industry. By comparison with previous disturbances, the center of gravity was shifting toward the mass-production industries, gradually, in step with other forms of contention and political activity, not in such a way as to call the miserable outsiders into the streets.

The bulk of the rebels had originally come from outside of Paris. That is truest of construction (as one might expect), and least true of printing. Just under a quarter of those arrested and a little less than a third of those convicted were natives of the Seine. As it happens, Louis Chevalier's data indicate that about forty percent of Paris' population of the time, including children, were natives.[16] The adult working population was surely well below that proportion. So there is no clear sign that outsiders were over-represented. Furthermore, the distribution of departments of origin follows Chevalier's estimates for the Paris of 1833 quite faithfully. In addition to the 2457 born in the Seine, we find 498 from Seine-et-Oise, 327 from Seine-et-Marne, 353 from Moselle, 262 from Nord, 230 from Creuse, 215 from Somme, 210 from Aisne, and so on through the list of regular suppliers of migrants to Paris. While these data do not make the point, Rémi Gossez, who knows the histories of the individual rebels of June far better than anyone else, remarks:

> The typical insurgent was an individual who, if a native of the provinces, came to Paris to settle or at least to complete his training and who in general was moving up in the world, a move blocked by economic change and crisis.[17]

Again the violent masses turn out to be those integrated into the setting rather than those at the margins of society.

That is the general impression these diverse observations give. The absence of the uprooted, the continuity of different forms of conflict, their gradual change in response to shifts in the collective conditions of work and community life, the sheer lack of correlation between rapid urban growth and mass violence all challenge the cataclysmic theories of urbanization. To be sure, the distance between the scattered observations I have made and the testing of the finer hypotheses now available is still great. That is to come. Furthermore, the alternative formulations I have to offer do not amount to much more than suggestions that collective violence flows out of routine political life, which is itself shaped by the scale and complexity of the city.

Through the chaos of living cities, what do we see? Certainly not the lawless disorder a romantic notion of urbanization has advertised. Not bucolic bliss, either. We see men held to their routines by commitments and controls, often dismayed by their routines, sometimes articulating and acting on their dismay, mostly singly, mostly in nonviolent ways, but occasionally being trained in another way of understanding and dispelling the evils of their present situation, and joining with other men to strike out against the situation itself. There is a kind of order to the city's collective disorder, if not the one the forces of order would like to see prevailing.

It takes another poet, Christopher Fry, to state the theme properly: "There's no loosening, since men with men are like the knotted sea. Lift him down from the stone to the grass again, and, even so free, yet he will find the angry cities hold him." Angry cities, but not mad. Violent cities, but not pathological. Living cities, and in the last analysis not nearly so chaotic as widespread sociological ideas imply.

Notes

1. The research reported in this paper has received support from the Center of International Studies (Princeton University), Social Science Research Council, Harvard University, the Joint Center for Urban Studies and Grant GS-580 of the National Science Foundation. Among the many people who have helped gather material and do analyses used here, I would like to offer special thanks to Karen Ambush, Lutz Berkner, Judy Carter, James Doty, Ronald Florence, Mohammed Khan, Lynn Lees, Ted Margadant, James Rule, Edward Shorter, Gerald Soliday, Cyrus Stewart and Sandra Winston.

2. Lewis Mumford, *The City in History* (New York: Harcourt, Brace & World, 1961), p. 43.

3. Philip Hauser, "The Social, Economic and Technological Problems of Rapid Urbanization," in Bert Hoselitz and Wilbert Moore, eds., *Industrialization and Society* (The Hague: Mouton for UNESCO, 1963), p. 212.

4. Louis Chevalier, *Classes laborieuses et classes dangereuses* (Paris: Plon, 1958), pp. 552–553.

5. Hannah Arendt, *On Revolution* (London: Faber and Faber, 1963), pp. 9–10.

6. As represented in Archives Nationales series BB^{18}, 1 through 1795.

7. Archives Nationales BB^{30}432.

8. Compiled from Jean-Pierre Aguet, *Contributions à l'histoire du mouvement ouvrier français: lés grèves sous la Monarchie de Juillet (1830–1847)* (Geneva: Droz, 1954).

9. George Rudé, *The Crowd in History* (New York: Wiley, 1964), p. 165.

10. Archives Nationales F^{1C}133.

11. Adeline Daumard, *La Bourgeoisie parisienne de 1815 à 1948* (Paris: SEVPEN, 1963), p. 578; David Pinkney, "The Crowd in the French Revolution of 1830," *American Historical Review,* 70 (October, 1964), 1–17.

12. Archives de la Préfecture de Police, Paris, A^a422.

13. Rudé, *op. cit.*, pp. 168–169.

14. The source of quantitative data is a huge register (Archives Nationales $F^7$2586) containing uniform descriptions of about 11,400 persons arrested for taking part in the June Days. The register has been drawn on before, by Rémi Gossez, George Rudé, and very likely Georges Duveau. See Gossez, "Diversité des antagonismes sociaux vers le milieu du XIXe siècle," *Revue economique* (May, 1956), 439–457; Rudé, *op. cit.;* Duveau, "L'ouvrier de 1848," *Revue socialiste,* n.s. nos. 17–18 (Jan.–Feb. 1948), 73–79. Gossez' forthcoming thesis on 1848 should set these arrests firmly in context. However, no one has so far reported the sorts of detailed counts and comparisons presented here. I am grateful to Lynn Hollen Lees, who supervised the preparation of these data for analysis, and Cyrus Stewart, who helped me design the machine procedures. This tabulation omits about 300 persons whose names are on sheets missing from the copy of the register used in our analysis. While this omission will certainly be corrected in further reports of this investigation, it could hardly affect the general conclusions materially.

15. Georges Duveau, *1848* (Paris: Gallimard, 1965).

16. Louis Chevalier, *La Formation de la population parisienne* (Paris: Presses Universitaires de France, 1950), p. 45.

17. Gossez, *op. cit.*, 449.

CHAPTER SIX

THE DYNAMICS OF URBAN CHANGE

INTRODUCTION

It should be amply evident by now that the city still is what it has always been, a landscape of change. Historically and cross-culturally, the nature of that change has, of course, manifested wide variability—as to rates, types, pathologies, and so on.

Although urbanization is itself a "process" word, denoting a set of sequences of change, we use "change" in the title of this volume in order to emphasize a particular purpose we had in assembling these readings: to utilize investigations and discussions of the city as a vehicle for theoretical consideration of the nature and problems of social change. That there is in contemporary sociology no general theory of social change is well borne out in these readings. Indeed, these selections on urban sociology share a characteristic in common with general sociology, the prevalence of a number of *perspective organizations* of social data. These perspectives are for the most part furnished by the institutional rubrics of the field. Certainly when we seek to describe and explain the "dynamics of urban change," we usually resort to established categories and contexts of analysis. Such certainly is true of the analyses in this present chapter.

The first three articles report and analyze social change in urban areas of the United States: Greenstein, from the viewpoint of party politics; Blood, concerned with urbanization and family structure and function; and Reissman, interrelating urbanization and development in the American South. The remaining four articles set forth a panoramic view of the urban scene in a variety of cultures outside the United States: Howton, viewing slums and the acculturative process in cities and developing countries in general; Carpenter, outlining the patterns, rates, and problems of social change in a recently but well industrialized country, Japan; and Gutkind and Mitchell, relating urbanization to the agents and processes of detribalization and stabilization in Africa.

These selections emphasize the fact that the city, wherever located geographically or culturally, is now perhaps more than ever in history a theater of intensive change. The reader will find in these, and in the other selections in this volume, no mature theory of social change. He will find that urbanization is a shorthand word descriptive of a universal dynamic whose face and form, style and future we are beginning to know somewhat better.

THE CHANGING PATTERN OF URBAN PARTY POLITICS

Fred I. Greenstein

Highly organized urban political parties are generally conceded to be one of America's distinctive contributions to mankind's repertory of political forms. Just as the two major national parties in the United States are almost universally described in terms of their *dis*organization—their lack of an authoritative command structure—the municipal parties have, until recently, been characterized by most observers in terms of their hierarchical strength. E. E. Schattschneider once summarized this state of affairs in the memorable image of a truncated pyramid: a party system which is weak and ghostlike at the top and solid at the bottom.[1]

This essay deals with the disciplined, largely autonomous local political parties which sprang up in many American cities in the nineteenth century. Much of the literature on these political configurations is heavily pejorative, concerned more with excoriation than explanation. Even the basic nomenclature, "boss" and "machine," is laden with negative connotations, although recently there has been a turn toward nostalgic romanticization of the "vanishing breed" of city bosses.[2]

Here, for reasons which I shall indicate, the attempt shall be to delineate rather than to pass moral judgment: What was the nature of old-style urban party organization? Why did this political pattern develop and how did it operate? What contributed to its short-run persistence in the face of reform campaigns? Under what circumstances have such organizations disappeared and under what circumstances have they continued into the present day—or even undergone renaissances? What are the present-day descendents of old-style urban party organizations?

Analytic delineation invariably involves oversimplification. This is doubly necessary in the present case, because our knowledge of the distribution of types of local party organization is scant. We have no census of local political parties, either for today or for the putative heyday of bosses and machines. And there is reason to believe that observers have exaggerated the ubiquity of tightly organized urban political parties in past generations, as well as underestimated somewhat their contemporary prevalence.

Old-Style Party Organization: Definitional Characteristics

Ranney and Kendall have persuasively argued that the imprecision and negative connotations of terms like "boss" destroy their usefulness. What, beyond semantic confusion, they ask, can come from classifying politicians into "bosses" versus "leaders"? Such a distinction leads to fruitless preoccupation with the purity of politicians' motives rather than the actuality of their behavior; it overestimates the degree to which figures of the past such as Richard Croker, William Tweed, and Frank Hague were free of public constraints; and it obscures the fact that *all*

Reprinted by permission of the author and publisher from *The Annals of the American Academy of Political and Social Science,* **353** (May, 1964), pp. 2–13.

effective political leaders, whether or not they are popularly labeled as bosses, use quite similar techniques and resources.[3]

Granting these points, it still seems that a recognizable and noteworthy historical phenomenon is hinted at by the venerable terms "boss" and "machine." If the overtones of these terms make us reluctant to use them, we might simply speak of an "old style" of party organization with the following characteristics:

(1) There is a disciplined party hierarchy led by a single executive or a unified board of directors.

(2) The party exercises effective control over nomination to public office, and, through this, it controls the public officials of the municipality.

(3) The party leadership—which quite often is of lower-class social origins—usually does not hold public office and sometimes does not even hold formal party office. At any rate, official position is not the primary source of the leadership's strength.

(4) Rather, a cadre of loyal party officials and workers, as well as a core of voters, is maintained by a mixture of material rewards and *nonideological* psychic rewards—such as personal and ethnic recognition, camaraderie, and the like.[4]

The Rise of Old-Style Party Organization

This pattern of politics, Schattschneider comments, "is as American as the jazz band . . . China, Mexico, South America, and southern Italy at various times have produced figures who played roles remotely like that of the American boss, but England, France, Germany, and the lesser democracies of Europe have exhibited no tendency to develop this form of political organization in modern times."[5] What then accounted for the development of old-style party organization in the United States?

The Crokers, Tweeds, and Hagues and their organizations probably could not have arisen if certain broad preconditions had not existed in American society and culture. These include the tradition of freewheeling individualism and pragmatic opportunism, which developed in a prosperous, sprawling new society unrestrained by feudalism, aristocracy, monarchy, an established church, and other traditional authorities. This is the state of affairs which has been commented on by countless observers, even before de Tocqueville, and which has been used to explain such disparate phenomena as the failure of socialism to take hold in the United States, the recurrence of popularly based assaults on civil liberties, and even the peculiarly corrosive form which was taken by American slavery.[6]

It also is possible to identify five more direct determinants of the form that urban party organization took in the nineteenth century, three of them consequences of the Industrial Revolution and two of them results of political institutions and traditions which preceded industrialization.

Massive urban expansion. Over a relatively brief span of years, beginning in the mid-nineteenth century, industrial and commercial growth led to a spectacular rise in the number and proportion of Americans concentrated in cities. A thumbnail sketch of urban expansion may be had by simply noting the population of urban and rural areas for each of the twenty-year periods from 1840 to 1920:

	Urban Population	Rural Population
	(in millions)	
1840	1.8	15.2
1860	6.2	25.2
1880	14.1	36.0
1900	30.1	45.8
1920	54.2	51.6

These statistics follow the old Census Bureau classification of areas exceeding 2,500 in population as urban. Growth of larger metropolitan units was even more striking. In 1840 slightly over 300,000 Americans lived in cities—or, rather, a single city, New York—with more than a quarter of a million residents; by 1920 there were twenty-four cities of this size, containing approximately 21 million Americans.

The sheer mechanics of supporting urban populations of this magnitude are, of course, radically different from the requirements of rural life. There must be extensive transportation arrangements; urban dwellers are as dependent upon a constant inflow of food and other commodities as an infant is on the ministrations of adults. A host of new administrative functions must be performed as the population becomes urbanized: street construction and maintenance, bridges, lighting, interurban transportation, sanitary arrangements, fire-fighting, police protection, and so forth. Overwhelming demands suddenly are placed on governments which, hitherto, were able to operate with a minimum of effort and activity.

Disorganized forms of urban government. The forms of government which had evolved in nineteenth-century America were scarcely suitable for meeting the demands of mushrooming cities. Governmental structures reflected a mixture of Jacksonian direct democracy and Madisonian checks and balances. Cities had a multitude of elected officials (sometimes they were elected annually), weak executives, large and unwieldy councils and boards. The formal organization of the cities placed officials in a position permitting and, in fact, encouraging them to checkmate each other's efforts to make and execute policies. Since each official was elected by appealing to his own peculiar constituency and had little incentive to co-operate with his associates, the difficulties caused by the formal limitations of government were exacerbated. In a period when the requirements for governmental action were increasing geometrically, this was a prescription for chaos.

Needs of businessmen. A third aspect of mid-nineteenth-century American society which contributed to the formation of old-style party organizations was the needs of businessmen. There was an increasing number of merchants, industrialists, and other businessmen, licit and illicit, who needed—and were willing to pay for—the appropriate responses from city governments. Some businessmen wanted to operate unrestrained by municipal authority. Others desired street-railway franchises, paving contracts, construction work, and other transactions connected with the very growth of the cities themselves.

Needs of dependent populations. The needs of the bulk of the nineteenth-century urban population were not for profits but for the simple wherewithal to survive and maintain a modicum of dignity. It is difficult in the relatively affluent society of our day to appreciate the vicissitudes of urban life several generations ago: the low wages, long hours, tedious and hazardous working conditions, and lack of security which were the lot of most citizens. Even for native-born Americans, life often was nasty and brutish. But many urbanites were first- and second-generation immigrants who, in addition to their other difficulties, had to face an alien culture and language. Between the Civil War and the First World War, the United States managed somehow to absorb 25 million foreigners.

Unrestricted suffrage. Urban dwellers were not totally without resources for their own advancement. The American tradition of unrestricted male franchise was, in the long run, to work to their advantage. Although it doubtless is true that few city dwellers of the day were aware of the importance of their right to vote, politicians *were* aware of this. Because even the lowliest of citizens was, or could become, a voter, a class of politicians developed building upon the four conditions referred to above: the requirements of organizing urban life, the inability of existing governments to meet these requirements, and the presence of businessmen willing to pay for governmental services and of dependent voting populations in need of security from the uncertainties of their existence.

The old-style urban party leader was as much a product of his time and social setting as was the rising capitalist of the Gilded Age. Building on the conditions and needs of the day, the politician had mainly to supply his own ingenuity and co-ordinating ability in order to tie together the machinery of urban government. If a cohesive party organization could control nominations and elect its own agents to office, the formal fragmentation of government no longer would stand in the way of municipal activity. The votes of large blocs of dependent citizens were sufficient to control nominations and win elections. And the financial support of those who sought to transact business with the city, as well as the revenues and resources of the city government, made it possible to win votes. The enterprising politician who could succeed in governing a city on this basis was a broker *par excellence;* generous brokers' commissions were the rule of the day.

The importance of out-and-out vote-buying on election day as a source of voter support can easily be overestimated. Party organizations curried the favor of voters on a year-long basis. In a day when "better" citizens espoused philosophical variants of Social Darwinism, urban politicians thought in terms of an old-fashioned conception of the welfare state. In the familiar words of Tammany sachem George Washington Plunkitt:

> What holds your grip on your district is to go right down among the poor families and help them in the different ways they need help. I've got a regular system for this. If there's a fire in Ninth, Tenth or Eleventh Avenue, for example, any hour of the day or night, I'm usually there with some of my election district captains as soon as the fire engines. If a family is burned out I don't ask whether they are Republicans or Democrats, and I don't refer them to the Charity Organization Society, which would investigate their case in a month or two and decide they were worthy of help about the time they are

> dead from starvation. I just get quarters for them, buy clothes for them if their clothes were burned up, and fix them up til they get things runnin' again. It's philanthropy, but it's politics, too—mighty good politics. Who can tell how many votes one of these fires bring me? The poor are the most grateful people in the world, and, let me tell you, they have more friends in their neighborhoods than the rich have in theirs.[7]

With numerous patronage appointees (holders not only of city jobs but also of jobs with concerns doing business with the city), party organizations could readily administer this sort of an informal relief program. And, unlike many latter-day charitable and governmental relief programs, the party's activities did not stop with the provision of mere physical assistance.

> I know every man, woman and child in the Fifteenth District, except them that's been born this summer—and I know some of them, too. I know what they like and what they don't like, what they are strong at and what they are weak in, and I reach them by approachin' at the right side.
>
> For instance, here's how I gather in the young men. I hear of a young feller that's proud of his voice, thinks that he can sing fine. I ask him to come around to Washington Hall and join our Glee Club. He comes and sings, and he's a follower of Plunkitt for life. Another young feller gains a reputation as a baseball player in a vacant lot. I bring him into our baseball club. That fixes him. You'll find him workin' for my ticket at the polls next election day. Then there's the feller that likes rowin' on the river, the young feller that makes a name as a waltzer on his block, the young feller that's handy with his dukes—I rope them all in by givin' them opportunities to show themselves off. I don't trouble them with political arguments. I just study human nature and act accordin'.[8]

This passage reflects some of the ways in which party activities might be geared to the *individual* interests of voters. *Group* interests were at least as important. As each new nationality arrived in the city, politicians rather rapidly accommodated to it and brought it into the mainstream of political participation. Parties were concerned with tthe votes of immigrants virtually from the time of their arrival. Dockside naturalization and voter enrollment was not unknown.

But if the purpose of the politicians was to use the immigrants, it soon became clear that the tables could be turned. In Providence Rhode Island, for example, a careful study of the assimilation of immigrant groups into local politics shows that, within thirty years after the arrival of the first representative of a group in the city, it began to be represented in the councils of one or both parties. Eventually, both of the local parties came to be dominated by representatives of the newer stocks. Thus, in 1864 no Irish names appear on the lists of Democratic committeemen in Providence; by 1876 about a third of the names were Irish; by the turn of the century, three-quarters were Irish. In time, the Republican party became the domain of politicians of Italian ancestry.[9] Perhaps the most dramatic example to date of urban party politics as an avenue of upward social mobility was in the antecedents of President Kennedy, whose great-grandfather was an impoverished refugee of the Irish potato famine, his grandfather a saloon keeper and a classical old-time urban political leader, his father a multi-millionnaire businessman, presidential advisor, and ambassador to the Court of St. James's.

When the range of consequences of old-time party organizations is seen, it becomes apparent why moral judgments of "the boss and the machine" are likely to be inadequate. These organizations often were responsible for incredible corruption, but they also—sometimes through the very same activities—helped incorporate new groups into American society and aided them up the social ladder. The parties frequently mismanaged urban growth on a grand scale, but they *did* manage urban growth at a time when other instrumentalities for governing the cities were inadequate. They plied voters, who might otherwise have organized more aggressively to advance their interests, with Thanksgiving Day turkeys and buckets of coal. But, by siphoning off discontent and softening the law, they probably contributed to the generally pacific tenor of American politics. It seems fruitless to attempt to capture this complexity in a single moral judgment. One can scarcely weigh the incorporation of immigrant groups against the proliferation of corruption and strike an over-all balance.

Why Reformers Were "Mornin' Glories"

Stimulated by high taxes and reports of corruption and mismanagement on a grand scale, antiboss reform movements, led by the more prosperous elements of the cities, became increasingly common late in the nineteenth century. Compared with the regular party politicians of their day, reformers were mere fly-by-night dilettantes—"mornin' glories." [10] They lacked the discipline and the staying power to mount a year-long program of activities. Perhaps more important, the values of the reformers were remote from—in fact, inconsistent with—the values of the citizens whose support would be needed to keep reform administrations in office. Reformers ordinarily saw low taxes and business-like management of the cities as the exclusive aim of government. To the sweatshop worker, grinding out a marginal existence, these aims were at best meaningless, at worst direct attacks on the one agency of society which seemed to have his interests at heart.

The Decline of Old-Style Party Organization

Although in the short run old-style party organizations were marvelously immune to the attacks of reformers, in recent decades the demise of this political form has been widely acclaimed. Because of the absence of reliable trend data, we cannot document "the decline of the machine" with precision. The decline does seem to have taken place, although only partly as a direct consequence of attempts to reform urban politics. Events have conspired to sap the traditional resources used to build voter support and to make voters less interested in these resources which the parties still command.

Decline in the resources of old-style urban politicians. Most obviously, job patronage is no longer available in as great a quantity as it once was. At the federal level and in a good many of the states (as well as numerous cities), the bulk of jobs are filled by civil service procedures. Under these circumstances, the most a party politician may be able to do is seek some minor form of preferment for an otherwise qualified job applicant. Furthermore, the technical requirements of many appointive positions are sufficiently complex to make it inexpedient to fill them with unqualified personnel.[11] And private concerns doing business with the cities are not as likely to be sources of patronage in a day when the franchises have been given out and the concessions granted.

Beyond this, many modern governmental techniques—accounting and auditing requirements, procedures for letting bids, purchasing procedures, even the existence of a federal income tax—restrict the opportunities for dishonest and "honest" graft. Some of these procedures were not instituted with the explicit purpose of hampering the parties. Legislation designed deliberately to weaken parties *has,* however, been enacted—for example, nomination by direct primary and non-partisan local elections, in which party labels are not indicated on the ballot. Where other conditions are consistent with tight party organization, techniques of this sort seem not to have been especially effective; old-style parties are perfectly capable of controlling nominations in primaries, or of persisting in formally nonpartisan jurisdictions. But, together with the other party weakening factors, explicit antiparty legislation seems to have taken its toll.

Decline of voter interest in rewards available to the parties. Even today it is estimated that the mayor of Chicago has at his disposal 6,000 to 10,000 city patronage jobs. And there are many ways of circumventing good government, antiparty legislation. An additional element in the decline of old-style organization is the increasing disinterest of many citizens in the rewards at the disposal of party politicans. Once upon a time, for example, the decennial federal census was a boon to those local politicans whose party happened to be in control of the White House at census time. The temporary job of door-to-door federal census enumerator was quite a satisfactory reward for the party faithful. In 1960 in many localities, party politicians found census patronage more bother than boon; the wages for this task compared poorly with private wages, and few voters were willing to put in the time and leg work. Other traditional patronage jobs—custodial work in city buildings, employment with departments of sanitation, street repair jobs—were becoming equally undesirable, due to rising levels of income, education, and job security.

An important watershed seems to have been the New Deal, which provided the impetus, at state and local levels as well as the federal level, for increased governmental preoccupation with citizen welfare. The welfare programs of party organizations were undercut by direct and indirect effects of social security, minimum wage legislation, relief programs, and collective bargaining. And, as often has been noted, the parties themselves, by contributing to the social rise of underprivileged groups, helped to develop the values and aspirations which were to make these citizens skeptical of the more blatant manifestations of machine politics.

Varieties of Contemporary Urban Politics

Nationally in 1956, the Survey Research Center found that only 10 percent of a cross section of citizens reported being contacted personally by political party workers during that year's presidential campaign. Even if we consider only nonsouthern cities of over 100,000 population, the percentage is still a good bit less than 20.[12] This is a far cry from the situation which would obtain if party organizations were well developed and assiduous. But national statistics conceal a good bit of local variation. A survey of Detroit voters found that only 6 percent of the public remembered having been approached by political party workers; in fact, less than a fifth of those interviewed even knew that there *were* party precinct officials in their district.[13] Reports from a number of other cities—for example, Seattle and Minneapolis—show a similar vacuum in party activity.[14]

In New Haven, Connecticut, in contrast, 60 percent of the voters interviewed in a 1959 survey reported having been contacted by party workers.[15] The continuing importance of parties in the politics of this municipality has been documented at length by Robert A. Dahl and his associates.[16] New Haven's Mayor Richard C. Lee was able to obtain support for a massive urban redevelopment program, in spite of the many obstacles in the way of favorable action on such programs elsewhere, in large part because of the capacity of an old-style party organization to weld together the government of a city with an extremely "weak" formal charter. Lee commanded a substantial majority on the board of aldermen and, during the crucial period for ratification of the program, was as confident of the votes of Democratic aldermen as a British Prime Minister is of his parliamentary majority. Lee was far from being a mere creative creature of the party organization which was so helpful to him, but he also was effectively vetoed by the party when he attempted to bring about governmental reforms which would have made the mayor less dependent upon the organization to obtain positive action.[17]

Further evidence of the persistence of old-style party activities came from a number of other studies conducted in the late 1950's. For example, in 1957 party leaders from eight New Jersey counties reported performing a wide range of traditional party services, in response to an ingeniously worded questionnaire administered by Professor Richard T. Frost.[18]

TABLE 1. SERVICES PERFORMED BY NEW JERSEY POLITICIANS

The Service [18]	Percentage Performing It "Often"
Helping deserving people get public jobs	72
Showing people how to get their social security benefits, welfare, unemployment compensation, etc.	54
Helping citizens who are in difficulty with the law. Do you help get them straightened out?	62

There was even some evidence in the 1950's of a rebirth of old-style urban party activities—for example, in the once Republican-dominated city of Philadelphia, where an effective Democratic old-style organization was put together. Often old-style organizations seem to exist in portions of contemporary cities, especially the low-income sections. These, like the reform groups to be described below, serve as factions in city-wide politics.[19]

Why old-style politics persists in some settings but not others is not fully clear. An impressionistic survey of the scattered evidence suggests, as might be expected, that the older pattern continues in those localities which most resemble the situations which originally spawned strong local parties in the nineteenth century. Eastern industrial cities, such as New Haven, Philadelphia, and many of the New Jersey cities, have sizable low-income groups in need of traditional party services. In many of these areas, the legal impediments to party activity also are minimal: Connecticut, for example, was the last state in the union to adopt direct primary legislation, and nonpartisan local election systems are, in general, less common in industrial cities than in cities without much manufacturing activity.[20] Cities in which weak, disorganized parties are reported—like Seattle, Minneapolis, and even Detroit (which, of course, *is* a manufacturing center of some importance)—are quite often cities in which nonpartisan institutions have been adopted.

Some New-Style Urban Political Patterns

In conclusion, we may note two of the styles of politics which have been reported in contemporary localities where old-style organizations have become weak or nonexistent: the politics of nonpartisanship and the new "reform" factions within some urban Democratic parties. Both patterns are of considerable intrinsic interest to students of local government. And, as contrasting political forms, they provide us with further perspective on the strengths and weaknesses of old-style urban politics.

The politics of nonpartisanship. The nonpartisan ballot now is in force in 66 percent of American cities over 25,000 in population. Numerous styles of politics seem to take place beneath the facade of nonpartisanship. In some communities, when party labels are eliminated from the ballot, the old parties continue to operate much as they have in the past; in other communities, new local parties spring up to contest the nonpartisan elections. Finally, nonpartisanship often takes the form intended by its founders: no organized groups contest elections; voters choose from a more or less self-selected array of candidates.

In the last of these cases, although nonpartisanship has its intended effect, it also seems to have had—a recent body of literature suggests[21]—a number of unintended side effects. One of these is voter confusion. Without the familiar device of party labels to aid in selecting candidates, voters may find it difficult to select from among the sometimes substantial list of names on the ballot. Under these circumstances, a bonus in votes often goes to candidates with a familiar sounding name—incumbents are likely to be re-elected, for example—or even candidates with a favorable position on the ballot. In addition, campaigning and other personal contacts with voters become less common, because candidates no longer have the financial resources and personnel of a party organization at their disposal and therefore are dependent upon personal financing or backing from interest groups in the community.

Nonpartisan electoral practices, where effective, also seem to increase the influence of the mass media on voters; in the absence of campaigning, party canvassing, and party labels, voters become highly dependent for information as well as advice on the press, radio, and television. Normally, mass communications have rather limited effects on people's behavior compared with face-to-face communication such as canvassing by party workers.[2] Under nonpartisan circumstances, however, he who controls the press is likely to have much more direct and substantial effect on the public.

Ironically, the "theory" of nonpartisanship argues that by eliminating parties a barrier between citizens and their officials will be removed. In fact, nonpartisanship often attenuates the citizen's connections with the political system.

The reform Democrats. The doctrine of nonpartisanship is mostly a product of the Progressive era. While nonpartisan local political systems continue to be adopted and, in fact, have become more common in recent decades, most of the impetus for this development results from the desire of communities to adopt city-manager systems. Nonpartisanship simply is part of the package which normally goes along with the popular city-manager system.

A newer phenomenon on the urban political scene is the development, especially since the 1952 presidential campaign, of ideologically motivated grass-roots party organizations within the Democratic party.[23] The ideology in question is liberalism: most of the reform organizations are led and staffed by college-educated intellectuals, many of whom were activated politically by the candidacy of Adlai Stevenson. In a few localities, there also have been grass-roots Republican organizations motivated by ideological considerations: in the Republican case, Goldwater conservatism.

New-style reformers differ in two major ways from old-style reformers: their ideological concerns extend beyond a preoccupation with governmental efficiency alone (they favor racial integration and improved housing and sometimes devote much of their energy to advocating "liberal" causes at the national level); secondly, their strategy is to work within and take control of the parties, rather than to reject the legitimacy of parties. They do resemble old-style reformers in their preoccupation with the evils of "bossism" and machine politics.

There also is an important resemblance between the new reform politician and the old-style organization man the reformer seeks to replace. In both cases, very much unlike the situation which seems to be stimulated by nonpartisanship, the politician emphasizes extensive face-to-face contact with voters. Where reformers have been successful, it often has been by beating the boss at his own game of canvassing the election district, registering and keeping track of voters, and getting them to the polls.[24]

But much of the day-to-day style of the traditional urban politician is clearly distasteful to the new reformers: they have generally eschewed the use of patronage and, with the exceptions of campaigns for housing code enforcement, they have avoided the extensive service operations to voters and interest groups which were central to old-style party organizations. For example, when election district captains and other officials of the Greenwich Village Independent Democrats, the reform group which deposed New York Democrat County Leader Carmine DeSapio in his own election district, were asked the same set of questions about their activities used in the New Jersey study, strikingly different responses were made.

The successes of this class of new-style urban party politician have vindicated a portion of the classical strategy of urban party politics, the extensive reliance upon canvassing and other personal relations, and also have shown that under some circumstances it is possible to organize such activities with virtually no reliance on patronage and other material rewards. The reformers have tapped a pool of political activists used by parties elsewhere in the world—for example, in Great Britain—but not a normal part of the American scene. One might say that the reformers have "discovered" the British Labor constituency parties.

TABLE 2. SERVICES PERFORMED BY NEW YORK REFORM DEMOCRATS [25]

The Service	Percentage Performing It "Often"
Helping deserving people get public jobs	0
Showing people how to get their social security benefits, welfare, unemployment compensation, etc.	5
Helping citizens who are in difficulty with the law. Do you help get them straightened out?	6

It is where material resources available to the parties are limited, for example, California, and where voter interest in these resources is low, that the new reformers are successful. In practice, however, the latter condition has confined the effectiveness of the reform Democrats largely to the more prosperous sections of cities; neither their style nor their programs seem to be successful in lower-class districts.[26] The areas of reform Democratic strength are generally *not* the areas which contribute greatly to Democratic pluralities in the cities. And, in many cities, the reformers' clientele is progressively diminishing as higher-income citizens move outward to the suburbs. Therefore, though fascinating and illuminating, the new reform movement must at least for the moment be considered as little more than a single manifestation in a panorama of urban political practices.[27]

Conclusion

The degree to which *old-style* urban party organizations will continue to be a part of this panorama is uncertain. Changes in the social composition of the cities promise to be a major factor in the future of urban politics. If, as seems possible, many cities become lower-class, nonwhite enclaves, we can be confident that there will be a continuing market for the services of the service-oriented old-style politician. Whether or not this is the case, many lessons can be culled from the history of party politics during the years of growth of the American cities—lessons which are relevant, for example, to studying the politics of urbanization elsewhere in the world.[28] In the nineteenth century, after all, the United States was an "emerging," "modernizing" nation, facing the problems of stability and democracy which are now being faced by countless newer nations.

Notes

1. E. E. Schattschneider, *Party Government* (New York, 1942), pp. 162–169.

2. Among the better known accounts are Frank R. Kent, *The Great Game of Politics* (Garden City, N. Y., 1923, rev. ed., 1930); Sonya Forthall, *Cogwheels of Democracy* (New York, 1946); Harold F. Gosnell, *Machine Politics* (Chicago, 1937); and the many case studies of individual bosses. For a recent romanticization, see Edwin O'Connor's novel, *The Last Hurrah* (Boston, 1956).

3. Austin Ranney and Willmoore Kendall, *Democracy and the American Party System* (New York, 1956), pp. 249–252.

4. This last definitional criterion explicitly departs from the characterization of a "machine" in James Q. Wilson's interesting discussion of "The Economy of Patronage," *The Journal of Political Economy,* Vol. 59 (August 1961), p. 370 n., "as that kind of political party which sustains its members through the distribution of material incentives (patronage) rather than nonmaterial incentives (appeals to principle, the fun of the game, sociability, etc.)." There is ample evidence that for many old-style party workers incentives such as "the fun of the game," "sociability," and even "service" are of central importance. See, for example, Edward J. Flynn, *You're the Boss* (New York, 1947), p. 22; James A. Farley, *Behind the Ballots* (New York, 1938), p. 237; and the passage cited in note 8 below. The distinction between "material" and "nonmaterial" incentives would probably have to be discarded in a more refined discussion of the motivations underlying political participation. So-called material rewards, at base, are nonmaterial in the sense that they are valued for the status they confer and for other culturally defined reasons.

5. *Op. cit.*, p. 106.

6. See, for example, Edward A. Shils, *The Torment of Secrecy* (Glencoe, Ill., 1956) and Stanley M. Elkins, *Slavery* (Chicago, 1959, reprinted with an introduction by Nathan Glazer, New York, 1963).

7. William L. Riordon, *Plunkitt of Tammany Hall* (originally published in 1905; republished New York, 1948 and New York, 1963; quotations are from the 1963 edition), pp. 27–28.

8. *Ibid.*, pp. 25–26.

9. Elmer E. Cornwell, Jr., "Party Absorption of Ethnic Groups: The Case of Providence, Rhode Island," *Social Forces,* Vol. 38 (March 1960), pp. 205–210.

10. Riordon, *op. cit.*, pp. 17–20.

11. Frank J. Sorauf, "State Patronage in a Rural County," *American Political Science Review,* Vol. 50 (December 1956), pp. 1046–1056.

12. Angus Campbell, Philip E. Converse, Warren E. Miller, and Donald E. Stokes, *The American Voter* (New York, 1960), pp. 426–427. The statistic for nonsouthern cities was supplied to me by the authors.

13. Daniel Katz and Samuel J. Eldersveld, "The Impact of Local Party Activity on the Electorate," *Public Opinion Quarterly,* Vol. 25 (Spring 1961), pp. 16–17.

14. Hugh A. Bone, *Grass Roots Party Leadership* (Seattle, 1952); Robert L. Morlan, "City Politics: Free Style," *National Municipal Review,* Vol. 38 (November 1949), pp. 485–491.

15. Robert A. Dahl, *Who Governs?* (New Haven, 1961), p. 278.

16. *Ibid.;* Nelson W. Polsby, *Community Power and Political Theory* (New Haven, 1963); Raymond E. Wolfinger, *The Politics of Progress* (forthcoming).

17. Raymond E. Wolfinger, "The Influence of Precinct Work on Voting Behavior," *Public Opinion Quarterly,* Vol. 27 (Fall 1963), pp. 387–398.

18. Frost deliberately worded his questionnaire descriptions of these services favorably in order to avoid implying that respondents were to be censured for indulging in "machine tactics." Richard T. Frost, "Stability and Change in Local Politics," *Public Opinion Quarterly,* Vol. 25 (Summer 1961), pp. 231–232.

19. James Q. Wilson, "Politics and Reform in American Cities," *American Government Annual, 1962–63* (New York, 1962), pp. 37–52.

20. Phillips Cutright, "Nonpartisan Electoral Systems in American Cities," *Comparative Studies in Society and History,* Vol. 5 (January 1963), pp. 219–221.

21. For a brief review of the relevant literature, see Fred I. Greenstein, *The American Party System and the American People* (Englewood Cliffs, N. J., 1963), pp. 57–60.

22. Joseph T. Klapper, *The Effects of Mass Communication* (New York, 1960).

23. James Q. Wilson, *The Amateur Democrat* (Chicago, 1962).

24. There is another interesting point of resemblance between old- and new-style urban party politics. In both, an important aspect of the motivation for participation seems to be the rewards of sociability. Tammany picnics and New York Committee for Democratic Voters (CDV) coffee hours probably differ more in decor than in the functions they serve. An amusing indication of this is provided by the committee structure of the Greenwich Village club of the CDV; in addition to the committees dealing with the club newsletter, with housing, and with community action, there is a social committee and a Flight Committee, the latter being concerned with arranging charter flights to Europe for club members. See Vernon M. Goetscheus, *The Village Independent Democrats: A Study in the Politics of the New Reformers* (unpublished senior distinction thesis, Honors College, Wesleyan University, 1963), pp. 65–66. On similar activities by the California Democratic Clubs, see Robert E. Lane, James D. Barber, and Fred I. Greenstein, *Introduction to Political Analysis* (Englewood Cliffs, N. J., 1962), pp. 55–57.

25. Goetcheus, *op. cit.,* p. 138.

26. DeSapio, for example, was generally able to hold on to his lower-class Italian voting support in Greenwich Village; his opponents succeeded largely by activating the many middle- and upper-class voters who had moved into new high-rent housing in the district.

27. Probably because of their emphasis on ideology, the new reform groups also seem to be quite prone to internal conflicts which impede their effectiveness. One is reminded of Robert Michels' remarks about the intransigence of intellec-

tuals in European socialist parties. *Political Parties* (New York, 1962, originally published in 1915), Part 4, Chap. 6.

28. On the significance of the American experience with old-style urban politics for the emerging nations, see Wallace S. Sayre and Nelson W. Polsby, "American Political Science and the Study of Urbanization," Committee on Urbanization, Social Science Research Council, mimeo. 1963, pp. 45–48.

IMPACT OF URBANIZATION ON AMERICAN FAMILY STRUCTURE AND FUNCTIONING

Robert O. Blood, Jr.

In the "good old days," most American families lived on farms, remote and isolated. Pioneer family members clung together with a desperation born of economic necessity. They depended on one another for most essential services. Survival required the cooperation of the entire household. The rudimentary nature of other social institutions imposed religious, political, and educational responsibilities on the family. Divorce was unthinkable, since neither man nor woman could afford to lose the services of the other. Childlessness or even limited childbearing was a hardship to be endured with regret.

The compulsory nature of family life on the frontier is indisputable. The controversial question is whether such family life was not only compulsory but "golden." To many Americans the past has a lustre which the present lacks. Pioneer families seem in retrospect to have found unique satisfaction in working and playing together. Family life then was rewarding and satisfying, vital, and meaningful. By contrast, modern family life seems brittle, tenuous, and often meaningless.

Is this picture true? Unfortunately it is impossible for the methods of social science to be used to measure the family life of the past. However, it is possible to examine contemporary rural and urban families to see whether the "golden past" still survives on the modern farm and whether urban family life is obsolescent. If contemporary rural and urban families do not differ greatly from one another and if urban families have a stable structure and perform vital functions for their members, then the past may not have been so golden, and the present not so tarnished.

Urbanization of the American Farm Family

A total of 178 farm wives were interviewed in southeastern Michigan (a random sample of three counties extending west of Detroit). The information they provided is fundamentally similar to that derived from the Detroit Area Study. For instance, the city and farm families are equally democratic in their patterns

Reprinted by permission of the author and publisher from *Sociology and Social Research*, **49** (October, 1964), pp. 5–16.

of making family decisions. When the urban families are arbitrarily divided into husband and wife dominated segments of equal size, the farm families have an equally large proportion of equalitarian cases.

The chief way in which these farm and city couples differ is in their division of labor. As tradition suggests, farm wives are more involved than city wives in practical tasks. Farm women engage in such outside tasks as raising poultry and vegetables. They also get less help in the home from their busy husbands. Since city wives are geographically separated from the husband's place of work, they can't assist him directly. Similarly, the fact that the commuter leaves his work behind when he comes home makes him more available to help with household tasks.[1]

Does this greater service of farm wives mean that rural families are better than city families? That depends on the criterion for what is better. If the criterion is divorce rates, farm families score somewhat better. But if it is the wife's satisfaction with her marriage partner, the rural advantage largely disappears. In these samples, farm wives are slightly more satisfied with their standard of living and the husband's understanding, less satisfied with the love and affection received and equally satisfied with the companionship. Since in the American scheme of values, companionship is the crucial test of marriage, the overall evaluation of family life by rural and urban wives is essentially the same.

This brief comparison of contemporary city and farm families suggests that in most respects their family patterns are similar. It gives no conclusive answer to the question whether farm family living in the past was more "golden" than in the present. It does suggest, however, that city and farm families shine with essentially the same hue today.

Contemporary farm families have become urbanized, at least in Southern Michigan. They read the same newspapers, listen to the same radio broadcasts, and watch the same telecasts as their urban counterparts. Their children attend consolidated schools in urban centers. Their cars and all-weather roads give them access to the city where they participate in community activities. Modern farming has become a business which happens to be located in the country and differs little from urban family businesses in its effect on family life. Viewed in the large, city families and farm families have more common characteristics than differences, for today the metropolitan community and its hinterland are a single social unit.

Vitality of the Modern American Family

If farm families resemble city families, perhaps that only proves that they, too, are decadent. Perhaps all American families and not just urban ones have disintegrated. It is not enough to compare city and farm families relative to one another. Some assessment of the actual level of functioning of contemporary families must be made. For the sake of simplicity, this assessment will focus on urban families, but in almost every case, the same findings characterize the farm families studied.

The vitality of family life can be looked at from two points of view. First, how sound is the structure of American family life? Secondly, how effectively do these families carry out their functions?[2]

Stability of Modern Family Structure

The structure of a family consists of the configuration of positions which the family members occupy. This paper is concerned with the positions which the husband and wife occupy in relation to one another. These positions (or statuses) and the roles attached to them may be analyzed in terms of the power structure and the division of labor in the family.

For present purposes, it is not enough to describe these structural characteristics since no evidence is available that one structure is inherently more stable than another. Rather, the question must be raised as to the basis for contemporary structural forms. Are they based on outmoded conventions undermined by changing times? Or, do they vary randomly with no rhyme nor reason, reflecting chaotic or meaningless social conditions? If, by contrast, family structures are determined by factors which produce efficient results, it may be assumed that they will be stable over a period of time. Efficient social structures create their own rewards, leading the participants to be satisfied with them rather than to wish for change.

An efficient power structure may be defined as one which produces "right" decisions. In the past, husbands were considered the best qualified to make decisions by virtue of being men. However, the improved status of American women has increased their contribution to the decision-making process. Some alarmists suggest that the American wife has already seized domestic power, not necessarily by wresting it from her husband but at least through his abdication of authority.

The Detroit data fail to disclose an American matriarchate. Rather, the general mode of decision-making is equalitarian. Around this mode, however, there are significant variations. In some marriages the wife is more dominant while in others the husband dominates.

What is the basis for these variations? Concrete factors which affect the power structure can be summarized under the heading of "competence." Whichever partner has the greater ability to make a decision usually does so. Sometimes competence results from the individual's experience in a certain activity. For example, husbands generally choose their own job and purchase cars whereas wives make decisions about food purchases. However, the crucial question is not the competences husbands generally share but rather the variations which occur between couples.

Table I provides one example of a source of competence affecting marital power structure. In this case, the resource is the time the husband and wife work outside the home. Taken by itself this might not suggest individual competence so much as an economic interpretation of marriage. However, other data show that unpaid participation in the community has a similar relationship to family power structure. For example, whichever partner attends church more often and whichever partner belongs to more organizations tends to make more of the family decisions. Taken together this suggests that participation in activities outside the home provides social experience and knowledge which carry over into marital decision-making. Even more directly reflecting personal competence is the evidence that whichever partner has more education makes more decisions.

TABLE I. HUSBAND'S POWER BY COMPARATIVE WORK PARTICIPATION OF HUSBAND AND WIFE

	Wife Not Employed—Husband Employed			Wife Employed—Husband Employed		
	Overtime	Fulltime	None	Overtime	Fulltime	None
Husband's mean power score	5.62	5.28	4.88	4.50	4.46	2.67
Number of families *	195	218	25	44	57	3

* white families only

If family decisions are made by the best qualified partner, family power structures are geared to the most efficient accomplishment of their objective. Apparently, therefore, these power structures are basically stable and unlikely to be a source of complaint or unrest.

An efficient division of labor gets tasks done with the least effort. This is precisely the pattern which Detroit families follow. In general, the division follows traditional sex lines, with women doing most of the housework and men concentrating on technical repairs and outside work. The fact that these are traditional sex roles does not mean that they are inefficient. Women's tasks are naturally associated with childbearing and child rearing and men's with muscular strength and mechanical aptitude.

In Detroit, the division of labor at home is drastically affected by the out-of-the-home work schedules of both husband and wife. Housework is primarily the province of the wife, but when she works outside the home, the time left for housework is severely limited. Under these circumstances, the husband tends to come to her rescue, unless he is preoccupied with responsibilities of his own.

It has already been suggested that farm wives do more housework and get correspondingly less help from their husbands because the latter's chores are readily accessible at all hours of the day and every day of the week. Since farmers are seldom far from exterior tasks needing their efforts, they tend to be perennially busy and unable to help around the house.

Although household tasks are generally done by whichever partner has the most time, tasks requiring special skill are less easily interchanged. In Detroit, a task closely linked to personal competence is keeping track of the money and bills. In some families, the wife "has the head for figures," while in others the husband is the better bookkeeper. In general, whichever partner has more education handles this responsibility, but in the higher income brackets this task is increasingly performed by the husband. Presumably as income exceeds the subsistence level, it is less limited to the wife's usual provinces of consumption and increasingly available for saving, investment, and tax options familiar to the husband from his business experience.

In general, then, the division of labor, like the power structure, is so organized as to accomplish the family's objectives. Hence the modern family's structure is usually stable, no matter what its form.

What about the functions performed by the urban family? They have changed drastically. Old functions have dwindled with the rise of specialized institutions.

TABLE II. EXPECTED NUMBER OF CHILDREN BY WIFE'S EDUCATION FOR WIVES UNDER AGE 45

	Years of Education		
	Grade School	High School	College
Expected number	2.51	2.64	2.86
Number of families *	50	318	40

* white families only

Protective functions are shared with the police and the army, religious functions with church and Sunday School, educational functions with the school, and recreational functions with the cinema. The once crucial function of home production has shriveled to vestigial proportions in Detroit. Food growing and processing are minority experiences in the metropolitan area, the former because of the unavailability of garden space, the latter because of the ready availability of processed foods at the corner store. Dressmaking has been taken over by the factory, and even the baking company is superseding the housewife in her kitchen. One sixth of our Detroit housewives report that they purchase all their bread and most of their cakes, cookies, and pies, while an additional 7 percent confess that they never bake at all.

At the same time that economic production has nearly vanished from the urban home, the production of children has dwindled, too. To some extent this results from the children's transformation from useful "hands" into dregs on the family labor market. Partly, however, the decreased number of children born has been offset by the increasing proportion who survive to maturity. Under pioneer conditions, the average family lost at least one child through sickness. Today childhood fatalities are so rare that childbearing can be reduced accordingly.

The emphasis with respect to children has shifted from childbearing to child-rearing, from the quantity of children produced to the quality of children raised. While the emphasis on quality began in the middle class, it is spreading to the masses. As a result of the growing homogenization of parental aspirations for children and of the filtering down of family planning practices to the working class, families at all levels of society are beginning to gear their birthrate to their "ability to pay." For the first time in American history, couples predict that those with greater resources will have more children. (see Table II)

People in other countries often wonder what the American wife does with the leisure time provided by her labor-saving devices. One of the important answers is that she spends more time on her children's social development. Whereas she used to be preoccupied with subsistence tasks, today she can focus on her children's personality problems and achievements.

This shift has occurred with respect to parents, too. Whereas the economic and biological functions of the family once monopolized the attention of the parents, today there is time left over for each other's subtler needs. As a result, new functions emerge.

When our Detroit wives were asked to rank several new functions in comparison with the traditional economic and child-bearing ones, the shifting pattern of functions appeared. Asked which of five functions they considered "the most valuable part of marriage," they most often chose "companionship in doing things together with the husband" (47 percent). "The chance to have children" was a poor second at 26 percent, leaving 13 percent who chose "the husband's understanding of the wife's problems and feelings," 10 percent for "the husband's expression of love and affection," and only 3 percent for "the standard of living" provided by the husband's income. Exactly how many functions the family performs depends on one's analytic framework but in the light of these statistics there can be no question of the emerging significance of several new ones.

Whereas traditional family functions were directed toward the welfare of the children or of the family as a whole, the new functions focus on the husband-wife relationship. Perhaps for the first time in history, the marriage bond has become important in its own right, even after children arrive. This reflects the emergence of a whole new stage in family living after the departure of the last child from the home.[3] Whereas a few decades ago the typical wife was widowed before her last child married, today's wives experience more than a decade of living alone with their husbands. Under these circumstances, the marital relationship increases in importance.

These new functions are oriented toward the personal needs of the marriage partners. The affectional function meets the need for acceptance and appreciation, the mental hygiene function the need for release from emotional tension, and the companionship function offsets the anonymity and loneliness of urban life.

Two empirical questions can be raised with respect to these functions. (1) How actively do the Detroit couples try to meet these needs? (2) How well do they succeed?

Companionship involves doing things for pure enjoyment through joint use of leisure time. While no overall measure of companionship is available from the Detroit Area Study, several specific facets were measured. A majority of Detroit husbands tell their wives every day or almost every day about things that happened at work. This "informative companionship" reduces the urban gap between the workplace and the home though it does not match the even higher communication level of farm husbands and wives about the business on which they depend for their livelihood.

Other types of companionship require more effort than just talking over the day's events, and therefore cannot be expected to occur so often. Nevertheless the median Detroit couple get together with relatives at least once a week, and with other friends several times a month. This joint sociability results in shared friendships, for most of the Detroit wives know at least half their husband's friends quite well.

In addition, the typical Detroit male goes to church once or twice a month, almost always with his wife, providing a significant amount of religious companionship. Joint participation in secular organizations, however, is rare beyond a small circle of high status couples.

In general, Detroit married couples engage in a considerable amount and variety of joint activity both inside and outside the home. As a result, 30 percent of the wives are enthusiastic about the companionship they have with their husbands while most of the rest express considerable satisfaction. Should such expressions of satisfaction be discounted as mere rationalizations? Certainly they are subjective evaluations of the marital situation. But they testify to the effectiveness of the marital relationship in meeting the wife's need for companionship.

While no measures of the frequency of expressing affection are available, the wives' enthusiasm about this marital function is even greater. Affection is the one aspect of marriage where urban satisfaction markedly exceeds the rural. Apparently urban husbands particularly excel in giving love. Perhaps they also perform better in the closely related sexual function. In any case, the average Detroit couple is bound together by mutual affection. This interpretation is reinforced by the fact that the majority of urban wives feel that their families are more closely knit than "most other families" they know.

Perhaps the newest family function dealt with is the mental hygiene function. At least this aspect of marriage has seldom been studied. Assuming that peace of mind is a basic human need, what contribution do marriage partners make to it? Particularly after a crisis has disturbed the individual's emotional equilibrium, how does the partner respond?

To be able to respond one must know about the difficulty. The typical Detroit wife tells her husband her troubles about half the time. The rest of the time, she deals with her tensions by herself or turns elsewhere for help. The problems she shares with her husband depend on his availability, his own frame of mind, and the seriousness of the problem. The typical wife relies on her husband for therapeutic assistance whenever she especially needs it and he is capable of giving it.

A majority of Detroit husbands respond with sympathy, advice, or help and the wives feel much relieved as a result. Only a small minority of husbands react so negatively that the wife feels worse or learns that it is better not to tell him at all. Apparently, the mental hygiene function operates effectively when it is really needed.

This brief exploration of three non-traditional functions of marriage reveals sources of strength in modern urban marriages which probably were less effective in the past under more arduous living conditions. In any case, they are rewarding aspects of contemporary family life which reinforce the stability inherent in the modern family's social structure.

Variation in Modern Family Patterns

While it is possible to generalize about "the urban family," there are significant differences between various segments of the population. Detroit's religious and ethnic groups differ little in most aspects of their family life. But educational, occupational, and income groups which involve differential social status produce varying patterns of family structure and functioning.

The Landecker-Lenski Index of Social Status provides a convenient combination of education, occupation, income, and the reported social esteem of ethnic background.[4] Table III shows the direct relationship which exists in Detroit between the husband's social status and the amount of power he wields in the family.

TABLE III. HUSBAND'S POWER BY SOCIAL STATUS

	Percentile Ranking on Social Status				Index
	0–19	20–39	40–59	60–79	80–99
Husband's mean power	4.39	4.79	5.00	5.33	5.56
Number of families *	41	147	204	177	86

* Entire urban sample (both white and Negro).

Although the difference between high and low status families in power structure is substantial, there is a regular progression over the social status continuum. Therefore, this is better described as a difference in degree rather than kind. Nevertheless, the difference is great enough at the extremes to become almost qualitative in nature.

Detailed analysis of the Detroit data suggests that high status contributes to the husband's power through increasing his knowledge and skill relevant to decision-making. His wife usually defers to him, recognizing his special competence, rather than being forced to submit to his arbitrary exercise of power. The low status wife frequently finds that she must take over the reins of the family as a result of her husband's incompetence, negligence, or indifference. Insofar as there are matriarchs in America, they are found at the bottom of the social scale. However, they rule by default rather than conquest.

Everything which applies to low status families generally applies in greater degree to Negro families. Table IV shows how much lower Negro husbands' power is than white husbands' within the same occupational category. Extra economic and social disadvantages undermine the Negro husband's morale with the result that he plays a marginal role in family decision-making. This difference in power structure between Negro and white families is correlated with the high incidence of divorce and desertion in low status families generally and Negro families in particular.

In general, high social status is associated with marital satisfaction, though the husband's community responsibilities sometimes conflict with his marital relationship. Especially when the husband is preoccupied with vocational success, com-

TABLE IV. HUSBAND'S POWER BY OCCUPATION AND RACE

Husband's Mean Power by Race	Occupation			
	Blue Collar		White Collar	
	Low	High	Low	High
White	5.07 (162)	4.98 (161)	5.36 (78)	5.52 (151)
Negro	4.31 (78)	4.60 (20)	—	5.00 (5)

Numbers in parentheses represent the number of families on which means are computed.

TABLE V. FREQUENCY WIFE TELLS HUSBAND HER TROUBLES AFTER A BAD DAY, BY HUSBAND'S OCCUPATION

	Husband's Occupation			
	Blue Collar		White Collar	
Frequency wife tells her troubles	Low	High	Low	High
Always	25%	23%	19%	17%
Usually	23	20	34	24
Half the time	23	26	30	32
Seldom	16	21	10	21
Never	13	10	7	6
Total	100%	100%	100%	100%
Mean	2.32	2.24	2.49	2.26
Number of families *	173	173	88	157

* White families only

panionship with the wife suffers. However, such preoccupation hardly mars the general positive correlation between social status and marital satisfaction.

High social status couples usually do more things together. On all the types of companionship measured in the Detroit Area Study, high status families report more sharing. However, in the mental hygiene area, high status wives are more selective about telling their troubles to the husband.

Table V shows that wives of high status men typically "bother" their husbands half the time whereas wives of low status men are more apt to tell them always or not at all. Perhaps low status extremism reflects greater impulsivity. If the wife is the impulsive partner, she unburdens herself every time. On the other hand, if the husband is the impulsive one, the wife learns it isn't safe to approach him with her troubles. Wives of professional and managerial husbands, by contrast, balance their own needs against the husband's in determining how often to approach him.

Conclusion

Variations between social strata (and the other changes which occur over the family life cycle) are important but fail to alter the basic generalizations about urban families as a whole. In general, data from the Detroit Metropolitan Area suggest that modern urban families possess structural characteristics which enable them to function effectively. The range of functions performed by the family has shifted with the rise of the metropolis, but the reduction of old functions has released time and energy for new ones.

Urbanization, then, has enabled the family to undertake new functions and to make structural alterations appropriate to a new division of labor between the family and other social institutions and to the growing equalization of external participation by the husband and wife. These urban influences extend beyond the metropolis to adjacent farm families with the result that contemporary rural and urban families closely resemble each other in most essential features.

Notes

1. See Robert O. Blood, Jr., "The Division of Labor in City and Farm Families," *Marriage and Family Living*, 20 (May, 1958), 170–74.

2. For a complete report and analysis of the Detroit Area Study data on marriage, see Robert O. Blood, Jr., and Donald M. Wolfe, *Husbands and Wives: The Dynamics of Family Living* (New York: The Free Press of Glencoe, 1960).

3. See Paul C. Glick, "The Life Cycle of the Family," *Marriage and Family Living*, 17 (February, 1955), 3–9.

4. Gerhard E. Lenski, "Status Crystallization: A Non-Vertical Dimension of Social Status," *American Sociological Review*, 19 (August, 1954), 405–13.

SOCIAL DEVELOPMENT AND THE AMERICAN SOUTH

Leonard Reissman

For many decades the American South [1] could be fairly described by the same characteristics used to describe underdeveloped areas anywhere: depressed living standards, a predominantly agricultural economy, widely discrepant social inequalities, traditional mindedness, and a social isolation from outside influence. History aside, the region was an anomaly: a backward area contained within the borders of one of the most developed nations in the world. Compared with the new nations in Africa or southeast Asia, it could be argued, the South generally was better off, although not all segments of the South's population would be covered even by that claim. In any case, the comparison ought not to be drawn in that direction, but rather toward a juxtaposition between the South and the rest of the United States. By that comparison, the South fared poorly. On almost every measure of social development the region has ranked well below the national average. The fact that the South is, after all, part of the nation could only serve to amplify the discrepancies. Clearly, the region was not sharing in the affluence or the social gains attained by the rest of the country. Illiteracy rates have been among the highest in the South, median incomes among the lowest, standardized mortality rates [2] among the highest, and levels of economic prosperity among the lowest. In general terms it could be fairly said for much of the South that it was a region distinguished by an oppressive rurality, by an unbalanced dependence upon agriculture, by an outmoded aristocratic social structure, by an expensive biracial caste system, and by a fierce dedication to sectional political units. Until quite recently, then, the South had committed itself to remain socially underdeveloped, restrained by the historic mold of its institutions and its traditions.

Reprinted by permission of the author and publisher from *The Journal of Social Issues*, **22** (January, 1966), pp. 101–116.

Left alone, the region probably would have continued into the present in much the same way, blunting or deterring any major force for change. As before, its politicians would invoke the filibuster, many of its talented men and women would leave an unreceptive social climate,[3] and its leaders would invoke that handy euphemism about the "southern way of life" when confronted by a possibility for change. Much of this traditional southern response, however, has been altered recently. Within the past decade the South has lost the option to choose the kinds of change it preferred, if any. The federal government, the large private corporations with federal support, and new leadership groups have gained more than a little control over the once closed affairs of the South. As a result, the South has been impelled into a massive social transformation that must bring the region more into line with the rest of the country. A number of complex, interrelated, and pervasive social forces has hit the South with enough impact so that the region has been unable either to avoid those forces or to assimilate them gradually into a traditional institutional structure. Increased federal expenditures have poured into the region in connection with the space program, and as such things go, have brought with them firmer federal intervention in the South than anything since Reconstruction. Similarly, a number of critical decisions by the federal courts on school integration, legislative reapportionment, and voting rights literally has forced a revision of traditional southern behavior. Of course, traditions die hard but there are signs that the historic defenses against outside intervention have given way to a more pragmatic and realistic recognition of the need for law and order. Finally, the successes achieved by an organized Negro militancy, coupled with the migration of Negroes out of the region and middle class persons into the region, have contributed importantly to the changes taking place in the South. The effects of these social changes, it now seems likely, will convert the South from a traditionally rural, agricultural, and aristocratic society into an urban, industrial, and class society.

Similar assessments have been made by a number of social scientists writing in several recent symposia. Even the titles, as is the case with this issue of the *Journal*, convey the strong emphasis upon change: *The Deep South in Transformation, The South in Continuity and Change, Change in the Contemporary South,* and *The American South in the 1960's.* Change is obviously the major feature of this article. More specifically, the emphasis here is upon the South as an area in the process of social development from backwardness to modernity. That process, whether in the American South or in underdeveloped areas elsewhere, can be analyzed by means of four variables: urban growth, industrial growth, the rise of a middle class, and the rise of nationalism as an ideology to replace narrower sectional loyalties. I have elsewhere described these dimensions and their interrelationships in the process of development (Reissman, 1964).

Each dimension specifies a critical element in the process of social development. Urban growth measures the ecological shift of population from farms and villages into cities, a shift that sooner or later requires that people also alter their attitudes and values to fit them for living in the urban environment. Industrial growth measures the shift from an agricultural to an industrial economy. With this growth must come new attitudes toward work, industrial discipline, consumer practices, and a wide array of industrially inspired values. The rise of a middle class to replace an aristocratic elite and thereby to alter the entire structure of stratification is a third critical element of social development. The shift from an aristocratic to a class structure means a redistribution of power and a redefinition of the legitimate bases of power. Finally, the rise of nationalism as an ideology requires that primary loyalties be focussed upon the nation rather than on any narrower social unit such as the region, a race, a religion, or an ethnic group. The purpose of that loyalty is to establish the nation-state as the legitimate and supreme arbiter of political disputes, with the consequent decrease in the political importance of smaller units.

These four dimensions or variables of social development make sense not only for the analysis of the admittedly backward countries in the world, but also for the analysis of changes that now characterize the American South. On every count, the deep changes that are moving the South toward a level of modernity comparable to the nation as a whole can be understood in terms of these four dimensions.

These four each account for an integral aspect of the process of social change. Urban growth specifies the locale where change is, in effect, generated. Cities have been historically the centers for social change because they provide a receptive environment. "City air makes man free" was a medieval edict that is still reflected today in the urban attitude of inquiry and experimentation with new social forms. Industrial growth specifies the character of contemporary development, not only in the economic sense but also in the broader value sense. An industrial economy builds the labor force it needs, and also fans out into other institutional areas, in what Roshwald has called the "confusion of spheres" (1965, p. 249). The importance of the middle class for development is to provide the agents to lead. This class, more than any other, is the reservoir of talented and motivated individuals who rebel against those older traditions that kept the society static. Finally, nationalism provides the rationale to legitimate the change. People do not willingly let go of the past in order to embrace the future. An acceptable explanation is needed that can endow changes with meaning and purpose.

Doubtless there are patterned sequences in the way each of these variables appears on the scene (Reissman, 1964; Chap. VII). The sequence will vary from one situation to the next, depending upon other factors such as available economic resources, the degree of leadership that is supplied, the level from which a country begins development, and the like. In the case of the contemporary South, all of the variables seem to come upon the scene at once, making it impossible now to separate out the effects contributed by each. Yet, even without knowing the precise causal sequence, we can learn much about the situation by seeing the consequences of each dimension for southern society today.

Urban and Industrial Growth

The subjects of urban and industrial growth in the South have received enough attention in recent years to require only a brief summary here (Nichols, 1960,

1964; Danhof, 1962; Reissman, 1965). So popular have these subjects become, that some analysts have tended to trace all changes in the South to one or both of these variables. Urban and industrial growth are unquestionably important for current developments, but they are not alone the causes of change. Rather, in concert with the other two dimensions that have been mentioned, urbanization and industrialization have produced important changes in social organization.

Comparative statistics for the period from 1930 or 1940 to 1960 show clearly that the South has been urbanizing and industrializing at a faster rate than has the rest of the nation. The gap that for so long has separated the region from the nation is closing, and closing rapidly. Nichols has summarized (1964a, p. 26) the industrial development of the South as follows:

> During 1930–60, as a percentage of the total gainfully employed, manufacturing employment grew from 14.5 to 21.3 percent in the South but only from 25.7 to 29.4 percent in the rest of the country. In the process, the South closed a major part of the gap between itself and the non-South in relative manufacturing employment—standing at 72 percent of the non-South in 1960 as compared with only 56 percent in 1930.

A similar trend is also evident in the growth of southern cities during the last two decades. In 1940, two out of every three persons in the U. S. were residents in urban places; i.e., an incorporated unit with a population of 2,500 or more. In that year, however, only one out of every three southerners was an urbanite by that definition. By 1960, the urban population in the South had increased from 36 percent to almost 58 percent, an increase of 22 percent. During the same twenty years, the urban population in the country as a whole increased by only nine percent. In 1940, there were almost ten million southerners living in the larger urban complexes called standard metropolitan areas, and they accounted for some 13 percent of all Americans living in those areas. By 1960, the southern population in metropolitan areas had doubled and accounted for some 17 percent of those residents. Although urban expansion has come to the South relatively late compared with other regions of the country, the rate of expansion has been more rapid.

Therefore, as regards urbanization and industrialization, it can be said that the South has closed the gap separating it from the nation as a whole very rapidly, even though the region is still somewhat below the national average. Yet, the forces that have produced these rapid gains in the region during only two decades will continue to function in the future. It is most probable that within a relatively short period of time—less than another two decades—the differences between the region and the nation as regards urban and industrial growth will have disappeared.

The Rise of the Middle Class

The significance of urban and industrial growth for recent developments in the South is matched by the rise of a middle class in the region to a position of social importance. The importance of the middle class for the process of change comes from the forced restructuring of society that this class sets into motion. The middle class in a developing area provides the leading personnel for social modernization. It is the social segment most committed to such development, for its future power and prestige depend upon it. I do not mean to imply that this is necessarily a conspiracy or even a deliberately organized movement. Rather, the driving aspirations of middle class persons push them toward social modernization as the means to realize their ambitions. In our own history, in the history of other western nations, and again today in the events in newly emerging nations, the middle class has assumed the pivotal role of promoting social development. Each successful step toward an urban and industrial economy, toward an open class society oriented toward achievement, serves to make the position of the middle class more secure. In return the middle class pulls the rest of society along with it toward higher living standards, broader educational opportunities, and wider participation in the society.[4]

In addition to these considerable functions, the rise of the middle class in a developing area challenges and, if successful, finally replaces the dominance of the aristocracy. It could not be otherwise. The values that the middle class seeks to legitimate are those that attack the traditional bases of aristocratic domination. Land as a source of wealth and power is challenged by money; ascribed status is challenged by status through achievement; and traditionalism is challenged by pragmatism. In brief, by its own rise the middle class broadens the basis for political, economic, and social participation. Later on in the process, the middle class may well seek to secure its power by the very elite practices it earlier sought to destroy.

As late as 1930, the South could be characterized as a regional society built upon aristocratic domination, aristocratic sentiments, and aristocratic traditions. The plantation and magnolia image of the antebellum South was somewhat tarnished as Tennessee Williams has informed us repeatedly, but aristocratic traditions did not die easily. The South's stratification structure was steeply pyramidal: a small, land-owning and commercial elite at the top; a relatively small middle class of professionals, managers, and public officials; a large segment including the small farmers, tenant farmers, and the urban poor; and finally, the whole of this structure resting upon the bulk of the Negro population bound to agriculture. The caste barrier separated Negro from white, and just as surely, the aristocratic barrier separated the elite from all others. Upward social mobility was relatively limited compared with the rest of the nation. Whatever mobility there was seemed to be confined largely to the cities, which were not yet sufficiently dynamic to support any widespread upward mobility. For the most part, those who held such aspirations chose to leave the region, thereby denying the South the necessary talent and support for change.

Under these restrictive conditions, political and social relations tended to remain traditionally static. With but few exceptions during most of the hundred years after the Civil War, political styles and social etiquette in the South continued to reinforce the *status quo*. The South had constructed an almost impenetrable barrier around itself during those decades that kept out most changes originating outside. Its insistence upon states' rights was a demand for autonomy to maintain intact the existing structures of social and political power. In time, that insistence became increasingly reactionary because it was so opposite to the direction in which the nation as a whole was moving. From the southern Bourbons to Governor Wallace, southern leadership well understood that any changes to modify the structure of stratification in the region must inevitably mean the alteration of the entire structure of power. This stance is quite clear as regards race relations, and although less apparent, is applicable as well to the challenges being made by the new, urban, middle class.

The rhetoric of segregation may be different from the rhetoric of aristocracy, but both are really comments on the same situation. Any gains by either the Negro or the middle class must be at the expense of those who have held power in the South. It is this type of change that the leadership in the South is attempting to stifle—by persuasion, by conformity to old traditions, and by violence if all else fails.

Evidence for the growth of a middle class to challenge the former aristocratic elite is hard to come by. For one thing, we are considering extremely subtle social changes that do not show up in the available statistics. For another thing, social scientists have not yet paid enough attention to this aspect of changes in the South, tending to restrict their attention to voting statistics or census reports. However, it would be a mistake to stop there. The theoretical orientation that I have suggested here strongly supports the logic of the social role that has been assigned to the middle class in the present period. There is really no other valid way to explain the revolutionary changes now taking place, since there must be human agents who are behind that change. There is some evidence that can be cited on this point, although it is less specific than one would ordinarily prefer. The relatively larger immigration of new middle class persons into the region as a result of increased skill demands by industry can be ascertained somewhat by the figures presented in Table 1.

Table 1 presents a classification of occupational categories arranged in four class groups in order to highlight the trend toward middle class expansion in the South. The new middle class includes professionals, managers, clerical and sales workers. The new working class includes operatives, service workers, and laborers. The old middle class consists of farm managers and craftsmen. The old lower class includes private household workers and farm laborers.

Table 1 reveals that in 1960 all southern states, except for Florida, Texas, and possibly Virginia, were still behind the national average in the proportion of what are here called the new middle class occupations. Contrariwise, nine of the twelve states had higher proportions—Georgia, Florida, and Louisiana excepted—in the old middle class, identified in this context with a plantation aristocracy. It is also evident from the 1960 distribution that every southern state had more than its share of those in the old lower class. In short, the South as late as 1960 was still lacking a middle class component of a proportion comparable to the nation as a whole.

Yet, these comparisons hide the rapid changes in the occupational distribution that have taken place in the South over the last decade. As the last columns of Table 1 reveal, every southern state showed a higher increase in the new middle class than that experienced by the nation as a whole. At the same time, the proportion in the old middle class decreased more sharply in all of the southern states, except Florida, than was the case for the nation. Almost the same conclusion is reached in the case of the old lower class as well. The rapidity and the pervasiveness of these class changes is the main key to understanding the social developments taking place in the South.

TABLE 1. CHANGES IN OCCUPATIONAL STRUCTURE IN THE SOUTH: 1950–1960

State	1950				1960				1960–1950			
	New Middle Class [1]	New Working Class [2]	Old Middle Class [3]	Old Lower Class [4]	New Middle Class [1]	New Working Class [2]	Old Middle Class [3]	Old Lower Class [4]	(5)–(1)	(6)–(2)	(7)–(3)	(8)–(4)
	(1)	(2)	(3)	(4)	(5)	(6)	(7)	(8)				
Alabama	26.0	32.3	26.4	13.8	33.8	35.1	18.8	9.7	7.8	2.8	– 7.6	–4.1
Arkansas	25.9	26.0	32.7	13.7	32.7	34.2	20.2	9.2	6.8	8.2	–12.5	–4.5
Florida	37.7	31.1	17.1	12.7	42.5	28.2	14.8	8.4	4.8	–2.9	–2.3	–4.3
Georgia	27.8	33.6	22.7	14.2	35.1	35.2	15.9	10.2	7.3	1.6	–6.8	–4.0
Kentucky	27.6	31.4	29.6	9.9	34.1	32.2	22.5	6.6	6.5	.8	–7.1	–3.3
Louisiana	32.7	32.6	21.8	11.6	37.8	33.3	15.7	8.9	5.1	.7	–6.1	–2.7
Mississippi	21.9	23.5	36.4	17.0	29.2	30.8	21.0	16.5	7.3	7.3	–15.4	–.5
N. Carolina	24.8	35.1	25.9	12.7	30.5	36.3	19.4	9.0	5.7	1.2	–6.5	–3.7
S. Carolina	23.1	34.5	23.9	17.2	29.6	37.6	17.3	11.9	6.5	3.1	–6.6	–5.3
Tennessee	29.7	31.8	27.3	9.6	34.9	33.9	19.6	7.1	5.2	2.1	–7.7	–2.5
Texas	36.3	29.8	22.6	9.9	41.2	29.2	17.5	7.0	4.9	–.6	–5.1	–2.9
Virginia	29.3	33.7	22.1	9.2	40.4	31.3	17.6	6.5	11.1	–2.4	–4.5	–2.7
United States	36.9	33.5	21.4	6.7	41.2	31.6	17.4	4.9	4.3	–1.9	–4.0	–1.8

[1] Includes professionals, managers, clerical, and sales.
[2] Includes operatives, service workers, & laborers.
[3] Includes farm managers, craftsmen.
[4] Includes private household workers & farm laborers.
SOURCES: *U.S. Census of Population: 1950.* Vol. II, *Characteristics of the Population,* Part 1, U.S. Summary. Table 79, *U.S. Census of Population 1960. General Social & Economic Characteristics.* U.S. Summary. Table 128.

The shifts that are documented in Table 1 have consequences. Not only do they find resonance in the altered tone of political and social dialogue in the region, but they also affect every institutional sector of southern society. Hence, educational facilities have been expanded and improved in most urban sections of the South because education is a dominant concern of the middle class and fits in with their goals and expectations. Similarly, the programs begun under the Economic Opportunities Act of 1964 have won acceptance among the middle class leadership in the region because the intent of those programs coincides with the middle class concern with social welfare and improvement. The emphasis of those programs upon education, job training, welfare services, and rational consumer patterns among the poor is basically an expression of middle class values.[5]

I am not arguing that the middle class holds a monopoly on virtue, but rather that these efforts are directed toward creating an environment that is acceptable to the middle class. Clearly, this new middle class cannot resort to the use of such total power formerly exercised by the aristocratic elite to keep social order. What is more, the aristocracy had the considerable support of tradition and institutionalized norms. The new middle class, however, must operate during this period of social transition in the very teeth of existing traditions. A major means of winning support, I am suggesting, is for the middle class to champion the cause of social improvement not only because it fits their definition of what is desirable, but also because it brings them the added support from those at the bottom of the social hierarchy. Their action is analogous to the demands of the new leadership in developing nations who push for land reform in order to weaken the power of the aristocracy and to strengthen the basis of their support. In the South's case, the middle class is seeking to create as stable a social order as possible and as quickly as possible. Fortunately, it has the nation's social ideology on its side.

Another indication of the role of the middle class in the South can be inferred from the changes in median family income over the period 1950 to 1960 as shown in Table 2. A pattern similar to that described in Table 1 results. Median family incomes in 1960 in every southern state were below the national median of $5660, varying from Mississippi's poor $2884 to Texas' relatively affluent $4884. However, when the changes during the decade are compared for the proportion of families earning less than $3000 a year, there was a greater decrease in every state (except Texas) than in the nation as a whole. Not so, however, in the gains of those earning $10,000 a year or more. I interpret these figures to mean that the South has moved to close the gap between itself and the nation as far as the poorest families are concerned, although it has not yet begun to move so dramatically in the case of the more affluent families.

One is tempted to account for the rapid rate of improvement by arguing that the South had so far to come. No doubt there is some truth in that. After all, wide discrepancies between the region and the nation in these aspects of social development had existed for a long time and, presumably, could have continued. The point is, however, that the discrepancies have been narrowed significantly and rapidly. Such gains have not been automatic because societies do not change so sharply nor so quickly without some impelling force. The only exception is a revolutionary situation, which is a characterization that is applicable to the South at present.

TABLE 2. CHANGES IN MEDIAN FAMILY INCOMES IN THE SOUTH: 1950–1960

State	1950			1960			1960–1950		
	Median Income	Under $3000	Over $10,000	Median Income	Under $3000	Over $10,000	(4)–(1)	(5)–(2)	(6)–(3)
	(1)	(2)	(3)	(4)	(5)	(6)			
Alabama	$1810	69.7	1.3	$3937	39.1	8.0	$2127	−30.6	6.7
Arkansas	1501	75.5	1.2	3184	47.7	5.5	1683	−27.8	4.3
Florida	2384	57.8	2.6	4722	28.4	11.1	2338	−29.4	8.5
Georgia	1898	67.0	1.6	4208	35.6	9.2	2310	−31.4	7.6
Kentucky	2032	66.7	1.5	4051	38.0	8.0	2019	−28.7	6.5
Louisiana	2122	62.5	2.2	4272	35.6	9.9	2150	−26.9	7.7
Mississippi	1198	79.2	1.0	2884	51.6	5.2	1686	−27.6	4.2
N. Carolina	2121	64.9	1.6	3956	37.2	6.9	1835	−27.7	5.3
S. Carolina	1921	67.1	1.3	3821	39.5	6.5	1900	−27.6	5.2
Tennessee	1983	66.2	1.6	3949	38.3	7.8	1966	−27.9	6.2
Texas	2680	52.8	3.1	4884	28.8	11.8	2204	−24.0	8.7
Virginia	2602	54.1	2.4	4694	27.9	13.2	2094	−26.2	10.8
United States	3073	46.0	3.0	5660	21.4	15.1	2587	−24.6	12.1

SOURCES: *U.S. Census of Population: 1950*. Vol. II. *Characteristics of the Population*. Part 1, U.S. Summary. Table 85. *U.S. Census of Population: 1960. General Social & Economic Characteristics*. U.S. Summary. Table 106.

The Rise of Nationalism

An accompaniment to middle class growth, urbanization and industrialization has been the change in political loyalties: from sectionalism to nationalism. One of the best descriptions of sectionalism is that by Frederick Jackson Turner as quoted in an essay by Odum (1964, pp. 181–182).

> I shall recognize as tests of sectionalism all of those methods by which a given area resists national uniformity, whether by mere opposition in public opinion on the part of a considerable area, or by formal protest, or by combining its votes in Congress and in presidential elections, and also those manifestations of economic and social separateness involved in the existence in a given region of a set of fundamental assumptions, a mental and emotional attitude which segregates the section from other sections or from the nation as a whole. Sooner or later such sectional influences find expression in politics and legislation, and they are even potential bases for forcible resistance.

Sectionalism, of course, has not been uniquely southern. Yet, it is an ideology that has remained longer and had more influence in the South than in other areas of the country. Sectionalism has been used to maintain and justify southern autonomy and thereby to resist national intervention in the region except on the terms acceptable to the South. So it has been until recently when sectionalism has been forced to yield to a broader nationalism.

Nationalism, among other things, is an ideology that emphasizes the nation as the primary focus for citizens' loyalties rather than any lesser unit such as regions or races. "The nation," according to Emerson (1960, p. 95), "is a community of people who feel they belong together in the double sense that they share deeply significant elements of a common heritage and that they have a common destiny for the future." In this sense, nationalism has been a vital component for the development of all nations.

Considering the South, the rise of nationalism and the decline of sectionalism has a particular application. Constitutionally, of course, the South has been part of the nation except during the Civil War. In sociological and psychological terms, on the other hand, the South has long persisted in maintaining its identity separate from the nation. Consider, for example, that only the South, unlike any other region, has its own flag and its own anthem to serve the purposes of sectional patriotism. Consider also that only in the South would local police powers be used to challenge and resist federal police powers, presumably with the support of significant segments of the South's population. I will not go so far as to claim that these examples are signs of a distinct southern nation, but at the very least, they do convey the strong and viable sectional loyalties that have gripped the region.

Sectional loyalties no longer have any future although nostalgia and inertia will keep them alive psychologically for a longer period of time. Sectionalism must decline because of the positive intrusion by the federal government and the federal judiciary into the affairs of the region. Additionally, the other social and economic changes that have been described have also destroyed the viability of narrow sectional loyalty. Like it or not, southerners have had to accept the reality of putting the nation ahead of the region.

The federal government, in the South and in other regions, has become the primary if not the sole decision-maker for those large-scale social, economic, and political affairs that matter most. The military program, the anti-poverty program, the space program, federal support for education, and many other federally supported programs indicate the high level of federal involvement in the administration of the separate states. Sectional autonomy and states' rights simply cannot withstand the impact of those forces, thereby pulling the South more and more into the national orbit.

One relevant way of considering the growing nationalization of the South is to analyze certain urban developments that have been taking place. Out of the formerly separate jurisdictions of states, counties, and cities a new set of functional relationships is now emerging in the South, very similar to those that have developed in other regions of the country. The name given to this phenomenon is "conurbation," which refers to the functional linkage of common social and economic interests that binds cities together. As Osman (cited in Mayo, p. 8) wisely discerned several years ago:

> In time, this country will become a federated civic system, instead of a union of states. . . . The South is a constellation of cities laced together in a growing industrialized agricultural area for which the towns and cities are intersections —concentrations in the Piedmont, in the triangle of Atlanta, Birmingham, and Chattanooga, and in the conurbation of Texas. A tremendous technological system has woven the area together and provides the plexus for mass production and mass distribution to a mass market, establishing conditions for a mass economy in the South. The age of the city has come late to the South, but now the lineaments of the urban future can be discerned.

There are at least two major consequences produced by these conurbations. First, they establish new functional relationships within the region that tie cities together without reference to existing administrative or legal boundaries, a condition that necessarily weakens traditional state and county boundaries. For example, the cities along the Gulf Coast crescent even now find that they have more in common economically and politically than each city has with the rest of the state where it is located. Houston, New Orleans, and Mobile are now tied more closely together into a mutual economic dependence than is likely the case for their intra-state dependence. Second, these conurbations pull the regional urban networks into the national orbit where the major decisions originate that affect them so heavily. This effect is accomplished, in part, because people move more easily than before throughout these networks and their ties to the locality become weaker.[6] In part, it is achieved because some conurbations are pulled into an orbit that extends outside of the region as, for example, Richmond which is tied into the conurbation along the northeast coast. This condition must come to mean that the South is not as isolated as before and must come to develop an outlook that harmonizes with the national outlook. I have covered some of these points in another article that I should like to quote at some length here (Reissman, 1965, p. 96).

> A major point to be emphasized is that the metropolitan pattern that has emerged in the South resembles the national patterns. A related point also needs to be reiterated. The metropolitan conurbations in the South mean the

end of the region as a homogeneous unity and the creation of a new alignment by which the older boundaries and older loyalties have less functional meaning. For most of the South this will come to mean, as it already has in some cases, the development of new chains of common interest and outlook.

Let me stress the point that these metropolitan constellations represent more than just an abstract neighborliness based on geographic proximity. Rather, they have reference to an emerging pattern of functional unity within the conurbation that is reflected in common political and economic interests as well as in a whole range of social conditions common to the conurbation. The existing legal and administrative boundaries, it is safe to say, will continue to stay for some time even though they will become increasingly disfunctional.

A final observation is perhaps in order concerning the role of the Negro in the social developments that I have described, for the Negro has been so much a part of the history of the region. There is little doubt that the emigration of Negroes out of the region coupled with the successes of an organized Negro militancy have played a significant role in the changes that have been described. As late as 1950, 61.5 percent of all Negroes lived in twelve southern states. Only ten years later, the proportion had dropped to 49.7 percent. It will continue to fall. Within the region, as elsewhere in the country, there has been a sharp increase in the urban migration of Negroes so that by 1960, eight out of the twelve southern states had a majority of their Negro population living in cities. In fact, four of the states—Florida, Kentucky, Tennessee, and Texas—were close to or exceeded the national average of 72 percent of the Negro population living in urban places.

The success of the Negro's struggle to gain equal rights in employment, voting, education, and consumer prerogatives has been of equal significance. Each of these gains, in turn, will stimulate further consequences that will broaden the area for Negro participation in the South. Hence, better educational opportunities will equip more Negroes to enter the labor market at a higher income level, just as the opportunity for more Negroes to vote will force substantial political concessions.

Even as one must recognize the importance of these trends, I believe there is a tendency to give them complete credit for shaping social developments in the South. Even migration patterns and civil rights gains should also be considered as effects of other social changes, not simply as initiating causes. Hence, the urban migration of Negroes can be traced in part to the changes in the economic balance of the region and the expansion of economic opportunities in southern cities. Coupled with those trends are the demands by the federal government for equal opportunities in a labor market that has been expanded largely through the efforts of that government. Similarly, the success of the civil rights movement depends in some measure on the presence of a significant middle class in southern cities. The earlier structure of aristocratic stratification had no flexibility to allow for a redefinition of the caste position of the Negro within southern society. The development of a stronger middle class, as I have argued, has significantly altered the aristocratic patterns and thereby prepared the ground for a redefinition of the positions of both the Negro and the white lower class. In other words, the presence of a middle class has made it more possible than before to honor the demands of civil rights organizations with much less violence than would have been predicted, say, twenty years ago. The middle class has the strongest commitment of any segment of southern society to the maintenance of political and social order. Although slower to act in some cases than one might prefer, the middle class has exerted leadership in many southern communities when the issue became one of law versus anarchy.

Quite clearly, then, the South is in the midst of a revolutionary social development that is greater and more significant than anything that has happened in the history of the region, including the Civil War. What will emerge finally is a region that will be almost indistinguishable from any other region in the country. For better or worse, the destiny of the South has now been joined with the destiny of the nation as a whole.

Notes

1. Although we speak of the South as if it were a single, homogeneous region, there are, in fact, differences between the twelve states here included. It should be kept in mind, therefore, that the generalizations made in this article are meant to apply in varying degrees to the different states in the region.

2. Standardized rates are calculated to allow for the relatively younger population in the region compared with the rest of the nation.

3. This point has been documented in the case of business leadership (Danhof, 1956). It is my impression that there has been an emigration of talent from the South over the years in other fields of endeavor as well. The point is that many of the potential leaders and spokesmen for change have left the region.

4. There is a related matter here as to whether the middle class in this process is inevitably an agent for political democratization. In the past, this has tended to be true, but there are no structural requirements that would guarantee that result. In the South at present, the middle class is exerting a democratic influence but it is impossible to predict how long that influence will remain.

5. Middle class participation in initiating and directing such programs seems to me to be very heavy. I suspect that an important motive behind that participation is to give members of the new middle class a means to gain prestige for themselves and to shape their environment. Without implying any denigration of these worthwhile efforts for social improvement, I would say that anti-poverty programs serve some of the same functions for the new middle class that *noblesse oblige* earlier served for the plantation aristocracy.

6. Consider that private corporations, utilities, and the military establishment follow a deliberate practice of moving their personnel around these conurbations with relative frequency.

References

DANHOF, C. H. "Business Leadership in the South," *The Journal of Business of the University of Chicago,* 1956, **39,** 130–137.

DANHOF, C. H. *Three Decades of Thought on the South's Economic Problem,* Report prepared for the Second Annual Conference of the Inter-University Committee for Economic Research on the South, 1962 (mimeo).

EMERSON, R. *From Empire to Nation.* Cambridge: Harvard University Press, 1960.

HIGHSAW, R. B., (ed.). *The Deep South in Transformation.* University, Ala.: University of Alabama Press, 1964.

LEISERSON, A. (ed.). *The American South in the 1960's.* New York: Praeger, 1964.

MCKINNEY, J. C. AND THOMPSON, E. T., (eds.). *The South In Continuity and Change.* Durham: Duke University Press, 1965.

NICHOLS, W. H. *Southern Tradition and Regional Progress.* Chapel Hill: University of North Carolina Press, 1960.

NICHOLS, W. H. "The South as a Developing Area," in Leiserson, *op. cit.* 1964a.

NICHOLS, W. H. "Industrialization, Factor Markets, and Agricultural Development," in *Regional Development and Planning,* John Friedmann & William Alonso (eds.). Cambridge: MIT Press, 1964.

ODUM, H. W. *Folk, Region, and Society,* arranged and edited by K. Jocher, *et al.,* Chapel Hill: University of North Carolina Press, 1964.

OSMAN, J. "The Coming Urban Age of the South," quoted in S. C. Mayo, "Social Change, Social Movements and the Disappearing Sectional South," *Social Forces,* 1964, **43,** 1–10.

REISSMAN, L. *The Urban Process: Cities in Industrial Societies.* New York: The Free Press of Glencoe, 1964.

REISSMAN, L. "Urbanization in the South," in McKinney & Thompson, *op. cit.,* 79–100.

ROSHWALD, M. "Confusion of Spheres: A Comment on American Civilization," *British Journal of Sociology,* 1965, **16,** 243–252.

SINDLER, A. P. (ed.). *Change in the Contemporary South.* Durham: Duke University Press, 1963.

CITIES, SLUMS, AND ACCULTURATIVE PROCESS IN THE DEVELOPING COUNTRIES

F. William Howton

Introduction

Big cities have always had slums. They receive the bulk of in-migrants and provide them with a stopping place until they are able to move up and out—which is to say, "in"—into the city proper. This is their prime function.[1] A fortunate few find something like Miss Liberty's "golden door" and pass directly through it, but the many do not and cannot and have to settle for the back door provided by the slums. The reasons are first of all economic, but beyond that they are cultural and social. The immigrant without resources has a better chance of finding the means of livelihood and ways of life he needs in the slum than anywhere else in the city, even if he could afford the rent.

Published by permission of the author.

The prime function of slums is therefore a constant, but their relative size and distinctive character are variables. Relative size is a consequence of volume of immigration, and rate of assimilation. Distinctiveness of character, the degree to which the slum differs in culture and social structure from the city whose offspring it is, varies in relation to the alienness of the immigrants.

Most of the developing countries today are experiencing a rush of movement of population from the hinterland to the urban centers that in sheer volume is without parallel in history. Moreover, the difference in cultural level and type between the established urbanite and the ex-villager just arrived in the slums is so great that the rate of assimilation is markedly low. The result is that the capability of institutions and agencies of control and service to do what they are supposed to do has fallen farther and farther behind the need, reflecting a condition of saturation and incipient breakdown. This has aggravated the already severe problem of heavy influx to the point that, in some instances, the aggregate absolute size of the civically and socially unintegrated slums is now close to the size of the city proper.[2]

This paper is concerned with some of the causes and consequences of a worldwide phenomenon: the overburdening of regulative and assimilative institutions in the urban centers of developing countries by excessive slum growth, and the threat this poses to the orderly and effective accomplishment of nation building.[3] Will the cities be able to stabilize and manage the flow of in-migrants from the traditionalist hinterland, and integrate them civically, bring them into the body politic fast enough to keep pace? Or will the present tense situation grow worse—perhaps to the point that something like Frantz Fanon's prophecy of "universal peasant revolt"[4] becomes an actuality, and the "backward" people of the countryside rise up and overwhelm the cities? In order to clarify the problem it will be useful to set forth a provisional explanation of why the slums exist and assume the character they have, and how the acculturative process works in them.

The discussion is organized by considering: (1) the "primate city" and the peripheral *barriada* and how they are related; (2) the role of mediating groups and associations in the acculturative process; (3) patterns of individual response to acculturative challenge; and (4) implications for sociological research.

City and Slum

The Primate City. It is a striking fact that throughout the "underdeveloped" world the cities are "overdeveloped."[5] In Asia, Africa, and Latin America, in spite of their many differences, there tends to be a single massive urban center of government, culture, and economic activity in each country. The metropolis stands as a sort of sociological island, or peninsula, an alien intrusion into a slumbering, stagnant, subsistence-minded hinterland. Surrounded on three sides by the countryside it serves, as capital and nerve-center, the city turns its fourth side, its "face," to Europe and North America. Often it fronts on the sea and depends for its existence on its locked-in place in the circuit of international, sea-borne commerce. (The geography is becoming less important, however, in the new age of air transport and large-scale, direct foreign subsidies than it once was. There are now overdeveloped inland cities as well.)

Such massively concentrated urban centers, abnormally large and complex and modern in relation to the countryside, are *primate* cities because there is a qualitative difference in cultural level and type between them and their hinterlands.[6] They are more than mere neutral *entrepots* between roughly equal social and economic orders. The goods they trans-ship are as much social and cultural as economic, and the way the trans-shipment is carried out reflects an endemic imbalance of power. Regardless of the city's intentions it is the middle-man in an unequal transaction, and its character shows this. The prototypic urbanite is oriented towards the distant metropole, however strenuous his efforts may be, personally, to remember, or perhaps discover, the interests of the "voiceless" back country.[7] The metropolitan center stands for power and enlightenment, however colonial (even neo-, semi-, or quasi-) it may still be, against what it sees as backwardness.

The native or non-European urbanite of the primate city, with few exceptions, finds that in the logic of his situation he relates to his country cousins in the village very much as the expelled European settler related to "the native" during the era of political colonialism. He has become a quasi-European. The irony is not easy to bear; [8] but the task is lightened, morally, by the manifest fact that the back country people show signs of wishing to become urbanites themselves [9] and as quickly as possible. They stream in so fast they threaten the foundations of social order.

The Peripheral Barriada. During the Great Depression of the 1930's in the United States quasi-permanent settlements of shacks and tents (called "Hoovervilles" in ironic tribute to the then President) grew up around the edge of cities and large towns in the agricultural regions of the far west. They were put up and occupied mainly by men and their families who had been small farmers in the Kansas-Oklahoma-Texas "dust bowl" region until they were driven off their land by the prolonged drought, falling prices, technical modernization, and foreclosure. They put up shanties and ragged tents on unused land just outside the city limits, beyond the jurisdiction of both law enforcement and service agencies of the city. If they were without utilities and amenities, they were also beyond the reach of building code, zoning, and sanitary ordinances. Those who lived there stayed on as illegal tenants, "squatters," as long as they could find some bare means of subsistence and as long as the county and state officials left them alone —which they frequently did, out of mixed motives of pity and fear.

The "Hoovervilles" never approached the size or posed the political threat of the squatter settlements (Latin Americans call them "barrios" or "barriadas," which means "quarters") [10] that characteristically ring the primate cities of the developing countries today. Moreover, the American dust bowl migration was never very large as a proportion of the whole population. The institutions and agencies affected by it were not saturated, except in exceptional and localized instances. In both respects the urban shanty towns in developing countries today are different.

The *barriada* (I shall use the Spanish term as a convenient rubric for the phenomenon as its exists universally) is peripheral in a two-fold sense. It is *ecologically* peripheral, in the first place. The squatter has the best chance of putting up and keeping a substandard dwelling on property not his own if he chooses for a building site land not in use (waste land, or land held for speculation, or publicly owned land acquired for some purpose to be realized in the future), preferably outside the city limits. An alternative is to settle on land within the city limits proper but considered unusable—steep hillsides, swampy areas, dry creek bottoms subject to flooding. Such lands are inside the city geographically, but functionally they are "outside" since it is not considered feasible to include them in the water, sewerage, electrical power, and other utilities networks.[11]

The *barriada* is *sociologically* peripheral as well. The squatter is a homeowner and yet he is not (he owns his house under common law, but he lacks title to the land it stands on); he gains his livelihood from the city but, excluded from full participation in its social life, he keeps his roots in the village; he is a citizen and yet he is denied the full benefits of citizenship (since he is an illegal tenant he is in a poor position to demand his rights). The *barriada* dweller is a good example of the "marginal man": he has his existence in each of two separate cultural and social orders and is fully and finally involved in neither.

The *barriada* comes into existence and continues to exist because it meets needs: the migrants from the pre-urban hinterland need a place to live, and the primate city needs them for their labor.

But in this situation the municipality is institutionally underequipped. Officials are often confused and demoralized and lack the will to act; migrants are sucked into the vacuum, as it were, and improvise their own institutional solutions. They put up shacks on unused land, and little by little, aggregatively, the shacks constitute settlements and the settlements constitute communities which function as ecological, sociological, and cultural zones of transition between the Europeanized city and the traditional peasant, peon, or tribalized hinterland. The Hoovervilles of North America in the early '30's grew up out of a roughly similar set of circumstances, but they rather quickly passed away, because the need was less sharp and the power of the established institutions to meet it was much greater. The *barriadas* continue to grow in the developing countries because the opposite conditions prevail. The acculturative process has to have a place to occur, and the *barriada* is it—by urban default.

The Acculturative Process

Acculturation is the taking on of culture. Every individual has to learn new roles from time to time, as his status and activities and interests and the expectations others have of him change with age, but only a relative few have to learn a whole new design for living in the course of doing so. The learning of roles of the sort not envisaged in one's native heritage, and therefore not patterned, calls for the acquiring of new modes of thinking, feeling, experiencing. To say that the *barriada* is a sociological zone of transition is to say that it is where acculturation takes place: the native arrives from the back country with the "wrong" kit of cultural baggage, and passes through it to enter the city as a new urbanite—if the process is successful—with the "right" equipage (skills, habits, attitudes, values) for coping with and eventually finding a secure place in the urban social order.

Migration and the *Dual Economies* Problem. Acculturation is an evolutionary process, if we understand by that term a patterned and irreversible movement from one mode of existence to another. One way to grasp the character of the "before" and "after," in the sense relevant to acculturation in the *barriada,* is to follow J. H. Boeke [12] and posit a situation of "dual economies" in the developing countries. This may help make clearer why migration from the pre-urban hinterland to the city does occur [13] and what its gross psycho-cultural consequences are.

Boeke [14] contends that money and acts of material exchange have a different meaning in the Westernized cities of underdeveloped countries than in their hinterlands. Economically and culturally they are two different worlds existing side by side—dual economies. The assumptions and postulates and theorems which serve to explain the level of prices and the movement of resources in a market economy are irrelevant and misleading when applied to the same problems in a non-market, or "traditional" economy. The classic example is the "backward-sloping demand curve" for labor. When workers are rational and hedonistic, the gross supply of labor increases in direct proportion to the level of wages offered. But in the traditional sector the "target worker," who works only as long as necessary to yield a certain fixed sum in wages decided upon in advance,[15] is typical. To the extent that the aggregate of individual targets is a constant sum, it follows that the gross amount of labor offered in the market *decreases* as the level of wages increases: the relationship is inverse rather than direct.

The dual economies thesis has been criticized as over-simplified, but of course it was never intended to be a literal description of reality. As a model it raises important questions. Why do villagers migrate to the city? What do they have to relearn when they cease being target workers and become irrevocably and wholly absorbed into the urban proletariat?

It seems clear that most *barriada* dwellers have the target worker mentality when they first arrive. Many actually do return to the village, even those who brought their families with them, after accumulating a certain sum of money and goods. But few remain there; the tendency is to return to the city, even to repeat the whole cycle and return yet again. Perhaps the village is overcrowded or slow, lacking in vitality. Perhaps the nurturance and warmth of kinship ties and the rituals evoking communal solidarity are now experienced as intrusive, even tyrannical, having been over-idealized during the period of absence. Whatever the reason the pattern itself seems clear: the typical migrant does not intend to settle permanently but in fact ends up doing so, even if it takes one, two, or even three visits "home" to bring him finally to make the commitment.[16]

The Role of Mediating Groups as Quasi-Stages. The individual is made fit and able to live in society through participating in the life of a group. As he moves from early childhood toward adulthood and the end of moral and economic dependency, he learns the roles appropriate to his changing age and status and destined life activity. In the course of doing so he becomes *enculturated:* he takes on the culture of the community into which he was born and in which it is taken for granted he will remain. Social pressure to learn to do the "right" things and develop the "right" understandings of what they mean makes itself felt through the actual, real group in which he participates.

The mediating group is no less important as the most important single agency of *ac*culturation for the adult who has migrated to the city than it was for the child and young adult during the process of his *en*culturation in the village of his birth. Moreover, in both cases it assumes a somewhat different character at successive stages of the process: the ideal movement is from small, intimate, family-type groups toward large impersonal, interest-based associations.[17]

What forms of mediating groups typically occur in the *barriada*? There seem to be five.[18]

1. The first type is very small, tightly knit and xenophobic, limited to the immediate family, close relatives, and perhaps one or two old and close friends from the home village. It is the associational pattern that best suits the "hick" or "greenhorn," the person without much experience with the urban scene and urban ways. The need such a pattern meets is to provide in microcosm something like the village *Gemeinschaft,* with its time-worn certainties of identity and obligation.[19]

2. The second type is larger, looser, and somewhat more extensive than the first. However, it resembles the first type in that the bond of solidarity is strictly communal, based on kinship or quasi-kinship. All real kinsmen are potential communicants, although only in rare instances are all who are eligible actual participants in the interlinked net of social circles that constitutes the functioning group. Certain categories of quasi-kinsmen are eligible as well: persons from the same village, caste, or tribe, or who speak the same dialect, or who are fellow cult communicants, depending on history and local circumstances. The important thing is that the constituent individuals feel themselves to be brethren regardless of the basis, and thus constitute a community—but it is a *new* community, reflecting in its character an awareness that life in the city is not and can never be much like life in the villages of the traditional society left behind.[20]

3. The third type is a hybrid form: half community, half voluntary association. It has a roster of members, an apparatus of officers, and an instrumental purpose of the self-help, mutual aid sort, so that it has the form of a voluntary association. But access is stringently limited, and the criteria are communal. It grows out of natural groupings (Types I and II) and is attuned to their ethos. Its organizational form is superimposed, and has to adjust informally to pre-existing patterns of communal association.

Examples include mutual aid, guild-like associations such as burial societies, "friendly societies," and neighborhood clubs of the sort that involve illegal forms of recreation and entertainment such as unlicensed drinking, gambling, cock fighting, and the like. Its membership and officialdom is rudimentary but does definitely exist. It has to, even though the ethos of bureaucratic arrangements is out of harmony with the predominantly communal ethos, because the association has at least some business to transact as a corporate entity. It has to have officials —however "unofficial" and informal their selection, work procedure, and personal, non-work conduct may be. It has to have "members" for the same reason. The transaction of corporate business demands, in logic, not only that there be some particular persons designated to carry it out in the name of all, but that the "all" in whose name the official acts be an actual collective body with determinate boundaries.[21]

4. The fourth type is based on common recreational and sociable interests. It is open to all and is indefinitely large in size; the spirit of interaction among members is comparatively casual, unserious, playful, superficial; the bond of solidarity is more associational than communal. Although it is treated lightly, a utilitarian interest is admitted. The primal totemic aura of sacredness is pushed into the background. It is legitimate to make light fun of the symbols of the corporate entity and *to be egocentric.* This is possible because nothing of much import is at stake.

Examples include clubs of all sorts: burial societies, self-help and protective organizations, and recreational associations of the sort that cut across communal and neighborhood boundaries. The Latin-American "sports club" is not very typical but it does serve to exemplify the logic of this type of formation. The sports club—which is somewhat like the American country club, in that it provides access to recreational facilities to "members only"—is based outside the *barriada* but draws much or even most of its membership from within the *barriada.* Its significance is that it provides a social setting within which the *barriada* dweller can interact casually, non-communally, with others of comparable status and also with full-fledged urbanites. It provides a bridge of sociability between the traditional and the urban society, directly, through casual contacts between the two different social types, and indirectly, by providing an opportunity to the "traditionalist" to practice playing—*playing*—the "urbanite" role.

5. The fifth type is also founded on common interests, and is bureaucratic and associational rather than communal in structure. Again, there is a real membership and a real officialdom. But the interests they are founded on are economic and political rather than sociable in nature. They are "serious." These associations seek to reach down deep into the individual's mind and heart and build a new core identity. The individual member's involvement is not necessarily more intense and passionate than in his sports club, but it is much more earnest, it brings out and gives form to interests at the center of his life as a new and still not yet established urbanite.

The classic example is the neighborhood improvement association of the sort Matos Mar describes in Lima, Peru.[22] It existed even before the beginning of settlement, and was in fact the instrument through which an organized invasion occurred which brought a new *barriada* into existence. Literally overnight five thousand people occupied a tract of unused land and put up shelters. (Under Latin-American common law an illegal tenant "with a roof over his head" is hard to evict.) More generally, the neighborhood improvement association as a form has a chance of coming into being and continuing in force only as long as there is a strong and recognized sense of common insecurity and the hope of betterment through action in concert. These conditions may or may not exist in a particular *barriada,* depending on circumstances. The important thing is that favorable conditions can exist, they sometimes do exist, and a mediating group of the neighborhood improvement association type does occasionally get formed. When it does it marks a significant terminus in the acculturative cycle: kinship or quasi-kinship communality as the basis of association has then been supplanted by association on the basis of rationally derived interests held in common, which makes possible a new and distinctively urban communal bond.

Types four and five serve to bring the *barriada* dweller directly into the orbit of urban life, but provisionally, tenatively. There is still enough looseness in the institutional linkage these formations provide between the *barriada* and the city proper to permit the individual some freedom of maneuver, in terms of role-playing and moral commitment. The mutual aid societies and sports clubs cannot function without becoming in some measure part of the institutional fabric of the city, whether this is the result of urban institutions "reaching in" to the *barriada* for members, as in the case of the sports clubs, or of "reaching out" by an indigenous *barriada* group formation such as the neighborhood improvement association.

To sum up: types one through five constitute points on a continuum of the *Gemeinschaft*-to-*Gesellschaft* sort. Types I and II are more communal than associational, type III is intermediate, and types IV and V are more associational than communal. As such they are quasi-stages in the evolutionary sense. The whole series is meant to describe one aspect of the acculturative pattern hypothetically typical of the *barriada* generally in developing countries throughout the world, in relation to the primate city.

The Role of Meliorative Institutions and Agencies. A modernizing society develops formally established institutions for social control and for the realization of welfare objectives, in the broad sense of the term, as the need becomes apparent and as the will and the means necessary to meet it become available. Typically the earlier ones are the product of private philanthropic enterprise rather than of government. Schools, dispensaries, hospitals, asylums and monasteries, meeting halls and houses of worship are the more obvious examples. Almost without exception they had their beginning,[23] in the developing countries of the past century or so, in Christian missionary projects—which is to say, in the "good works" of proselytizers of the religious faith of the "advanced countries" in what were called, until recently, the "backward countries."

Welfare institutions began and to a considerable extent still remain [24] in what we have become accustomed to call the private sector. Control institutions (law courts, the police, the military), on the contrary, have always been in the public sector in post-feudal social orders.[25]

Both welfare and control institutions are formally meliorative. Moreover, both have a socializing and acculturating mission. What is their effect in the *barriada*? How does their role in the acculturative process compare with that of the mediating groups discussed above?

The question is exceedingly hard to answer generically, because state policy and the state's will and ability to carry out its policy is such a large factor and varies so greatly from situation to situation. However, it is possible to make some tentative observations:

1. The whole complex of mission activities on the village level, and the mission school in particular, play an important acculturative role in loosening the bonds of tradition and in making life in the city seem attractive and realistically attainable.

2. The operation of control agencies in the villages tends to be politicized rather than bureaucratic, and therefore to favor the interests of one group at the expense of another. This creates a disgruntled minority group of "outs."

3. The welfare and control institutions set up and run by big, labor intensive industrial establishments such as mines and lumber mills, usually rural in their location but drawing labor from villages hundreds of miles away, introduce the native to the ways and rewards of the "cash economy" in contrast to the "subsistence economy."

In all three instances the net effect is to foster migration to the city, which means to the *barriadas.* Once there the individual finds that the relatively bureaucratic, non-discriminatory administration of justice and enforcement of law can be just as onerous as the partisan-politicized mode he fled from in the village: there are more laws to break and less chance of pleading extenuating circumstances or bringing pressure to bear for leniency. At the same time the valued amenities of urban life, education, material comfort, medical care, are tantalizingly near although often hard to reach and use.

The *barriada* creates a visible need for bureaucratically organized meliorative institutions and agencies because of the concentration of people with problems. But the physical and juridical characteristics of the *barriada,* typically a jumble of squatters' huts along narrow, winding pedestrian paths, sometimes without even the most elementary utilities, makes it hard to do anything about them. Individuals are not easy to locate because very often that is their preference. Municipal government functionaries appear to them as hostile interlopers, the Enemy (equivalent to "the Man," in American Negro ghetto parlance).

One may conclude that the sheer concentration of people with problems, which favors rationalized meliorative intervention, is largely neutralized by the *barriada's* characteristic ecological disorder and suspicious attitude toward functionaries. If bureaucratic procedure is frustrated it would seem unlikely that meliorative institutions can play a very significant acculturative role.

But note the tentativeness of this conclusion. It depends on the nature of the state. A regime bent on total mobilization would find the disorder—normative and social as well as physical—of the *barriada* to be a distinct advantage, if it had a program with mass appeal and the cadres to carry it out. The same applies to a revolutionary movement. The content of its "revolutionary work with the masses" would certainly include the promotion of self-help organizations, and, in the later stages, the direct provision of welfare services. In effect the movement would pre-empt the functions of meliorative intervention as a means both of showing the power it has and of garnering more. The general point is that a situation virtually impossible for an ordinary welfare bureaucracy to deal within the developing countries can be highly favorable ground to cultivate from the standpoint of a totalitarian venture in establishing institutions with grass roots anchorage.[26]

Patterns of Individual Response to Acculturative Challenge. Mediating groups and meliorative institutions are positively acculturative in a gross sense: if they work they pull and push the individual through the *barriada,* thus providing it with its zone-of-transition character. The raw immigrant settles in, he is "processed" over a period of time, and then finally he emerges "finished" into the urban polity.

But this is a simplified description of an ideal pattern. Actual patterns in any given instance are much more complex. The acculturative mechanisms they embody vary not only in form, reflecting the need to adapt to local circumstances, but also in functional adequacy: in some *barriadas* most people become successful graduates and speedily move out, "onward and upward" into the city proper, while in others they do not. The first pattern makes for a healthy and hopeful climate by providing models for those still struggling, and by making room for newcomers. In other circumstances there is relatively slow movement up and out, and a relatively rapid rate of in-migration. New *barriadas* spring up and the older ones stagnate; the effect is likely to be growth of symptoms of disillusionment and frustration, such as anger, apathy, or withdrawal.

It will be useful to consider how the acculturative process works or fails to work by examining three hypothetical patterns of individual response to acculturative challenge: (1) "success," (2) "failure," and (3) "rebellion." [27]

1. Success. The successful product of the molding and remolding characteristic of the new life experiences of the *barriada* first learns a new and different discipline of interpersonal relations: how to accept relatively impersonal authority, how to relate to another person as an instrument or a convenience for one's own purposes, how to accept and even enjoy light banter (socializing) with neighbors or work mates who are virtual strangers without letting it involve the whole person. Secondly, he learns a new and different kind of *self*-discipline. This means building into the self distinctively urban standards of conduct and the values and attitudes that validate them. The new urbanite becomes time-conscious and learns to value reliability; he becomes money-conscious and values thrift; he becomes self-conscious and values individualism and ethical universalism. Thirdly, he learns a marketable skill, some sort of "know-how"—even common labor involves "knowing how to work"—that makes it economically as well as psychologically possible to sever his ties with the village. Finally, he learns to want to sever those ties and to take on a new identity.[28]

2. Failure. Failure is both more and less than the simple absence of success. A person who lives in the *barriada* for some years is necessarily changed by the experience, acculturated, and so we cannot mean by a pattern of failure an insufficiency acculturation. It is a question of kind, not amount. Something went wrong. The acculturative process either did not "take" or else there was a "negative reaction."

The person who fails is one who is unable to learn new techniques or unwilling to accept restructuring of his values and attitudes such learning makes necessary, or both. What happens then? One response is to return to the village and the ways of traditional society. In North America, for example, the phenomenon as it exists among educated American Indians is called "going back to the blanket." Another response is to adapt to the *barriada* as it is, to learn to accept it and one's place in it as a permanent life situation. This involves a certain surrender of self-respect. Typically the individual becomes a "drunk" or a "bum" or a "hustler." The objective meaning of such a pattern is that it reveals the conduct of a man who has "given up" and lives day-by-day, in apathy, withdrawal, self-alienation.

3. Rebellion. Rebellion differs from failure in two ways. First of all the character of the rebel's response reflects lack of opportunity, not incompetence or psychological incapacity to adjust to the city. He has learned his technical and social lessons. He knows how to get and hold at least some sort of job, to cope, to get by, but he is dissatisfied. For some reason he cannot seem to find a really suitable place in the urban social order, one that would take him out of the slum. His past term stay in the *barriada* he sees as a case of simple injustice: "they won't let me in." (The "failure" is willing to concede that "I can't make it.")

Secondly, the rebel is unique in that he is willing to accept the renovation and restructuring of the values and attitudes that validate urban technique—but with a twist. He is an innovator. He accepts the urban spirit but, prompted by festering *ressentiment,* he comes more and more to reject the concrete mode in which he finds it manifested around him. He sees a good thing gone bad, corrupted. He wants his rights. He wants justice restored. The less he is able to find legitimate channels through which to express his sense of being aggrieved, and to work with some hope of success in righting wrong and securing a tolerable level of civic morality, the more likely he is to become not a self-alienated retreatist but a disaffected proto-revolutionary.

The rebel therefore is an acculturative mutant—the remolding process "took" but the results were not as intended. This is understandable as a sociological possibility because acculturation is a two-way process. The individual is not passive. He reaches out and forms his own provisional interpretation of what his experience means, and then he tests these new meanings through interacting with others sharing a common group life. The situation of each, especially each "rebel," is unique but not absolutely so; if it were, communication would be impossible. Depending on the course and outcome of his communal involvement with peers, the disaffected proto-revolutionary may be either deflected toward "adjustment to failure" or "acceptance of scaled-down success"—redefinition of his situation—or else developed further—"brought out"—as a real revolutionary. It depends largely on the weight of influence exerted by his mediating group experiences, modified as they may be by the impact of mass communications and organized "agitprop" work carried out by revolutionary groups.

Implications for Research

The account of the acculturative process as it is found in the peripheral *barriadas* has been set forth here in the declarative voice, even though there is only in part a factual warrant for doing so. Some statements are grounded in evidence no one would dispute. But others rest on assumptions which have varying degrees of plausibility, and still others are deduced from sociological axioms, and thus as statements of fact are conjectural. Given the goal of understanding the present more clearly by relating it to the known past and the predictable future this procedure is useful, however, because it raises questions about what we do not know that we need to know. What are these questions?

1. *Is the primate city universal throughout the developing world?* There can be little doubt that it is, in some form and to some degree. The next step is to move down to a lower level of generalization and establish what types of primate cities

there are, and then inquire into the conditions that favor the growth of one type over another and account for the differentials in rate of growth the various types have experienced. One possible strategy would be to relate different types and growth rates to different types and degrees of *colonization,* direct or indirect, "settler" or "bureaucratic," mercantile or industrial, economic or political, because this is one common experience the developing countries have undergone. The hypothesis implied is that colonization is a necessary although not a sufficient condition for the appearance of primate cities.

2. *Is the peripheral barriada universally associated with primate cities?* One can easily think of negative instances, primate cities without *barriadas* as here defined and *barriadas,* or something like them, squatter shanty towns, without primate cities. But it is very hard to deny a universal tendency for *barriadas* to form in consequence of primate city growth. If they do not in any given instance, it ought to be treated as a deviant case and analyzed as such. What factors unique to that situation (political, economic, cultural) prevented the "normal" course of development? In the Union of South Africa, for example, the policy of *apartheid* has tended to politicize and thereby deflect processes of change that would ordinarily be governed by economic and ecological forces. In Argentina the lack of a significant dual economies problem has made an acculturative zone of transition much less necessary.

3. *Is there an acculturative continuum in the peripheral* barriada *constituted by mediating groups and voluntary associations arranged in a quasi-evolutionary series?* Again, it seems quite plausible to assume that there are graded way stations in the acculturative process, and that they take the form of institutionalized opportunities for interacting with others as a participant in group activity. And yet it is quite likely that one or more of the way stations, or quasi-stages, is altogether lacking under certain circumstances, and that even where they exist certain types of people skip several steps while others get stuck on one level and find it hard to move on to the next. The whole idea is presented here as a rather sketchy hypothesis, and stands in need of the sort of fleshing out that could be done adequately only by means of comparative and cross-cultural studies.

4. *Is there a "rebellion" pattern, or does acculurative failure overwhelmingly tend to take the form of personal disorganization?* The inference that there is a rebellion pattern generally found in the peripheral *barriada* is an even sketchier hypothesis; there are no facts known to this writer that could be cited as direct evidence to support it. And yet the theory that the marginal quarter functions as an acculturative bridge between dual social structures leads us to expect to find it. There must be some individuals who succeed in making the transition in every way except the one that is decisive, the actual move "up and out," and who resent it greatly enough to become politically disaffected and yet have the strength to resist being crushed into a pattern of retreatism. Moreover, the existence of clandestine revolutionary political organizations in many of the developing countries with roots and an operational base in both city and country means that they must have active underground agents or at least sympathizers in the urban region. We know that some are alienated bourgeois intellectuals, some are disgruntled independence-party militants (in the post-colonial situation), and

it seems quite likely that others are indigenous *barriadistas* of the type we have called "rebels." Research ought to be done on the extent to which there are such individuals, and on the combination of conditions that generates the greatest likelihood that the politicized discontent they represent will appear.

5. *Is there a possibility that government sponsored or aided meliorative programs can materially effect the acculturative process?* At first glance, it would seem that the answer is a simple "no" if government or quasi-government agencies lack either the will or the means to carry out such programs, and a simple "yes" if they do have the will and the means. But the question is much more complex. A program right for one situation (some combination of housing, family planning, community development, information and referral services, legal aid, adult education, reception centers, vocational guidance and training) may be wrong for another. What if it speeds up the "revolution of rising expectations" unrealistically in relation to actual opportunities which are a function of the urban social structure's absorptive capacity? What if it has the effect of cutting people off from their roots in the pre-urban social structure too precipitately, making it hard for them to go back if and when they need to?[29] The consequence may be a rise in the rate of social and political disaffection (rebellion) in the case of the first, and of personal disorganization (failure) in the second.

Even a well-planned program—well-planned in that it rests on a sound diagnosis and does not overreach itself in terms of the level of technique and the ability to utilize it which is available—is bound to generate unintended consequences. One task of research is to establish what these are likely to be, both in relation to conditions peculiar to the developing countries generally and also to the widest possible range of particular type situations. Again, this calls for comparative and cross-cultural research instead of isolated, mutually unarticulated studies case by case.[30]

Summary and Conclusions

The impact of more developed upon less developed societies has resulted in "overurbanization," which appears in the form of the primate city whose hinterland remains relatively traditional and pre-capitalistic. This condition gives rise to the dual economies problem, or, more generally, the problem of dual social structures and cultures. The growing need the villager has for sustenance, security, services, and urban amenities has pushed him and pulled him to the city, where he tends to settle as a squatter in the slum shanty towns that ring it. These *barriadas* function as an acculturative zone of transition between the dual social structures. Mediating groups and associations spontaneously take root there, and form a rough, quasi-evolutionary series of acculturative stages. Efforts at meliorative intervention by formal institutions of government and of private agencies close to the government—they are usually two parts of a common establishment—may or may not show some success in affecting the process, depending on how effective they are in mobilizing participation. The individual responds to acculturative challenge by learning new ways of thinking, feeling, and behaving, which fall into one of three patterns: "success," "failure," or "rebellion."

Implications for sociological research include the need to establish the generality of the primate city and the peripheral *barriada* as universal phenomena and to study how they grow out of conditions peculiar to the developing countries, especially in relation to the type of colonization experienced; the need to determine the grounding in fact of the posited quasi-evolutionary series of acculturative stages formed by mediating groups and voluntary associations; the need to test the hypothesis that patterns of "failure" and "rebellion" can and do result from the acculturative process; and, finally, the need to explore the unintended consequences of programs of meliorative intervention. These various but related research objectives can best be met by designing projects to be comparative and cross-cultural to the greatest possible extent.

A theme basic to the analysis that ought to be reiterated here is: *under conditions of rapid modernization slums are functional and in this sense "normal."* This does not mean that slums are desirable, any more than the fact that human mortality is functional and normal makes it desirable; it does mean that the absence of slums indicates either that little or no modernization is going on, or else there is a totalitarian regime—perhaps both. In the developing countries of today it is not the presence but the absence of the primate-city-peripheral-*barriada* syndrome, in the general sense, that is surprising and calls for explanation.

Beyond that, however, there is the larger question of how the acculturative process is affecting the character of the emerging nation. Modernization is not a one-way street. Traditional society is surely being destroyed by the Europeanized primate city. But in enacting its role as destroyer it is itself being transformed. It cannot continue with its face fixed gazing toward the West; it is under pressure to look within, even to look to the rear to find its identity. The social scientist will want to search for clues to the outcome in the despised and embarrassing *barriada,* for it must be there, in that tension-ridden zone of transition, that the culture and institutional forms of the future are taking shape.

Notes

1. The prime function is not the only one, of course. Slums also house and provide a social existence for permanently depressed population groups (the ghetto function), and for downwardly mobile groups and individuals from the general population (the "wastebasket" function). However, from the standpoint of our interest in rapid social change in the developing countries the acculturative function is the most important one. A good textbook example (still rare) of the newer interest is to be found in Noel P. Gist and Sylvia F. Fava, *Urban Society,* N. Y., Thomas Y. Crowell Co., 1964, 5th ed., pp. 273–77. See also David R. Hunter, *The Slums: Challenge and Response,* N. Y., Free Press of Glencoe, 1964, esp. pp. 15–19.

2. Hauser, especially, expresses the sense of urgency found in a good many writings that the situation is getting beyond control. Cf. Philip M. Hauser, "The Social, Economic, and Technological Problems of Rapid Urbanization," in Bert F. Hoselitz and Wilbert E. Moore, eds. *Industrialization and Society: Proceedings of the Chicago Conference on Social Implications of Industrialization and Technical Change, 15–22 September, 1960,* N. Y., UNESCO, 1963.

3. Reinhard Bendix, *Nation Building and Citizenship,* N. Y., Wiley, 1964. Nation building involves *modernization* (social and political development) plus *industrialization* (economic development), conceived of as interrelated but quasi-autonomous processes. See esp. pp. 5 ff.

4. Frantz Fanon, *The Wretched of the Earth,* trans. Constance Farrington, N. Y., Grove, n.d. First published (French ed.) 1961. Fanon projects an apocalyptic vision of an "inevitable" clash between the rural "native" and the new "nationalist bourgeoisic" *after* the settlers have been expelled. He writes: "The men whom the growing population of the country districts and colonial expropriation have brought to desert their family holdings circle tirelessly around the different towns, hoping that one day or another they will be allowed inside. It is within this mass of humanity, this people of the shanty towns, at the core of the *lumpen-proletariat,* that horde of starving men, uprooted from their tribe and from their clan," that is to be found "one of the most spontaneous and the most radically revolutionary forces of a colonized people." (p. 103.)

5. Hauser, for example, refers to "the hypertrophy of capital cities" resulting from the fact that they "developed as links between the colonial and mother country." (Hauser, *op. cit.,* p. 202.) Moore discusses the "over-urbanization of principal cities" in Latin America in particular. (Wilbert E. Moore, "Industrialization and Social Change," in Hoselitz and Moore, *op. cit.,* p. 343.) The concept of the "primate city" was developed first by Mark Jefferson.

6. This is recognized by scholars, natives, and colonial administrators. Brandao Lopez cites Lambert's conception that there are "two levels of Brazilian civilization." (Juarez Rubens Brandao Lopez, "Aspects of Adjustment of Rural Migrants to Urban-Industrial Conditions in Sao Paulo, Brazil," in Philip M. Hauser, ed., *Urbanization in Latin America,* N. Y., UNESCO, 1961, p. 234.) Pons notes that Africans distinguish between *Kizungu* (of or with Europeans) and *Kisendjii* (of or with countrymen), and that this is quite close to that drawn by colonial administrators between *coutumiers* and *noncoutumier* populations. (W. G. Pons, "The Growth of Stanleyville and the Composition of its African Population," in the International African Institute, London, *Social Implications of Industrialization and Urbanization in Africa South of the Sahara,* N. Y., UNESCO, 1956, p. 241.)

7. J. H. Bocke, *The Interests of the Voiceless Far East: Introduction to Oriental Economics,* Leiden, The Netherlands, Institute of Pacific Relations, 1948.

8. Fanon (*op. cit.,* p. 91) bears down hard on the "turncoat" character of the "nationalist bourgeoisie."

9. This is the central thesis of Daniel Lerner, *The Passing of Traditional Society,* N. Y., Free Press, 1956. Because of the mass media, many people in "traditional societies" are acquiring a "mobile sensibility," an "empathic readiness to try on a new way of life."

10. The term "perpheral *barriada*" and much of the concept as I use it here is taken from Jose Matos Mar, "Migration and Urbanization," in Hauser, *loc. cit.,* pp. 170–90. He defines it as a "marginal quarter" formed by a population which takes over waste land typically situated on the perimeter of a municipality.

11. The *barriada* is "peripheral" ecologically and sociologically even though it may exist, spatially, as an enclave within the city rather than as part of a more or less continuous perimeter around it. For example, the Brazillian type (*favela*) is a settlement of shacks built on a steep hillside or in lowlands subject to flooding. Such areas are called "non-urbanized" in Brazil, even though they are situated deep within the major city, Rio de Janeiro. What is crucial is that they are treated as wasteland and excluded from the street and utilities grid. Cf. Andrew Pearse, "Some Characteristics of Urbanization in the City of Rio de Janeiro," in Hauser, ed., *op. cit.*, p. 191.

12. *Op. cit.*

13. Demographers and economists often refer to "push" and "pull" factors. Those who are interested in motives and in social-psychological types have posed the question of whether those selectively drawn to the city—or pushed out of the village—are "dropouts" or "golden boys": are the city-bound migrants the cream of traditional society or its cast-offs? The issue is explored at length in Moore, *op. cit.*, in Hoselitz and Moore, *op. cit.*, esp. pp. 334 ff.

14. *Op. cit.* Bocke's thesis has been critized by E. J. Berg, "Backward-Sloping Labor Supply Functions in Dual Economies—The Africa Case," in Immanual Wallerstein, ed., *Social Change: The Colonial Situation*, N. Y., Wiley, 1966, pp. 116–22.

15. Melville J. Herskovits, *The Human Factor in Changing Africa*, N. Y., Knopf, 1962, pp. 386–7. An interesting example is the new nation of Botswana. According to a report in *The New York Times*, October 1, 1966, p. 10, three out of four of its gainfully employed males, or 18% of its entire population, were non-resident workers in mines and other industrial enterprises of its white-supremicist neighbors at the time it gained independence in 1966.

16. Matos Mar (*op. cit.*, pp. 186–8) conjectures that, in Latin America, at least, the pull factor is very strong. There is greater security against major risk in the city, and simply by being in the city one achieves a higher social status.

17. Cf., Kenneth Little, *West African Urbanization: A Study of Voluntary Associations in Social Change*, Cambridge, Cambridge University Press, 1965.

18. This conceptualization is a variation of the *Gemeinschaft*-to-*Gesellschaft* theme—closest, perhaps, to Redfield's folk-urban continuum than to any one other of the major versions. The difference is that the conception presented here of a set of types of mediating groups connected in a series and having the character of quasi-stages incorporates a time dimension, and posits a situational dynamic that tends to move the individual along the continuum. Does this make it "neo-evolutionist"? A useful discussion of the larger issue may be found in Bendix, *op. cit.*, p. 299 ff. In addition, see Herbert R. Barringer, George J. Blanksten, and Raymond W. Mack, eds., *Social Change in Developing Areas*, Cambridge, Mass., Schenkman, 1965.

19. Cf. William J. Goode, "Industrialization and Family Change," in Hoselitz and Moore, *op. cit.*, pp. 237–58. Extraordinarily vivid documentation of the impact of urban social structure and culture is presented in Oscar Lewis, *The Children of Sanchez*, N. Y., Random House, 1961.

20. In Africa, tribalism is frequently transplanted to the city, sometimes in the modified form of "super-tribalization." (Daryl Forde, "Social Aspects of Urbanization and Industrialization in Africa: a General Review," in International African Institute, *op. cit.*, p. 38 ff.) The corresponding pattern in Latin America is the village or regional grouping, and in Southeast Asia it is the cult or sect, usually some variant of Buddhism. Separatist sects and chiliastic cults flourish in Africa as well. (R. L. Rotberg, "The Rise of African Nationalism, 1962," in Wallerstein, ed., *op. cit.*, pp. 512–15.)

21. See esp. R. Mugu Gatheru, *Child of Two Worlds,* N. Y., Praeger, 1964, and J. Abun-Nasr, "The Salafiyya Movement in Morocco: The Religious Basis of the Moroccan Nationalist Movement," in Wallerstein, ed., *op. cit.*, pp. 489–502.

22. *Op. cit.*

23. This is true of the pre-industrial phase. Once industrialization takes hold European, or European trained plant management plays a large role in providing welfare services to its native employees. Cf. Hortense Powdermaker, *Copper Town: Changing Africa,* N. Y., Harper, 1962.

24. The strong and rising current of nationalism generally opposes these arrangements as a form of "cultural imperialism." Their role seems bound to decline.

25. Except, of course, in colonized countries. For an account of how a private corporation, the British East India Company, for a long time assumed the functions of sovereign government, see John W. Davis, *Corporations,* N. Y., Capricorn, 1961, pp. 114–18.

26. This of course alludes to the Marxist-Leninist-Maoist technique, which is quite different in the beginning, before the state is seized, than the technique of nationalist, vaguely socialist demagogues such as Mossadegh, Nasser, Sukarno, or even Castro in his more recent actions. Once the state is seized, however, the classical Leninist "agit-prop" principles of organization building become just as important for consolidating power as they were—or may have been—for gaining it in the first place. For an excellent analysis of Bolshevik strategy and tactics in the '30's and '40's, see Philip Selznick, *The Organizational Weapon,* N. Y., Free Press, 1962, (First published 1952.) Selznick's treatment is pre-Maoist, however. The supplement urgently needed is yet to be written.

27. These categories are loosely derived from Merton's typology and analysis of means-end relationships, which first appeared nearly 30 years ago. Robert K. Merton, "Social Structure and Anomie," *American Sociological Review,* 1938, pp. 672–82.

28. One of the more common subtypes is the *potential self-dependent.* For example, Brandao Lopez describes the Brazilian factory worker, typically a recent migrant from village to city, as one who dreams of escape from factory discipline: "I'd like to work *por minha conta* [on my own]." *Op. cit.*, p. 241.

29. These possibilities and the dilemmas they pose for planning are discussed in Bureau of Social Affairs, U.N., "Some Policy Implications of Urbanization," in Hauser, ed., *op. cit.*, pp. 294–324.

30. Moore, in Hoselitz and Moore, *op. cit.*, p. 366.

URBANIZATION AND SOCIAL CHANGE IN JAPAN [1]

David B. Carpenter

This paper reports on some interrelationships between urbanization and social change in Japan since 1600. The writer's concern with the case of Japan is one facet of his continuing attempt to understand the role of urbanization in the course of social change in the modern world.[2] It would be presumptuous to present the following observations as other than tenative and exploratory.

Japan is proposed as a laboratory for the investigation of some possible interrelationships between urbanization and social change for several reasons. In the first place, Japan is the most highly industrialized and urbanized of the major nations of Asia. In Asia lives the bulk of the world's population, a population which is now in the midst of major social, economic, and political transformations of enormous consequence to the rest of the world. Japan is not only a key part of rapidly changing Asia, but its earlier experience with industrialization and urbanization provides important clues to understanding the rising tide of Asian aspirations, unrest, and power.[3]

In the second place, Japan lends itself to the testing of hypotheses regarding social and cultural change which have been primarily documented with data on European and European-dominated peoples. Japan is of particular interest because of its isolated island location off the Asia mainland, its long history as an independent cultural entity, and its sharply alternating periods of rapid change and relative stability.

Third, Japan is an appropriate concern of Ameircan scholars because of close past and present relationships between the two countries. The United States played a major role in ending Japan's self-imposed isolation a little more than one hundred years ago; it shared in the events which led to the emergence of Japan as a world power; it engaged Japan in a mounting conflict which culminated at Pearl Harbor and war; it undertook the leading role in the post-surrender occupation and military government of Japan; and it has now based its foreign and military policy in Asia on close cooperation with the Japanese.

It is the central argument of this paper that Japanese history since 1600 may profitably be regarded in terms of three remarkable experiments in planned social change undertaken by powerful, centralized governments which were relatively free to exercise unlimited authority. In each of these three instances the regime consciously set out to fashion Japan's national life after a preconceived pattern; and in each case the planned change was in substantial degree realized. However, these planned changes were in part *not* realized because of factors in social change which apparently were not susceptible of successful manipulation even by great centralized authority. In each case urbanization was an important factor in planning failure.

As a backdrop to the proposed analysis, a brief account of pre-1600 Japan and its development may be helpful.[4] Slightly larger than the British Isles or Italy, Japan is a rugged, mountainous land with not more than 20 percent of its land

---

Reprinted by permission of the author and publisher from *The Sociological Quarterly* (July, 1960), pp. 155–166.

area suitable for cultivation. Settled by a hunting and fishing people, the Ainu, in the north and east, and by a village-dwelling, agricultural people in the south and west, Japan early came to occupy a position on the fringe of Chinese civilization at a time when, between 200 B.C. and A.D. 200, China rivaled the greatness of Rome. The Yamato clan, emerging dominant in the third and fourth centuries, came to provide the ancestors of the imperial family in their hereditary priest-chiefs, descended, according to clan mythology, from the Sun Goddess.

Like Britain's legacy from ancient Rome, Japan's heritage from China became a principal civilizing force. During the seventh and eighth centuries, China was the richest, most powerful land in the world. The Yamato Court, by then asserting its imperial prerogatives, set out to reproduce in Japan a carbon copy of T'ang China. Profound though these Chinese influences were, they directly affected only the capital city, Kyoto and its environs, and they were severely modified as they reached out into the provinces. There a feudal society was developing, dominated by provincial warrior aristocrats managing their estates and peasants, with less and less control from Kyoto.

Wars between the two strongest cliques of provincial aristocrats in support of two quarreling court factions led in 1185 to the emergence of a century and a half of unified rule of Japan from Kamakura (near present-day Tokyo), the military headquarters of the triumphant faction. Using the title *Shogun*, "Generalissimo," the new ruler of Japan maintained the fiction that the Emperor in Kyoto ruled and that the Shogun was merely commander of the Emperor's army. The rule of Kamakura, depending upon personal loyalty of feudal knights to the Shogun, proved inadequate to the government of a growing and changing Japan. In 1333 Kamakura was destroyed as a city and a regime, and there began 250 years of declining imperial fortunes and power, rising localism, and increasing unrest and civil war.

Though political confusion and civil strife followed the Kamakura overthrow, the so-called "dark ages" actually were years of impressive commercial and industrial development. By the end of the sixteenth century Japanese ships, traders, and products were in vigorous competition with those of the Chinese and Europeans, and Japanese warrior traders had come to dominate the water-borne commerce of East Asia.[5]

A notable feature of the period following the collapse of the Kamakura regime was the rise of the provincial lord, the *daimyo*, as the key figure in the political and social system. In the local conflicts and civil wars of the period, more powerful *daimyo* tended to absorb the realms of the less powerful. In 1568, Oda Nobunaga, *daimyo* of three provinces around Nagoya, gained control over central Japan, including Kyoto and merchant-dominated Osaka—by then the two principal cities of Japan. In 1587, Hideyoshi, Oda's ablest general, won control by force of all Japan, but failed in his attempt to conquer China, Japan's first major imperialist adventure. In the struggle for power after Hideyoshi's death, Tokugawa Ieyasu, chief Hideyoshi deputy in eastern Japan at Edo (present-day Tokyo), emerged dominant in 1600.

As the first of the three remarkable experiments in controlled social change offered by modern Japanese history, the Tokugawa regime presents the attempt, in large measure successful, of an authoritarian national government to freeze a consciously selected mold upon a people through highly organized regimentation and deliberate national isolation from the rest of the world.

Impressed with the previous 250 years of political disunity and with the inability of the heirs of Oda and Hideyoshi to retain political control, Tokugawa Ieyasu set out to build a political structure which would survive his death. The Tokugawa rulers established headquarters in their Edo castle, which they built into a vast fortress, a portion of which remains as the palace grounds in central Tokyo. They and their military allies held directly the rich central portion of Honshu, Japan's main island. These allied "hereditary *daimyo*" were differentiated from the "outer *daimyo*" of northeast and southwest Japan whom the Tokugawa had forced into submission. Both sets of *daimyo* were subject to ingenious Tokugawa controls: limitations on castle building and repairs; required periods of residence in Edo, with wife and children held as virtual hostages in the absence of the *daimyo* from Edo; and the *metsuke,* the highly organized Tokugawa secret police and civil censors.

The Tokugawa Shogunate continued the fiction of imperial rule, generously subsidizing the Emperor and his court but keeping them under strict surveillance. A strong, complicated, centralized administration was established, including a small Council of State and a highly efficient core of well-trained civil administrators, backed and checked by the ever-probing *metsuke*. High offices tended to be restricted to the families of the hereditary *daimyo*.

In pursuit of political stability, an artificially imposed system of social stratification was buttressed by a deliberate revival of traditional Confucianism. At the top of the system were the Shogun, the Emperor, and the *daimyo;* second were the *samurai,* the reconstituted class of feudal knights who were given sole right to bear arms; third were the peasants; fourth were the artisans; fifth were the merchants, in Confucian theory a parasite class; and at the bottom were the *eta,* the outcasts.[6]

Most drastic of the Tokugawa policies was that of deliberate isolation from the rest of the world. By the beginning of the seventeenth century the Japanese were the dominant trading and seafaring people of Asia. An active commerce with Europeans had developed. Nearly half a million Japanese had been converted to Christianity as a result of vigorous Jesuit missionary work which began with Francis Xavier's two-year residence in Japan from 1549 to 1551. The obsessive Tokugawa search for political stability, the not irrational fear of increasing European colonial imperialism, and the distrust of alliances between Europeans and the outer *daimyo,* led to progressive restrictions on foreigners and foreign travel. By 1638 only limited and closely supervised trade through Nagasaki with the Dutch and Chinese remained. The following centuries of national isolation, peace, and authoritarian control have had a lasting effect on Japanese society. The adventurous, trading, fighting Japanese of the sixteenth century had become by the mid-nineteenth century a disciplined, orderly people accustomed to firm rule from above. A feudal order, already maladapted to the world of 1600, had been maintained in disciplined isolation far longer than it could have survived under any other circumstances.[7]

Although the Tokugawa government was successful in creating social and political stability, it did not succeed in stifling change. The years of peace brought great prosperity, industrial development, and domestic trade. With this economic development came a rise of cities and towns and an increase in the power of the merchant class. The castle headquarters of the *daimyo* came to be surrounded by administrative and commercial towns. The size and importance of each castle town was related to the wealth and power of the *daimyo*. The great cities of modern Japan had already developed as major urban centers during this period. Edo, center of the complex bureaucracy, had by 1800 a population of about one million. Osaka, center of domestic commerce and handicraft industries, was only slightly smaller. Kyoto, the ancient imperial capital, was a populous center especially for court nobles and their functionaries, priests, artisans, and craftsmen.[8] Reischauer notes that "Japan in 1800, though an outwardly feudal land, was almost as urbanized as were the leading industrial countries of the West at that time." [9]

As urban tastes emerged in patterns of life, Spartan-like military virtues languished during centuries of peace. Shinto students with a revived interest in Japanese history increasingly questioned the legitimacy of Tokugawa usurpation of imperial prerogatives. Through the port of Nagasaki, Dutch books brought to small intellectual circles some knowledge of the exciting changes occurring in the outside world. Events were, by the mid-nineteenth century, to link against the archaic Tokugawa order urban merchant discontent, loyalist restorationist sentiment, outer *daimyo* aspirations, and foreign intervention.[10]

In a succession of events beginning with the arrival of Admiral Perry's warships in Tokyo Bay in 1853, United States and European military power forced the Tokugawa regime to sign treaties of commerce which were not acceptable to the Kyoto court and to the majority of the *daimyo*. Unwittingly the Americans and Europeans forced the Edo government to discredit itself and expose its helplessness. The last Tokugawa Shogun relinquished power to the Emperor in 1867, and the restoration of imperial rule became a reality in 1868.

The Meiji Restoration and imperial expansion which occurred between 1868 and 1945 provide the second of the three experiments in planned social change. Coming to power and ruling in the name of the fifteen-year-old Emperor Meiji in 1868 were a remarkable group of young *samurai* from southwestern Japan. Most of them had staunchly opposed the Edo treaties with the foreigners and helped bring the Tokugawa regime to an end. Yet they all had been deeply impressed and humiliated by the helplessness not only of the Edo government but also of the restorations in the face of foreign force. As the Tokugawa in the early 1600's had been obsessed with political stability, so Japan's new ruling oligarchy was obsessed with the desperate need to create a Japan strong enough to maintain itself militarily in the modern world.

Moving the imperial headquarters from Kyoto to Edo, renamed Tokyo, "the eastern capital," the new regime set upon a most remarkably successful program of modernizing and strengthening Japan. A great asset in the process was the strong and reasonably efficient governmental machinery of the Kokugawa bureaucracy which was largely intact and which the new regime utilized with little change.

The *daimyo*, led by the example of the lords of Satsuma and Choshu, were persuaded to renounce their feudal fiefs and offer their domains to the Emperor.

Feudal obligations, such as those to the *samurai,* were paid off in government bonds, and ranks of nobility were awarded to the *daimyo* and key figures in the new oligarchy. By 1872 universal military service displaced the tradition of the hereditary warrior caste, and a modern army was modeled on that of the German victors in the Franco-Prussian War. The process of selective Westernization was efficiently and speedily carried forth with primary concern always for strengthening an independent Japan. As Borton has emphasized in his careful account of the process "Japan had met the challenge of Western civilization by *adopting* the basis elements of Westernization." [11]

So successful was the process of planned change in achieving its major objectives, that by 1895 Japan had overwhelmed its ancient mentor, China, and won Formosa; by 1905 it had defeated Czarist Russia and won a privileged position in Manchuria and Korea. In 1919 Japan participated as one of the Big Five at Versailles, gaining territory and privileges in China and the Pacific. The expansion—economic, military, and political—reached its peak during World War II and came to an abrupt halt and reversal in 1945.

For the second time in modern Japanese history an all-powerful central government mobilized the nation toward achieving a desired goal. In this planned program of change, an astute oligarchy, ruling in the name of an artificially strengthened imperial institution, succeeded in building from a state of relatively complete helplessness to major military and economic strength. Only the combined might of the United States and its allies blocked the realization of a Japan-dominated Asia.

Yet the attempt of the Japanese oligarchy to gain military and economic strength without basically changing the homogeneous patriarchal social structure did not succeed. The leadership in Japan, as elsewhere, found in militarization and industrialization a veritable Pandora's box. With military and economic changes came urbanization, and with urbanization came fundamental changes in Japanese culture and social structure which were neither planned nor desired by the leadership. As a growing proportion of Japan's population became residents of great cities, familism began to be corroded by individualism; cultural homogeneity began to be replaced by cultural heterogeneity; National Shinto began to be subject to doubt and skepticism; the traditional patriarchal organization of the business and the factory began to be challenged by such radical concepts as those of collective bargaining. War, defeat, and disillusionment accelerated these processes of change and bred uncertainty and disorganization as old norms and values succumbed in the painful rise of the new.[12]

General Douglas MacArthur's remarkable regime provides the third experiment in planned social change.[13] As supreme commander for the Allied powers, General MacArthur exercised dominant authority in Japan from August 14, 1945, when his appointment was approved by President Truman, Prime Minister Attlee, Generalissimo Stalin, and Generalissimo Chiang, until April 10, 1951, when he was removed from his post by President Truman. Acting under the general policy laid down in the Potsdam Proclamation, General MacArthur played major roles as both policymaker and executive.

The two basic objectives of the Allied powers were defined to be prevention of any future Japanese military threat to world peace and formation of a responsible, democratic government in Japan. Means of achieving these were defined in general terms in the Potsdam Proclamation, issued on July 26, 1945, by the governments of the United States, China, and Great Britain.[14]

When Allied forces landed to begin the Occupation, they found that the Japanese food supply was desperately low, far lower than had been reported by Allied intelligence agencies. The Allied regime from the beginning had, in addition to demilitarization and democratization, to address itself to pressing food, health, and economic problems.

The MacArthur policy was one of indirect military government. Most Japanese civil officials, including police, were continued in office, and Japanese governmental structure and laws, with only specified exceptions, were maintained. General MacArthur was determined to see that governmental and legal machinery in this complex, highly industrialized society did not break down and that change was introduced gradually and in ways consistent with legal continuity and a minimum of social disorganization.

In his Tokyo headquarters, General MacArthur had a dual staff conforming to his dual role as military commander and military governor. In his role as military governor he achieved remarkable success in winning the respect and confidence of a majority of the Japanese people. Particularly welcomed in Japan were the MacArthur program of food imports, his attention to health needs, his espousal of Japan's necessities in foreign trade and fishing, and his resistance to reparations programs which would jeopardize a minimum level of recovery in the drastically reduced Japanese economy.

As in the two other massive experiments in planned social change in Japan, great success was achieved in carrying through the MacArthur objectives—interrupted though the program was by the Korean incident. The Japanese military establishment was dismantled; 6,000,000 overseas Japanese were returned to the homeland; a parliamentary government on the English model was securely established; a vigorous labor movement developed; land reforms greatly reduced farm tenancy; minimum food and health needs were met; civil liberties were strengthened; and groundwork was laid for a peace treaty and an end to military occupation.

And yet, as in the two other experiments, there were also impressive failures. Efforts at breaking up large industrial combines have not had a lasting effect. School reformers failed in their attempt to establish in Japan something like the kind of local district control common in the United States. The extensive purges of prewar leadership in public and private life have had only very temporary effects. The MacArthur-imposed constitutional renunciation of war and of a military establishment seems destined for limbo.

Again we note the limits within which the most absolute of governmental authorities can manipulate social change to a desired end. Again urbanization emerges as a variable subtle and difficult of control—not even the massive destruction of Japanese cities during World War II basically changed the relentless march of urbanization. Insofar as the MacArthur reforms countered social and cultural changes implicit in growing urbanization—as in attempts at revival of localism in government or of small scale in industry—the reforms had little continuing effect.

TABLE 1. RELATIONSHIP BETWEEN URBANIZATION AND 24 SELECTED SOCIAL, ECONOMIC AND POLITICAL MEASURES, 46 PREFUNCTURES, JAPAN

	Spearman Rank Correlation Coefficient between 1950 Percentage of Prefectural Population Living in Urban Places of 30,000 or More Population and Specified Measure
Percentage of population not living on farms (1947)	+ .71
Mean cinema attendance per capita (1948)	+ .66
Percentage of labor force employed in commerce (1947)	+ .64
Percentage of labor force (1947) labor union members (1949)	+ .64
Percentage of population in the age range 15 to 49 years (1947)	+ .60
Number of hospital beds per 1,000 population (1949)	+ .55
Percentage of labor force employed in manufacturing (1947)	+ .54
Number of physicians per 1,000 population (1948)	+ .50
Percentage of population professing Christianity (1949)	+ .48
Percentage of population civilian foreign nationals (1950)	+ .46
Number of divorces per 1,000 marriages (1949)	+ .43
Number of dental surgeons per 1,000 population (1948)	+ .42
Number of males per 100 females (1948)	+ .42
Percentage of House of Representatives vote Socialist or Communist (1949)	+ .34
Percentage of House of Representatives vote Communist (1949)	+ .27
Percentage of House of Representatives vote Socialist (1949)	+ .17
Number of registered radio receivers per 100 families (1948)	+ .16
Number of suicides per 1,000 population (1948)	+ .02
Children age 0 to 4 years per 1,000 population age 15 to 49 (1947)	− .24
Percentage of Population age 65 years or older (1947)	− .25
Infant deaths per 1,000 live births (1949)	− .32
Percentage of population age 0 to 14 years (1947)	− .37
Percentage of dwelling units owner occupied (1948)	− .51
Mean number of persons per ordinary household (1948)	− .52

Source: Calculated from data published in Bureau of Statistics, Office of the Prime Minister, *1950 Japan Statistical Yearbook* (Tokyo, June, 1951).

The pace of urbanization has continued unabated in Japan. In her authoritative study of population, Taeuber has provided the facts of recent urban growth in spite of massive urban destruction in the closing years of World War II. Cities of a million population or more lost more than two-thirds of their population in casualties, refugees, and other out-migrants in 1944 and 1945. Cities between 100 thousand and a million lost 30 percent. Yet the tenacious march of urbanization in Japan is vividly underlined in the speed with which great cities were rebuilt and repopulated. Cities of 100,000 or more had a total population of 21,291 thousands in 1940, declined to 11,014 thousands in 1945, rose to 21,326 thousands in 1950, and reached an all-time high of 31,141 thousands in 1955. Between 1950 and 1955 population in cities of one million or more increased 39.3 percent, in cities of one hundred thousand to one million increased 51.4 percent, in cities of fifty to one hundred thousand increased 49.1 percent, and outside cities of fifty thousand or more *decreased* 12.6 percent.[15]

Although Japan as a whole is highly industrialized and urbanized, there are significant differences between regions in the degree of industrial and urban development. In a heretofore unpublished study, the writer, utilizing selected prefectural data from the *1950 Japan Statistical Yearbook,*[16] analyzed social, economic, and political correlates of urbanization. Table 1 summarizes results of Spearman rank correlation coefficients [17] run, with the 46 prefectures of Japan as reporting units, between percentage of 1950 population living in urban places (*shi*) of 30,000 or more population and twenty-four social, economic, and political measures.

In general, data of Table 1 are consistent with the view of the city as a focal point in innovation, secularization, individualization, and breakdown in traditional patriarchal social structures as represented by the extended family and the paternalistic business or factory. The correlations suggest that the impact of the city is maximum: (1) at the level of market place and job; (2) in the availability and use of such facilities as cinemas, hospitals, and physicians; (3) in the rural-to-urban migration of young adults; and (4) in reduction of family size. Middle range correlations document the impact, significant but less marked, on traditional values occasioned by such urban-associated phenomena as Christianity, presence of foreigners, higher divorce rates, leftist political sentiment, and lower birth and death rates.

The correlations of Table 1 are all in directions expected by the student of comparative urbanization with two notable exceptions. First, the positive relationship between urbanization and the sex ratio is quite the reverse of the pattern to be found in a nation like the United States. Explanations of this reversal have been made both in terms of the industrialization of Japan more recent than that of the United States and in terms of contrasts in the role and status of women traditional in the two countries.

The second of these exceptions to the general urbanization pattern is provided by the apparent lack of relationship between city living and suicide rates. To the Japanese student this finding will not be surprising in view of the place of suicide in traditional Japanese culture. One might hypothesize that our statistics confuse two different phenomena: forms of traditional suicide which may be more frequent in rural areas and forms of suicide symptomatic of personal and social disorganization which may be more frequent in urban areas.

Although our statistical analysis confirms familiar hypotheses concerning the social impact of urbanization, it also suggests significant variations of the Japanese pattern. Just as in other periods of Japanese history innovation was adapted and modified in a unique amalgam of the old and the new, so urbanization and industrialization seem to have acquired distinctive qualities in Japan. Our findings are consistent with Taeuber's conclusion (p. 170): "Not only migration but industrialization itself was adjusted to the underlying culture, the difficult resource situation, and the increasing population."

Notes

1. Revised version of a paper read before a joint session of the Conference on Asian Affairs and the Missouri Sociological Society at Columbia, Missouri, October 18, 1958.

2. For the writer's general approach to urbanization, with particular reference to the United States, see Stuart A. Queen and David B. Carpenter, *The American City* (New York: McGraw-Hill, 1953).

3. See Philip M. Hauser (ed.), *Urbanization in Asia and the Far East* (Calcutta: UNESCO, Research Centre on the Social Implications of Industrialization in Southern Asia, 1957).

4. This account is based primarily upon: Edwin O. Reischauer, *Japan, Past and Present* (2d ed.; New York: Knopf, 1958); G. B. Sansom, *Japan, A Short Cultural History* (New York: Appleton-Century, 1943).

5. Reischauer, *op. cit.*, p. 76.

6. A helpful analysis of strains inherent in the Tokugawa class system is presented in Robert N. Bellah, *Tokugawa Religion: The Values of Pre-Industrial Japan* (Glencoe, Ill.: Free Press, 1957), pp. 24–25.

7. Reischauer, *op. cit.*, pp. 94–95.

8. Irene B. Taeuber, *The Population of Japan* (Princeton: Princeton University Press, 1958), p. 25. This definitive study of Japanese population places demographic facts in historical perspective and provides important insights into the interplay of demographic processes with economic and other socio-cultural phenomena.

9. Edwin O. Reischauer, *The United States and Japan* (Cambridge, Mass.: Harvard University Press, rev. ed., 1957), p. 82.

10. Sansom, *op. cit.*, p. 524. Sansom notes also the serious financial difficuities of the mid-nineteenth century Tokugawa regime as well as the discontent of other groups in the population than those mentioned above.

11. Hugh Borton, *Japan's Modern Century* (New York: Ronald, 1955), p. 195.

12. For a careful documentation of the demographic facts of Japanese urbanization during this period see Taeuber, *op. cit.*, especially p. 71 and p. 167.

13. The writer supervised the statistical analyses in a majority of the 35 volumes of the *Summation of Non-Military Activities in Japan* (Tokyo: Supreme Commander for the Allied Powers, Sept.–Oct., 1945, to Aug., 1948), which give an official MacArthur statement of objectives and achievements.

14. The Soviet Union did not join in the issuance of the Potsdam Proclamation since it was still at peace with Japan on July 26, 1945, the date of issuance. See Borton, *op. cit.*, pp. 387–96; 485–86.

15. Taeuber, *op. cit.*, p. 72.

16. Bureau of Statistics, Office of the Prime Minister, *1950 Japan Statistical Yearbook* (Tokyo, June, 1951).

17. This coefficient has a range from a maximum of +1.00 (when the ranks of the two correlated series are identical) to 0.00 (when the ranks of the two series are completely unrelated) to a minimum of −1.00 (when the ranks of one series are the complete opposite of the ranks of the other series).

AFRICAN URBAN CHIEFS: AGENTS OF STABILITY OR CHANGE IN AFRICAN URBAN LIFE?

Peter C. W. Gutkind

In some of the literature on urban Africa, which has appeared during the last fifteen years, the traditional and modern functions of tribal chiefs or headmen, in both the older or newer urban areas in Africa, have been given some attention. Most of this data is in relation to urban administration, i.e. local government, and, in particular, the administration of justice through specially constituted, official or unofficial, urban African courts. This judicial function has engaged these chiefs in relatively structured activities usually defined under the terms of various ordinances. Less attention has been paid to their less formalized activities which are, nevertheless, of considerable importance. Generally we know little about urban chiefs, a reflection, perhaps of the declining importance of chieftainship generally (Mair 1958) and in particular of the difficulties of its operation in urban Africa. Nevertheless some observers are agreed that the newly arrived migrant, in particular, as well as some urbanites who have lived in towns for a considerable time, turn to the chiefs for help. (Banton 1957:160), for example, points out that "the tribal immigrant has been conditioned to a way of life largely dependent upon the institution of chiefship . . ." Likewise Skinner, writing about Mossi migrants in Ghana, points to the important functions of expatriate Mossi chiefs although his discussion does not deal explicitly with urban chiefs:

> The Mossi chiefs in the Gold Coast played an important mediating role between the migrants and the local population. Very often they functioned as labor recruiters for Ashanti chiefs and cacao farmers, since many migrants sought them out in order to find food, lodging, jobs, protection, and companionship. Even when most Mossi migrants found jobs on their own, they established relationships with Mossi chiefs so that they might have someone to protect them and look after their welfare in the event of trouble, sickness or death. The migrants visited the chiefs whenever they could, giving them a few shillings and occasional help if the chiefs had cacao farms. The Mossi chiefs in turn we expected to—and did—come to the aid of migrants who had disputes over wages with their employers. (Skinner 1965:76)

To understand the operation of urban chieftainship it is important to recognize the varied contexts in which it operates. A major distinction exists between urban chieftaincy in the south and central African towns and such west African towns as Ibadan (Comhaire 1953:14–21). In the former the role and activities of headmen or chiefs are closely regulated by ordinances drawn up by non-African authorities exercising control "felt to be much more direct" than over the rural areas (Mayer 1961:51). In west African towns chieftainships have operated for a considerable time in an indigenous context. Yet another distinction is to be found between the pre- and post-independence situations in which urban chiefs have found themselves. In the pre-independence period the colonial administrations delegated special authority to chiefs who functioned in urban areas (or created chieftaincies where none existed before—Gutkind 1963—with the result that the

Reprinted by permission of the author and publisher from *Anthropologica*, 8 (1966), pp. 249–265.

basis of their power was rejected by Africans) and used them as a link with the African population while often refusing to give them official recognition (Banton 1954b; Mathews 1940). Urban chiefs frequently represented major tribal groups in town while in some areas no particular provisions were (or are) made for tribally based representation.[1]

Contemporary urban administration based on the authority of tribal representation and leadership continues in some areas such as Monrovia (Fraenkel 1964:70–109) and in Ghana among the Mossi migrants (Skinner 1965). The same situation has been described by Acquah for Accra (1958:92:107) and by Busia (1950:74) who wrote about Sekondi-Takoradi (on the basis of a 1948 study): ". . . old tribal loyalties persist in the new situation of urban life, and put a brake on the development of municipal government along Western lines." (All the members of the Sekondi-Takoradi Council were, then, members of the indigenous Ahanta tribe.) Thus, Acquah writes (1958:97):

> The staff of the [Accra] Council is inter-tribal in composition. In theory, when posts are advertised, the applicant most qualified, irrespective of tribal considerations, is appointed, but whenever there is a sufficiently qualified Ga, the non-Ga does not stand a good chance of being selected. Whenever an important post in the Accra municipality is given to a qualified non-Ga there is regret expressed on the part of Gas that no member of their tribe had the qualifications required.

In the immediate pre-independence, and certainly in the post-independence era, urban populations have come increasingly under modernized township, municipal and city administrations with the objective of unifying and centralizing urban administration (Acquah 1958:98–101). Hence tribal aspirations and pressures have generally found new expression in a large number of political, economic and social associations which are viewed as "adaptational devices" (Little 1965; Morrill 1963). Urban administration based on tribal authority and representation certainly has its supporters—not only among urban chiefs and headmen but also among educated young men (Banton 1957:159). Although today political office is often contested on party lines, few leaders would dare ignore the need to give adequate representation to the major urban tribal groups and those in the immediate hinterland (Acquah 1958:94).

Within the formal structure of local government, councillors, nominated or elected, are replacing urban tribal chiefs and headmen with the result that the status of chiefs is much reduced. This change is favoured by the new African governments, firstly because the forces of African nationalism seek more radical changes than those supported by chiefs, and, secondly, because the complexity of urban life cannot readily fit into the kind of authority which is rooted in chieftainship which draws its strength from particular (tribal) segments of the urban population (Banton 1957:159, 161). Nevertheless, the system of authority, the enforcement of law and order, the resolution of conflict and all manner of assistance needed by the African urbanite still rests heavily on the shoulders of traditional, and modified traditional, authority. In this sense African urban chieftainship provides an anchorage for social stability and adjustment to urban conditions while at the same time the chief's withdrawal from many traditional functions prepares the urbanite to develop and accept new types of authority.

This function is brought out clearly by Banton (1957:160):

> . . . it would appear that the indirect contribution they [tribal headmen] make to good order is greater. The existence of recognized Tribal Headmen and their many officials undoubtedly helps the native immigrant to orientate himself to life in Freetown and prevents his being exploited; it gives him a certain security and preserves that informal control of public opinion which is often drowned in the re-adjustment to unfamiliar surroundings.

Most observers are agreed that the functions of urban-based tribal chiefs extend beyond the judicial. Thus, Banton (1957:143), writing about Freetown, notes:

> . . . it soon became apparent that the position of Tribal Headmen had a social importance far exceeding the judicial power of the incumbent. The political structure of each tribe centered round the headman because he was the only recognized tribal official having any authority to represent the tribe, and because the immigrants expectations of the chief's role were largely transferred to him.

The fact that urban chiefs deal with a large number of disputes, most of them of a minor nature, not only relieves the courts of what otherwise would be a very heavy load but without their "controlling influence . . . social disorder [would be] greater." (Banton 1957:150)

The activities of the *muluka* (parish) chief and his *batongole* (stewards, assistants) in the peri-urban area of Mulago (one of a number of parishes surrounding the town of Kampala) have been described in detail by Southall and Gutkind (1957:183–214). In this study it was pointed out that the parish chiefs "draw upon an undefined reserve of traditional powers" which do not fit easily into the more formal mechanisms of authority and control required under urban conditions. The problem of social control was analysed as follows:

> There are two major facets to this problem. In what may be called the primitive situation there are always well organised small scale groups based on the family, descent groups, neighbourhood units and associations of a very localised type. All of these groups have a large stable core, the personnel of which changes comparatively slowly and mainly in accordance with the natural cycle of birth, mating and death, the cultural interpretation of which is closely integrated with the structure of the social groups and their recruitment. Hostilities and tensions engendered within these small groups are usually projected with considerable success outside them. This creates a high degree of internal cohesion. It is difficult for the average individual to commit what are considered as major wrongs on fellow members of his own group, and such outbreaks as may occur are provided for by generally accepted formal procedures of restitution and reconciliation, which are easily enforced by the weight of opinion of those on whom the individual relies for his own security. The projection of hostilities outside the small groups increases the frequency of breaches between them, but here too, there is in such systems some recognition of mutual bounds and responsibilities, and breaches are healed by methods which have the sanction of familiar and jointly accepted custom and tradition. Although this type of system is inadequate for the maintenance of order over wide areas, it evidently provides individuals with the minimum security considered necessary for the leading of a normal life in a very

> small-scale society. But it is a system that inhibits change, and is in fact destroyed by it.
>
> In more complex societies the mechanisms continue to operate, but are supplemented by more specialised means of enforcement. Chiefs, nobles and other persons with some degree of concentrated power are able to maintain order over much wider areas. This wider order is accepted by the community as a whole because both the institutions and the persons through which the order is enforced and maintained are recognised as belonging to the same social and beliefs and general values there is a community of sentiment which renders this enforcement of order acceptable to the majority as a morally right and desirable supplement to the traditional small group system which continues to operate within the wider framework. (Southall & Gutkind 1957:211–12)

While this analysis appeared to be particularly appropriate in the context of Ganda society, the literature on urban Africa gives this particular theoretical formulation wider applicability. Everywhere urban local governments are forced to work within the "primitive situation"—the social cohesion of the tradition-oriented small scale groups—while at the same time the African urbanite, urban administrator and African urban associations create institutional arrangements more appropriate to the particular conditions now characteristic of town life. For urban chiefs and headmen these circumstances produce a complex and ambiguous situation. On the one hand they must continue to exercise their duties within the context of tradition—itself no longer always clearly understood—while at the same time they are faced with wholly non-traditional urban conditions. These conditions are well known and by far the most significant are the considerable ethnic heterogeneity, the instability brought about by constant mobility in and out of the town and the difficulties facing marriage and the family. A central problem is therefore how people socialized in a traditional context adjust to and manipulate urban conditions over which they have little or no control.

During a period of eleven months, from June 1957 to April 1958, while I was engaged in research in the peri-urban parish of Mulago, the chief of this parish kept—most conscientiously—a diary of his daily activities. In studying the events in which he was engaged, it became quite evident that as a chief he sought to act as a source of traditional stability while at the same time acting as an agent of change and modernization. The most obvious demonstration of this is a rather remarkable entry in his diary in which he describes his difficulties in being "both a good chief and a chief able to help his people in modern times." (Luganda: *unaku zino ebiro*).

> I think that it is no good being a chief now. My father was a *muluka* (parish) chief before me and he had less trouble. He did not have to take orders from so many people. He was respected and I am not. Town people abuse their chiefs and do not listen to them because chiefs know better than ordinary people (*abakope* = peasants). Chiefs can help people to understand modern times but in modern times everybody wants to do what is best for them and they think that chiefs want to keep them always in the past so that the chiefs are always powerful. But I do not want to do this. Our Government [the Buganda Government] has told us that we must all get an education because we need money. I always tell all the people in this parish that if they want to live in the past they will harm their children because everybody needs an education.

> Mr. H. and Mr. P. came to see me last week and they asked me to settle a problem between them because Mr. H. had accused Mr. P. of stealing his wife which he had not married according to the rules of the Ganda—I knew that. So I said to them that if they were educated they would not fight and quarrel like this and told them to come back to me when they had decided to live like educated men [*okugunjuka abantu*].
>
> I always read in the newspapers about people in other countries and I learn that they have become big and powerful because they have set apart [*okutereka*] their traditions from the new life they now have. I think that that too is our duty as chiefs of the people. (September 19th, 1957)

On another occasion he wrote about his advice to the people of Mulago to impress upon them the need to get smallpox vaccinations:

> Today I and my *batongole* (headmen) visited many houses in Mulago. I was told to tell the people that if they did not wish to get smallpox then they should all go to the Mulago Hospital to get vaccinated [*okusala emikono*] against this terrible disease. Some people listened to me and I gave them a piece of paper to take to the Medical Officer in Charge. But many other people were very ignorant and stupid [*esirusiru*] and I know that they won't go.
>
> So I told them that they can keep their old ideas but they should then not come to me for any help when they are in trouble. This shows what a difficult time I am having in doing my job. I have told the *omukulu we kibuga* (chief of the town) how very stupid many people are in my parish. He asked me whether they were Ganda or other people and I told him that Ganda are always more educated than the visitors [*omigenyi*] i.e. non-Ganda.
>
> I have a great deal of trouble with people who are not Ganda. They do not have the same customs as we do. They do not know how to live in towns because they have always lived in the wilderness [*eddungu*]. But I think that the chief must also tell them how to live in the town because now that they are here they are the cause of a great deal of trouble. If they do not respect a Ganda chief they must leave and build their own town somewhere else. (January 27th, 1958)

On another occasion the chief writes vividly about how difficult it is for him to be a chief in the town.

> To be a chief in the *kibuga* (town) is very difficult. It is not the same as in the village. There are many people who live in the town and I do not know all of them. I do not think that I will ever know them all but my father once told me that he knew everybody in his village. I can go from door to door in Mulago and see new people I have never seen before. Many of them do not come to see me when they first come to Mulago. If they respect the chief they should come. There are some people who do not speak Luganda so they do not understand what I tell them. I must then go to another person of his tribe who does understand Luganda. All this takes time and I do not get paid well enough for all this trouble.
>
> There are many people living in Mulago who do not have a marriage and they just pick up women whenever they can find one who wants food and nice clothing. These young men abuse women but there are also some bad women who abuse the men. I have much trouble in the *lukiko* (council) every week about men and women who fight each other.

> I think if we had better conditions in our parish our troubles will be over. We have little water and it is far away and our shopkeepers do not serve us well. Many people do not buy in Mulago but they go to Kampala to the European shops. You can only buy matches and bananas in our shops and some of the shopkeepers are rude and they swindle the people.
>
> I have been in Mulago now for two years and so many people have come and so many have gone. I hear my cases every Saturday, unless I am on other official duties, but the people are not getting better. They always fight and they steal and they often abuse each other. (February 7th, 1958)

These extracts will, I think, suffice to make the point that African urban chiefs are tied into a complex system which they find immensely difficult to handle. The tensions which arise are not easily resolved within the structure of traditional authority as the events and circumstances which give rise to these tensions spring from conditions which have no referant in traditional methods of resolving conflicts and maintaining unity. As a consequence urban chiefs devise their own informal means of handling complex situations—means which are not acceptable to many urbanites as the following comments made by an association of Ganda shopkeepers in Mulago clearly indicate:

> We, the Ganda shopkeepers in Mulago, wish to protest at the way the chief is enforcing his authority over us. He abuses us and tells us that we must do what he tells us. He has told us that he will withdraw our permits [to sell] unless we keep our shops clean and give honest trade. This is no business of the chief. He does not give us our permit. We get these from the *omugulu we kibuga* and he has more authority than the parish chief. We know how to do our business and the previous chief never interfered in our work; that is why the people of Mulago come to our shops. But now all the people are going to shops of the Europeans in Kampala and that is because he has told the people of this village that our shops are bad and dirty. He has also told us that we are stupid and don't know anything about commercial subjects.
>
> We are sending a copy of this letter to the *omukulu we kibuga* and to the *saza* (county) chief so that they may know of our complaints. We do not object to paying taxes, which the chief must collect, but we do object that Mr. S. [the parish chief] always lectures to us and tells us what to do.
>
> Mr. S. is a Muganda and he should know what our customs are. He always talks badly about us. We think that a good chief will be liked by the people because he is like a teacher. But Mr. S. is not a good teacher because he does not understand us.

These conflicts arise largely because urban chiefs in particular are tied to two types of social systems—the modern and the modified traditional. Furthermore, in heterogeneous urban situations their authority must be acceptable to a large number of tribal groups and as this is often unacceptable, tribally-based authority develops. In addition, the chief's authority, whether it be over a tribally mixed group or over his tribal group alone, rests largely on the amount of support he can muster—a fact which is recognized in the various ordinances designed to legitimize his authority. A chief who is helpful in formal and informal situations is no doubt more popular than a chief who simply defines his duty as enforcement of the law even though he attempts to strike a careful balance between his prerogatives and the expectations of the ruled.[2] The difficulties which arise stem largely from the fact that boundaries between traditional and non-traditional situations are nowadays most unclear. When a chief is asked for help and advice in the context of what could be defined as a traditional situation, his authority is generally accepted largely because the traditional relationship between a chief and his people has been maintained. However, as urban Africans are drawn into commercial and industrial activities tribal authority is no longer relevant. Mair (1958:198–199) has pointed out that:

> The chief has ceased to be the ultimate source of protection to the humble, aid to the needy and advancement to the ambitious. It is not simply that the superior government has taken his place, but that the new world offers opportunities which depend on the creation of relationships right outside the traditional system. People can attain success in commerce, or eminence in the professions, without being beholden in any way to their political superiors, and in these fields the chiefs often could not compete with them. In these circumstances, resentment against the rule of chiefs is something more than a protest against injustice, even though it may express itself in that form. It is part of a wider demand: the demand for full participation in the institutions which control the destinies of Africans.

Epstein (1958) has shown clearly where the authority of the Tribal Elders on the Copperbelt ended and where that of the trade union leaders, for example, began. A primary school teacher living in Mulago brought out this distinction very clearly in an interview:

> To me, and lots of other people who have had some education, a chief is still an important person. I will go to the chief when other authorities cannot help me. When I wanted to send some money to a friend of mine who lived close to the village in which the chief had lived I went to him and asked whether he knew of anyone going that way. I did this because I knew that I could trust a person recommended by the chief to be honest and to deliver the money safely. But there are not many occasions like that. When recently there was a bad fight in our area and people were knifing each other, I ran to the local police station for help because I knew that the chief's actions would be useless. I am more educated than the chief and the work I do is not understood by him. He cannot help me in my profession or to get me a better job. The political leaders are more important. Modern government is not always understood by small chiefs who will never become important. When I have a disagreement with a neighbour who accuses me of terrible things I don't go to the chief for help. I just ignore my attacker or try to solve it in the best way I can myself. If the chief gives me some instructions what to do, such as clearing up my courtyard or not playing my radio too loudly, I try to obey his instructions but I do this only because I know myself that I ought to do these things.

Even less educated residents of the parish draw a clear distinction between traditional and contemporary functions of the urban chief. Thus a Ganda woman with only four years of primary education, who came about once a month to visit her husband, a carpenter, put it this way:

> In my village we all accept that the chief is there to help us. It would be very foolish to fight the chief because he has prestige and power. He knows us and we know him. When we have trouble we go to him and he helps us. He knows

> what everyone is doing all the time *because we all do the same things all the time* (my italics).
>
> But in the town it is different. Many people come to the town because they want to do what they really like. The town chief cannot allow that. In the town you do not ask a chief to protect you or to solve your fights with other people. The police are here to help you. My husband is a carpenter and this is a big and important work but the chief only knows about cultivators. He does not know about skilled work.
>
> There are now some political parties in Kampala and I think they are more important than the chiefs because chiefs cannot get us more money but the political leaders can.

Thus the chief is caught in a difficult situation. Mair (1958:199) sums it up as follows:

> In this situation the chief can be looked at in two ways. He is an individual doing his best to retain the advantages which his status used to bring him, and sometimes coming into conflict with the new leaders in the process, but he is also a symbol, a rallying point for likeminded persons. At different times the chiefs have been found to symbolize different aspects of the complex modern situation. This is the reason why the same chiefs may be objects of hostility at one moment and of vociferous loyalty at the next, and also why the same persons may appear to be successively, or even simultaneously, opponents and supporters of the recognition of hereditary authority.

Non-Ganda are in quite a different position in Mulago. Being treated as rather unwelcomed visitors they have to submit to the authority of the Ganda parish chief who treats them with stern authority which invariably causes considerable difficulties (Gutkind 1962). To them urban chiefs appear all powerful as is indicated in these comments by a Toro office messenger who lived in Mulago for fourteen months:

> I am far away from my country and have not been home for a long time. I live here among my other Toro friends and we look after each other. When we have trouble among us we first decide what to do and if we are still fighting then we go to Mr. S. [the parish chief]. He does not speak our language but we understand him because we can speak Luganda. He is very sharp with us but he tries to help us. He first tells us that as foreigners we should not cause so much trouble and stop abusing and fighting each other. Mr. S. often threatens us with the police and says that he will ask the *omukulu we kibuga* to send us home. We know that he cannot do that against us, but he says he can.
>
> The other day I had to go to him because a thief had broken into my house. I reported it to him but he kept me waiting all Sunday afternoon before he spoke to me. He then told me that he could not give me a letter to the *omukulu we kibuga* because I had no witnesses. He just told me to find someone to prove that I had owned the things which were stolen.
>
> My [Toro] friend met a Ganda woman in a bar last week and she agreed to come to live with him. She stayed one night and in the morning asked for Shs. 10/—. But this was not the agreement my friend made. He wanted her to cook for him. The lady went to the chief and reported that my friend had beaten

her. Mr. S. came to his house in the evening and asked him for an explanation. He told my friend that he had no business beating a Ganda woman and that if this happened again he would be reported to the [then] Protectorate Police.

Some of the non-Ganda groups have their own tribal associations, notably the Luo and the Rwanda. Non-Ganda often lodge complaints with their associations about the treatment they receive from their Ganda hosts. Thus in December 1957 the Rwanda Association wrote to the parish chief of Mulago about the complaint of one of their members who claimed that he had been refused a hearing by him. The Rwanda wanted to lodge a complaint against a Ganda shopkeeper who had given him short weight. The letter concluded as follows:

> We ask that you treat us fairly and that you show us the same respect that you show the Baganda men and women. Our people respect the law as well as others. If you visit our country you will be welcome. We shall not hate or despise you. (Gutkind 1957, fieldnotes)

All this perhaps says no more than to note the fact that the functions of chiefs are changing and that urban chiefs in particular are called upon to carry out their duties knowing that a large section of the population pay scant attention to them while some are outright antagonistic. As the African urbanite generally obtains his living in a different manner from the rural dweller and hence must seek different solutions to the problems he faces, he progressively turns to those authorities and leaders who hold before him the prospect of social, economic and political advancement. Unless the chief uses his formal and informal authority to aid the urbanite to advance within the urban system, his position will increasingly be relegated to a ceremonial role.

But even this position is no longer respected by many urban Africans. Mafeje (1963), in a particularly insightful documentation, has shown how the visit of a Tembu chief to Cape Town aroused violent opposition by many migrants who felt "that chieftainship is an anachronism." Some said that "they had no time to waste on chiefs . . . [and] are no longer prepared to receive a chief." Chieftaincy in urban areas has to battle with the forces of westernization which have—

> completely undermined the position of the chief and other tribal dignitaries. In the urban areas, the breeding place of African nationalism, this process is so advanced that it cannot be reversed. In town in his daily life, the African is in contact with modern civilization, and shows great readiness to accept it. So, the African society is following a path of development that is very similar to that of most of the European societies. (p. 96)

The inability of chiefs, as chiefs, to understand the difficulties urban Africans face was brought out clearly by one agitated speaker at the meeting called to welcome the chief: "It is a good thing that you have come to town so that you may see for yourself what is happening; go home and tell them that we are still surviving, though between the flesh and the nail (i.e. in a tight corner)." (p. 93) Another speaker appeared to challenge the view that chiefs exist in their own right:

> The people are convinced that there are no more chiefs. I want to ask you, as a chief, do we exist? I would like to remind you that, traditionally, it is not the

> people who are made for the chief, but it is the chief who is made for them. In fact, the chief is a chief by the grace of the people. I want to be frank with you. You should not listen to all the flattery you have been subjected to this afternoon. Take it from me, the Thembu are not at all happy about your presence here. Do you think that if they were pleased, there would be so few of them here today? Please, let us not fool ourselves, we are not children. (p. 93)

Pauw (1963:26), on the other hand, reports a case of a rural chieftainness who was cordially received in East London.

These attitudes, and divisions, in African urban society help to explain the present position of the urban chief. Theoretically a number of recent studies have drawn a sharp distinction between those who are committed to urban life and see their future in salaried or wage employment, and those who reject change and modern ways of the town either out of choice or because they are unable to reach above the lowest levels of employment and earning power (Mayer 1961; Pauw 1963; Powdermaker 1962:291–305). Powdermaker (1962:292), for example, has suggested the following hypothesis:

> Individuals committed to the new moral order have faith in eventual rewards from it and an ego sufficiently strong to accept the risks and anxieties which always accompany change; they have a desire for the more personal autonomy inherent in the new order and do not always think in terms of opposing polarities. Conversely, the intransigents do not have the same characteristics or possess them to a much smaller degree.

It might be possible to apply a typological analysis to various types of urban chieftainship. In a forthcoming article I set out some of the main educational and attitudinal differences of fourteen parish chiefs in the peri-urban area which surrounds Kampala. It is clear from this data that at least nine of these chiefs interpreted their functions in a traditional or neo-traditional manner. The remainder saw their functions rather like the parish chief of Mulago referred to earlier in this paper. Preliminary study of the data also showed that residents in those parishes furthest from the centre of Kampala, i.e. within a three to four mile radius, looked to the chief in much the same manner as in rural Buganda. This is so because the political and economic basis of chieftainship prevailing in these parishes is not basically different from that of the rural areas (Richards 1960; Southwold 1961). In contrast, in those parishes contiguous with or within a one to two miles radius of the centre of Kampala, the chiefs viewed their duties in a more modernist manner simply because typical urban conditions prevailed. The view the residents had of what a chief should be and do also varied considerably. However, simply because they took a more modern approach to their duties did not necessarily make them more popular or better chiefs.

Thus the future of African urban chiefs appears to be primarily determined by two important sets of variables: 1) their ability to meet the needs (both in traditional and modern terms) of an increasingly heterogeneous, and increasingly stratified, urban African population and 2) the attitudes of the latter towards the urban chiefs. To the traditionalist, or as Mayer has characterised such people—the incapsulated—, the urban chief will continue to provide a major social and political anchorage. This is likely to be particularly so in such urban areas dominated by one or two major tribal groups which have captured economic, political and social power at the expense of smaller tribal groups. Among them occupational mobility is generally low and their commitment to urban life is less certain. Such groups comprise a far larger percentage of highly mobile migrants. Under such conditions, as among the Mossi, the urban chiefs can, and usually do, offer the migrant the kind of help he wants and needs. Banton (1954b:141–142) states quite explicitly:

> In most of the tribes represented in Freetown the institution of chiefship plays a central role. The natives look to their chief or headman for a variety of services and it will be a long time before other institutions can take over all his functions.

This is so because "the indirect contribution they [headmen] make to good order is the greater, for the infrastructure of tribal institutions is better adapted to the needs of the people than office-made rules can ever be."

Whether or not the migrant turns away from acceptance of the authority of the chief seems to depend not only on situational factors and on the economic, social and educational niche the migrant is in (Acquah 1958:103–104), but also on the "determinants that lie behind the choices" he makes as to whether or not to be an urbanite.[3] Thus Mayer (1962:591) writes:

> It seems sometimes to have been implied that prolonged residence in the "atmosphere" of town will automatically tend to "change" people and make them "urbanized." East London does not bear this out. There, while some are born "urban," and others achieve urbanization, none can be said to have urbanization thrust upon them. There is a power of choice; some of the migrants begin to change; but others voluntarily incapsulate themselves in something as nearly as possible like the tribal relations from which their migration could have liberated them. The study of urbanization of migrants . . . is a study of such choices and of the determinants that lie behind the choices.

The position of urban chiefs, as agents of stability or change must therefore be analysed closely within the total context and the specific patterns of urban life. Chiefs, rural or urban, represent an important feature of African society (or their counterparts in non-chiefly societies) whose functions are embedded in the basic rules of obedience and authority, social control and administrative action and ritual and ceremonial activities. To many urban Africans, chiefs and headmen continue to give expression to these functions but progressively the former live and work in an institutional complex which compels them to look to the type of leadership and authority able to deal effectively with the wholly non-traditional conditions characteristic of most of the newer African towns. Thus, in 1958 Acquah observed:

> Today, in Accra, the chiefs' functions are mainly ceremonial. They play a major role in tribal festivals. In some measure they assist in the maintenance of law and order through their position as arbitrators. In spite of the fact that the municipal council is now the sole authority, many Gas and non-Gas in Accra take their troubles and grievances to the chiefs for them to settle. . . . Whether they have as deep an influence on the lives of their subjects today as they had before . . . is a wide field for study . . . (p. 101)

Likewise, Mayer (1961:54) reporting on the position of headmen in the urban locations in East London, writes:

> Lacking confidence in the effectiveness of the official "intercalary" authorities [of location headmen], the migrants in town are tempted to turn to others who act the part unofficially or even illegally. In the seats of White power . . . a number of Xhosa are employed in subsidiary capacities as clerks, constables and so forth. Because of their nearness to the source of power, these are regarded by many location people as key figures. Most migrants appear to be firmly convinced that the good will of the man who actually wields the rubber stamp is vital . . .

At the same time Mayer (1961:72) also reports that migrants are frequently at odds with the established urbanite because the latter completely reject the authority of the chiefs. Extensive case studies should now be carried out to determine the conditions under which the functions and authority of urban chiefs are rejected and those conditions under which they are acceptable to urban Africans.

Notes

1. The "use" of tribal elders as the basis for the organization of a council of industrial workers (miners) has been well described by Spearpoint (1937).

2. Fallers (1955:302) has pointed to the "high casualty rate among chiefs" as they are expected to be both civil servants and kinsmen. The urban chief appears to be particularly exposed to this dilemma as he is constantly called upon to add new administrative functions on top of traditional ones. In this sense Fallers is right when he says: "Institutions are constantly getting in each others' way, and individuals are constantly being institutionally required to do conflicting things". (p. 292) In the racially more complex situation in southern Africa the position of African chiefs has been characterised as "intercalary" i.e. "those positions occupied by persons who link two opposed parts in an authoritarian system" (Mitchell 1959:16). See also: Gluckman 1949:93–94 and Wilson and Mafeje 1963:143–152.

3. A good deal of the above discussion is, of course, closely related to the functions of tribalism in urban social organization and social interaction. The significance of tribalism as a particular kind of social interaction is perceptively analysed in a number of publications by Mitchell (1959, 1960), Gluckman (1960a, 1960b, 1961) and Mercier (1961).

References

Acquah, I., Accra survey. London, University of London Press, 1958.

Banton, M. P., The origins of tribal administration in Freetown. Sierra Leone Studies N.S., 2, 109–119, 1954a.

——Tribal headmen in Freetown. Journal of African Administration, 6, 3, 140–144, 1954b.

——West African city: a study of tribal life in Freetown. London, Oxford University Press (for International African Institute), 1957.

BUSIA, K. A., Report on a social survey of Sekondi-Takoradi. Accra, Government printer, 1950.

COMHAIRE, J. L. L., Aspects of urban administration in tropical and southern Africa. Communications from the School of African Studies (New Series), 27, Cape Town, University of Cape Town, 1953.

EPSTEIN, A. L., Politics in an urban African community. Manchester, University Press (for Rhodes-Livingstone Institute), 1958.

FALLERS, L. A., The predicament of the modern African chief: an instance from Uganda. American Anthropologist, 57, 2, 290–305, 1955.

FRAENKEL, M., Tribe and class in Monrovia. London, Oxford University Press (for International African Institute), 1964.

GLUCKMAN, M., The village headman in British Central Africa. Africa, 19, 2, 89–94, 1949.

——Tribalism in modern British Central Africa. Cahiers D'Etudes Africaines, 1, 55–70, 1960a.

——From tribe to town. Nation (Sydney), 53, 7–12, 1960b.

——Anthropological problems arising from the African industrial revolution. *In* Social change in modern Africa, A. W. Southall ed. London, Oxford University Press, 67–82, 1961.

GUTKIND, P. C. W., Diary of an African urban chief. Ms. in possession of P. C. W. Gutkind, 1957–1958.

——Accommodation and conflict in and African peri-urban area. Anthropologica, N.S., 4, 1, 163–173, 1962.

——The royal capital of Buganda: a study of internal conflict and external ambiguity. Series Maior, 12, Institute of Social Studies, The Hague, Mouton, 1963.

LESLIE, J. A. K., A survey of Dar es Salaam. London, Oxford University Press (for East African Institute of Social Research), 1963.

LITTLE, K., West African urbanization: a study of voluntary associations in social change. Cambridge, University Press, 1965.

MAFEJE, A., A chief visits town. Journal of Local Administration Overseas, 2, 2, 88–99, 1963.

MAIR, L. P., African chiefs today. Africa, 28, 3, 195–206, 1958.

MATHEWS, A. B., Report on the tribal administration in Freetown. Sessional paper No. 4 of 1940, Freetown, Government Printer, 1940.

MAYER, P., Townsmen or tribesmen. Cape Town, Oxford University Press (for Institute of Social and Economic Research, Rhodes University), 1961.

——Migrancy and the study of Africans in towns. American Anthropologist, 64, 3, 576–592, 1962.

MERCIER, P., Remarque sur la signification du 'tribalisme' actuel en Afrique noire. Sociologie, 31, 61–80, 1961.

MITCHELL, J. C., The Kalela dance. The Rhodes-Livingstone Papers 27, Manchester, University Press (for Rhodes-Livingstone Institute), 1959.

——Tribalism and the plural society. London, Oxford University Press, 1960.

MORRILL, W. T., Immigrants and associations: the Ibo in twentieth century Calabar. Comparative Studies in Society and History, 5, 4, 424–448, 1963.

OTTENBERG, S., The development of local government in a Nigerian township. Anthropologica, N.S., 4, 1, 121–161, 1962.

PAUW, B. A., The second generation. Capetown, Oxford University Press (for Institute of Social and Economic Research, Rhodes University), 1963.

POWDERMAKER, H., Copper town: changing Africa. New York, Harper and Row, 1962.

RICHARDS, A. I., The Ganda. *In* East Africa chiefs, A. I. Richards ed. London, Faber and Faber (for East African Institute of Social Research), 41–77, 1960.

ROBINSON, R. E., The administration of African customary law. Journal of African Administration, 1, 4, 158–176, 1949.

SKINNER, E. P., Labor migration among the Mossi of the Upper Volta. *In* Urbanization and migration in West Africa, H. Kuper ed. Berkeley and Los Angeles, University of California Press, 60–84, 1965.

SOUTHALL, A. W. and P. C. W. GUTKIND, Townsmen in the making: Kampala and its suburbs. East African Studies 9, Kampala, East African Institute of Social Research, 1957.

SOUTHWOLD, M., Bureaucracy and chiefship in Buganda. East African Studies 14, Kampala, East African Institute of Social Research, 1961.

SPEARPOINT, F., The African natives and the Rhodesian copper mines. Supplement to the Journal of the Royal African Society, 26, 1937.

WHITE, C. M. N., The changing scope of urban native courts in Northern Rhodesia. Journal of African Law, 8, 1, 29–33, 1964.

WILSON, M. and A. MAFEJE, Langa: a study of social groups in an African township. Cape Town, Oxford University Press, 1963.

URBANIZATION, DETRIBALIZATION, STABILIZATION AND URBAN COMMITMENT IN SOUTHERN AFRICA: A PROBLEM OF DEFINITION AND MEASUREMENT: 1968[1]

J. Clyde Mitchell

Introduction

One of the many consequences of the introduction of the Western economic system to Central and Southern Africa has been the growth of large towns. The existence of these large agglomerations of the population, where previously there had been none, has brought in its train a host of social and administrative problems. Some of these problems are associated with city life all over the world; some of them are due to the fact that many thousands of Africans are being thrown into a situation for which there is no set of prescribed behaviour in their traditions; others derive from a conflict of political dogma and economic neces-

Reprinted by permission of the author and publisher from *Social Implications of Industrialization and Urbanization in Africa South of the Sahara,* UNESCO, 1956, revised and extended for this volume.

sity. As a result a considerable volume of literature dealing with *urbanization, detribalization* and *stabilization* has come into being.

A brief glance at the literature, however, reveals that there appears to be a good deal of confusion about the use of these three terms. It seems that the time is ripe for an examination, however cursorily, of the way in which these words are used and some of the implications behind them.

Demographic and Sociological Frames of Reference

In Southern Africa the three terms are frequently used interchangeably. This arises because of a hidden assumption in all three words which, as I hope to demonstrate, is an implicit value-judgment and should be recognized as such.

Urbanize, according to the *Shorter Oxford English Dictionary,* was first used in 1884 in the sense of "to make of an urban character; to convert into a city." In sociological usage however urbanization refers to the "process of becoming urban; the movement of people or processes to urban areas; the increase of urban areas, population, or processes." [2] In this definition there are clearly two themes. The first of these refers to the increase of urban populations as such. The other refers to the increase of urban "processes." The word process here refers to "any change in which an observer could see a consistent quality or direction to which a name is given." [3] It is clear, therefore, that the word urbanization has a meaning in a demographic frame of reference as the "movement of peoples to urban areas." It is this sense that Thompson has in mind in his article in the *Encyclopedia of Social Sciences* when he writes: "Urbanization is characterized by movements of people from small communities concerned chiefly or solely with agriculture to other communities generally larger, whose activities are primarily centred in government, trade, manufacture or allied interests." [4]

But urbanization may also have a meaning within a sociological frame of reference when it implies change in behaviour as a result of living in town. Beals has this in mind when he refers to "the modification of human behaviour imposed by the urban way of life"; or later in the same article when he writes: "within the framework assumed by the concepts of urbanization and acculturation we are dealing with processes which, if not identical, at least form a related continuity of social phenomena." [5]

The word *detribalization* does not appear in the English dictionary. But in sociological usage this word too is used in two different frames of reference. Wilson, although he uses the word in the title of his essay, does not use it as a crucial variable.[6] The theme of his study is the age and sex disproportion of the population in town and country in Northern Rhodesia (now Zambia), the causes of this disproportion, and its concomitants in the life of African town dwellers. Therefore Wilson uses the word primarily in the demographic sense, that is, to describe the movement of population out of rural areas into urban areas. Hellman, on the other hand, has a distinctly sociological view of detribalization. For example, she lists three criteria of detribalization:

1. Permanent residence in an area other than that of the chief to whom a man would normally pay allegiance.

2. Complete severance of the relationships to the chief.
3. Independence of rural relatives both for support during periods of unemployment and ill-health and for the performance of ceremonies connected with the major crises of life.[7]

In other words, Hellman is concerned primarily with the social relationships among people and not the correlation of the attributes of categories of people. She is also concerned with "westernization" [8] or "Europeanization" [9] so that she takes the same point of view as Beals in considering detribalization as part of acculturation.

From both the sociological and demographic points of view urbanization and detribalization are not the same thing. From the sociological point of view, urbanization implies participation in social relations in urban areas. Detribalization, on the other hand, implies the dropping or the rejection of tribal modes of behaviour, and the lapse of social relationships with people living in tribal areas. Hellman's studies show that very few Africans in urban areas drop their association with their tribal areas completely, and that it is quite possible for people to continue to follow tribal modes of behaviour in some respects and participate in urban social relations in others. At the same time tribal modes of behaviour may be eschewed by some people living in rural areas, though as Hellman points out, it is very difficult for a man living in a tribe not to have social relationships with them.[10] A man living as a trader in the area of a foreign tribe could by these criteria be "detribalized" but he is clearly not "urbanized." From the demographic point of view also, urbanization and detribalization are not the same. People who leave tribal areas do not necessarily go to towns.

The word *stabilization* is frequently used in referring to problems of African urbanization. It is used, however, almost exclusively in a demographic frame of reference, and it is significant only against the background of labour migration. A population becomes stabilized in town when people no longer make intermittent journeys back to their rural homes. Wilson uses the term to mean permanently resident outside the rural areas. For example, he says: "When I speak of a relatively stabilized group I mean one stabilized in town, but not necessarily in the same towns and still less the same jobs all the time." [11] Frequently the words detribalization and urbanization are used in the same sense. When the Native Economic Commission in the Union of South Africa reported for example: "The increase of females in an urban area is some indication of the urbanization of the native population" [12] it meant, not that Africans are currently living in towns, but that Africans are settling in towns. The fundamental idea behind stabilization is the achievement of some demographic balance between rural and urban areas. Industries, as for example the copper mines in Zambia, select workers in the age groups 20 to 35. The effect is to denude the rural population of men and their wives in these age categories. Urban areas, therefore, show a concentration of population in the working age categories and a correspondingly lower proportion in other categories. This is what Wilson calls *disproportion*.[13] This disproportion is maintained by the circulation of population between town and country. As Wilson expressed it: "Circulation of population is the keystone of the unstable arch of present-day Northern Rhodesia economy." [14] The young men spend several years of their working lives in towns and return to the rural areas when they get older. The result is that there is a greater proportion of young adults in the towns than in rural areas. This has direct effect on the national economy which Wilson has analysed so admirably.

The implication of the fact that the words "urbanization" and "detribalization" may be used within different frames of reference is the danger that the user may slip unwittingly from one frame of reference to the other. He may assume, in other words, that if a man is "urbanized" in the demographic sense he is also "urbanized" in the sociological sense. It is all too easy to assume that the longer a man has been in town the more disorganized he is, the more severe his state of *anomie.* In fact, there is a certain amount of evidence that *anomie* is most severe among those who have lived in town for longer periods, and who accept certain standards of behaviour and conform to them.

To avoid this danger I suggest that, in scientific writings at least, the words should be used with due care and that stabilization be used for the settled residence of Africans in town, urbanization for the development of modes and standards of behaviour peculiar to urban areas, and detribalization, if it is used at all, for the general change from tribal to Western standards of behaviour.

It seems to me that the first task of urban sociology in Africa is to establish correlations, if there are any, between stabilization and urbanization. To do this we need some objective methods of measuring stabilization. It is to the discussion of this task that the rest of this paper is devoted.[15]

The Content of "Stabilization"

Stabilization refers essentially to the change over from the circulation of people between town and country to the settlement of people in towns. But a *stabilized population* is not easy to define in quantitative terms.[16] The difficulty arises from trying to apply discrete categories to a continuous variable; it is similar to the difficulty in defining "old age" or "adulthood." Ageing or growing-up is a continuous process through gradual stages, so that it is not possible to say at one point in the lifetime of a person that he is "adult" or "old." For practical purposes certain conventional ages are taken to be socially significant, as for example, the full age at 21 years, or the conventional retiring age of 60, which could represent a point at which people are "adult" or "old." In the same way "stabilization" is a continuous process. People are less and less likely to leave urban areas the longer they have been living there, so that the problem boils down to an estimate of the chances of a person's returning to his rural home within any given period.

For administrative purposes some arbitrary definition must be made. Stent gives a list of examples of these under different laws in South Africa. For example, the Representation of Natives Act No. 12 of 1936 [Section 37 (2)] defines an African as "urbanized" when he has made his permanent home in an urban area for at least three consecutive years.[17]

For purposes of description, therefore, we may assume that labour is normally migratory and estimate the degree of stabilization by measuring how much this hypothetical pattern of migration is departed from. A dangerous trap however exists in the word "normally." It could be taken to imply on the one hand an empirically determined most frequent or modal type of behaviour. We cay say that of 2393 adult males 68 percent had spent less than two-thirds of their adult life (i.e. since turning 15 years of age) in towns. We can say then that, since the majority of adult males still spend a considerable proportion of their time in rural areas, "migratory labour" is "normal." From this point of view the other 32 percent who spent more than two-thirds of their time in town could be considered abnormal—they constitute by one definition, therefore, the "stabilized" population.

But if we say that African labour is normally migratory, we might also mean this in a normative sense. We may imply, in other words, that it *should* be migratory and that the population should not be stabilized. The stabilized population here is also abnormal, but in the sense that it should not be in the town at all, and presents a problem to the Administration. This essentially political view of the problem is familiar in South Africa and has led to the provision of legislation to "repatriate" unproductive urban population.[18]

In Southern Rhodesia basically the same assumption was made in the Land Apportionment Act, the Native Registration Act (1936), and the Native (Urban Areas) Accommodation and Registration Act (1946). Under the Land Apportionment Act, "Urban areas generally are 'European Areas'," and the other two acts "accept this principle and make provision and decide where Africans shall live in urban areas and how control shall be exercised over them there." [19] In other words, in Southern Rhodesia "Africans in law are within municipal and other urban areas not in their own right, but as employees of Europeans and European concerns." [20] In Northern Rhodesia in 1951 it was held that the law was different but the practice in almost all respects was the same.[21]

Needless to say, when we attempt to design a measure of stabilization, and in doing so take account of the migrant labour system, we do not of necessity accept that this system is "normal" except in the statistical sense I have just pointed out.

Measures of Stabilization

If we define *stabilization* therefore as the process whereby Africans are becoming permanent dwellers in urban areas, we can devise certain measures of stabilization. But the initial assumption should be explicitly stated, namely the assumption that Africans normally, in a statistical sense, live in rural areas and that any African living in an urban area is likely to return to his rural home at some time or another. The measures that we derive on this basis will be based on a dichotomy of town and country which is to some extent artificial. "Stabilization" in effect will refer to rural depopulation and not to the growth of urban population.

Once we have accepted this as a working hypothesis, two distinct problems arise. These are the problems of the availability and the significance of the data. It may be possible to define exactly what is meant by detribalization or urbanization, yet virtually impossible to apply a scale of measurement. For example, the Commission of Inquiry into Industrial Legislation defined "permanently urbanized" as (a) having severed all ties with the rural areas of his origin, and (b) being solely dependent upon the labour performed by him in some industry in an urban area.[22] Theoretically, the definition is perfectly sound. But difficulties arise when we try to measure the categories isolated by the definition because of the practical problem of deciding, in a social survey, when all ties with a rural area are severed and when a man is solely dependent on the income derived from his labour in an urban industry.

In the same category is the definition of a Detribalized Native used by the Transvaal Chamber of Mines in their evidence to the Native Laws Commission of Inquiry. By this definition a detribalized native is one "who has been born and brought up in an urban area, or who is permanently settled in an urban area and has no intention of returning to the Native Reserves." [23]

At the other extreme it is possible to use some simple criterion of urbanization, stabilization or detribalization which is easy to measure, but we may find its relevance problematical. For example, we may use the length of residence out of rural areas as a measure of stabilization, but we all know that some men have labour histories with constant visits to rural areas for twenty years and more.[24]

A Predictive Measure

If we accept that our measure of stabilization should be based on objective and easily observed criteria, then it appears that our measures can be prepared in two different ways. In the first we can try to arrive at some measure of the flow of labour in and out of urban areas. This type of measure, which ideally should be computed for different categories of migrants, would measure the chances under prevailing conditions (i.e. assuming that the flow will remain constant) that a person just arriving in town will stay there for any given period of time.

In the second type of measure we can use the characteristics of town dwellers to distinguish those who have maintained close contact with their rural homes from those who have not.

For the first type of measure we need the following type of information:

1. A breakdown of all departures from town to the country over a given period, by the length of residence in town.
2. A breakdown of all those left in town at the end of that time by length of residence in town.

This information could be available for any community for which records are kept—as, for example, a housing area for which registers must be kept. But the resulting measure would of course relate to the stability of residence in that particular area and not in the town or country as a whole. I do not see any way in which the requisite information can be gathered for towns and country as a whole, because there is no way of knowing accurately who has left a town in a particular area or to what place he has gone.

There is some possibility that this measure may be computed from the rural side of the picture. If we make the assumption that the majority of those who leave town, return to their area of origin, then we can collect the following data for small groups in rural areas, for example in villages, where data derived from kinsmen ensure that most absentees are included in the sample. The categories

TABLE 1. CUMULATIVE PRODUCT TO COMPUTE PROBABILITY OF RETURN OF LABOUR MIGRANT WITH A GIVEN PERIOD

Years Absent	Date Left	No. Left	No. Stayed	Proportion Stayed	C.P.
Less than 1 year	1953	x_1	y_1	$\frac{y_1}{x_1}$	$\frac{y_1}{x_1}$
1 year to 2 years	1952	x_2	y_2	$\frac{y_2}{x_2}$	$\frac{y_1y_2}{x_1x_2}$
2 years to 3 years	1951	x_3	x_3	$\frac{y_3}{x_3}$	$\frac{y_1y_2y_3}{x_1x_2x_3}$
:	:	:	:	:	⋮
$(n-1)$ years to n years	?	x_n	y_n	$\frac{y_n}{x_n}$	$\frac{y_1y_2y_3 \cdots y_n}{x_1x_2x_3 \cdots x_n}$

of information needed are these:

1. The number of men who left this particular area for labour markets over the last, say, 30 years and the years in which they left.
2. An analysis of those returning over, say, the last five years by the years in which they left.

The procedure in computation would be as follows: Suppose that for each year in Table 1, "x" represents the number of men who left in that particular year and "y" represents the number who had not returned at the time of the investigation. Then y/x represents the proportion who did not return for that particular period. The value (y_1y_2) (x_1x_2) represents the proportion of 100 men who will still be away at the end of the second year after departure. The value $(y_1y_2y_3)$ $(x_1x_2x_3)$ represents the proportion of 100 men who will still be away at the end of three years.

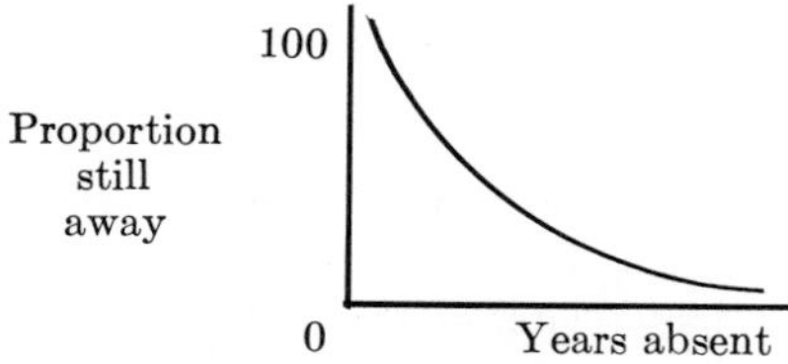

If the values of these expressions are plotted as a curve, a typical evaporation curve results.

The area under this curve represents the total number of man-years that the original 100 men would spend away, so that if this figure is divided by 100 we arrive at a figure which represents the number of years a man may be expected to stay away from his rural area under present economic conditions. The difficulties in this measure lie not in its computation, but in acquiring the requisite categories of information. No rural community is likely to be able to recall those who left a long time ago. On the other hand, the proportion of these away is likely to be so small that their exclusion would not make much difference to the computation.

The cumulative product gives an estimate of how long on the average a man is likely to stay away from his tribal area. Since the statistic is derived from data relating to a large number of men from a particular area it is, an average measure and it can be used to compare the stabilization of communities. If we were able to compute the mean expectancy of length of residence in a number of communities we could say that since the mean expectancy of residence in one community is longer than in another, the first is more stabilized.

Static Measures

In the absence of the requisite data to compute this predictive type of measure, however, we must rely on other measures of stability, either by individuals in communities or by communities as a whole. These measures must be based on information that can be derived from the social survey results. One such indicator sometimes used is the age and sex composition of the urban population as compared with the rural. Diagram I shows the estimate age and sex structure of the African population of Rhodesia in 1961.

The structure of the urban population reflects that males of working age have been attracted to the town to a greater extent than women of the same ages and

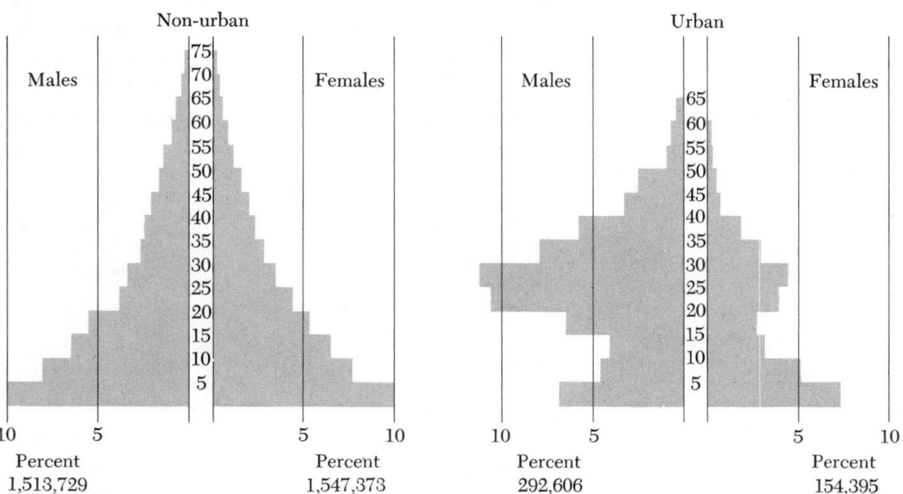

Diagram I. Age and Sex Structure: Urban and Non-Urban African Population: Rhodesia, 1961.

Source: Estimated from *Final Report of the April/May, 1962 Census of Africans in Southern Rhodesia,* Salisbury 1964; *Report on the Salisbury Demographic Survey August /September, 1958,* Salisbury 1959; *Report on Bulawayo African Demographic Survey held in May, 1959,* Salisbury 1960; *Report on Umtali and Gwelo African Demographic Surveys held in August/September, 1959,* Salisbury 1960.

that both men and women are strongly selected from the young adult age range. The age distribution of the children also suggests a population of young married couples at an early phase of the family cycle. An age and sex distribution as different from the overall structure as this could be maintained indefinitely if young people were to migrate to towns, spend the early years of life there, to send some of their children back to their rural homes when they reached puberty, and finally to return to their rural homes themselves when they reached the mid-forties in age.

Clearly, if the circulation between town and country were to cease entirely then the age and sex distribution of the towns would approximate the proportions in the population as a whole [26]—as in fact is the case in countries such as England and Wales where there has been a long history of urban growth. It is on this basis that the Native Economic Commission argued in the passage quoted earlier that the increase in the number of females in an urban area is some indication of the stabilization of the native population. The same argument was used by the Industrial Research Section of the Department of Commerce of the University of Witwatersrand which wrote of the population in so-called native areas, "This portion had an age-sex composition characteristic of a stable urbanized population." [27] This was 55,000 adults "divided more or less equally into male and female and 74,000 children under 18 years of age—the outward evidence of family life." In other words, there were 21.3 percent adult males, 21.3 percent adult females, and 57.4 percent children under the age of 18.

On exactly the same basis the South African Census Department argues that "judging from the ratios of males to females and the proportions of persons in the different age groups, it appears that the native populations of Port Elizabeth, East London, Kimberley, and Bloemfontein were comparatively stable." [28] The proportions in the age groups selected by the Industrial Research Section for these towns are: [29]

	Adult Male	Adult Female	Children
Port Elizabeth	36.4	31.4	32.2
East London	36.8	37.5	25.7
Kimberley	32.7	29.0	38.3
Bloemfontein	28.8	35.4	35.8

In the native population of South Africa, excluding those born outside the Union, there were, however, 22.4 percent adult males, 25.0 percent adult females and 52.6 percent children.[30] It appears that the Industrial Research section was justified in assuming that in the areas for which they have the information these broad age and sex categories give outward evidence of family life. But there were far more children in the sample quoted by the Industrial Research Section than in the populations of the towns considered by the Census department to be the most stable. A basic question arises, however: To what extent may we assume a stabilized urban population because the age and sex structure is the same as that of the general population? It is possible that the circulation between town and country could occur in all age groups and in both sexes in such a way as

TABLE 2. YEARS ABSENT FROM RURAL AREAS

	Local Authority Housing Areas		Mining Company Housing Areas		Industrial Housing Areas		Domestic Housing Areas		Private Housing Areas	
	M	F	M	F	M	F	M	F	M	F
0–4	31.0	50.3	46.0	58.6	50.4	60.6	61.7	61.1	14.8	29.1
5–9	20.5	16.3	19.6	19.5	17.0	17.3	16.4	12.6	12.5	19.9
10–14	21.2	15.6	16.6	11.0	15.4	9.8	11.4	8.1	23.9	19.4
15–19	11.7	8.3	9.0	6.7	5.7	5.7	4.2	10.8	21.0	13.4
20–24	9.6	7.7	5.3	2.9	6.0	5.5	3.2	4.4	18.1	13.4
25–29	3.3	1.2	2.0	1.1	2.7	0.9	1.5	1.1	4.8	1.7
30–34	1.5	0.6	0.9	0.1	1.8	0.2	1.4	1.9	2.4	3.1
35–39	1.2	—	0.5	0.0	1.0	0.0	0.2	0.0	2.5	—
	100.0	100.0	100.0	100.0	100.0	100.0	100.0	100.0	100.0	100.0
No information	1.1	0.8	0.4	0.6	1.2	0.5	0.2	1.0	1.2	0.0
Number of respondents	1236	824	3015	1805	742	440	487	93	83	61
Median years absent	9.6	5.0	6.0	4.3	5.0	4.1	4.1	4.1	14.7	10.3

Based on occupants of a random sample of premises occupied by Africans in Ndola, Luanshya, Kitwe, Mufulira, and Chingola 1951–1953. The housing areas refer to those under the control of Local Authorities, Mining Companies, various industrial concerns, employers of domestic servants and local township authorities such as Twapia, Fisinge, etc.

to maintain the main proportions. The population could hardly be called "stabilized" if this were true. The similarity of the age and sex structure of an urban population with the population of a country as a whole if a necessary but not a sufficient condition for inferring stability in the urban population. We may not assume stability until it has been demonstrated.[31] While the age and sex composition by itself can tell us something of the probable stabilization of an urban population as a whole, it cannot tell us anything about the individual and in particular about his circulation between town and country. For this information we need to go to more specific data.

One of the simplest measures of stabilization is the length of time away from the tribal area. For example, Table 2 is derived from the Rhodes-Livingstone Institute social surveys on the "line-of-rail" towns of Zambia. As measured by this index, men are more stabilized than women and those living in Private and Local Authority housing areas are more stabilized than those living in other housing areas. To some extent, however, these figures are artificial since they include those who have been born and bred in town. In themselves they do not constitute a measure of the probability that people in any category are likely to stay in town longer, though independent evidence suggests that in fact the longer a man stays in town the more likely he is to remain.[32] This measure of stabilization, furthermore, is crude because it obscures the differing age structures between the sexes and among different urban communities. The older a person is, the more years he has lived, so that it is likely that he will have spent a longer period in town than a younger person.

If we are to measure stabilization then, we must relate the number of years lived to the number of those spent in town. Wilson has done this in his four categories of town dwellers.[33] Wilson, it will be recalled, worked on a sample of 198 African males. Of these, one-quarter, say 46, had been out of their villages for less than three years. This category Wilson put aside. He then computed the proportion of time each of the remaining 152 had spent in town, and divided them arbitrarily into four categories. These were:

1. Those who had spent less than one-third of their time in town since they had first left the rural areas. These he called *peasant visitors.*
2. Those who had spent between a third and two-thirds of their time since first leaving rural areas, in town. These he called *migrant labourers.*
3. Those who had spent more than two-thirds of their time since leaving rural areas, in town. These he called *temporarily urbanized.*
4. Those who had been born and brought up in town. These he called *permanently urbanized.*

Having established the proportions in each of these categories, Wilson now distributed the original 46 proportionately amongst them. Wilson derived the following proportions: peasant visitors, 8.5 percent; migrant labourers, 20.5 percent; temporarily urbanized, 69.9 per cent; permanently urbanized, 1.0 percent.

Wilson's proportion of permanently urbanized must be taken with a certain amount of caution. This figure was estimated because his survey did not include single men in the location or plots, and it is among these that most permanently urbanized men are found.

The weakness in Wilson's method is that it does not take into account the age at which the men first left the rural areas. On page 46 of his first essay, Wilson defines temporarily urbanized as those who "have spent most of their time in long periods, in the towns, since the age of fifteen and a half." In his Table IV, page 41, we see that the average age of leaving the rural area was 15 years, 10.5 months. We are left in doubt whether Wilson was making a generalized statement on page 46 where the average age of leaving the tribal area becomes 15.5 and not 15 years 10.5 months, or whether, in fact, he assumed in making his computations that each man left the tribal area when he was 15.5. It seems clear that a man who leaves his tribal area when he is, say, 45 and spends 4 of the ensuing 6 years in town, is less likely to remain in town than a man at the age of, say, 20 who does the same thing. If we are comparing the degree of stabilization in communities of roughly the same age structure, then Wilson's measures are satisfactory. But if we wish to compare the degree of stabilization in populations of differing age structures, some method must be devised for controlling the age variable.

For this purpose I have proposed an index of stabilization based on the proportion of time spent in town since the age of 15.[34] The argument here is that each adult, at the age of 15 approximately, must make the decision to go to town or to stay away. The index of stabilization then becomes

$$\frac{\text{Years in town since turned 15}}{\text{Years lived since turned 15}} \times 100.$$

TABLE 3. AGE OF FIRST LEAVING TRIBAL AREAS

Age	Number	Age	Number
-4	26	25–29	116
5–9	17	30–34	40
10–14	38	35–39	20
15–19	169	40 and over	6
20–24	212		
Total			644

The advantage of this method over Wilson's may be gathered from two hypothetical instances. If a man Z, now aged 30, left his tribal area at the age of 15 and has spent say 10 years in town, in Wilson's scheme he would be classified as temporarily urbanized, i.e., he has spent $^{10}/_{15}$ years = ⅔ of his time, in town. If a man, Y, also aged 30, came to town when he was 25 and spent 4 years in town, he is also classified as temporarily urbanized, i.e., $^{4}/_{5}$ = 80 percent of his time in town since leaving rural area. By the index of stabilization, however, Z has a score of $^{10}/_{15}$ = 66.7, whereas Y has a score of $^{4}/_{15}$ = 26.0 which reflects the greater stabilization of Z. I consider that the fact that Z has been in contact with town since 15, whereas Y did not come to town until he was 25, should be taken into consideration.

Furthermore, in Wilson's method the date of coming to town is not related to the age of coming to town. Wilson, as we have noted, found the mean age or coming to town as 15 years 10.5 months. He gives no age distribution, but there must have been some variation round the mean. The age distribution for first coming to town of a Broken Hill sample (adult males) in 1953 is shown in Table 3. The median age of this series is 21.7 and arithmetic mean is 24.8 years. Wilson recorded that the average of the men in employment was 24 years 7 months.[35] In the 1953 survey, however, the age distribution of men over the age of 15, i.e., almost entirely all those in employment was as shown in Table 4. The median age for this sample is 31.2 years while the arithmetic mean is 31.6 years. This rise in the mean age of the working population is a natural concomitant of the stabilization of the urban population, but it is clear also that Wilson must have included in his sample some men who were mere children when they left their tribal homes. Thus the years spent in town as a child count in his measure as much as the years spent as an adult.

The index of stabilization thus takes into account the number of years spent in tribal areas since the attainment of working age. The indexes in Table 5 are taken from the Rhodes-Livingstone Institute surveys in Zambia. As measured by

TABLE 4. AGE OF MEN IN EMPLOYMENT

Age	Number	Age	Number
15–19	47	35–39	84
20–24	120	40–44	59
25–29	129	45–49	31
30–34	149	50–54	25
Total			644

TABLE 5. PROPORTION OF ADULT LIFE SPENT IN TOWN (Index of Stabilization)

	Local Authority Housing Area		Mining Housing Area		Industrial Housing Area		Domestic Housing Area		Private Housing Area	
	M	F	M	F	M	F	M	F	M	F
Less than a third	33.5	32.1	45.7	41.5	50.6	42.1	42.1	44.7	14.9	33.8
Between one- and two-thirds	27.6	25.5	31.6	29.4	26.3	28.0	24.4	18.3	34.5	20.8
Over two-thirds but less than whole life	21.1	15.3	15.4	13.1	13.8	12.6	10.9	12.5	26.4	25.8
Whole life	17.8	27.1	7.3	16.0	9.3	17.3	22.6	24.5	24.2	19.6
	100.0	100.0	100.0	100.0	100.0	100.0	100.0	100.0	100.0	100.0
No information	1.4	0.5	0.7	0.9	1.6	0.7	0.4	2.8	0.1	0.0
Median proportion spent in town	0.53	0.56	0.38	0.43	0.33	0.42	0.44	0.43	0.68	0.59

Based on same sample as in Table 2.

this index, those living in Private and in Local Authority housing areas are shown to be more stabilized than those in other areas, but whereas measured by numbers of years of absence from rural areas those living in domestic quarters are more stabilized than those living in mining housing areas, as measured by the index of stabilization the order is reversed. The "ratio" effect of the age distribution, however, has not been eliminated.[36]

This can be demonstrated most easily through two hypothetical cases. If a man Z comes to town at the age of 16 and is 18 at the time of survey, his index of stabilization will be

$$\frac{18-16}{18-15} \times 100 = 66.$$

A man *Y* who is 45 at the time of the survey and who has been in town continuously for 20 years has the same index,

$$\frac{45-25}{45-15} \times 100 = 66.$$

It is clear that a man who has been in town for 20 years and is now 45, is much less likely to return home than a boy of 18 who has been in town for two years. Thus this index takes into account the age of coming to town, but does not take into account the present age of the respondent. It would seem that the only way in which effective comparisons between populations can be made is by comparing the index of stabilization in various age groups.

The Approach Through Attitudes

A more direct approach to the problem may be through asking respondents what their intentions are. During the Rhodes-Livingstone Institute social surveys of the line-of-rail towns of Zambia, an attempt was made to elicit the attitude of respondents to continued residence in town. They were asked simply whether they intended to stay in town or not. The response was fitted into one of eight categories which are arranged in a scale of attitudes showing increasing stabilization in town. These responses were:

1. Will return home as soon as possible.
2. Working so as to go home soon.
3. Will return home as soon as specific object is attained, e.g., money for sewing machine, to buy cattle for bride-wealth, etc.
4. Will return home at some unspecified future date.
5. Will stay, but will keep contact with the village.
6. Will return home on retirement.
7. Thinks he will always be on the Copperbelt.
8. Born and bred in town. "It is as if it were my village."

These categories of responses may be classified into:

A. Typical *labour migrant* responses, i.e., they are in town for a specific purpose and have no intention of staying longer than necessary. (Responses to 3 above.)

TABLE 6. ATTITUDE TO CONTINUED URBAN RESIDENCE

	Local Authority Housing Areas		Mining Housing Areas		Industrial Housing Areas		Domestic Housing Areas		Private Housing Areas	
	M	F	M	F	M	F	M	F	M	F
Labour Migrant	51.4	64.7	59.6	67.0	59.5	72.7	60.7	69.2	34.7	45.9
Temporarily Urbanized	37.8	23.5	36.9	27.0	32.7	15.6	34.0	16.9	38.7	15.8
Permanently Urbanized	10.7	11.8	3.5	5.9	7.8	11.7	5.2	13.9	26.6	38.3
	100.0	100.0	100.0	100.0	100.0	100.0	100.0	100.0	100.0	100.0
No information	16.8	49.0 [a]	2.3	27.0 [b]	2.3	18.6 [b]	1.5	10.1 [b]	4.8	33.5 [b]

Based on same sample as in Table 2.

[a] The relevant questions were omitted from the first survey made in the Luanshya Local Authority housing area resulting in a high proportion of cases where no information is available.

[b] Includes those women who said that they would do as their husbands did.

B. Typical attitudes of *temporary stabilization*. That is they intend to leave town some day, but when is quite uncertain—not in the immediate future. (Responses 4, 5, 6 and above.)

C. Responses of *permanent stabilization*. These people have no intention of returning home. (Responses 7 and 8 above.)

Table 6 sets out the proportion of adult males giving the type of responses in five urban samples. The expressed attitude to urban life correlated well, but not perfectly, with the index of stabilization. Table 7 refers to males aged 20–29 in all the line-of-rail towns of Zambia. The greater numbers evincing attitudes of permanent stabilization as the index of stabilization goes up is quite clear and to be expected. A surprising proportion (78.7 percent) however, who had been in town before the age of 15 expressed the wish to return to the rural areas, so that the correlation is not perfect. Many Africans accept the proposition that their rightful home is in some rural area, as, for example, an Ngoni lad I knew, who had never been to Fort Jameson, having been brought up on the Copperbelt, where his father, an Ngoni from Fort Jameson, was a government clerk. Yet this lad insisted that his home was in Fort Jameson.

Measures of Urban Commitment or Involvement

A respondent's expressed intention to stay in town, or not, may be looked upon as one manifestation or a more general disposition which may be reflected in other actions or expressions of attitude. This more general disposition may be constructed within a psychological framework as "urban commitment," i.e., an individual's subjectively experienced preference for living in town as against elsewhere. Alternatively, the general disposition may be construed within a sociological framework as "urban involvement," i.e., as the individual's participation in social relationships which are centered in urban institutions. Insofar as measurement is concerned, much the same indicators in fact are used to measure both commitment and involvement; the distinction lies essentially in the explanatory frameworks in which the measures are subsumed.

TABLE 7. PROPORTION OF ADULT LIFE SPENT IN TOWN BY ATTITUDE TO CONTINUED RESIDENCE IN TOWN

			Over Two-Thirds	
Labour Migrant	66.2	61.2	44.5	41.5
Temporarily Urbanized	32.3	34.0	47.7	37.2
Permanently Urbanized	1.5	4.8	7.8	21.3
	100.0	100.0	100.0	100.0
No information	2.6	3.9	5.0	6.4

Based on interviews with 3457 males aged 20–29 in all the line-of-rail towns in Zambia.

Hellmann in 1935 had indicated three characteristics which might be used to identify "commitment" or "involvement" in this way (see pp. 471–472 above), but found that she could not easily use these characteristics to classify any individual as "committed" to town life or not. Subsequently, in a study of the African employees of a commercial firm she adopted three criteria which were amenable to quantification. They were:

(i) A period of ten years' continuous residence in town, allowance being made for holiday visits.
(ii) Permanent residence of the wife in town.
(iii) No land rights in Native Reserves or in other rural areas.[37]

On the basis of these characteristics she classified the individual in her survey as "urbanized" and "non-urbanized," although the method she used to do this is not clear from her account. Subsequently, Glass in an extensive study of African industrial labour expanded and modified the criteria used by Hellmann. Glass determined an "index of urbanization" from the following indicators.[38]

(i) Period of continuous residence of 10 years or more in urban area.
(ii) Present place of residence of wife and children (mother for unmarried men), i.e., whether in rural or urban area.
(iii) Whether worker possesses land rights in rural areas.
(iv) Place of birth, i.e., whether in rural or urban area.

She then combined these indicators to achieve a classification of workers into seven ordered categories of commitment from completely urban through non-committed to completely rural. It is not clear from the published material, however, how she reduced these indicators to the single dimension of rural-urban commitment. In subsequent publications she has indicated that she used three main indicators (continuous residence in town, the urban residence of wives and kinsfolk, and the lack of land rights in rural areas) to determine high urban commitment,[39] but the exact procedure remains obscure.

Factor analysis is one technique which could be used to reduce measurements on several indicators to a single dimension,[40] though the dichotomous character of some of the data involved presents some difficulties.[41]

Briefly, the rationale of the procedure is that indicators of an underlying commitment to urban life (or involvement in urban institutions), if they indeed reflect the same general phenomenon, must be correlated one with another. Furthermore, the amount of intercorrelation among the indicators may be looked upon as a measure of the extent to which they reflect their common factor, i.e., urban commitment. The correlation of each indicator with this common factor may be viewed as a measure of the extent to which that particular indicator reflects the common factor, and may be used as a weight to combine it with other indicators, weighted in the same way, to derive a measure of urban commitment.

To illustrate this procedure, indicators of urban commitment (or involvement) were taken for 1850 men aged between 25–29 who were interviewed in the towns of Zambia in 1951–1954. These attributes, with the arguments for using them are as follows:

(a) *Proportion of time spent in town during adulthood.* Following closely Wilson's argument we accepted that if a man has spent more time in urban than in rural areas since he turned 15, then he is more committed to urban life than a man of the same age who has spent more time in the country than in the town during the same period.
(b) *Period of continuous residence in one town.* If a person has spent a comparatively long time living in one town (in this case, more than 5 years) then this is evidence that he has settled in that town.
(c) *Wife present in town.* If a man has brought his wife to live with him in town or has married in the town, this is evidence that his stay is likely to be a prolonged one.
(d) *Occupation.* If a man has an occupation of a skilled type associated with industrial or other urban activities then he is more likely to be rooted in town life than in country life.
(e) *Level of education.* Since economic opportunities for those with some education are greater in town than in the country, those with better than average education are more likely to be committed to town life than those with poorer education.
(f) *Attitude to town life.* Those who express an attitude which reflects an intention to stay in town are more likely to be committed to town than those who express a desire to return to the country.
(g) *Wage level.* If a person is earning a relatively high wage in town, he is more likely to remain in town than if he were earning a low wage.

Some of these indicators, such as length of continuous residence in town and wage, could be considered to be continuous variables, but others, such as occupation or the presence or absence of the wife, could better be thought of as discrete variates. For the purpose of this analysis, therefore, each continuous indicator was converted into a discrete variate by dichotomising it at its median value. A set of 2×2 tables was prepared in which every indicator was tabulated against every other indicator. The association between indicators was measured by the "standardized cross-product," that is,

$$a_{ij}/N - a'_{i.}a'_{.j}/N^2.$$

The matrix of these "standardized cross products" was analysed using the centroid method.[42] The residuals after three factors were extracted were negligible.

The loadings on the indicators after the axes had been rotated by the varimax procedure are set out in Table 8. Clearly, the factor relevant to a measure of urban commitment is the first, with high loadings in the proportion of time spent in town and on the period of continuous residence in town. Factor coefficients can be estimated from these loadings,[43] as in Table 9. The estimation of a score for an individual exhibiting a particular pattern of attributes is simple. The scores are arranged so that a person who exhibits all the appropriate at-

TABLE 8. LOADING ON FACTORS AFTER ROTATION OF AXES

	F_1	F_2
Proportion of time in town	0.302	0.059
Period of continuous residence	0.265	0.014
Wife present	0.157	0.098
Attitude to town life	0.101	0.031
Occupation	0.063	0.270
Education	0.044	0.198
Wage level	0.037	0.204
Percentage of variance explained	68.5	29.0

TABLE 9. WEIGHTS FOR ESTIMATION OF URBAN COMMITMENT SCORE

X_1	Proportion of time in town	30.3
X_2	Period of continuous residence	47.2
X_3	Wife present	11.5
X_4	Attitude to town life	8.1
X_5	Occupation	1.4
X_6	Education	0.6
X_7	Wage level	0.9

Commitment score $= 30.3(X_1) + 47.2(X_2) + 11.5(X_3) + 8.1(X_4) + 1.4(X_5) + 0.6(X_6) + 0.9(X_7)$, where x_i may be 0 or 1 depending on whether the characteristic is absent or present.

tributes for a positive rating on the measure will achieve a score of 100, while a person who exhibits none will achieve a score of 0. Persons who exhibit a combination of attributes will receive a score which is merely the sum of the weights for the positive attributes. This is done most simply by preparing "response patterns" showing the presence and absence of attributes. Each response pattern has an associated score. Hence the pattern (1111111) has a score of 100.00 and the pattern (0000000) a score of 0, but the pattern (1010101) for example has a score of $30.3 + 0 + 11.5 + 0 + 1.4 + 0 + 0.9 = 44.1$, say 44.[44] A person is given the score appropriate to his particular pattern of attributes. The larger the number of indicators used in the determination of the score the greater will be the number of response patterns and the finer the gradation of individual scores.

The index may be validated by computing scores for categories of persons who are known to differ sharply in their degree of urban involvement. Migrants from the Zambian districts of Fort Rosebery and Kasama and those from Malawi and Tanzania provide suitable categories. At the time when the survey was made it was common knowledge that the Tanzanian and Malawian people on the Copper-mines were essentially "target workers" in contrast to those from Fort Rosebery and Kasama who were known to be more orientated to town life. The results are shown in Table 10.

TABLE 10. COMMITMENT SCORES OF MALES AGED 25–29 FROM SELECTED AREAS

	Fort Rosebery	Kasama	Malawi	Tanzania
High (70–100)	34.6	27.0	16.1	7.2
Medium (30–69)	34.5	35.4	22.8	8.3
Low (0–29)	30.9	37.6	61.1	84.3
	100.00	100.00	100.00	100.00
Mean Commitment Score	49	43	29	13

The scores seem to reflect the known difference in urban commitment of the men from these districts. Table 11 sets out for comparison with Tables 2, 5, and 6 the commitment scores of men aged 25–29 in the different housing areas in the Copperbelt towns of Ndola, Luanshya, Kitwe, Mufulira and Chingola.

There are obviously some difficulties in the computation and use of a score of this kind. There clearly can be no fixed set of weights that can be used indiscriminately for computing a commitment score. The weights would need to be computed for each set of data for which the scores are going to be computed. Unless the same attributes can be used for men and women no score can be computed which would allow comparison between the sexes. Since occupation and wage were both included in the set used in the example quoted, these attributes could not be used for women as well as men. Because of the influence of age on such variables as the proportion of time spent in town, and the correlation of age with the life cycle and occupational careers, the distribution of variates is likely to differ from one age group to another. Different weights, therefore, would need to be computed for different age groups, and the scores would be comparable only within age groups, not between them.

The utility of such scores of commitment and involvement lies not in any supposed power based on the measure of "commitment" and "involvement" in

TABLE 11. URBAN COMMITMENT SCORES FOR MEN IN HOUSING AREAS ON THE COPPERBELT *

Commitment Score	Local Authority Housing Areas	Mining Housing Areas	Industrial Housing Areas	Domestic Housing Areas	Private Housing Areas
High (70–100)	25.2	23.2	13.7	18.8	24.9
Medium (30–69)	39.0	24.4	34.6	43.2	50.2
Low (0–29)	35.8	52.4	51.8	38.0	24.9
	100.0	100.0	100.0	100.0	100.0
Mean Commitment Score	43	35	33	34	51
Cases Used	261	648	152	88	4

* Based on characteristics of 1153 men aged between 25–29 in Ndola, Luanshya, Kitwe, Mufulira and Chingola.

any absolute way, but rather in the fact that we are enabled to distinguish categories of persons who share attributes associated with urban commitment so that correlation with other characteristics may be examined. An index of this sort has been used, for example, in examining the effects of distance and origin of migrants to the Copperbelt in relation to their involvement in an urban way of life.[45] Mrs. Glass has used the index she has devised in this way also.[46]

The purpose of establishing correlations of this sort is to deepen our understanding of the general processes through which people who are being swept into newly established but rapidly growing towns are, either by choice or by force of circumstances, maintaining social links that bind them to their rural homes or establishing new links which instead hold them firmly to the towns. It is only in this context that measures of urban commitment or involvement—or indeed of urbanization and stabilization as defined here—have any meaning. They are means to an end and not ends in themselves. The end, the study of the processes of urban growth in countries where towns are a relatively novel phenomenon, demands a marriage between measurement and interpretation.

Notes

1. This is an expanded and amended version of a paper first published in C. D. Forde, (Ed.) *Social Implications of Industrialisation and Urbanization in Africa South of the Sahara,* Paris, UNESCO (1954): 693–711. The statistical material has been brought up to date, a section on commitment to urban life added, and the section dealing with factor analysis rewritten in the light of subsequent work.

2. H. P. Fairchild (Ed.), *Dictionary of Sociology,* New York City, 1944, p. 330.

3. *Ibid.,* p. 234.

4. Warren S. Thompson, "Urbanization" in *Encyclopedia of Social Sciences,* Macmillan, 1935, XV, p. 189.

5. R. L. Beals, "Urbanism, Urbanization and Acculturation," *American Anthropologist iii,* 1 (Jan.–Mar. 1951), p. 5–6.

6. G. Wilson, *An Essay on the Economics of Detribalization in Northern Rhodesia,* Rhodes-Livingstone Institute (Livingstone, 1941–2) papers 5 and 6.

7. E. Hellman, *Roolyard: A Sociological Study of an Urban Native Slum Yard,* Cape Town, Oxford University Press, 1948, *Rhodes-Livingstone Institute Paper,* No. 13, p. 110.

8. *Ibid.*

9. E. Hellman, "The Native in the Towns" in I. Schapera (Ed.) *The Bantu-Speaking Tribes of South Africa,* London, George Routledge, 1937, p. 429 ff.

10. *Ibid.,* p. 430.

11. G. Wilson, *An Essay on the Economics of Detribalization in Northern Rhodesia,* p. 58.

12. *Report of the Native Economic Commission,* Pretoria, Government Printer, 1932, para. 406.

13. G. Wilson, *An Essay on the Economics of Detribalization in Northern Rhodesia*, p. 36 ff.

14. *Ibid.* For some incisive comments on the same theme see W. E. Moore, "The Migration of Native Labourers in South Africa," *The Millbank Memorial Fund Quarterly*, xxiv. 4 Oct. 1946.

15. Since this paper first appeared Philip Mayer has discussed the problem in some detail in several of his publications. In particular he describes the way in which a certain type of Xhosa tribesman "incapsulates" himself among fellows in town and so resists becoming involved in urban practices and behaviour even though his residence in town may be extended. In this way he argues against too close an association between "urbanization" and "stabilization" as here defined. See Mayer, P., *Townsmen or Tribesmen: Conservatism and the Process of Urbanization in a South African City* (1961), Cape Town, Oxford University Press; and Mayer, P., "Migrancy and the Study of Africans in Towns," *Amer. Anth.*, xliv (1962), 576–592.

16. Not used here in a more specialised demographic sense.

17. G. A. Stent, "Migrancy and Urbanization in the Union of South Africa," *Africa* XVIII, 3 July 1948, p. 172.

18. Section 10 of the Natives (Urban Areas) Consolidation Act of 1945 requires local authorities to estimate their labour requirements for any period and to repatriate the surplus population. Certain classes of "detribalized" natives, however, are exempt from this section of the law.

19. Committee appointed by the Governments of Southern Rhodesia, Northern Rhodesia, and Nyasaland in March, 1950, consisting of the Secretaries for Native Affairs in the three territories, under the chairmanship of the Chief Secretary of the Central African Council. Central African Territories: *Comparative Survey of Native Policy*, Cmd 8235, London, HMSO, 1951, para. 154.

20. *Ibid.*, para. 155. See also *Report of the Urban African Affairs Commission Plewman Report* (1958) Salisbury, Government Printer, para. 172.

21. *Ibid.*, para. 156. Except perhaps that under the regulations of the Municipal Corporations Ordinance (Cap 119), and the Mine Townships Ordinance (Cap 121) no adults could remain within these urban areas without employment unless they had a visitor's pass. Visitor's permits lasted for one year.

22. *Report of the Industrial Legislation Commission of Enquiry.*

23. Quoted by Stent, *op. cit.*, p. 171.

24. See, for example, the case histories in Hobard D. Houghton and Edith M. Walton. *The Economy of a Native Reserve* (*Keiskammahoek Rural Survey*, vol. 11), Pietermaritzburg, Shuter and Shooter, 1952, pp. 120–124.

26. Assuming that the intrinsic rate of growth of the urban population did not differ too much from that of the rural population.

27. Industrial Research Section, Department of Commerce, University of Witwatersrand. *Native Urban Employment. A Study of Johannesburg Employment Records, 1936–44*, duplicated, 1948, p. 887.

28. *Report on the Sixth Census of the Population of the Union of South Africa,* 5 May 1936, vol. ix, *Natives (Bantu) and other Non-European Races,* p. xiii.

29. *Ibid.,* Table 5.

30. *Ibid.,* Table 12 (i), pp. 68–9. The classification is 10-year groups so that children here means those 19 years of age and under.

31. We could, however, predict what the age and sex distribution of an urban population would be after a given period on the basis of its natural increase and assuming no circulation between town and country and then compare this distribution with what is actually the case. The difference between the two structures would give us some indication of the effects of in and out migration on the age and sex structure of the town. I am at present experimenting with this approach.

32. J. C. Mitchell, *African Urbanization in Luanshya and Ndola,* Table XVII, Rhodes-Livingstone Communication No. 6 (1954), Lusaka, Rhodes-Livingstone Institute. See also J. C. Mitchell, "A Note on the Urbanization of Africans on the Copperbelt," *Human Problems* xii, 1951, 20–27, where it is suggested on the basis of the number of shifts between towns and an analysis of attitudes to town life, that if a person has been out of his rural area for ten years or more he is unlikely to return. This view is confirmed in J. D. Rheinallt Jones, "The Effects of Urbanization in South and Central Africa," *African Affairs,* iii, 206, Jan. 1953, 37–44.

33. G. Wilson, *An Essay on the Economics of Detribalization, Rhodes-Livingstone Institute Paper,* No. 5, 1940, p. 42 ff.

34. See J. C. Mitchell (1954), p. 15. This measure is there called "index of urbanization."

35. G. Wilson, *op. cit.,* Table IV, p. 41.

36. Measures of this kind have been used by D. Reader, *Black Man's Position: History, Demography and Living Conditions on the Native Locations of East London,* Cape Province, Cape Town, Oxford University Press, p. 62 and Table 14, p. 158, though Reader does not standardize his measure by relating to a base of "number of years lived since age 15." See also "Demographic Stabilization in the East London Locations, Cape Province," *S. A. Journal of Science* (1963 lxx: 269–272; D. G. Bettison, *Numerical Data on African Dwellers in Lusaka, Northern Rhodesia* (1959) Rhodes-Livingstone Communication No. 16. Lusaka, Rhodes-Livingstone Institute: Table 47(a). S. Alverson Hoyt, has suggested some modifications to this measure in "Time Series Analysis of Migratory Stabilization" *African Studies* (1967) xxvi: 139–144.

37. E. Hellmann, 1953, *Sellgoods: A Sociological Survey of an African Commercial Labour Force,* Johannesburg, S. A. Institute of Race Relations, pp. 64–65.

38. Y. Glass, *The Black Industrial Worker: A Social Psychological Study,* Johannesburg National Institute for Personal Research: p. 21.

39. Y. Glass, and S. Biesheuvel, "Urbanization among an Industrial Labour Force," paper presented to a CSA meeting of Specialists in Urbanization and Urban Development. Abidjan 23–31 August, 1961; Y. Glass, "Industrialization

and Urbanization in South Africa," in J. F. Holleman, (Ed.), *Problems of Transition.*

40. This was raised in the earlier version of this paper written in 1954. This section represents a development of the idea set out there. Obviously, latent structure analysis could also be used but with seven indicators the amount of arithmetic computation would be prohibitive.

41. The findings discussed here were presented to the Central African Scientific and Medical Congress in Lusaka, North Rhodesia in August 1963. They are published in J. C. Mitchell and J. R. H. Shaul, "An Approach to the Measurement of Commitment to Urban Residence" in G. Snowball, (Ed.), *Science and Medicine in Central Africa,* London, Pergamon Press (1965): pp. 625–633.

42. The standardized cross-products are in fact covariances between indicators. If the value $(a_i/N) - (a_i/N)^2$, for any variable is entered in the appropriate position of the leading diagonal of the matrix of standardized cross-products, the resulting variance-covariance matrix may be analysed by principal components on the assumption that all factors are common factors. I am indebted to Mr. Peter Burrows of the Agricultural Research Council in Salisbury, Southern Rhodesia, who pointed this out to me. In fact this procedure resulted in large unique loadings on several factors. This analysis, unlike that published in Mitchell and Shaul (1965), uses values in the leading diagonal which are the sum of squares of the given variable explained by the remaining variables. This procedure in effect provides estimates of the commonalities which exclude the unique factors. The results reported in Mitchell and Shaul (1965) were analysed by the centroid method.

43. H. H. Harman, *Modern Factor Analysis* (1960), Chicago, University of Chicago, Chapter 16. The weights are applied to the standardized value of the variables, i.e. $(x_i - \bar{x}_i)/\sigma_i$, and subjected to a linear transformation to locate the commitment scores between the extreme values of 0 where the respondent has none of the attributes and 100 where he has all. I am grateful to Mrs. A. Kitchen who has done the programming and assisted me with the mathematics of this operation.

44. This procedure was proposed by the late Mr. J. R. H. Shaul. The mathematical validity of the procedure was clarified for me by Mr. Peter Burrows.

45. J. C. Mitchell, "Distance and Urban Involvement in Northern Rhodesia." Paper given at a Wenner-Gren Symposium, Cross-Cultural Similarities in the Urbanization Process, Burg Wertensten, Aug. 27–Sept. 8, 1964.

46. Y. Glass, *The Black Industrial Worker. A Social Psychological Study,* Johannesburg: National Institute for Personnel Research.

CHAPTER SEVEN

THE MANAGEMENT OF THE URBAN FUTURE

INTRODUCTION

Viewed in a purely physical and financial sense the modern industrial city is an expression not only of a sense of its future but also of the importance of the management of its future: one thinks readily of bonded indebtedness, home mortgages, public utility investments, traffic and transport systems, corporate investment in capital equipment, public and civic buildings, and so on. Control of its growth in well-determined directions is increasingly vital to expanding populations. The problem of the urban future, however, is not so much a matter of management as a matter of what kind of management. Management there indeed is, but in such great variety, in such variable quality, so typically lacking in coordination, consensus, and sharp vision of dominant developmental direction that the resulting duplication, wastefulness, and neglect amount to no management at all.

This is the reason there is so much attention given to the idea and the process of planning. In its simplest form, planning is the forethoughtful determination of purpose and means. It is a determination based upon a canvass of consequences flowing from possible specific actions. For this task of determining optimum options and actions, there are at hand today a number of resources: information in great quantities covering an incredible range of interests, and an increasingly large body of professionally trained personnel both in government and private firms. We have in this country today a national awareness of the strategic significance of the urban sector in the total economic and political life of the country, and a growing willingness to allocate more and more economic, governmental, and human resources to renewal and rehabilitation as well as to the developmental management of the metropolis *and* its region. As a major social and political process, management of the urban future is perhaps our best illustration of the limitations and possibilities, the challenge and complexity of the planning process.

This last chapter concludes our survey of the changing urban scene with what is unquestionably the most urgent aspect of contemporary urbanism. Questions about planning continue to emerge, and the answers remain incomplete although significant progress is being made. The selections included here are designed to give the reader a sense, first, of the range of possibilities in the idea and process of planning (articles by Peterson and Godschalk and Mills); second, of the administrative complexities involved in the management of the city (Campbell and Sachs); third, of the human dimensions of urban management and planning

(Gans); and finally, of two contrasting political and administrative patterns of urban planning, developed in Russia and in the United States (articles by Pióro *et al.* and by Lowi).

ON SOME MEANINGS OF "PLANNING"

William Petersen

One need have only a casual acquaintance with the twentieth-century world to know that more and more of its social processes are "planned." Five-year plans, once restricted to the Soviet Union, have now spread not only to other Communist states but to such diverse countries as India and Brazil. In the United States, which is featured in Communist propaganda as the last capitalist redoubt, the whole social-economic structure was altered by the government's response to the depression of the 1930's and to World War II. And city planners have extended their purview to regions and then—through local, national, or international agencies—to the whole physical-social environment of human life.

This seeming ubiquity of "planning," however, depends largely on the application of a stylish word to modes of thinking and behavior that differ as radically now as they ever did.

> The word "planning" . . . has been known to cover the shooting of those who disagree, as under Stalin, or it may mean nothing more than consultation, making sure that all interested parties are properly informed, as in Ireland. It may involve the setting of targets with no compulsion to achieve them, but with certain inducements to try, as in France; or it may involve the setting up of targets with a large number of physical controls to back them up, as in India. And it can mean no more than the attempt to work out what consistency requires, to investigate what needs to be done if a given objective is to be achieved, as in England.[1]

Are there common elements that link these meanings and, if so, what are they?

When a preliminary draft of this paper was delivered to a class in planning theory at Berkeley, the response it evoked among these planners in the making was a curious combination of naiveté and cynicism. Of course, they told me, what they are doing is precisely the opposite of what planning was a generation ago and still is among certain middle-aged laggards. Everyone in the profession knows of this difference. But at the present time, while the new ideas are still evolving, they believe it would be unfortunate to distinguish the two schools too precisely, for the present lack of clarity affords practitioners a greater range of legitimate activity. So long as "planning" can mean almost anything, planners can

---

Reprinted by permission of the author and publisher from the *Journal of the American Institute of Planners,* 32 (May, 1966), pp. 130–142.

both use the approbation the concept brings and avoid the limitations imposed by any single designation of function.

There is a parallel between the present ubiquity of "planning" and the conquest of eighteenth-century thought by "reason," or of nineteenth-century thought by "sciene." Darwin's *Origin of Species* excited the last major battle between the defenders and the opponents of scientific analysis. For a certain period intermediate disciplines underwent a painful, and largely sterile, self-analysis; a half-century ago the *American Journal of Sociology,* for example, was obsessed with whether or not sociology is a science. Today, when we have the "science" of psychoanalysis, even the "science" of metaphysics, members of "the social sciences" seldom see any reason to question whether they are correctly subsumed under so broad a designation. The victory of "science" has been all but total—not over nonscience, but over the clear thinking that is based on meaningful distinctions, which constitute an indispensable prerequisite to an efficient choice among policy alternatives.

Deductive Planning

The average lay person, perhaps, is likely to understand "planning" in the deductive sense, following what is still the only dictionary definition. The planner draws up a blueprint on a flat surface or, in Latin, *planum;* and the design is completed before the first steps are taken toward its realization. "Planning results in blueprints for future development; it recommends courses of action for the achievement of desired goals." [2] This conception of planning was an extension to larger and more complex entities of the architect's design of a building or, less obviously, of the landscape architect's design of a park.[3] "The Essence of City Planning is City Designing. . . . It is landscape designing in a larger phase." [4] The closest parallel to an architect's blueprint, of course, is the master plan. In the words of one practitioner, "the preparation and maintenance of the general plan is the primary, continuing responsibility of the city planning profession, . . . our most significant contribution to the art of local government." [5]

But the overall detailed design, a useful instrument to plan a building, is less appropriately applied to whole cities or national economies. In order to bring the dynamic complexities of such larger units within the restricted compass of his design, the planner is forced to choose between a drastic restriction of his function and a narrowed perception of the matter he deals with. When he picks the second alternative, he generally evolves one or another monistic theory to reconcile his broad purpose with the limited realization possible to him. City planning is thus both the control of cities' growth by a "master" or "general" plan and also, by one common definition, the control merely of the city's physical elements—streets, parks, transportation, and the rest. The resolution of the contradiction is by what one analyst, after a study of more than a hundred master plans, termed "the physical bias"—the notion that the physical factors are the key determinants of all others.[6] In the words of Alfred Bettman, "the comprehensive master plan of city, town, region, state, by determining the appropriateness of place or location, and the program of urgency or priority, by determining the element of time, are instrumentalities for the creation of social values." [7]

* * *

Planners of national economies, since they try to cope with a yet larger and more complicated system, are even more prone to squeeze their subject into manageable simplicity. America's entire program of aid to underdeveloped areas is based, at least in part, on a belief in crude economic determinism: ignoring the counter examples of Nazi Germany, the Soviet Union, and prewar Japan, our policymakers apparently believe that industrialization brings with it a full cornucopia of associated benefits, from greater democracy to a richer mass culture. The notion that changes in the economic base determine the movement of the rest of the society, the noneconomic "superstructure," while it derives partly from Marx, is not limited to Marxist analysts. All who use the term "economic development" to denote the precursor to general social advance follow this line of thinking.[9]

In an important sense, planning was foreign to Marx's thought. The doctrine that the inner workings of capitalism would lead to its inevitable collapse, and thus to the inevitable establishment of socialism, was in Marx's mind what distinguished his "scientific" socialism from "utopian" varieties, which depended on man's rational will rather than economic laws as the main impetus to change.[10] Engels could not have been more contemptuous of the "crude theories" of his socialist predecessors:

> The solution of the social problems . . . the utopians attempted to evolve out of the human brain. Society presented nothing but wrongs; to remove these was the task of reason. It was necessary, then, to discover a new and more perfect system of social order and to impose this upon society from without. . . . These new social systems were foredoomed as utopian; the more completely they were worked out in detail, the more they could not avoid drifting off into pure phantasies.[11]

In Marx and Engels's own writings, thus, the nature of the socialist future is barely suggested, and this refusal to specify the society they advocated became a mark of orthodoxy among Marxists of all schools.

In the socialist parties of the West, the main—one might almost say, the sole—criterion of a socialist society used to be the public ownership of the means of production. In the 1951 Frankfurt Manifesto, which marked the postwar rebirth of the Socialist International, the emphasis shifted to "democratic planning" in a mixed economy as the basic condition of socialism. After more than a century of unremitting propaganda for nationalization, the argument was abandoned by the dominant factions in both Germany's Social Democratic Party and Britain's Labor Party. As Crosland wrote in *Encounter*, paraphrasing the opening sentence of *The Communist Manifesto*, "a specter is haunting Europe—the specter of Revisionism." The "first and most obvious" reason for the new stance was that when industries had been nationalized, "the reality proved rather different from the blueprints. Some of the anticipated advantages did not materialize, while certain unexpected disadvantages emerged." [11]

Though Lenin adhered to historical materialism in theory, in practice he did not depend on the spontaneous reaction of the working class to "immiseration." The decisive element in taking power would be the Leninist party, a small, tightly knit organization of professional revolutionaries. In 1917 the Bolsheviks took power not in order to create a specified kind of society; they took power in order to have power. Apart from general socialist slogans like "Production for use," their program consisted of "Peace," "Land," "Bread," "Workers' Control"—rallying cries that reflected accurately enough what the Russian mass wanted but in part contradicted Bolshevik principles and subsequent practice. When Lenin announced, the day after he established control, "We shall now proceed to construct the socialist order," [13] he could lead the government only to the destruction of the capitalist economy, a few catastrophic attempts at economic rationalization, and the eventual retreat to the mixed economy of the New Economic Policy. Planning in Russia did not begin really until 1928; its progenitor was not Lenin but Stalin.

The goals of the First Five-Year Plan, the methods by which they were to be achieved, and the complex allocations of human and material resources, were spelled out in three large volumes, which proved to be a grossly inadequate tool for guiding the whole economy and society through a period of forced rapid change. The details included in the following plans were successively reduced, so that by the time of the Fourth Five-Year Plan, the first after the defeat of Nazi Germany, the general directive consisted of a single pamphlet. Its function was to incite enthusiasm for the broad goals that were to be achieved—to restore prewar levels of production, to overtake and surpass the capitalist nations, to move from socialism to communism. More and more, the actual guide to the development of the economy was in the quarterly plans, which were loosely drawn and adjustable to unforeseen circumstances. More recently, a number of economists in both the Soviet Union and other Communist countries, trying to overcome their ideological encumbrances, have advocated that the half-surreptitious use of the market be recognized and extended.[14] For if the market is admitted as a legitimate tool of a planned economy, then Western economic theory, that powerful analytical instrument, can be used to improve the quality of the planning. In short, even in the original home of the planned economy "planning" has been consistent only as a highly successful propaganda facade. The five-year plans, originally conceived as end-state portraits, were gradually converted into a relatively loose program of economic development.

Utopian Planning

A deductive plan, when applied to a large, complex, dynamic system, tends thus to break down into more manageable parts, or to be broken down by a systematic distortion of reality. Alternatively, a planner with ideas too grandiose for his practical world may take off into fantasy. Though planning ordinarily connotes the introduction of a greater rationality into social policy, it can mean also the abandonment of reason. My impression is that utopian thought has undergone a certain revival during the past decade. Not only have such works as the Goodmans' *Communitas* and Howard's *Tomorrow* come out in new editions, but one of the better recent texts on urban sociology offers, as a new departure, a generally sympathetic chapter on "The Visionary," [15] and the dean of one of our more important schools of city planning has suggested that "planners ought to recognize the value of utopian formulations in the depicting of the community as it might be seen through alternative normative lenses." [16] To analyze utopianism is not, as it might have seemed to be some years back, beating a dead jackass.

1. A utopian formulation is, most obviously, the statement of a purpose so broad, so lofty, that if anything at all it denotes an unattainable goal. "The nurture of life is the main aim of collective endeavor"; [17] the goal of planning is "substantial gains in human happiness." [18] (It is true that both Mumford and Riesman define such aims as—in the latter's words—"a realistic possibility, not a mere idle dream"; but then what utopian has ever seen his own fantasy as such?) Such grandiloquent purposes are supposed to be useful as a goad. As Mumford puts it, while adaptations will be necessary as the plan "encounters the traditions, the conventions, the resistances, and sometimes the unexpected opportunities of actual life," it would be a mistake to anticipate these necessary changes. Only "overbold" plans will "awaken the popular imagination: such success as totalitarian states have shown in their collective planning has perhaps been due to their willingness to cleave at a blow the Gordian knot of historic resistances." [19]

Comment: Whether holistic utopian schemes act as a leaven to workaday dough is an empirical question, and one that to my knowledge has never been seriously examined. Some important points suggest that the thesis is invalid. Frequently, perhaps typically, the utopia is seen not as an incentive but as an alternative to social reform. Such aims as "a chicken in every pot or a car in every garage," which *can* be achieved, are therefore in Riesman's perspective no more than ideological pressures of business enterprise.[20] By a utopian criterion, anything that is feasible is by that fact not worth attempting; every revolutionary party has always devoted its major effort to fighting reformists. Both extremes of the political spectrum attack the center and its relatively modest aims and the moderate means of achieving them; the wild charges that the radical right and the extremist left seemingly make against each other are mutually supportive.[21] Among both city planners and Soviet administrators, the contrast between The Plan and actual planning typically induces chronic frustration, and a consequent search for a scapegoat—those persons or institutions that have not fully cooperated in furthering The Plan. One need hold no brief for either real estate boards or Western governments to find this devil view of social processes naive and, in a totalitarian context, the prelude to terror. Very often the details that are omitted from the utopian's broad vista relate to the attitudes and desires of the people who will be affected. Those who oppose The Plan, then, are depersonalized into Mumford's "historic resistances," while those who impose it acquire special license from the splendor of the world they are creating.

2. Perhaps an even more characteristic stance of the utopian than his demand for the vague and unattainable Good is his denunciation of the equally vague Evil—"the system," "the establishment," "the power elite," and so on. As always, Mumford provides a convenient example: "the debris of these dying systems" includes, by his broad compass, "Orthodox Christianity, Protestantism, individualistic humanism, capitalism, humanitarianism, and libertarianism." [22] The utopian is simply "for" planning; "the irrational and planless character of society must be replaced by a planned economy" in order that "self-realization for the masses of the people" may be achieved.[23] Apart from planning there is, in this perspective, no order in society. Capitalist production is "anarchic." Any unplanned city is "this chaos of congestion, this anarchy of scatteration." [24] Alternatively, whatever

the consistent patterns in the unplanned social world may be, their effect is mainly noxious. Almost any plan, it follows from such a premise, is better than no plan at all.

Comment: It is a remarkable procedure to begin a more rational control of society by blithely dismissing the whole subject matter of the social disciplines. If outside the planned sectors there is nothing but anarchy and chaos, then economists, sociologists, and political scientists have certainly been adept at inventing the recurring patterns they study. For Marx, the "anarchy" of capitalist production was no more than a journalistic gloss on a life's work in trying to establish the "laws" of capitalist development. The laws of social behavior are not, it is certainly true, as absolute as he depicted them. Many are not well established, and those that are better known are sometimes difficult to interpret. But inadequate as our knowledge of society may be, it is a better basis for control than a self-imposed ignorance.

The market, to return to that recurrent example, is an efficient mechanism for distributing commodities in order to achieve the maximum overall utility. One may object that this is not the only social goal to be sought, that labor and land are not commodities and should not be subjected to market conditions, that often so-called markets are half-disguised monopolies, and so on. But the point remains that the market is a good tool for certain important purposes. As we have noted, it has been deemed necessary even in Communist countries to introduce the market principle, to the degree that the utopian heritage of Marxian thought permits.

The tendency of planners to depreciate all social regularities is important enough to make another example appropriate. In *American Skyline,* Tunnard and Reed demonstrate with a wealth of fascinating detail that "definite forces" (with city planning among the least of them) have molded the physical patterns of urban America, but they do not spell out the implications of this fact for present-day efforts to control these forces. As in the work of many other planners, the main burden of their excellent study is to contrast "city efficient" with its unplanned and therefore inefficient counterpart.[25]

3. An engineer operates on the assumption that if he lowers cost, he *generally* sacrifices quality; if he has to cut the weight of his material, he *usually* loses some of its strength; and so on. The expectation of the typical social engineer is the contrary. Family sociologists almost to the man are deeply concerned about family instability, yet few seem to recognize that this is in part the consequence of social trends that they support. In a society where women have minimal legal rights and no possibility of earning their own living, wives are less likely to consider divorce no matter what the provocation; and in a society where young men routinely follow their fathers' occupation, with no opportunity to rise above it, the link between generations is apt to be strong. Women's rights, social mobility, and family stability are three elements of an interrelated system. To maximize any one of these goals is a feasible project, but an attempt to realize all three goals totally is a form of utopianism to which all too many of us succumb in our enthusiasm for particular projects. Few proponents of "family harmony" presently oppose the right of married women to a job, but even fewer see that

the divorce rate is relatively high in this country in part because this right is better established than elsewhere.

A recurrent dilemma for democratic city planners is that their professional efforts to structure space into functional units may result in the hierarchical social ordering of the persons occupying the space. Perry's neighborhood principle, designed to create a "community in which the fundamental needs of family life will be met more completely," was based on the doctrine that the elementary school should be the neighborhood's focus.[26] For a period his thesis was generally accepted—until "de facto segregation" became an issue; then some began to assert that "the 'neighborhood unit' is an instrument for segregation." [27] It is not necessary here to argue the comparative worth of reinforcing social units intermediate between the family and the city, and of facilitating the movement of ethnic minorities more fully into the general society. The point is only that by our values both goals are desirable and that they are partly incompatible. A planner who propounds one or the other course should at least be aware that its cost includes a relative sacrifice of the other. In particular, he should try to avoid advocating a full realization of both at the same time. In a recent article, Bernard Frieden (in my opinion, one of the more perceptive writers on city planning) at least implicitly accepts the commonplace that a prime fault of metropolitan structure is that the central city, which carries the main burden of providing services for the whole region, has lost much of its tax base. However, a policy of rebuilding central cities by attracting some of the more prosperous back to them, "far from assisting low-income families, . . . is a threat to their welfare." [27] As before, the intent here is not to argue for one course or the other but only to point out that they are incompatible, and thus to raise the question of whether the welfare of the poor is wholly enhanced if they are encouraged to remain segregated in central cities, even if in public housing.

Comment: While often only one of several related goals can be fully realized, sometimes indeed the interaction is mutually supportive. Perhaps the best known case is what Myrdal termed "the principle of cumulation."

> White prejudice and discrimination keep the Negro low in standards of living, health, education, manners and morals. This, in its turn, gives support to white prejudice. White prejudice and Negro standards thus mutually "cause" each other. . . . If either of the factors changes, this will cause a change in the other factor, too, and . . . the whole system will be moving in the direction of the primary change, but much further.[29]

It would be useful to distinguish, other than ad hoc, between the two broad types of equilibrium. Myrdal's example, though used by many as a general model, is in several respects a special case. The inferiority of Negroes is not innate, and can thus respond fully to an ameliorative environment. Consider, in contrast, the "social problem" of the aged. All too much written about it is based on a refusal to accept the fact that here the physiological distinction *is* crucial. If the reality of the Negro's situation improves, moreover, the persistence of irrational prejudice must combat a value system so strong that Myrdal termed it *the* American creed—that is, the belief in equality of opportunity irrespective of race. In contrast, even if all of the *real* problems of urban life were completely solved—traffic congestion, smog, slums, excessive crime, and so on—these victories would probably not affect the irrational anti-urban animus, dating from Washington and Jefferson, that colors most of our urban policy.[30] Those city planners who now plan *against* the city could still feed their prejudices from this tradition.

Inductive Planning

Thus far, in our effort to bring order into the variety of meaning given to the word *planning*, we have looked at two main types, deductive and utopian. The third type, inductive planning, constitutes, as a minimum, attempts to coordinate public policies in several overlapping economic and social areas. In the words of Gunnar Myrdal, for example:

> Coordination leads to planning or, rather, it *is* planning as this term has come to be understood in the Western world. . . . The need for this coordination arose because the individual acts of [government] intervention, the total volume of which was growing, had not been considered in this way when they were initiated originally.[31]

Planning in this sense is "pragmatic and piecemeal and never comprehensive and complete"; plans usually constitute "compromise solutions of pressing practical issues."[32] It is no criticism of such policy-making per se to ask if it is coordination, if it is administration, why then is it useful to term it "planning"?[33] We are like Molière's *bourgeois gentilhomme* when he discovered he was speaking prose: for more than forty centuries we have been planning without knowing it.[34] The answer to the question, presumably, is that "planning" is a special kind of prose, different indeed from the classic iambs of blueprints and the free verse of utopians, but different also from the prose of earlier bureaucratic operations. To specify these latter differences is not easy at this time, but some of the main ideas now evolving can be discerned. Those who have been working for the past dozen years in reaction against the two earlier traditions have produced enough to start one thinking of how these several strands can be brought together.

In such a synthesis, one would begin with the most apparent elements of the developing new consensus:

1. Planning concerns process and not state; it pertains not to some idealized future but to the mode of moving from the present.

2. The traditional concentration on the physical plant (city planners) or on the economy narrowly defined (national planners) is a false emphasis. "A plan for the physical city has utility only as a step in a means-ends continuum that causally relates the artifactual city to the social-economic-political city."[35]

3. As a corollary, the relevant skills are not exclusively architecture, landscape architecture, sanitation engineering, and the like (for city planners), or economics, economic geography, formal demography, and the like (for national planners), but rather the full range of social sciences, especially some of the newer emphases or subdisciplines. These include the study of political determinants of social stability and of decision-making, systems analysis (with the computer as

the fundamental tool and model-building as a routine step), sociology (insofar as this departs from the Chicago ecological tradition and concentrates on the social setting of ethnic relations, poverty, education, labor-force recruitment, and similar policy fields).

4. An attempt to realize a broad, overall plan (or, in the new language, to move forward on a broad front) is likely to be successful only if a "middle-range bridge" is built of specific functions assigned to particular agencies.[36] In a history of planning from this point of view, five-year plans would get no more attention than phlogiston in a history of science, and the analysis of city maps by a Reps would be amply supplemented with a McKelvey's account of the rise of municipal bureaus.[37]

5. The choice among competing goals, a key problem that is beyond ultimate solution, can sometimes be reduced to manageable scale by extending the principles of the market and of cost accounting to new uses. For example, the so-called Victoria Line of the London underground, though manifestly needed by reasonable criteria, was ruled out because it could not "pay its way." But if one brought into the calculation such secondary benefits as the relief of traffic congestion on the streets and the saving of time to commuters, the investment could be shown to have a return of more than 10 percent.[38] On this basis the project was started. This type of analysis is most useful when there is general consensus on the social benefits to be attained, and when they can be quantified without too great a strain on credibility.

There are also several fundamental areas that, as I see them, need further clarification. I shall restrict myself to two: facts and evaluation.

Facts

Wesley Mitchell, who like all of the institutional economists was a forebear of the American social planners of today, believed that tested factual knowledge is a prerequisite to adequate policy-making. On the face of it this may seem to be a reasonable point of view, but it was widely attacked as visionary and reactionary.[39] Indeed, our ignorance in many areas is so great that if we demanded an adequate empirical base for planning, in many cases we could hardly begin to plan. For example, one list of "research needs" for metropolitan planning runs to 63 items, and includes everything from "Why do people move to the suburbs" to "How to devise a system of metropolitan government which is expandable with its area growth."[40] What information exists, moreover, is seldom available in a coordinated, up-to-date, usable form to the agencies that need it. One important "middle-range bridge" would be intelligence centers to process facts and provide inventories and forecasts to interested persons and groups.[41] If in the meantime those with various kinds of authority intervene in citizens' lives with "a healthy pragmatism," "an appropriately experimental approach in the face of many unknowns," is this altogether "on the positive side"?[42]

The horns of this moral dilemma are sharp for a democratic empiricist. If administrators act on the basis of incomplete knowledge, they may do serious harm to those affected by their policies. But if they fail to act, the state of our knowledge will remain inadequate. For typically the facts we need are precisely those in a human rather than a technical context, what John Dewey termed "social facts." His theory of how knowledge and action interact, which pervades all of his enormous body of writings, is most succinctly stated in a two-page article:

> It is a complete error to suppose that efforts at social control depend on the prior existence of a social science. The reverse is the case. The building up of a social science, that is, of a body of knowledge in which facts are ascertained in their significant [human] relations, is dependent upon putting social planning into effect. . . . The assumption is generally made that we must be able to predict before we can plan and control. Here again the reverse is the case. We can predict the occurrence of an eclipse precisely because we cannot control it. . . .
>
> If we have no social technique at all, it is impossible to bring planning and control into being. If we do have at hand a reasonable amount of technique, then it is by deliberately using what we have that we shall in the end develop a dependable body of social knowledge. . . . Forethought and planning must come before foresight.[43]

For Dewey, the resolution of the dilemma is to use our intelligence. No simple answers, no formulas, no blueprints, will suffice.

We have spoken of "facts" as though this were a nonproblematic term. "Factual statements and their analysis invariably reflect the values of their makers, if only in the importance attached to them or the sequence in which they are studied." [44] It is a measure of the harm that simplistic positivists have done to the social disciplines that it is still necessary—and it *is*—to make this kind of elementary rejoinder. It is also necessary to develop the point a good deal farther. Is the word "invariably" appropriate? Does the statement, for example, that the population of the United States in 1960 was almost 180 million reflect, in any sense or to any degree, the values of the director of the Census? People have many values, sometimes in conflict. Which ones are reflected in factual statements? One important value is to strive to tell the truth; when a scientist thoroughly imbued with the ethics of his calling reflects this value, does he give "true" facts? In short, those who wander into the social disciplines in order to get some guidance on how to plan should acquire an understanding beyond the level of simple antipositivism.

Moreover, if planning is seen as processual, then the empirical base required is not merely isolated facts, but facts in correlated moving systems, or projections. If a model is constructed showing how land use, transportation, and people's behavioral patterns interact, then it is possible to build the most efficient highway relative to the other two factors and, if the system is projected into the future, to provide a continuing basis for public decisions on the matters.[45] I gladly accept this as an advance in an area about which I know nothing, but I am less certain that the method can be extended to matters about which I am more knowledgeable.

Population forecasts are a good test of the general utility of projections: the data are excellent, and the trend in the number of people affected is basic to virtually any kind of planning. The record of success has not been one to inspire confidence; the U. S. Census Bureau abandoned the use of the word "forecast" for "projection" and then began to use what are termed "illustrative projections."[46] For local areas, where migration is often an important determinant of population growth, many projections are hardly even illustrative—except of our ignorance. One important reason that population projections often fail, one should remember, is that they are automatically tested—in a sense that is never true of the hypothesis that this transportation system is the most efficient, or the cheapest, or the most whatever, out of all the systems that might have been built. Another reason is that what we know of human behavior pertains mostly to that portion of it defined by "economic man"; the motives that lead parents to decide whether to have another child are still largely a matter of speculation.

Evaluation

When planning introduces a greater rationality into an area of life, planning is in this respect akin to science. A scientific proposition is one that can be proved fallacious by comparing it with the empirical world, and thus a scientist constantly shuttles between his hypothesis and his data, between the model he constructs and the pattern he observes. The analogous process is the evaluation of plans, which would be equally routine if planning were scientific in the same sense. It is no novelty to remark that, on the contrary, evaluation is atypical and often inadequate if made.

With respect to utopian plans what can evaluation signify? If the purpose of the plan is one or another paraphrase of Riesman's "substantial gains in human happiness," it will never be possible to determine in any precise sense whether this has been achieved. Since such a utopian goal *keeps receding* as we approach it, the goal cannot be used to measure progress along the road toward it. Nor has the supposed proximate value of a utopia, to furnish the incentive that aids one in achieving realizable goals, ever been more than supposed. The evaluation of utopian plans, then, is ruled out as impossible or meaningless, and one must remember that many nonideological plans contain a utopian element.

Evaluation of processual inductive plans is obviously difficult since ordinarily the measuring stick and the thing to be measured constantly interact. The most efficient type of operation when it is feasible, a feedback system, means that evaluation in one sense takes place constantly,[47] but not the determination of whether any operation is successful in realizing a given fixed goal.

Let us restrict ourselves here to the relatively simple case of deductive planning, since even that involves problems of what we mean by "evaluation." A schematic typology may help in differentiating the situations to be discussed:

TABLE 1

		Actual Change: no	Actual Change: yes
Planned Change	no	*1. "Natural" stability*	*2. "Natural" change*
	yes	*3. "Unsuccessful" planning*	*4. "Successful" planning*

We shall consider each of these quadrants in turn.

1. "Natural" stability, one might think, is irrelevant to the problems of planning. But though no policy has been initiated because a process is seen as "natural" (that is, beyond the realm of policy), that definition of it may change at any time. To the degree that planning connotes an attempt to establish rational control over social processes, in other words, it results in a contraction of "nature." At one time, when children were seen in Western countries as "gifts of God," fertility was in fact regulated by institutional patterns (such as the postponement of marriage from puberty to some "appropriate" age), but no type of birth control was seen as legitimate. Since the "modernization" or "westernization" of the world usually means an extension of rational control, no present designation of "nature" can give a clear indication of what it will be in the future.

In other cases the "lack" of policy is rather a conscious, deliberate decision not to act. The existence of the Tennessee Valley Authority and the nonexistence of a Missouri Valley Authority are both consequences of policy decisions. If the first represents an important influence of the federal government on one region, the second does also. Another example: perhaps the most effective way to inhibit the overrapid growth of cities in underdeveloped areas is to cut down the overrapid growth of the general population, and governments that attempt to control the first but do nothing about the second are in the most meaningful sense acting in both fields. Logically, then, we ought to include some types of nonplanning in a survey of planning; but with such a definition the subject would become almost coextensive with the social world. In practical terms we must omit decisions not to act from a useful definition of planning.

2. "Natural" change should be a nul category for the true utopian; is there any segment of society that one could leave unplanned in order to attain "self-realization for the masses"? A meaningful goal, however, ordinarily pertains to only a small segment of social life, and its success largely depends on how it fits in with the larger, more significant, unplanned sector. Success in planning thus depends on our knowledge of the whole society, which—to repeat—is quite poor.

3. "Unsuccessful" planning, in theory, is of fundamental importance. The true test of a plan, as we have noted, is its failure, which is parallel to the negation of a scientific theory. For it is principally by proved deficiencies in specific plans (or theories) that planning (or knowledge) as a whole can advance. To carry through the parallel, the test of success ought to be made independently, not by the man with a personal stake in demonstrating a success.

4. "Successful" planning means, at a simplistic level, planned change that is congruent with actual change; the question is when may we reasonably substitute "the determinant of" for "congruent with." In any but the least complex social policies, establishing a causal link between purposive acts and their possible consequences involves a full-scale analysis. If there are multiple purposes to a policy, as is usually the case in actual instances, some may be realized and others not; is the policy then successful?

Such points can be made better in terms of examples. The Venezuelan government's housing agency supervised the construction of apartments in Caracas to accommodate an estimated 180,000 persons. In mechanical terms the project was completed: 97 15-story buildings were erected at a total cost of some $200 million. However, 4,000 families invaded the apartments and lived there illegally, while others squatted in the community facilities or in shacks built on the project site; unpaid rents totaled $5 million; losses in damage to property amounted to $500,000 monthly; delinquency and crime rose appreciably; tenant associations, controlled by agitators, impeded control measures and built up a potentially explosive atmosphere. An international interprofessional study team recommended that "the government should suspend all construction of superblocks until there exists a defined housing policy related to the economic and social development of the country and within a process of national planning and coordination. It was found that the massive construction programs in Caracas had served to attract heavy migration to the city from rural areas and, therefore, severely intensified the housing problem in the capital.[48]

Sometimes the effect of planning is not less but greater than was envisaged. The most important effects of city planning in the United States have been on the construction outside the framework of specific plans, much of which has nevertheless reflected (sometimes as a kind of caricature) the planners' dicta of earlier years: the superblock, the abolition of the gridiron pattern, the stress on low density or what is now called "scatteration."

> A generation ago most experts saw great crowded cities as a destructive anachronism, to be drastically altered by some form of decentralization. But suburban sprawl is clearly no solution, and the big centers have survived despite decay and mounting congestion. Now the new generation of experts and critics tends to glorify the economic and cultural virtues of the Great City, scorning decentralization in any form.[49]

It would be an exaggeration, but one with more than a germ of truth, to say that the plan of one generation becomes the social problem of the next. Such "success" as planning has had is sometimes an embarrassment.

As a final example let us glance once more at that thoroughly worked theme, Britain's new towns. A discerning British town planner tells us that the project was "mainly successful," and in this opinion he joins in "the almost universal support" now given it in Britain. The towns exist and are the homes of thousands. The Conservative Political Centre adjudged the new towns "a financial success"; and *Socialist Commentary*, published by a group well to the left of the Labor Party, said they have been "a striking financial success." [50] But surely the program was not instituted to make money; on the contrary, it was started because the operation of the market system led to a number of specified social ills that the project was supposed to ameliorate. To judge whether it was successful in this sense, we must look first at the goals with respect to the large cities from which the people were transferred, and then at the new towns themselves.

Perhaps the most authoritative and succinct expression of the first goal is the statement of purposes of the Barlow Commission, out of whose report the new-towns program developed. The Commission's assignment was—

> to inquire into the causes which have influenced the present geographical distribution of the industrial population of Great Britain and the probable direction of any change in that distribution in the future; to consider what social,

> economic or strategical disadvantages arise from the concentration of industries or the industrial population in large towns or in particular areas of the country; and to report what remedial measures, if any, should be taken in the national interest.[51]

The Commission inquired, considered, and recommended; and their policy *was* a success in the minimal sense that the new towns exist. But have "the social, economic, or strategical disadvantages" of industrial concentration been mitigated? In particular, has London stopped growing, or has it even grown less than it would have without the plan? To answer such questions fully would require another study on the scale of the one the Commission used as the basis of its recommendations. In the opinion of Peter Self, writing in 1957, the answer is negative. "All available evidence suggests that the drawbacks to the indefinite growth of the conurbations, and particularly of London, are in fact much greater" than before World War II.[52] I am in the process of trying to test his conclusion with the most recent available data, which seem to indicate that it still holds, particularly if one takes into account what might have been done in the metropolitan areas themselves with the vast amounts of energy, money, and skill used to move factories and people out of them.

Perhaps the intention with respect to the new towns can be stated best by citing the final report of the Reith Committee.[53] Once again, beyond the facts that the towns exist and that they are paying their way, what is there that could be denoted a success?

"There should be a full latitude for variety and experiment," the Reith Committee declared, with no "standardized pattern of physical or social structure." Most commentators, even including those like Madge who are inclined to a friendly view of the program, are disappointed that it has done so little to disturb the physical monotony of Britain's old towns and suburbs.

The "optimum normal range" of population was given as "30,000 to 50,000 in the built-up area," with a total of 60,000 to 80,000 in the town plus its immediate environs. In most cases it seems the question is not *whether* these limits will be breached, but only *when*.

The Reith Committee was willing to congratulate itself for its realism in acknowledging that social classes still exist in Britain ("some would have us ignore their existence"), but the notion that the provinciality of the provinces can be legislated out of existence is no less strange. "So long as social classes exist, all must be represented in [the new town]. A contribution is needed from every type and class of person; the community will be the poorer if all are not there." The factory workers are accommodated with their factories, but if their sons, taking advantage of Britain's new emphasis on higher education for a larger proportion of the population, seek to rise to different skills, will not many of them be induced to move to the centers of British civilization?

In short, no matter which of such details one picks, there is serious question whether the goals have been realized in the new towns. Their destiny, like that of the Radburns in the United States, is undoubtedly to merge into the generality of other places of their region and size, with no more idiosyncracy than any locality is likely to retain from its specific past.

More broadly, the new towns represent the most massive and important effort to progress within the framework of dynamic urban-industrial system by reversing the trend toward greater urbanization, emphasizing the "community" and "harmony" of preindustrial society. Sometimes these are offered not merely as superior goals but as the aims of planning altogether: planning is *defined* as a means of directing change "toward the ultimate objective of orderly and harmonious community processes,"[54] or as "methods and techniques to coordinate and bring into harmony" the uses made of land and the structures on it.[55] Harmony, one must note, equals stagnation, or lack of progress. Change takes place because a disjunction arises among the parts of an interrelated system, and a planner who wants to bring about more or different changes cannot dispense with this motive power. Only in the final stage of development, in the utopia where no ills remain, is harmony entirely a useful characteristic. But there planners will be unemployed.

Notes

Author's Note: *Aaron Cicourel, Lewis Feuer, and Melvin Webber were kind enough to comment on an earlier draft, and I have incorporated some of their suggestions into this version.*

1. Maurice Zinkin, *Growth, Change and Planning: Economics of Developing Countries* (London: Asia Publishing House, 1965), p. 28. For a more complete and systematic comparison of planning in various countries, see Jan Tinbergen, *Central Planning* (New Haven: Yale University Press, 1964), pp. 104 ff.

2. John C. Bollens and Henry J. Schmandt, *The Metropolis: Its People, Politics, and Economic Life* (New York: Harper, 1965), p. 278.

3. See Frederick J. Adams and Gerald Hodge, "City Planning Instruction in the United States. The Pioneering Days, 1900–1930," *Journal of the American Institute of Planners,* XXXI (February, 1965), 43–51.

4. Crawford, in *City Planning* (1927); quoted in Charles M. Haar (ed.), *Land-Use Planning: A Casebook on the Use, Misuse, and Re-use of Urban Land* (Boston: Little, Brown, 1959), p. 45.

5. T. J. Kent, Jr., *The Urban General Plan* (San Francisco: Chandler Publishing Co., 1964), p. 2.

6. David Farbman, "A Description, Analysis, and Critique of the Master Plan," unpublished study cited in Paul Davidoff, "Advocacy and Pluralism in Planning," *Journal of the American Institute of Planners,* XXXI (November, 1965), 331–338.

7. Quoted in Frederick J. Adams, "Recent Trends in Town Planning in U. S. A.," *Urban and Rural Planning Thought,* I (January, 1958), 7–11.

8. John P. Dean, "The Myths of Housing Reform," *American Sociological Review,* XIV (April, 1949), 281–288. According to the now famous—or, in the view of some critics, notorious—Baltimore study, lower class Negroes who moved to better housing, as compared with those who remained behind in the slum, showed remarkably few improvements in physical, mental, and social health. One need not accept every detail of this study's elaborate methodology to be struck by this overall conclusion. See Daniel M. Wilner *et al., The Housing Environment and Family Life: A Longitudinal Study of the Effects of Housing on Morbidity and Mental Health* (Baltimore: Johns Hopkins Press, 1962).

9. See, for example, W. W. Rostow, "Non-Communist Manifesto," *The Stages of Economic Growth* (Cambridge: University Press, 1960).

10. For an excellent discussion, see Robert V. Daniels, "Fate and Will in the Marxian Philosophy of History," *Journal of the History of Ideas,* XXI (October-December, 1960), 538–552.

11. Frederick Engels, *Socialism, Utopian and Scientific* (New York: International Publishers, 1935), p. 36.

12. C. A. R. Crosland, *The Future of Socialism* (London: Jonathan Cape, 1956), p. 316. A more telling break was made by Richard Crossman, a prominent Labor Party left ideologue and thus a frequent opponent of Crosland's. "What we describe as the Welfare State," Crossman wrote in 1956, "has been immensely successful and immensely popular, whereas nationalization has not changed the lives of the workers in the industries affected in the way they expected." Even more amazing was the general conclusion from this experience: "Socialism cannot and should not be based on any particular economic theory." R. H. S. Crossman, *Planning for Freedom* (London: Hamish Hamilton, 1965), pp. 61–62.

13. Merle Fainsod, *How Russia Is Ruled* (Cambridge: Harvard University Press, 1957), p. 84.

14. See, for example, several of the essays in Gregory Grossman (ed.), *Value and Plan: Economic Calculation and Organization in Eastern Europe* (Berkeley: University of California Press, 1960). A good article on the trend in the Soviet Union is Leon Smolinski and Peter Wiles, "The Soviet Planning Pendulum," *Problems of Communism,* XII (November-December, 1963), 21–34.

15. Leonard Reissman, *The Urban Process: Cities in Industrial Societies* (New York: Free Press of Glencoe, 1964), chap. iii.

16. Martin Meyerson, "Utopian Traditions and the Planning of Cities," *Daedalus,* (Winter, 1960), pp. 180–193. To cite as another example, Dahl and Lindblom: "As models, utopias . . . indicate directions in which alternatives to existing reality might be looked for, . . . help one to focus on long-run goals, . . . function as aids to motivation." Robert A. Dahl and Charles E. Lindblom, *Politics, Economics, and Welfare* (New York: Harper, 1953), p. 73.

17. Lewis Mumford, *The Culture of Cities* (New York: Harcourt, Brace, 1938), p. 377.

18. David Riesman, *Individualism Reconsidered and Other Essays* (Glencoe, Illinois: Free Press, 1954), p. 73.

19. Mumford, *loc. cit.,* p. 380.

20. Riesman, *loc. cit.*

21. As a migrant from the more consistently democratic East Coast, I have been struck by the way this principle operates in California politics. Both of the major parties in this state are seriously infected with utopian factions that, each in its own manner, would like to go beyond the orderly processes of legal change—and is reinforced in the conviction that this is necessary by those seeking quasi-legal methods to move in the contrary direction.

22. Mumford, *loc. cit.,* p. 378.

23. Erich Fromm, *Escape from Freedom* (New York: Rinehart, 1941), p. 272.

24. Victor Gruen, "How to Handle this Chaos of Congestion, this Anarchy of Scatteration," *Architectural Forum,* CV (September, 1956), 130–135.

25. Christopher Tunnard and Henry Hope Reed, *American Skyline: The Growth and Form of Our Cities and Towns* (New York: Mentor, 1956).

26. Clarence Arthur Perry, *Housing for the Machine Age* (New York: Russell Sage Foundation, 1939).

27. This is the title of an article by Reginald R. Isaacs in *Journal of Housing,* V (August 1948), 215–219. See also Nathan Glazer, "The School as an Instrument in Planning," with a "Comment" by John W. Dyckman, *Journal of the American Institute of Planners,* XXV (November, 1959), 191–199.

28. Bernard J. Frieden, "Toward Equality of Urban Opportunity," *Journal of the American Institute of Planners,* XXXI (November, 1965), 320–330.

29. Gunnar Myrdal, *An American Dilemma: The Negro Problem and Modern Democracy* (New York: Harper, 1944), pp. 75–76.

30. See, for example, Morton and Lucia White, *The Intellectual versus the City: From Thomas Jefferson to Frank Lloyd Wright* (Cambridge: Harvard University Press and MIT Press, 1962) and Henry Nash Smith, *Virgin Land: The American West as Symbol and Myth* (New York: Vintage Books, 1957).

31. Gunnar Myrdal, *Beyond the Welfare State: Economic Planning and Its International Implications* (New Haven: Yale University Press, 1960), p. 63.

32. *Ibid.,* p. 23.

33. In a rather good book on economic development—written, it so happens, by a socialist administrator—the item under "Planning" in the index reads as follows: "*See* Government (administrative functions); Investment criteria; Price mechanism." W. Arthur Lewis, *The Theory of Economic Growth* (Homewood, Illinois: Richard D. Irwin, 1955), p. 448.

34. "In this sense there has always been economic planning— . . . in the days of the Pharaohs of old, in ancient Greece, in the Roman Empire. . . . There has always been town planning, planning in relation to great public works." Ferdynand Zweig, *The Planning of Free Societies* (London: Secker & Warburg, 1942), p. 11.

35. Melvin M. Webber, "The Prospects for Policies Planning," in Leonard J. Duhl (ed.), *The Urban Condition: People and Policy in the Metropolis* (New York: Basic Books, 1963), pp. 319–330.

36. Martin Meyerson, "Building the Middle-Range Bridge for Comprehensive Planning," *Journal of the American Institute of Planners,* XXIII (Spring, 1956), 58–64.

37. John W. Reps, *The Making of Urban America: A History of City Planning in the United States* (Princeton: Princeton University Press, 1965) and Blake McKelvey, *The Urbanization of America, 1860–1915* (New Brunswick: Rutgers University Press, 1963). McKelvey's work is the only one I know of that discusses

the muckrakers (the utopians of that era) against a background of rising professionalism in city government and related social agencies.

38. C. D. Foster and M. E. Beesley, "Estimating the Social Benefit of Constructing an Underground Railway in London," *Journal of the Royal Statistical Society*, Series A, CXXVI, Part 1 (1963), 46–78.

39. Forest G. Hill, "Wesley Mitchell's Theory of Planning," *Political Science Quarterly*, LXXII (March, 1957), 100–118, n. 24. Lynd, for instance, asserted that the research under Mitchell's direction at the National Bureau of Economic Research, since its purpose was to establish empirical relations in the world as it exists, had "a general bias in favor of the going system." Robert S. Lynd, *Knowledge for What? The Place of Social Science in American Culture* (New York: Grove Press, 1964), p. 121.

40. Emil J. Sady, "Notes on Research Needs, Compiled from the Conference Records," *Proceedings of the National Conference on Metropolitan Problems Held at Kellogg Center, Michigan State University, East Lansing, Michigan, April 29–May 2, 1956* (New York: Government Affairs Foundation, 1957), pp. 87–89. For an intelligent variation on that common theme, "more research is needed," see Resources for the Future, *A Report on Planning, Policy-Making, and Research Activities* (Washington, D. C., 1961).

41. Melvin M. Webber, "The Role of Intelligence Systems in Urban-Systems Planning," *Journal of the American Institute of Planners*, XXXI (November, 1965), 289–296.

42. Harvey S. Perloff, "Social Planning in the Metropolis," in Duhl (ed.), *loc. cit.*, p. 331.

43. John Dewey, "Social Science and Social Control," *New Republic*, July 29, 1931, pp. 276–277.

44. Paul Davidoff and Thomas A. Reiner, "A Choice Theory of Planning," *Journal of the American Institute of Planners*, XXVIII (May, 1962), 103–115.

45. Britton Harris, "Plan or Projection: An Examination of the Use of Models in Planning," *Journal of the American Institute of Planners*, XXVI (November, 1960), 265–272.

46. A good critique, even though its examples are now out of date, is Harold F. Dorn, "Pitfalls in Population Forecasts and Projections," *Journal of the American Statistical Association*, XLV (September, 1950), 311–334. A more general discussion is given in William Petersen, *Population* (New York: Macmillan, 1961), chap. xi.

47. See Britton Harris, "New Tools for Planning," *Journal of the American Institute of Planners*, XXXI (May, 1965), 90–95.

48. Eric Carlson, "High-Rise Management Design Problems as Found in Caracas Studied by International Team," *Journal of Housing*, XVI (October, 1959), 311–314.

49. Catherine Bauer Wurster, "Framework for an Urban Society," in American Assembly, *Goals for Americans* (New York: Prentice-Hall, 1960).

50. John Madge, "The New Towns Program in Britain, *Journal of the American Institute of Planners,* XXVIII (November, 1962), 208–219.

51. Royal Commission on the Distribution of the Industrial Population, *Report* (London: H. M. Stationery Office, 1940; Cmd. 6153).

52. Peter Self, *Cities in Flood: The Problems of Urban Growth* (London: Faber and Faber, 1957), p. 27.

53. New Towns Committee, *Final Report* (London: H. M. Stationery Office, 1946; Cmd. 6876).

54. Noel Gist and L. A. Halbert, *Urban Society* (New York: Thomas Crowell, 1956), p. 480.

55. Mary McLean (ed.), *Local Planning Administration* (3rd ed. Chicago: International City Manager's Association, 1959), p. 10.

A COLLABORATIVE APPROACH TO PLANNING THROUGH URBAN ACTIVITIES

David R. Godschalk and William E. Mills

Urban services and facilities are largely consumed and paid for by the local community. The total community is thus the planner's ultimate client. However, instead of a simple, monolithic structure, the urban community consists of a number of multifaceted, overlapping, and interdependent subcommunities. A successful democratic planning process, like a successful democratic government, must allow for representation of the interests and identities of its subcommunities.

To achieve this representation, we propose an expanded planning process based on three premises. First, the process is *collaborative,* bringing citizens and planners together in a common effort. Second, the process focuses on *human activities* as well as land use. And third, the process stresses *two way communications* between planners and their client publics. After developing these premises and drawing them together in the concept of an *activities base,* a pilot study of household activities in a medium sized community is presented.

Planning As a Collaborative Process

It is our first premise that democratic planning must be based on involvement with the client public. In this way society participates in planning rather than being manipulated by planning. This is not a new idea; the HHFA has been demanding "citizen participation" in local Workable Programs for years. Acceptance of the idea on other than a superficial basis, however, has been rare. Only a

Reprinted by permission of the authors and publishers from the *Journal of the American Institute of Planners,* **32** (March, 1966), pp. 86–95.

few planning programs have recognized a responsibility to a total community and not just to its wealthy or powerful members.

By a collaborative planning process we mean one in which there is genuine interchange between planners and citizens from all walks of life throughout the course of the process. The working relationship with the community is *with* rather than *for*. In this approach the planner's role may be compared to that of a counselor, whose job is to assist the community in discovering and achieving its objectives. This does not mean attempting to sell a prepared plan, nor simply seeking the blessing of key people.

Collaborative planning is similar to the collaborative marketing approach which assumes that the consumer is not sure of his exact desires but would be interested in defining them with the help of a skilled counselor who knows the range of possible alternatives. Nelson N. Foote has contrasted this more advanced marketing approach with the early "persuasive" or hard sell approach, and the more recent "listening" or poll taking approach.[1] The parallels with planning are obvious.

The planner gains several advantages by defining his role as a public counselor. First, he demonstrates that he considers the citizens of his community to be intelligent, able to think, decide, and grow. Counter to the trend toward quantification and abstraction, he sees his community, not through a computer, but across a table. Second, with a systematic public consultation process, the planner is able to stay abreast of social change. Finally, and perhaps most important, the planner gains a vital understanding of the people and groups for whom he works, with their specific limitations and potentials. If planning is to be judged in terms of the effectiveness of plan implementation rather than solely the efficiency of plan preparation, these will be important gains.

An interesting phenomenon in some areas where there has not been public-planner collaboration has been the rise of counter planning agencies, which employ planners and prepare plans. SPUR, the San Francisco Planning and Urban Renewal Association, is an example, calling itself "a nonpartisan citizens organization, working for a better planned and more attractive San Francisco."[2] These agencies usually are supported by businessmen or citizens groups that do not feel the official planning agency adequately represents their interests.

The collaborative planning process attempts to include the interests of all community groups. It attempts a complete realignment of approach outward toward the community. By bringing society into the planning act, traditional American individualism can be reconciled with the pressing need for planning.

> . . . the crisis of planning is a crisis of society, of which the planners, in spite of honest self-criticism, are not yet conscious; they are looking for the shortcomings in their own ranks while in fact they seem to be the scapegoats of a society which cries out for planning, and yet repels it as incompatible with its tradition and the sacred principles of unlimited individual freedom and opportunity.[3]

A Human Activities Focus

Our second premise holds that planning must be concerned with the objective analysis of human activities. This is a relatively new idea, but one which has been increasingly stressed in theoretical planning literature. Activities analysis refers to a continuing planning survey of the activities of individuals, households, firms, and institutions. In the case of individuals and households, the survey is conducted through interviews of a representative sample of the population. Such an analysis seeks to identify subcommunities and to understand their values and activities. It is concerned with attitudes as well as factual data, with the *why* as well as the *what* and the *where* of activities. In the case of firms the survey consists of interviews with managers concerning business activities, with arrangements for updating data periodically. Institutions are surveyed both through interviews with officers and through discussion meetings with members. As the planning program advances, these institutional discussions become more important as forums and sounding boards for proposals and issues.

Chapin and Hightower have described a technique for analyzing activities systems which they define as "behavior patterns of individuals, families, institutions, and firms which predispose to disposition in space." [4] Our approach differs primarily in its emphasis on qualitative aspects of activities systems, in its use of activities analysis interviews as planning—public contacts, and in its less rigorous study methodology. We feel that a focus on spatial structure, or disposition in space, is somewhat limiting. The quality of activity seems as important as the quantity and pattern of activity. Chapin and Hightower, themselves, state that the distinction between spatial and nonspatial activities is not perceived by respondents. A further difference is our use of activities analysis interviews as a community consultation and involvement technique in addition to use as an urban research method. This is a direct outcome of our operational planning commitment as participants in the process of social change as well as observers and predictors. The interviews are the starting point for a continuing dialogue. A final important difference is the study design itself. Rather than a rigorously tested and applied activities questionnaire, we chose an unstructured, open-ended interview technique. While this placed a larger burden on the analyst, it encouraged free conversational exchange, particularly with people of lower income groups who were unaccustomed to, and suspicious of, questionnaires.

Once established within the planning process, activities analysis can provide continuing contact with the pluralistic urban context. It can be used on a total community basis or for areas in transition or under special stress. Whatever the scale, the activities analysis is needed for an understanding of the local context, without which planning proposals are usually ignored. As Henry Fagin has observed, "we plan within a particular context, and the context validates the particular methods we use." [5]

Two-Way Communications

Our third premise is that meaningful and effective planning must be based on a two-way communication flow between the public and the planning agency. Communications between planner and client are conceived as dialogues rather than monologues. In this way planners not only learn about their communities, but the communities also learn about themselves and their potentials.

Of the wide range of available communication devices, face-to-face conversation is still the most useful. Discussion with individuals and groups allows the give and take vital to collaboration. Supplementary communication methods may be used to trigger public thinking and feedback. Mass media can be effective for reaching large groups over a period of time. Television and films are especially under-utilized devices for dramatizing community issues.

A look at the use of communications in some progressive planning programs in various locations will illustrate the possibilities. In reviewing other contemporary planning programs three kinds of citizen consultation methods were noted: the attitude survey; the organized discussion group; the continuing consultation within the planning process.

The Joint Program for the Twin Cities Metropolitan Area has used a home interview *attitude survey* to find out what the residents liked and disliked about the area; what they thought the image of the area was; and their attitudes toward environmental problems, the local power structure, information sources, home choice, the neighborhood, and facilities for recreation.[6] The survey, conducted by a private firm under contract with the Metropolitan Planning Commission, included both specific and open-ended questions. This technique is valuable as a first step in an overall collaborative process, but unless repeated and expanded, its information becomes dated. Also the use of a professional interview firm imposes an addition filter in the communication process.

The Regional Plan Association of New York experimented with a variety of communications techniques through *organized discussion groups* in its Goals for the Region Project. RPA's information director, William B. Shore, has suggested that existing political and electoral processes are not effective in registering community preferences on planning issues, and that, "planners should try to formulate a system through which personal preferences can be considered in the developing metropolis." [7]

The Goals for the Region Project attempted to provide information about choices open in the region to 5,600 participants, who were divided into small discussion groups for five weekly meetings. Communication techniques included five televised films dramatizing central issues, background booklets, small group discussions, and questionnaires on environmental preferences. Unfortunately, the participants were not representative of the diverse regional population but rather were primarily middle class people whose civic consciousness prompted them to participate in the program.

Although this was a pioneering communications effort for planning, all of the devices used are actually standard features of adult education programs. However, by recognizing the citizens of the region as participants, the Goals Project was collaborative in nature; it was an especially impressive undertaking in light of the large number of people involved.

A promising initial basis for a *continuing consultation within the planning process* has been established through area workshops by the East Central Florida Regional Planning Council in the counties around Cape Kennedy. Citizens' ideas about the future development of the region were solicited by planners in public workshop meetings prior to preparation of the preliminary plan. Officials and decision-makers were briefed on specific issues raised by the preliminary plan on the part of the citizens. The next phase of the planning process will include another round of community workshops to inform citizens of the consultant findings and to receive further comments. Citizen involvement is planned on a continuing basis as full scale land use and transportation plans are developed. Although it is too early to evaluate the effectiveness of the local workshops, if fully utilized they could become a valuable institutional means for developing and testing community objectives is an unstable and dynamic region.

A mature planning program which perhaps most effectively demonstrates *continuing consultation within the planning process* is that of the City of Toronto Planning Board. The process begins in one of the City's 25 planning districts with a detailed study of the conditions and problems of the district compiled by planners with the assistance of district citizens, institutions, and officials. Results are then summarized in a preliminary district plan which is distributed to every district household and business establishment. Public meetings are held within each subarea of the district to discuss the appraisal and plan proposals in small groups. Local comments and suggestions coming from the discussions are recorded and reviewed by the planning staff. Finally the proposed plan, amended in the light of citizen reaction, is transmitted to the elected officials with a report of citizen comments and a supplementary staff report produced after the public discussions.

The Chairman of the City of Toronto Planning Board recently reported that six district plans had been prepared using this process and that the results well justified the effort and expense in establishing a good spirit of collaboration.[8]

Composite Activities Base

As a kind of conceptual container for the various community issues, social orientations, and life styles discovered through collaborative planning with its emphasis on human activities and two-way communications, we propose an *activities base*. Just as the economic base study describes the significant economic conditions of a particular community, the activities base study describes the significant local activities and social context.

In preparing the study, activity is considered in two dimensions—quality and quantity. Quantity is examined through such traditional studies as land use and traffic movement. Quality is studied through interviews and discussions with individuals, households, institutions, and firms. Throughout, there is recognition of the interaction between the relatively static physical structure and the more dynamic activities structure of the community.

Preparation of the activities base begins with the earliest research of the planning agency, and continues throughout the life of the collaborative planning process. In the traditional three phase comprehensive planning process of research, plan and policy preparation, and implementation, the activities base enters into all phases. Thus, during studies of population and economic activities, interviews are conducted with households and firms. Findings of these early studies are transmitted back to the community through short reports, news releases, workshops, forums, films, and television programs—depending on local communication channels available. During plan and policy preparation another round of interviews and group discussions tests draft proposals. Completed plans are subjected to public review before final legislative approval. Again, in the implementation phase the various subcommunities concerned are involved

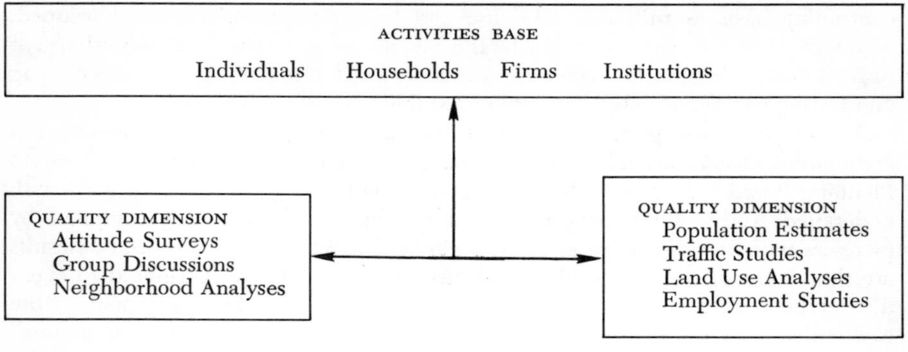

FIG. 1

through forums and workshops. The complexities and changes inherent in urban areas should ensure continuing opportunities for public consultation as plans and policies are revised over time.

A Pilot Study of Household Activities

In the course of establishing a planning program for Gainesville, Florida, the authors conducted a pilot household activities survey as a first step toward a collaborative process. Given the commitment to democratic planning with the total community as client, we felt a strong responsibility to understand the many subcommunities that made up the city. Information on attitudes, values, neighborhoods, and life styles seemed an essential prerequisite to proposals for planning concepts and strategies. The activities survey was conducted concurrently with a program of land use mapping and data collection, and a study of population and housing.

Our research method consisted of a series of open-ended tape recorded household interviews as well as neighborhood field observations. The sample was evenly distributed throughout the city. In the interviews two types of information were sought—basic household activities and household composition characteristics. The interviews, which lasted about an hour, covered 350 households, a sample of about 2.3 percent. Interviews and field reports were analyzed and compiled into a staff report on household activities.

Interviewers were furnished with a check list of basic activities to be discussed in the course of the interview, but were instructed to let each situation spontaneously dictate much of its own order and direction. They were asked to discover the activities in which each household participated and the qualitative responses to these activities. Respondents were encouraged to talk about their attitudes and aspirations as well as time spent and locations for activities such as shopping, education, religion, recreation, transportation, and communication. Neighborhood and city livability were also discussed.

Use of the somewhat unconventional loosely-structured, open-ended interview was considered important in developing a rapport of free conversational exchange. Respondents were encouraged to express themselves in a discussion rather than a question-answer situation. Although this procedure lacks statistical objectivity and demands a high degree of skill and sensitivity on the part of the interviewer, it was considered justifiable in terms of the comprehensiveness of the responses.[9] It also avoided built-in biases found in standardized questionnaires. We judged reproducibility and predictability to be less important than a more complete human understanding of social and cultural environment.

Our procedure also demanded a disciplined and objective analysis. A small analytical staff listened to all interview tapes and read interviewers' field reports. Geographic neighborhoods, attitudes toward community life, and basic life styles were categorized only after interview tapes had been heard in order to let the results emerge from the materials. Conferences between the analysts and the interviewers maximized the interchange of information on survey results. Interviewers were local residents with graduate education in anthropology or experience in social work. Analysts were planning staff members.

As a result of the survey the planning agency obtained a great range of quantitative and qualitative information and insight about the subcommunities of the city. A second possible output—increase in the level of self awareness, concept of possibility, and propensity for action within the subcommunities themselves—will depend upon continuation of the collaborative planning process over time.

Outputs obtained by the planning agency have relevance primarily for local planning. They are not presented as having implications of universal significance, but as illustrations of the collaborative process. Locally, the pilot activities survey provided basic information for a neighborhood analysis and some valuable guidelines for land use and zoning policies; it triggered a joint university-city study of student housing policies, and served as a starting point for census tract delineation. It was also used for background information by the new local anti-poverty agency.

Gainesville has changed in the past twenty years from a small north Florida town to a medium sized city of about 55,000. It has grown along with the University of Florida, its main source of employment, exchanging many elements of a rural culture for a more diverse and sophisticated urban social character. Its social matrix contains university students, country people, professors, businessmen, laborers, professionals, and retired people.

Superimposed on occupational and class differences the activities survey discerned three primary cultural outlooks. The *North Florida rural culture* has emerged from years of trying to eke out a meager existence from harsh soil and unpredictable weather. This culture is oriented toward property and friends, face to face relationships, concrete and specific things and ideas. It is suspicious of impersonal abstract ideas like the public good, esthetics, or comprehensive planning. The *traditional middle class culture* is inclined toward a static and institutionalized order based on status, measured by such things as income, residence, occupation, education, and club memberships. Although this kind of social orientation potentially has great utility in community improvement programs, its local impact has been weakened through diffusion over numerous social groups with diverse objectives. The *contemporary middle class culture* is evolving from the experiences of younger adults whose approach to status is through a dynamic concept of value. They tend to emphasize style and experience above fixed status symbols. Often highly mobile students and younger faculty or professionals, they seek opportunities for activity rather than long term stability. Conflicts between these three cultural outlooks lie at the root of many of the planning and development problems of Gainesville.[10]

Findings of the Pilot Study

As expected, the information from the survey was voluminous and inter-related. Only a few illustrative findings are presented here, along with the classifications developed. Each interview was classified in three ways: attitude toward life in the community, basic life style, and neighborhood designation.

1) Attitude Toward Life in the Community. The *positive* attitude was basically satisfied with life in the community even though having some specific complaints. Most of the positives came from the rural cultural orientation (who liked the remaining small town character), or the traditional middle class orientation (who enjoyed living in a small university city which was clean, free from crime, and a good place to raise children). Those positives from the contemporary middle class outlook liked the easy casual style and academic atmosphere.

The *acceptors,* either for reasons not associated with the city itself, or lack of choice, accepted life in the community. The first group was composed of students and other temporary residents whose presence depended on the university or some other local organization. They did not specifically choose the city. The second group were primarily those low income residents whose judgment of the city as an environment was purely academic since they had neither the ability to influence changes nor to move away. Their community involvement could go no further than a day-to-day struggle to provide for themselves and their families.

The *negatives* were basically dissatisfied with community life even though they had some specific satisfactions. This group was composed of two extremes —those from the rural culture who felt the city had become too large, urbanized, and impersonal, and those from the contemporary middle class culture who considered the city too small, rural, and unsophisticated.[11]

2) Basic Life Style. These categories were used: *Student, Retired, Lower class, Working class, Middle class, Upper middle class.* Each class designation was further broken down by race. Within the middle class, "traditional" and "contemporary" life styles were distinguished primarily by whether status was perceived in terms of fixed symbols such as a "good address" or in terms of dynamic experiences and style. A distinction was made between married and unmarried student life styles, and between active and inactive retired life styles (a class designation was also used with the retired category since the retired tended to preserve their former class associations and values). Although the multiplicity of classifications complicated the analysis, it more fairly represented the diversity of the community. One broad distinction which cut across other lines was whether or not middle class values were accepted. Thus, a student might either be striving toward middle class values or might have rejected them, while a mechanic might or might not aspire to features of a middle class life style.

3) **Neighborhood Designations.** The *older established neighborhoods* were the centrally located areas now often in transition to other uses. Built up around the turn of the century, some of the fine old houses dated back to 1890. The *established neighborhoods* were the "suburbs" of the 1930's and 1940's. These areas were the second ring of growth, still near the center of the city. *Newer established neighborhoods* were in the middle and upper income categories, distinguished from more recent subdivisions by their stable, established character. Developed since World War II, they contained many professionals and faculty members. *Suburban neighborhoods,* developed since the mid 1950's, were recognizable by their newness and appearance of having been built as a unit. Located in outlying areas of the city, they had a predominance of middle and upper income residents. *Student neighborhoods,* located near the university for the most part, contained a high proportion of university students and their families, along with faculty and others associated with the university, and a number of older established residents.

Combining characteristics of both established areas and informal suburban areas, the *combination neighborhood* primarily housed working class families, often with small town or rural backgrounds. Some of these neighborhoods were in transition to student apartment uses. Development had gone on from the 1930's to the present. *Suburban Negro neighborhoods,* built between 1957 and 1965, were in developing suburban districts adjacent to newer schools. *Older Negro neighborhoods,* dating back to the 1890's, had many housing and environmental problems. Although most residents had low incomes, there were also some middle income and professional residents. Mixed areas consisted of combinations of commercial or industrial uses and lower income residential uses. They were generally in transition to nonresidential development. *Apartment neighborhoods* had concentrations of apartments planned or underway. Probably most of them will be student neighborhoods when they are occupied.

In matching neighborhoods and life styles, it was generally true that the various Established and Suburban areas were inhabited by middle and upper middle class residents; that the Combination areas housed working class families; and that the Mixed areas had lower class residents. Low income was apparently responsible for a certain amount of racial integration and there were small groups of temporary Negro houses on land slated for future nonresidential use, but the major Negro neighborhoods were segregated. A recent apartment building boom had preempted several areas for apartment construction, geared mainly to university students.

There was a problem of overlap between life styles and geographic neighborhoods, only partially solved in the designated neighborhoods. Also, several neighborhoods were well along in transition from one life style to another. Thus, some of the Older Established areas were changing from middle class to student occupancy, while in some Combination areas part of the working class population was adopting a middle class life style. The Older Negro areas were particularly difficult to classify since historically race had obviously been a stronger determinant of residential patterns than occupation or income. The ambiguity of the neighborhood designations thus reflects a resistance to simple categorizing inherent in the residential patterns of the city. Urban physical order and social order are too complex to fit neatly into categorical systems, even when these systems are worked out from a study of a particular city.

Significantly, the outputs of the pilot survey were not tabulated in percentages or abstract schemes of order but were shown as a sense of the diversities and unities of a complex living community and the real issues which confront its people. As previously mentioned, these are the context of the city which must validate planning efforts before they are effective.

The importance of this context may be illustrated by an example of a conflict discovered during the survey. A general city wide shortage of rental housing had caused a sizable invasion by university students into several of the rural working class neighborhoods some distance away from the campus. Most of the working class residents occupied older single family dwellings while the students either lived in similar old rental dwellings or in groups of small new apartments which took over land often formerly occupied by old houses. The result was not only displacement of working class residents further down the housing scale, but also considerable social disparity within the neighborhoods.

Conflict between the conservatism of the rural working class culture and the "swinging" style of the student culture was apparent. The working class people resented the social advantages, better housing, irregular hours, parties, and lack of friendliness of the students. On the other hand, students generally regarded their temporary working class neighbors as socially undesirable inhabitants of the unpainted houses and littered yards which they passed on their way to classes.

Located along a major thoroughfare, these neighborhoods were part of a larger working class district which had experienced considerable pressure for zoning change. Without some overall policy which recognized the needs of both groups, it was probable that real estate speculators eventually would have secured rezoning of most of the district for further student apartments. The majority of working class residents would have been forced to seek other locations, abandoning their stable and convenient (though unaesthetic by middle class standards) neighborhoods for new locations in the rural-urban fringe outside the city. Those remaining would have faced increasing social tension.

In working out planning objectives for this area, the Plan Board studied the interview results and neighborhood field reports. That neighborhood which appeared to have irreversibly passed the tipping point from working class to student residents was designated for high density, multiple family zoning. Those still predominantly working class, single family parts of the district were maintained with single family zoning. These proposals were incorporated into a land use plan for the district which was approved by the City Commission.

Another important issue raised by this conflict concerned the future location of off-campus student housing in the overall city plan. A forum was held with the Plan Board and university housing officials to discuss this matter. Among the preliminary conclusions reached were that student housing should be encouraged near the campus rather than in outlying low income neighborhoods and that development regulations and planning policies should reflect this conclusion.

The relevance of this example is not in its particular outcome but rather in the way in which a community activity issue was discovered and transmitted through planning channels. Without household interviews this issue would probably have received little or no attention, especially since the groups concerned, students and rural working class people, do not have established communications linkages with the city government. Also, the informal and somewhat rural physical appearance of the working class neighborhoods would have caused them to be rated as rundown or even blighted by the average planning windshield survey of neighborhood conditions. Thus, zoning changes leading to displacement of the working class residents might have proceeded without full understanding of their overall impact. Through discussions with households in affected areas, the issue became a part of the context of the city, expressed in the activities base.

Spotlighted by the pilot activities survey were many other issues, each presenting planning and policy questions of its own. These lead naturally and directly into continuing community participation in planning. Thus, in the collaborative approach the activities analysis is not simply another project whose results are observations at one point in time, but an ongoing basis for community involvement at all levels—from the individual to the institution.

Problems of the Collaborative Approach

In spite of obvious advantages, the collaborative approach poses a number of problems. These include the influence of the analysts' values on the resulting activities base, the difficulties of deriving a useful synthesis from the massive and unstructured data, the ratio of survey costs to planning area scale, and the apparent political character of the planner's role in consulting with the community.

Without minimizing the effect of these admitted problems, which need little elaboration, the process appears nevertheless possible. It is not suited to all planning programs nor to all communities. It will be too costly for some, too risky and/or too difficult for others.

Perhaps the apparent political nature of the process will prove to be its greatest drawback in many areas. Where planning is attempting to remain a technical activity outside of controversial matters, a program of vigorous citizen involvement will not seem feasible.

Conclusions for Planning

Three primary conclusions have appeared from our preliminary experiences and our overview of other programs:

1) The necessity for, and evidence of a trend toward, a new *collaborative* planner-client relationship.

2) The potential for realizing this relationship through a community consultation process based on human *activities.*

3) The importance of full utilization of available *communication* technology to ensure a valid exchange between planner and community.

The collaborative relationship makes the planner a direct participant in the community. In stressing planning with people rather than for them, the role of the planner could be considered as similar to that of the psychotherapist who works with each conception of his patient. He does not pretend to know the "truth" about the patient, but instead acts as a backboard and mirror for the patient's own ideas. Similarly, the planner becomes a counselor-participant in community life rather than merely an observer-recorder or an aloof "master planner." [12]

In proposing a human activities base for planning, we conclude, along with others, that the realm of human experience is as important to the planner as land use. A pilot survey of household activities in a medium sized city has demonstrated the possibility and value of tying activities surveys into the planning process. Further applications will undoubtedly produce refined measurement scales and techniques. In addition to other advantages the activities base approach offers a workable basis for collaboration since the language of activities is easily understood and discussed by citizens.

Naturally, the process will stand or fall on its communications. All available channels will be needed—from the face to face interview to the interpretive film or television debate. An over reliance on written reports and abstracted terminology obstructs two-way communications, reducing public feedback. It is precisely this feedback which is necessary to record the actual performance of plans and policies as opposed to their expected performance, and the actual nature of subcommunities as opposed to their stereotyped images.

Based on our observations and work, we suggest that there will be increasing application of the collaborative approach. Not only should it be useful for overall planning, but also for project planning and Community Renewal Programs. The activity analysis is merely one means to realization of a democratic planning process, but one with excellent promise for creative community decisions when it is generally understood and accepted.

> The best defense against planning—and people do need defense against planners—is to become informed about the plan that is indeed existent and operating in our lives; and to learn to take the initiative in proposing or supporting reasoned changes. Such action is not only a defense but good in itself, for to make positive decisions for one's community, rather than being regimented by other's decisions, is one of the noble acts of man.[13]

Notes

1. Nelson N. Foote *et al., Housing Choices and Housing Constraints* (New York: McGraw-Hill, 1960), p. 308.

2. San Francisco Planning and Urban Renewal Association, *SPUR Annual Report: 1964* (San Francisco, Calif., 1965).

3. Thomas Sieverts, "Readers Write," *ASPO Planning News,* (April, 1965), p. 33.

4. F. Stuart Chapin, Jr. and Henry C. Hightower, "Household Activity Patterns and Land Use," *Journal of the American Institute of Planners,* XXXI (August,

1965), 223. See also F. Stuart Chapin, Jr., *Urban Land Use Planning* (2d ed; Urbana: University of Illinois Press, 1965), pp. 69–106, and pp. 221–253.

5. Henry Fagin, "Planning for Future Urban Growth," *Law and Contemporary Problems,* XXX (Winter, 1965), 9.

6. "The People Look at Their Area," *Program Notes,* Newsletter published by The Joint Program (St. Paul, Minn., March, 1965), I, 1–2.

7. William B. Shore, "Public Opinion and Goals for Planning," (Panel) American Institute of Planners: 46th Annual Conference, *A Report of the Milwaukee Proceedings* (Milwaukee, Wis., 1963), p. 188.

8. W. Harold Clark, Paper delivered at "Public Consultation in the Planning Process," (Panel) American Society of Planning Officials and Community Planning Association of Canada Joint Planning Conference (Toronto, Canada, 1965).

9. For a demonstration and defense of the open-ended interview technique, see John F. Cuber, *The Significant Americans* (New York: Appleton Century, 1965).

10. For a background study of local conflicts as expressed in the political arena, see Ruth McQuown, William R. Hamilton, and Michael P. Schneider, *The Political Restructuring of a Community,* Studies in Public Administration No. 27 (Gainesville, Fla.: Public Administration Clearing Service, 1964).

11. Cross relationships between life style and attitude toward life in the community were not necessarily consistent. Thus some working class members were enthusiastic about the community while others were negative. More often, the positives were from the traditional middle class; the acceptors from the contemporary middle class, students, and the lower class; and the negatives from the working class.

12. An example of the ineffectual nature of master planning which is out of touch with community objectives is described in Edward C. Banfield and James Q. Wilson, *City Politics* (Cambridge: Harvard University Press, 1963), pp. 192–196. These authors also briefly discuss planning as community decision making on p. 200.

13. Paul and Percival Goodman, *Communitas: Ways of Livelihood and Means of Life* (New York: Vintage Books, A Division of Random House, 1960), pp. 10–11.

ADMINISTERING THE SPREAD CITY

Alan K. Campbell and Seymour Sacks

Since the end of World War II increasing attention has been paid to the spatial redistribution of the American people. The urbanization and metropolitanization of the country have been widely discussed and its implications for the nature of American society vigorously debated. The full ramifications of this fundamental change defy summary since the change involves nearly all aspects of man's behavior. In fact, it has been argued that ". . . now, when the last rural threads of American society are being woven into the national urban fabric the idea of city is becoming indistinguishable from the idea of society.[1] Urban man has become "every man."

While philosophers, statesmen, social critics and journalists debate the merits of this revolution with a colorful but imprecise language, day-to-day decision-makers must try to cope with the new reality. Among those most directly concerned are the local government administrators who daily make decisions which reflect the revolution and, to some degree, influence its course.

Of the names this new environment is called, a few are flattering, most are damning, hardly any are value-free: urban sprawl, scatteration, cancerous growth, and slurbs are but a few of the value-loaded names which have been given to it. Perhaps the phrase "spread city" is as nearly a neutral one as is likely to be found although even it is likely to have a negative ring in the ears of most readers since a city is normally pictured as being compact rather than spread. The New York Regional Plan Association's definition of the term is, by implication at least, negative rather than positive: "It is not a true city because it lacks centers, nor a suburb because it is not a satellite of any city, nor is it truly rural because it is loosely covered with houses and urban facilities." [2] Others view the phenomenon in a more positive way, arguing that it provides a range of choices in living conditions and styles never before possible. They find ". . . in the dissolution of the urban settlement a liberation of human energies and a proliferation of opportunity for human interaction." [3]

Whether good or bad the urban future of this country is a "spread-city" future. It may be "less" rather than "more" spread if policies are geared to this end, but when compared to the compact city of the past it will be spread. For the local official the result is a new decision making environment. Even under the simplifying assumption of a single governmental jurisdiction for the entire spread city area, the problems he faces will be new, if not in content at least in dimension. For a given level of services many of the infrastructure cost advantages possible through economies of scale in a compact city, for example, will not be realized in a spread city, whatever the jurisdictional pattern. Further, the spatial distribution of welfare, health and education needs would probably not be much altered by a one-jurisdictional governmental system.

Although the decision environment of the spread city, even with the assumption of a one-jurisdictional local system, will be vastly different from that of the

---

Reprinted by permission of the authors and publisher from *Public Administration Review*, **24** (September, 1964), pp. 141–152.

compact cities, the reality is not one jurisdiction, but many. The fact of many jurisdictions operating in the same area has resulted in many defining *the* metropolitan problem as governmental fragmentation.[4] Whether this is *the* metropolitan problem or if the situation is better described as problems in metropolitan areas is not the issue here. Rather it is the nature of the impact of spread city, plus governmental fragmentation, plus the state-local governmental system on the decision environment of administrators. The result is that no single set of officials within a spread city is responsible for the entire area or even a very large part of it.

The fact of fragmentation as a general feature of local government in the United States has led to the development of a variety of generalizations about its impact on policy-making at this level of government. These generalizations usually point to a lack of coordination, inequity in tax burdens, distortions in land-use patterns and unhealthy competition among local jurisdictions as the inevitable results of the fragmentation. It is normally assumed that these criticisms apply with equal or nearly equal validity to all spread cities in the country.

It is the lack of validity in this assumption of uniformity of impact which is the concern of this analysis. Governmental systems operative in spread cities across the country are not the same in every spread city area. Nor are these systems enough alike to assume that generalizations can be made about the impact of fragmented government on the nature and quality of public decisions.[5]

State-Local Governmental Systems

The first step necessary, therefore, is an analysis of the significance of fragmentation for local decision making in the spread city is to describe the kinds of governmental systems from which the decisions emerge. There are 50 state-local governmental systems and the District of Columbia system in the United States, each with its own unique characteristics; and within each state-local system there are distinct local sub-systems, usually more than one within each state. Alongside these state-local systems and their sub-systems is the federal government with its state-local aid programs and, of particular relevance to spread city governmental systems, its recent efforts to encourage planning in urban areas.

Although there are various ways in which these systems can be described and classified, one of the most useful is to base the classification on fiscal characteristics. The relevant fiscal characteristics for describing state-local systems are: the allocation between state and local governments of general expenditure and general revenue responsibilities,[6] the extent and character of state aid, variation in local revenue sources, and the nature of the property tax. To illustrate the widespread variation in these factors the following table indicates the interstate differences within and between regions for each of the fiscal characteristics.

The allocation of expenditure responsibility to local government varies greatly from state to state although there are regional patterns. In 1962 local government expenditures ranged from 39.4 percent of total state-local expenditures in Vermont and 42.3 percent and 44.9 percent in Kentucky and West Virginia, respectively, to highs of 77.8 percent in New York, 74.8 percent in Wisconsin, and 74.4 percent in New Jersey. The state average expenditure allocation has remained

TABLE 1. STATE AND LOCAL FISCAL CHARACTERISTICS BY STATE FOR CONTINENTAL UNITED STATES: 1962

UNITED STATES	General * State-Local Expenditures Per Capita $	Local General * Expenditures as Percent of State-Local Expenditures %	Local Taxes as Percent of State-Local Taxes %	State Aid as Percent of Local Taxes %	Local Property Taxes as Percent of Total Local General * Revenue %	Assessed Value of Commercial and Industrial as Percent of Assessed Value of All Property %
NORTHEAST						
Maine	271.78	50.7	54.9	19.1	75.4	39.6
New Hampshire	302.33	52.6	62.5	8.5	78.5	N.A.
Vermont	372.66	39.4	44.6	30.0	70.8	N.A.
Massachusetts	343.25	72.0	60.8	37.6	63.3	32.3
Rhode Island	292.98	53.7	49.4	29.7	66.8	N.A.
Connecticut	367.37	59.4	53.4	23.0	70.1	N.A.
New York	398.26	77.8	56.9	49.7	44.4	N.A.
New Jersey	301.68	74.4	71.1	19.0	87.6	34.6
Pennsylvania	272.41	61.3	41.7	41.9	44.6	28.9
Delaware	335.37	49.3	22.2	159.8	31.2	31.6
Maryland	318.32	69.4	43.4	84.0	41.5	37.8
NORTH CENTRAL						
Michigan	343.25	65.7	47.0	68.4	51.3	N.A.
Ohio	290.52	72.0	55.3	45.1	49.7	51.9
Indiana	290.37	67.2	55.6	44.9	59.1	N.A.
Illinois	315.06	70.2	57.8	26.3	58.4	33.9
Wisconsin	350.78	74.8	53.1	63.4	50.4	36.5
Minnesota	362.81	70.5	53.5	56.8	53.1	35.2
Iowa	325.58	64.1	56.7	34.2	61.4	N.A.
Missouri	266.39	59.1	51.4	33.7	50.0	29.5
North Dakota	378.66	52.7	53.6	32.6	58.4	27.3
South Dakota	329.29	48.7	61.9	13.8	70.4	18.1
Nebraska	280.49	65.3	64.4	25.9	58.9	20.9
Kansas	321.35	66.6	55.8	40.7	58.4	N.A.

* See footnote 6, page 142.
Sources: U. S. Bureau of the Census, Governments Division, *Governmental Finances in 1962* and Census of Governments 1962, *Property Values*.
N.A. = not available

remarkably constant over time: 59.1 percent in 1962 and 59.2 in 1957, with standard deviations of 9.1 and 9.2 for the same two years.

For tax allocation to local government, the range for individual states is from

TABLE 1 (*Continued*)

UNITED STATES	General * State-Local Expenditures Per Capita $	Local General * Expenditures as Percent of State-Local Expenditures %	Local Taxes as Percent of State-Local Taxes %	State Aid as Percent of Local Taxes %	Local Property Taxes as Percent of Total Local General * Revenues %	Assessed Value of Commercial and Industrial as Percent of Assessed Value of All Property %
SOUTH						
Virginia	249.26	60.2	42.3	65.4	38.4	N.A.
West Virginia	250.95	44.9	30.6	77.8	40.6	N.A.
Kentucky	293.01	42.3	33.2	80.5	33.6	42.9
Tennessee	238.70	59.8	37.5	86.1	36.9	N.A.
North Carolina	229.38	62.1	37.1	121.8	30.4	39.9
South Carolina	202.11	50.8	26.4	125.4	32.3	53.9
Georgia	256.71	59.4	35.3	92.4	33.3	N.A.
Florida	282.68	67.8	48.6	46.9	42.6	N.A.
Alabama	244.81	52.4	30.3	122.9	18.3	N.A.
Mississippi	248.69	55.4	35.4	114.3	29.9	N.A.
Louisiana	332.78	47.8	25.8	152.4	26.6	N.A.
Arkansas	221.10	49.1	31.1	95.2	37.0	34.9
Oklahoma	290.52	48.2	32.5	81.4	40.5	N.A.
Texas	269.17	65.3	46.6	51.2	48.4	N.A.
WEST						
New Mexico	326.92	52.8	26.4	185.5	21.6	N.A.
Arizona	354.14	59.5	44.6	64.4	44.2	N.A.
Montana	350.93	52.4	55.6	24.9	62.4	N.A.
Idaho	310.82	54.4	46.3	52.3	51.4	46.6
Wyoming	497.60	53.0	46.2	64.6	44.3	N.A.
Colorado	362.19	67.8	51.5	58.2	48.1	43.7
Utah	332.71	55.2	53.5	53.3	45.2	55.5
Washington	385.15	57.8	31.2	110.5	29.8	N.A.
Oregon	382.63	55.0	48.8	48.6	51.5	41.0
Nevada	496.40	57.9	40.7	63.7	33.9	N.A.
California	429.34	71.8	54.2	58.8	47.0	N.A.

71.1 percent in New Jersey to Delaware with 22.2 percent. The average state allocation for 1962 was 45.8 percent as compared to 44.9 percent in 1957, with standard deviations of 12.0 and 11.8 for the same two years.[7]

In general, the major determinants of allocation are state and federal aid and the degree of urbanization. The most important determinant of this difference in allocation responsibility is the division of public welfare expenditures between state and local governments.[8] There are 31 states in which state governments take primary responsibility for this function and 17 in which local government is given such responsibility. Another determinant of allocation is the rather random year-to-year differences of federal grants for the interstate highway programs.

Another difference in state-local governmental systems revolves around state aid. The already discussed allocation of expenditures is greatly influenced by the amount of state aid. In 1962 this source of local revenue varied from $10.54 per capita in New Hampshire to $96.81 per capita in California, or a variation from 6.6 percent of local expenditures in New Hampshire to 52 percent of local expenditures in New Mexico with California's high per capita figure equivalent to 31.4 percent of local expenditures. These differences in state aid require the development of distinct local strategies by public officials if they are to maximize their benefits from this source of revenue. In Wisconsin, for example, the state aid system takes the form, in part, of shared taxes and this kind of system demands different local public finance decisions than the more usual pattern of having aid inversely related to fiscal resources.

It is a combination of the allocation of responsibility for state-local services, and the extent of state aid which determines, in part, the amounts of revenue which must be raised from local tax sources. As would be expected, the variations are very great. Per capita local taxes varied from $35.97 in South Carolina to $175.85 in New York, a substantially greater proportional variation than in the differences in local expenditures which varied from a low of $103 to a high of $310 per capita.

The chief source of local tax revenue is the property tax; this tax produced, in 1962, 88 percent of all local tax revenues. It is in spread cities, or portions thereof, where local nonproperty taxes have been most widely adopted. Although these taxes add a new dimension to the decision environment, the property tax usually remains the chief source of local taxes. In the case of New York City, even with its almost $600 million of non-property tax revenues, the property tax still contributed 69.6 percent of all local tax revenue in 1962.

The property tax varies greatly, too, in the content of its base. In all but four states both real and personal property are taxed, but even in these four the content of the base is by no means completely explained by the term "real." When both real and personal property are included in the base there is no way of knowing what property is taxed without examining the assessment rolls themselves.

Of particular significance is the proportion of the assessed base made up of different classes of property, for it is through these proportions that the contribution of different classes of property to total tax revenue is determined. In this instance assessed value is much more meaningful than "true" value. It is through specific assessment practices that it is possible to shift heavier fiscal responsibility from one class of property to another. There is, for example, great variation in the proportion which commercial and industrial property constitutes of total assessed value in different states. For the 22 states for which figures are available, commercial and industrial property constitute only 18.1 percent of the base in South Dakota, while the comparable percentage in South Carolina is 53.9.

These variations in fiscal characteristics, as between state and local governments and among local sub-systems, define a part of the differences among governmental systems. There are, however, at the local level, other significant differences which must be fitted to variations in fiscal characteristics before a complete classification is possible.

The Non-Fiscal Characteristics of Local Sub-systems

Each state-local system has operating within it a number of local governmental sub-systems. These local sub-systems can be classified by a number of characteristics. The most useful, perhaps, are functional inclusiveness, size of jurisdiction, and the jurisdictional assignment of land-use controls.

Functional inclusiveness is a measure of the generalness of governments operating in spread cities. The empirical fact of overlapping governments in metropolitan areas is well known but the actual variations in the extent of this phenomenon is often overlooked.

TABLE 2. GENERAL EXPENDITURES PER CAPITA IN CENTRAL CITY AREAS MADE BY CENTRAL CITY GOVERNMENTS AND OTHER OVERLYING GOVERNMENTS AND THEIR RELATIVE PROPORTIONS IN THE 24 LARGEST METROPOLITAN AREAS—1957.

City	Total General Expenditures Including Overlying Governments in Central City Area (Per Capita)	Central City Expenditures (Per Capita)	Central City Expenditures as a Percent of Total General Expenditure in Central City Area (Percent)
Atlanta	$158	$ 72	45.6%
Baltimore	199	189	95.0
Boston	273	258	94.5
Buffalo	193	142	73.6
Chicago	203	96	47.3
Cincinnati	246	138	56.1
Cleveland	180	88	48.9
Dallas	175	86	49.1
Detroit	202	111	55.0
Houston	155	61	39.4
Kansas City	157	86	54.8
Los Angeles	261	77	29.5
Long Beach	320	122	38.1
Milwaukee	229	101	44.1
Minneapolis	182	80	44.0
St. Paul	189	125	66.1
New York	257	237	92.2
Newark	243	181	74.5
Paterson	160	132	82.5
Clifton	141	113	80.1
Passaic	166	138	83.1
Philadelphia	165	109	66.1
Pittsburgh	188	88	46.8
St. Louis	147	91	61.9
San Diego	191	65	34.0
San Francisco	218	146	67.0
Oakland	231	89	38.5
Seattle	174	73	42.0
Washington, D. C.	234	224	95.7

Source: Bureau of the Census: Local Government Finances in Standard Metropolitan Areas, Vol. III, No. 6, *1957 Census of Governments*, U. S. Government Printing Office (Washington, D. C.), 1959.

One measure of functional inclusiveness is the proportion of total general governmental expenditures made in a particular jurisdiction by that jurisdiction itself. The central cities in metropolitan areas are among the most inclusive jurisdictions in the country but there is great variation even among these. The central cities in the 24 largest metropolitan areas vary in the proportion of general expenditures for which they are responsible within their own jurisdictional area from a low of 29.5 percent in Los Angeles to a high of 95.7 percent in Washington, D. C., with Baltimore, Boston, and New York all having proportions over 90 percent. Table 2 indicates the total per capita general expenditures in

TABLE 3. THE ALLOCATION AMONG GOVERNMENTAL JURISDICTIONS OF TAXES COLLECTED IN MUNICIPALITIES AND URBAN TOWNSHIPS OF OVER 50,000 POPULATION IN THE NEW YORK METROPOLITAN REGION—1962

	Allocation of Taxes Collected in the Municipalities and Urban Townships to:			
Cities/Villages	The Municipality Itself	The County	The School District	Per Capita Total Local Taxes
New York				
Mt. Vernon	44.1%	14.4%	41.5%	$163.42
New Rochelle	41.6	15.4	43.0	225.69
New York	100.0	—	—	219.87
White Plains	38.4	15.8	45.8	278.43
Yonkers	83.1	16.9	—	148.77
Connecticut				
Bridgeport	100.0	—	—	126.74
Norwalk	100.0	—	—	162.80
Stamford	100.0	—	—	192.55
New Jersey				
Bayonne	71.0	29.0	—	172.37
Clifton	77.3	22.8	—	139.08
East Orange	80.3	19.7	—	176.51
Elizabeth	89.1	10.9	—	144.15
Jersey City	82.4	17.6	—	191.47
Newark	85.2	14.8	—	194.89
Passaic	88.2	11.8	—	165.03
Paterson	88.5	11.5	—	130.95
Union	81.8	18.2	—	182.01
Urban Townships				
Connecticut				
Greenwich	100.0	—	—	221.76
New Jersey				
Bloomfield	74.9	25.0	—	167.34
Irvington	76.6	23.4	—	147.93
Union	23.7	19.9	56.5	155.50
Woodbridge	19.2	18.3	62.6	142.60

Sources: U. S. Bureau of the Census, *Compendium of City Government Finances in 1962*. Government Printing Office: Washington, D. C., 1963. New Jersey Taxpayers Association, *Financial Statistics of New Jersey Local Government*, September 1962. The Department of Audit and Control, State of New York. Unpublished data.

the central city areas and the proportion of these for which the central cities themselves are responsible for 1957.[9]

Functional inclusiveness also is related to local fiscal interdependence since the more governments operative in the same area the more taxing units there will be drawing on the same tax base. For any specific piece of property in a spread city the result may be the imposition of from one to a dozen tax rates on variable tax bases. Because of the multiplicity of special districts it is impossible in many areas to measure fiscal burden by any areal unit larger than individual parcels of property. Where there is greater functional inclusiveness or where the multiple units of government tend to be coterminous, it is possible to calculate burden by governmental unit rather than by individual pieces of property.

This characteristic is reflected through the substantial differences, even within the same spread city, in the division of taxes collected in a particular area by jurisdictions in that area. In the inclusive jurisdictions all taxes will go to the jurisdiction itself, while in other cases it will be divided among various jurisdictions operating in the same area. Table 3 shows the division of taxes collected within each municipality and urban township of over 50,000 population in the New York Metropolitan Region. In the case of the functional inclusive jurisdictions of Connecticut, all of it goes to the municipality; in New York it may all go to the municipality or may be shared by the municipality, the county and the school district.[10]

Jurisdictional geographic size is separate from but related to the characteristic of functional inclusiveness. Jurisdictions may be small but inclusive or large but fragmented. There are regional patterns, with exceptions, for this characteristic. New England (towns) and the South (counties) tend to have small but inclusive jurisdictions. The rest of the country combines large and small jurisdictions in the same area with a tendency to non-inclusiveness.

Finally, there are vast differences across the country in the jurisdictional assignment of land-use controls. In fact, in some instances these controls may be divided between these smaller jurisdictions and the county, with the addition power may be assigned to municipalities or towns while the planning power is divided between these smaller jurisdicitons and the county, with the addition recently of many regional planning agencies, usually advisory. The mix of these fiscal, structural and power characteristics will probably be different for every spread city in the country. Each particular mix carries with it implications for the public official who must seek the interest of his jurisdiction within the framework of the system within which he is operating.

One very clear example of the impact which differences in just the fiscal system may have can be shown through its impact on land-use zoning. A great deal has been written in recent years about fiscal zoning, i.e., the adoption of zoning practices which attempt to maximize the revenue gain from new land uses. The practice is usually deplored on the grounds that fiscal criteria for zoning are inferior to other criteria.[11]

Whatever the merits of fiscal zoning there are some situations where it is more attractive than in others. Where there is a high allocation of local expenditure responsibility and low state aid, the pressure on the local tax base will be very great. Fiscal zoning in this situation makes a great deal more sense than in the case where both state responsibility and state aid are high.

Other examples of the impact of the fiscal variables could be provided, but the addition of the governmental variables—functional inclusiveness, size of jurisdictions and land-use control—presents a more realistic picture of the decision environment. In one kind of situation these variables can reduce the complexity of the environment. Again using fiscal zoning as the policy area, the larger a local government jurisdiction is and the wider the range of governmental functions it performs, the simpler (although still difficult) is the calculation of possible financial gain from fiscal zoning. Further, the impact on other local governments drawing from the same tax base is eliminated when there are no other local governments operating in the same area.

The more common situation of small and overlapping jurisdictions presents a more complex picture. Assume the existence of several jurisdictions relying on the same tax base combined with high state aid for one type of jurisdiction. Another type jurisdiction in the same area, perhaps the county, may receive relatively little state aid while possessing high fiscal responsibility for those functions which it does perform, thereby placing a rather severe strain on its tax base. For the county, therefore, it may make good fiscal sense to zone heavily (if it possesses the zoning power) for land uses which are fiscally productive or, even if it does not have zoning power, to vigorously promote new industries for the area.

In the same area, however, the school districts may receive substantial state aid and this aid will normally be inversely related to property value per student. While the county, therefore, is increasing the tax base to improve its fiscal position, the school districts drawing on that same base will find that their property value per student is going up and, as a result, state aid will decline. The losses to the school district might well exceed the net gain which the county experiences through the improvement in its revenue base. Of particular interest is the lack of any governmental mechanism below the state able to even consider this kind of conflict situation, to say nothing of resolving it.

Governmental Systems in the New York Metropolitan Region

The existence of quite different state-local governmental systems is well illustrated by the neighboring states of New York, New Jersey and Connecticut, all of which have within their boundaries a part of the spread city of New York. Relative to the rest of the country, these states are all strong local-effort states as measured by per capita local taxes, but the similarity stops with this characteristic. In terms of local expenditures per capita, New York and New Jersey rank considerably ahead of Connecticut, while New York and Connecticut are considerably stronger state-aid states than New Jersey. Connecticut and New Jersey tend to have small general governmental jurisdictions; while the New York system is characterized by a fragmented governmental system with a great amount of overlapping.

Some of the differences in the assignment of functional responsibilities to municipalities and urban townships is shown in Table 4. All of the jurisdictions listed provide the normal municipal functions of fire, police, street maintenance and sanitation but here the similarity ends. Of the other functions included in the table only New York City provides them all, while some provide none beyond

Table 4. Assignment of Functional Responsibilities and Per Capita Expenditures of Municipalities and Urban Townships over 50,000 Population in the New York Metropolitan Region—for Selected Functions—1962.

	Per Capita General Expenditures (own)	Education	Higher Education	Categorical Public Welfare	Non-Categorical Public Welfare	Sewerage and Sewerage Disposal	Hospital	Housing and Urban Renewal	Utilities Water	Utilities Other
Cities/Villages										
New York State										
Mt. Vernon	$113.56	−	−	−	−	+	+	+	+	−
New Rochelle	170.31	+	−	−	−	+	+	+	−	−
New York	332.34	+	+	+	+	+	+	+	+	+
White Plains	139.90	−	−	−	−	+	−	+	+	−
Yonkers	200.89	+	−	−	−	+	−	+	+	−
Connecticut										
Bridgeport	158.55	+	−	−	+	+	+	+	−	−
Norwalk	251.89	+	−	−	+	+	−	+	−	−
Stamford	246.76	+	−	−	+	+	−	+	−	−
New Jersey										
Bayonne	150.05	+	−	−	+	+	+	−	+	−
Clifton	155.17	+	−	−	+	+	−	−	−	−
East Orange	161.45	+	−	−	+	+	+	−	+	−
Elizabeth	155.90	+	−	−	+	+	+	+	+	−
Jersey City	204.17	+	−	−	+	+	+	+	+	−
Newark	230.66	+	−	−	+	+	+	+	+	−
Passaic	166.13	+	−	−	+	+	+	+	−	−
Patterson	164.36	+	−	−	+	+	+	−	−	−
Union	156.88	+	−	−	+	+	−	−	−	−
Urban Township										
Connecticut										
Greenwich	294.57	+	−	−	+	+	+	−	−	−
New Jersey										
Bloomfield	162.13	+	−	−	−	+	−	−	+	−
Irvington	152.95	+	−	−	−	+	+	−	−	−
Union	76.30	−	−	−	−	+	−	−	−	−
Woodbridge	58.97	−	−	−	−	+	−	−	−	−

Source: U.S. Bureau of the Census, *Compendium of City Government Finances in 1962.*

the basic municipal services. A great deal of the differences in per capita total expenditures are explained by these differences in functional assignment which, in turn, have an influence on the nature of the decision environment.

In a study of state aid in New York State,[12] six distinct sub-systems of local government were found to exist. These six systems are in stark contrast to the two which exist in Connecticut and the three in New Jersey. Since all of these systems are operative in the spread city of New York, it means that for this area there are three state-local systems and eleven sub-systems.

Each of these systems carries its own imperatives for the local official administering it. The overlapping situation in New York, for example, might well cause jurisdictions to follow conflicting policies in relation to their common tax base. In contrast, the small functionally inclusive jurisdictions in New Jersey and Connecticut would be able to follow consistent intra-jurisdictional policies. Area-wide consistency in these states, however, would be unlikely while large area coordination is a possibility in New York because of its relatively strong counties. However, even here the lack of zoning power at the county level reduces the potential for such coordination.

The point is simply that it is not particularly useful to try to analyze the decision-making system in metropolitan areas on the assumption that the determinants of the environment are the same in all spread cities or even are alike in all parts of the same spread city. The need, as expressed by H. Douglas Price in discussing the politics of state-local government, is for comparative studies. He says, "The study of state and local politics is, of necessity, a problem in comparative government." He deplores the fact that "it has been treated as almost everything else: a problem in administrative organization, a matter of constitutional law, a question of 'power elites' or no 'power elites,' and so forth." [13] The need is no less urgent for comparative studies of state-local governmental systems and their local sub-systems, especially as they operate in urban areas.

Governmental Systems and the Local Official

For the local official, in contrast to the student of government, the need is not to understand all the governmental systems in the country but rather to understand his own jurisdiction and its relation to those of his neighbors. His role is to fit the policies for his jurisdiction to his own system in a way which will promote the interests of that jurisdiction. In one situation this might require him to push very hard for an increase in the industrial base of his community; in another his emphasis might better be placed on increasing state aid; in another his interest might be better served by trying to move a function to a higher level of government.

The only meaningful generalization possible is that he will try to serve the interest of his particular jurisdiction as he sees it. That interest is likely to be seen in terms of maximizing services and minimizing costs (however inconsistent these goals may be, both are sought), and maintaining an environment which fits the jurisdiction's image of itself.[14] To accomplish these ends will require very different decisions in different jurisdictions. For example, it is likely that the public finance differences already discussed may well cause the New Jersey portion of the New York spread city to emphasize fiscal zoning much more heavily than the New York portion. In Connecticut, with categorical welfare a state function, but with small functionally inclusive jurisdictions competing for revenue base, the pressure for fiscal zoning probably would rank between New Jersey and New York.

There are situations, of course, which lead to inter-local cooperation. Certain problems cannot be solved by an individual jurisdiction acting alone. In the areas of water supply, sewerage disposal, air pollution control, and transportation, the need for inter-local cooperation is most obvious. To the extent that local jurisdictions performing these functions in the same area can see a gain for themselves in inter-local cooperation, it is predictable that after a due amount of negotiation some form of inter-local cooperation will take place. The form of the cooperation can vary from an actual inter-local contract or agreement for the performance of the service to the movement of the service to a higher level of government or to the creation of a special jurisdiction specifically for that function.[15]

The possibility of gain relates, in part, to the governmental system operative in an area. For example, cooperation in sharing welfare costs is unlikely when the welfare function is assigned to municipalities rather than to a larger jurisdiction. Welfare needs tend to be concentrated in the core area of the spread city, although it can be argued that the financial responsibility for the function ought to be region-wide. As Harvey Brazer says, "To the extent that suburban communities, through zoning regulations and discriminatory practices in rentals and real estate transactions, contribute directly to the concentration in the central city of socio-economic groups which impose heavy demands upon local government services, they are in fact, exploiting the central city."[16]

It seems unlikely, however, that the central city could convince its suburban neighbors that they should assume a part of the fiscal responsibility for these costs. The city, of course, is left the political alternative of attempting to have the function performed at the state level and, as already pointed out, in a good number of states it has been moved to this level. Another alternative is to retain the expenditure responsibility at the local level and yet reduce the direct costs to the local taxpayer by having the service more generously aided by the state.

Again, the significant calculation for the local official is the determination of the interest of his local jurisdiction. Because of the different governmental systems which surround each local official, it is not possible to predict the impact of the sum of the decisions made by all local officials in a particular urban area on the general well-being of the whole area. The only accurate generalization is that if the interests of the whole area are served it is a result of chance rather than design.

On the other hand, it should not be assumed, as it often is, that the general interest of a spread city is necessarily damaged by a fragmented decision environment. The outcome depends, of course, on how that interest is defined. For example, it is quite possible that the multiplicity of school districts in a spread city causes competition among these districts to provide high quality education. The result could well be a higher average quality of education for the area than would result from a one-jurisdiction education system. On the other hand expenditures might be lower in a one-jurisdiction system. For other functions the result could be the opposite. In the case of fire protection, for example, it would often be the case that quality of service over the whole area would be improved if there were a one-jurisdiction system, but expenditures probably would be higher. These results would follow from the professionalization of the service and the water supply requirements it would impose throughout the spread city area.

Jurisdictional Conflict and the County. These illustrations point up again one of the major characteristics of most spread-city governmental systems: the impact of decisions by one jurisdiction on the neighboring jurisdictions. The present system has no decision-making focus below the state to resolve conflict situations which emerge from this system. The potential for conflict has led many to advocate the adoption of some kind of metropolitan-wide government.

There is neither space nor the inclination to argue the merits or demerits of this proposal. It is enough to say that it is politically impossible, in most of our metropolitan areas, to accomplish this kind of fundamental change. Further, apart from the political issue surrounding metropolitan government, there are some positive virtues in attempting to adjust present local governmental systems in a way which will make it possible for them to resolve their conflicts of interest.

The unit most able, outside of New England, to assume a large role in performing this responsibility is the county. This unit is the most encompassing jurisdiction in many of America's spread cities. Leaving aside the special New England situation,[17] the county does include all the other types of local jurisdiction: towns, municipal corporations, school districts, special districts and authorities. There are, of course, metropolitan areas which include more than one county and emerging from this fact is the necessity for inter-county cooperation in multi-county spread cities. Within these larger areas the counties are sufficiently diverse within their own boundaries that the leaders are more likely to understand the interdependence of the area than is true with small urban town and village officials who, of necessity, see their jurisdiction's interests in provincial terms. Their social and economic homogeneity makes such provincialism inevitable.

Another advantage is that the county is a strong unit politically. The party system is normally based on the county committee. This relationship of the county to the political party system should enhance its ability to accomplish changes through the state legislature.

Despite the county's advantages in jurisdictional and political terms it has disadvantages relative to its power and structure. The county is weak, structurally, in a variety of ways. First, and perhaps most important, it often lacks an executive head. It is governed, in some parts of the country, by a board made up of representatives from the townships within the county and these representatives are likely to take their township responsibilities more seriously than their county obligations. In other sections of the country the county board, although representative of only county interests possesses some of the weaknesses of the city-commission form of government. Another structural weakness is caused by the election of many administrative officials. Such elections provide these officials with independent political bases and restrict the board's potential for county-wide administrative leadership. In terms of power the county's primary role to date, as agent of the state and its rural background, has tended to restrict the amount of general legislative power granted to it by the state.

If reform is needed a means should be found of capitalizing on the county's jurisdictional and political advantages while overcoming its power and structural weaknesses. The role of the federal government through its planning grants could help with this strengthening as could appropriate state policies.

Summary

The spread city does impose a new environment on the local administrator. His task of finding the interest of his jurisdiction is made immensely complicated by this new form of human settlement. Further, the fragmentation of government within the spread city guarantees that policies for the area will be the sum of the individual policies of the jurisdictions which exist within it, plus whatever policy imposition is made by the state or encouraged by the federal government.

The federal government has an increasing role in these areas but thus far has developed no coherent policy orientation toward them. It is possible that there is beginning to emerge at the federal level some concern for such coherence—as expressed, for example, in the recently imposed planning requirements in many substantive programs,[18] plus the potential role of the Senate-passed bill requiring advisory metropolitan-wide planning agencies.[19]

As the federal government moves more and more into the provision of aid to local governments and develops planning requirements to qualify for such aid, its role in the state-local systems and local sub-systems will be enhanced. Its impact will obviously vary from system to system.

Over-all, the present systems of government in the United States lack uniformity. For the local administrator this characteristic requires the development of a strategy and a set of tactics which fit his own system. For the student of government the need is to develop a way of classifying governmental systems which aids in understanding the public policies that emerge from them. The variables which must be included in such a classification (there undoubtedly are others) are:

(1) The allocation of expenditure and revenue responsibilities between state and local governments and between local governments
(2) The system of state aid
(3) The nature of the property tax
(4) The degree of functional inclusiveness
(5) Geographic size of local jurisdictions
(6) The jurisdictional assignment of land use and other controls

A realistic analysis of the behavior of local officials and the policies they pursue in the spread city must take into account the unique mix of these factors. It is this mix which constitutes the decision making framework of state-local governmental systems.

Notes

This article is based on a paper delivered at the American Society for Public Administration Annual Meeting in New York, April 15–18, 1964. Professors Campbell and Sacks are currently engaged in an analysis of the effects of state aid on taxes in metropolitan areas sponsored by the Brookings Institution and being carried out at the Maxwell Graduate School of Syracuse University. Assisting in this study are Woo Sik Kee and Yong Hyo Cho, who also contributed to this article.

1. Melvin M. Webber, "Order in Diversity: Community Without Propinquity" in *Cities and Space: The Future Use of Urban Land* (Lowdon Wingo, Jr., ed.), The Johns Hopkins Press, 1963, p. 23.

2. Regional Plan Association, *Spread City: Projections of Development Trends and the Issues they Pose: The Tri-State New York Metropolitan Region 1960–85.* Bulletin 100, September 1962, p. 3.

3. Melvin M. Webber, *op. cit.*, p. 18.

4. Council of State Governments (John C. Bollens, Director of Study): *The States and the Metropolitan Problem,* 1956. "The basis of the problem is the absence of general local government organizations broad enough to cope with metropolitan matters." p. 17.

5. For a discussion of the implications of fragmentation which does not accept the easy assumption of a need for area-wide government see Vincent Ostrom, Charles M. Tiebout and Robert Warren, "The Organization of Government in Metropolitan Areas: A Theoretical Inquiry," *The American Political Science Review,* Vol. LV, No. 4 (December 1961), pp. 831–842.

6. General expenditure and revenue, rather than total, are used throughout this analysis in order to avoid comparing non-comparable packages of public services. Following the Census Bureau's definition, general expenditures include "all expenditures other than (a) benefit and refund payments of public-employee-retirement and other social-insurance systems and (b) spending for state and local liquor stores and for local water, electric, transit, and gas utilities." General revenue includes all revenue "except utility and liquor store revenue and insurance trust revenue."

7. A comprehensive analysis of the impact of the allocation systems on fiscal behavior at the national and metropolitan levels will be provided in the forthcoming Brookings-sponsored study. As a part of this general study a Ph.D. dissertation by Yong Hyo Cho is attempting to measure the determinants of the allocation systems.

8. Selma J. Mushkin, "Intergovernmental Aspects of Local Expenditure Decisions" in *Public Expenditure Decisions in the Urban Community* (Howard G. Schaller, ed.), The Johns Hopkins Press, 1963.

9. In a forthcoming Ph.D. dissertation done as a part of the Brookings study, Woo Sik Kee has analyzed the local fiscal patterns of all central cities in terms of their functional inclusiveness.

10. It should be noted that this comparison understates the complexity of the governmental pattern in New York State since it omits the unincorporated areas.

11. Regional Plan Association, *op. cit.* "Tax considerations, in short, will play an expanding role in land development decisions, weakening the chance of planning for the best possible use of the land, unless the sources of local government revenues are modified." p. 3.

12. Seymour Sacks, Robert Harris, and John Carroll. *The State and Local Government. . . . The Role of State Aid,* Comptroller's Studies in Local Finance, No. 3, 1963.

13. "Comparative Analysis in State and Local Politics: Potential and Problems." Paper prepared for delivery at 1963 Annual Meeting of American Political Science Association. (Mimeo)

14. This image is a product of objective socio-economic characteristics as well as community aspirations. A comprehensive picture of the behavior of local officials would have to include both these classes of variables.

15. For a comprehensive description of the cooperative techniques which are emerging in metropolitan areas see Roscoe Martin, *Metropolis in Transition,* Housing and Home Finance Agency, Washington 1963.

16. Some Fiscal Implications of Metropolitanism" in *Metropolitan Issues: Social, Governmental, Fiscal,* Guthrie S. Birkhead, ed. (Syracuse University, Maxwell Graduate School, 1962), p. 77.

17. It is interesting to note that Connecticut, since abolishing its counties, has found it useful to establish regional planning units.

18. See Advisory Commission on Intergovernmental Relations, *Impact of Federal Urban Development Programs on Local Government Organization and Planning*. 1964, Government Printing Office, Washington, D. C.

19. For a discussion of the implications of this bill see *Metropolitan Planning:* Hearings Before the Subcommittee on Intergovernmental Relations of the Committee on Government Operations, U. S. Senate, Eighty-Eighth Congress, First Session, 1963.

THE CITY AND THE POOR: THE SHORTCOMINGS OF PRESENT HOUSING AND ANTI-POVERTY PROGRAMS, AND SOME ALTERNATIVE PROPOSALS FOR ELIMINATING SLUMS AND POVERTY

Herbert J. Gans

A hard and realistic look at any American city in 1965 indicates that little has so far been done to improve the physical environment or the living conditions of the low-income population. Everywhere most poor people inhabit poor neighborhoods, and more often than not, slums. They must endure overcrowded apartments in rotting buildings, located in areas inadequately supplied with municipal services—from ancient schools to ineffective garbage removal and vermin control. It is no wonder, then, that these areas rank high in all the indices of poverty and deprivation: infant mortality, mental illness, crime, delinquency, alcoholism, and narcotics addiction.

The Shortcomings of Present Housing Programs

Federal and local housing policies to do away with the slums and with poverty have not yet become effective. Waiting lists for public housing are long in many cities, but very few new units are being built: only 60,000 are authorized by Congress annually. The existing public housing projects have undoubtedly improved physical living conditions, but they have not helped people socially or psychologically. Too often, they were built as huge high-rise complexes which are unsuitable for families with small children. Also, they are located in ghettos and thus increase racial segregation, and by being limited to poor people, they publicly mark their tenants as unworthy and inadequate. This differentiation is reinforced by a variety of regulations which restrict the activities and associations of the tenants, and require them to practice standards of housekeeping and decorum higher than those expected in a luxury apartment house. Finally, in many cities, pubic housing does not admit the very poorest people, and it excludes families with illegitimate children or delinquent teenagers. These restrictions are partly to prevent political opponents of public housing from attacking it for sheltering "undesirables," but they add to the tenants' feelings that society considers them less than first-class citizens.

Urban renewal is a vital and still growing program, but in most cities, its impact on the low income population has been even more negative than that of public housing. Slums have been torn down, of course, but more often than not they have been replaced by high-priced housing which the slum dwellers cannot afford, or by shopping centers and public or semi-public facilities which rarely invite or benefit the poor. This pattern of rebuilding the cleared sites would have

---

Prepared for a symposium, "The Troubled Environment," Washington D. C., December 1965, sponsored by the ACTION Council for Better Cities. Portions of this paper were printed as "Slum Housing: Doing Something About the War on Slums," *Commonweal*, 83 (March 1966), pp. 688–693. Reprinted by permission of the author and *Commonweal.*

been acceptable if it has been preceded by proper relocation of the displaced in decent inexpensive housing, but so far, this has usually not been the case.

Studies made of renewal projects completed during the late 1950's and the early 1960's show clearly that urban renewal in most instances worsened the lot of the slum dwellers.[1] Because of the slowdown in public housing and the absence of other federal programs to construct more low-income units, the net effect of urban renewal was to reduce even more the already scarce supply of housing that poor people could afford. Most displaced slum dwellers had to relocate in other slums, and if they were Negroes—as they were in two-thirds of the cases—to overcrowd the ghetto even further. Those who found decent relocation housing—and even those who moved to other slums—usually had to pay higher rents. Many had to pay a third or more of their income for shelter, even though because of their poverty and instability of income, they should be paying less than the 20 percent of income usually considered an equitable rent. When clearance destroyed entire neighborhoods, the displaced were also saddled with social and emotional burdens, for they lost institutions that had served them well, and were separated from family members, old friends, and long-time neighbors.[2] Storekeepers suffered as well, for relocation payments were inadequate, and about a third are known to have gone out of business.[3] In short, these studies indicate that the slum dwellers were paying high financial, social, and emotional costs so that affluent people and affluent institutions, subsidized by generous federal renewal grants, could move on to the cleared sites.

Since 1960, the promiscuous use of the bulldozer has been slowed down, and in some cities, urban renewal has come to a virtual halt. Rehabilitation is now replacing clearance, sometimes without requiring relocation. In most instances, the net effect has been the same as clearance, however, for when rents in rehabilitated dwellings rose, their poor occupants were priced out. Where clearance still takes place, relocation procedures have improved, but in cities where there is a shortage of inexpensive housing and where Negroes are restricted to the ghetto, it is doubtful that the improvement in procedures has helped the displaced slum dwellers. The 221 (d) program for building low-cost housing and the recently passed rent supplement legislation will make it possible to create more relocation housing, but both programs are new and small in scale, and Congress has not yet appropriated funds to implement the rent supplement measure. Thus urban renewal is not improving the living conditions of the slum dwellers, and in too many cities, it is still making them worse.

This conclusion is at variance with official reports by the Urban Renewal Administration, which claim that about 80% of the relocated are rehoused properly, and with a recent Census Bureau survey of relocation in 132 cities, conducted for the Housing and Home Finance Administration, which reported that 94% of the relocatees had moved into standard housing. Unfortunately, however, the study was inadequate in many ways, and its conclusions must therefore be questioned.[4] For one thing, it surveyed only people *relocated* by local agencies, not all those *displaced* by the renewal project, thus leaving out of the study the people who leave a project area before they can be contacted by renewal officials. These sometimes constitute up to half the project population, and the available evidence suggests that many of them flee to other slums. Also, the sample of cities used in the survey was unrepresentative of the typical large or medium sized city, for fully 53% of the relocatees were reported to have moved into single family housing. This would be possible only in small cities and towns. The definition of standard relocation housing used in the study was quite liberal, including units considered deteriorated but not dilapidated by Census criteria. Moreover, half the relocatees were now paying 28% or more of their income for rent.

Until more reliable studies are made of current relocation practices, one must conclude that urban renewal is still not helping the slum dwellers except in those cities where inexpensive good housing is plentiful. Moreover, the urban renewal program is still too small to stem the creation of new slums.

Even a larger urban renewal program with adequate relocation provisions would not resolve the main problems of the low-income population. Studies among people moved from slums into public housing projects indicate that they benefit only minimally from the move. New units improve their housing conditions, of course, and raise their morale a little, but they do not reduce their poverty or the deprivations and pathologies associated with it.[5] Housing schemes can do little to help the poor—the real need is for effective anti-poverty programs to allow the low income population to share in the rights and opportunities of their more affluent neighbors. Such programs can be carried out in conjunction with improved renewal and other housing activities, but they are much more urgent than efforts to improve the physical environment.

There are several reasons for this conclusion. First, it should be obvious that giving a poor person good housing does not eliminate his poverty, whereas removing his poverty enables him to obtain good housing and the other attributes of the American standard of living. Second, two decades of experience with public housing suggest that constructing housing specifically for poor people publicly stigmatizes them as disadvantaged, and reduces further their dignity and their ability to live as they choose. In a democratic society which stresses freedom of choice, federal policy ought to improve the economic and social conditions of the disadvantaged so as to enable them to select the housing they want and can afford like other Americans. In other words, poor people should not be relegated to ghettoes but should be enabled to participate in the housing market like everyone else.

Third, it can be shown that effective anti-poverty programs will do more in the long run to improve the physical environment than urban renewal and other housing and planning efforts. If one runs through the catalogue of urban problems, it is apparent that most of these problems are caused not by the city and its physical environment, but by poverty and racial discrimination. Slums and the pathological social conditions within them are not the result of the aging or deteriorating housing, for when there is demand for such housing from affluent buyers, it is quickly turned into middle- and upper-income dwellings. This has recently happened in many American cities, for example, in Washington's Georgetown, Chicago's Old Town, and New York's Greenwich Village and East Village. Rather, slums come into being when poor and nonwhite people cannot afford to participate equitably in the housing market and are forced to overcrowd buildings and areas, thus creating blighted conditions.

Similarly, downtown retail districts are running down because the poor people who live near them cannot afford to shop in their stores. Municipal services are so often inadequate because they are neither adapted to, nor well enough financed to meet the needs of low income people. For example, urban schools are poor because they have not yet learned how to teach children from deprived homes, and because they lack the funds to establish the smaller classes and to hire the numbers and kinds of teachers needed to teach their disadvantaged students. Tax revenues are insufficient to maintain and modernize the city because the middle class exodus to the suburbs is in part, though only in part, a reaction to the failure of the city to assimilate the large and increasing proportion of poverty-stricken city residents. Finally, crime, delinquency, drug addiction, and similar pathologies are not produced by the city or its physical environment, but are self-destructive and socially destructive expressions of the lack of opportunity and hope in the lives of the poverty-stricken. In short, the physical and social deterioration of the city can be traced largely to the effects of poverty and discrimination.

Over the past decade, cities have attempted to cope with this deterioration through urban renewal, downtown modernization, and by other development schemes intended to bring the middle class back to the city and to increase municipal revenues. These efforts are likely to fail, for physical methods of dealing with social problems always fail, as do solutions which do not attack the root causes of these problems. The attractions of suburbia are too strong to bring significant numbers of the middle class back to the city, and indeed, studies of people's residential aspirations indicate that yet more want to go to the suburbs.[6] The stores which have moved out to serve the new suburbanites will not come back either, and nor will industry, which needs larger and more adequately located sites than the city can provide. Thus, in the long run, residential and commercial renewal plans for downtown will not hold back the shrinkage of the central retail areas or the deterioration of its older blocks, and they will not produce enough middle class returnees or tax benefits to hold back the further deterioration of the city.

If the sources of the city's problems are principally those of poverty and racial discrimination, the best solution is to eliminate both these evils. When poor people can afford to live in decent houses and decent neighborhoods, they will also be able to afford and want a decent city. Indeed, they will want very much the same kind of city which planners and architects are now seeking to achieve through policies of environmental improvement alone. Consequently, the best way of improving the physical environment is to bring the living conditions of the poor up to the American standard. This requires a comprehensive anti-poverty program, complemented by an equally comprehensive urban rehousing program designed to support the anti-poverty effort. The remainder of the paper will describe briefly some proposals for both programs.

Proposals for an Effective Anti-Poverty Program

Like urban renewal, the programs of the War on Poverty have not yet begun to meet the needs of those for whom they are intended. At present, the anti-poverty effort emphasizes education job training, and improved social services;

programs which seek to change the poor, rather than those which will eliminate poverty. Job training programs which cannot offer jobs to the trained are ineffective, however; and the Job Corps and other new educational techniques cannot induce much interest in learning if the children have no assurance that they will be able to find work after graduation. Better social services are helpful, but so far, these have not often reached the really poor. Community action programs may begin to organize poor neighborhoods, but they cannot do away with the fact that the poor are an economic and racial minority in a political system in which the affluent white majority is as yet unwilling to provide them with a greater share of the society's wealth.

The present anti-poverty program has been in existence for little more than a year, and like urban renewal, it will undoubtedly improve with age. Yet progress must not only be faster than in the case of renewal, now fifteen years old, but it must also include a drastic change toward schemes that will do away with poverty.

Such a program must have at least four basic components: abolition of unemployment, raising of incomes, elimination of racial discrimination, and improvement in municipal and social services. The most important component is the abolition of unemployment. If people have good and well-paying jobs, they can participate more equitably in the affluent society, including its housing market. Since many of the unemployed are unskilled and semiskilled, and automation and other technological changes are reducing the demand for low-skill jobs, such jobs will have to be created in new ways. And since the new technology increases productivity without increasing employment, private enterprise can no longer be counted on to create new jobs.

As a result, this function will have to be taken over by the government, and I am sure the day will come when job-creation will be a regular and accepted role of local, state, and federal governments. One way of creating jobs is by a massive rehousing program to replace urban renewal. This will be described in the next section of the paper. Another is to set up a giant public works program to improve the cities and the quality of municipal services for everyone by building the schools, hospitals, clinics, libraries, recreation facilities, mass transit systems, pollution control installations and other facilities which every city needs. A third is to upgrade the quality of all public services by hiring more people for them. A fourth is to improve the quality of the helping professions—education, social work, medicine, recreation and others—by hiring "subprofessionals" who can assist the overworked professionals.[7] Once subprofessional jobs are available, and job training methods are perfected, low income and unemployed people can be trained for subprofessional work. They can be particularly useful in improving the quality of professional services to other poor people, because unlike middle class professionals, they can communicate more easily with poor clients, and adapt the professional services to their needs. This may make it possible to end the present under-utilization of health, welfare, and other services by the people who need these services the most.

Second, decent incomes must also be provided for those who cannot work. This means income subsidies, and the best way of providing these is through direct income grants, perhaps in the form of the negative income tax. Such grants are not only a more effective way of reducing poverty than welfare or dependency payments, or unemployment compensation, but they are also less punitive and degrading. Public welfare payments are based on the assumption that their recipients are unwilling to work, and must therefore be punished by low payments; by regulation which prescribe how the payments must be spent, and how their recipients ought to live; and by investigators who invade their lives and their privacy to make sure the regulations are enforced. In a society where poverty is largely a result of job scarcity and racial discrimination, such treatment is unjustifiable. Dependency programs such as Aid to Families with Dependent Children are equally undesirable because they encourage families to separate in order to obtain payments. Since the money is given to mothers rather than to families, the results are particularly undesirable in the Negro community, for this system maintains the superior economic and familial role of the mother, and thus helps to keep the Negro man in the inferior and marginal familial role he has occupied since slavery. Unemployment compensation is too low as well and too short in duration, and it does not increase with family size. Finally, the minimum wage, which is another form of income subsidy, is also too low, for the people who earn such a wage cannot possibly support a family, particularly in the cities. Therefore, the minimum wage must either be raised, or complemented by federal wage supplements which function like the recently approved rent supplements. In the long run, however, all these subsidies ought to be replaced by direct income grants.

The third component of an effective anti-poverty program is the elimination of racial discrimination. Much of the urban low income population is nonwhite, and many of its problems are the result of exclusion from good jobs, decent neighborhoods, good schools, and equitable political representation at the local level because of race. Racial discrimination is not easily abolished, although where effective legislation is available and enforced, it is at least being reduced. However, much of what appears to be racial discrimination is really class discrimination, resulting from middle and working class fears of lower class people and the pathological behavior associated with poverty. If jobs and higher incomes are available, these class fears will be reduced, and the white society will find it easier to accept nonwhites as equals.

The fourth component is the improvement of municipal and social services to the low income population to help it overcome the ravages of poverty, and take advantage of economic and other opportunities. Schools must not only be desegregated, for segregated ones teach inferiority by their very existence, but they must also be improved so that children from low income families are able to learn. Even so, their willingness to learn is not likely to increase until they are sure that jobs will await them when they finish their education. Similar improvements must be made in medical care, mental health, social work, recreation, and all other public services which have so far been unable to reach the core of the poverty-stricken because they have not hired the kinds of staff members who can adapt the services to the needs of the poor and can then persuade them to make use of these services.

Proposals for a Comprehensive Rehousing Program

The fifth component of an effective anti-poverty program is the improvement of the physical environment *for the low income population.* I underline the words for the low income population, because any schemes for environmental improvement that do not affect it are useless, and indeed harmful, because they only increase the constantly widening gap between the poor and the affluent. Unfortunately, most present planning programs have this effect. For example, the construction of expressways help the suburbanite and the car-owning city dweller, but not the low income population which relies on mass transit. Central business district modernization caters to the affluent residents who use its stores; and civic or cultural centers benefit the middle classes who make use of such facilities, but they are almost entirely irrelevant to the poor. Similarly, industrial parks provide jobs mainly for highly skilled workers; the nonwhite low income population works more often in loft industries which are now frequently condemned as slums and are torn down without adequate relocation provisions.

We cannot argue, as we have in the past, that if poor people have to live in overcrowded slums, one way of improving their condition is to give them a beautiful city or more open space as a substitute for decent housing. They may want a beautiful city as much as everyone else, but given their poverty many other improvements are of higher priority. People who are too poor to shop downtown are not impressed by shopping malls, and people who see city hall as a source of deprivation cannot appreciate a new city hall or an award-winning civic center. More open space is also of low priority, particularly if it would require the clearance of yet more inexpensive housing. In the eyes of a poor beholder, the attractive city that architects and planners propose is a mirage that makes his own desert even more degrading and unbearable.

A program for improving the urban environment must therefore deal with the environment of the poverty-stricken, and in this environment the feature most urgently in need of change is the slum. Not all dwelling units that look like slums to the middle class observer are actually slums, but some are a danger to health and all are a source of discomfort to their occupants.[8] Similarly, not all low income neighborhoods are slums, but in some, the presence of drug addicts and other sick people exposes residents to theft and violence, and also tempts those predisposed to drugs and delinquency by their constant availability on the street. As I noted before, moving people out of slums cannot by itself improve their living conditions, but as part of an anti-poverty effort, it is the first priority of an urban improvement program.

The shortcomings of public housing and urban renewal require a replacement by a large, federally supported *rehousing program* with three major features: the construction of new housing for slum dwellers, low-income people, and others; the expansion of the rent supplement scheme to allow them and yet others to leave the slums, both for new and for better older housing; and the *subsequent* clearance or rehabilitation of the slums themselves.

The first step in such a program is the building of new housing for low income people. Instead of public housing, the new units should be like those now being built for middle income buyers and tenants, including single family homes and apartments, whether subsidized by F.H.A. or by direct federal, state, and local grants. Such housing should be open to middle and low income people alike, and a certain proportion of the units should be reserved for the latter. Poor people should be enabled to rent them by a greatly expanded rent supplement program. The present program should also be revised, first by letting tenants eventually buy the units if they wish, and more important, by providing supplements when rents are beyond 20% of income, rather than the unreasonably high figure of 25% of the present scheme. This housing and rent supplement program, when combined with the other anti-poverty measures I described previously, should make it possible for poor people to choose the same kinds of housing in the same way as all other Americans.

The new housing must be built on vacant land in the city, on presently commercial or industrial land that would be better used for housing, and most important, on vacant land beyond the city limits. It must be provided in the suburbs and also in the new towns which are now being developed near some cities, and proposed for many others. Needless to say, the new housing must be racially integrated wherever it is put up.

Building integrated housing in the suburbs and the new towns is difficult, for not only do many middle class whites want to keep out nonwhite neighbors, but until job opportunities for nonwhites are available, few of them will be able to move out of the city. However, it must be done for those who can move out, in order to begin to reduce ghetto densities, and to make it possible eventually to eliminate the ghetto through urban renewal.

Actually, the difficulties are not so great as they seem. Until more jobs for nonwhites are available, the people who will be able to move to such new housing will be principally middle class nonwhites, and being middle class, they are accepted much more easily by middle class whites. Indeed, this is already happening in some suburban areas.[9] Moreover, if the rehousing program is massive enough, and the housing is built on many sites in small projects, or better still, as part of normal suburban subdivision and new town development, then it can be put up everywhere, and no suburb can continue to attempt to remain racially "pure."

In addition, the federal government can make the rehousing program attractive to the suburbs by including in it provisions for schools and other facilities and even tax subsidies for municipal services so that suburban tax rates can be reduced. Beyond that, the government would also have to exert its power on the suburbs to accept the rehousing scheme, for example, by arguing that as long as *de facto* segregation exists in suburban schools, they will not be entitled to federal educational subsidies. At the same time, the government, private enterprise, and the unions must make greater efforts to integrate industries located in the suburbs so that job opportunities for nonwhite workers will be available.

Even so, the vast majority of poor nonwhites will neither be able nor, perhaps, willing to move behind the city limits in the foreseeable future, for this requires not only occupational security, but also the emotional skill and courage to live in predominantly white surroundings. Since most poor nonwhites will probably remain in the city for perhaps another generation, a significant proportion of the rehousing program must be located in the city, and particularly in the so-called grey areas outside the ghettoes. In addition, a vastly increased rent supplement program, combined with rehabilitation efforts, and even the acquisition of older housing by urban renewal agencies for relocation purposes would make it possible for many more poor nonwhites who want to get out of the ghetto but do not want to leave the city to raise their children in better surroundings.

Once the supply of housing available to poor and nonwhite people is increased in this way, it would then be possible to begin to clear or to rehabilitate the slums, either for their present occupants or for any other land uses determined by city-wide planning considerations. As soon as a significant supply of new housing is available, the slums will begin to empty automatically; an adequate relocation program can then be set up in order to carry out urban renewal. It might even be desirable to revive public housing, not for low income people generally, but as a kind of therapeutic community for those people who need help in overcoming the social and emotional ravages of past poverty and deprivation, provided, of course, that such a program is voluntary, and is not used as a way of imprisoning the people who cannot adapt to new opportunities. Actually, once an effective anti-poverty program is established, I suspect we will discover that the proportion of poor people who cannot accept the new opportunities will be quite small, and that the need for social and psychological therapy will be minimal.

The rehousing scheme, the expansion of rent supplements, and the renewal of the slums should be carried out in such a way that poor and nonwhite people can make housing choices like everyone else, without being punished by special regulations because of their poverty. Although private enterprise has failed to provide housing for the poor in the past, except in the slums, it does have the advantage of treating its customers as equals if they have the ability to pay. Consequently, as much as possible of the program should be carried out through private enterprise, or through public agencies, semi-public institutions, foundations, and labor unions who will treat the subsidized purchasers and renters as customers.

Such a program will require a large increase in federal expenditures for housing, both in subsidies to builders and communities and in rent supplements. This, however, is one of its major virtues. Since the most important component of an effective anti-poverty program is the abolition of unemployment, and since construction is a highly labor-intensive industry, a massive rehousing program would create millions of new jobs, particularly for unskilled and semiskilled workers. Many other new jobs would be created in the construction and staffing of new community facilities.

Just as public housing was set up during the depression to create new jobs, a prime justification for the housing effort is its job-creating potential. The program must be massive enough not just to employ present workers in the building trades, but to bring many more new jobs into being. In addition, the federal government night require that a certain proportion of unemployed people be hired before federal subsidies are made available. These job opportunities would of course have to be made available on a racially integrated basis, and the present job discrimination in the building trade unions would have to be eliminated, but if enough jobs were available, white union members would no longer be so opposed to admitting nonwhites as members. Indeed, if a shortage of skilled construction workers developed as a result of the program, the presently employed might become supervisors and training officers for the presently unemployed. Ideally, the slum dwellers should be hired to build the new housing they and their neighbors will occupy, and to clear or rehabilitate the slums which they have left behind. Such a program could learn much from Israel, where untrained newcomers from African and Oriental countries are being employed to build a huge amount of new housing for themselves and their families, and are thus creating full employment in a much less affluent economy than the American one.

There is no doubt that the rehousing program I have proposed would increase further the proportion of nonwhites in the city. Even if it could begin to integrate the suburbs, its immediate effect would be to move more nonwhite people into the city neighborhoods outside the ghetto, which in turn would at first increase the white exodus to the suburbs. This is not so undesirable as it may appear to be, and more important, it is bound to happen anyway if present housing programs and current population mobility trends continue. The migration of nonwhites from the rural South to southern and northern cities is likely to go on and perhaps even to increase as industrialization of agriculture and southern racial persecution is stepped up. Moreover, the increasing affluence of the white city dwellers is almost certain to attract more of them to the suburbs.

Present housing, anti-poverty, and public welfare policies are only making sure that the nonwhite people of the city will become what Gunnar Myrdal calls the underclass, a poorly housed, poverty-stricken and unemployed urban proletariat. If white affluence increases further, and if the promise of anti-poverty legislation is not matched by results, the nonwhite poverty-stricken city dwellers will become angrier and more hostile to the whites who run the city's economy and political life. If their living conditions are not improved and their needs not met, political protests and riots are likely to become commonplace.

Once effective anti-poverty and rehousing programs can be developed, however, and the economic and social condition of the poverty-stricken is visibly improved, crime, delinquency, and other forms of pathology and protest will be reduced significantly. Not only will the nonwhite population be much less hostile toward the whites who remain in the city and those who commute from the suburbs, but more important, they will be able to want and to afford better municipal services and a better physical environment, and they will have the political strength at city hall to put power behind these demands.

At the same time, the white fears of the predominantly nonwhite city will be reduced, because at bottom these fears are based not on race but on class; the fear is of a city of angry poor people. If they are not poor, they will not be angry, and then, like all the previous immigrants to the city, they will be able to make a positive contribution to the quality of urban life. When this happens, the fact that the city is predominantly nonwhite will no longer be of much relevance, and indeed, those suburbanites who would prefer the city but shun it now because they do not want to live among the poor and deprived may return to the city to take advantage of its urbanity.

The Costs and Benefits of Effective Programs

The anti-poverty and housing proposals I have made will be expensive to carry out, and will necessitate many changes in the economic, social, and political arrangements of the city. They will require higher federal subsidies for the city; perhaps a rise in city tax rates; much more federal and state intervention in city activities, particularly in enforcing desegregation; and increased political representation for the poor and nonwhite residents of the city.

Yet if all the subsidies were costed out, I doubt that they would be significantly higher than the costs of present programs to help the poor, and those which seek to protect the middle class from the poor. To the billions of dollars now spent for welfare and for other programs that do not really eliminate poverty must be added the many other millions expended for efforts to alleviate the pathologies of poverty, like narcotics addition, and the further millions spend for policemen, prisons, hospitals, and other institutions for "containing" the poor. As long as these expenditures do not really get at the root causes of the problem, poverty and racial discrimination, they are virtually wasted. Moreover, when the tensions developed by poverty and racial discrimination boil over into riots, hundreds of millions in property damage are "spent" at once. If we could adequately measure the emotional and social costs of poverty and discrimination for those who suffer from it directly, and for those who suffer from it indirectly through deteriorating cities, crime, unsafe parks, and the like, the total cost of the present measures of dealing with the poor would rise vastly above the cost of the subsidies I have mentioned. And if we could similarly cost out the rising hostility between the rich and the poor and the nonwhites and the whites who live in the city and commute from the suburbs, the expenditures required by new programs are an obvious bargain.

Economic rationality alone would therefore dictate the urgency of an effective anti-poverty and housing program. But other goals are also urgent: the ending of social injustice and inequality, the opportunity for a decent life for every city dweller, the achievement of a freer and more democratic urban community, and the establishment of social peace in the city. These are vital benefits that justify considerable costs. The sooner this is realized, the more quickly we can get down to the task of creating a better social and physical environment in our troubled cities.

Notes

1. See e.g. Herbert Gans, *The Urban Villagers,* New York: Free Press, 1962, 1965, Chapters 13–14; Peter Marris, "A Report on Urban Renewal in the United States," in Leonard J. Duhl, ed., *The Urban Condition,* New York: Basic Books, 1963, pp. 113–134; Martin Anderson, *The Federal Bulldozer,* Cambridge: M.I.T. Press, 1964; and Chester Hartman, "The Housing of Relocated Families," *Journal of the American Institute of Planners,* November 1964, pp. 266–286.

2. Marc Fried, "Grieving for a Lost Home," in Duhl, *op. cit.,* pp. 151–171.

3. See e.g. Advisory Commission on Intergovernmental Relations, *Relocation: Unequal Treatment of People and Businesses Displaced by Governments.* Washington: Advisory Commission, January 1965.

4. For a more detailed critique of the Census bureau study, see Chester Hartman's reply to Edward Logue in the November 1965 issue of the *Journal of the American Institute of Planners,* and his letter in the November 1965 issue of *Commentary.*

5. Daniel H. Wilner and others, *The Housing Environment and Family Life,* Baltimore: John Hopkins University Press, 1962; see also Irving Rosow, "The Social Effects of the Physical Environment," *Journal of the American Institute of Planners,* May 1961, pp. 127–133.

6. See e.g. Lansing, E. Miller and W. Barth, *Residential Location and Urban Mobility,* Ann Arbor, Michigan: Survey Research Center, 1964.

7. See Arthur Pearl and Frank Riesman, *New Careers for the Poor: The Nonprofessional in Human Service.* New York: Free Press, 1965.

8. For a more detailed analysis of the distinction between the slum and the low-rent dwelling, see Gans, *op. cit.,* Chapter 14.

9. See e.g., H.H.F.A. *Equal Opportunity in Housing,* Washington: Government Printing Office, June 1964.

SOCIALIST CITY PLANNING: A REEXAMINATION

Zygmunt Pióro, Miloš Savić, and Jack Fisher

In a special issue of the *AIP Journal* on city planning in Europe (November, 1962), Jack Fisher wrote an interpretation of planning goals and achievements in the socialist countries of Eastern Europe. His article, "Planning the City of Socialist Man," received widespread attention in both the United States and Europe. In Western countries, it helped fill a serious gap in our awareness of postwar planning in Europe. At the same time, it offered an opportunity for a fuller exchange of views with planners from Eastern Europe. Two distinguished planners from Yugoslavia and Poland—the countries covered most fully in Fisher's article—were invited to write comments on the article for publication in the *Journal.* Arh. Miloš Savić, planning director of Novi Sad, Yugoslavia, and Dr. Zygmunt Pióro of the Institute of Town Planning and Architecture in Warsaw, agreed that an exchange of this kind would be valuable and responded with comments from their own points of view. To round out the discussion, Jack Fisher was invited to supply a further note expanding his earlier contribution along lines suggested by the reactions of Arh. Savić and Dr. Pióro. Hopefully, this series of papers will encourage further interchanges on a professional level between Eastern and Western countries. B. J. F. [Jn. Ed.]

Comment by Zygmunt Pióro (Institute of Town Planning and Architecture, Warsaw, Poland)

The views of a foreign observer on planning and urban development are often most valuable in identifying elements and relationships that may be invisible to people closer to the scene of events. Recognizing and becoming conscious of these relationships may lead planners to improve their work. In this spirit, Polish

Reprinted by permission of the publishers from the *Journal of the American Institute of Planners,* 31 (February, 1965), pp. 31–42.

city planners have read with great interest the article "Planning the City of Socialist Man," in which Dr. Jack Fisher attempts to present the aims and methods of urban planning in the countries of Eastern Europe, especially Yugoslavia and Poland, and to interpret their effects.

Dr. Fisher has perceived correctly the relationships of a planned economy with Marxist philosophy, of physical planning with economic planning, and of urban planning regulations or directives with certain specific effects. An attentive reading of his article by a person involved in Polish planning, however, may arouse some fear as to whether a foreign reader is given a proper perspective on the nature of Polish urban planning. Some of the cause and effect relationships are not adequately established, or are selected at random, both of which may have resulted from linguistic difficulties. In addition, the works that Fisher cites are not fully representative of the theory and practice of contemporary urban planning in Poland, since many important programs were not under way until after the completion of his article.

To complete and correct the picture—solely for Poland—it is worthwhile to indicate the fundamental tenets of the theoretical and legal basis of urban planning in Socialist Poland. Professor Boleslaw Malisz, Director of the Institute of Urban Planning and Architecture, in an address delivered on the fortieth anniversary of the Society of Polish Town Planners, defined the place of physical planning in the socio-economic life of Poland:

> The Socialist Revolution had affranchised the forces which, following Soviet Russia's example, have pushed many countries on the road to socialist development. Owing to this, Polish town planners, while realizing their aims, rely on the universal principles in socialist countries: the socialization of the means of production and the accessibility of land for the needs of national economic development. In this way, physical planning in this country has been included in the system of a planned economy. Regional plans are worked out for all areas of the country, and they constitute an integral part of long-range economic planning. The plans of cities and villages ceased to be an expression of one's subjective views and ideas and became, to an ever-increasing degree, the instrument of economic and investment policy on urban areas in the hands of city councils. Gradually, due to methodological efficiency, the recommendations of these local plans begin to influence the formation of long-range economic plans. The political changes connected with the development of socialism in this country have given new sense and new content to physical planning and have created real possibilities for the realization of plans.

This new content and the guaranteed implementation of physical plans have been codified in the Physical Planning Law of January 31, 1961, which provides:

> 1. The object of physical planning is to insure proper development of individual areas of the country, taking into account all their mutual relationships and the interests of the entire country, and to establish the correct spatial interrelations in these areas between production and service facilities, and thereby to create conditions for the development of production which would meet in every aspect the people's needs and which would protect the natural resources and values of the country.

> 2. The task of physical planning is to provide for every territory the land use and methods of development, considering actual and future needs resulting from the program of economic and social development.
>
> The above dispositions should be based on the short- and long-range national economic plans, on the results of geographic, demographic, economic, and social-scientific research for particular territories and indispensable technical analysis.

From this abstract, one can easily summarize the intention of the law, as it discusses the correct spatial development of the particular territories of the country. The aim is to utilize available facilities and activities in planning the universal development of human activity, and the exploitation of the natural resources of particular areas. The objectives for development in this country are determined by scientific research, the resolutions of the Party, cultural anthropology, the philosophy of Marxist-Leninism, the Athens Charter of CIAM, and the Council of Mutual Economic Assistance. The general concepts of the Law are made concrete depending upon each particular situation.

Polish city planners are aware of how difficult it is to find proper spatial relations between different functions of the urban community. These difficulties result from the chaotic development of Polish cities in the capitalist period, from the rapid industrialization and accompanying urbanization during the post-war period, and from the lack of reliable and exact knowledge of the factors determining the ecological structure of our cities under a planned economy. Last but not least as an impediment to planning the proper conditions of human life in the cities, has been the lack of experience in the new political situation and of a clear, rational picture of what the socialist city should look like.

This remark leads us to the problem of identifying those elements of the city that are specifically socialist and of differentiating the characteristics of Polish cities developed under the conditions of a planned economy from western cities. In addition, we must try to determine the methods for forecasting a model of the future socialist city.

Here, once again, it is advisable to look at a report Professor B. Malisz delivered at the UN seminar on Urban Development Policy and Planning in Warsaw in September, 1961:

> The creation of a model or a vision of a future city has been the main problem vexing the minds and engaging the efforts of people concerned with the development of contemporary town planning ideas. . . . There is no other way of visualizing the future than assessing the human needs which can be detected today.
>
> By judging the degree to which the level of urban organization in the given town meets present-day needs, we obtain an almost infallible basis for determining the requirements of man and society today and in the near future . . . .
>
> In conditions of a planned economy, the town planner is considerably aided at this point by something that can be called an official vision of the future: the national economic plan. In certain conditions this official forecast can also fail to comply with the facts of everyday life. However, its unquestioned superiority over the visions created by the individuals lies in the fact that it stands the greatest chance of being applied in practice.

> And when it turns out that the difference between such a vision of the future and the needs of reality have become too great, there is always the possibility of introducing gradual changes and corrections by applying the method of balance, and at the same time maintaining the proportions in the development of all branches of the national economy.
>
> In contemporary Poland, the visions of future developments of our towns, city concentrations, and conurbations are basically in accord with the perspectives of economic development and the tasks thus resulting.

On the basis of the above formulated aims and methods of Polish city planning, one can perhaps see which points Fisher neglected or selected arbitrarily.

Let us now consider the objectionable points in his article. One of the characteristics of the Socialist city, according to Fisher, is "urban uniformity" in its social and physical aspects. Fisher supposes that the norms and standards necessary to realize this rule are widely applied in Polish town planning practice. I would rather define the rule as the "principle of equal possibilities." This meaning is much nearer to the ideology of socialism which predicates social justice on the basis of a classless society and equal chances of opportunity for every working man. Of course, this principle should be considered as one which will be accomplished gradually. Thus, if Mr. Fisher looked for "urban uniformity" he would not find it. But he could easily, if impartially minded, find "the principle of equal possibilities" at a certain stage of realization. The postwar development of Polish cities is the expression of the national endeavor to meet differentiated and constantly growing human needs. If, as the result of spontaneously working ecological forces, there are internal migrations in the city that bring about concentrations of people in particular social categories, nevertheless housing equipment, services, and transportation facilities are equal or are intended to be equal.

In the spatial structure of the socialist city, two elements have attracted his attention: the neighborhood unit and especially the city-center. The first element is presented correctly, but the second demands careful correction. According to Fisher, the socialist city-center "functions not as an area of retail concentration, but as the political-cultural-administrative center in which troops parade and in which the masses of the population have little need to venture except for state holidays" and occasional visits to the one department store, the restaurant, and the coffee shop. I realize that the proper conception of the modern city center is exceptionally difficult to present. In the Polish Institute of Town Planning, a team of prominent town planners have worked on this problem for a year with as yet modest results. Up until now, we are not sure how the future centers of our cities should look. But one thing is certain: those glimpses of ideas which have served as the basis for the program and design of city centers in places such as Nowa Huta, Nowe Tychy, and Warsaw cannot be reduced to the concept of "a political-cultural-administrative center." When we look upon the newly realized city centers, we see that their primary function includes providing services for the inhabitants, commuters, and others who are there not as "Sunday visitors" or "parading troops," but everyday people shopping and utilizing services, as well as passing their leisure time in various central facilities which are unique in their functions and location: theatres, museums, art galleries, big department stores, and luxurious restaurants. Besides these, offices of several kinds have taken over the previous role of the business center and are located appropriately in the core of the city. Thus, central districts of Polish cities are full of life in the day as well as in the night.

Fisher charges that Polish planners and administrators have failed to limit the growth of cities. In Poland, there is only one case, Lublin, in which dynamics overpassed the provisions of the plan. This was due to an error in the evaluation of the strength of spontaneous ecological forces of immigration from the country to the city. Generally, we have made efforts to provide in our plans all the conditions necessary for developing cities with moderate concentration. Even if our endeavours of active deconcentration were not fully successful, they slackened the speed of growth of different cities. Nowa Huta, Nowe Tychy, Pyskowice, Swidnik and other new cities serve as good examples of this process. There is no reason to ascertain that urbanization in Poland has not been directed by a conscious policy of rational concentration.

A serious misunderstanding has crept into Fisher's appreciation of the development of housing in Poland. He states, "a substantial improvement in housing norms does not appear to have taken place. On the contrary, the effect has been one of consistently *decreasing* the per capita urban 'living space' throughout Eastern Europe." In support of this interpretation, he cites Warsaw as an example: "In Warsaw, from an estimated 'living space' per capita average of 7 square meters in 1955–57, the average fell to a current 5.5 square meters." This statement is erroneous, as it concerns the provisional measure of Warsaw's Council to regulate space allocation in new state buildings. The aim of this regulation was to liquidate substandard, slum dwellings. This norm will be obligatory up to 1965. This administrative measure does not, however, in any way support Fisher's conclusion. The quality of housing cannot be measured by spatial indices only. It is necessary to take into account such factors as dwelling equipment, spatial layout, and external service facilities.

In Polish housing policy, the small living space is compensated for by the high standard of service equipment—electricity, gas, water, toilet, wash-basin, central heating, and outdoor utilities. The modern spatial layout of the buildings provides open spaces for children's recreation facilities, and there are neighborhood service centers with commercial and handicraft shops, youth clubs, and a post office. All these taken together represent the real value of housing condition; at most, measures of floor space present only a half-truth. The exact data which could verify or falsify Fisher's contention of "*decreasing* living space" are not actually available in Poland. But we have comparative data for urban areas in Poland showing that the proportion of dwelling units without electricity was reduced from 12 percent in 1950 to 4 percent in 1960; without running water, from 58 percent to 46 percent; without toilet, from 74 percent to 64 percent; and without washbasin, from 86 percent to 73 percent.* These figures show real progress in improving dwelling conditions in urban areas, on the supposition that living space per capita has not been lowered.

* W. Litterer-Marwege, *Housing Condition of Nonfarm Population* (Warsaw: Institute of Housing, 1963).

In concluding his observations, Fisher poses the question, "Have the present [socialist] planners failed?" and answers with a "No," followed by a series of reasons for failure which nearly cancels this "No." Polish town planners cannot accept his view of the situation, however. There is no clash between physical and economic planning in Poland. As a rule, city plans are realized according to the accepted standards and modern pattern of city structure. If specific parts of our city plans were not fully realized, the main reason was economic difficulties resulting from the "cold war" and other international economic forces such as the common market. Impartial observers should understand this background in order to have a comprehensive picture of such an extremely complex activity as town planning.

In this short commentary, I have not been able fully to present the nature of Polish city planning. I have been able only to comment on some points of Dr. Fisher's article which must be objected to. However my critical remarks should not be taken in any way to diminish the role of Fisher in his fairly objective attempt to present the characteristics of socialist town planning. In fact, his personal role can only be praised, as he is now concluding the editing of a detailed, serious study of Polish city and regional planning written by leading Polish planners and soon to be published in the United States. The problem of city planning in all countries of the world is very complex and the fullest exchange of ideas is the only means of eliminating misunderstanding.

Comment by Miloš Savić (Director, City Planning Commission, Novi Sad, Yugoslavia)

City planning as a new discipline has fundamental economic and human goals which are achieved through a variety of technical tools. Its central concern is with man, and with the problems of agglomerations that he creates.

Although ideological principles are the driving forces of social systems and create great differences between them, every discussion of this universally important problem is useful. The exchange of opinions and the use of all experience to solve a particular problem is part of the working method of Yugoslav planners. Every objective evaluation and criticism is welcome. Professor Fisher's article is among those which attempts honestly and objectively to represent Yugoslav methods and city planning practice. Although the article discusses planning in several of the socialist countries of Eastern Europe, this commentary refers only to Yugoslav planning and experience, focusing particularly upon the examples of one city, Novi Sad. The comment follows the order of the article.

Part I: The Theoretical Basis of Socialist City Planning. Fisher's introduction correctly emphasizes that city planning is an integral part of economic and regional planning. Since our practice is inseparable from the social system of our country, the following additional points should be added to the discussion for Yugoslavia specifically.

Land ownership in the urban areas has been regulated by nationalization. The former landowners received compensation. By resolutions of the communal assembly (the highest organ of local government in the commune), land is assigned for the use of individuals or organizations. Utilization of land is based on a zoning policy which assigns the land a value in relation to its proximity to the center of the settlement. The rent charged to the occupant of the land depends upon the value of the building and thus, in reality, upon the investor's financial capacity. The cost includes and insures the provision of communal installations (sewage, water, electricity, telephone service, streets, and green areas); these costs are higher when it is necessary to destroy existing buildings on the site.

Fisher has noted the socialist goal of integrating the cities with rural areas. In Yugoslavia, the character of rural settlement and the relations between the villages and the cities are changing significantly through the development of better transportation. The inherited situation reflected previous backwardness in agriculture. Economic activity was concentrated in the cities, and communication was poorly developed.

Part II: The Operational Principles of Socialist City Planning. The article correctly indicates that the leading principles which characterize socialist planning are concerned with: standardization, the proper size of the city, the city's center, and the neighborhood unit concept. In addition, another important distinction is the division of the city into functional areas of residence, employment, and recreation. These areas are, of course, connected by transportation routes, the fifth basic factor.

The significance of these principles, according to Professor Fisher, was to provide a means for achieving efficiency and the ultimate maximization of impact from limited investments, while at the same time securing urban uniformity. To this I would add only that they are also a means of maintaining an established standard.

In distinction to an early period which had *maximum* permissible housing space and norms for construction in order to use the scarce materials to alleviate the ills inherited from the past, the fundamental law today in Yugoslavia establishes only a *minimum* housing norm which must be respected. These minimums are: living room, 16 square meters; bedroom 12 square meters with a height of 2.50 meters; an apartment with two beds, 35.0 square meters; an apartment with 4 beds, 45.0 square meters. Such facilities as electric current, telephone installations, and an equipped bathroom are also required.

Determining the proper size of the city within the framework of regional and city planning is still in a phase of research verification. The regional factor, is only an important consideration economically. Regional plans have been completed for only a few areas of Yugoslavia. The expansion of industry has produced an uneven migration and constant pressure on urban development. As a consequence, certain regional centers have already reached an optimum size, with a 10:1 ratio between the number of inhabitants of the region and the city. With planned economic development, it is possible to influence (within certain limits) the natural phenomenon of urban growth. Novi Sad has not yet reached its optimum size as a regional center (for 2,000,000 people of Vojvodina), but it has had too rapid a growth: 1948—75,158; 1953—83,180; 1961—110,798; 1963—120,000.

The relationship between the employed and total population is a means for establishing the structure of the population of the city and its optimum size. The norm $(N = K \cdot 100)$ P, which Fisher cites, refers only to the minimum of employed.

The center of the city is the administrative-cultural-political core, and the city at large is the commercial center of the region. In reality there are two functional considerations. The first of these—the city as the administrative-cultural-political center—in fact epitomizes the nature of the socialist city. The second, commercial function, represents a distinctive problem which differs from that in Western countries. The city center is not oriented solely toward retail trade. Besides department stores and specialized retail stores, there are also tourist and service activities, various public agencies, and cultural institutions.

If the city center is understood to include all those institutions or activities which exist in the center of a region, then our definition must be expanded to include schools, health facilities, and so on. These activities are usually not located within the physical center of the city but rather in the lower-order service centers of the neighborhood units. This network of service centers within the neighborhoods makes it unnecessary for us to build separate shopping centers as in the United States.

Neighborhood Units. The neighborhood unit as the fundamental unit in the planning of urban residential zones is explained in Fisher's article with exceptional insight and understanding. It is perhaps in this regard, despite the short time since its implementation, that we in Yugoslavia can speak somewhat more fully.

Each of the land use categories has its own internal breakdown. The zone of residence, for example, consists of neighborhoods (*mesne zajednice*) as fundamental units. These are grouped in a city region (three to five neighborhood units), which is part of the still larger housing zone (more than one region). The structure of neighborhood units and residential zones differs with the size of the city. Novi Sad has neighborhood units, other districts, and a city center. Zagreb has further subdivisions. There is no segregation of married couples or particular age groups into special housing areas. On the contrary, every effort is made to avoid creating such special units, which would only create special problems in providing facilities and services. There are public discussions about each new neighborhood before construction begins. These discussions have become an important psychological and social element of our planning.

Part III: The Cities of Socialist Man. The rapid economic development which occurs in Yugoslavia and the countries of Eastern Europe has brought consequences other than increased urbanization. Nevertheless in the article the existence of three types of urban complexes is correctly presented. It is important for all these three types to be developed according to a plan which entails the describing principles of city planning. The first type—the new cities—most easily satisfy this condition. The second type, which is the expansion of an existing city so that both a quantitative and qualitative change takes place, involves the most difficult problems resulting from the city's heritage. The third type which Fisher calls "cities which experience no change," is in reality rather rare. If by this type, we mean cities which have not had an explosive development, but which nevertheless have expanded, then they are of course developing according to some plan, though more gradually.

The most common is the second type of city. This type is the expression in one sense of the natural development of society. Here implementation of elementary planning measures requires major intervention in the growth of the city. In the first place, transportation routes, the location of railroads, and new streets must satisfactorily connect the various zones within the city and the city with the region. The construction and expansion of the city's center demand new space. Since the center includes buildings of historical and cultural value, these objects must be incorporated and preserved in the new plan. In such conditions, economic considerations are less important than preserving historic areas.

Sociological Situation. The consequence of industrialization and modernization of agriculture was the movement of the peasant into the cities. This movement is significant, particularly in view of the fact that cities have had great difficulty in maintaining and increasing the urban standard in general, let alone adding to the infrastructure or service facilities. Yugoslav practice was exceptional in that a number of "reception centers" for newcomers were constructed. The recommendation of several experts, however, that this be the major means for increasing the general culture of the population was not put into general practice.

There are several categories of apartments and homes which allow for the economic possibilities of different families. The important fact is that in a spatial sense there is no separation of family types. Within one residential area or neighborhood unit are built apartments of various categories. Since there is no administrative division of apartments, old or new, it is impossible for the inhabitants of any residential zone or district to belong to a single segment of society.

Standardization and Urban Uniformity. Yugoslavia has introduced a system of standardization (called JUS) which includes both entire buildings and various parts of buildings, with several industrial systems of prefabrication. Most residential construction, however, is along traditional lines adapted to local conditions and needs.

The attainment of spatial harmony in cities via planned neighborhood development is an ambitious undertaking. Fisher observes correctly that there has been a concentration of investment in the productive economy, and that only during the last few years has there been a significant increase in housing and various service facilities. As a result, it is too early to offer any conclusions on the attainment of equal space and facilities for all residents. It is possible, however, to evaluate the plans that have been prepared and the buildings constructed to date. The completed buildings reveal remarkable qualitative improvements from year to year.

The tempo of urbanization of Yugoslavia and the varying levels of development is such that it is difficult to generalize about the problems of urban planning. For Novi Sad, the following problems are important: the reconstruction of transport and underground utilities, the preparation of low-lying areas for construction, and the specific character of the center for an agriculture region.

Within one article and still further within the limits of a commentary such as this, it is difficult to cover such a complicated problem as city planning. This review has covered only a few points which it is believed will give the reader a fuller picture of Yugoslav planning. For a more complete picture the evaluation of an economist, an architect, and a sociologist would be necessary.

In its entirety, the article by Professor Jack C. Fisher captured and showed most of the characteristic problems of the practice of city planning with exceptional insight and understanding. As an illustration and criticism of our practice it undoubtedly has many positive qualities and represents a contribution to the exchange of thoughts within the complex discipline of city planning.

Comment by Jack C. Fisher (Department of City and Regional Planning, Cornell University)

The ideals expressed for socialist utopian cities during the late 'forties and early 'fifties appear today to be in sharp contrast with the existing reality of urban life in most East European cities. This difference does not signify a change of policy: questions concerning the proper land use structure for a socialist city and the nature of the urban center have never ceased to occupy the thoughts of planning theoreticians. It is clear, however, that economic priorities of industrialization during the 'fifties necessitated the imposition of minimal housing standards and other measures designed to maximize the impact of very limited investments. Concern for the ideal was relegated to the background in order to make the best use of the meager resources available for housing and urban development. During the entire period of the cult of personality (the Stalinist Period) the belief persisted that there is a difference, or at least that there should be a difference, between socialist cities and those of the non-socialist world. The lack of adequate resources made it almost impossible to construct cities that would in any way approximate the philosophical dreams of the early postwar years.

Increased industrial production, the easing of the cold war, and the gradual negation of the worst features of Stalinism permitted increased investments in housing and urban facilities and thus made possible a reexamination of the theoretical basis of socialist city planning. Russians, Poles, and other East Europeans are again beginning to examine the philosophical tenets of Marxist-Leninism and its implications for operational city planning and future urban development.[1] This statement is not intended as a criticism: for just as it is necessary for us to measure our continuing urban expansion against increasing physical mobility and improved technology and the resulting social and administrative problems, so socialist planners must examine their planning mechanism and urbanization process in the light of their social goals and improved investment possibilities.

Three operational factors contributed to deficiencies in city planning in Eastern Europe during the 1950's:

One, planning and design proposals were rarely related to the economic realities of the urban area or its region. The spatial aspects of projected economic programs were neither properly studied nor adequately anticipated.

Two, city planning, due in part to its isolation from economic planning, consisted more or less of a set of formal alternatives or a series of sporadic plans. One contributing factor was the time variation between physical and economic plans: most city plans were for twenty to thirty years, while economic plans were for a maximum of seven years, and usually for far shorter periods with much revision and occasionally total alteration of the plan.

Three, even where there was an urban master plan, a capital investment program for its implementation was often lacking. In many cases the city planning authorities would draw up the plan without either the financial resources or administrative apparatus necessary to carry it out.

The difficulties arising from these three factors were recognized and gradual corrective action began to be applied after 1959. In Yugoslavia, city planning developed as a serious professional discipline concerned with more than urban design only after 1959. Though city planning offices existed prior to 1959 they were generallly composed of architects or at best urban designers. Governmental legislation in 1959 and 1961 provided the necessary legal basis and stimulation for the evolution of sound city planning practice in Yugoslavia. In Poland, though the year 1960 and 1961 introduced new and important measures, subsequent economic difficulties and the failure of many high officials to recognize the importance of physical planning tended to minimize the intended goals of the Physical Planning Law of 1961. It need only be noted that the Committee for Construction, Architecture, and Town Planning—the main Polish administrative and coordinative body—was eliminated without replacement in October, 1963.

Mr. Savić has described in his commentary some of the operational features and legal controls relevant to the city planning process. While agreeing with Mr. Savić's remarks, I must point out that the overall system of planning in Yugoslavia is basically not comparable to that existing in other socialist countries.[2] In particular, Yugoslavia lacks a regional planning apparatus between the central planning authority and the local township or commune or, in larger agglomerations, the city planning commission. Activities which may be designated "regional planning" are for the most part conducted by the central organs and directed to designated underdeveloped areas. The sole exceptions to this are the comprehensive territorial studies of the former Kotars (counties) of Krapina and Split in the Republic of Croatia. In the Republic of Slovenia, which lacks any semblance of a regional planning body, the need has been expressed in a publication of the Republican City Planning Institute which discusses the theoretical nature of regional planning, implying both its utility and current necessity. True regional planning does not exist in Yugoslavia today.

Dr. Pióro's comment makes an important point that was omitted from my discussion of housing. Though I would continue to maintain that per capita living space has declined in Eastern Europe, it is equally important to point out that new housing construction includes all the necessary features of contemporary life, such as electricity and fully-equipped kitchens and bathrooms. Yet for many peasants the addition of improved—and for many, completely new—equipment does not simplify the severe readjustments in life-style required by the smaller area of the new apartments.

One further objection of Dr. Pióro concerning the city's center requires comment. There is no question that a non-commercial urban center was initially considered necessary for a socialist city. Pióro is correct in implying that discussion on this subject declined and is only now becoming a major subject of study among planners. The character of the center of a socialist city is a fundamental problem which is as yet unresolved. It is equally true that most Polish cities do not correspond with the stated ideal of a cultural, administrative, and political functional center. This did not result from a desire on the part of Polish planners to create a central business district in our sense of the word, but rather from the need of supplying cheaply and efficiently the commercial services planned, but never constructed, in the new residential districts. By the late 1950's, the lack of adequate services in these districts created pressures for an immediate soution. It was considered more economical to concentrate the services in one central area rather than disperse them through the neighborhood units. The resulting commercial developments may well give the urban centers of smaller cities a permanent commercial character which will prove financially and functionally impossible to eliminate.

In retrospect one of the most significant points of my November, 1962 article was the stress on the importance of the neighborhood unit concept. In Yugoslavia the term was changed from *stambena zajednica* (housing) to *mesna* (local) *zajednica* by the new Yugoslav Constitution of April, 1963. The "local community" (the technical translation) is "a self-governing community of citizens of rural and urban settlements," in which "the citizens directly participate in self-government in activities that satisfy the basic communal, cultural, health, social, and other needs and desires of the community."[3] Kardelj has observed that *mesne zajednice* (local communities), have primarily three functions: first, the *mesna zajednica* is a unit of the city plan; second, it is a unit and form of self-government in the commune; and third, it is a means of widening the material-technical base for the everyday life of the family and the individual."[4]

Though varying in certain technical details, the neighborhood unit is an element of city planning in all socialist countries.[5] Significantly, in Yugoslavia the concept has evolved from a unit of urban planning to broader social and political significance. Dr. Pióro's suggestion that my term "urban uniformity" should be replaced by "the principle of equal possibilities" is significant in this regard. The *mesna zajednica* or *microrayon* as it is evolving within the framework of socialist city planning today is less concerned with the "social categories" of the inhabitants of the neighborhood and more with the provision of equal services, utilities, and transport facilities to all individuals regardless of the neighborhood unit in which they reside. Though there may be differences among the neighborhoods in the social categories or income levels of the inhabitants, the application of the "principle of equal possibilities" ensures that their service centers will be equal. This conforms with the Marxist thesis that "each will receive his share according to his work." Thus at this stage of development differences in the economic means of individuals will undoubtedly lead to differences in housing quality but not, in theory, to variations in neighborhood services and facilities. Here we see an important shift from a desire for equality of every person's life-style to a concern that each residential unit, regardless of the income level or social category of the inhabitants, will have an opportunity to obtain equal services.[6]

In closing, I should like to thank the *AIP Journal* for providing the opportunity for this unique exchange of comments on city planning in Poland and Yugoslavia. This is a significant development and an important contribution to the improvement of understanding between East and West.

Notes

1. Recently B. Michael Frolic examined in detail the newest utopian ideals of Soviet planners: "The Soviet City," *Town Planning Review, XXIV* (January, 1964), 285–306. My month-long review of Czechoslovak city and regional planning facilities in 1963 indicated that many of the general conclusions expressed here and in my article in the November, 1962 *AIP Journal* are equally valid for Czechoslovakia. I was impressed by the extremely high professional level of many of the Czech city planners. The research being carried out at a federal city planning institute in Brno is comparable in quality with research in this field in America.
2. This paragraph of my discussion is adopted from my article: "A Need for Regional Planning," *Nazi Razgledi* (Ljubljana, Yugoslavia), January 11, 1964. The purpose of the article was to point out the difficulties that the lack of a regional planning mechanism would produce in subsequent years.
3. *Mesne Zajednice u Komunalnom Sīstemu i Zadaci Socijalistickog Saveza* [The Local Community in the Communal System and the Goals of the Social Alliance], Subotica, December, 1962, p. 1.
4. Edvard Kardelj, *Samoupravljanje u Komuni* [Self-Government in the Commune], Materijali sa Godisnje Skupstine Stalne Konferencije Gradova Jugoslavije, Nis, 30 Oktobar—1 November, 1961 (Belgrade, 1961), p. 19.
5. Frolic, *op. cit.*, pp. 287–306.
6. The Yugoslav Constitution of April, 1963 made the township or commune the foundation of the political system. In another publication I have described the evolution of the communal system in Yugoslavia and illustrated its operation in practice through a discussion of the city planning mechanism: "The Yugoslav Commune," *World Politics,* XVI (April, 1964), 418–441. The general development of the communal system along with the role of the local associations (*mesne zajednice*) leads me at present to the tentative conclusion that we may well be seeing the evolution in Yugoslavia of the basic institutional forms of government anticipated for the stage of "full communism." Recent statements by Yugoslav officials makes this a subject deserving further study and explanation.

MACHINE POLITICS AND THE LEGACY OF REFORM

Theodore J. Lowi

The political machine is an institution peculiar to American cities. Like the militant party elsewhere, the American machine as a classic type is centralized, integrated, and relatively ruthless. But there the similarity ends.

Machines have been integrated from within, as fraternities; they do not arise out of opposition to the state or to a hostile class. The power of the machine rested upon being integrated in a dispersed, permissive, and unmobilized society. Integrated, however, in a special American way.

The most militant parties of Europe have depended upon homogeneity—enforced if necessary. Machines have developed ingenious techniques for capitalizing upon ethnic and racial heterogeneity. Militant parties have typically been based on common ends at the center, holding the periphery together by fear. The machines were based upon a congeries of people with uncommon ends, held together at the center by logrolling and at the periphery by *fraternité, egalité,* and ignorance.

As to the significance of the machine for the development of the American city, the returns are still not in. Typically, it was the European observers who were the first to appreciate this unusual, American phenomenon. Ostrogorski, Bryce, Weber, Michels, Schumpeter, and Duverger each in his own way made an outstanding effort to appreciate the peculiarities of urban democracy in America. Harold F. Gosnell, in *Machine Politics: Chicago Model* (1937), was one of the very first Americans to join that distinguished company with anything approaching a systematic treatment of the subject. (By this standard, the muckrakers do not count.)

However, Gosnell was limited by the fact that there was in his time, insufficient experience with alternative forms of big city politics. Too few big cities in the United States had been "reformed" in sufficient degree to provide any basis for comparison.

In the 1960's, sufficient time has passed. The machine is nearly dead, and we have experienced lengthy periods of Reform government. We can now see the machine in perspective.

How does it shape up?

Chicago and New York

We can begin to introduce perspective by immediately setting aside Gosnell's claim that the Chicago experience on which his book was based is representative. It is the very uniqueness of Chicago's experience with the machine that gives his study such value. It is New York that is the representative big city, not Chicago.

Reprinted by permission of the author and publisher from *The Public Interest,* **9** (Fall, 1967), pp. 83–92. For an extended version of these and similar ideas see Theodore Lowi, "Introduction," to Harold F. Gosnell, *Machine Politics,* Chicago: U. of Chicago Press, 1968, revised.

Its representativeness derives from the fact that it has experienced Reform in a way that Chicago has not. In 1967, political power in Chicago still has an extremely strong machine base; political power in New York has an entirely new and different base. As New York was being revolutionized by the New Deal and its successors, the structure of Chicago politics was being reaffirmed. When New York was losing its last machine and entering into a new era of permanent Reform, Chicago's political machine was just beginning to consolidate. New York became a loose, multi-party system with wide-open processes of nomination, election, and participation; Chicago became a tight, one-party system. New York sought to strengthen a weak mayor who already operated under a strong-mayor government; Chicago has had the opposite problem of an already strong mayor in a weak-mayor government.

To evaluate the machine we must ask whether, by surviving, machine politics in Chicago in any way distorted that city's growth and development. How much change would there have been in Chicago's history if the nationalization of politics had made possible in Chicago, as it did in virtually every other big American city, ways of "licking the ward boss" and altering precinct organization, means of loosening the hold of the county organization on city hall, power for liberating the personnel and policies of the professional agencies of government? We cannot answer these questions for Chicago because the basis of machine strength still exists there, and the conditions for its continuity might well continue through the remainder of the century. However, we may be able to answer them, at least better than before, by looking at Chicago from the vantage point of New York's experience.

Populism and Efficiency

New York city government, like government in almost all large American cities except Chicago, is a product of Reform. It is difficult to understand these cities without understanding the two strains of ideology that guided local Reform movements throughout the past three-quarters of a century. *Populism* and *efficiency*, once the foundation of most local insurgency, are now almost universally triumphant. These two tenets are now the orthodoxy in local practice.

Populism was originally a statement of the evils of every form of bigness in the city, including big business, big churches, big labor, as well as big political organizations. Decentralization was an ultimate goal. In modern form, it has tended to come down to the aim of eliminating political parties, partisanship, and if possible "politics" itself.

Efficiency provided the positive program to replace that which is excised by populist surgery. The doctrine calls essentially for the centralization and rationalization of government activities and services to accompany the decentralization of power. Some Reformers assumed that services do not constitute power. Others assumed the problem away altogether by positing a neutral civil servant who would not abuse centralized government but who could use it professionally to reap the economies effected by rationalization and by specialization. That was the secret of the business system; and, after all, the city is rather like a business. ("There is no Republican or Democratic way to clean a street.")

While there are many inconsistent assumptions and goals between the doctrines of populism and efficiency, they lived well together. Their coexistence was supported by the fact that different wings of the large, progressive movement they generated were responsible for each. Populism was largely the province of the working class, "progressive" wing. Doctrines of efficiency were very much the responsibility of the upper class wing. Populism resided with the politician-activists. Efficiency was developed by the intellectuals, including several distinguished university presidents, such as Seth Low, Andrew Dickson White, Harold Dodd, and, pre-eminently, Woodrow Wilson, who, while still a professor of political science, wrote a classic essay proclaiming the virtues of applying Prussian principles of administration in the United States.

These two great ideas were, by a strange and wonderful chemistry, combined into a movement whose influence forms a major chapter of American history. Charters and laws have been enacted that consistently insulate city government from politics, meaning party politics. It has become increasingly necessary, with each passing decade, to grant each bureaucratic agency autonomy to do the job as each commissioner saw fit, as increasingly appointments were made of professionals in each agency's fields.

On into the 1960's, the merit system extends itself "upward, outward, and downward," to use the Reformers' own rhetoric. Recruitment to the top posts is more and more frequent from the ranks of those who have made careers in their agencies, party backgrounds increasingly being a mark of automatic disqualification. Reform has succeeded in raising public demand for political morality and in making "politics" a dirty word. A "good press" for mayors results from their determination to avoid intervening in the affairs of one department after another. The typical modern mayor is all the more eager to co-operate because this provides an opportunity to delegate responsibility. Absolution-before-the-fact for government agencies has become part of the mayoral swearing-in ceremony.

Reform has triumphed and the cities are better run than ever before. But that is, unfortunately, not the end of the story, nor would it have been the end of the story even had there been no Negro revolution. The triumph of Reform really ends in paradox: *Cities like New York became well-run but ungoverned.*

The New Machines

Politics under Reform are not abolished. Only their form is altered. *The legacy of Reform is the bureaucratic city-state.* Destruction of the party foundation of the mayoralty cleaned up many cities but also destroyed the basis for sustained, central, popularly-based action. This capacity, with all its faults, was replaced by the power of professionalized agencies. But this has meant creation of new bases of power. Bureaucratic agencies are not neutral; they are only independent.

Modernization and Reform in New York and other cities has meant replacement of Old Machines with New Machines. The bureaucracies—that is, the professionally organized, autonomous career agencies—are the New Machines.

Sociologically, the Old Machine was a combination of rational goals and fraternal loyalty. The cement of the organization was trust and discipline created out of long years of service, probation, and testing, slow promotion through the ranks, and centralized control over the means of reward. Its power in the community was based upon services rendered to the community.

Sociologically, the New Machine is almost exactly the same sort of an organization. But there are also significant differences. The New Machines are more numerous, in any given city. They are functional rather than geographic in their scope. They rely on formal authority rather than upon majority acquiescence. And they probably work with a minimum of graft and corruption. But these differences do not alter their definition; they only help to explain why the New Machine is such a successful form of organization.

The New Machines are machines because they are relatively irresponsible structures of power. That is, each agency shapes important public policies, yet the leadership of each is relatively self-perpetuating and not readily subject to the controls of any higher authority.

The New Machines are machines in that the power of each, while resting ultimately upon services rendered to the community, depends upon its cohesiveness as a small minority in the midst of the vast dispersion of the multitude.

The modern city has become well-run but ungoverned because it has, according to Wallace Sayre and Herbert Kaufman, become comprised of "islands of functional power" before which the modern mayor stands denuded of authority. No mayor of a modern city has predictable means of determining whether the bosses of the New Machines—the bureau chiefs and the career commissioners—will be loyal to anything but their agency, its work, and related professional norms. Our modern mayor has been turned into the likes of a French Fourth Republic Premier facing an array of intransigent parties in the National Assembly. These modern machines, more monolithic by far than their ancient brethren, are entrenched by law, and are supported by tradition, the slavish loyalty of the newspapers, the educated masses, the dedicated civic groups, and, most of all, by the organized clientele groups enjoying access under existing arrangements.

Organized Decentralization

The Reform response to the possibility of an inconsistency between running a city and governing it has been to assume the existence of the Neutral Specialist, the bureaucratic equivalent to law's Rational Man. The assumption is that, if men know their own specialties well enough, they are capable of reasoning out solutions to problems they share with men of equal but different technical competencies. That is a very shaky assumption indeed. Charles Frankel's analysis of such an assumption in Europe provides an appropriate setting for a closer look at it in modern New York; ". . . different [technical] elites disagree with each other; the questions with which specialists deal spill over into areas where they are *not* specialists, and they must either hazard amateur opinions or ignore such larger issues, which is no better . . ."

During the 1950's, government experts began to recognize that, despite vast increases in efficiency flowing from the defeat of the Old Machine, New York city government was somehow lacking. These concerns culminated in the 1961

Charter, in which the Office of Mayor was strengthened in many impressive ways. But it was quickly discovered that no amount of formal centralization could definitively overcome the real decentralization around the Mayor. It was an organized disorganization, which made a mockery of the new Charter. The following examples, although drawn from New York, are of virtually universal application:

1) Welfare problems always involve several of any city's largest agencies, including Health, Welfare, Hospitals, etc. Yet during more than 40 years, successive mayors of New York failed to reorient the Department of Health away from a "regulative" toward a "service" concept of organization. And many new aspects of welfare must be set up in new agencies if they are to be set up at all. The new poverty programs were set up very slowly in all the big cities—except Chicago.

2) Water pollution control has been "shared" by such city agencies as the Departments of Health, Parks, Public Works, Sanitation, Water Supply, and so on. No large city, least of all New York, has an effective program to combat even the local contributions to pollution. The same is true of air pollution control, although for some years New York has had a separate Department for this purpose.

3) Land-use patterns are influenced one way or another by a large variety of highly professional agencies. It has proven virtually impossible in any city for one of these agencies to impose its criteria on the others. In New York, the opening of Staten Island by the Narrows Bridge, in what may be the last large urban frontier, found the city with no plan for the revolution that is taking place in property values and land uses in that borough.

4) Transportation is also the province of agencies too numerous to list. Strong mayors throughout the country have been unable to prevent each from going its separate way. To take just one example: New York pursued a vast off-street parking program, at a cost of nearly $4,000 per parking space, at the very moment when local rail lines were going bankrupt.

5) Enforcement of civil rights is imposed upon almost all city agencies by virtue of Federal, state, and local legislation. But efforts to set up public, then City Council, review of police processes in New York have been successfully opposed by professional police officials. Efforts to try pairing and busing on a very marginal, experimental basis have failed. The police commissioner resigned at the very suggestion that values other than professional police values be imposed upon the Department, even when the imposition came via the respected tradition of "legislative oversight." The Superintendent of Education, an "outsider," was forced out; he was replaced by a career administrator. One education journalist at that time said: "Often . . . a policy proclaimed by the Board [of Education], without the advice and consent of the professionals, is quickly turned into mere paper policy . . . The veto power through passive resistance by professional administrators is virtually unbeatable. . . ."

The decentralization of city government toward its career bureaucracies has resulted in great efficiency for the activities around which each bureaucracy was organized. The city is indeed well-run. But what of those activities around which bureaucracies are not organized, or those which fall between or among agencies' jurisdictions? For these, as suggested by the cases above, the cities are suffering either stalemate or elephantiasis—an affliction whereby a particular activity, say, urban renewal or parkways, gets pushed to its ultimate "success" totally without regard to its importance compared to the missions of other agencies. In these as well as in other senses, the cities are ungoverned.

The 1961 Election

Mayors have tried a variety of strategies to cope with these situations. But the 1961 mayoralty election in New York was the ultimate dramatization of the mayor's plight. This election was a confirmation of the New York system, and will some day be seen as one of the most significant in American urban history. For New York, it was the culmination of many long-run developments. For the country, it may be the first of many to usher in the bureaucratic state.

The primary significance of the election can be found in the spectacle of a mayor attempting to establish a base of power for himself in the bureaucracies. The Mayor's running mate for President of the City Council had been Commissioner of Sanitation, a position which culminated virtually a lifetime career of the holder in the Department of Sanitation. He had an impressive following among the sanitation men—who, it should be added, are organized along precinct lines. The Mayor's running mate for Comptroller had been for many years the city Budget Director. As Budget Director, he had survived several Administrations and two vicious primaries that pitted factions of the Democratic Party against one another. Before becoming Director he had served for a number of years as a professional employee in the Bureau. The leaders of the campaign organization included a former, very popular Fire Commissioner who retired from his commissionership to accept campaign leadership and later to serve as Deputy Mayor; and a former Police Commissioner who had enjoyed a strong following among professional cops as well as in the local Reform movement. Added to this was a new and vigorous party, the Brotherhood Party, which was composed in large part of unions with broad bases of membership among city employees. Before the end of the election, most of the larger city bureaucracies had political representation in the inner core of the new Administration.

For the 1961 election, Mayor Wagner had put his ticket and his organization together just as the bosses of old had done. In the old days, the problem was to mobilize all the clubhouses, districts, and counties in the city by putting together a balanced ticket about which all adherents could be enthusiastic. The same seems true for 1961, except that by then the clubhouses and districts had been replaced almost altogether by new types of units.

The main point is that destruction of the machine did not, in New York or elsewhere, eliminate the need for political power. It simply altered what one had to do to get it. In the aftermath of twenty or more years of "modern" government, it is beginning to appear that the lack of power can corrupt city hall almost as much as the possession of power. Bureaucracy is, in the United States, a relatively new basis for collective action. As yet, none of us knows quite how to cope with it.

What If. . . ?

These observations and cases are not brought forward to indict Reform cities and acquit Chicago. They are intended only to put Chicago in a proper light and to provide some means of assessing the functions of the machine form of collective action.

Review of Reform government shows simply and unfortunately that the problems of cities, and the irrational and ineffectual ways city fathers go about their business, seem to obtain universally, without regard to form of government or type of power base. All cities have traffic congestion, crime, juvenile delinquency, galloping pollution, ghettos, ugliness, deterioration, and degeneracy. All cities seem to be suffering about equally from the quite recent problem of the weakening legitimacy of public institutions, resulting in collective violence and pressures for direct solution to problems. All cities seem equally hemmed in by their suburbs and equally prevented from getting at the roots of many of their most fundamental problems. Nonpartisan approaches, even the approaches of New York's Republican mayor to Republican suburbs and a Republican governor, have failed to prevent rail bankruptcy in the vast Eastern megalopolis, to abate air or water pollution, to reduce automobile pressure, or to ease the pain of the middle-class Negro in search of escape from his ghetto.

The problems of the city seem to go beyond any of the known arrangements for self-government. However, low public morality and lack of what Banfield and Wilson call "public-regardingness" may be a function simply of poor education and ethnic maladjustment. The Old Machine and its abuses may just have been another reflection of the same phenomena. If that is so, then passage of more time, and the mounting of one socio-cultural improvement after another, might have reformed the machines into public-regarding organs, if they had been permitted to survive.

Are there any strong reasons to believe that real reform could have come without paying the price of eliminating the popular base of political action? Intimations can be found in the last of the machine-recruited leaders of Tammany, Carmine DeSapio and Edward Costikyan. Each was progressively more public-regarding than any of his predecessors. Indeed, Costikyan was a model of political responsibility for whom the new New York had no particular use. However, for this question the best answers may lie in looking afresh at Gosnell's Chicago. With a scientific rigor superior to most political analysis of the 1960's, his book goes further than any other single work to capture what political behavior was like under Old Machine conditions. The sum total of his findings, despite Gosnell's own sentiments, does not constitute a very damning indictment of the Chicago machine—if contemporary experience is kept clearly in mind.

Chicago in Perspective

Even amidst the most urgent of depression conditions, the machine in Chicago does not seem to have interfered with the modest degree of rationality distributed throughout the United States. Take for instance the case of voting behavior on referendum proposals, the most issue-laden situation an electorate ever faces.

Gosnell criticized the referendum as generally subject to fraud and other types of abuse, and most particularly so in Chicago during the 1920's and '30's. But even so, his figures show that the electorate, despite the machine, did not behave indiscriminately. The theory that universal suffrage provides no check against the irresponsible acceptance of financing schemes which pass the real burden on to future generations is simply not borne out in Chicago. Conservative appeals by the propertied were effective. Over a twelve-year period, including six fat years and six lean years, 66 local bond issues were approved and 48 were rejected. Those rejected included some major bond issues offered for agencies whose leaders had become discredited. Other types of issues show responsiveness to appeals other than local precinct or county organizations. As the antiprohibition campaign began to grow, so did the vote on the prohibition repealer. Clear irrationalities tended to be associated primarily with highly technical proposals involving judicial procedure or taxation; but this is true everywhere, and to much the same degree.

In a bold stroke, Gosnell also tried to assess the influence of the newspapers, the best source for rational—at least nonmachine—voting decisions. For this particular purpose Gosnell's data were weak, but fortunately he was not deterred from asking important questions merely for lack of specially designed data. Factor analysis helped Gosnell tease out of census tract data and newspaper subscription patterns a fairly realistic and balanced sense of the role of the local newspapers. Gosnell was led to conclude that the influence of news media is limited, but that this was a limitation imposed far less by the machine than by the extent to which newspapers were regularly read. Newspaper influence on issues was measurably apparent wherever daily readership was widely established—the machine notwithstanding. Here again is suggested the possibility that real machine domination rested upon a level of education and civic training that was, at the very time of Gosnell's research, undergoing a great deal of change.

Taking all the various findings together, and even allowing for abuses that were always more frequent in cities than towns, and probably more frequent in Gosnell's Chicago than other cities, we can come away from Gosnell's analysis with a picture not at all at odds with V. O. Key's notion of the "responsible electorate."

Gosnell felt his book to be an indictment of machine politics. But today, looking at the Chicago experience from the vantage point of New York's, one feels less able to be so sure.

AUTHOR INDEX

SUBJECT INDEX

ABCDE69